DAVID VICHNAR

joyce
against
theory

Prague 2010

Litteraria Pragensia Books
www.litterariapragensia.com

Published 2010 by Litteraria Pragensia
Univerzita Karlova, Filozoficka fakulta,
Centre for Critical & Cultural Theory,
Náměstí Jana Palacha 2
116 38 Praha 1, Czech Republic

 Published 2010 by Univerzita Karlova v Praze
Filozofická Fakulta

Litteraria Pragensia Books
Centre for Critical & Cultural Theory, DALC
Náměstí Jana Palacha 2
116 38 Praha 1, Czech Republic

The publication of this book has been partly supported by research grant MSM0021620824
"Foundations of the Modern World as Reflected in Literature and Philosophy" awarded to the
Faculty of Philosophy, Charles University, Prague, by the Czech Ministry of Education.

Cataloguing in Publication Data

Joyce Against Theory, by David Vichnar—1st ed.
    p. cm.
  ISBN 978-80-7308-315-1 (pb)
      1. James Joyce. 2. Literary Theory. 3. Cultural Studies. 4. New Media.
      I. Vichnar, David. II. Title

Printed in the Czech Republic by PB Tisk
Typesetting & design by lazarus

Acknowledgements

There are two people without whom the present book would have been unrealisable, if not inconceivable. Louis Armand, mentor and friend, provided the idea of a dissertation mapping some of the present-day theoretical approaches to Joyce's writing. Fritz Senn provided the stuff which the dreams of the present study are made of—access to the most comprehensive Joyce book collection in Europe—well beyond the scope of the two-month "Friends of the Zürich James Joyce Foundation Scholarship" in August-September 2007, during which the groundworks of the project were lain. His hospitality, wit, patience and encouragement gave as much as the books themselves. Over the subsequent two years of work, other people have been of help and assistance and should be thanked, as it were, in order of appearance: Jean-Michel Rabaté, John Bishop, Jed Deppman, David Spurr, Sam Slote, Finn Fordham, Martin Procházka and Sebastian Knowles—all have provided useful tips for further research or correctives of work already done, and are all thankfully remembered. It is not just an idle phrase to say that whatever merit the present study might claim to have is their due; the author can only claim the mistakes as his own.

I would like to dedicate this book to my parents, who have inspired my interest in reading Joyce in my young youth by claiming Joyce to be "an unreadable author." I hereby hope, with fondness and gratitude, to have proven them right.

Prague, June 2010

Contents

INTRODUCTION
Joyce Against Theory

I

This work sets out to map the genealogy of a possible location of "Joyce" and "theory" in present-day Joyce studies and, equally important, to think of the meanings of the copulative conjunction *and* which separates/unites the two. The phenomenon of the contagious "Joyce and…" to be found in a plethora of book and, even more so, lecture titles is significant in its own right, bespeaking not so much a lack of imagination on the part of the scholarly community, as a central tendency of Joyce's writing, variously described as its (all-)inclusiveness. Joyce's writing method, itself based on addition and expansion, produced texts whose semantic reference, more than in the case of any other writer, is extra-textual as much as intertextual. This tendency in turn solicits a repetition in the response of Joyce's readership (from the earliest projects of textual annotation to the complex genetic examinations of some contemporary Joycean scholarship), whether of the individual exegete or—again to a degree paralleled by few other writers—of a reading group. Joyce's texts, from the floating signifiers of "paralysis," "gnomon," and "simony" in the first paragraph of "The Sisters" to the possibly inexhaustible allusive potential of almost all "words" in *Finnegans Wake*, call for expansion, extension and addition. In approaching Joyce's text, the reader finds it always already supplemented by some "and"—such that every critical work that unproblematically operates within the syntactic construction of "Joyce and …" re-enacts a gesture already performed by Joyce's text about which it purports to be. More of which later—at this point, suffice it to say that one of the aims of the present work is to demonstrate the intangibility, if not impossibility, of employing the copulative conjunctive in the case of "Joyce" *and* "critical theory."

Hence, Joyce *against* theory. In its usual sense, "against" implies oppositionality, and thus also distancing in space. Though this is not without relevance for some of the cases examined here, the belief underlying what follows is that Joyce's writing is itself theoretical through and through, and much can be gleaned from mapping the developments in Joyce studies that have, in their own variously focused theoretical readings, identified, analysed, evaluated and creatively re-enacted the crucial gestures of Joyce's texts. As long as the problem with the Joyce of meta-discourse is not distance, but proximity, the "against" of the title is meant to refer precisely to the distinct character of Joyce's writing, which seeks to pre-empt its own meta-discourse and thereby thwart any attempt at saying something *about* it that is not already *in* it. More importantly for my purposes here, this "against" also implies what might be seen as the other direction of the exchange, in which Joyce's writing impacts upon, re-shapes, or challenges the conceptual frameworks whose utilization it solicits. Thus, in a more playful yet no less serious sense, the etymological and formal connection of "against" with "again" serves to refer precisely to this paradoxical double-bind in which the encounter between Joyce and theory changes the what and the how of reading, producing both a Joyce-again of theory and Joyce-inflected theory.

II

This paradox found some of its most fruitful formulation(s) in Derrida's renowned plenary address at the 1984 Frankfurt International James Joyce Symposium. His *"Ulysses* Gramophone: Hear say yes in Joyce"—an intriguing, humorous, ironic, and above all, deliberately provocative foray into a whole array of topics as diverse as (un)translatability, experience, performativity, and telephonics—traces the textual effects of the word "yes" in Joyce's *Ulysses*, "which says nothing and asks only for another yes, the yes of the Other, which [...] is analytically implied in the first yes," since "the self-affirmation of yes can address itself to the Other only in recalling itself to itself, in saying to itself yes, yes."[1]

For Derrida, the signature of "Joyce," which every interpretation (his own including) seeks to countersign, is first and foremost the encyclopedic, all-inclusive character of his texts, by means of which it becomes the "hypermnesiac machine" (48) and "the sum total of all sum totals" (57). Hence, on a general note,

> [t]he effects of this preprogramming, you know better than I, are admirable and terrifying, and sometimes of intolerable violence. One of them has the following form: nothing can be invented on the subject of Joyce. Everything we can say about *Ulysses*, for example, has already been anticipated, including, as we have seen, the scene about academic competence and the ingenuity of metadiscourse. (48)

The all-inclusiveness is amusingly played out in the example of Derrida's interweaving his discussion of the various *Ulysses*-related issues with a seemingly irrelevant digressive story of his purchasing postcards in a Tokyo Hotel, only in order to demonstrate that

> [e]verything that happened to me, including the narrative that I would attempt to make of it, was already foretold and forenarrated, this unusualness being dated, prescribed in a sequence of knowledge and narration: within *Ulysses*, to say nothing of *Finnegans Wake*, by a hypermnesis ma-

[1] Jacques Derrida, *"Ulysses* Gramophone: Hear say yes in Joyce," *James Joyce – The Augmented Ninth*, ed. Bernard Benstock (New York: Syracuse University Press, 1988) 63; 66.

chine capable of storing in an immense epic work, with the Western memory and virtually all the languages in the world including traces of the future. Yes, everything has already happened to us with *Ulysses* and has been signed in advance by Joyce. (48)

If this be the case, Joyce's all-inclusiveness brings about the subversion of several important binaries, including the one of Derrida's standing against the community of Joycean scholarship, which implies the destabilization of the issue of competence:

> When you call on incompetents, like me, or on allegedly external competences, knowing full well that these do not exist [... it is because] you are at once very sure and very unsure of your rights, and even of your community, of the homogeneity of your practices, your methods, your styles. You cannot rely on the least consensus, on the least axiomatic concordat among you. Basically, you do not exist, you are not founded to exist as a foundation, which is what Joyce's signature gives you to read. And you call on strangers to come and tell you, as I am doing in replying to your invitation: you exist, you intimidate me, I recognize you, I recognize your paternal and grandpaternal authority, recognize me and give me a diploma in Joycean studies. (51)

What is at stake in this rhetoric gesture, and the speech as a whole, is Joyce's pre-emptive inclusion, a "yes" in advance which paradoxically bespeaks a certain denial of the other while at the same time appearing to affirm it. This affirmation in turn is revealed as reflecting man's awareness of being in the world as "always already" aimed toward this other. Derrida's mock-Heideggerian (since paralleling his *Dasein* as *der Angerufene*) being-at-the-telephone (40), as manifested through the many technological means which Derrida follows throughout *Ulysses*—including the phonograph, gramophone, telephone, print, photography, or indeed, the rudimentary technology of inscription itself—bears witness to its all-pervasiveness. These technologies of telecommunication are further on traced within the repetitive doubleness which marks all of (particularly Joyce's) literary language, relying as it does, not on any simplistically conceived mimeticism, but rather on the creation of the different by means of a reiteration (with a difference) of the same. It is precisely within this doubleness that the absent and distant other at the heart of the self (whether that of the individual or of the literary text) lies, bringing about this double gesture of both affirmation and denial (just as Joyce spoke of Molly as of *das Fleisch, das stets bejaht*, reversing *der Geist, der stets verneint* of Goethe's Mephistopheles).

Ulysses and its discussed pre-emptiveness also appears, in Derrida's concern with the inexhaustible potential of merely its one word, to participate in "the relationship of a *yes* to the Other," which, "with or without words [...] demands *a priori* its repetition, its own memorizing" (68). It follows that what this very account of Derrida's talk, and the present work itself, perform is precisely this repetition which is the implicit *yes* of affirmation—and denial.

III

To be sure, all or most of this is well known. The famously professed relation of *supplementarity* between Joyce's "primary" text and its critical commentary, intermingling with and contaminating each other, has been documented and commented upon from various positions by the three meta-meta-critical works whose informative influence upon the present endeavour should be affirmed.

Alan Roughley's 1990 *James Joyce and Critical Theory: An Introduction*[2] has provided the present work with both form and content, insofar as its format of a chapter-by-chapter exposition of individual works prefaced by brief introduction to the general movement they come to represent within Joyce studies is followed here. It should be noted that the contents of my thesis are crucially formed by the advances in Joyce studies emerging after 1990 (thus falling outside the scope of Roughley's work chronologically) or those preceding the 1990s that fell out of Roughley's framework (therefore falling outside the scope of his study conceptually).

Roughley maps the wide gamut of critical approaches running from the broad stream of Saussurean and Lévi-Straussian structuralism to post-structuralism, whether emergent (in Margot Norris' seminal study)[3] or full-blown (in the Attridge-Ferrer co-edited collection).[4] Among the most significant additions to Roughley's otherwise thoroughly informed and detailed account are my discussions of the Lacanian psychoanalytical approach, cultural studies of Joyce, studies of Joyce's (post)modernism, and textual genetics, all of which, though culminating during the 1990s or in the present day, can be traced well before 1990yet seem to have fallen outside Roughley's focus. Nevertheless, the points of continuity—in my chapters on e.g. deconstruction, feminism, the various strands of politically committed criticism, or the early psychoanalytic approaches to Joyce—remain equally important, and Roughley's book presents a formal paradigm for, and a thematic precursor to, the present investigation.

A more recent and therefore up-to-date study, Joseph Brooker's *Joyce's Critics: Transitions in Reading and Culture*,[5] negotiates a more chronological and *ad-hominem* approach. Rather than Roughley's strictly delineated categorization of Joyce criticism into several individual critical frameworks, Brooker centres his discussion around the two various at-

[2] Alan R. Roughley, *James Joyce and Critical Theory: An Introduction* (Exeter: Harvester Wheatsheaf, 1991).

[3] Margot Norris, *The Decentered Universe of 'Finnegans Wake'* (Baltimore: Johns Hopkins University Press, 1974).

[4] Derek Attridge and Daniel Ferrer, eds., *Post-structuralist Joyce* (Cambridge: Cambridge University Press, 1984).

[5] Joseph Brooker, *Joyce's Critics: Transitions in Reading and Culture* (Madison: University of Wisconsin Press, 2004).

tempts at "de-nationalizing" the Irish Joyce (undertaken by Joyce's fellow-modernists T.S. Eliot and Ezra Pound within the rubric of "International Modernism," and by the two famous figures of post-war Joyce criticism, Richard Ellmann and Hugh Kenner, as part of its "Americanization"). He also examines the two more recent alternative national affiliations of Joyce's writing, the one conducted by the French theory of the late 1960s/early 1970s (with a marked influence upon the radical proponents of the "68 thought" in Britain), and the other in Joyce's native Ireland about a decade later (under the banner of postcolonial studies).

The second half of Brooker's study (the first half has little relevance for this work) presents a useful, gracefully written, if at times somewhat sweeping overview of the two recent re-nationalizations of Joyce's work, and deserves to be discussed in some detail. The "French" chapter swarms with identifications of the paradoxical gesture identified with Joyce by deconstructionists, understood rather negatively:

> On the one hand, Joyce's quality of anticipation offers criticism a guarantee of relevance [...]. On the other hand, Joyce is credited with superhuman powers: criticism, in effect, abases itself before him. One apparent implication of the Derridean pronouncements on Joyce is that Joyce knows everything and can never be wrong. (Strictly, the Derridean claim refers to the operation of Joyce's writing, not the man himself: but this makes little practical difference.) (169)

Without intending to delve into much detail in regard to these reservations, one of the aims of my first chapter will be to show that the distinction between Joyce-the-man and Joyce-the-writer matters a good deal, and that implications as to the nature of personal all-knowingness and always-being-right are simply not within the compass of Derrida, deconstruction, or indeed literary theory. What is of relevance, rather, is the technology (whether stylistic, rhetoric, narrative, etc.) of inclusion (and exclusion) of certain discursive practices; in other words, how Joyce's works affirm, at the same time as they deny, the other of their critical supplement. However, personal tastes aside, both Brooker's further connections between French theory and Anglo-American feminist, cultural theory, or political thought, as well as his broadly conceived final chapter on the Irish perception of Joyce's works, competently lay the groundwork that has informed the conceptualization of these topics in the present exploration.

The last work, Geert Lernout's *The French Joyce*,[6] is the least present here in text form, yet all the more present in the person of its author, and it is also a study whose critical objections to its subject matter were coterminous with, and to some extent also catalysed, the early1990s turn from (particularly French) critical theory in search of different paradigms, thus playing a role within the massive transformation which forms the

[6] Geert Lernout, *The French Joyce* (Ann Arbor: University of Michigan Press, 1990).

overarching subject of this work. Here it will suffice merely to pinpoint two of its most important features as a text: one, the encyclopedic exhaustiveness of its treatment of Joyce's (mis-)appropriation at the hands of French theorists (including Derrida the deconstructionist, Jacques Lacan the psychoanalyst, Hélène Cixous the feminist, but also the more strictly Joyce-oriented Jean-Michel Rabaté, Daniel Ferrer, Jacques Aubert, and others), spanning the period from the revolutionary year of 1968 to the late 1980s; and two, the uncompromisingly negative attitude to its subject, Lernout's explicit disagreement with the theory and practice of poststructuralism, whose failure to engage with Joyce is seen as particularly strong in its "overinterpretation of minor details of the text, on the one hand, and factual reading errors, on the other hand" (195).

The first is then regarded as a direct outcome of the unhealthy deconstructionist obsession with interpretation, and the latter as having to do with the critics' sense of self-importance that leads to negligence as regards the text's formal proprieties. Throughout, Lernout positions his critique from the perspective of traditional philology, among whose most outspoken adherents he counts himself. Thus, the text points to its author and Lernout will make several important appearances in various places in this study (most notably, in the final chapter on the textual genetic studies of Joyce) as a powerfully inquisitive, and usually dissenting voice. It is ultimately Lernout's own turn away from deconstruction—narrated in both the introduction and conclusion of his study—to the more concretely text-grounded criticism (such as, though not wholly so, the one of textual genetics), that the present work sets out to examine within the context of the whole of Joyce studies.

IV

Where then can one say consists the merit of this work, much as it is a follow-up of previous critical projects, with which it can compete neither in the breadth of their scope (Roughley, Brooker), nor in the fruitfulness of their informed dissent (Lernout, Brooker), nor in the relevance of their temporal moment, marking an end of an era (Roughley, Lernout)? Moreover, how can one attempt to categorize contemporary literary thought, marked as it is by eclecticism and the interbreeding of specific positions rather than a strict adherence to one discreet movement or another, without at the same time severing and devaluating lines of development, points of connection and spheres of affiliation?

In terms of formal arrangement, I have aimed both at drawing dividing lines and at preserving continuities: therefore it proved necessary not only to focus my investigation on five of the most influential contemporary theoretical approaches to literature (deconstruction, psychoanalysis, feminism, cultural studies, and postcolonial theory), but also to single out five types of "studies"—approaches to Joyce centred around specific topics relevant to his writing, as it were from within, rather than theories or methodologies brought from without—in terms of which to discuss the shared points of the former five: Joyce vis-à-vis: (post)modernism; historicism; politics; media, technology, and hypertext; and finally, the textual genetic studies of Joyce, which forms a sort of a synthetic anomaly with which to conclude. Textual genetics combines amore or less clearly defined methodology with amore than less clearly defined subject (the *Ur*-texts of Joyce's canon) and presents the most fruitful approach to Joyce in current critical practice, as confirmed by its almost monopolistic (insofar as this word can be understood positively) presence in recent Joyce symposia, summer schools and workshops. It is in its attention to the plurality of contemporary critical approaches (which exceeds even the scope of Brooker, who covers only two of the five major currents identified here) that the particular merit of the present study might be said to lie.

"Theory," the other term in the title which does require at least a tentative definition in any work with a purpose such as mine—assuming, of course, that some sort of a definition of the third term, "Joyce," shall surface somewhere along the way—is understood in its historico-etymological sense. As the editor of the Paul de Man reader (whose subtitle, *Resistance to Theory*,[7] would well apply to the present work) reminds us, *theoria* were originally of a plural number, denoting the procession of officially chosen witnesses that bore their testimonies to whether or not such or such event had happened. In this work, too, several witnesses shall be called upon to testify how and why certain transformations have taken place. These transformations can be said to have uncannily re-enacted the originally political (steeped as it was in the public life of the Greek polis) and historical (consisting as it did in the varying accounts of irretrievable yet re-iterable past events) nature of theory, insofar as the crucial double-movement of Joyce studies over the past quarter of a century has been precisely one engaged with the historicisation and politicisation of his writing.

This attention to the polyvocity of Joycean criticism has a formal ramification for the way the contents of this work are informed—more so than in the three cases mentioned above— by the wish to present the critical text as objectively as is possible in such projects, to let the critical text speak in its own words, and to reserve the presenter's own judgment to his selection of particularly relevant passages over others, as well as to allow for occasional expressions of strong agreement or mild doubts. The aim here, in other words, is not so much to present an opinionated critique from a staunchly maintained position—like the one of Lernout's study—as to give an account of the historical roots, genealogies, and current state of the most significant critical advances in Joyce studies from over the last quarter of a century. This has impacted upon the form in two ways: in its preference for direct quotation rather than roundabout

[7] Wlad Godzich, ed., *Paul de Man – The Resistance to Theory* (Minneapolis: University of Minnesota Press, 1986).

paraphrase or commentary, and in its chronological progression through the individual critical developments. For this work, in a way similar to that of Derrida's Joyce (or Joyce's Derrida), to quote is to say yes, to affirm, to accept. This work seeks to, above all, accept.

However, as part of the same gesture, it also denies. For, as already explained above, it posits a Joyce *against* theory, a Joyce whose writing stymies, precludes, evades, or (in the least radical case) problematises the conceptual framework brought to bear upon it. Joyce's "yes" to theory in its affirmative sense is too obvious to need much brooding over. From Joyce's own construction of a critical reply to his work, or even recircula- tion of the criticism of his earlier works in his later ones, to the peculiar quality of his writing which has ever since the beginnings of modern liter- ary theory in the early days of structuralism and semiotics exhibited a special proneness to critical examination, Joyce's work has always mes- merised literary theory. This special status of Joyce's writing within criti- cal theory has been famously captured in Terry Eagleton's contention that "[i]t is always worth testing out any literary theory by asking: How would it work with Joyce's *Finnegans Wake*?"[8] What has, however, not been dealt with to a sufficient degree (excepting deconstruction, and a few privileged moments of critical self-examination within all the other major approaches), is Joyce's "yes" in its pre-emptive, self-affirmative sense, with which it reduces its Other (the critical text) to a mere repetition of its own self-affirmation. This study, relying on the above-mentioned supple- mentary relation of the two, and well-aware of the double nature of the yes proclaimed by the Joycean text vis-à-vis its critical Other, thus fo- cuses on both directions of the Joyce-theory exchange: on how the cata- lytic reaction between Joyce and theory non-reversibly changes both the texts we read at the same time as it changes the methods by and through which we read them.

V

At this point, it appears appropriate that two genuinely introductory voices[9] be heard, the one thematising the wider context of the historical era, the other addressing issues pertaining to the subject matter, dealt with in the present work. This study will also concern itself, on a broader level, with what Attridge terms "Joyce effects," that is, "the effects pro- duced by his work [...] upon the way we think about a number of signifi- cant topics, and upon our involvement in other cultural (and more than cultural) activities" (Attridge: xiii). Yet more specifically, it will also focus on what Milesi regards as "unanswered—and perhaps unanswerable— questions to the nature of (re)reading as a historically motivated act of external (re)appropriation, itself not devoid of ethico-political or at least

[8]   Terry Eagleton, *Literary Theory* (Oxford: Basil Backwell, 1983) 82.
[9]   Derek Attridge, "Introduction" to *Joyce Effects: Language, Theory, History* (Cambridge: Cambridge University Press, 2000). Laurent Milesi, ed., "Introduction" to *James Joyce and the Difference of Language* (Cambridge: Cambridge University Press, 2003).

ideological implications, or 'genuine' heuristic discovery" (Milesi: 20). A re-reading which here is another word for theory.

Attridge's "Introduction: On Being a Joycean" casts some historical light on what has been one-sidedly presented as the theoretical explanation for the otherwise always arbitrarily selected point of beginning. As his book is a collection of essays garnered from over twenty years of his Joycean career, its organization and progression is of much use in documenting the make-up of the period's progression. If the 1982 Dublin symposium marked its humble beginnings, the 1984 Frankfurt symposium marked the moment French theory became "the dominant approach to Joyce's writing" (8). The early 1980s as a whole are seen as "a watershed [...], after which Joyce criticism would never be the same," yet also one that did not stop other new critical trends from arising (9). Thus, the mid-1980s saw the poststructuralist text-based criticism "enriched by an increasing concern with historical contexts and changes," as evidenced by Attridge's participation in the 1986 Copenhagen panel on "Joyce and History."

With the impact of historical approaches on Joyce studies during the 1980's, the influence of feminism increased, to which Attridge's essay on "Molly's Flow" presented in Venice in 1988 bears witness, alongside the issues connected with postmodernism (Monaco 1990). By the early 1990s, "the most rapidly growing research area in English departments was cultural studies, [which] found a fertile new terrain in Joyce's relation to popular and consumerist culture" (11). The other remarkably influential critical domain of the mid-1990s were colonial and postcolonial studies, whose poststructuralist founding was reflected in the fact that "questions of marginalization, alterity, and difference ha[d] been crucial to these discourses since the 1960s" (12).

In addressing the *so what* rather than the mere *what* of the changing courses of Joyce criticism, Attridge first poses the dissenting view (one that Lernout also voices):

> The academic marketplace [...] it is pointed out, thrives on rapid obsolescence [in which] all stand to gain from a cycle of critical fads, each rendering last year's ideas, books, and courses out of date as it stakes its own (equally short-lived) claims. (13)

But where Lernout stops and refuses, Attridge goes on to view the conclusions to be drawn from this set of facts as not quite clear-cut and accepts by claiming that underneath this "razzmatazz of competing isms and posts" there rests "some solid, abiding, dependable approach to literature" (13). Although the sundry Joyces of the various critical allegiances "all necessarily entail easily parodiable, formulaic applications of what at their best are insightful and rigorous ways of reading," it is to Attridge's mind precisely the overproduction of such applications that partly incites the development of new critical approaches. Therefore a completely different deconstruction from the one of Lernout's emerges in Attridge's account. Here, it is regarded as

an approach to literature which did a great deal more justice to the complexity and internal disjunctions of the works I read than the habits of interpretation and evaluation to which I had becomes accustomed,

even though, in the same breath, the hindsight in which it is viewed (and which we shall encounter elsewhere as well) now reveals

more value in some of the critical methods I then regarded as entirely superseded, and I see limitations in the new thinking I endorsed that were then invisible to me but which I am attempting to overcome in my current work. (15)

We can see that from the new, historical perspective maintained by the Attridge of 2000 the changes in styles of Joyce criticism

provide evidence that modes of literary criticism, and more generally the ways in which books get read and talked about, are historical through and through. Not only are the normative judgements that are made about literary works dependent on time and place, but so are the very meanings that readers find in them; in a quite real sense, therefore, the works themselves keep changing. (16)

Critical fashions, however important, are found to be more transient than "critical values," featuring "rigour, accuracy, honesty, originality, and responsibility" (16); and yet even what appears to be a single mode of criticism "will always serve many different purposes, and its value will be correspondingly complex"—an example being, quite tellingly, the examination of Joyce's drafts and notebooks (17).

It thus follows that the purposes served by Attridge's historicizing perspective fall within the agenda of markedly postcolonial approaches to literature: the present (2000) imperative for "good" Joyce criticism is to respond to "the pressing need today to reassess the system of assumptions and values that have dominated [...] Western thought, Western politics, Western ethics, and Western culture." As long as

there is no set of values which can be taken as merely given, the task of refashioning social, philosophical, cultural, economic, and ethical tools is an urgent one. Accompanying [...] the process of decolonization [...] has been the technological revolution which has broken down many of the barriers that insulated the West for so long; these changes, too, demand new practices and new modes of thinking. (19-20)

In conclusion, when addressing the issue of the future of Joyce criticism, Attridge regards unpredictability as being at the heart of both the artistic and the critical project, and stresses the necessity of hindsight for any serious evaluation. Finally, the only certainty about future critical responses is that "they will be significantly different from the ones that command our attention as the millennium ends" (21).

VI

Milesi addresses Joyce's oeuvre from what he considers the best perspective, as "constantly trying to inform an evolutive linguistic poetics," one which "conditions, and therefore should remain central to, whatever interpretive avenue we choose to explore" (1). The "revolutionary" nature of Joyce's project, as well as the project of his criticism, is therefore to be viewed in its etymological sense of "coming round full circle," rather than "as an acclaim à la Jolas of Joyce's linguistic breakthroughs" (1-2). Joyce's re-fashioning of language is occupied with transcending national languages as well as national(ist) ideologies, and thus "cannot simply be seen as a purely aesthetic gesture," but rather as "a politicized pluridialect 'idioglossary' [...] with a universalist, translinguistic and well as transcultural, slant" (3-4). For this "joint poeticization and foreignization" of normative English goes hand in hand with

> a "political" awareness of the coerciveness of the "native" tongue, and exposing its own repressed foreign dimension through etymological recalls or syntactical manipulations conveying the idiosyncratic rhythms of *Dubliners'* speech was Joyce's way of devising a middle course of literary action between the imposed rigours of an English tradition and the artificially revived nationalist orthodoxies of Irish Gaelic. (5-6)

Joyce's is a middle ground between aesthetics and ethics, poetics and politics because paradoxically purity has, by the time of *Finnegans Wake*, become a thing of "mediation, with its political, ethical and even critical extensions" (6).

It is to these critical extensions that Milesi's argument turns here, echoing Derrida in his point that "one of the most original, "self-reflexive" traits in Joyce's last novel is its ability to pre-empt [...] the interested speculativeness of our various interpretive biases and the ideologies that underpin them," a canonical example of which would be I.5, the "Mamafesta" chapter, of the *Wake* (8). More concretely, the pre-emptive, anticipatory quality of Joyce's own artistic evolution is seen to have uncannily prefigured the gradual shift in Joyce scholars and readers from "an earlier focus on the mimetic powers and programme of/in Joyce's fictional language" to an recognition of "the assumptions underlying such a naïve belief in language's illusory mimetic and organic ability, including the ability to be the spearhead of fictional experimentation" (8-9). The revolutionary aspect of Joyce's writing, according to which its path of development could be seen as continuously revisiting, and re-writing, its previous stages, could be regarded as the critical "opening up within his literary idiom: for example, the self-conscious rewriting of Stephen Hero, the self-recyclings of Ulyssean prose in the novel's "second half," the *Scribbledehobble* Notebook and the Ur-project of reworking earlier texts as well as their critical receptions for *Finnegans Wake*" (9). What the Joycean reader, "poised halfway between Joyce's narrative insights and our critical afterthoughts, between production and consumption," is confronted with is "the necessity to set up a dialogue or 'translation' between Joyce's writings and our reading practices, a middle voice between Joyce's idiom and our own Joyceanized idioms" (10). An example of such a Joyceanized idiom, a critical vocabulary taking the "strategic middle course of action" already mentioned, is Fritz Senn's established practice of reading-as-translation, in which

> the stereotyped application or sounding out of the latest theories, soon to become new-fangled critical orthodoxies, would be profitably offset by the rewards from paying heed to the specifically Joycean exempla, which not only "oblige" us to devise methodological tools from the Irish writer's own verbal arsenal [...], but also empower us to do just that to creative and critical ends for theory "itself," in ways that overreach the usual osmotic moulding of one's critical language on the chosen writer. Only on these conditions can literature bounce back on/against "theory." (10)

What, for Milesi, is at stake in Joycean criticism, is that the critical discourses procured to come to terms with Joyce's texts must be "capable of taking the reading of the Joycean corpus beyond the imposition of preconstructed analytic grids and allowing the "theory" to be influenced and permeated by Joyce's own sophisticated idiom" (11).

Milesi proceeds to discuss three of these *critical idioms*—those of gender, nation and history, demonstrating what he terms the "Hermetic" importance of Joyce's "language with a difference" as a heuristic tool:

> just as Hermes stood at the crossroads as a mediator, messenger and agent of the Gods, holding the key to communication and interpretation, so can Joyce's innovative literary language be placed at the intersection of various critical fields (philosophy, linguistics/philology, gender, psychoanalysis, politics, postcolonialism, intertextuality, etc.) in order to challenge their demarcations and... cast their exemplarity into a different light. (11)

More specifically, Joycean feminist criticism, founded on the assumption of "the question of woman" as a touchstone of the issue of literary representation (as well as its critical mediations), has developed from "early considerations of women's representations within the Joycean corpus [...] to more rounded analyses of the whole palette of plural gendered and sexual positions occupied by both sexes in Joyce's texts"—a case in point of what Milesi identifies as the structural property of the critical movement "from patterns [...] to ambivalences" (11). This shift in focus is grounded in careful attention to the workings of language:

> The radicalization of sexual positions and gender constructions could not have been achieved without an exposure of stereotyped gendered language and the ruse of pronominal and syntactical indirections (12).

An illustrative instance of this would be "the ostentatious play on 'male' (consonantal) and 'female' (vocalic) rhythmic patterns in *Finnegans Wake*," where a more mature feminist and gender criticism must subvert this comfortable binary and take into account "the subtler inscriptions of "femininities"/"masculinities," homo- or bisexuality," understood "as performative effects in/through textuality" (12).

Milesi discusses the 1990s "critical shift towards issues of culture, history, ethics and politics, away from aesthetic reflections or considerations of 'textuality'" as sometimes sadly entailing "a waning attention to/awareness of the political constructedness of discursive effects in literature" and creating an unhealthy environment in which "reaffirming the centrality of language may wrongly be perceived as a reactionary step to the heyday of a supposedly depoliticized 'poststructuralism.'" Milesi insists on keeping in mind that

> [for] Joyce, politics (or ideology and history, for that matter) first and foremost materializes as "style", and to note how his exploration of the plurality of discourses within his fiction's intracritical vein [...] evinces the inescapably ethico-political dimension of artistic experimentation. (13)

The Joyce that emerges from within this critical reorientation (the most extreme example of which Milesi adduces is Emer Nolan's *James Joyce and Nationalism*) is one whose modernism forms a discourse "significantly analogous" to that of Irish nationalism, an overlap which is seen as "awkward" and "aporetic" in that it links "Modernism (with its felt tensions between cosmopolitanism and localism) or modernity (and its complicity with colonialism), and postcoloniality's ambivalent appeal to a politically problematic nationalism for purposes of emancipation" without taking into account "the issue of the 'linguistic politics' of Joyce's increasing polyglotism within his imagined fictions of an Irish community" (14), a synthetic idiom which apart from staging issues of (post)colonial supremacy can also be seen

> to perform the ambivalent condition of a lingua franca, at once bearing an uncanny affinity with the artificial tongues whose reductionist claims to universalism it also derides in the name of an avant-garde (modernist) aesthetic and recalling the dominant status of the English "language of the oppressor" for communicative, trading purposes. (14-5)

Milesi's positive example of a Joyceanized postcolonial approach would be the collection *Semicolonial Joyce*, where the restricted correspondence "between the neo-canonized postcolonial agendas and Joyce's texts fostered the need to inflect the mature Joycean advocacy of middle grounds in yet another direction: the Wakean semicolonial" (15).

Another relatively recent shift in Joyce criticism, the flourishing field of Joycean studies of popular culture, re-enacts Joyce's own evolution from the "detached, incorporeal aestheticism of Stephen" to "an openness towards, and re-embodiment of, popular consumer culture through a more earthy ad canvasser" in *Ulysses*, culminating in "the generalized collapse of low- and highbrow spheres in the transcultural polyphony of *Finnegans Wake*" (16). However, despite its avowed consubstantiality with Joyce's own career, Milesi's linguistic perspective raises one important reservation about the current practice of materialist studies of Joyce's culture, pointing out that

> there remains a more "linguistic" flavour of culture that new concerns with the socio-historico-economic realities of everyday consumption and popular culture fail to acknowledge: the indissociability of the cultural-ideological substrata from Joyce's processing them through variously thematized languages and idioms [in the Wake]. (16)

Finally, the thematic criticism of Joyce's complex, yet immensely significant relation to history, is a category placed by Milesi

> at the crossroads of the recent explosion of discourses on the excluded (sexual, colonial, racial, class, etc.) "Other," inter- or trans- disciplines/perspectives, hybridity and difference, and, in a more simplistic, dualistic scheme, envisaged as a patriarchal, imperialist logos to be subverted by the muthos of a reinventive writing by an androgynous artist. (17)

Particularly fashionable with the stream of New Historicism, or indeed of all "broadly cultural" perspectives, is the practice of re-positioning literary texts beyond their authors' own historical and fictional realities—examples of which are Robert Spoo's *James Joyce and the Language of History* which "details how nineteenth-century ideologies, rhetorics and styles of history impacted Joyce's early intellectual formation and are both figured and resisted in the Joycean text" (17), James Fairhall's *James Joyce and the Question of History*, or the edited volume entitled *James Joyce and the Subject of History*, whose "seductively ambivalent title" seeks to "encompass at once our primordiality as subjects of a process shaping our 'life stories' and the individuation of history 'itself' as subject beyond the prismatic distortions through which it is reductively apprehended" (18). However, for Milesi, this historicizing externalization yet again strays away from "the paradoxical historicity" at the core of the general (and Joyce's in particular) experience of fiction writing which "demonstrates how history is indissociable from its recreations as/in fictional narratives. History may well be (also) language but language is definitely not history..." (19).

The question remains whether these "increasingly hybrid theoretical reconfigurations" of Joyce's writing were the natural extensions of "a broadly interdisciplinary, more pluralistic, critical climate," or whether "Joyce's own texts demonstrably stimulated such fruitful cross-fertilizations," a question unsolvable in terms of the narrowed perspective of Milesi's edited collection. However, he remains an outspoken opponent of the practice of recent discourses that "risk reducing the issue of performance and process back to thematic representations and reference," an example of which would be Joseph Valente's *Quare Joyce*, a collection that "remains operative at the level of a singular programmatic catchword" (19).

In conclusion, Milesi notes that what fundamentally all these variegated theoretical concerns come down to is a continuous engagement in raising

> unanswered—and perhaps unanswerable—questions to the nature of (re)reading as a historically motivated act of external (re)appropriation, itself not devoid of ethico-political or at least ideological implications, or "genuine" heuristic discovery. (20)

The one most prominent question begged by this process of theoretical commodius vicus of revisionism is "whether, in renewed protocols of reading, each generation of critics domesticates literary works in order to vindicate its own critical agendas or whether it (also) exhumes so far hidden traces inherent in the artist's productions that had gone unnoticed until the emergence of the appropriate critical slant" (20). It is ultimately theory as *bearing witness*, producing a *testimony*—in the sense mentioned above—to the textual operations and historical conditions of the Joycean text, that emerges as the imperative of Milesi's sustained analysis.

VII

This study then informed as it is by Attridge's and Milesi's succinct, far-reaching and yet internally consistent examinations, sets out to add one important particularizing corrective to the general view sketched above by claiming that all of the major approaches (criticized by Milesi on grounds of their shared ignorance of their own blind spots and oblivion of the essentially linguistic character of the object of their study) are, in the best work they have yielded, always already aware of the importance of being "Joyceanized."

As mentioned above, the work is split into two parts, the former engaged with major theoretical conceptual frameworks, the latter focusing on crucial thematic concerns, of the Joyce criticism of the last quarter of a century. Since all of the following chapters deal solely with Joyce criticism (mostly) after 1984, it also remains for this introduction to serve as a general overview of the genealogy, terminology, and methodology of the theoretical discourses brought to bear upon criticism's coming to terms with Joyce. In accordance with the supplementary function it seeks to have, this introduction will be utterly indispensable in that it will outline a broader picture in which to view the contemporary concerns of Joyce studies, while at the same time being perfectly dispensable, since all of the works discussed in individual chapters shall introduce their own theoretical apparatus in their own right. This broader picture will be provided by synthesizing and summarizing the work done in a variety of secondary critical literature, referenced in the concluding bibliography. It is necessary at this point to single out one particularly useful source relied on throughout: the ground-laying work done by the many contributors to the *Johns Hopkins Guide to Literary Theory* must be acknowledged as informing the following overview.[10]

The first chapter aims to assess how Joyce has fared when exposed to the particular method of textual analysis known as deconstruction which when practiced by its leading practitioner Jacques Derrida would be marked by a focus on binary oppositions within a (literary or other) text, with the threefold intention of showing how those oppositions are structured hierarchically, of overturning these in preferring the underprivileged term, and of displacing this reversed hierarchy in a non-hiearchichal relation of "difference."

Difference in the broadest sense is meant to oppose the concept of *presence* on which Derrida perceives Western metaphysics to have founded its crucial notions such as truth, being, identity and reality, all of which are constituted by the presence of voice (as opposed to writing based on absence), consciousness (as opposed to the repressed unconscious determination), and subjectivity (opposing the disregarded other). The relationship of difference undoes hierarchy, installing instead the relation that Derrida calls *supplementation*, by which he understands the process of how every privileged member of such binaries defers its meaning, or indeed comes to be constituted by what it suppresses in opposition; in other words, how every presence comes into being by making possible, at its very heart, a lapse into its seeming opposite. An example of this would be Derrida's critique of Ferdinand de Saussure, taken by many to herald the advent of poststructuralism at the end of the 1960s. However, Derrida has not been concerned with postulating, let alone promulgating a new law of sorts with which to substitute the laws of the past; rather, what he aims to show is how Saussure's discourse *deconstructs itself* in the first place.

Saussure's linguistic system has been famously theorized as conceiving of language on the basis of three fundamental assumptions: the *systematic* nature of language (*langue versus parole*); the *relational* conception of the elements of language (*signifiant versus signifié*); and the *arbitrary nature* of linguistic elements. Derrida's poststructuralist critique of this structure lies not only in his subversion of de Saussure's privileging of speech over writing by the introduction of the term *différance* (relevant in this context because of how writing contains a differentiation that is absent from speech, thus gaining precedence). More importantly, Derrida's intervention can be explained within the methodological framework of structuralism first fully articulated by Saussure by its emphasis on how the *relational* and *arbitrary* characteristics of signifying phenomena both

[10] Michael Groden and Martin Kreiswirth, eds., *Johns Hopkins Guide to Literary Theory* (Baltimore and London: Johns Hopkins University Press, 1994).

call for and also breach the third assumption of structuralism, its *systematicity*. Given that language can use *anything* to articulate its meanings, any "structure" can be recontextualised (relationally and arbitrarily)—Saussure's binary of the signifier and the signified (where the latter is preferred at the expense of the former) does not hold, for the signified can be taken for another signifier, and from there *ad infinitum*. Provided that signs acquire linguistic value only insofar as they are opposed to, and differentiated from other signs, then the binary relation disintegrates into a plurality of differences, and every word's "reference" must necessarily take into account its own "difference"; which, however, is already included in Saussure's theory itself, positing as it does language as composed of *differences without positive terms*. In this light, the two global aims of language described by Saussure—the "articulation" and "communication" of meaning, the structural "processes" and "products" of language—are mutually incongruent and incompatible.

The reason for treating this matter in such detail is to highlight what Derrida has repeatedly stressed himself, that deconstruction comes into being *with*, or better still, *within* the workings of textuality, by means of the double action of identifying and overthrowing the binary oppositions on which what Derrida terms the *logocentrism* of Western logic relies, seeking not to destruct (as it has been accused) meaning, but to expose it as an arbitrary effect of writing, understood as difference-making. The most influential "application" of Derrida's philosophy (insofar as what it does is to show that philosophy's reliance on systematicity, the notion of there being "a philosophy" is highly problematic) has taken place in the USA, within the so-called Yale School of criticism, whose key proponents have taken different cues from Derrida in order to analyze the particular nature of literary discourse: most prominently, Geoffrey Hartman (the priority of the signifier over the signified, the textualisation of consciousness, and the rhetoric of form); J. Hillis Miller (entering deconstruction through language itself, the "groundless ground" of words) and Paul de Man, perhaps the most radical deconstructionist preoccupied among other things with the "allegory of reading," meaning the text's reflexive awareness of itself as a system of rhetorical figures. It follows that given its very nature (that is, within texts of all sorts of origins, ideologies, or purposes), deconstruction has impacted the whole spectrum of critical discourses, most importantly feminist thought (deconstructing the male/female binary on precisely these terms), psychoanalysis (the conscious/unconscious binary), postcolonial discourse (colonizer/colonized, hybridity). It also might have been precisely due to its omnipresence that some of its radical impact had been felt by the early 1990s as having worn itself out, as if neutralized by its omnipresence, and its seeming ignorance of what had come to be increasingly perceived, in the decolonized, increasingly globalised world, as criticism's imperative attention to historical and material embeddedness of literature within the broader social processes and mechanisms.

It was precisely this self-inquisitive character of the deconstructive forays into Joyce's writing that has spurred its most fruitful engagements with a writer increasingly perceived (and acknowledged as such by Derrida himself on a number of occasions) as engaged, in his dealings with and appropriation of literary discourse, with exactly the deconstructive practices which Derrida identified in his philosophical and theoretical predecessors. Chapter I will be devoted to the work following (and in one exceptional case preceding) Derrida's seminal 1984 Frankfurt address, exploring how (a point raised by Derek Attridge) "deconstructive criticism of Joyce," just like Stephen's *amor matris*, involves a genitive that is undecidably double. The history of deconstructive criticism of Joyce after Derrida's personal intervention, followed in Chapter I, starting with the seminal collection *Poststructuralist Joyce*, involved a flurry of both theoretically sound and merely fashionable deconstructive criticism throughout the 1980s, culminating with the 1988 publication of Attridge's *Peculiar Language*. The "Irish turn" of the mid-1990s marked also a turn away from deconstruction, which was not revisited until the end of the decade—a revision both scathing and appreciative. However, the chapter concludes by surveying two recent contributions to the discussion, both of which convincingly voice the belief that much work still can and hopefully will be done in the field.

Chapter II charts out how the psychoanalytic approach was impacted upon by a crucial poststructuralist intervention into Joyce (or, which amounts to the same thing, a crucial Joycean intervention into poststructuralist psychoanalysis): the Lacanian psychoanalysis. Since not all of the approaches examined in the chapter deal exclusively with Lacan, a brief genealogy of psychoanalytic theory and criticism will contextualize Lacan's allegiance with, and his radical break from, the tradition preceding his intervention.

Psychoanalytic theory and criticism evolved in three roughly distinctive periods. The early traditional period was marked by its assumption of a relative transparency between the text and the author, the former being read as expressive of the latter's unconscious make-up. Such is the overriding supposition of the vast critical work of for example Ernest Jones, the author of the seminal Freud biography and his prominent English translator (*Hamlet and Oedipus*, 1948). The middle period (understood thematically rather than chronologically) was devoted to the revision of some of the implications of this central assumption of transparency. In identifying what might be called a psychoanalytic observer paradox, Simon O. Lesser was among the first American critics who argued that the experience of reading (that is interpreting) should be grasped in psychoanalytic terms, by means of the dyad of fantasy and defence. This was taken a step further by Norman N. Holland (in *The Dynamics of Literary Response*) in the devising of a reader-response theory based on the central postulate that the reader experiences literature as a transformation of the material of unconscious fantasy.

Finally, Lacan's intervention was undertaken with two primary goals: to rebel against the approach of the prevalent ego psychology and its stress on the ego as a stable entity (seen as a betrayal of Freud), and to redefine the ego on linguistic-semantic grounds, re-conceiving the unconscious in semiotic terms as structured *like* a language. In literary theory, Lacan's approach was quick to resound in feminist criticism, especially due to its emphasis on sexual difference and Freud's mismanagement of the non-Oedipal development of the female ego (proponents of which shall be discussed later on), as well as Marxist cultural studies criticism, dealing as it did with the material(ist) constitution of the human ego, the human subjectivity as centred around a lack, and the complex implication of the desire of the self within the desire of the other. As proponents, one should at least mention Shoshana Felman, whose *Jacques Lacan and the Adventure of Insight* aims to bring pedagogy into psychoanalysis by showing the importance of teaching in relation to the pupil's *unmeant knowledge*, and Gilles Deleuze and Félix Guattari's vastly influential project of critiquing psychoanalysis as such in order to transform it, or better still, destroy it by unmasking its ideological embeddedness within the bourgeois culture from which it sprang. This is done by and large through a threefold critical agenda: exposing the nature of repression and castration as intrinsic to psychoanalytic machinery; critiquing the psychoanalytic conception of the unconscious as static being instead of a dynamic *becoming*; and exposing the situatedness of discourse within the hegemony of the Oedipal narrative.

Let us however remain with Jacques Lacan for a while, and introduce his work in at least some further detail with regard to his late forays into Joyce. It is not without significance that his earliest psychoanalytic work focused on the treatment of patients suffering from what psychiatrists call "automatism" or *délires à deux*, a condition in which it was supposed that their speech or writing was governed by an unseen but omnipotent force beyond their control. In his seminal paper on "The Function and Field of Speech in Psychoanalysis," Lacan postulates his two famous strategies of psychoanalytic treatment, the "short session" and the "analyst's abstention," both of which are meant to evade what he discerned as the fundamental danger of psychoanalytic praxis: the patient's liability to identify with the analyst and to attribute an independent objectivity to that identification, or what Lacan elsewhere refers to as transference, which must be contested on account of its sustenance of the ego's illusionary coherence. Lacan's revision of Freud takes place on a poststructuralist revision of de Saussure (as charted out above) in that the unconscious, famously said to be "structured like a language," is governed entirely by the order of the signifier rather than by some independent realm of what has undergone repression. In this light, even the Oedipal moment constitutive of sexual identity happens linguistically, as an option of either accepting or rejecting the signifier in place of the object or the imaginary other, a displacement possible due to, as de Saussure had identified it, its

entirely arbitrary relation to the signified. This split or necessary substitution, structured along the subject's passage from the pre-Oedipal order of
the Real unity with the (m)other, to the mirror-stage of the Imaginary self-
(mis)identification, to the Symbolic order of permanent linguistic displacement and deferral by its very nature, introduces lack as the defining
principle, not only of subjectivity as such, but of its fundamental relation
to the other, its desire of the other.

In the present context, then, Chapter II presents what critical activity
has been elicited by the late Lacanian intervention into, and preoccupation
with Joyce, which is at once a crucial Joycean intervention into Lacan. In
this respect, what Lacanian psychoanalysis had come to term the *symptomaticity* of Joyce's writing (which, in order to distinguish it from the
key pretext of its rewriting, the Freudian symptom, Lacan has in a consciously Joycean fashion renamed *le sinthome*); its exploration of the
Wake-an idiom in terms of the *lalangue*, the language of the mad; and
most importantly, its reconceptualisation of the missing connecting link
that ties together the three Borromean knots of the three orders of experience—the Imaginary, the Symbolic, and the Real—not as the Name-of-
the-Father of Lacan's earlier phase, but as Joyce's name, the symptom
(or, *le sinthome*).

All these brought about essential changes within Lacan's own theory
and practice of psychoanalysis, and considerably contributed to a groundbreaking departure from the traditional practice of literary psychoanalysis.
As has been convincingly shown by (among others) the recent work of
the Lacanian Joycean Luke Thurston, Lacan's notion of Joyce as *pas-à-
lire*, not-to-be-read, designates a radical break from the common practice
of psychologising literature from various vantage points—most notably, of
the biographically authorial, or generally linguistic—and shakes the very
foundations of psychoanalysis, reminding it of its own complicity with
literature as a practice embedded in and inseparable from language, both
in its spoken (therapeutic) and written (theoretical) form. It has been the
field of Lacanian psychoanalysis that has posed perhaps the most radical
challenge to the all-too-simple *and* "between" Joyce and theory.

Another significant theoretical current crucially informed by deconstruction during the 1980s is Joycean feminism and gender studies, as it
too underwent a major shift under the impact of French theory and the
work of its French practitioners (both female—Julia Kristeva, Hélène
Cixous, or Luce Irigaray—but also male: most crucially, Derrida). This
major transformation marked a decisive departure from literary feminism's
early concerns with on a basic level the writing and personal careers of
female writers or, even more essentially, the personal opinions on the
"female issue" of the individual authors (particularly exasperating in
Joyce's case), or more sophisticatedly with examining the issues of literary representation of the oppressed female and the degree of its self-
awareness of its own complicity with or subversion of the ideological
instruments of that oppression.

Joyce ranked highly in some of the earliest feminist literary criticism as one of the few male voices to be summoned to relate the familial, vocational, and artistic experiences of women characters in a period marked by such influential projects as Elaine Showalter's gynocritics, establishing a "female framework" for the analysis of women's literature in order to develop new models for the study of specifically female experience, in refusal of the hitherto dominant male ones (a self-contained platform regarded as problematic by later critics). To say that "Joyce ranked high" is to commit an unwitting pun, however, for his place in the work of prominent early feminists Sandra Gilbert and Susan Gubar—*The Madwoman in the Attic* (1979) and *No Man's Land* (1988)—is anything but a place of honour: Joyce is scathingly criticised for his avowed misogyny and his crippling, reductive representation of female characters.[11]

However, a radical turn in evaluation comes with the feminist adoption of poststructuralist deconstruction, taking as its cue the premise that gender difference dwells in language itself rather than the referent (Lacanian influence is palpable here as well) and proceeding to conduct a series of interventions from within what has come to be redefined as phallogocentrism, with the aim of resisting and contesting the patriarchal discourse of phallic authority. This is most radically done in the work of Luce Irigaray, especially her theoretical departure (however much betrayed by some of her practical applications) from the stressed impossibility of any "evasion" (as Showalter would believe) of male discourse, and the imperative need to "infect" it from within.

The very influential and oft-mentioned concept of *écriture feminine*, as coined by Julia Kristeva and developed by Hélène Cixous (both of whom have had direct dealings with the writings of Joyce)—even though it does reflect the linguistic turning away from the lived empirical "real," together with Monique Wittig's project of "lesbianisation of language" or Irigaray's own exploration of "anti-scopophilism" of the female desire—can be (and has been, most prominently by Hélène Wenzel or Toril Moi) criticised on the same grounds: as an essentialisation rather than deconstruction of the male/female binarism, reinstating what it sets out to dismantle. This in turn has led to a redefinition, or rather de-definition of the woman, which for Julia Kristeva has ceased to "exist" as a gender category, as a mode of being, turning into a processual series of variously (psychologically as well as socially) shaped identifications. It is also on these grounds of the female as a socially determined (and individually adopted or resisted) product that the various materialist feminisms, succeeding the feminism of the 1970s French theory, have conducted their historico-theoretical analyses, oftentimes adopting a politically committed stance, whether it be either a traditionally outright Marxist (Juliet Mitchell already in the 1960s), or a more contemporarily influential postcolonial one (Donna Harraway, Gayatri Chakravorty Spivak in the 1990s).

---

[11] For more see Roughley's *James Joyce and Critical Theory*, 122-6.

Chapter III details how Joycean feminism dealt with the crucial feature of the impact of deconstruction (as well as of Lacanian psychoanalysis), along with the broader transformation under the sweeping wave of materialist cultural criticism toward the previous feminist positivist slant, reverting, however, after a revolution which prevented any simplistic return to the former state of affairs. The historical framework of the chapter begins in Frankfurt again with the keynote address on "Joyce the Gracehoper" by none other than Julia Kristeva, and then goes on to trace the deconstructivist tradition of the late 1980s, culminating in the 1990 publication of Suzette Henke's main work followed by the postcolonial/historical "turn" toward more materialist readings of how Joyce's texts interrogate the social and political givens of female status, especially as part of the Irish postcolonial situation.

The crucial questions and concerns of feminist criticism shall be "Joyceanized" below. No longer is the main issue what Joyce said or thought about women nor how his depiction is or is not faithful and objective. Instead, we might outline the most pressing questions as follows. How does the patriarchical dominance of male characters over the repressed female bespeak the broader agenda of Joyce's socio-political critique? How does Joyce's exploration of "polymorphously perverse" sexuality work toward the same? What purposes does Joyce's preoccupation with homosociality and homosexuality serve? Perhaps most significantly of all, we must ask ourselves whether his often-praised masterful depiction of the female other is an act of its violent appropriation and subjection to the male order of his art, or on the contrary an act of respectful preservation of the other as other and its liberation? Indeed, does this "preservation" really entail liberation? Even more fundamentally, can and should one even speak of the male and the female in any productive or even legitimate way when dealing with a work whose main protagonist is hailed as "the new womanly man"? Bearing these key questions in mind, Chapter III strives to provide an overview of the current state of debates within feminist and gender studies, and the varied ramifications of his peculiar treatment of sexuality.

Crucial in the critical reorientation of the late-1980s and early-1990s toward a historico-materialist criticism was the wide stream of cultural studies, divided into two broad branches—English and American—whose genealogies and agendas should be at least briefly overviewed at this point. Taking its crucial impetus from Raymond Williams' 1958 groundbreaking work, *Culture and Society: 1780-1950*, the key argument of which was that the *whole* of its production is indispensable for any study of culture, the British cultural studies project has been concerned from its inception with bringing the hitherto underprivileged field of so-called popular (or, in a tellingly pejorative way, *low*) culture within the scope of critical analysis.

Despite its later anti-deconstructivist turn, the incipient challenge to the binary opposition between high and popular was conducted from significantly poststructuralist perspectives—here, the film theory of the journal *Screen* and its main proponents, Stephen Heath and Colin Mac-Cabe (both prominent Joyceans, instrumental in introducing the French Joyce of deconstruction into the English-speaking Joyce studies) would be an obvious point of reference. Its theoretical outlook was also crucially formed by a fusion of Marxism and psychoanalysis, as delivered in the reading of Lacan through Marx in Louis Althusser's *Ideology and Ideological States Apparatuses*, whose crucial concept of "interpellation" became a most useful tool in analysing the dialectical relationship between the workings of ideology upon the illusorily independent individual subjectivity. In the art-focused discussion, then, the question was how a (literary) work of art (itself seen as an ideological construct) addressed its recipient and what subject positions it offered. In this connection, Stuart Hall's influential 1980 essay "Cultural Studies: The Two Paradigms" identified the two prevailing traditions as "culturalist" and "structuralist," where the former gives prominence to the empirical subject (in the present context, the "actual" reader), whose dealing with the text participates in a broadly-conceived social and historical process, whereas the latter's emphasis is on the other direction: on how the text´s participation in—or subversion of—ideology addresses, or interpellates, the reader. Ideology here is related to Antonio Gramsci's concept of *hegemony* as an ideological set of practices *negotiated* between the ruling class and subordinate blocs of society. However, this dual conception of meaning as (culturalist) *event* and/or (structuralist) *structure* cannot be levelled and is to remain in disjunctive tension, which is restraining at the same time as it is productive.

The American branch of cultural studies, apart from the many commonalities, differed from the British approach in that unlike its institutionalized structure (the CCCS in Birmingham, founded in 1964 by Richard Hoggart), American cultural studies evolved by means of critical inquiries into the broad cultural gamut undertaken by individual, and usually apostatical figures. Indeed, one possible marker of American criticism is its sustained analysis of institutionalism as ideological agent, both productive and disseminative of knowledge and instrumental in its officialisation. Leslie Fiedler's deconstruction of the concept of the "Great American Novel" or Edward Said's courageous if controversial blend of cultural studies with the emergent field of postcolonial theory (his 1978 *Orientalism*) would be examples of this shared effort. However, the launch at the end of the 1980s of the new journal *Cultural Studies* under the guidance of a broad international editorial board indicates best how—unlike in the case of the Anglo-French divide in feminist studies—the differences along the Atlantic divide are rather of degree than of kind.

Analogously, the crucial project of the cultural studies of Joyce was a revision of the view of Joyce (furthered mainly by his contemporaries and the New Critical or broadly humanist wave of the 1930s and 1940s criticism) as the high modernist aesthete serving with devotion and resolution his own artistic project with nothing but contempt for the mass popular, into a Joyce-the-high-priest-of-popular-culture, including its technological progress and ideological apparatuses. Its anti-deconstructionist contextualization of Joyce's text within the historically positivist reality is, however, challenged not only by its re-enactment of Joyce's own textual gesture, as Milesi has observed. To take just one example here, its project engaged in a re-reading of Joyce within the critical framework of Mikhail Bakhtin is undermined both by its deceptive easiness and fitness on the one hand, and by the strange omission of Joyce within the Bakhtinian corpus on the other—two issues of most relevance for any serious Joyce-Bakhtinian engagement.

Questions that should be further dealt with include among others those concerning the ideological purport of Joyce's employment of the popular culture of his time. Is it, as has been rather facilely suggested on various occasions, merely a corroboration of his democratization of culture, or can there be residua of hierarchisation present within this popular context? Furthermore, how is this democratization to be accounted for in the context of Joyce's modernity? These issues are addressed in Chapter IV.

Contextualizing Joyce within the popular culture of his time led to a recontextualisation of Joyce at the turn of the 1980s within the culture, society, and politics of his space, particularly the space he desperately escaped from in his life, yet gratefully inhabited within his art—Ireland. Chapter V traces the general transformation of Irish studies into studies of the (post)colonial status of Ireland, and its marked impact upon Joyce studies.

Postcolonial studies, according to a wide consensus, constitutes a momentous intervention in the widespread revisionist project that has impacted academia since the 1960s, and has come to dominate the field in the late 1980s. It countered the post-WWII academia the Western preoccupation with the institutionalisation of modernism with a dissident voice raised from the "third world." Chinua Achebe's 1958 *Things Fall Apart* was instrumental in sparking the major developments in this critical formulation in the 1960s, together with Franz Fanon's prominent work *The Wretched of the Earth*. In regard to Walter Rodney's famous observation that "to be colonized is to be removed from history," the central project of postcolonial studies can be described as a continuous effort to reinstate the dissident voice of the colonised back into Europe-fashioned history. Given the sheer breath of both its methodology and specific (geography-related) agenda, postcolonial studies appears not so much a discipline as a distinctive problematic, centred around structural resemblances of such discourses as Latin American, African, or Caribbean studies, as well as minority discourse, studies of subalterity and so on.

Following the seminal collection representing the state of the debate at the end of the 1980s, *The Empire Writes Back: Theory and Practice in Post-Colonial Literatures* (1989), one can identify the broader purpose of the studies in a critical examination of the totality of texts that participate in hegemonising other cultures, as well as of texts that write back to correct or undo this hegemonisation. The *post*-ness of Postcolonialism, as is the case with many other such prefixes, is a problematic notion serving—if one were pressed to assign it a function—to align the stream with the overall post-ness of poststructuralist theoretical currents. In this respect, of interest is the often-stressed fact that key figures such as Sartre, Althusser, Derrida, Lyotard, and Cixous were all either born in Algeria or became personally involved with the war.

This general *post*-ness however poses problems regarding the political valency and effectiveness of the approach, since every homogenization involves a blurring of lines of difference from which to conduct critique. Thus, two branches can be discerned, one that homogenizes and treats postcolonial writing as resistance (Spivak or Said), and the other which foregrounds the irreducibility of local difference and opposes any unitary treatment of postcolonial writing (most notably, Homi Bhabha). However, a more relevant division line is to be drawn between the Euro-American academia which also comprises originally Third-World thinkers (such as Spivak, Said, or Bhabha) and the "authentic" Third-World thinkers who adamantly defy their homogenizing tendencies (Aija Ahmad's critique of Said's *Orientalism* is a case in point). In its ideal form, thus, postcolonial studies performs a dialogue presenting an important corrective to the Occidental paradigm of ideologically constructed and politically effected supremacy, a dialogue in which, contrary to postmodernist concerns with the end of history, the discourse of the historically specific aims to oppose what it perceives as the prevalent aestheticisation of postmodern politics and the poststructuralist lack of critical political engagement.

Chapter V presents an overview of the various postcolonial repositionings, the likes of which Milesi has discussed above, whose value as either enriching re-interpretations or dogmatic misappropriations must be ascertained on a case-by-case basis. However, the purpose of the chapter lies in paying close attention to a few cagey voices which raise questions as to the legitimacy of the whole postcolonial project as "applied" to Joyce's case. In what sense can an author of Joyce's stature be claimed for the cause of minor literature? What is the ideological justification for it, and which sides benefit from the exchange? Does not Joyce's status of in-betweenness do disservice to postcolonial studies, obscuring as it must through its overwhelming influence the work of other, genuinely subaltern voices? Furthermore, what is a genuinely subaltern voice—and how can it be addressed by the methods and tools of the institution of literary criticism based in the West?

These then are the five different critical approaches to Joyce that have shaped Joyce criticism over the last quarter of a century. The second part of the work examines how these various critical positions have viewed some of the thematic concerns of Joyce's work. First, its concern with and departures from the artistic and ideological framework of its own literary period—Chapter VI on (post)modernist Joyce—with the crucial figures of the theoretical (as well as directly Joyce-related) debate being Ihab Hassan and Jean-Francois Lyotard. This is then followed by an investigation into Joyce's sustained engagement with the issue of history as shaping both his contemporary condition and his artistic vision (Chapter VII)—the contemporary influence of the New Historicist movement on the study of history is palpable in the selected examples. Chapter VIII examines the critical work dealing with Joyce's own personal and artistic commitments within the field of literary politics and the response they have solicited from politically committed literary criticism—whether along the lines of the avant-garde "revolution of the world," or as part of outright Leftist or Marxist interventions. Chapter IX on "Technicity, Media & Hypertext" presents theoretical work that has revisited Joyce's modernity and his artistic project with a particular sensitivity to its embeddedness in the increasingly technological condition of his era, an aspect of modernity regarded as anticipating the hyper-technologised condition of our contemporariness—the high-priest of digital culture, Marshall McLuhan, as well as his colleagues from the field of media and hypertext theory (Walter J. Ong, David Jay Bolter, and others) leave discernible traces on the overall debate. Departing from the stress on the particularly technological nature of Joyce's modernity, Chapter X maps out the specifically technological nature of Joyce's writing itself, mapping the currently prevalent approach to Joyce's texts, textual genetics—a sustained critical attention to the creative process and textual development of Joyce's works before they became "works"—in their pre-publication state.

Textual genetics it will be argued has become so dominant recently not only due to the sheer vastness of Joyce's notebook and manuscript archive, but also because of the way it synthesizes, in perhaps the Joyceanized way called for by Milesi, the attention to the very material, technological condition of Joyce's art—the word in its constant movement away from and back toward itself in the endless deferral of its meaning on the semantic level, and the word in its state of always already being someone else's, Joyce's word as quotation with a difference on the literary level—with a broad concern with the cultural gamut of its era from which it springs, both attesting to the particular anomaly of Joyce the creator, as well as to the great potential of Joyceanized theory in a critical coming to terms with his art.

Zürich-London-Genève-Zürich
August 2007 – August 2009

1. Deconstruction

I

Arguably, the most important herald within the Anglo-American Joyce studies of the to-be-dominant deconstructionist practice of reading Joyce's texts in the early 1980s was Colin MacCabe's 1978 Cambridge doctoral dissertation, *James Joyce and the Revolution of the Word*.[1] Its fundamental presupposition, already inherent to the work's title which echoes Eugène Jolas' seminal 1929 essay, is that "the relation between politics and language [...] is of relevance to the works of James Joyce [...], for Joyce's writing produces a change in the relations between reader and text, a change which has profound revolutionary implications" (1). MacCabe points to the difficulty which Joyce's writing presents for the practice, or indeed the sheer possibility, of literary criticism, its "metamorphosis and displacement" presenting critical discourse "with its own impossibility," since "interpretation as the search for meaning must cease when both meaning and interpreter become functions of the traverse of the material of language" (2). Thus, in MacCabe's view, it is through the encroachment upon the relation between reader and text, one "on which literary criticism is predicated," that Joyce's writing renders literary criticism ineffectual. This very binary in turn rests on the central category of critical discourse, that of the subject, for literary criticism "depends on a theory of the subject in order to carry out its task of interpretation." However, Joyce's texts "refuse the subject any dominant position from which language could be tallied with experience" in that *Ulysses* and *Finnegans Wake* for example deal not with the representation of experience through language, but rather with the experience of language by means of destroying representation. For MacCabe, "if the literary critic is interested in meaning, Joyce's texts are concerned with the various positions from which meaning becomes possible" (4). It should be clear by now that the literary criticism whose impossibility vis-à-vis Joyce's writing MacCabe seeks to thematise is the one rooted in the modernist New Critical tradition, the humanistic criticism of the Leavisian "great tradition" that sought to do away with Joyce's experimentalism in the first place.

However, MacCabe does not postulate the crisis of the meta-literary critical mimesis only from the position of a Derridean deconstruction of

---

[1] Colin MacCabe, *James Joyce and the Revolution of the Word* (New York: Palgrave, 1978; 2003).

the reading subject. Just as Margot Norris' pioneering study[2] had combined its structuralist (and in its last chapter poststructuralist) method with Freudian treatment of the dreamwork in poetic terms, the other important theoretical anchoring of MacCabe's argument is Lacanian psychoanalysis, which had already made its formative impact on Joyce studies at the Paris symposium in 1975. The particular kind of Lacanianism used by MacCabe employs its "talking cure" to reveal the unconscious as an unavoidable effect of the human subject's entry into the symbolic order of signification—thus, its primary relevance to James Joyce studies is seen as consisting in its sustained attempt "to redirect attention to language as the primary material of the psychoanalytic method" (5). If for Freud the unconscious appears a secondary result of a conscious decision to repress the conscious experience, and moreover, the importance of the fundamentally linguistic relation between the analyst and the analysand, for Lacan, the unconscious is

> a necessary consequence of the fact that the conditions of the possibility of language are both present and absent in any moment of speech [...]; present as the differences that constitute the existence of meaning, the system of language is necessarily absent from that meaning (that moment of consciousness). (6)

It is this interplay between meaning as presence and absence (what Derrida, in another context, has termed *différance*), which ensures the functioning of language, and shapes human subjectivity as a desiring one. A crucial Lacanian moment of MacCabe's interpretation is his insistence that the text be conceived of as "the articulation of the possibilities of experience, these possibilities being another name for the limits of our language" (7). It is precisely on the basis of this Lacanian typology of texts according to the positions offered to the reader that MacCabe posits the effect of Joyce's texts in their thwarting a meta-critical position.

Difficulties with MacCabe's sound oppositional approach arise when he pitches Joyce's writing practice against what he all-too-reductively regards as "classic realism" (and for whose illustrative example he picks the all-but-classically-realistic George Eliot), formed as it was "in those multitudes of contemporary practices which reproduce and sustain an ideology of realism" (27).[3] Against this, MacCabe posits Joyce's constructed absence of such a dominant discourse "which places such emphasis on the reader," thereby reinstating the clearly defined boundary his argument had sought to dismantle (28). To support this statement, MacCabe turns in a surprisingly biographical gesture to Joyce's letters to Richards. According to MacCabe the dialogue in his "Ivy Day in the Committee Room" is "suspended in a vacuum of sense, a vacuum that must

[2] Margot Norris, *The Decentered Universe of 'Finnegans Wake': A Structuralist Analysis* (Baltimore: Johns Hopkins University Press, 1974).
[3] For more on the critique aimed at MacCabe's reductionism in this issue, see Brooker, 160-5.

be filled by the reader" (29), and that therefore the whole of *Dubliners* comes to be seen as a collection of "stereotypes without any discourse that will contain or resolve them" (30).

Perhaps more convincingly, MacCabe discerns a Joycean tendency of augmentation of ambiguity (and "perversity," for in a side-note later on echoed in many a sustained analysis of Joycean sexuality[4] MacCabe observes that "perversion is the fundamental mode of sexuality in Joyce") by looking at the pre-publication history of his early *Dubliners* stories, especially "The Sisters." In his later addition of the famous opening paragraph with the by-now notorious floating signifiers of *paralysis*, *gnomon*, and *simony*, Joyce introduced "a set of signifiers for which there is no interpretation except strangeness and an undefined evil"—this lack of the possibility of interpretation also thwarting any sort of meta-language which would mediate "the gap between the utterance, the act of signification [...], and the proposition, what is signified" (34). To sum up, there is no position within Joyce's texts where "the reading subject can insert itself to consume some paralysed reality," and thus the reading subject must "follow the positions taken up by the writing subject and in the split thus instituted can begin to read its own discourses [...] as a set of significant oppositions in which the subject's world is constituted and in which [...] it can hear its desire speak" (37). It is this dangerous proximity, verging on indiscernibility, between the writing and the reading subject, that prevents an analysis of his text from being "constructed in terms of some external truth which the text represents or embodies," but rather in terms of the lines of force constitutive of the text, which engage with those same forces in our own discourse—or, in MacCabe's words, "truth is no longer correspondence but struggle" (38).

Having laid out his crucial main points and charted out their theoretical background, MacCabe proceeds to discuss the individual instances of the creation of various subject-positions within the Joycean text. Regarding Joyce's earliest novelistic attempts he observes that in *Stephen Hero*, "the neutral narrative is time and again interrupted by discourse and these interruptions destroy the very possibility of narrative," but what is regarded as a difficulty here becomes "the constitutive principle of *A Portrait*," a text which is in itself a "montage of discourses" and "refuses to tell stories" (64). It is this structure of self-contradiction that MacCabe identifies with "the structure of perversion" (66). *Ulysses* is dealt with first through the prism of "The Sirens" episode, whose famous opening 58 phrases (only 57 of which are repeated later on in the episode's text) stage "the interplay of letters and words as material" which "refuse all possible meaning," since "words without context cannot be read in terms of meaning because words derive their meaning [...] from their position in regard to other words." What, to MacCabe's mind, the overture to "The

[4] Most consistently, in Richard Brown's *James Joyce and Sexuality* (see Chapter III "Feminism, Sexuality & Gender Studies," section III).

Sirens" brings to the fore is the differential definition of the word to which it defers for its meaning:

> [A] word is defined in terms of difference: the different letters that go to make it up, the different words that surround it, and this difference is a difference which is activated across time and space through reading. (80)

Despite its musical technique of *fuga per canonum* and its concern with the aural properties of words (as uttered and/or sung), "The Sirens" is seen as decomposing the power of the voice and sound into the play of material (textual) difference—it is Bloom whose writing (his clandestine letter to Martha Clifford) stages "a dramatization of the materiality of language" which "subverts any notion of a full presence in the act of reading through an attention to, and dramatization of, the exteriority and the materiality of writing" (83-4). This complex interaction between the discourses of the reader and those of the text finds its poetic expression in the episode's metaphor of the shell: "just as it is the interaction of the shell and ear produce the roar that the drinkers hear," so it is the interaction between the two kinds of discourses "which produces the meanings that we can extract" (85). If the last (and non-repeated) overture bit ("Begin.") is "already caught up in the flow of signifiers (86)," the last word of the whole episode ("Done."), belonging as it does contextually both to the Robert Emmet quote and to Bloom's farting, performs a "fissuration" which

> ensures that there is no final end to the text from which a one-to-one relation between signifier and signified can be imposed and this refusal of an ending is further emphasised by the fact that the "Done" refers back to the command "Begin." (88)

As long as "The Sirens" thematises the lack of a simple origin of writing and textuality, "The Cyclops" is composed of "a montage of texts" which "works around a basic division between the narrative of the 'I'... and the way this narrative is taken up and "explained" by other discourses" (90). The different representations are recognized as representing the same event only through a third discourse, which identifies the two as such: "the third discourse is the reader's own and the reader is thus involved in the play of the text" (92-3). This meta-narrative is, however, again decomposed in the episode's ending, where the two hitherto alternating discourses are found conflated into one. Bloom's position within this episode is seen as threatening the area of the Citizen's representation "because he cannot be identified," and this impossibility of identification is what evokes violence "for, in the threat to the Citizen's area of representation, Bloom poses a threat to the Citizen himself," since at the very heart of violence is "the struggle against [...] displacement" (102).

On a more general note, MacCabe regards the first two triads of chapters as two introductory paths to the text, paths which cross in "The

Aeolus" chapter, where "the text no longer provides a centre for itself." Insofar as in the first six chapters Bloom's or Stephen's consciousness could be taken as central, "this is no longer the case in the newspaper office" (114). This decentring of the written consciousnesses also precipitates the introduction of the writing consciousness, that is, the author— "as if in acknowledgement, it is in this section that the text begins a set of humorous references to Joyce as the author," such as MacHugh's reference to Antisthenes, or the appearance of Gabriel Conroy (116). Stephen's Shakespeare theory, aiming as it does to rule out the possibility of chance, invests in the concept of necessity, and yet "it is only the acceptance of chance that will allow him to write, because his fixed position is incompatible with writing itself." Stephen's resistance to chance is of a profoundly neurotic nature, since both "threaten identity, leaving it at the mercy of others' actions and others' voices" (122), and opposed to it is Bloom's willing submission to writing and writing functions in "The Sirens" episode: "If the voice of the singers in the Ormond Bar affirms a presence and an identity that Stephen longs for, Bloom is the ear that deconstructs the presence into difference" (124).

Other *Ulysses* passages examined in MacCabe's text include "Circe," where the contradiction of the neurotic lived out by Stephen (in which "the demand of the mother, which should bury her desire, bears witness to it") is solved through "the experience of the writing," evoking as it does "a raising of the dead which allows the possibility of life" (129), and "Penelope," of which MacCabe observes that its "speaking of female desire through a male pen" has Penelope herself "as the destroyer of the phallic pretensions of the suitors" and thus "continues the process of the work" (132).

In accordance with his opening thesis, MacCabe's reading of *Finnegans Wake* is self-professedly "political." This slant, as we have seen, points to the earliest Wakean criticism: MacCabe invokes Beckett's famous maxim about Joyce's words not being "about something" but rather "that something itself," which he interprets as pointing "not to an empty formalism but to an encounter with those constitutive processes that render us sexed and civil subjects," as Joyce's writing is seen to focus on "the relations of language, desire, and power; of discourse, sexuality and politics." It is these relations that are considered as productive of "the incessant repetitions of *Finnegans Wake*, the inevitable return to a network of significations which are different but the same, mobile but static" (133). Furthermore, the *Wake*'s most fundamental signifying operation is considered as having much to do with the concept of the Freudian lapsus, in turn embedded in the Derridean differential conception of the sign on which MacCabe relies throughout. Freudian lapsus occurs "at that moment when the subject loses control of his or her discourses that something else can be heard: 'it' speaks there where 'I' have lost control" (143).

The political concerns of MacCabe's argument come to prominence in his discussion of language as law—once ALP "breaks with all forms of law, be they secular or religious," she "cannot use language; she cannot write down her secrets" (146). It is here that MacCabe makes a highly problematic identification of the absent dimension within meaning with the feminine:

> Through its constant demonstration of the differences and absences with which language is constituted, writing allows a constant openness to the feminine. *Finnegans Wale* lets the unconscious speak by investigating the very act of writing; it tells us the mother's secrets. (147)

More convincing than this somewhat spurious moment of gender-essentialisation is MacCabe's discussion of the double—boy's and girl's—narcissism. This split is due to the asymmetry in the girl's Oedipal development, in which before taking up her Oedipal relation with her father "she must separate herself from her mother," yet this separation receives no such single determination as does the small boy's does (that is, a severe blow to his narcissism and a renunciation of the mother's imperfect body). In other words, whereas "Shaun's narcissism is always a defence involving aggression," Issy "just looks in the mirror" (149-50).

The political dimension of Joyce's work then is contained within the questions it poses about the reader/text relation, a relation in which "[t]he reader is transformed into a set of contradictory discourses, engaged in the investigation of his or her own symbolic construction," a transformation marked by "the production of a separation between the signifier and the signified and the consequent de-naturalisation of signification" (152-3). However, as long as the political question for any text is "whether it addresses a specific identity or identities and whether it confirms these identities in an imaginary exchange or whether it transforms them into a network of relations which thus become available for knowledge and action," then to MacCabe's mind, Joyce's texts are shown as "politically ineffective because they lack any definite notion of the audience to which they are addressed" (156). This observation is another of MacCabe's barbs at literary critics, for it is they who have resurrected "the notion of the individual at the limit of texts dedicated to the subversion of that notion" and thereby "recuperated" Joyce "so easily." MacCabe concludes:

> In order to place ourselves in the position from which the processes of separation in *Finnegans Wake* can be experienced, it is necessary to have a commitment to Joyce. The only section of society that shares an imaginary identity with Joyce are the Joyce scholars and it is they who form his only audience. (157)

The unanswered questions remain the one of agency behind this process of critical misappropriation—for it cannot be only due to the evildoings of literary critical establishment—and the very notion of "commitment," solicited as it was not only by the peculiar nature of Joyce's writing, but also by his very own project of critical self-fabrication—what Derrida refers to as the ambiguous "being in memory of Joyce."

MacCabe then proceeds to discuss specific issues from a broad variety of critical perspectives, bringing on board Noam Chomsky's linguistic concepts of competence and performance to discuss the subversiveness of Joyce's Wakese, Benjamin's analysis of mechanical reproduction in the context of Joyce's interest in communication technology and newspaper culture, and concludes on a general note of discussing Barthes' work on Balzac (especially *S/Z*), which presents a thorough discussion of the problem of realism in terms of the famous five codes of signification, thereby supplementing his previously rather sketchy treatment of the topic. But we shall leave MacCabe's argument here, reserving a more detailed discussion of his conception of Joyce's politics for the appropriate place,[5] and conclude with a metaphorical note on which he himself chooses to end:

> Theory is always closing the stable door after the horse has bolted. Theory's usefulness may lie in reminding us that this is not a stable to which we can return. My own pleasure is an increasing conviction that we are now closing one particular door very firmly and we can now, once again, take off after the horse. (231)

II

As said before, MacCabe's early attempt at a politically committed analysis of Joyce's writing informed by contemporary poststructuralist theoretical approaches was a pioneering one, falling in between the pompous entry of Lacanian psychoanalysis into the field of Joyce studies in Paris, 1975, and Derrida's plenary address at the 1984 Frankfurt symposium. In his introduction to the edited volume of the symposium proceedings,[6] Bernard Benstock describes the symposium as one which "forced a confrontation of sorts between members of the Joyce "establishment" [...] and those philosophers, linguists, psychoanalysts, and literary historians whose own writing has been influenced by Joyce's texts and has in turn influenced recent approaches to Joyce's texts, but who are not "Joyce specialists" per se" (4).

In the light of the previous discussion here, it appears that rather than a confrontation between two opposing groups, what was at stake in Frankfurt was a deconstruction of the boundary between them, as one of the objectives of Derrida's address was to question, in a way analogous to MacCabe's critique of the "all too easy recuperation" of Joyce's texts on the critics' part, the very concept of a "Joycean competence." Apart from the deconstructive approach, the essays collected here fall into three

---

[5] See Chapter VIII "Politics," section I.
[6] Bernard Benstock, ed., *James Joyce: The Augmented Ninth* (Syracuse: Syracuse University Press, 1988).

other kinds of critical approach—the psychoanalytic, the Marxist, and the feminist—which, taken together, attest to the diversity of the "post-traditional" schools. Thanks to the variety of these approaches

> [t]he Frankfurt symposium holds a special place among Joyce meetings precisely because it openly addressed that which is usually repressed by the very organization of such meetings—the bringing together, under the auspices of the James Joyce Foundation and in the name of Joyce, of Joyceans in a sudden encounter with the Joycean "other." (22)

Derek Attridge's piece "Criticism's Wake"[7] opens up the panel on "Deconstructive Criticism of Joyce" by pointing to the double nature of the genitive in the panel's title. Just as the *amor matris* is a subjective/objective genitive, the deconstructive criticism *of* Joyce must, in Attridge's view, meditate on their undecidable two-way exchange:

> What if the body at the wake, splashed by some hermeneutic whiskey, should wake, to the embarrassment of the mourners? What if the critical text should find itself addressed by the writing on which it comments? (80-1)

As long as traditional criticism is seen as *epitaphic* in its "keeping the literary work alive in memory while reasserting and ensuring its death as text," deconstructive criticism, on the other hand, would be a critical practice which acknowledges that "*its* life is dependent on the continued life of the text it helps to keep alive, and which attempts to work through, or at least with, that enigma" (81-2). It follows that the traditional criticism is identified with the objective genitive, operating as it does "according to the model of testable hypotheses" and "the accumulation of ever more precise and detailed knowledge," that is, the scientific model (82). Deconstructive criticism, on the other hand,

> would weave itself through the text being read, and weave that text through itself, and thread other texts through both [...], exposing and destabilizing [...] the boundaries and hierarchies that have enabled the text to be pinned into [...] an ideology or a metaphysic that denies it its specificity, its inexhaustibility, its unrecuperable otherness. [...] [It] would offer no insights, conclusions, or detachable propositions, but would instead have the character of an *event* [...]. [It] would offer a unique conjunction or coincidence [...] of cultural traces, existing only by virtue of, and in anticipation of, an answering event, destined to repeat it and to change it with every occurrence: its reading. (83-4)

It is important to note along with Attridge that this general openness of the literary to the deconstructive is by far *not* a quality exclusively Joycean: to a certain extent, the name Joyce could "be replaced by that of

---

[7] Republished more recently as "Deconstructive Criticism of Joyce" in *Joyce Effects: On Language, Theory, and History* (Cambridge: Cambridge University Press, 2000.

any writer of literary texts." Where then lies Joyce's *specific* relevance for deconstruction, and vice versa?

For Attridge, Derrida's reading encapsulates the exceptional proneness of Joyce's writing to a deconstructive engagement with the governing ideological system of our day, particularly by means of its "simulacrum, or parody, of the scientific model of cumulative knowledge," designed to produce both "an endless series of coincidental effects that are not at all random (or whose randomness is in advance programmed by the laws of the text)" and "an unparalleled field in which the ruling principles of scientific knowledge can [...] be made to reveal their dependence on the aleatory, the excluded, the counter-rational, and the contingent," and therefore be exposed to a laughter, "not the irreverent laughter of the carnival [...] but the laughter that pre-exists, and presupposes, all the efforts of the scientific or analytic tradition to erect laws that protect the territory of the 'serious'" (85-6). Thus, the Joycean competence which Derrida's speech so powerfully called into question is seen by Attridge as not only a parody of "the dominant post-Renaissance model of knowledge," but also a locus of powerful resistance to its more recent—and more totalitarian—adjunct, i.e. the urge towards "technological efficiency and the maximization of profit." What Attridge calls for in his conclusion, and what to his mind is the right sort of Joycean deconstruction, is "a criticism which is able to turn this discourse against itself, to tease out the wastefulness and internal differences of its own premises and procedures, in a gesture [...] of parody, of laughter, of excess" (86).

Christine van Boheemen-Saaf opens her contribution by defining a deconstructive reading simply as "an analysis of a text which demonstrates its dependence on logocentric preconceptions." Her paper, "Joyce, Derrida, and the Discourse of the Other," proceeds to map the special interest which *Ulysses* has for Derrida, and sees it resting on the text's "paradoxical double movement of affirmation and denial" which "pre-empts the validity of any analytic attempt at mastering the text," and foregrounds its own all-inclusiveness. For Derrida, writes van Boheemen, in *Ulysses*, "all knowledge, all religious doctrines and philosophical positions have been preinscribed, to preclude the possibility of mastery by a metalanguage" (88). Her paper's aim is to elucidate *Ulysses*, while also addressing the question "about the function of the personification of the 'other' in the discourse of deconstruction." The very discussion of the notion of the other seems to run counter to the deconstructionist emphasis on the Joycean all- and pre-inclusiveness, bringing up the questions of "whether it is merely the fact of preinclusion in itself which, beyond pre-empting future articulations, also invalidates them" and of whether "[t]here may be more to Joyce's texts than all-inclusiveness" (89). In the ambivalent Joycean gesture of all-inclusiveness, invalidating appears coupled with maintaining, either one of them denied prevalence over the other in the way *Ulysses* "blurs the difference between *imitatio* and parody in its rewriting of the epic" (91). Through this practice, Joyce's novel is seen to subvert Aristotle's logic of the excluded middle, the effect of which is twofold: "It precludes the possibility of reading the text as mirroring a stable, unified reality outside itself" and "moreover, the semantic ambivalence of the text, its deconstruction of the traditional logos, subverts, beforehand, the validity of all interpretations, all metalanguages or discourses in which an interpretation of *Ulysses* might be rendered" (92-3).

Once the mimetic understanding of the text as a doubling of some external real is abandoned, what comes to the fore are "endless instances of doubling within the structure of the text itself: repetitions, inversions, metonymies, analogies." Van Boheemen-Saaf's example of such doubling is "Penelope," a textual *ricorso* of a sort, which

> comes almost as an afterthought, an ek-static supplement to the main body of *Ulysses*. If the novel has a story, "Penelope" forms no part of it. Still, even if "Penelope" stands outside and apart, the flow of its language — transgressing the boundaries set by syntax and decorum — continues the stylistic practice of the text as a whole. (93)

One instance of such continuation is Molly's translation of *metempsychosis* as "met him pikehoses," whereby "Molly turns Greek into the speech of an Irish housewife, just as Joyce turns the Greek epic into an Anglo-Irish novel" (95). Molly's discourse comes to be labelled as "her (m)othertongue" and is claimed to subvert the pretensions of presence and voice by pointing to the dependence on the physical and the material, thereby becoming an "emblem of otherness" (96). However, despite its status of otherness, Molly's speech reveals this otherness as never absolute, "never truly Other," but rather "always a variant of, and within, the dominant discourse" (97). Hence, the irresolvable ambiguity at the heart of the *Ulyssean* all-inclusiveness is the following one:

> *Ulysses* seems *at once* to suggest the futility and logical impossibility of a discourse of the Other, *and* to depend on the viability of the idea of making the Other present in language for the coherence of its structure as fiction. [...] *Ulysses* may be based, not on the illusion of presence, but on the illusionary dream of the realization of otherness through and within language. (97)

It is by this means that the *locus* of origin and authority comes to be shifted from a phallocentric logos to an hypostasis of the idea of the Other, "thus inverting the practice of Western metaphysics" (98).

III

The unprecedented prominent presence of deconstructionist practice at the Frankfurt symposium was not the only long-overdue debt paid in the year of 1984, which also saw the publication of the seminal collection of essays from the French, *Poststructuralist Joyce*.[8] This book has already been subjected to an extended analysis,[9] and will thus be dealt with here rather briefly from the particular perspective of the main concern of the present discussion: the mode in which the mutual contamination between the primary text and the meta-text comes to be theorized. Attridge and Ferrer's "Introduction" provides a useful starting point as it contains what might be argued the crucial argument of the whole collection that "there is no metalanguage: the text reads the theory at the same time as it is read by it" (10). Here, it suffices simply to point out how some of the essays' crucial concerns depart from this central thesis: Derrida's is perhaps most poetic, likening the theory/text relation to the interaction of two computer softwares; Stephen Heath constructs an argument outlining how the *Wake* grants the reader freedom to apply to it various different interpretive contexts, only to destroy these through its ability to generate yet other, different ones; Jacques Aubert delivers a sustained analysis of the last and first words of the *Wake*, whose interrelatedness undermines their very status as such, and motivates his insistence on the necessity of reading both with and against their flow; and last but not least Jean-Michel Rabaté's distinction between structural and serial thought brings forth an oscillation between the critical duality of discovery and invention. However, for an analysis that would do justice to this volume, the reader is asked to consult the above-mentioned critical works, for the purposes of the presentation here will be served by just this short overview.

IV

In the introduction to her edited collection of essays from the 1985 James Joyce Conference held in Philadelphia, the prominent feminist Joycean, Bonnie Kime Scott explains the title, *New Alliances in Joyce Studies*,[10] as reflecting the attempt "to make newer theory accessible by eliminating needless jargon, seeking clarity of terms, and calling for an abundance of textual references" (15). If MacCabe's attempt, undertaken a mere seven years ago, was pioneering in its revisitation of the avant-garde political Joyce of the earliest *Wake*-criticism from the poststructuralist perspective(s), now, "one pronounced pattern in the present essays is an awareness of political forces in life and language, the ways power operates in the social contexts of family and nation" and a "sensitivity to various feminist critical options has become a given," even though the feminism presented here is still marked by the Anglo-American versus Continental Europe divide (16).

---

[8] Derek Attridge and Daniel Ferrer, eds., *Poststructuralist Joyce: Essays from the French* (Cambridge: Cambridge University Press, 1984).

[9] Especially in Roughley's *James Joyce and Critical Theory*, Lernout's *The French Joyce*, and Brooker's *Joyce's Critics*.

[10] Bonnie Kime Scott, ed., *New Alliances in Joyce Studies* (London: Associated University Press, 1988).

Here, decisively influenced by the Frankfurt discussions, Christine van Boheemen-Saaf's "Deconstruction after Joyce" calls for a re-conceptualization of the relationship between critical theory and the literary text, according to which "both literary and philosophical discourses can express the same insights," and points to "the affinity between Derrida's *praxis* of writing philosophy and Joyce's play with language and identity" as an "effect of direct influence" (29-30). Derrida's Frankfurt address is found to be "most important in what it did *not* articulate," the deconstructive reading which it did not offer. In its emphasis on "the affirmative nature of *Ulysses*," as well as the suggestion of "its pre-emptive all-inclusiveness," Derrida is considered as pointing to Joyce as his own precursor (30). This is further corroborated by the continuous, if seemingly marginal, presence of Joyce within Derrida's philosophical works, ranging from the earliest texts such as his introduction to Edmund Husserl's *The Origin of Geometry* to his mature works such as *Dissemination* ("Plato's Pharmacy") or *La Carte Postale*. Yet again, van Boheemen-Saaf does not fail to note that despite their immense usefulness Derrida's central insights, for example his critique of (phal)logocentrism, his decon-struction of the Aristotelian axiom that A cannot be A and B at the same time, or his unsettling of the notion of meaning as self-presence, are all "foreshadowed in *Ulysses*, and especially in *Finnegans Wake*." Unlike Blake or Hegel, but very much like Derrida, Joyce does not conceive of opposition as a prerequisite step toward transcendence, but rather as a "'fact' inherent in human consciousness" and dependent on "language opening the circle of self-identity" (32). The crucial question arising from this affinity is then how does the knowledge thereof affect the Joycean reader and/or critic?

A possible indication, if not a direct answer, is provided in van Boheemen-Saaf's fourfold typology of strategies for reading both Joyce and Derrida. First, following the New Critical approach, meaning can be seen as residing in the structural features of the text with the focus on "the processes of interaction and flow, the systems of exchange and recircula-tion" (33). A second possibility is provided by a more sophisticated, less positivist kind of feminist approach, which understands the categories of the "masculine" and "feminine," "paternity" and "mothering," not as "*presences* or ideas necessarily embodied in male or female bodies," but as "culturally defined and mutually dependent qualities or functions" (33-4). Third, one can regard Joyce's oeuvre as "the reflection of one con-tinuous development from a primarily text-external (referential) ap-proach... to a primarily text-internal semiotics." Fourth, and last within this categorization, is the practice of reading "readerly texts like *Dubliners* with the writerly outlook demanded by *Finnegans Wake*," which leads to the recognition "that the Joycean and Derridean understanding of polar opposites as having "identity" by virtue of their mutual dependence also holds for critical approaches" (35). Strangely enough for a discussion of the Derridean deconstruction, the Barthesian distinction between the *readerly* and the *writerly* as categories of the reader's mind-actualizations of the text functions as the concluding note of van Boheemen-Saaf's paper, where it is only a combination of the two that enables one "to see Joyce" as a "'whole'" (36).

V

The co-editor of the *Post-Structuralist Joyce*, and also later on Derrida's interviewer on the subject of literature who thereby gave rise to the much-influential volume, *Acts of Literature*, Derek Attridge was also the author of one of the most sophisticated as well as accessible studies of the deconstructed/deconstructive Joyce to see the light of day in the 1980s. His *Peculiar Language*[11] deals with the three crucial modes of peculiarity by which the "poetic" language differentiated itself from its "ordinary" counterpart, in the Renaissance, Romantic, and Modernist periods of its development. The particular double-bind of the normative aesthetics of such peculiarity are its two mutually inconsistent demands "that the language of literature be recognizably different from the language we encounter in other contexts, and that it be recognizably the same" (3). Attridge's is an argument formed against what he sees as two major recent theoretical interventions in this problematic issue: first structuralism, a project premised "on the convertibility of any cultural judgment into explicit rules," and yet one whose theoretical foundations "are themselves open to question, for they assume a model of transcendent objectivity"; and second, sociology, the analysis of "the social and institutional structures within which literature is constituted and controlled," which nevertheless, "for all its value in exposing the social and political dimension of literary judgments," still operates "in terms of the same model of transcendent objectivity as structuralism" (5-7).

The three turning points in the debate have each their theoretical/critical text on which Attridge documents their agenda: Puttenham's *Arte of English Poesie* for the Renaissance period, which focuses on the idea of *decorum*; Wordsworth's *Preface to "Lyrical Ballads"* for Romanticism, attempting to ground poetic language in "the real language of men"; and Saussure's *Course in General Linguistics* for Modernism, a text which "both marks and participates in the shift from the historically based philological studies of the 19th-century to the linguistic theory of the 20th," thus liberating language from "a certain myth of transparency and dependence upon the real," with the focus lain on "the opposition between synchrony and diachrony, with particular reference to its function in the discussion of etymology" (9). Joyce's last two novels are used as quarries for an inquiry into "some of the frequently adduced characteristics of literary language" (11). These include the variance between Saussure and Jakobson on the issue of onomatopoeia, played out within the context of

[11] Derek Attridge, *Peculiar Language (Language as Difference from the Renaissance to James Joyce)* (Ithaca, New York: Cornell University Press, 1988).

"The Sirens," Attridge's analysis of which proposes a new conception of the long-discussed operations of onomatopoeia (Chapter 5); the issue of linguistic deviation, illustrated by Joyce's manipulation of expected language formations on the syntactic level (Chapter 6); or an examination of the positivist and structuralist accounts of literary language with *Finnegans Wake* as their ultimate test case, regarded not as an easily dismissible marginality, but as the fullest manifestation of the defining properties of the literary tradition (Chapters 7 and 8). Together these different forays share the goal of showing

> why the domain of literature and of literary theory cannot provide its own self-sufficient and lasting answers to the question of the distinctiveness of literary language, [and why], if art [...] always exceeds the rules and codes adduced as its determinants [...], the judgments that control its status and function as art must be related to the wider context in which they are formed, sustained, and modified. (16)

It is precisely in the various strategies of undermining critical control and mastery it deploys that Attridge's work implicitly aligns itself with the deconstructive practice.

Let us discuss the latter Joyce-focused part of Attridge's book in more detail, albeit only briefly. His "Literature as Imitation: Jakobson, Joyce, and the Art of Onomatopoeia" takes Jakobson's 1958 paper "Linguistics and Poetics" as a starting point for a discussion of two very different conceptions of poetic language which follow from an careful consideration of Jakobson's distinction between the "context" and the "message":

> if meaning is largely the preserve of utilitarian discourse, poetry may be said to be a linguistic practice that specially emphasizes the material properties of language in certain organized forms [...; but if] the task of poetry is to heighten attention to the meanings of words and sentences, the distinctiveness of poetic language must lie in the particular forcefulness with which it presents its semantic content. (130)

If for Jakobson it is precisely by means of traversing this dichotomy, by healing "the breach between signifier and signified," that poetic function comes into being (132), then it would also lie somewhere between the two possible accounts of the role of speech sounds, where according to one, "the sounds of language draw attention to themselves and their configuration, independently of their referential function" (thereby preferring the signifier), or "they tend to disappear in an enhanced experience of referentiality" (thereby privileging the signified) (133-4). However much he would like to share Jakobson's sense that the reading of poetry evokes a feeling of intensified referentiality coupled with (and inseparable from) an enhanced notion of the aural properties of language, Attridge nevertheless argues that what mars Jakobson's account of this response is "an attachment to an unexamined concept of art as *imitation*" — and an example by which he seeks to demonstrate the insufficiency of Jakobson's account is the reading of onomatopoeia in "The Sirens" episode (specifically, passage *U* 11.1284-97).

In these instances of non-lexical onomatopoeia, the notion of onomatopoeic "imitation of sound" is complicated by no fewer than eight factors (among others, the prerequisite knowledge of the phonological system of the English language, their certain semantic admixture, their visual effect of the supposed "sound-painting," or a prior familiarity with the sound required of the receiver), meticulously listed by Attridge, which together seem to justify Jakobson's double emphasis "at least as far as nonlexical onomatopoeia is concerned: the series of linguistic sounds *and* their referents receive simultaneous, if separate, enhancement," if for a different reason than Jakobson would have, for "this pleasurable double foregrounding is achieved by something other than the art of imitation" (147). Attridge proceeds to illustrate this by looking at the text's lexical onomatopoeia, where "the experience that nonlexical onomatopoeia does not offer [...] is one of *heightened meaning*" (150). He takes as his example the sentence, "Shebronze, dealing from her oblique jar thick syrupy liquor for his lips, looked as it flowed," whose "richness of texture, the fluidity, the way it is moulded and savoured by the lips and other organs of the mouth" he does not deny (152), but still points to the fact that

> the particular aspects of this complex physical process which function in a given example of onomatopoeia depend less on the specific configurations of the phonetic sequence in question than on the meaning of the passage. (154)

It is then only seemingly paradoxical that the illusion of a more direct involvement in those qualities that language normally attains is created, not by any directness of experience, but precisely by an enhancement of our apprehension of language, the medium that stands *between* us and direct experience itself: "Understood in this way, onomatopoeia might be seen as a model for all literary language" (154). Attridge concludes:

> If onomatopoeia is to be judged in terms of the accuracy with which it enables the sounds of language to reproduce the sounds...of the nonlinguistic world, then the more successful it is...the more it is bound to come into conflict with the necessarily abstract nature of the language system, foregrounding the physical properties of speech (and writing) and drawing attention to itself as a rhetorical device instead of melting away in a presentation of unmediated reality. The more it succeeds, the more it fails. (156)

"Literature as Deviation: Syntax, Style, and the Body in *Ulysses*" turns yet again to the contrary demands the cultural tradition makes upon literary language, in other words that "such language be both clearly distinguishable from and closely related to the language of the quotidian world," and how *Ulysses* fails to meet either (158). If one can pair "Cyclops" and "Penelope" on account of their "convincing" faithfulness to "real language," and oppose them to "Nausicaa" and "Oxen of the Sun," whose overtly literary styles could never have existed in the streets, then "The Sirens" and "Eumaeus," the two objects of Attridge's attention, prove much harder to categorize, for they challenge "the norms of both 'literary' and 'nonliterary' language" (160).

The poetic procedure focused on in "The Sirens" episode is the independence it gives to the organs of the body: more specifically, the no fewer than nine examples of "six different pairs of lips, all engaged in activities we normally regard as the proper province of the whole individual acting under the command of a central will: they say, titter, lisp, hum, trill, laugh, coo, blow, and murmur" (163). This synecdochic substitution of the part for the whole can be regarded as a means of liberating the body from the dictatorial will of the self, but, from a psychoanalytic perspective, one can also see this substitutability as underlying every individual's libidinal development toward the varied richness of human sexual life. This sexual substitutability of organs (most notably the repeated analogies between the tympanum and the hymen) is, then, tracked throughout the whole chapter, which as a whole seems to be under the domination of "Boylan's organ," staging a process of verbal deformation whose result is "not to reinforce the stability and certainty of the norm, and the sharp distinction between literary and nonliterary language that depends upon it", but rather "to put in question the norm itself" (172).

The "Eumaeus" chapter, on the other hand, is often seen at the opposite end of the linguistic spectrum, due to its employment of "all-too-familiar clichés, [...] sense spread thinly across a seemingly endless flow of words, [...] pedantic adherence to conventional forms [...], flaccid and sprawling prose." (172). This "un-literariness" of the chapter demonstrates for Attridge that

> any extended literary text is involved in a double process: it constantly evokes norms that pre-exist it in the cultural community, but it also constantly establishes its own norms, which it then challenges and confirms as it goes on. (179)

Attridge analyses the "Molly's photography" passage in detail, a particular instance of where the fluidity and instability of the chapter's inappropriate language are "effective in ways that go beyond comedy" (180), the argument being that this passage actually stages Bloom's interest in arousing Stephen's desire for Molly, and thus clichés of aesthetic conversation, such as "drink in" or "treat," suddenly take up their involvement with the literarily physical:

> What the style of "Eumaeus" achieves, for all its attempts at propriety, is a vivid demonstration of the impossibility of fixed boundaries and significations when the structures of language are permeated by the dissolving energies of erotic desire. (182)

Despite their obvious differences, in both "The Sirens" and "Eumaeus" the processes of displacement, sliding, and exchange launch an interpenetration of the categories of "form" and "content," exceeding, if not utterly undermining, all simple notions of mimesis. These processes, moreover, are also involved in laying bare what Attridge terms "the ideology of the body" in that they resist the processes of naturalization "which lead us to assume that the distinctions and continuities given in our language or languages are 'normal' or 'real,'" conveying the fact that

> the parts of the body acquire their meanings through a specific set of signifying systems, which is possible only if the relation between these meanings and their actual physical properties of the organs in question is, in part at least, arbitrary [...] in just the same way every item of speech or writing has its own sound and shape independent of its authorized function in the language system, and this material specificity and independence prohibit complete transparency, fixity, and singleness of meaning. (186)

Both linguistic and physical signifiers are thus revealed as having an arbitrary relation to their signifieds, whose "naturalness" is of a purely ideological nature, and the materiality with which they are endowed hampers the efficient transmission of meaning from one consciousness (or body) to another, "a transmission that relies on the illusion of words which perfectly serve their meanings, without slippage and without residue," where in fact, however, it is slippage and residue that make the functioning of language possible, in the first place (186-7). Neither language nor the body can be seen, in the light of the textual practices of these episodes, as "merely secondary and subservient to a nonmaterial, transcendent, systematic, controlling principle, whether we call that principle "meaning" or "the self." More important, they demonstrate some of the pleasures, sexual and textual, that we owe to this fact" (187).

Equally stimulating is Attridge's discussion of the Wakean "pun" in "Unpacking the Portmanteau; Or, Who's Afraid of *Finnegans Wake*?" He identifies the pun's power as its ability to undermine our underlying assumptions about the effectiveness of communication, according to which, in Attridge's Saussurean formulation:

> for each signifier there is an inseparable signified, the two mutually interconnected like two sides of a sheet of paper. [In contrast], the possibility of the pun is a mark of out fallen condition—our language, it seems, like every other aspect of our existence, is touched with imperfection. (189)

This peccable nature of the pun brings about its marginalization in the most common uses of language:

> Outside the licensed domains of literature and jokes, and the uncontrollable manifestations of parapraxes and dreams, the possibilities of meaning in any given use of a word are stringently limited by context. The more that

context bears down upon the word, the less the word will quiver with signi-fication. (191)

However, the pun can be seen as aberrational only as long as one sup-poses the independence of meaning from its material representation—an illusory independence the challenging of which presents one of the pri-mary tasks of poetry, where the pun is merely "a particularly extreme case of such articulation at the level of the signifier, relying as it does on *complete* coincidence of sound between two words." In Attridge's decon-structive gesture, the pun "turns out to be not an aberration of language but a direct reflection on its 'normal' working" (192-3). The particular working of the pun falls into two modes, either as "one signifier with two possible signifieds, which in a particular context are simultaneously acti-vated," or as "two identical signifiers, which in a particular context are made to coalesce" (193).

Here Attridge turns to the *Wake*'s deployment of the portmanteau, which is similar to the pun in that "there is no escape from its insistence that meaning is an *effect* of language, not a presence within or behind it, and the effect is unstable and uncontrollable." However, the portmanteau is crucially different since it cannot be as easily contained by being treated as a symptom of an imperfect language in the ways a pun can, but instead must be viewed as "the defining feature of language itself," derived as it is from the fact that the same segments can be "combined in different ways to encode different meanings" (197). It therefore follows that the portmanteau's history of exclusion from official and proper dis-course is a much harsher one than in the case of the pun, having existed "chiefly in the form of malapropism and nonsense verse—the language of the uneducated, the child, the idiot." Not surprisingly, it is to the same area that the literary establishment has often relegated *Finnegans Wake* (198). However, its all-pervasive presence within the *Wake*'s deconstruc-tion of the oppositional structures of thought has rendered the portman-teau something akin to Derrida's *pharmakon*, since its very power renders it ineffective. As long as like the pun the portmanteau is context-dependent, and in *Finnegans Wake*, the context itself is *made of* portman-teaus,

> a "contextual circle" is created whereby plurality of meaning in one item in-creases the available meanings of other items, which in turn increase the possibilities of meaning in the original item. (202)

A circle, akin to the undecidable intertwining of part and whole in the hermeneutic one, is equally inescapable insofar as there is no single privi-leged item that would yield its meaning apart from the system which contains it. This working of the portmanteau (both an aberration from and a possible paradigm for the operation of language) is seen as a *pars pro toto* of the working of *Finnegans Wake* (both an aberration from and a possible paradigm for the operation of literature) in showing that "*every* text [...] is ultimately beyond the control of its author, *every* text reveals the systems of meaning of which Derrida speaks in his consideration of the word *pharmakon*" (207). Attridge ends here by focusing on the problematic nature of the *Wake*'s status and the slippery nature of its acceptation into the literary canon, which can easily turn into a debilitating containment within it:

> When the *Wake* is welcomed [...] it is often by means of a gesture that simultaneously incapacitates it, either by placing it in a sealed-off category [...], or by subjecting it to the same interpretative mechanisms that are applied to all literary texts, as if it were no different. (209)

The issue of the critical reception of the at once anomalous *and* paradigmatic *Wake* is taken up in Attridge's last chapter, "Deconstructing Digression: The Backbone of *Finnegans Wake* and the Margins of Culture." Anthony Burgess' early attempts at "aiding the reading public" by means of his "backbone" accounts of the plot and characters of the *Wake*, for all their *bona fide* usefulness, are ultimately regarded as doomed to failure due to the nature of the *Wake*'s narrative that dispels the illusion of there being a clear-cut distinction between events and individuals and their secondary representation;[12] in the *Wake*,

> events, people, places, times are clearly constructed by the text [...] and attention is focused on the process of linguistic fabrication itself; [and yet], at the same time, *Finnegans Wake* could be said to glory in the *secondariness* of language, in its never-ending and never-failing attempt to point to something beyond itself. (216)

As long as the *Wake* does away with the idea of a centre, it also discards the idea of digression: it is a book "without anything that can be skipped, taken in at a glance, or read rapidly to get the gist," which, however, is also to say that "*everything* in it is capable of being skipped, because the book has no life-giving heart that might be injured" (217). The crucial question, then, for Attridge, is whether Joyce's *Wake* is best seen as a digression from the central tradition of the novel. The supplemental nature of digression, combining its secondariness and dispensability with its inseparability from and coterminousness with its supposed opposite—centre—needs no further specification, for

> [the] functioning of digression as a structural principle clearly depends on its double nature—at once necessary and dispensable, part of the novel and excluded from it, inside and outside at the same time. (220)

---

[12] This argument is further, examined in far greater detail in Peter Mahon's study, discussed at the end of this chapter.

Texts such as *Tale of a Tub*, *Tristram Shandy*, or *Moby Dick* thematise "the hierarchical opposition between progressive and digressive" as "deconstructed by the text itself" (228).

In a typical deconstructionist twist, returning to the issue of the "backbone" of the *Wake*, Attridge in turn asks of this third part of his essay to show whether "the first part was a digressive prelude in *Finnegans Wake* in an essay on digression or the second part a digression in an essay on *Finnegans Wake*" (231). The crucial claim made in this third part combines both of the preceding ones in viewing *Finnegans Wake* as "the *exemplification* of the literary [...], namely, the impossibility of ever being limited by originating intention, or external reference, or constraining context" (232). The reversal of *Finnegans Wake* not as a periphery but as a centre of the canon has important consequences. More specifically, it induces "a close attention to the linguistic detail of the novel hardly encouraged by the search for psychological subtlety or moral significance or by the rush to a 'represented' world of character and event." It also undoes "the opposition between narrative centre and digressive periphery in every novel we read" (234), and regards "any work of literature" as partaking of "the modes of textuality which have been variously described in terms of *écriture*, genotext, *signifiance*, heteroglossia, dissemination, rhetoricity, performativity, *scriptibilité*," and so on (236). Turning Burgess' metaphor back on him, Attridge asks:

> Which, after all, is the centre of the fish on our plate, the backbone we fillet out or the flesh we eat? [...] As long as we need centres and digressions [...] we will find them. The lesson of the *Wake* is that we do not stop finding them, and building on them, when we know that they are our own productions. (237)

Attridge's insightful, gracefully written, and rigorously, yet also accessibly thought-out examination of the question of difference and the practice of making different thus manages to convincingly show these as a potentially useful instruments for "the critical reconsideration of any homogenizing characterization of language, a reconsideration whose implications go well beyond the problematic and pleasurable domain of the literary" (238).

VI

The next work discussed here directly juxtaposes the names "Derrida" and "Joyce" in its title. Claudette Sartiliot's *Citation and Modernity: Derrida, Joyce and Brecht*[13] begins by observing how modernity rests on a different understanding of the status of quotation:

---

[13] Claudette Sartiliot, *Citation and Modernity: Derrida, Joyce and Brecht* (Norman and London: University of Oklahoma Press, 1993).

A traditional definition of quotation derived from classical rhetoric no longer pertains to the role of quotation in modernist texts. Retrospectively, and under the influence of poststructuralist literary theories, one notices by the end of the nineteenth century a change in the status of quotation that should call for a new definition and theory of citation. (3)

Despite its novelty, Sartiliot does not subscribe to the widespread view that sees the classical writers as free of "the problematic of quotation as it reflect[ed] on the status of their texts as well as their own status as authors." She instead argues throughout that

> the task of writers has been to present themselves as "original" rather than derivative, as different from, but also equal to, their predecessors. Quotation, as defined by classical rhetoric, supplied the ground for such a contest to be performed. (4)

Quotation for Sartiliot has traditionally had a twofold function: that of "illustration," when used as "*auctoritas*," or as "ornament," something seemingly superfluous used as "a stylistic exemplum." Flaubert (and his *Bouvard et Pécuchet*) here is regarded as an inaugural figure in the shift within the "erotics of literary production," from "a metaphysical rivalry for priority and prestige" to "an amorous devotion to the supposedly lost virgin body of language" (5). It is only in Flaubert's *Bouvard* (other texts examined by Sartiliot include Longinus' *Essay on the Sublime* and Montaigne's *Essays*) that "clichés are no longer the characteristics of characters or professions: they are the characteristics of language itself. Quotation becomes intrinsic to language" (12). Like Flaubert himself, reported to have read fifteen hundred books in preparation for this novel, "the two clerks (paradigms for the modern writer and reader) are lost in a maze of books that has taken the place of 'reality,' or outside referentiality" (12-13). The notion of resemblance in the way both *Bouvard* and *Ulysses* dismantle the distinction inherent to quotation between the primary and secondary text, and thereby pose the act of writing as repetition, copying, or even plagiarizing, was already noted by the perceptive Ezra Pound:

> Pound had noticed in Joyce's *Ulysses* a dismantling of traditional characterization similar to Flaubert's *Bouvard et Pécuchet*. It is such a crossing of languages, cultures, and texts that renders the traditional definition of citation inadequate and outmoded. (15)

Helpful here is Mikhail Bakhtin's theory of heteroglossia and polysemia as opposed to the notion of univocity and the concept of unified verbal communication from the standpoint of a Marxist critique of bourgeois ideology, according to which, Bakhtin contends in his *Dialogic Imagination*, "the dialogic orientation of discourse is a phenomenon that is, of course, a property of *any* discourse" (16). Even though by maintaining that "the word in language is half someone else's," Bakhtin still clings to the notions of *intention* and *accent* in literary appropriation, he fails to show how these can be tracked down, let alone theoretically assessed:

> If, therefore, Bakthin's theory seems to provide a useful tool for an analysis of citational procedures in modernist and postmodernist texts, one realizes that his own application of his theories to literary texts reintroduces the classical categories that he first seemed to do away with. (17)

Roland Barthes, like Bakthin, deals with the ideology inherent in language, but, unlike Bakhtin, "his emphasis on culture, the endoxal, leads him to dismantle and resituate the notions of subject and context" (18). At this point, Sartiliot introduces Barthes' famous distinction (from his late text *S/Z*) between *readerly* and *writerly* text, and stresses his preference for the latter. It was also he who was instrumental in introducing and theorizing (together with Kristeva) the notion of *intertextuality*:

> from the moment one can no longer recognize a quotation as an insertion separated typographically from the "main" discourse, the relationship between one text and another becomes a form of complicity. (20)

Sartiliot then plunges into some of the implications of the etymological roots of citing and quoting, noting that the former (from the French *citer*—"to summon or appear in court") has strong legal connotations, while the latter (from the Latin *quota*, "how many," "as many") is related to the concept and convention of number and measure. The German concept of *Geflügelte Worte* (itself a borrowing from Homer's *epea pteroenta*), of quotations as "winged words," and other connections between quotation and flying or birds, "seem to remind us, as Derrida points out, that writing and citing, writing and grafting, are closely related" (24).

As opposed to these frequent organic metaphors, according to Derrida's own of "the clothespins" in Ponge's texts (his text on Ponge, *Signsponge*), quotation becomes "the pins used to dry photo negatives, thus linking quotation marks with technological reproduction ad infinitum." In Joyce's *Ulysses*,

> those clothespins become the pins in Molly's hair, which Joyce decides to remove as he puts both Molly and language to sleep. Taking the hairpins out of a woman's hair and taking the quotation marks out of a discourse is a sign of "letting one's hair down." (28)

Joyce's intertextuality requires a conceptual turn to Derrida, who is seen as developing "a *post*classical theory of quotation as dissemination based directly on the practices of modernist texts" (dissemination as opposed to Bakhtin's polysemia), which "both forbids formalization and closure and negates the notion of context as origin." This theory in turn derives from Derrida's recognition of the necessary iterability of the mark (whether written or spoken), according to which "the capacity of any linguistic mark to function—to be understood—depends on its iterability, that is, on its capacity to function in the absence of both addresser and addressee" (29), and therefore "outside of the intentionality, the "meaning to say" (*vouloir dire*) of the addresser, as well as outside of the anticipated response of the addressee." What is reproduced in this quoted repetition can never be identical to itself — in Derrida's view, there is always a remainder (*un reste*) that divides identity, intention, and meaning: "Language always says something else or something other than what the subject of utterance means to say" (30). Thus, Sartiliot summarizes the two complementary moments in Derrida's theory of quotation as dissemination: first, the irreconcilability of saying and meaning, "the impossibility of the signifier to arrest itself on, to correlate with, one signified"; and second, "the impossibility for a text to be a closed system uncontaminated by other texts" (31).

This is where the significance of Derrida's *Glas* for Sartiliot's argument surfaces, for it is here that

> Derrida does not only confront two texts (Hegel's and Genet's) in order to show how each column contaminates the other, he also practices a new kind of reading meant to take into account what is inevitably left out, excluded, and repressed by hermeneutic systems of interpretation. (32)

Glas is the work that reveals deconstruction as "habitation within texts," explaining its strange beginning as well as its typographical arrangement:

> The reader of *Glas* cannot produce a complacent linear reading; he or she is rather called upon to do the joining, the stitching, between the texts at hand. [...] the reader must follow the zigzag line of sewing and stitching; he or she is caught in a maze of texts [...] in a labyrinth, forever looking for an absent center and an origin. (42)

The beginning of *Glas* is likened to that of "The Sirens" episode in that it "assembles words intent on hiding their meaning, or more precisely, on deferring their meaning" (43). The confrontation between Hegel and Genet presents the reader with a double bind, making him feel "forced to read two texts at once — which is physically impossible"; by the same token, "it proves just as impossible to read one for very long without being tempted to jump over to the other side" (44). In *Glas*, not even the proper name is excluded from "the basic and generalized disseminative process which reveals that words hide other words in themselves" (47). Thus, Hegel becomes *aigle*, and Genet *gênet*, a practice which "links dissemination to decapitation, emasculation, and emajusculation" (48). By drawing a parallel between "échec de la traduction" (the failure of translation) and "l'échec de la philosophie" (the failure of philosophy), as represented in the non-concept of *pharmakon*, Derrida "demonstrates, through anasemia, how words quote one another in a nonsaturable fashion" (57). Throughout *Glas*, Sartiliot's close analysis reveals,

[m]eaning and interpretation are not rejected, but they no longer rely on the equivalence (or translation) between the signifier and the signified; rather, they depend on a citational process inscribed within each signifier; they depend on the allosemic relation between words. (58)

This citational process is traditionally conceived of metaphorically as castration, treating the quoted text or author as castrated by the quoting author/text. Sartiliot's reading of Derrida, however, shows that paradoxically, "the quoted author retains his authority, and the quoted fragment appears as fetishized" (67). In this respect, the quoting author appears a fetishist, fetishising the authors he quotes through the ambiguous practice of both undermining and confirming their authority — which is precisely what Derrida himself is doing when he vacillates between Hegel and Genet:

Derrida's discussion of castration and the fetish allows him to theorize his attempt to inscribe his own text in the hymen between two other texts [...] between philosophy and literature. [...] As such, Derrida's text is situated between incorporation, the internalization of Hegel's *Aufhebung*, and introjection, the encrypting nature of Genet's writing. (73)

Here, Sartiliot's argument turns to *Finnegans Wake*, from the perspective of the question of whether a quotation is still a quotation "when it has become distorted beyond recognition, when one no longer knows with any certainty whom to attribute it to, if the boundaries between text and intertext, if the notions of closure, paternity, totality have themselves been subverted" (74). This also has an important bearing on Joyce's criticism, the paradox being that

while Joyce was doing away with quotation marks in his own texts, he was forcing his critics to surround most of their critical terms with quotation marks, as a sore sign of their inability to find the right word to describe what he was doing. (75)

More generally, the notion of reception becomes central to Joyce's project, for

[e]ven though Joyce was obsessed with the reception of his works and read all the criticism on them, he also insisted on mentioning his sources and revealing his schemes to his commentators, who become characters in *Finnegans Wake*. In so doing, he was already doing the critic's work, sometimes inventing sources and sending the critic on a wild-goose chase. (75-6)

Specifically in the *Wake*, the practice of writing and quoting is paralleled with eating and digesting, the connection being the relationship between self and other:

Eating is taking the body of the other into the self; this process then follows a kind of combination and transformation out of which, the self and the other, after being combined, separate again—and both self and other of course go through a transformation in the process. (78)

What Joyce learned "from his own body, from writing and then from Vico, Bruno, and Quinet" was that there is no *creatio ex nihilo*, that "there is neither creation nor waste, only an infinite recycling" (78). Entering into his *Wake* thus resembles entering into language itself:

If [...] there is no entrance into *Finnegans Wake* because of its circular form without beginning or end, it might be because there is no entrance into language, no privileged beginning where the subject can create a place for himself. In the same way that the story of the *Wake* seems to have started before we have started reading [...] language has always already started without us. (80)

This peculiar nature of Joyce's text has to do with what deconstructionists and Lacanians have termed its *unreadability*—"if reading is 'understanding,' then *Finnegans Wake* is an unreadable text." From this perspective,

Joyce's *Finnegans Wake* can be seen as an extreme example of [the] Derridean notion according to which interpretation (reading and writing as a complementary process) is an endless process of dissemination. (81)

Analogously to Walter Benjamin's notion of reading the text as a translation that refuses to be translated, Derrida exposes the text "as an *Aufgabe*, that is, an indebtedness to its future translation," as well as "a *Gabe*, a gift, which desires to be received and this calls for its translation as a means of ensuring its survival, its afterlife." On the other hand, the text wants "not to be received, that is, it refuses its translation, the kind of translation that would exhaust it, consume it, and thus cause its death as text." According to this double-logic, the force and fascination of a text

is what is neither translatable nor untranslatable, namely an excess, a remainder that cannot be recuperated, predicted, or calculated, a force that prevents its message (the letter) from ever coming to its destination and death. (82)

At this point, Sartiliot approaches Derrida's examination of the peculiar quality of Joyce's letter, its "hypermnesiac" quality, can be "forgiven" when one realizes that one is "in the same position as he is when confronted with language, a language that was always there before us, always saying, signifying before our intentions, or even without our entrance into it" (87). Joyce's *Wake*, among other things, might teach us what De Man called the impossibility of reading [...] without repeating, without quoting, without necessarily transforming, shuffling, and reshuffling the marks on the page, letting semes agglutinate the way they do in language in general before our entrance into it. (88)

Here, Sartiliot turns to the "only typical example of a classical quotation" in the *Wake* — the Quinet quotation in II.2. Classical though its presentation might be from the formal viewpoint, its purpose is anything but traditional:

Joyce does not present the Quinet quotation as an origin, as an original text, to which the variations would be subordinated. On the contrary, the Quinet passage, which Joyce disseminates through the pages of the *Wake*, is itself submitted to the general law of dissemination. (89)

Furthermore, Sartiliot discerns the disseminative process to which Joyce subjects the passage within the passage itself, especially through its flower imagery. Like Derrida in *Glas*, Joyce "discloses not what flowers represent or symbolize, but what they hide and encrypt" (90). In the layout of the nightlessons chapter itself (to which *Glas* has been oftentimes compared),

the sexual theme is reflected in Shem's annotation in the left-hand margin [...], whereas the relationship between writing [...], seduction, and war is expressed in Shaun's annotation in the right-hand margin. (92)

A similar process of dissemination and re-circulation throughout the *Wake* is launched in the famous ALP letter, which also appears only after it has been commented on, and is also subjected to scholarly study. Here, Sartiliot focuses on the section of the *Wake* devoted to the reading of the letter, I.5, examining a series of related topics, ranging from the question of quotation marks (*FW* 108.29-36), the question of signature (*FW* 115.6-11), or the issue of inseparability of form and content (*FW* 109.12-36). On the whole,

section 1.5 opposes all hermetic systems of closure (and enclosure) that rely on the supremacy of the transcendental signified [...] and thus attempt to arrest or recuperate the force or energy of the signifier. This is why *Finnegans Wake* insists on its surface: the page appears as a field of syntactic and semantic interplay that defies analytic reduction. (105)

Another example of the *Wake*'s self-quoting disseminative processes would be the Buckley and Russian General story (*FW* 353.22-32), where Beckett's is a helpful interpretation, making it possible to read the story's multiple versions "as Joyce's attempt to understand, read, appropriate, misappropriate, and deconstruct the story, the joke of the father, as an attempt to kill the father, to bracket the father's name and authority" (110). Ultimately, Heath's understanding of reading as aggressive appropriation of the other (in his "Ambiviolences" — see above) is brought on board as describing the role of the reader of *Finnegans Wake*, "who is forced to reduplicate through his reading the kind of scattering and gathering, disseminating and recollecting, already involved in the writing process" (113).

After her informed reading of Brecht in the context of "praise of plagiarism," Sartiliot concludes her study by revisiting the Derridean understanding of citation in relation to "hypermnesis." Of Derrida, she observes that if he is to be regarded as a philosopher, then only as a special kind of philosopher: "He must be the first 'philosopher' who makes such abundant use of citation that his books read like critical works rather than like 'philosophy.'" However, unlike traditional philosophy, Derrida

> reinscribes the discourse of the other within his own, lets the other speak within his discourse, as a way of reinscribing the past, and of making the past survive albeit in a new medium and within a different frequency. (153)

Derrida's avowal that "mon désir premier n'est pas de faire oeuvre philosophique ou oeuvre d'art, c'est de garder la mémoire" is recalled, as corroborating his belief that the act of citation

> represents the presence of the other, as other, but also as other in myself to whom my text is addressed and without whose presence there could be no writing, no thinking, and perhaps even no being. (155)

Derrida's concept of "the impossibility of non-telepathy" between the self and other "describes the postmodernist venture whereby writers present themselves as being unable not to repeat, not to copy." Derrida's is a marked desire for the words of others as well as for the survival of their words: "Such works, and citation in general, are, as Derrida implies, set against forgetting" (156). To sum up, Sartiliot's excellent study offers an innovative and productive perspective on what it means to be, in Derrida's words, to be "in memory of Joyce."

VII

The impact of deconstructive practice upon feminist studies (already adumbrated in the last piece of van Boheemen-Saaf's examined above), which marked the field in the late 1980s, as well as the early-1990s would-be turn away from theory toward historicising cultural approaches, will both be examined later. It is enough here simply to note that Derridean approaches to Joyce were not revisited until ten years after Attridge's major contribution in two shorter essays by Christine van Boheemen-Saaf and Mark Currie which looked back on (and criticized on varying grounds) deconstruction as a long-abandoned practice, and in a major retrospective study mapping the whole of Joyce-related Derridean corpus, written by Alan Roughley.

Within the context of the present examination, it will be sufficiently illustrative of the shift as a whole to compare the 1985 van Boheemen-

Saaf celebratory piece discussed above with her 1998 re-visitation from an explicitly "cultural-historical perspective" of the post-structuralist Joyce of French theory in her "Purloined Joyce."[14] Her attention turns to "the *psychodynamics* of French use of Anglo-American styles of textuality during a period when [...] the ideal of political revolution and what Eugène Jolas called 'the revolution of the word' were seen as one indistinguishable mission," producing a necessarily historicizing approach to the whole poststructuralist problematics. Here Derrida's *La Carte Postale* is "the doubly privileged site of inquiry," interweaving as it does Joycean references with comments on Barbara Johnson's response to Lacan's reading of Poe, and Derrida's own critique. In doing so, it participates in "the scenario of 'purloining' (misplacement which ends in displacement)" (246-7).

Derrida's main objection to Johnson is levelled at her decision to turn "Lacan and himself into the Shem and Shaun of French post-structuralism," which leads her to reverse his or Lacan's statements (248). Although this may be a familiar scenario which illustrates the cliché of the French/American divide in academic scholarship , it is worth noting that "this psychological condition would seem to have had its pre-textual beginning in Poe's story, set in Paris, in which, it will be remembered, Dupin blames the French for their subversion of logic" (249). In a similarly subversive gesture, van Boheemen-Saaf turns to *The Post Card* from a Joycean perspective, since the occasion of the text's origin was Derrida's visit to Joyce's Zürich grave:

> At the heart of this text about the dissemination of the postal system and the transatlantic shuttle lies a dead body, the body of a precursor who...has for ever pre-empted the possibility of full self-presence of his successors. "He has read us all—and plundered us." (249)

Analogous here is the relation between Plato and Socrates, the son-figure "writing from out of the death of Socrates who had condemned writing as a form of parricide." A Derrida text thus stages a confrontation between literature and philosophy, in their struggle for originality end up perpetually at stalemate since "the 'work' (the transferential, purloining effect of literature) pre-empts the philosopher's revision of truth. Philosophy is 'caught in Joyce's net'" (249-50).

In light of this, the visit to Joyce's grave at the heart of Derrida's text is not so much an act of reverent mourning as "a perverse attempt to incorporate the dead father by the appropriation of his signature and style, his intellectual displacement, his irony and his laughter," and to set this spectre working as Plato does with Socrates. The title, *The Post Card*, referring as it does to the "postal situation without ultimate destiny or origin," dramatizes the emptiness springing from the lack of self-presence

[14] Christine van Boheemen-Saaf, "The Purloined Joyce," *Re-Joyce. Text, Culture, Politics*, eds. John Brannigan, Geoff Ward, and Julian Wolfreys (London: MacMillan Press, Ltd., 1998).

at the heart of the linguistic subjectivity as central to the modern human condition. This incorporation, however, is not without important political effects as it "guarantees the continued intellectual hegemony of Paris over an increasingly influential Anglo-American culture" in staging the mock-oedipal situation of "father-son, Joyce-Derrida, philosophical litera- ture over against philosophy with literary features" (251).

Van Boheemen-Saaf's observations aim to distil from this structure of similarity the possibility of ethical differentiation within the repetition of the same gesture—in order to answer the question, "Are all critics pur- loiners?," she turns to Lacan as the "facteur de la vérité" (252). After a general discussion of Lacan's late-life fascination with—and appropriation of—Joyce, resulting in the 1975-6 change in his structural topology of the psyche which introduced as a stand-in term for The-Name-of-the-Father, the famous and influential "sinthome,"[15] van Boheemen-Saaf focuses on this pun which for her illustrates how "the historical example of Joyce's peculiar linguistic modernity figures to Lacan's as a case which generated a revision of his understanding of psychoanalysis" (253). Lacan's discus- sion of transference is mentioned, which also refers to Socrates, whom he calls "the first philosopher," thereby "implicitly denying Derrida's dis- tinction between the oral and the written, patient and analyst" (254). A Lacanian perspective enables van Boheemen-Saaf to view Johnson's ver- sion of deconstruction as "a performance of a technique, the demonstra- tion of mastery, where, as in Poe's story, the rational operations of the medium have become the message," and to read American deconstruction itself as "at once 'imaginary' and 'symptomatic' in psychoanalytic terms, perhaps a belated version of American transcendentalism and its repres- sion of the Puritan or English Symbolic Father" (254-5).

These transcultural adoptions of intellectual father-figure raise the question of their role and function in the project of the constitution of a national cultural identity: "Poe and Joyce for the French, just as Derrida and Lacan for Johnson?" (255). In a reversed gesture, the heritage of the Joyce purloined by the French critics plays itself out in the critics who introduce the French Joyce to the Anglo-American Joyce community. Van Boheemen-Saaf observes that Attridge's introduction to *Poststructuralist Joyce*, in addition to overt echoes of Derrida, "presents a programme of reading which deliberately excludes all reference to the historical deter- minisms of both reader and text." Pointing out Attridge's South African heritage, van Boheemen-Saaf asks whether his agenda presents "the umpteenth English move to erase the specificity of Joyce's cultural heri- tage." This is surely a rhetorical question raised only due to Attridge's antagonistic stance towards Geert Lernout, whose "solidly documented history of the reception of Joyce in France[16] plays Shaun the Post to At- tridge's Penman," disapproving of post-structuralism and stressing the

---

[15] For more, see Chapter II "Psychoanalysis."
[16] I.e., Lernout's *The French Joyce* (for more, see "Introduction").

absolute historical self-identity of Joyce's works, which "need archival and editorial attention—true scholarship, in his view—not exegesis or interpretation" (256). Ultimately, the Lacanian "return of the real" within the academic reception of the "French Joyce" takes place in the scenario of the purloined letter where "the situation of oppositional splitting which represents a severance at the point of origin itself, like the radical dispossession of the Irish by the English." Van Boheemen-Saaf concludes her provocative critique by asking whether it is not high time that "Joyce criticism turned over a new leaf, to pursue the Joyce of the purloined self, rather than the author of the purloined letter?" (257). Her own attempt to do so, published one year later is an eclectic study which synthesizes deconstruction, Lacanian psychoanalysis with a postcolonial perspective on Joyce's relation to history, will be discussed later.[17]

Currie's "Revisiting Poststructuralist Joyce"[18] is a self-purportedly retrospective piece, offering a powerful critique of what Currie regards as the poststructuralist legacy: "a tendency toward literariness in criticism, toward intertextual modes of commentary such as parody, and above all a new cult of the untheorized critical metaphor" (258). The starting point of his analysis is the way in which this cross-contamination of the literary and the critical is theorized in the *Post-Structuralist Joyce* collection, which Currie identifies with "the kind of contempt for cause and effect that Derrida would call *supplementarity*," according to which "poststructuralist theoretical perspective is not only something that came later in the revision and rereading of Joyce, but that it was there in the first place" (259). More broadly, Currie regards poststructuralist writing as marked by "Barthes's idea of the *theatralization* of language," according to which "language stages itself as the object of its own discourse at the same time as it refers unproblematically to things other than itself," and which occasions within the critical language an oscillation between discovery and invention which resists satisfactory logic and which, moreover, is "itself an imitation of Joyce's own oscillation between the poles of naturalism and symbolism in *Ulysses*." This *myth-fact paradox*, to Currie's mind, has never seemed particularly subversive:

> [To] make visible the conditions that make reference possible is not the same as to make reference impossible; to embed extratextual reference within a system of intertextual reference does not subvert the referential function of language; to incorporate critical discussion of Shakespeare does not appropriate further critical discussion; and to explore the consciousness of an artist among others does not render the representation of that consciousness helplessly self-referential. (262)

---

[17] See Chapter VII "Historicism," section IV.
[18] Mark Currie, "Revisiting Poststructuralist Joyce," *Re-Joyce. Text, Culture, Politics*, eds. John Brannigan, Geoff Ward, and Julian Wolfreys (London: MacMillan Press, Ltd., 1998).

Here, Currie identifies what he terms a collusion between reading and text, which in the case of Derrida's reading of *Ulysses* is due to the theoretical content in *Ulysses* "which is not entirely generated by Derrida's reading, and which is enacted rather than explicitly stated by both: a performative and not a constantive knowledge of referential theory" (263). It is with the authority of this theoretical collusion that Derrida's strategy in *"Ulysses* Gramophone" is seen to be invested, relying as it does on the theoretical metaphor which "assigns theoretical knowledge ambiguously between the object text and its reading" (264).

In the increasingly critical stance of Currie's piece, Derrida's legacy comes to be evaluated as "an untheorized confusion between subject and object which underpins rather than undermines the authority of criticism," which consequently "recruits Joyce for theoretical fiction, constructing him as a proto-poststructuralist," undermining the subversive power of deconstructive reading. Currie concludes:

> Poststructuralist readings of Joyce […] establish a new theoretical competence to guide the performances of criticism, placing Joyce's texts the more firmly in the sphere of this academic competence by constructing them as philosophical and theoretical performances themselves. (264)

Derrida's project, questioning the concept of Joycean competence thus appears in Currie's account to re-instate this very competence by means of its own position of theoretical questioning and therefore becomes a deconstructive snake biting its own tail.

VIII

Van Boheemen-Saaf's and Currie's critical articles in *Re-Joyce*, both of which (irrespective of how different their approaches) presented deconstruction in a retrospective arrangement as an approach long-forsaken and discarded within the field of Joyce studies, were followed shortly by the most comprehensive study of the Joyce-Derrida intertext to date, Alan Roughley's *Reading Derrida Reading Joyce*.[19] Roughley explains the peculiar timing of his study by stating his conviction that, contrary to the received notion that Joyce scholarship has moved on to "exploring Joyce from the perspectives of cultural studies," there still remains much work to be done in "understanding the full impact of Derrida's use of an aesthetic, literary language in his philosophical investigations" (xi), and that such "progress" could have only taken place at the cost of "closing off or ignoring the conceptual ruptures and textual spaces opened up in the writings of both Joyce and Derrida" (xii). Among the most prominent of these ranks the term *being*, understood by Derrida as "an ongoing process of becoming" and by Roughley as

[19] Alan Roughley, *Reading Derrida Reading Joyce* (Miami: University Press of Florida, 1999).

one of the reasons why Derrida finds Joyce's writings such a powerful attraction, [for] the concept of being at work in "Literature" is continually investigated and called into question to remind us that the questioning of being is a primary, pressing, ongoing, and unfinished matter for philosophy
and "Literature" alike. (xiii)

The contemporary critique of Derrida's Joycean interventions is viewed as
ill-grounded, resting as it does on the confusion of Derrida's writing with
programs of systematic literary deconstruction, and on a misunderstand-
ing of Derrida's conception of history. Whereas most critics have tended
to link Derrida's work with nihilistic anti-historicism, Derrida himself outspokenly defies the claim that his work is not historical. Instead, "his
work reveals serious reservations about any historicism that fails to consider the vital tool of language with which historicism gathers its evidence
and then represents this evidence and the arguments premised upon it"
(xiv). The focus of Roughley's study is what Currie has dubbed rather
derogatorily as a "collusion," here redefined as

> Mimesis and the production of an always-at-least-double meaning sustained
> by the tension between the signified object and the very process of signifi-
> cation itself: these are the operations between Derrida's writings and his
> readings and re-marking of Joyce's texts. (xv)

The central double-bind of Roughley's approach, often previously identified as such, springs from the sense of a failure to comprehend "all of the
polysemous meanings and complex textual operations of either of the two
writers," a sense which, in Joyce's case, is "intensified by the feeling that
anything one might try to say about Joyce's writing has already been said
by that writing itself." The prime example of this is of course *Finnegans
Wake*, "a book that we can never finish reading in the same way that we
can finish reading a book by other authors" (xvi-xvii). The way out of this
deadlock taken by Roughley consists in "occupying some of the marginal
positions inscribed by Joyce and re-marked by Derrida in order to uncover
some of the intertextual relays and circuits between the projects of these
two writers," for it is these that offer "new interpretative strategies as
well as insights into the deconstructive operations within specific texts"
(xviii-xix).

   To map Roughley's analysis is to follow his chronological discussion of
Joyce's presence within Derrida's works (ranging from his 1967 "Introduction" to Edmund Husserl's *The Origin of Geometry* to the 1992 inter-
views with Attridge in *Acts of Literature*), which I do here in a necessarily
eclectic manner. In his early critique of Husserl, Joyce's writings provide
Derrida with a perspective opposite to Husserl's goal of phenomenological
univocity. Derrida then draws on Joyce as an alternative model for the
complex network of culture, language, and history, examined by Husserl
from the hierarchical three-level stratification of linguistic "ideal objectivity": a primary level, on which "a specific word can be 'free and therefore

ideal,' compared with its sensible, phonetic, or graphic incarnations only within a 'facto-historical' language'"; a *secondary* level, where "a word's sense can be available in different languages through differing signifiers," and the ideal concept thus achieves a degree of independence from its utterance or expression; and finally a *tertiary* level of "absolute ideal Objectivity," the level of "the free, ideal geometrical forms that are the ultimate object of Husserl's investigations" (2-3). It is within this split between the ideal content and the functions of language as its vehicle that "Derrida compares the respective projects of Husserl, which insist on univocity, and of Joyce, which insist on equivocity" (4). As long as Husserl "tries 'to reduce or impoverish empirical language' to the point where its univocity is transparent," Joyce attempts "to bring the past into the present of a writing that seeks to collapse the chronological distance between specific historical events, myths, and narratives" (5). Thus, Derrida's deconstruction of Husserlian univocity, which is revealed as ultimately unattainable, posits Joyce's writings as a corrective to the limitations of its aspirations.

Discussing the marginal Joyce in *Writing and Difference* and *Dissemination*, Roughley repeatedly insists on Joyce's movement from the margins toward the centre of Derrida's concerns. It follows then that the *Ulysses* quote ("Jewgreek is greekjew. Extremes meet.") concluding Derrida's analysis of Lévinas in "Violence and Metaphysics," is seen to encapsulate the whole work. As long as Hebraism comes, in Lévinasian ethics, to represent the central relation between the self and the other in that its "renunciation of hope is an ethical movement toward the totally other, and the relation of separation from the totally other is the ethical relation which Being has with the totally other," then "Hebraism and Hellenism and Jewgreek provide the frame of the entire work" (19). In other words, as long as "Plato's Pharmacy" claims to be 'nothing but a reading of *Finnegans Wake*,' then Joyce's final text can be seen as informing the central concerns of the whole of *Dissemination*, among which Roughley identifies "the structure of the book as an *ideological* structure, the relationships between speech and writing, the relationships between fathers and sons, and the operations of desire in writing" (20).

The *Wake*'s formal destabilization of the traditional book-structure is evident, first and foremost, from its fusion of the beginning with the end, which has important consequences:

> The same is true for the number of "books" into which the *Wake* is divided. The traditional view that it consists of four books must be modified if the last section is a part of the first section because of the sentence fusing them together. Joyce, in fact, makes us think the impossible formulas $17 = 16$ and $4 = 3$, for his text has both sixteen *and* seventeen chapters as well as three *and* four sections. (24)

Derrida's contemplation in *The Post Card* of postcards and the postal system as well as the addressor/addressee relationship inherent in all writing, whose "enigmatic and playful messages inscribed on the back of Derrida's fictitious, philosophical, and literary postcards" solicits traditional philosophical discourse, is seen as haunted by "the *Wake*'s identification of itself as a letter, rather than a book, written by Shem the penman and carried by Shaun the post" (32). In *Glas*, Derrida's writing "deconstructs the form in which that writing is presented in ways that continue his investigation of such notions as presence, existence, unity, and mimesis as they are articulated in language" (44), and is thus seen to foreground three *Wake*-an techniques: "(1) a radical exploitation of paronomasia, (2) the use of a circular structure for the text, and (3) the construction of pages from columns and marginalia engaged in a textual interplay like that of the Talmud and the intertextual structure Joyce constructed for section II.2" (46). Throughout these, Roughley observes,

> Derrida does not claim to have "read" Joyce or to have "proposed a general reading of [his] texts." His interest lies elsewhere: in the "singularity" of Joyce's work, a singularity to which Derrida "tries to respond" or "countersign." Joyce's is an example of an equivocal writing against a limiting historicity and a reductive empiricism. (57)

In his discussion of Derrida's Frankfurt address, Roughley sees this question of "reading" as one of mastering as opposed to "responding" as refusing to master played out in Derrida's concern with competence. The irony unravelled in his argument against the very possibility of such competence attests to his refusal to "submit to any existing Joycean body for an evaluation of his competence" (59). This idea is toyed with further on when Derrida addresses the present Joycean scholars as "Elijah":

> Because the Joyceans whom he addresses are "Elijah," Derrida can count himself among their number; because he bears Elijah's name, he is even more Joycean than they; because the name does not appear on his "official documents," he, like they, lacks legitimate support for a claim to Joycean expertise. (72)

More interestingly, Roughley notes the curious moment of Derrida's identification of "*the* definitive book" as "*two* texts by Joyce," whereby Derrida

> keeps in play both the singularity he stresses as a hallmark of the event of Joyce's writing and the double structure (of Joyce's texts, of his own countersigning of those texts, and of his own writing as a counterexample to Joyce) by which this singularity doubles and unfolds, as if by chance, in Joyce's two texts. (61-2)

Although this may seem to be a minor detail, Roughley convincingly shows that yet again the marginal in Derrida is found at the very heart of the central. "*Ulysses* Gramophone" is therefore seen as being "organized by a series of circular relays operating around the doubling divide of a fold or crease," where

> [the] first part of this double structure takes the form of a confession in which Derrida admits his fears, his intimidation, and his apprehension at speaking on Joyce to an audience of experts on Joyce's works; the second part consists of a denial of the possibility of any kind of Joycean authority or expertise that reveals the irony of the initial confession. (73)

It is in the last text by Derrida within Roughley's focus, "'This Strange Institution Called Literature': An Interview with Jacques Derrida," that the issue of historicity, crucial to the supposed "anti-theoretical turn" of the 1990s, is dealt with fully. Returning to his earlier dealings with Joyce, Derrida sees his value as a counterexample to Husserl or Lévinas in that his texts "offer a model of history attempting to free itself from the empirical and historicist ideas of history that we saw deconstructed by Derrida's readings of those philosophers." Joyce's writing, particularly in the *Wake*, stages the paradoxical historicity of writing,

> produced by the opposition between history as a series of empirical, objective past events, which is the historian's duty to record, and the vital, fictive re-creation of those events within the presence of a narrative that sets them to work in the re-creation of a necessary but unmotivated account of history as the source for fictive narratives.

Ultimately, against "the nightmare of history" which they thematize in a plethora of ways, Joyce's texts evoke "laughter" as a means of awaking from it "by loosening the repressive, historical, and empirical, linear suppression of the play of language's inherent polysemy" (79). Roughley concludes by observing Derrida's engagement with Joyce from a feminist perspective, dealing with how Joyce's *writings* (as opposed to his *statements*) produce "a criticism of phallocentrism and deconstruct their own phallocentric effects" (82). This double movement within Joyce's writing of "both" a critique "and" effectuation of phallocentrism is not to be split into two as

> [the] *Wake* clearly has both phallocentric and antiphallocentric impulses. The reader can attempt to separate the two, but in so doing, he may be producing the results of a critical operation carried out under the restrictions of the logic of the either/or rather than re-markıng the *Wake*'s (con)fusion of the two. Joyce's writing already says anything that we could possibly say about it. (88)

It is here then, pointing to the potential of deconstructive practice within feminist studies (to be returned to later), that the present exposé will leave Roughley's examination of the Joyce/Derrida exchange. Before that is done, his two-chapter glossary of Derrida's "Undecidables" deserves mention, containing key notions of his deconstructive practice, analysed with a keen eye to their indebtedness to Joyce's writing (90-115) — a useful summary of the specific conceptual points of contact between the two, which also serves as a *commodius vicus of recirculation* of Roughley's main arguments.

IX

The 2003 collection of essays, *James Joyce and the Difference of Language*, the editor's introduction to which provided an invaluable backdrop for some of my argument in the "Introduction," offered a fresh perspective on Derrida's other full-length attempt at coming to terms with Joyce. Sam Slote's "No Symbols where None Intended: Derrida's War at *Finnegans Wake*"[20] conceives of the Derrida piece "Two Words for Joyce" as a critique of Martin Heidegger's concept of Being. The connection between the two is presented by Derrida's emphasis on the Germanic overtones of the "He War" passage, according to which "*war* (the past tense of the verb *sein*) and also *wahr* (true) and *wahren* (to guard and preserve)" suggests "Heidegger's characterization of the presencing of presence with the German word *war* in 'The Anaximander Fragment'" where "Being belongs to an *ek-static* temporality registered in the manifold sense of the archaic *use* of the German word *war* (clearing, securing, protection)." Derrida's critique of Heidegger would, then, consist in considering "the event of Being's linguistic self-appropriation (*Ereignis*)" impossible unless "remarked through a *trans*linguistic trace that is not present in the present" (197). As Derrida's remarking of the Greek Heideggerian primordiality takes place by means of a Babelian reinscription (where "Babel" would denote the lack of equivalence between any two languages), the Hellenic is, not for the first time in Derrida, translated into a Hebraic register. However, the *he* of "he war," in Derrida's essay, is not only the God of Babelian confusion, but also Joyce himself: "Derrida characterizes reading the *Wake* as '*être en mémoire de lui*': being stranded within the memory of James Joyce, the locodaedalus: an affirmative hear-say (*l'ouie*)" (199). Slote then proceeds to discuss a different locus in the same *Wake*-an passage (258.2-3: "The timid hearts of words all exeomnosunt"), pasting the rearrangement of *exeomnosunt* into *exeo*, carrying a variety of meanings to do with departing, and the *sunt* that names the plurality of situations that *are*, and the remainder — *mn*: *men* or *man* — which also suggests *mneme*, and by extension "*Mnemosyne*, the mother of the muses — since memory has been the poet's chief gift before the pharmacopoeic gift of writing" (201). Slote then goes on to discuss the "*re-sounding* laughter" which ends II.1 ("Loud, heap miseries upon us yet entwine our arts with laughters low! Ha he hi ho hu. Mummum." 259.7-11). This laughter, met as it is by a murmur, is voiced "preparatory to being silenced," with the end "always forthcoming." Slote's enlightening exploration of Derrida's

---

[20] Slote, Sam, "No Symbols Where None Intended: Derrida's War at *Finnegans Wake*," *James Joyce and the Difference of Language*, ed. Laurent Milesi (Cambridge: Cambridge University Press, 2003).

conceptualization of the Wakean translinguistic war as posed against a totalized Heideggerian Being shows that what emerges at the heart of his engagement with Joyce is Derrida's ethics of responsibility:

> The *Wake* remains an awaiting of a forgetting, the awaiting of hearing a failed or exeomnosunt being. In *hearing* this silence of the translinguistic lapse of Being, Derrida rigorously finds a complex ethical call to respond; hearing this passage otherwise we have found a cunningly babelian Shema of silence and exile. (204)

X

The most recent highly stimulating attempt at "imagining Joyce and Derrida" has taken place "between *Finnegans Wake* and *Glas*."[21] In the introduction, Peter Mahon sketches the Joyce-Derrida intertextuality on the basis of their shared project of disrupting and reinscribing "the philosophical understanding of the process of *mimesis*" through its substitution with what the *Wake* terms *immargination* (4.19): "a sort of unlimited imagination which tries to picture the ever-receding figure of Finnegan, who is lost in a past that has never been present or a future that never arrives," and therefore one which "imitates 'nothing.'" Mahon's examination of the Wakean imagination derives its conceptual rigour from its reconsideration of "some of Derrida's earlier, so-called more philosophical texts" (3), aiming to broaden the so-far mapped Joyce-Derrida intertext through "building upon and generalizing Derrida's contribution to Joyce studies by considering those texts where Derrida does not explicitly address Joyce" (4). In so doing, Mahon's study, despite acknowledging its indebtedness to Sartiliot, Roughley, or Slote, differs from all the previous efforts in that by theorizing "a broadened conception of Joyce-Derrida intertextuality," it aims to address the situation that Laurent Milesi describes in *James Joyce and the Difference of Language* in terms of a "gap" — "It is precisely the 'gap' that Milesi alludes to here that this study seeks to supplement" (5).

Mahon starts out by pointing out that Derrida's critique of Platonic mimesis (particularly in "The Double Session" and "Plato's Pharmacy") has "a profound bearing on what is called 'literature,' since it has traditionally been understood to 'copy' pre-existent 'reality.'" Once, however, the order of appearance (by which Derrida understands "the very process of appearing in general" where the precedence of the imitated "governs the philosophical or critical interpretation of literature") is subjected to the sort of literary experimentation undertaken in *Finnegans Wake*, a "displacement" occurs which "prevents one from considering the *Wake* as literature in any simple sense" (6). It is in the sense of Hegelianism as philosophy "anticipating its exterior" that Derrida's statement about Joyce "the most Hegelian of writers" is to be understood, where the peculiar type of Joycean anticipation is denoted by the term "hypermnesia." The

[21] Peter Mahon, *Imagining Joyce and Derrida: Between "Finnegans Wake" and "Glas"* (Toronto Buffalo London: Toronto University Press, 2007).

Joyce/Derrida relation is then "at its most complex" precisely "with respect to this Joycean [...] variant of Hegelian appropriation," since this
perspective requires a reconceptualization of reading Joyce together with
Derrida (7).

The special mode of Derrida's non-exteriority and non-appropriation
vis-à-vis Joyce is approached in two different ways: first, by "employing
the motifs of *différantial* spacing, doubling, and catachresis utilized by
Derrida to disrupt other 'hypermnesias'" to treat them as "a guide for
disrupting the structure of hypermnesia *itself*" (8), and second, by using
the motifs that constitute "the theoretical matrix of the spacing inherent
in the laughter of the *yes, yes* that Derrida elaborates in both '*Ulysses*
Gramophone' and 'Two Words,'" a laughter which is "always multiple,
dialogical, and directed to another" since its *yes* is always "non-
appropriative" (9). This twofold approach

> will try to avoid seeing Derrida's work [...] as a mere moment of the Joy-
> cean text. It seeks to view the Joycean and Derridean texts in a double re-
> lationship, where their writing is open-endedly "selfpenned to one's other
> ... neverperfect everplanned" (489.33-4). (9)

Mahon's work proceeds from sketching its theoretical groundwork by
detailing the particular deconstructive strategies—*différance*, catachresis,
doubling—which underpin the Joycean/Derridean *yes*-laughter (Chapter I).
This is done in order to test the general applicability of this approach by a
comparative analysis of *Finnegans Wake* and Derrida's "most overlooked
text" *Glas*, chosen primarily because "it is Derrida's most sustained analysis of the Hegelian philosophical system" and because "it can be read as
Derrida's most sustained meditation on the imagination, time, and the
body" (11). Chapter II focuses on the issue of imagination in the celebrated hen's letter of I.5, which is seen—in the context of one of the
Wake's most important intertexts, Giambattista Vico's *New Science*—as a
parody of the practice of augury, which is of momentous import in Vico's
analysis of the constitution of human institutions. Later, the operations of
imagination within the hen's letter are metonymically related to the operations of the *Wake* as a whole, offering a parodic double to the workings
of the philosophical logos (from *legein*, to gather, to collect), and the
Wake/*Glas* intertext is then examined on the basis of the two's joyful
fusion of both writing and reading with the scatological processes and
rhythms of bodily discharging (Chapter III). These rhythms are subsequently connected with what Vico terms "the topics" (Chapter IV), and
the process of bodily writing is revisited within the context of *Glas*'s thematization of "repression" (Chapter V). Finally, the elaborations of time in
both the *Wake* and *Glas* are juxtaposed as part of a reconsideration of the
relevance of the previous discussions of rhythm to a critical examination

of time within the peculiar Wakean temporality of the "not yet" (Chapter IV).[22] This temporality provides

> an important context for the imaginative framework that underlies this study's broadened understanding of the shared intertextual "laughter" of both *Glas* and *Finnegans Wake* that resists being appropriated by philosophical meaning. (13)

At this point, lacking the space to faithfully follow Mahon's extensive argument in its entirety, I shall content myself with charting out Mahon's critical framework as adumbrated in his first chapter, and end on a note of general evaluation.

"'Immargination': The Site of the Imagination" commences with Derrida's attack on Platonism, which for him stands in for all of Western philosophy, on account of what he terms "eidetic reality," a philosophical conception of the real in which the *eidos* is constitutive of "the order of appearance" and thus always interpreted in terms of the undisturbed presence, preceding its imitation. Or, in Mahon's own summary:

> To the extent that both the signifier and writing are expelled outside in that they merely "represent" the meaning of the spoken signified, the relation of the signified to the signifier remains governed by the Platonist order of appearance. Derrida gives the name "logocentrism" to all the forms of present meaning that bear this privileged relation to thought understood as speech. (16)

However, Mahon follows Derrida in listing three reasons why the Platonic *eidos* is NOT immediate or intuitive: 1. the order of appearance "already entails an understanding of 'reality' that is itself already predetermined by a concept of presence derived from the *eidos* understood as meaning or sense"; 2. the interpretation of reality within the order of appearance is further "dependent upon an interpretation of the *eidos* derived from the role that meaning and speech play in the philosophical understanding of the *logos*"; and, 3. through a consideration of the *eidos*, "the order of appearance is further revealed to be dependent upon a covert interpretation of the process of creation or production as a guiding metaphor for interpreting and ordering the relations that obtain between the *eidos*, the *logos*, and the *res*" (17).

The focus of Mahon's study then is on how the *Wake* displaces this Platonist order, and, more specifically, on "how this displacement of presence permits the *Wake* to *avoid* simply rejecting Platonism by considering how it offers its reader a non-Platonist 'double' for the *eidos*, which gives rise to alternative modes of textual practice" (17). Among these alternative modes, the above-mentioned *immargination* ranks high, suggesting itself "as a site for theorizing, and therefore guiding, a more detailed comparative exploration of Wakean textual practice and the radical Derridean

[22] Here, I follow the author's own summary of the work on 11-13.

textuality that interminably deconstructs the philosophy of presence." By foregrounding the deferral and displacement of its own protagonist, Finnegan, *Finnegans Wake* becomes "a text that is no longer adequately understandable in terms of the order of appearance that constitutes the literary-philosophical conceptions of *mimesis*, evidence, consciousness, truth and sense" (18). Finnegan is therefore regarded as a structural principle underlying the concept of sign, akin to the Derridean *différance*:

> since he is not reducible to any on signifier in the text, he must act as a sort of transcendental signified that offers the possibility of an eternally present meaning/truth that would remain outside of the plays of the signifier, thereby regulating and maintaining the structure of the sign [...], and guaranteeing that the "signified" [...] is never to be reduced to a mere "signifier." (20)

Finnegan's "non-presence, or non-presentness, in the sense of nearness or proximity" is connected to its other sense—"temporal presentness or presence," thematized in the *Wake* through the famous formula *passencore*, "not yet":

> The events [in *Finnegans Wake*] have not happened yet, even though they are said to have *already* happened. The deferred temporality of the "not yet" is therefore allied to what Derrida calls the trace—"a past that has never been present"—which is to say, a textual "past" since the present only comes after the written text, which nevertheless lies somewhere in the future since these traces "always remain, as it were, to come—come from the future, from the *to come*." (25)

This displacement of the order of appearance does not bring about any simple *loss* or *rejection* of meaning associated with *mimesis*—in its stead comes what Mahon terms "the double," which functions as the structuring principle in the text. This doubling structure, which proceeds by causing to be repeated what it has made *before*, is manifest on the thematic level of the *Wake* as the motif of "building / bildung / buildung" (28-9):

> Buildung is therefore indissociable from the double to the extent that it proceeds by using what it has made as its material to make what it has already made, with the result that it is impossible to discern here the order of appearance: where is the "buildung" to be imitated if it is already part of the "imitation"? (30)

This making and unmaking of the *Wakese*, after a long and complicated analysis which moves from the discussion of the inherent metaphoricity of language to an investigation of the philosophical dwelling (and Wakean non-dwelling) in metaphor, is further linked to Derrida's conception of catachresis, by means which this metaphoricity is denied, since it concerns the violent and, forced, abusive inscription of a sign, the imposition of a sign upon a meaning which did not yet have its own proper sign in language. So much so that there is no substitution here [...], but rather the irruptive extension of a sign proper to an idea, a meaning, deprived of their signifier. (43)

At the heart of Derridean catachresis is the process by which language and words are called upon to name the idea believed to precede them, and yet in fact coming into existence only *through* this operation of naming. Mahon goes on to discuss a few scenes of writing and composition (*FW* 288.1-14, *U* 1.160-75), noting how the process they depict "is purely imaginative insofar as it cannot be said to arise out of any particular past-present or present experience" (48), and connects this to Derrida's analysis of Mallarmé's "Mime" in his "Double Session," which he sees as "imitating nothing," and therefore the most subversive of all (even derived) Platonism. As Mahon observes, "[if] it is text that is imitated, then the one imitating it imitates nothing, and stays within the space of the non-Platonic *eidos*" (52).

Mahon's argument regains consistency and concreteness when he relates the above-said to Vico's *New Science*, especially its principles of *verum = factum* and *creatio ex nihilo*. The former tenet, "the made is true," posits that since "the produced object is known and knowable completely only by its maker," then human history made from scratch by the human mind which "acts without imitating anything," is in turn knowable only to the Vichian man (55). The latter springs from Vico's belief that "God tells man to contemplate as he does, without a model. In offering that model, he withdraws as model of imitation, and this leaves man free to experience the divine model of creation without model, *ex nihilo*" (56). It is then this "detailed staging of the Vichian origins of man as writing" which "allows *Finnegans Wake* to both participate in and reinscribe Vico's productive method" (57).

Together, Roughley's and Mahon's critical projects exemplify the two prevalent tendencies within Joycean deconstructive criticism — one following the line of Derrida's own explicit engagement with and reference to Joyce's works, and one imagining other possible points of connection, contention, or conflict. Together, though on different grounds, they both insist on the far-from-exhausted potential of deconstructive approaches to Joyce. Perhaps they also attest to their inexhaustibility, paving the way for the work yet to be done.

2. Psychoanalysis

I

The intervention of French theory into Joyce studies at the 1975 Paris symposium (where Lacan delivered a plenary address) had taken another decade to gradually make itself felt within the field of psychoanalytic approaches to the Joycean oeuvre. The most prominent exception to this was Colin MacCabe's pioneering work, *James Joyce and the Revolution of the Word*,[1] the main essence of which already been discussed in the previous chapter. Here my purpose will be to outline the most interesting features of its deployment of Lacanian theory.

In the introduction to his attempt at mapping how Joyce's textuality deconstructs the supposed self-presence of meaning within the signification process, destabilizes the reader/text dichotomy, and therefore questions the very possibility of a meta-critical position, MacCabe makes heavy use of a Lacanian psychoanalytic approach. When charting the theoretical preliminaries of his work, MacCabe raises two important objections to the very possibility of a psychoanalytic approach to literary criticism. Responding to the first— "how can one use psychoanalytic concepts to investigate the very different linguistic order that obtains between reader and text?"—MacCabe points to Lacan's reformulation of the *cogito*. As long as according to Lacan, "I think where I am not and I am where I do not think," then the unconscious is an effect of language "which escapes the conscious subject in the distance between the act of enunciation (in which the subject passes from signifier to signifier) and what is enunciated (in which the subject finds him or herself in place as, for example, the pronoun 'I')" (9). Needless to say, this division characterizes all uses of language but the literary one most prominently. The other objection, "how can one use psychoanalysis outside the context of symptom and cure?", is addressed by MacCabe in terms of the Freudian concept of "deferred action," which postulates that it is essentially impossible "to fix conflicts in the past independently of their articulation in the present," and the ensuing impossibility "to hold apart conflict and symptom," a collapse which has to do with the necessary introduction of the concept of fantasy (9-10).

For MacCabe, insofar as traditional psychoanalysis conceives of itself as a science of human behaviour, "literature can be treated as a form of

[1] Colin MacCabe, *James Joyce and the Revolution of the Word* (New York: Palgrave, 1978; 2003). For more, see Chapter I on "Deconstruction," section I.

that behaviour and thus as an object of study," a subject-object relation of "applied psychoanalysis" whose deeply problematic nature cannot be overstated. However, if Lacanian psychoanalysis "considers itself as the science of the construction of the subject in language," then its relation to literature can be posed "not as that of science to object but as that of theory and practice." Of note is also Lacan's own writing practice, which "displaces reading as a passive consumption of a signified (meaning) and transforms it into an active organization of signifiers (material images)," and is marked by a very similar kind of text appropriation typical also of Joyce's writing (11). Finally, Lacanian psychoanalysis steers clear of a biographical psychologizing, so frequent in early Freudian literary criticism, for it "denies to a life that independence which could allow it to function as origin for the work," marked as it is by its "interweaving of forms, which constitutes the writer as it constitutes the text" (12). Furthermore, in MacCabe's account, psychoanalysis offers an important perspective on the issue of interpretation. As long as all signifying systems might be said to generate texts susceptible to a practically infinite number of readings, then "psychoanalysis locates the limit on interpretations not in any feature of the dream but in the progress of the analysis," in which the correctness of an interpretation is not dependent on ideal homology but on the process of the cure: "it is the extent to which an interpretation provokes new material that it will validate itself" (26).

Later in his discussion of *Ulysses*, MacCabe refers to Lacan's reversal of the causal connection between desire and unconsciousness, quoting Lacan to the sense that

> there is not an unconscious because of some unconscious desire [...]: completely on the contrary, there is desire because there is unconsciousness, that is to say language which escapes the subject in its structure and its effects, and because there is always at the level of language something which is beyond consciousness and it is there that one can situate the function of desire. (105)

This linguistic effect of unconscious, and the concept of the unconscious-as-Name-of-the-Father, is linked to what Freud saw as the motive behind the child's hatred of the father in the third stage of the Oedipus complex: "the father's failure to fill the role assigned to him by the child: to be the cause of its own desire" (108). This fact of absence at the heart of desire, the failure of its ever possible presence then creates what has come to be known as the Lacanian phallus:

> in order to grasp the fact of absence, the child must contrast it with the presence of its own penis. But to do so is to admit the possibility of that penis's absence. This interplay of presence and absence turns the penis into a signifier, the signifier of sexual difference. (109)

Turning to *Ulysses*, MacCabe uses this Freudian-Lacanian framework to comment on Stephen's entrapment. In the opening of the book, "within the speechless world of the neurotic," it is the *mother* "who lies as a barrier across Stephen's entry to this world." Stephen's "I" is conceived of here as full (simply and not so much so full of himself), but MacCabe adds, "it is exactly this full 'I' which can know nothing of language: of the experience of lack and difference." Stephen's writing on the beach is therefore "invisible," as

> within this section writing exists only as repressed possibility: an insistence on materiality and difference, absence and lack, which [...] will disrupt the clear subjectivity of this section and make language and desire possible. (112)

II

It was again the 1984 Frankfurt symposium that marked the first major impact of Lacanian thought upon Joyce studies. The Bernard Benstock edited collection, *James Joyce: The Augmented Ninth*,[2] bears witness to this by reprinting, in what is a considerable section of the whole book, the papers from the "James Joyce / Jacques Lacan" panel.

In an introduction to this panel/section, Patrick Colm Hogan employs the Lacanian term "Other scene" to describe the entire drama of Bloom's day, "the point around which all his thoughts turn, the center of his concentration" as that which "he does *not* think about"—his wife's adulterous tryst (181). He then goes on to document on several examples how, with the *post facto* meeting between Bloom and Molly drawing nigh, "the narrative intellect becomes more and more disturbed, more and more distracted, more and more prone to error" (182).

Albert Sonnenfeld ("Desire and Fantasm in Joyce/Lacan") examines the issue of desire, and more specifically "its relation to the creation of the stream-of-consciousness technique in the work of James Joyce, its relation, if you like, to the whole notion of poetic invention, poetic imaginings, *Einbildungskraft*" (184). An analogy is drawn between Lacan's conceptualization of desire as lack or absence pictured as presence, and the scene of artistic creation in *A Portrait*, where (in the famous villanelle scene), "the desire for the embodiment of womanhood—an embodiment who populates Stephen Dedalus' reveries and phantasms throughout the novel—has stimulated a vision and that vision flows in this liquid fashion through his brain." This phantasmatic stimulation gives rise to ejaculation-as-creation, "the ejaculation through the pen as, in the words of the text, "Fearing to lose all," Stephen Dedalus reached for his pencil and paper" (185).

On a more general note, Sonnenfeld observes of the relation between psychoanalysis and literary theory that the stuff they are made on, as it were, is one and the same—textuality: "The psychoanalyst is, in many ways, a *reader* of someone else's text, the text being the dream that has

[2] Bernard Benstock, ed., *James Joyce: The Augmented Ninth* (Syracuse: Syracuse University Press, 1988).

been verbalized in the commentary made by the patient, and the dream that has been deliberately obscured" (186). Sonnenfeld does not fail to address the fundamental question of the two-way process of reading, the question of agency: who or what is it that becomes analysed when psychoanalytic methods are applied to a literary text? A character? The author? Or even (with the famous fork-holed letter from the fifth chapter of *Finnegans Wake* in mind) — the reader? The answer provided here, one that draws on the definition of Bellemann-Noël, is accordingly a rather general one: "a kind of vast world which is a combination of character (to the lowest degree), and (primarily) author and work." Returning to the main theme of his paper, Sonnenfeld concludes by providing what seems a more satisfactory answer. As long as desire, the unfulfilled wish, functions as the locus for the production of fantasies, it "leads directly to the stream-of-consciousness technique" which calls for an analysis "not only as poem and artifice but also as the psychological or psychoanalytical monologue of that superpatient who is the creator of that monologue — James Joyce. Not James Joyce the person, but James Joyce the linguistic voice" (187).

Nate Clark's "Joyce and Lacan" deals with Lacan's emphasis on the Word. Its generation, however, is considered to have taken place "not in a patient but rather in a text, with the Lacanian potentialities and implications the Word has for both subject (the text, or author/analyst) and object (the consumer of the text)" (188). Lacan's famous dictum that "every word calls for a reply" is related to the reader's practice of lending an ear to "the text's *said* as well as its *non-said*, approaching it with what the *Wake* describes as an 'aural eyeness,'" whereby the process is launched in which "the free play in the Word is perpetually creating the world" (189). The special kind of the Word which Joyce created in his *Finnegans Wake*, "dredged up out of his 'muttheringpot memory' served his 'rejovinating' purposes well because his wordcraft resists categorization and consequent castration" (192). Ultimately, Joyce is regarded as a creator of a particular kind of discourse, subconscious in nature because forged in the smithy of the dreaming mind, and thus endowed with "the power of transformation" (193).

If the three papers discussed so far have in one way or another attempted to "apply" individual Lacanian notions to Joyce's text and have to a varying degree demonstrated both the difficulties and potential usefulness of such psychoanalytic readings, it is only Geert Lernout's intervention that poses the fundamental questions about the very notion of this "application." Lernout's provocative paper calls into question the polyvalent slash that stands in between Joyce and Lacan in the title of the panel (an in-betweenness which, as I tried to show in the Introduction's discussion of Derrida's Frankfurt address, is far from unproblematic in any meta-discourse *about* literature). In "Joyce or Lacan," Lernout sets out by proposing no fewer than four different ways of reading the panel's title. The first one is, "What do we learn about Joyce when we read what

Lacan wrote about him?" and Lernout's reply "must be disappointing to Joyceans" for in his view, "Lacan never actually *read* Joyce" (195). The second question to be posed about the title is, "What do we learn about Lacan when we read his comments on Joyce?" In a footnote, Lernout refers to Jean-Michel Rabaté in proposing that "Lacan attempted to combat his own neuroses by trying to find in *Finnegans Wake* how Joyce overcame his madness by writing the *Wake*," a theory which seems "very convincing and makes the second reading of the title an even more interesting area of research for Lacanians" (202). The third, "What does Lacanian theory teach us about Joyce?" is an even harder question "because nobody seems to know what Lacanian theory is." For argument's sake, however, Lernout takes what he believes is "the most popular and widespread Lacanianism: that of the sixties, based largely on the crucial essays in *Ecrits*" (196). Here, he identifies two sources for Lacan's thought: "an anti-rationalist reading of Freud and an equally anti-rationalist interest in Heidegger" (197).

The problem shared by both of these allegedly anti-rationalist interpretations is seen as lying in the question of authority. With Freud, that of the analyst, it derives from his ability to eschew the impact *his own* unconscious bears upon his examination of the unconscious of others (and Freud's famous remark about a cigar sometimes being only a cigar is dismissed as "unacceptable [...] for those who really believe in the unconscious"). In Heideggerian existentialism, the notion of the unsaid is essentially nebulous, for "if the unsaid is all that the said is not, it is unlimited and any statement about it is by necessity incomplete." Thus, both Freud's and Heidegger's authority is seen as merely subjectively asserted rather than objectively demonstrated:

> In the classical Freudian tradition and in Lacanian practice, an analyst's authority is based, through a training analysis, on that of his analyst, whose authority is based on that of his analyst. If a Freudian analyst's authority is given to him, or is ultimately based on the *person* of Freud, where did Freud get it from? [...] I can only agree with Theodor Adorno who has shown convincingly that Heidegger bases his authority on the assertion that he has that authority. (198)

The fourth way of reading the ambiguous slash separating Joyce / Lacan, the last one proposed by Lernout, is a direct juxtaposition of the two. Their commonalities include both having "a strong sense of what they wanted to do," both revolutionizing their respective idioms, gathering a network of people and showing "a particular liking for Catholicism" (199). The influence which either exerted (and exerts posthumously) upon the gathered group of disciples is likened to Freud's theory of primitive society espoused in his *Totem and Taboo*: "Both Joyce and Lacan are primal fathers, who, even after their deaths, lead Churches of their own." From this also springs what Lernout argues is a necessity: a choice of one over the other: "By definition, one cannot belong to two primal hordes at the same time and a Joycean will have to choose between Joyce and Lacan" (200). Here, Lernout digresses to raise an objection against what he regards as a common problem of Lacanian (and Lacan's own) readings of *Finnegans Wake*: "if it is true as Lacanians claim that every word in the *Wake* can mean anything at all, how is it that when they quote from the text, it only means one thing?" The poststructuralist notion of the unreadable, the *illisible*, is countered by the author's claim that "the strange thing is that *Finnegans Wake* is *lisible*, it can be read." Lernout then concludes by sharing a personal experience of his own coming-to-terms-with *Finnegans Wake*, his gradual discovery, over the years, of "what every Joycean must have found at some point: that *Finnegans Wake* was about *me*." This discovery in turn led to another: that "you can belong to only one primal horde." Needless to say, Lernout "preferred Joyce's" (201). However debatable this direct connection between the idiosyncrasy of each and every reader's personal reading of the *Wake* and the need to choose *either* Joyce *or* Lacan (as if purity or ideological integrity were categories easily applicable to the discussion of literary interpretation), Lernout's contribution presents the very fundamental problems of applied psychoanalysis, informedly and provocatively.

In a brief response to Lernout's paper, Jean-Michel Rabaté voices similar misgivings as regards attempts at "any vague synthesis" — "I do not believe that Lacan should be 'applied' to Joyce" (204). Rather, what any Joycean can glean from Lacan rather is the critical rigour with which he examined his famous precursor: "If I do find, for my own part, that Freud, more than Lacan, is the necessary reference prior to any deep understanding of Joyce, it is because I allude to a Freud whose violence has been reactivated by Lacan." Rabaté concludes by touching upon the importance of Lacan's emphasis on the importance of the symptomatic quality of Joyce's work, which "presents us with the materiality of the symptom as language, as letter, letters, and litters" and thus "speaks to us insofar as it makes us speak or write from it, about it, within it." This symptomaticity of Joyce's writing recalls what Derrida described as its "hypermnesiac" quality in that it, according to Rabaté, ensnares the reader in a similar double-bind:

> The elaborate machinery of *Ulysses* and *Finnegans Wake* is both a gift obliging its recipients to produce in it and for it more and more sense and glosses, and also a kind of trap that refuses to conclude on any certainty. (205)

The following two papers variously elaborate on Rabaté's central points. Catherine Millot's "On Epiphanies" addresses the contradictorily twofold function of Joycean epiphanies, as "testimonies of a fundamental spiritual experience" for their author, as well as a "mere transcription of some insignificant incidents" for their reader. This ambivalence is accounted for by the essentially metonymical nature of these textual snippets, "the blind and useless witnesses of the inexpressible" (207), devoid of meaning, while pointing beyond it:

> The lost meaning comes back in a way in the Real under the form of this obscure revelation. The epiphanies have the same function as neologisms, just like words of the fundamental language. Joyce dedicated his life to the creation of this fundamental language, and his achievement is *Finnegans Wake*. (208)

This fundamental language is, then, in turn seen as the ultimate goal of Joyce's life-time devotion to purification of language. As long as the emptied space of the epiphany gapes open for the impossible meaningless enjoyment, then "[t]he brilliance of *claritas* is the return of the void of phallic significance into the Real." It is to this void, then, to this "unbearable space of the enjoyment," that Joyce's writing is seen to set limit (209).

In "Sur le sinthome," Jean Guy Godin examines the famed Cork trip episode in *A Portrait* (*P* 91-4), in particular, the scene in which at the precise moment "when the father brings up the question of transmission between generations, father to son, his voice falters [...], breaks down in a sob, which produces a cascade of effects" (210). The most significant effect is that the Lacanian Borromean Knot tying the three registers of the Imaginary, the Real, and the Symbolic, disintegrates and the task is "to hold them together by using either an artifice or a fourth ring" (211). Godin sees the fundamental advantage of "reading Joyce with Lacan" (yet another prepositional relation) in that Joyce's writing is helpful in understanding the appropriateness of the term "sinthome" as referring to the symptom. This spelling alteration suggests, in Godin's understanding, that "if the unconscious in a language is centered on its written word, in Joyce's case the unconscious *is* the written word, the writing." (212) Insofar as the symptom on which Joyce's works consists of "the voice, the fault, and the letter, each linked in its way to this object which concerns the desire of the Other in a privileged manner: *the look*," then in the sinthome of his writing, "Joyce will treat the fault via faults in writing, writing the fault" as a *lapsus calami* (213). This symptom is seen as peculiar to Joyce and starkly different from the analytical symptom, neither to be interpreted, nor to be dissolved by cure.

III

The next major Lacanian foray into Joyce studies was penned by the well-established psychoanalytic scholar (*Joyce Between Freud and Jung* /1980/, *Joyce the Creator* /1985/),[3] Sheldon Brivic. *The Veil of Signs: Joyce, Lacan and Perception*[4] takes as its subject matter the issue of

---

[3] Discussed in Roughley's *James Joyce and Critical Theory*, 189-201.
[4] Sheldon Brivic, *The Veil of Signs: Joyce, Lacan and Perception* (Chicago: University of Illinois Press, 1991).

perception, placing special emphasis on its processing through language, as can be seen from the opening contention that perception in Joyce "operates as a circulation of signifiers between the self and its field, and it usually derives its insight from recognizing this circuit" (1). This circulation implies that words be seen (or, perceived) as dynamic as much as static:

> Every word, then, combines a stable component that can be seen clearly with a dynamic one that cannot, but we are trained to disregard the dynamic aspect. Convention makes us "see" words as static, logocentric structures, but this is not what we see at all. Even if I stop reading to focus on a single word, I can never see the word sitting on the page. What I see is the word coming into my eyes, received at a certain angle in a given light by a particular mind in a specific, unstable state. (2)

Brivic's primary figure of this circulation is the loop, revolving as he does around several kinds of circular movement where "the actual conversations [...] are only part of the spectrum of dialogic circulation in Joyce's texts," for the primary dialogue of every self is conducted with what is termed, with the Lacanian intention "to emphasize the alterity of the unconscious"—the Other, recognized here as a central narrative agency behind the framework of interior monologue (2-3). Lacan's work, whose particular relevance for Brivic's project is briefly discussed at this point, is based on Freud's in that it too regards "libido, the energy of desire, as continually being sent toward its object and then drawn back." It follows from this that "the Lacanian subject [...] is the unconscious basis of the self," knowable "only through the stages of the movement of desire outward and back that constitutes personality," and therefore "neither existence nor perception can take place [...] except as a looping involvement of words," which renders the field of desire equivalent to that of perception. This linguistic construction of personality (the signifier) is first formed by reflection from one's parents, whose function is to "convey the social structure of language." Subjectivity, in this light, appears "constituted by the interchange of speech with another, so that identity is a process of return, just as a word has meaning only by relation to other words"—the subject "exists only by relation to an unknown external agency" (3).

This has direct bearing on Brivic's understanding of the Joycean epiphany, the "sudden spiritual manifestation" concerned with perception of the objectified or linguistic other: "[W]hen the 'spiritual eye' adjusts its 'vision to exact focus,' an epiphany can be received from 'the clock of the Ballast Office'" (*SH* 211). Even though "for Stephen the artist's goal is to express himself," this self "can only appear as an interaction with objects." Yet truth as expressing the human subject can be regarded as not so much residing *within* objects as passing *through* them. Brivic notes, "there is no truth without the subject and its Other, without the looping of narration" (4). The Stephen of the "Scylla" episode has advanced from a romanticized expressivity toward the complex metaphor of "weaving and unweaving" (*U* 9.376-8), which, in Brivic's argument, has to do precisely with "the looping or weaving of signification that makes physical reality in Joyce" and that "always suggests an invisible force behind it," which is described as the Other. What is woven in *Ulysses* is "a tissue of signs into which perception loops, a curtain of appearances" which both conceals and suggests "the Other that can never be seen." It is precisely "the arrangement of this veil and its operation in *Ulysses*" that form Brivic's main concern (5).

Among the most prominent sources of possible inspiration for Joyce's notion of the loop and the veil are Giordano Bruno, the early Joyce's favourite thinker, whose *coincidentia oppositorum* suggests experience and sensation as a constant circular movement. This also has implications for the Saussurean understanding of language as a set of differences, as well as G. W. F. Hegel (whom both Jacques Aubert and Derrida identify as an informative influence on Joyce). The sources of Brivic's conceptualization of this problematic are Lacan's "integrative and disintegrative dialectic," as well as M. M. Bakhtin's dialogical principle which operates between the author and his character (6). In Lacan, it is the "linguistic dynamism" of his dialectic and phenomenology, in which "the subject involved is not identifiable with consciousness," which itself is a process of perpetual displacement where "the Other is identifiable as whatever slips beyond formulation." Being "the manifestation of the unconscious," it becomes for Lacan "the source of truth" (7).

The Lacanian understanding of the subject as being split and containing its own Other implies an address inherent to any kind of discourse— indeed, "discourse cannot exist without an aim"; throughout Joyce, "with regard to logical communication, rarely does anyone change anyone else's mind by speaking intentionally" and "when characters speak to each other, the emphasis is on how little is understood" (8). Even though possibly constituted without any other person present, there is within the Lacanian field of the Other "an imagined consciousness implied," which turns every perception into *interception*, a shared experience (9). Within the specifically literary text, the Other can assume two locations: either within the author himself (as is the argument of Patrick McGee's *Paperspace*[5]), or in the role of the reader. Here, Brivic echoes deconstructionist claims about the all-inclusiveness of the Joycean text, permeated by "the effort to expand the range of his written implications so that as many as possible would be processed by his personality" (11).

Brivic proceeds to glance through the whole of Joyce's corpus, making the overall claim that "the narrative agencies of Joyce's fiction are always contrary on an active level to what they narrate." Thus, in *Dubliners*, a principle of opposition is identified in that "each of these stories constitutes a dialogue between the central character and a narrator who

---

[5] See Chapter VIII "Politics," section IV.

sees beyond her or him" (examples of which would be the epiphanies in *Araby* and *The Dead* whose protagonists perceive the Other by seeing themselves as others see them); in *A Portrait*, the duality is inherent in the fact that "the narrator is a future version of the protagonist" and so "Stephen contrasts with the narrator by being an artist who is not mature"; in *Ulysses*, neither Bloom nor Stephen would be "the same without the other to counterpoint him"; and, in the *Wake*, the opposition is between Shem and Shaun, where "Shem is usually viewed with disapproval by narrators who tend to resemble Shaun, while Shaun is presented with mockery from points of view that are Shem-like" (12-3).

Bloom's "depth" comes from his being inserted "dialogically into 'other' discourses," which illustrates Lacan's idea that "depth comes from the otherness." The truth of Bloom's experience then, "is a dialogue between the convention of actuality that tries to enclose him and connections that come from beyond him to exceed 'actuality.'" At this point Bakhtin is referred to with his understanding of the artistic image of language as created by two consciousnesses: "the one being represented" and "the one doing the representing." As long as the place of the Other in Lacan may be identified with the place reserved for God by religion, then Joyce can be viewed as the God of his creation: "rather than pretending the need for God does not exist, Joyce co-opts it blasphemously by synthesizing God's functions" (15).

In a useful discussion of what he terms "linguistic mysticism," Brivic notes that it was the issue of Joyce's authority that has so impressed both Lacan and Derrida in his work. The view of Joyce's presence in his work as "a series of powerful effects in language" is identified — via a reference to the God of the "Oxen" chapter as the "Beneficent Disseminator" (*U* 14.766) — with the belief of the mystical tradition in "God as a principle of creative differentiation" (15). An opposite strategy to this self-effacing strain is Joyce's practice "of projecting himself as a source of transcendent knowledge that shifts and turns out to be a step beyond comprehension," linked, in turn, with what Lacan puts in the place of God: "*la jouissance*, a feminine effect of going beyond any particular form" (17). Lacan's symptom, in the context of Brivic's interest in the circulative movement of perception, is characterized as "a principle of repetition that constitutes identity," in relation to which Lacan's idea of the real, the moment of the impossibility onto which both the symbolic order (language), and the imaginary (ego and its identifications) are grafted. Within these orders, the unconscious is found "in the ambiguity of words, an uncertainty that can yield multiplicity and plenitude" (18). Analogously, the artist is regarded by Lacan as "suspended in otherness, suspended among alternatives" of which only one "can differentiate itself into enunciation, but the others have to be left to define it." Thought, it therefore follows, is "always the contrary end" (20).

There are other ways, however, in which the God-like stature of Joyce can be (and has been) conceptualized — Brivic references Derrida's famous "he war" discussion of God's signature, countersignature, and the self-referentiality of the *Wake*. Some of the most effective examples of Joyce's "movement beyond form" are found in "woman as a figure of displacement, a verbal flow that cannot be contained." According to this view, attempts to see the perspective of women at the ends of Joyce's works "are another way in which he puts himself in the position of the Other" (23). Thus, the topic of "gender as language" gains momentum in Brivic's argument, which is connected with Lacan's belief that "masculine and feminine are actually veils of language" (27). This also relates to his broader argument regarding the respective roles of the parents in the constitution of a linguistic subject:

> the infant has a closeness to the mother in which feelings flow freely in imaginary language until the father imposes phallic authority which separates the child from direct pleasure and forces it to use determinate symbolic language as its substitute. (28)

As long as Joyce's textual effects entail the creation of certain linguistic veils, then the aim of Brivic's book is to "think through" these in seven stages where individual discussions thematically centre around the following concerns. In the first chapter, the cyclical structure of *Portrait* is looked at, presenting the movement of Stephen's mind outward and inward and delineating the field of the Other. The second chapter then addresses the question of "the author" as "the Other" by means of "providing his characters with a channel into the unconscious that they use whenever their language goes beyond their understanding." Brivic's third chapter focuses on the "Proteus" episode, where the world is explicitly a veil of signs, a tissue Stephen wants to penetrate. The fourth chapter depicts the operations of the gaze *between* Stephen *and* Bloom, followed by "a series of scenes in which Stephen and Bloom get fleeting senses of going through the veil late in *Ulysses*." In the fifth and sixth chapters, Joyce's treatment of "Penelope" where "Molly weaves the veil that Stephen and Bloom see because the movement of her thought as woman is the object of their perception through desire" is examined and finally the seventh chapter consists of an extended discussion of the *Wake*, whose interacting figures are regarded as parts of one mind.[6]

Brivic's conclusion, "Reweave: The Gift of Tongue," revisits the three images of the field of desire discussed throughout (*Portrait*'s flux of artistic creation, *Ulysses*' veil of signs, and the *Wake*'s wall of language) from the perspective of the early emphasis on movement:

> Movement, which is equivalent to feeling, is the only way to penetrate the veil (or wall) because when the obstacle is shifted, it loses its solidity and contact is made with the other side. At least the space on that side answers the movement on this one. (184)

---

[6] In this summary, I closely follow the author's own groundwork plans of his work on 30.

This movement beyond the field of linguistic desire and toward the Other receives its most prominent treatment in the *Portrait* motif of "the kiss," the object of Stephen's first voiced question ("What did that mean, to kiss?" *P* 15), which not only indicates the "dependence of Stephen's thought on the feminine," but also raises "questions on the political level about the social reality involved in this gift" (188). This early question is linked to "one of [Stephen's] most penetrating insights into woman" in his villanelle of the temptress, where he repeatedly asks, "*Are you not weary of ardent ways?*" (*P* 223), indicating that the "woman must be tired of playing the role of the Other" (189). Brivic's innovative, insightful, and accessible Lacanian analysis ultimately yields a revelation of the social realities that have shaped his symbolization of the kiss as an affirmation, "not of discrete individuals," but "of circuits of interchange," enacting "the loop that Lacan locates at the rim in the field of the Other" (191).

IV

Brivic's seminal work marked the beginning of a sustained analysis of Joyce's work in the early 1990s from the positions offered by poststructuralist, but also historically and politically oriented psychoanalytic thought. *Joyce: The Return of the Repressed*,[7] edited by Susan Stanford Friedman, bears witness to a surge of activity in this latter field, whereas Garry Leonard's book-length study, to be discussed at a later point, presents a suitable example of the former.

In her introduction to the collection (which originated in a cluster of panels organized for the 1988 Joyce symposium in Venice), Friedman discerns the unifying theme of the essays culled here as being an examination of the ways in which Joyce's texts can be read as "sites of repression and insistent return." The interconnections looked at here span those "between the psychic and the political, the textual and the historical, the erotic and the linguistic" (1). Friedman proceeds to postulate the poststructuralist moment of the collection's publication by pointing out what she sees the two main reasons why Joyce seems "ideally suited" to poststructuralist readings. First, Joyce's texts

> anticipate and perform with an increasingly dazzling display many basic tenets of recent critical theory—most specifically the deconstruction of the Cartesian subject and the linguistic reconstitution of the subject as forever in process and unknown to itself; the materiality of language in all its thickness, density, opaqueness, undecidability, and ephemerality; the endless play of words in chains of reference that signify not "meaning" but indeterminate processes of meaning; and the binary of masculine/feminine as the master plot of pallo(go)centrism in Western culture. (3)

7 Susan Stanford Friedman, ed., *Joyce: The Return of the Repressed* (London and Ithaca: Cornell University Press, 1993).

However, Friedman's is an implicitly dissenting attitude, for she warns in one breath against the potential unproductiveness of the central double-bind of deconstructed/deconstructive Joyce:

> at their weakest, such readings remain caught in a hermeneutic circle: Joyce becomes the ideal terrain upon which to prove the theories that his texts themselves anticipate [...whereby] the poststructuralist reading becomes its own confirmation [...and] the theory that privileges unpredictability produces a repetition of readings in which Joyce...signifies the truth of Derrida or Lacan. (3)

The second reason for his proneness to deconstruction is that Joyce has become "something of an icon of and for modernity"—this in complex ways and for contradictory reasons:

> for some, Joyce is *the* canonical writer of the 20th century [...], the supreme avatar of modernity and its most brilliant practitioner[;] for others, Joyce serves as metonym for modernity, a fragment of the whole that stands in for the deconstruction of the very notion of icons and canons, [...writing] not in the language of the high priests of Western culture but rather speaks the problematic of these discourses: [...] the feminine, the unconscious, the radical Other[;] for a third group, Joyce is neither an idol not metonym for modernity [... but] rather, he is read dialogically as a voice containing many competing discourses—some in league with ideology, some subversive to it [... −] within this framework Joyce remains one voice, however multilayered and conflicted, among many other voices. (4-5)

Within these different outlooks, Joyce is read as either "the supremely modern writer, the inventor and technologist of modernist and postmodernist poetics," or "the inscription of modernity's fragmentations," or "the site of contestation between authoritative and marginalized discourses, [...] the textualization of modernity's discontents." Many critics, it need not be emphasized, treat aspects of all three, interweaving them into "dialogic representations of Joyce wherein different strands of his modernity compete with and often undermine one another" (5-6).

The present volume then seeks to combine these three in order to highlight the significance of *rupture* within Joyce's writing, here "premised on the psychoanalytic notion that nothing is completely lost, only 'forgotten,'" and engaged in adapting "Freud's concepts of repression, return, and interpretation to the project of reading Joyce's texts" (6). Therefore the collection itself, due to its concern with Freud emerges as a sort of "a return of the repressed Freud" at one of the highest moments of Lacanian psychoanalysis within Joyce studies in the early 1990s.

Their shared emphasis involves the essays' preoccupation with Kristevan intertextuality, and their common historicising endeavour, since intertextuality presupposes a context of "the historical and social text": the psychoanalytic essays in this volume thus "include an analysis of history and the politics of repression and return in Joyce's oeuvre" (6-7). In relation to Stephen's outcry that history is a nightmare, it is not in fact "the erasure of history," but rather "its insistent return as nightmare and desire" which appears to mark "modernity's stance toward the stories of the past" (7). The essays, whose foci range from the psychodynamics of repression and return or the social and political history as repressed discourses to the questions of desire, female subjectivity and the inscriptions of incest and narcissism in the figure of Joyce's late work (8-11), seek to integrate psychoanalytic and historical methods while exploring not only how "the psychodynamics of repression and return are represented textually in Joyce's oeuvre," but also the way "they inscribe processes and positionalities that return us to pressing questions of literary, cultural, and political history" (13).

Among the most prominent shared motifs is the figure of the mother who, "whether as historical subject or as image of the desired maternal body forms a matrix in the volume that draws like a magnet all the other issues examined in the volume," and the collection therefore marks a shift from the earlier Joycean paternalist criticism focusing on the problematic of the father toward maternal constellations (16). The volume as a whole ultimately hopes to open the debate concerning the question of "how fully Joyce was aware of or intentionally explored the processes of repression and return," and leaves it as a suggested task for the psychoanalytic criticism of the future

> to learn to read the dialogue (indeed polylogue) of cultural voices in Joyce's texts: both revolutionary and reactionary, both critiquing and subject to critique, both oppositional and ideological, both marginal and central. (16-17)

Thus, Alberto Moreiras "Pharmacononomy: Stephen and the Daedalids" remains the only palpable trace of deconstruction upon the psychoanalytic thought presented here, treating as it does the repressed resonances of Stephen's artistic formation in relation to Derrida's discussion of writing as *pharmakon* The collection's overall historico-cultural slant is best represented by such essays as Friedman's own "(Self)Censorship and the Making of Joyce's Modernism," which discusses the production of Joyce's modernity as documented in the shifting representations of Stephen's character, Robert Spoo's "Uncanny Returns in 'The Dead,'" which adapts the Freudian understanding of the uncanny as a site of repression in which to read Joyce's short story and Marilyn L. Brownstein's ambitious piece titled "The Preservation of Tenderness: A Confusion of Tongues in *Ulysses* and *Finnegans Wake*." In it Brownstein regards incest as involving a "confusion of tongues" between the infant's language of tenderness and the parent's language of passion and uses it for a convincing reading of father-daughter relations in Joyce's texts.

V

Another crucial study to emerge in 1993, one which as we have observed aimed to follow the Lacanian stream of psychoanalytic literary theory, was Garry Leonard's *Reading Dubliners Again: A Lacanian Perspective.*[8] This supplemented the merely marginal interest of *Dubliners* awarded to Brivic's argument by offering a book-length, story-by-story, Lacanian reading of the whole collection. Given the book's broad scope and acute attention to textual detail, it will be possible here to merely do justice to its introductory and concluding parts, with a cursory yet illustrative glance at its reading procedures.

Leonard opens his "Introduction: Spilling Whiskey on the Corpus" by seeing Joyce's fascination with "the mystery of the conscious" as having been behind the creation of *Dubliners*, aiming to "make the phenomenon of consciousness uncomfortably problematical for his readers" (1). Lacan's fascination with Joyce in turn is seen as having sprung from the fact that

> in his fiction the letter so revealingly collapses into litter and leaves the subject (the reader) with the uncertain sense that to be conscious is to be a signifier in relation to other signifiers, ad infinitum, with no genuine signifieds that are not self-generated myths. (2)

An important part of Leonard's argument is to call into question the commonly invoked "transcendence of experience" in *Dubliners*, usually linked to the stories' *epiphany*:

> the readers of *Dubliners* are encouraged by Joyce to enjoy transcending the limited perspective of the fictional selves (characters) in the stories but only at the price of becoming uneasily aware that the stories of their own lives also operate as texts that maintain their unity and coherence by forgetting, excluding and marginalizing whatever contradicts the myth of the self. (3)

Leonard's Lacanian position leads him to view the human subject as "an endlessly pliable version of reality carefully narrated to hold at bay all knowledge of the irreparable fragmentation and disharmony at the base of consciousness that is incontrovertibly Real" (3). This makeshift nature of the self, and the essential incompatibility at the bottom of consciousness, preclude from his approach any claim to essentialism. Instead, they enable him to lay claim to

> an antiessentialism [...] that sees reality, gender, personality, and so on, as the reality effects of a subject seeking to deny a lack-in-being that exists alongside of and, thus undermines the mythic ideology of unified consciousness. (4)

This informs his treatment with an essentially sympathetic attitude towards the characters caught up within Joyce's stories, balanced against a desire to master them from a convenient space of an outside meta-

[8] Garry M. Leonard, *Reading 'Dubliners' Again: A Lacanian Perspective* (New York: Syracuse University Press, 1993).

discourse. Rather than following the traditional critical project of "filling-in-the-gaps" or "seeing-through-the-masks," which entails the self-congratulatory gesture of arriving at interpretive discoveries inaccessible to the characters under observation, Leonard proposes to take account of the fact that "rarely in fiction do characters suffer as exquisitely for the benefit of a reader as they do in *Dubliners*" by urging the readers to "explore their kinship with the characters' moral paralysis rather than self-righteously suggest various cures for it." Any such exploration must take as its prime subject the human ego, whose Lacanian understanding underpins Leonard's argument.

Lacan's ego varies from the Freudian in the linguistic nature of its split, divided as it is "between a narcissistic, objectlike total being (*moi*) and a speaking subject (*je*) who tries to validate this (fictional) unity of being by seducing the objective world (the Other) into declaring it authentic," where the *moi* is seen as inherently paranoid because "its existence is dependent upon, and solicitous of, outside validation" (6). Beyond this split lies

> the Real subject of the unconscious that cannot be represented in imagery or signified in language […] the rem(a)inder of the lack-in-being that the *moi* is intended to paper over with fantasies of autonomy that constitute what it perceives as reality. [Thus], truth orbits beyond […] representation in the Real (invisible, but not ineffectual) and can only be glimpsed in those decentering moments during which the *je* fails in its task of linguistic seduction and momentarily experiences the terrifying fact that the *moi*, the subject's truth, which it desires to serve, is fiction. (6-7)

It follows that the Joycean *epiphany* as presented in *Dubliners* would be this terrifying experience of fictionality of one's truth rather than an interpretive discovery of a more deeply hidden one. The structure of ego-as-symptom, presented throughout Joyce's fiction as incurable—for example within the structure of *A Portrait*, where a tentative cure at the end of each chapter poses as the backdrop (if not cause) for another more serious crisis—substantiates Leonard's claim that Joyce refuses psychoanalysis "because he has already faced the terrifying and exhilarating fact that the structure of consciousness *is* 'the mental illness of man,'" and makes into the central purpose of this study the intent

> to "Re-Joyce" *Dubliners*, that is, to present this collection of "easy Joyce" as an exploration of the mystery of consciousness that is both invigorating and unsettling for the reader. (8)

Leonard's brief section introducing Lacan focuses on "the Phallus," defined rather obscurely as "a (nonexistent) transcendent signifier, presumed to bestow monadic self-sufficiency and mastery of the Symbolic Order on the masculine subject," which emerges from Lacan's understanding of the infantile development into subjectivity, marked by a substitution of the real with the imaginary wholeness of ego, and its subsequent re-identification with the endlessly substitutive processes of signifi-cation. During this process, the masculine subject, renouncing the mother's body as different from his own, "guarantees this fiction that he is 'all' by designating the 'feminine' subject as 'not all.'" However, the natural enough fact that a man has a penis is not to be confused with the ideologically constructed idea that he possesses "the Phallus". This phal-locentric dimension of Lacan's theory is compensated for by the special privilege he accords woman in retaining a "supplementary *jouissance*" that "ex-ists beyond a masculine subject's truth," functioning "as the ultimate limit upon phallocentric discourse" (9). Woman functions as man's symptom in that she

> serves a function similar to that of the ego, or *moi*; she validates the truth-fulness of the fictional construct of masculinity by acting out the fiction of femininity […] as being the phallus so that he, in desiring to have it, will desire her. […] the result of this comedy of desire is a strange dance of misrecognition wherein the woman pretends to lack what the man can only pretend he possesses. (10)

It is precisely "the absolute belief in the fraudulent authority of the phallic signifier" and the ensuing "abject dependence on the feminine subject as a symptom" that provide the masculine subject of *Dubliners* with the veil necessary for the Phallus to perform its (symbolic) function" (10).

In the light of these introductory forays into Lacan, Leonard proceeds to show their potential usefulness for reconceiving the whole collection which is seen as

> replete with representations of patriarchal authority teetering on the edge of the void: dying, dead, and long-absent priests, obtuse or drunken uncles… or older men with perverse desires, or abusive fathers, or fathers who feel out of place in their own homes. (11)

Furthermore, this opens up feminist vistas for approaching Joyce's short stories whose feminine subjects

> come to grief in their own gender paradox because if they slavishly support the validity of the Phallic Order, they will eventually be spurned and pushed aside; after all, of what use to the masculine subject is the confirmation and admiration of a slave? (14)

Leonard's book reserves a clearly demarcated section for each story, trying "to preserve the complexity of Lacanian theory" as well as "to make its interplay with Joyce's fictions as rich as possible," an example of which might be the very first analysis of "The Sisters" in terms of the three Lacanian orders and "how the text negotiates the realm between the unconscious and the structure of consciousness, between the inac-cessible truth of the real and the fiction of reality" (16). There is on an experiential level a parallel drawn between Lacan's seminars, "famous not because they were alternately brilliant and obscure but because their brilliance necessitated their obscurity," and Joyce's stories where "the experience of incomprehension" is seen as "the lesson of *Dubliners*" (17). Furthermore, the famously and frustratingly abrupt endings of the stories are likened to Lacan's notorious "short sessions," in which "the analyst purposely aborts the analysand's discourse by leaving before the end of the session," which in Joyce finds its equivalent in his strategy of interrupting a thematic pattern every time Joyce discerns one, and of "[dwelling] on the resulting rip in reality through which the Real momentarily shows through" (19). Leonard's own experience with the ending of "The Sisters" is one of being

> thrown back into what Lacan calls "the lumber-room of the mind," that cluttered room with restricted access, just behind the place where one stages one's existence: the room of scrap parts out of which one first constructed the myth of oneself,

an experience which allows the reader to reveal

> through the interplay of consciousness and text that the ego one holds so dear is a symptom, and the text cannot cure this symptom (fortunately!), but it can isolate some of the various threads that form the know of the "self" and show their inextricable relationship with the Real that informs the texture of reality. (20)

Informed by this radical practice, Joyce's writing is found to be an "aggressively subversive of the reading subject because it manipulates or frustrates any impulse on the part of the reader to strengthen the illusion of mastery by discerning the meaning of the story" (21). Thus, Leonard qualifies his previous statement about the nature of epiphany, where the "realization that the object of desire is once again a substitute" is found to be "precisely [the] sort of overhasty discovery of truth that allows the text to expose reality as a fictional construct" and therefore to permit "the split subject to misrecognize the actual indifferent and subversive power of the unrepresentable Real as the imagined benevolent gaze of the Other" (22-3). In perhaps more accessible words,

> To merely point out the mistakes of the characters of *Dubliners* or to regard them [...] as unique victims of the ineffable disease of moral paralysis, is to fantasize one's unity as a literary critic. To feel sorry for them is to avoid feeling sorry for ourselves. (23)

This central mode of Leonard's approach to *Dubliners*, one which discards the traditional "steady accumulation of 'meaning'" in order to "explore the gaps, silences, elisions, deferred actions, self-delusions and false consistencies," seen "as the dominant discourse of this collection" has consequences for the critic's pedagogical concerns which are revisited in his conclusion (309-10). Leonard's crucial concern throughout his psychoanalytic readings that tried to attest to their subversive textual practices is revealed to have been pedagogic all through. In his opinion,

> what teaching Joyce's fiction should teach everyone is that the "truth" about his fiction is not what one comes to understand, but what defies explication. [...] Benign acceptance of another's point of view is the sincerest form of complete dismissal. Education, both for analysts and their analysands and for teachers and their students, should generate resistance. (310)

What is unsettling about reading Joyce is that it entails, in a phrase *Ulysses* borrows from Mallarmé, "reading the book of oneself" — "a frightening, invigorating experience, impossible to sustain (and, therefore, akin to Joyce's epiphany)" (311). This in turn is linked to the anti-humanist (yet Leonard adds most decidedly pro-human) strain in Lacan's theory, which protests against humanism on account of its being "a school of thought that denies the complexity of the human condition it purports to examine" (313). Joyce's own admission to Grant Richards that he heard voices while working on *Dubliners* is seen as "his most profound comment concerning the collection," as it reflects Joyce's self-claimed ability "to become a mouthpiece for the extant voices of the Symbolic Order" (317).

However, there are other far less profound comments made by the author with which Leonard comes to terms in the end of his book. Joyce's letter concerning his "intention... to present... arranged... order" seen as a ploy or as "music to soothe the nervous ears of Grant Richards," for, "if Dublin is the center of paralysis, what is the periphery?" The four stages into which Joyce categorizes the collection are found to be "remarkably unhelpful" and "intended to be reassuring," turning the schema into "a dense parody of the paralysis that occurs when meaningless phrases are imposed in order to give 'definite form' to a subtly odiferous work" (320). The dialogue between Richards and Joyce is ultimately seen as having been re-enacted in Leonard's theoretically sound and textually attentive approach:

> Where Richards has said, in an apprehensive tone, "There is a heavy odour in the room," Joyce has reassuringly replied, "the flowers." In this book, I have tried to Re-Joyce *Dubliners* by reopening this reassuring statement of the facts:
> – The Flowers...yes...but something else... (321)

VI

One of the most sophisticated, innovative, and theoretically informed voices in present-day Joyce criticism, Jean-Michel Rabaté, has developed an approach that idiosyncratically blends deconstructionist practice and psychoanalytic theory with the frequent deployment of analysis of the notebooks — a blend which remains very difficult to categorize within the framing of the present work — allowing him to discuss a vast range of theoretical issues with a competence paralleled by few other Joyceans.

Since their concerns are too varied for all three of them to be presented within one chapter, here I outline the latest of Rabaté's three crucial essay collections, *James Joyce and the Politics of Egoism*,[9] with respect to its original use of Lacan in its first chapter.

Centred (like the two other essay collections) around a series of interrelated topics rather than aligning itself with one discrete critical methodology or agenda, this book's twelve chapters aim to

> look like a dodecaphonic series harping on a handful of key motifs—the ego as symptom of literary modernity; the pervasive tension between egoism and hospitality; late Modernism defined less by formal innovation than by an emphasis on a new reader; the curious interactions, antagonistic and yet parallel, between Joyce's esthetic program and the emergence of Irish nationalism, to name but a few. (vii)

From within this complex and wide-ranging series, three major concepts are singled out—"first egoism, then hospitality, and finally the concept of a self-generating and organic language" (vii)—and an axis of "the shift from *The Egoist* [...] to *transition* [... which] seemed to allegorize the entire trajectory of what we call Modernism" that, combined together, form the backbone of the entire collection (viii). Here the focus will be on Rabaté's engagement with Lacan.

The first chapter "Après mot, le déluge: *the ego as symptom*" investigates the opening suggestion that "Joyce's ultimate literary gamble [...] has to do with a collective utopia blending language and politics, a radical utopia with avant-gardist and anarchistic overtones shared by the *transition* group led by Eugène Jolas" (2). Ever since the *transition* group, the critic "who has done the most to restore the meaning of enjoyment as a verb to Joyce's name is Jacques Lacan," whose terms "provide a strong frame of reference allowing for a general assessment of Joyce's works." Rabaté returns to Lacan's 1975 plenary address at the Paris symposium, the most striking feature of which was that "Joyce did not appear essentially as the author of *Ulysses* [...], but as the writer of *Finnegans Wake*, a text described as his 'major and final work'" (5).

Of crucial importance is Rabaté's discussion of Lacan's key idea, that "the major 'symptom' was contained in Joyce's name, a name embodying *jouissance* (a key Lacanian concept compounding 'enjoyment' in all its meanings, along with sexual bliss and property rights)," which received its full treatment in Lacan's famous 1975-6 "Sinthome" seminar, where his confrontation with Joyce led him "to overhaul his theory of the three interlocking circles of the Real, the Imaginary and the Symbolic to show that their knotting depends on the function of a fourth circle, called Sigma for the Symptom." In the last seminar, Lacan goes on to describe Joyce's

[9] Jean-Michel Rabaté, *James Joyce and the Politics of Egoism* (Cambridge: Cambridge University Press, 2001). For the other two works, see Chapter VI "Modernism & Postmodernism," section V, and Chapter X "Textual Criticism & Textual Genetics," section V.

ego "as occupying the place of the fourth circle [...], identical with the symptom" (6-7). Rabaté makes clear that this presents a radical departure from Lacan's early system, which postulates language as constitutive of the ego and as situated in the dimension of delusion. Later, Rabaté finds Lacan at pains to prove affiliation between "the texts of psychotics" and "the linguistic experiments produced by the Surrealists"—a practice analogous to Jolas and Gilbert's publishing endeavour, busy as they were at the time "collecting and publishing some of these 'inspired writings' for *transition*," thereby "hoping to establish links between Joyce's new language and the language of the mad" (9).

The question of the parallel between Joyce's art and the psychotic structure of mad writing remained "a haunting one for Lacan, and for the generations of Lacanian psychoanalysts who started reading Joyce in the hope of understanding psychosis." Joyce's *Wake* was a structure resulting from several interconnected factors:

> a systematic linguistic deregulation, a re-knotting of the four circles providing a new place for an ego that occupies a crucial but fragile position since it depends entirely upon language to "hold," and more importantly perhaps, the determination of the whole structure by a *jouissance* of language experienced as raw material yielding enjoyment but produced outside the social norms of accepted meanings. It is indeed the "crazy" Joyce of the *Wake* who is given as a model for the new millennium. (10)

An important shift in Rabaté's overall concern is the identification of the Lacanian *jouissance* as "fundamentally egoistical," occupying as it does the very opposite pole of a desire marked by the Other. This identification in turn is linked with Freud's "intrepidation of our dreams" (*FW* 338.29-30), whose structural account of the dream-work depicts it as egoistical through and through. It follows, though a few important reservations need be made, that the day-dreaming that is the creation of art assumes an egotistical character in Freud's account of poiesis:

> Freud's theory of literature has often been called reductive; yet his insight, although almost brutal, is powerful: the function of art is a mere means to an end, which consists in the overcoming of the barriers that separate one ego from other egos with the ultimate aim of releasing a deeper egoism of fantasy that can be shared by all. (13)

Joyce's art of egoism is then paralleled, with that of Ayn Rand, "a very popular novelist who also happened to have invented a whole philosophy of egoism" (13). However, to return again to Joyce, his "genius of egoism" is seen as having had a powerful influence upon Lucia, the "egoist's daughter," the disavowal of whose "real life psychic condition" is regarded as having common traits with "the almost fantastic avoidance of any mention of politics by Joyce in the late twenties" (20). Joyce's egoistic genius is seen as the motivation behind several features of his private biography, such as his alleged "indifference" to human issues (all viewed, it seems, if not *sub specie aeternitatis*, at least as some manifestations of recurrent universal patterns), his determination to let his world shrink to that of an extended family, and his stubborn denial of psychoanalysis in spite of an intellectual proximity with Freud. (21)

Lacan's abiding interest in the *Wake* as a text with curative potential, attacking as it does "the linguistic root of psychosis by enhancing the poetological functions of the polyglotic and punning Word," is ultimately seen as reiterating the underlying be-all and end-all of Joyce's composition. This leads Rabaté to make the bold proposition that "Lucia should not appear merely as Joyce's 'anima inspiratrix,'" but rather as "the main addressee of the *Wake*." Rabaté concludes:

> Joyce's hope is that if he manages to reach through her multiple levels of allusions, to inhabit the darkness of a monstrous language long enough and the can still return to light in the morning, he will gain some therapeutic leverage on his daughter's condition. [...] In fact, Lucia became the ideal reader of *Finnegans Wake* — whose pathos increased as it became obvious that she could not read the text and ended up reproducing her mother's "indifference" to *Ulysses*, but for quite opposite reasons. (22)

VII

Kimberly J. Devlin's study, *James Joyce's "Fraudstuff*,"[10] deserves mention on account of the consistency of its argument in which it examines the whole of Joyce's canon from the perspective of its "increasingly complex representation of what Lacan calls the scopic drive" (173), as well as its overall feminist concerns, evident already from its title. Although taken from the *Wake*, 'fraudstuff' is symptomatic of a general move within Joyce's fiction "from the early concern with epiphanic self-revelation to an obsessive celebration of selfhood as imposture and sham — and as an ultimately unknowable entity" (xi). This claim could lead one to suspect a reading of *Dubliners* which would, *pace* Leonard, see the stories as concerned with "revelations" of "selfhood," but Devlin does not fail to add the important qualification that

> One notable dimension of the epiphanic moments in *Dubliners* involving a flash of insight about the self (as opposed to a revealing gesture that betrays a truth about an other) is how frequently they are imbricated in fraudulence itself. (xii)

Her example thereof is "The Dead," where the vision ultimately leads, "not to a coherent sense of self, but rather to its dissolution, as unified being is briefly experienced as an illusion." Joyce's early fictions as "explorations of insight and its consequences" are therefore paradoxically

10 Kimberly J. Devlin, *James Joyce's 'Fraudstuff'* (Miami: University Press of Florida, 2002).

seen as being "inseparable from a nascent interest in fraud: moments of self-revelation turn into realizations of shameful sham and sensations of fictionalized coherence" (xii). Thus, Joyce's "fraudstuff" functions as a critical metaphor for examining a number of motifs or general tendencies within the Joycean corpus: first, the three portraits of Stephen as presented in *Stephen Hero, A Portrait*, and *Ulysses*, where the general shift is from an initial obsessive inquest into the fraudulence in others to an increasingly ironic awareness of the fraudulence within the self.

Turning to *Ulysses* allows Devlin to enrich the context of her discussion with various theoretical speculations on gender as performance, particularly an examination of how the novel supports the concept of femininity as masquerade and masculinity as virile display linked to the castration complex.[11] In this context, a discussion of Gerty MacDowell is most relevant, with a stress on its logocentric structure, which turns femininity as an identity construct into an impossible double-bind with contradictory ideological valences. The constructedness of identity is further documented by a discussion of the "Circe" chapter, presenting *Ulysses* as a police novel, comprising "the domestic and social police, the political police, and the gender police: under the gaze of each, Bloom's self dissolves into multiple constructed identities, all 'fraudstuff' in increasingly transparent forms" (xiv). It is in Chapter 5, "Guilty Visions: Bloom, Mary, and Martha," that Devlin's analysis gains in psychoanalytic momentum as it deals with visual symptomology, a psychoanalytic examination of how visual images give latent thoughts an indirect mode of expression. The last section examines what Devlin terms "the fantasmic body," that is, "the body distortionally perceived through the lens of various psychic *méconnaissances*," by way of another foray into "Circe," combined with an analysis of the "Tavern Chapter" of the *Wake*.

It is certainly worth examining here the theoretical manoeuvre of the "Afterword," where the whole book's discussion is re-inscribed within Lacanian discourse, namely his concept of the *scopic drive*. Devlin conceives of this drive by referring to Lacan's implication that "the human sense of lack in the visual field, which creates the scopic drive, is not—at least on one level—a delusion," since there is an inevitable gap which splits the symbolic order, the systems of representation that structure perception (systems always ideologically inflected) off from the inaccessible real. In a statement echoing Brivic's work, Devlin observes that "Joyce emphasizes this gap in *Ulysses* by highlighting his characters' perceptual screens, the visual filters which shape their sense of others and externality in general" (174). The scopic drive is that by means of which the gaze aspires to position itself—and although the connection between gaze and power is a common one (for to see is to know), the innovativeness of Joyce lies "in his understanding that its proxies can

11 This part, included in Richard Pearce's edited collection *Molly Blooms*, will be discussed in detail in Chapter IV "Cultural Studies," section IV.

sometimes, by default, be found in unexpected and elided perspectives," as well as in his reluctance to draw the link between gaze and the masculine, for "the visual desire behind it is not gender specific (as the figure of Molly Bloom makes clear)." Equally subversive is Joyce's seemingly most scopically driven text, where he launches a process of textual deferral which "creates a sense of the dreamer's compulsion to see more by hearing more, to bring into focus somehow a picture of the cause of his fall; and a provocative visual diagram, of course, plays a crucial role in the chapter about childhood scopic curiosity" (175). However, the paradox of this voyeuristic desire is that it is fuelled by that which cannot be seen:

> The central paradox of Joyce's final fiction is that, even though HCE is recurrently accused of voyeurism, the truth of his transgression is precisely what he can never clearly see: it is the epiphany that refuses to arrive. (176)

The scopic drive consumes itself in an excess of knowledge "that turns, ultimately, into blindness" (176).

VIII

Two other publications dating from 2002 deserve to be discussed together, and not only because of their origin—despite the "Joycean presence" of Luke Thurston—outside of Joyce studies proper. Both *Re-inventing the Symptom: Essays on the Final Lacan*[12] and *How James Joyce Made His Name: A Reading of the Final Lacan*[13] deal with Lacan's very late seminars, and thus with his views on Joyce and literature. Due to the vastness of the works' scope and mostly "purely" psychoanalytical concern, the present discussion will have to content itself with the loci of Joyce's most palpable presence.

Thurston's introduction to *Re-inventing the Symptom* is a meditation on the Lacanian notion of *pas-à-lire*, literally *not-to-be-read*. First of all, Thurston examines the ambivalent status of the late period of Lacan's teaching as perceived in current psychoanalytic thought, with some of his followers praising "this period as his grand finale [...], amounting to a crucial *aletheia* that allows us to re-think the whole course of Lacanian theory," while others seeing in these last theoretical adventures "merely signs of an old man's decline, symptoms [...] of terminal anecdotage" (xiii-xiv). Both concur that Lacan's 1970s seminars present a "radical 'epistemological break'" from his earlier work, though the question of its value remains a thorny one. This is reflected in the main arguments of the collection's contributions. While Dominiek Hoens and Ed Pluth's piece treats *le sinthome* as, according to their essay's title, "A New Way of

[12] Luke Thurston, ed., *Re-inventing the Symptom: Essays on the Final Lacan* (New York: Other Press, 2002).
[13] Roberto Harari, *How James Joyce Made His Name — A Reading of the Final Lacan*, trans. Luke Thurston (New York: Other Press, 2002).

Writing an Old Problem," relating Lacan's late forays into Joyce with his earlier examination of Claudel's *L'Otage*, Roberto Harari's "The *sinthome*: Turbulence and Dissipation" argues that a genuine innovation takes place in Lacan's final stage on another level: "that of thinking itself, of the specific modality of psychoanalytic theory." Harari demonstrates how chaos theory and quantum mechanics have impacted upon the crucial moment of late Lacan's thought—its decisive break from the dialectical logic governing its earlier phases. Taken as a whole, Thurston has collected *Reinventing the Symptom* "to show how [the] familiar—and often notorious—notions (The Woman, the Name-of-the-Father, the phallus, etc.) are, precisely, reinvented in the last period of Lacan's work" (xv).

The rest of Thurston's introduction strives to clarify the position and role of Joyce's writing within this late transformation in Lacan's thought. He outspokenly resists the received notion of Lacan speaking "on" or "about" Joyce in his late seminars, by way of what is commonly held to be "a variety of the 'applied' psychoanalysis invented by Freud, with his oedipal *Hamlet* and so forth." What these accounts fail to take into consideration is

> Lacan's central claim about the Joycean *écrit*: that it is, precisely, something untheorizable, indeed the very *other of theory*. Joyce's texts were *pas-à-lire*, "not-to-be-read," insisted Lacan; turning to those texts offered him a way to show forth, not a confirmation of some preestablished doctrine or interpretative method, but an exemplary *resistance* to interpretation. And Lacan saw this resistance not as merely a baffling theoretical dead-end, but rather as a provocation to reconceive, to reinvent his psychoanalytic thinking. (xvi-xvii)

The question remains of how the problematic of the unreadable *écrit* as formulated in *Le sinthome* can be related to wider questions of literary interpretation and cultural analysis. For Lacan, Joyce stands as an extreme example of a general trait of the literary, a "specifically writerly or textual dimension of language that must always remain *intraduit*, 'untranslated'" (xviii). With reference to Lacan's favourite pun, *poubellication*, linking the book trade with the dustbin (*poubelle*), the anecdotal character of Lacan's late writing is resurfaces, from the Greek *anekdotos* meaning "secret, private, hidden." This anecdotal character resists any "wholesale textual enlightenment" and requires that one remains attentive to that "something *untranslatable* at the center of [Lacan's] work, a disruptive excess that no topology can finally reduce or master." It remains for us to corroborate here that the aim of Thurston's collection, "to engage with that irreducible excess without simply translating it," is achieved in a book that is, despite its primarily psychoanalytic orientation, of considerable relevance for Joyce studies.

One of the contributors to the Thurston collection, Roberto Harari, made his presence within Joyce studies felt even more markedly through Luke Thurston's 2002 translation of his study, *How James Joyce Made*

His Name: A Reading of the Final Lacan. This book-length close analysis of Lacan's 23rd seminar on *Le sinthome* is of great relevance for the field of Joycean psychoanalysis. However, its overtly psychoanalytic focal point and vast scope make it impossible for me to do justice to its entirety, and thus limit the present discussion to the work's first chapter, "Joyce and Lacan: A Quadruple Borromean Heresy," which maps out the overall project and presents a very lucid introduction to the Joyce/Lacan interrelation.

Lacan's interest in Joyce, Harari shows, can be shown to be both typical and unique. As long as "psychoanalysis is connected to literature through its work with spoken language" and analysts are "inevitably located on the borders of the literary field," then "Lacan uses his engagement with Joyce to set in motion transformations that are *without precedent* in any writer" (1). Essential to an understanding of these transformations is Lacan's early (and abiding) interest in topology, a "branch of geometry defined by the existence of nonmetric relations," and therefore preoccupied with an examination of surfaces (3). As early as Seminar 9 at the beginning of 1960s, Lacan radically transforms one of the fundamental binaries that defines our conceptualization of space, "inside" and "outside," by describing space as *imaginary*. To pronounce space as imaginary is to posit that

> it is only from within a space where we can immediately recognize ourselves that we are ready to believe that we have—and can master—an interiority; and it is only on this basis that we can easily posit a matching exteriority. (4-5)

This interconnectedness, this relationality of space is at stake, at least in its incipient state, in Lacan's deployment of the triple Borromean knot as illustrating the imbrication of the three registers of experience, Real, Symbolic, and Imaginary (in his *R.S.I.* seminar of 1974 which directly preceded the one on Joyce). Its pictorial representation by means of three intertwined circles is, for Lacan's purposes, of a purely conventional character:

> The decisive property of the triple knot is something else—precisely what causes anyone eagerly trying to draw it, or tie it, to make boo-boos, as Lacan puts it, alluding to the awkwardness attending any attempt by a speaker to produce a Borromean. He becomes a booboo-rromean, because of the ineptitude revealed in our capacity to imagine and in the way we handle our bodies. (9)

What is at stake in a Borromean is the interrelatedness of the three rings, each of which supports an identical relation with its neighbours, functioning, in fact, as their only connecting link. Furthermore, what the visual schema foregrounds is the ability of the orders to penetrate, through displacement, one another, giving rise to symptom (an advance by the Symbolic into the Real), anxiety (situated in the zone where the Real invades the Imaginary), and inhibition (belonging to the overflowing of the Imaginary into the Symbolic) (15-16). It is only later in the *R.S.I.* seminar that Lacan begins to depart from this trinitarian model (based on a rewriting of some of the trinitarian models already established by Freud), deploying a quadruple-Borromean model instead. The fourth circle, meant to ensure the interrelatedness of the other three, had previously been identified with the Name-of-the-Father and defined by Harari as "a psychical agency that, above all, serves to separate the Desire of the Mother from the phallicized son" (19). At this point, however, Lacan introduces *nomination* as a "fourth term that could be at once real, symbolic, and/or imaginary," and thus markedly different from the Name-of-the-Father in that it is no longer an agency, but rather "entails suppletions when the latter agency is lacking" (20-1).

This finally receives a full-fledged treatment in the following seminar, *Le sinthome*, where the shift from *le symptôme* to *le sinthome* (as reflected by the fact that Lacan's 1975 Paris symposium address was still called "Joyce le symptôme") bears witness to Lacan's employment of "different nomination in order to account for different constellations." What this different constellation aims to challenge most fervently is "the usual procedure adopted by psychoanalysts"—"applied psychoanalysis" (24). Lacan attempts something completely different:

> to engage with Joyce's work, with the deployment of that work and its role in the author's life. This entailed the sweeping away of the subject's constitution in language; and if this was so, it entailed a consideration of how the subject had been undone, and how it was refounded, in language. (25)

Thus, Lacan's *sinthome* is a new approach to matters already approached during the period of his relations with the Surrealist movement, particularly with Dali's "critical paranoia" which Lacan converted into the "controlled paranoia" of the psychoanalytic method. However, Harari insists that, despite the commonalities with Lacan's previous forays into the literary, in approaching this seminar we are "dealing with a category that lies outside the dialectic of general and particular: the *sinthome* is singular" (30). To expose the peculiar meaning that Lacan attributes to this adjective, Harari evokes his famous refutation of Aristotle's notorious syllogism concerning the mortality of Socrates the man. In claiming that "all men are mortal / Socrates is a man / Socrates is mortal," Aristotle is wrong about the second premise, the commonsensical character of which breaks down under Lacan's scrutiny. Socrates is not a particular case of a generality, and therefore is not *a* man. Since he preferred death to life, his choice to die is governed "not by a suicidal melancholia, but by a wish that the act should inspire horror in the living after his death" (31).

In the psychoanalytic domain, conversely, the singular figure is—Lacan himself. Yet, Harari maintains a view of his triple Borromean knot as "too balanced, too oriented toward the general-particular dialectic; and in fact he did not wish to see his clinical work give rise to subjects of, and through, such a condition" (33). Lacan's paradoxical remark in the sense that he was sorry not to have been more psychotic as that would have made him more logical is recalled and related to what is termed "rational madness" or paranoia, especially the paranoiac's *excess* of logic as opposed to being "normal," which indicates a lack of passion. In this light,

> the introduction of the quadruple Borromean knot overturns the firm balance between the three Borromean registers by breaking up the system as conceived in an Apollonian, harmonious manner with a quasi-aesthetic quality. With the fourth register, a point of discordance is introduced through the singularity of the *sinthome*. (34)

Thus, it is as an irreducible singularity tying together, and therefore unbalancing the three orders of experience that Lacan examines the perversion (or, *père-version*) of Joyce's writing, and in turn is examined by Harari's immensely useful psychoanalytic study. In this respect, it can be seen as informing the following book of Joyce criticism, focused as it is on the joint topics of singularity, excess, and paternity.

IX

A major work of Joycean psychoanalytic criticism which takes on board not only Lacanian discourse, but also makes use of the psychoanalysis of Joyce's day as well as broader intertextual dialogue on the psychology of literary creation, is Luke Thurston's *James Joyce and the Problem of Psychoanalysis*,[14] which merits detailed analysis.

The prologue opens with a note on Nietzsche's non-concept of eternal recurrence, "the highest formula of affirmation that can possibly be attained," seen by Blanchot as a "limit experience" in which "thought itself becomes untenable, as the impossible affirmation of affirmation 'itself' sends Nietzschean thought spinning into fatal self-deconstructive turbulence." This is paralleled by a reading experience of the *Wake*, "a stifling confrontation with the same-as-new, the reader being well-aware that in his search for semic novelty he 'moves in vicous circles'" (*FW* 134.16) (2). There is also the co-incidental overlap between Joyce's birth and the "birth" (year of publication) of *Fröhliche Wissenschaft*, a fact which was no doubt of potential significance for the superstitious Joyce. Joyce's superstitiousness, in turn, is linked to "the central ambition" of his art:

> to re-invent the historical status of the "I," to grasp and body forth in writing an instance of human *poesis*, the power to name and make a world through artistic "factification" (*FW*496.34). (5)

Time and temporality are seen as crucial themes in Joyce's writing, presenting (that is, *re*-presenting) "the fundamental ambiguity of a time lived

[14] Luke Thurston, *James Joyce and the Problem of Psychoanalysis* (Cambridge: Cambridge University Press, 2004).

'outside' history," either through a temporal *paralysis*, "the failure to re-member or symbolize properly" (where psychoanalysis can provide "a semantic solution"), or through the instant of "madness" identified by Joyce "with an escape into the literary 'thing itself,' the radical affirma-tion of *poesis*: what Nietzsche calls 'a sacred yes-saying'" (5-6). This bears a strong resemblance to what we have seen Derrida pun as *oui-dire*, which for Joyce, Thurston argues, "entails entering into the Other's fan-tasy, taking up a position inside another's dream" (6). The particular chal-lenge to literary criticism posed by Joyce then is also of a temporal na-ture, as it has everything to do with "the *integrity* of the now in literary interpretation," a problem that is due to "the eccentric temporality of the human subject itself, as a self-theorizing 'I' both caught up in and irre-ducible to language and history" (7). Here, Thurston speaks of "the coin-cidence of literary and critical excess."

Thurston's approach strictly opposes two tendencies: that of an ap-plied psychoanalysis, and that of the so-called dialogue between Joyce and psychoanalytic theory. Speaking of the former, Thurston refers to Lacan's seminar on *Le sinthome* as decisively *not* "a seminar *on* Joyce," but an investigation aiming "to get involved in a *writing* practice that exceeded [Lacan's] theoretical discourse, touched on a problem irreducible to the psychoanalytic representation of the subject" (9). The notion of *applied* psychoanalysis is thus utterly dismissed. Speaking of the latter, Thurston calls into question the whole notion of a "dialogue" as concep-tualized by a strictly delineated corpus of Joyce's writing and (so it is implied) an equally definable corpus of psychoanalytic writing. The prob-lem with psychoanalytic intertextuality thus conceived is that

> just as the "I" is both manifested in and irreducible to language, so psycho-analysis itself is both transmitted by a given set of texts and institutional practices and yet in the end remains *irreducible* to that discursive corpus.

Hence, the problem of psychoanalysis in Joyce "corresponds to some-thing that emerges first of all in an encounter: one between an 'I'—as well as an eye—and a particular manifestation or unveiling"; "this encoun-ter...is always an aesthetic experience involving an untranslatable, bodily singularity" (11).

Trifling though the difference between a dialogue and an encounter might seem at first glance, Thurston's account of the contents of his work articulates the importance which should be attached to it: in the first part of the book, "we explore a series of shocking encounters" that are "both interior and radically alien to Joycean and psychoanalytic texts, and beyond them to the general relation between text and reader" (11-12). The primary text here is "An Encounter," which is investigated within the broader context of the "various efforts to utter the unspeakable through translation—both in the literal translation of psychoanalytic texts into English and in the ostensible transference of theory to literary criticism" (12). That which is lost in such a literal and metaphorical translation, that *thing*, forms the major theme of Part II. Here Thurston examines "how Lacan's encounter with Joyce amounts to a deliberate break with the traditional attempt by psychoanalysis to translate itself into and through the aesthetic." This *non serviam* to translation is what Lacan famously termed the *unreadability* of Joyce (12). The conclusion finally reformulates the questions raised by Joyce "in seemingly *theological* terms" and examines "its simultaneous hindrance to and renewal of our reading practices" (13). But let us backtrack for more detail.

Thurston sets out to "explore what takes place in an encounter, both the evolving textual encounter between literature and psychoanalysis," as well as "the 'real' one between James Joyce and Jacques Lacan,"[15] which forms part of a larger, and more far-reaching project, "to argue the case against the currently fashionable urge to exclude psychoanalysis from literary studies," and also to show that "the encounter of psychoanalytic thinking with the unspeakable enjoyment of aesthetic experience still harbours crucial lessons for our critical engagement with Joyce" (17-18). The discussion of the "Encounter" story departs from the "unseen enormity" mentioned by Joyce to his publisher, where it is this "not seeing" which for Thurston is "what comes under the sign of 'as if,'" and thus forms the "key" to the text, in which "the thing taking place is precisely not reducible to an event in the ordinary sense" (24). The "enormity" remains invisible:

> it is thus at once too little—an element missing from the account we are given by the boy—and too much, the force of its obscenity [...] too powerful for it to be included in the narrative, translated and made legible for the narrator and for us [...] this problematic of the alibi intersects with—but perhaps also undermines—psychoanalytic theories of identity and fantasy. (25)

This project of undermining motivates Thurston's main argument that "An Encounter" dramatises, "an encounter of the *reader* with Joyce's writing" in that the event unfolded in the story "involves the desire of the Other in this double sense—as both the anonymous transmission of language and its enigmatic, non-transmissible act" (27). It therefore "dramatises this general condition of discourse—that is, the split between the diacritical signifier and the singular instance of the voice" (28). Thurston concludes:

> In "An Encounter," then, Joyce gives us an early indication of how his writing will pre-empt and challenge our theoretical response to his work: how, above all, it will undermine any response that would ape the story's narrator by striving to re-establish a fantasy of consistent, fully legible authority. (30)

---

[15] The "literalness" of the encounter between Lacan and Joyce is derived from Lacan's famous Paris Symposium address, in which he recounted the story of having, aged 20, encountered Joyce at Adrienne Monnier's Paris bookshop.

The first theorist to conceive of this sense of fantasy as the sight of an undecidable, inappropriable doubling being Freud, Thurston goes on to explore some of his "crucial encounters with the aesthetic in order to approach the relation they stage between fantasmatic revelation and theoretical discourse" (30).

In "Freud's Mousetrap," Thurston presents an innovative reading of the Freud-*Hamlet* intertext, arguing that it is its "dramatisation of a specific institutional crisis—relating to paternity and the law, to the question of signifying legitimacy" that attracts Freud's attention to Shakespeare's play (35). What Thurston sees at the heart of *Hamlet* is precisely the authority of the father, or the answer to the question "whether the call for vengeance is authentic, justified or tainted by sin, compromised by some hidden self-interest" (41). *Hamlet*'s "Mousetrap," is therefore the vindication of the father by the staged doubling of his murder directed by his son:

> We might characterise the Freudian traduction of art, then, as a consistent theoretical effort to *redeem* the father, to rescue the symbolic function of paternity from its flawed embodiment. (46)

Analogously, or by contrast, a Lacanian (what Thurston terms "anamorphic") reading would emphasize "what the play stages as an insistent crisis of meaning, a struggle to resolve and restore to signifying consistency what has been left 'out of joint' by the withdrawal of paternal authority" (51).

In "The Pleasures of Mistranslation," Thurston defines how his term "traduction" operates in his wider framework:

> In this study we have borrowed an anachronistic term, *traduction*, to designate this movement by which a subject or a theory transforms and appropriates—in effect, incorporates—something radically alien to it, beyond its language, something illegible or intractable. [...] Traduction at once translates and misinterprets, transfers and traduces, what it appropriates. More specifically, it renders semantic what it thus simultaneously purges of a disruptive otherness: an insoluble or non-analysable, intractable or untreatable *jouissance*. (64-5)

This notion of reading-as-translation (and mistranslation) stems from Fritz Senn's *Joyce's Dislocutions*,[16] one of the representative examples of a textual hermeneutic trying to come to terms with Joyce. In contrast,

> The notion of an intraducible Joyce—one whose writings, being *pas à lire*, would not lend themselves to facile theoretical appropriation, and would even undermine the representational architecture of any such theorising— clearly fits in with Lacan's attack on any easy transaction between the lit-

---

[16] Fritz Senn, *Joyce's Dislocutions*, trans. John Paul Riquelme (Baltimore: Johns Hopkins University Press, 1994).

erary and the psychoanalytic. But in what sense can explaining art "with the symptom" really differ from the classical Freudian approach? (71)

The last question is what the second part, "Unspeakable Joyce," seeks to answer. The fourth section, *"How am I to sign myself?,"* describes Joyce's relation to Shakespeare as *"père-version,"* employing the pun by which Lacan combines "father version" and "turning to the father":

> What the subject seeks in turning to the father, according to psychoanaly-
> sis, is a certain consistent institution or legality of signification; paternity
> would thus be a legal fiction in an active sense, that of instating a law-
> governed framework to render legible the vagaries of the subject's aesthetic
> or bodily experience (and notably [...] its fantasy). (78)

In "Scylla and Charybdis," Thurston observes "a crucial Joycean reversal," in which Shakespeare becomes for Stephen "the site of an 'unremitting intellect' identified with 'the hornmad Iago ceaselessly willing that the
moor in him shall suffer'" (*U* 9.1023-3). It is this last gloss on Shakespeare's name that allows Thurston to grasp Joyce's investment in "William Shakespeare and company" (*U* 9.729) "without falling back on the
tired old formula of Oedipal identification and rivalry" (79). Here Thurston
notes Vincent Cheng's observation concerning Joyce's interest in "notably fouled-up Shakespearean performances," citing as an example a performance of *Othello* in which "green-eyed monster" became "green-eyed
lobster," a point at which "a regime of representation collapses and something monstrous appears — something that precisely does not belong to
discourse, that breaks the chain of signifiers" (91). Iago's invocation, "I
am not what I am," comes to mind here, implying as it does that "if the
ego is to be relocated at the point where meaning collapses," then "it
must have undergone some radical transformation," since in as much as it
"coincides with the imaginary," the ego is "the locus *par excellence* of
semantic mastery" (95).

Another conflation of Shakespeare with Iago is Deasy's "what does
Shakespeare say?":

> The reflexive question of Joycean quotation returns here as another version
> of the preoccupation with debt, responsibility, and ownership. What does
> Shakespeare actually say? Who is to say who speaks in this line, spoken, in
> a play signed by Shakespeare, by a character called Iago, who defines him-
> self as not identical with himself? (100)

Deasy's reading is a *traduction* in that it "cuts out [the voice's] constitutive performative dimension, completely erasing the uncanny jouissance of
Iago's seductive villainy, his insidious ear-poisoning" (101).

In the fifth section, "Egomen and women," the "hornmad Iago" returns
as Circe's cuckolded Shakespare saying "Iagogo!" Thurston observes:

The line from Dumas might thus have to be revised, so that Shakespearean creation would be not so much divine as diabolic; or perhaps the very act of creating "after God," seeking to rival or double the original *ex nihilo*, would be a defining characteristic of the devil. [...] Iago's faceless knavery, an essentially unaccountable or asubjectal act, resembles nothing so much as Joycean paternity, at least as it is explicitly theorised by Stephen in his discussion of Shakespeare. (106)

The discussion then turns to the relation between Joyce and Jung, or in an amusing reversal on Thurston's part, to the relation between Jung and Joyce, where Jung's "*Ulysses:* A Monologue" is seen as marking "a crucial point in the relation between Joyce and psychoanalysis, on which it sheds both light and shadow" (133), mentioning as it does "the magic words that sent me to sleep." This attests to the fact that Jung continuously fell asleep while bored by *Ulysses* (136). However, Jung also performs a *traduction* by identifying Joyce's Elijah with a *Bejahung*, his "way of saying yes to *Ulysses*," assuming "the mantle of averting Joyce's biblical apocalypse, of saving the book from its own disastrous act, its transgressive revelation" (148).

"*God's real name*," the last chapter of the book, returns to the literary *thing*. As long as Lacan's very late work demonstrates "that the Name of the Father is *not* the only way of organising or knotting together the psychical orders of the real, the symbolic, and the imaginary," Joyce's relation to Shakespeare and to the literature of the double makes visible "a language-thing" which "exceeds representation" and takes place "not in the domain of eternal legibility but as actual performance" (161). Thurston then asks, "what kind of symbolic exchange do we partake in by accepting the gift or vocation of Joyce's work?", and points to the Joycean epiphany as discussed by Catherine Millot (see above), which "marks an uncanny coincidence of insignificance and signifying tautology, at once the evacuation and the over-determination of meaning," thus functioning as "Joyce's first declaration of faith in language to body forth the essential dimension of being" (166). The fact (again following Millot) that epiphanies arise mostly out of the mouths of women should be seen as marking "precisely an interminable movement between the Other" and "the revelation of lack in the Other, a revelation with disastrous effects on the stability of psychical and sexual boundaries"(168) instead of simply aligning Joyce's work with 'feminine' writing. This is further related to the God of the mystics as pure negativity, and humorously commented on in a reference to Stephen's early conclusion in *A Portrait* that "God's real name was God."

Lacan's analysis finally appears as "the encounter of Wakean 'anticollaborators': participants in an interpretive essay that refuses to operate by means of mutual collusion, imaginary oneness." In a final twist, Thurston suggests a reading of "this Lacanian anticollaborator as an 'antic collaborator': a reader who, like the fool censured by Hamlet for his 'pitiful ambition,' will not stick to the script but uses it as a pretext for his own rhetorical performance" (198). Thurston concludes:

> If Freud first looked to art as a confirmation of the truth of the unconscious, the *force* of his discovery took it beyond that traductive gesture, and towards a moment when psychoanalysis would attempt to learn from the aesthetic new ways to write what lay beyond its discourse of truth. (199)

Thurston's "Conclusion" revisits the starting point of a general sense of institutional exhaustion and interpretive redundancy within Joyce criticism, and attempts to suggest ways of resisting this possible closure of reading. In his comparison of Freud and Lacan, Thurston observes that

> while Freud strives to dissolve the symptomatic opacity of an artwork, and so restore the efficacy of the paternal signifier to govern meaningful narratives, Lacan takes the aesthetic thing as evidence of the terminal collapse of such meaningfulness, the emergence of an untranslatable jouissance, something impossible to theorise. (200)

In this connection, the first instance of *Hamlet*'s presence in *Ulysses*, Haines's "the Father and the Son idea" gains momentum. Thurston points out "how careful Haines is to disclaim any ownership of the idea, attributing it to a safely anonymous authority," facing a "predicament of non-originality" akin to that of any reader in search of "an authoritative solution or 'theological interpretation' of *Hamlet*—and now of *Ulysses*," with the desire "both to guarantee the integrity of the textual origin and to redeem himself from the sinful novelty, the fallen waywardness, of his present reading" (201). It is no coincidence of course that the art of "Telemachus" is theology. The other instance of "at-one-ment" in Joyce's corpus, his 1932 poem "Ecce Puer," is mentioned as Joyce's seeming "renunciation of sinful literary extravagance," a renunciation complicated however by the poem's "recitation of another sacred text"—the Bible:

> As we have argued, at first glance "Ecce Puer" reads as a plea for atonement written in the simplest, least Joycean language; but a more attentive reading discovers in it an act of "transluding" (*Finnegans Wake* 419.25), of parodic allusion and translation, in which we hear the blasphemous voice of the forsaken son.

Thus, Joyce's literary act is ultimately viewed as "something irredeemable or unrepresentable in a position of textual *extimacy*, somewhere beyond or beneath the text's characters" (205). God in this sense is the "Eloi, Eloi" of "pure tautology" which "eludes the network of human discourse" and is "impossible to integrate with the realm of the signifier," a point already brought home by the encounter of Moses with the burning bush which has "shown how the unspeakable tautology of God's absolute identity could be translated into an utterance of the 'I,' a *sum*." The central point of relevance for Joyce is here again, the name of God: for I AM, as God names himself in Exodus, is both a *sum* and a pun on the Latin *iam*, "now." In other words, the problem of reincarnation or re-presentation involves both the cogitating ego and its punctual manifestation in time, the bodily but also the temporal condition of the "I." (207)

It is first and foremost in Shakespearean *femininity* that "Joyce finds the trace of the pure literary act," which makes conspicuous the fact that literary criticism has "established itself as a traduction: an attempt, that is, to echo Hamlet's advice to the players by banning laughter, eliminating the unnecessary turbulence of jouissance from the space of interpretation." This however is related to the notion that Joycean writing "is above all a Dionysiac celebration, a gale of Rabelaisian laughter"—a critical commonplace in its own right. ALP's final appeal, "mememormee," "remember me!," evokes not only Ophelia, "the one who 'acts'" in *Hamlet* in the sense of "sacrificing the 'I' to an absolute, suicidal jouissance," and her "pray you, love, remember" is "likewise disfiguratively remembered at the end of the *Wake*." It is her brother Laertes' response to Ophelia's madness, "this nothing's more than matter," that provides the best gloss on this Joycean remembrance: "What is remembered, in other words, is precisely the excess of the Shakespearean performance: an act beyond identity, more than me, more than 'same.'" In turn, it is ultimately this writing excess, "at once something lacking, irreducible to the text, and yet 'more than matter'" that "makes the Joycean *thing* impossible to read or remember in terms dictated by a solitary 'I.'" The destruction of this 'I' is what "may seem its most repetitive feature," as well as "something unspeakably innovative" (210).

Thurston's re-visitation and re-mapping of places visited and mapped many times, but rarely seen with such informed and perceptive eyes, remains one of the most "innovative" studies within the field.

X

A more closely Joycean look at the concerns of Lacan's Joyce-seminar has been written by Louis Armand and published in a collection of his essays entitled *Incendiary Devices—Discourses of the Other*[17] and will serve as a piece that lucidly pinpoints Lacan's relevance for Joyce studies, and vice versa. Armand departs from a view on Lacan's *mirror stage* as describing "a moment in the inauguration of the subject into language, linking subjectivity to a certain type of subjection, which is characterised as a 'subjection to the signifier,'" which emerges from within "the field of the *Other*" (37). This emergence brings about a sense of indebtedness in language, by which it is said to *refer* or *respond* to the Other. Thus, what Lacan terms the "dialectic of identification" comes close, for Armand, to what Gilles Deleuze and Félix Guattari call the "machinic" as the constitutive relation of desiring-production. This, in turn, comes to be associated

[17] Louis Armand, *Incendiary Devices: Discourses of the Other* (Prague: Karolinum, 2004 [1994]).

with Viktor Tausk's exploration of the psychopathology of "the artist," most famously conceptualised as *la machine à influencer*:

> Transposed onto Lacan's mirror apparatus, this machinic element describes a structural matrix, an apparatus or programme in which the ghosting of the signifier in the illusion of a signified marks a pseudo-schematics of destination: an horizon effect of the mirror which gives the subject's desire back to it under the guise of the translated image of its own truth (as specular double). As Lacan points out, this dialectico-cyclical apparatus can also be seen as being structured as a *symptom*—a schematic of recursive *aphanisis*. (39-40)

This machinic apparatus, or *symptom*, comes to be associated in Lacan's late work with the workings of signification in Joyce's *Finnegans Wake*. Armand's etymological excursion proves useful here:

> Following from its etymology (Gk. *sumptōma*: occurrence, phenomenon; from *sumpiptein*, to fall together, fall upon, happen), Lacan links the Freudian notion of "symptom" as a condition of the unconscious (of the Oedipal entanglement), to the notion of the unconscious as structured like a language, to the reversion of Joyce's language and ultimately to Joyce himself (as "Shemptôme"), in whom all of these figures intersect as a kind of Borromean knot or "Borumoter" (*FW* 331.27). (41)

After paralleling Lacan's earlier emblem for the three orders, the triangle, with Joyce's use of triadic systems in general, and his use in the *Wake*'s Nightlessons chapter of the figure of *Vesica Piscis*—which is found out with reference to Roland McHugh's *Sigla* to be an ancient symbol of the feminine procreative organ—Armand goes on to show how Lacan's later reconceptualisation of the mutual embeddedness of the three organs, the Borromean knots, entails a turning toward the father, a *père-version*:

> What the topological metaphor of the Borromean knot suggests, then, is the *synthetic* nature of the psychoanalytic subject, which, *as subject*, is the unique "solution" to the problem of the incommensurability of what is named by these three terms. [...] In this way, Lacan argues: "It is not the division of the imaginary, symbolic and real which defines perversion, but rather that they are *already* distinct." (43-44)

The necessarily twofold situatedness of the Borromean know begins to emerge here: as the symptomatic *"topos"* of the encounter of the three orders, and as their *"tropological* linkage" which Lacan refers to as *le sinthome*, a topological entanglement which is regarded as "describing (by a process of metonymy) the radical condition of language as such (and exemplified for Lacan by the paronomasia of *Finnegans Wake*)" (45). Armand concludes by observing how this central insight of Lacanian psychoanalysis influenced the Joyce criticism of Philippe Sollers which focused on the $3+1$ structure of the *Wake*, relating this Lacanian structure to "a phonological rendering of 'the ... riverrun' as 'THREE VER UN, three towards one,' a 'constant state of triadicity, *plus one*' or $3 + 0/4 = 1$, which reads 'three plus nought which makes four equals one'" (48).

XI

Jen Shelton's *Joyce and the Narrative Structure of Incest*,[18] returns to the earlier Freudian tradition combining (extra)textual analysis with an examination of authorial biography and in this case focusing both on the particular topic of incest. In the "Introduction: 'Dadad's Lottiest Daughterpearl': Incest and Modernism," Shelton takes a broader view on the literary, or specifically modernist, interest in "incest," departing from the contention that

> Joyce's peculiar use of the power dynamic of incest is, of course, an outgrowth of his particular cultural moment — that period around the turn of the century when psychological theorists and anthropologists investigated incest's cultural functions. (2)

The particular potential of incest as a literary theme lies in how its corporeal dimension is bound with a narrative dimension, where competing and mutually exclusive stories clash with one another: "The child's narrative seeks to make known the sexual approaches of the adult, while the adult's narrative seeks to dismiss or explain away the child's story." Thus, incest is here treated as

> more than a set of physical acts one kind of body can perform on another kind of body, [in that it] exemplifies a specific, gendered power relation in which the father makes use of his greater physical, social, and narrative powers in order to coerce the girl to accede to his will. (3)

The specificity of the literary as opposed to the real-world narrative then lies in a different distribution of authority. Along the lines of this opposition, Joyce's literary deployment of the theme can be contrasted with Freud's casuistry insofar as Joyce's text seeks and celebrates the voices of girls:

> This study is especially interested in voices of daughters in the Joycean text: not the masterful speech that asserts dominance, but rather the subversive and chaotic emanations of those usually seen as silent and disempowered. [...] Because I see incest here as a thematic with roots in the real world that also helps to shape the real world, biography is implicated in my argument. (4)

For Joyce, what Shelton terms "the narrative structure of interest" is useful in that it "provides the mechanism through which he can test the boundaries of control and mastery" and allows him to "build into his text both the mastery readers need if the text is to be intelligible at all and the

---

[18] Jen Shelton, *Joyce and the Narrative Structure of Incest* (Miami: University Press of Florida, 2006).

subversion of that control that makes space for new voices and new stories" (7). The central argument of Shelton's study can therefore be seen in the following statement:

> [Incest] describes narrative contests of control and resistance as well as contests over meaning that structure the interplay of erotic transgression, accusation, and defense visible in all of Joyce's works. Understood as a narrative structure as well as a theme, incest pervades, indeed helps to constitute, the Joycean text.

Central to the book then, just as in the earliest works in the psychoanalytic tradition, "is the question of control: narrative control, control over one's body, control over cultural tropes and discourses" (9). Shelton's "reading through incest," therefore

> offers not only a novel approach but also one that is predicated on a refusal to resolve the conflict in favor of one or the other side. Like deconstruction, my method inquires more into tensions than resolutions; unlike that methodology, though, it takes a feminist political approach. (9)

The political commitment of this approach, as with other feminist approaches (discussed in the next chapter), lies in its attention to how Joyce has "given voice" to the hitherto unheard:

> The narrative structure of incest allows readers to hear anew voices that seemed familiar or unimportant; it helps us recognize voices we have heard all along without understanding their power. (13)

The first chapter, "Theorizing Incest," presents the theoretical vantage point of Shelton's study, and thus deserves to be discussed in detail. As already stated in the "Introduction," Freud's praxis of psychoanalysis serves as a counterpoint to Joyce's use of the "girl's story":

> Sigmund Freud's insistence on the analyst as a better reader of the patient's story than the analysand could ever be contrasts sharply with Joyce's gleeful deployment of girl's stories to disrupt the possibility of mastery in his narrative. (14)

Shelton provides a useful summary of how psychoanalysis emerged as a consequence of Freud's revision of his original reading of the causes of hysteria (the seduction theory), which held that "actual sexual trauma in early childhood [...] caused the problems he saw in the hysterical women he treated," interpreting the hysterics' stories as "incestuous childhood fantasies that had been followed by repression of the (presumed male) child's urges because of feared punishment from the father." By substituting the oedipal model of the development of subjectivity for the seduction theory, "Freud revised the problem of incest from an abuse of paternal power to an abuse of origin" (16).

Freud's research based on Frazer led to his famous articulation of incest as the one universal taboo on which culture was based. This shift toward incest as an abuse of origin created "a mechanism through which any story of incest can be denied and professional inquiry redirected from the abusing father, the focus of the daughter's narrative, to the incestuously desiring daughter, the focus of culture's enforcement." It is through this shift that psychoanalysis "came into being" (16). Insofar as Freud "offers a move through which to displace threatening female speech," Joyce thus renders incest as inextricably bound with what "Freud would silence: the dissident speech of incestuously abused girls" (17). Shelton's reliance on Foucault proves useful here, especially Foucault's suggestion that "incest occupies a keystone location between two systems of power: the 'regime of alliance' and the 'deployment of sexuality,'" a location implying that "the family has become an obligatory locus of affects, feelings, love; that sexuality has its privileged point of development in the family; that for this reason sexuality is 'incestuous' from the start'" (19).

The reason why incest is a public sexual act, and therefore threatening for culture, is that "culture uses it as a firewall against uncontained sexuality." This means that "incest that is not publicly narrated is acceptable, while incest that creates an open narrative of any kind must lead to disciplinary action," one where "fathers tell stories society wants to hear," whereas "daughters say what society does not want to hear, naming incest and rape in the face of their fathers' contradiction" (19-20). While psychoanalysis views incest from the point of view of "the child who desires a forbidding and forbidden parent," feminist discourses of incest strive to see it "in more 'real world' terms, which is to say anti-Freudian ones" (20). Among the feminist thinkers on whom Shelton relies are J. L. Herman, E. Bass and L. Davis, who all in their own particular ways, "alter Freud's terms only by allotting power and desire differently." It is Sandor Ferenczi's distinction between the child's tenderness and the adult's passion which is most crucial to Shelton's argument allowing as it does for the treatment of incest as a problem of misreading: "a mistake fathers make because they fail to understand children's stories" (22). Analogously, Shelton treats incest not so much as "an act in which one party is a victim and another is a criminal," but rather "as a structure of conflict over control of a child's body and narrative" (23).

Returning to Freud, Shelton examines the case of his patient Dora. First, however, the general rule of upbringing is mentioned which has bearing on the problematics:

> a long-running theme in Western child-rearing practice has been that children should not say "no" to adults in any context, that compliant children are good children, and that parents' job is chiefly that of making naturally rebellious children acquiescent.

Freud's privileging the unconscious over conscious desire is seen to have emptied the social *no* of meaning in that insofar as the unconscious according to Freud's definition knows no *no* as it can speak only endless desire. Freud therefore "makes violation an impossibility" (24). A case in point is Freud's "Fragment of an Analysis of a Case of Hysteria," where his treatment of Dora shows "the process of analysis to be an act of violence":

> In essence, Freud attempts to empty Dora's words and actions of any significance whatsoever: agreement and disagreement alike will equally confirm that the father-analyst, not the daughter-analysand, has understood Dora's case. (26)

Analogously, Foucault's argument that resistance to power never takes up any position of exteriority in relation to it is recalled to show that "for a child who experiences violation by a parent, 'no' is a word that has meaning only when uttered by authority figures." Therefore, for the speaking parent, "'no' is a functional word, for it is backed up by physical and legal power" (29).

The issue of authority links Shelton's critique of Freud and the overall theme of incest with modernist literature:

> Modernist writing is obsessed with authority: who controls narrative and how, how power structures shape stories, how different experiences of power and authority create divergent stories. (30)

An exemplary instance of this are the last two chapters of *Ulysses*, which offer contrastingly authoritative narratives, "one based on a 'dispassionate,' 'distant,' 'clinical' form of 'truth,' the other based on the 'truth' of feeling, memory, and self-making" (30). Hence, the entire project of the *Wake*—a representation of the most inchoate and polysemic part of existence—is marked by Joyce's practice of using girl's voices in order "to dramatize the disruptive energies of resistance, intentionally making himself vulnerable to that which he cannot master" (31).

How this "exposure to the unmasterable" comes about is further examined in the second chapter, "Subverting the Father's Discourse," where particular narrative practices in the Joycean text exemplifying the incest narrative structure are brought to light. Here also emerges Shelton's Bakhtinian conception of the resistance on the part of the incest structure to any stable synthesis, which is derived from Bakhtin's understanding of "novelistic fools," characters "whose naiveté allows them to notice the hidden rules of society" (36). Although in Joyce, "the position of the counter-speaking fool is often filled by a female or feminized character such as Issy in *Finnegans Wake* [...] or Milly in *Ulysses*," it is not restricted to characters who are literally female: "a writer who can switch characters' sex in 'Circe' understands the mutability of gender and its social constitution" (37). It therefore follows that even Stephen or Leopold can be thought of as Joyce's daughters.

Here the argued subversiveness of Joyce-generated voices must be questioned. If Molly's case presents us on a stylistic level with what has been perceived as "no style" by Kenner and proven by Attridge to be in fact a high *stylization* incorrectly passed on for a "flow" in Joyce criticism, then in creating Molly Joyce can be said to "[deflate] style through apparent stylelessness, typical of his strategy of debunking mastery through its own devices" (39). However, Molly stands already at the end of a long path leading up to her creation in *Ulysses*. Joyce's overcoming of his own anxiety regarding women's speech is reflected in the transition from *Stephen Hero* to *A Portrait*. Then,

> by the time Joyce writes *Ulysses*, his displacement and deferral of women's narratives begin to be replaced by his overt interest in women's storytelling, so that [...] it is female writing, not male, that is presented as complete: Joyce shows us all of Milly's letter to her father and all of Martha Clifford's letter to Bloom. Male writing is fragmentary and incomplete, whether it is Stephen's poem [...] or Bloom's sand-writing. (42)

This showing has to do with male voyeurism, thematized most outspokenly in the "Nausicaa" episode, where the juxtaposition of Gerty's and Bloom's discourses "highlights the insufficiency of narratives allotted to women: Gerty's discourse suggests that she can only see herself as object of the male gaze" (44). The voyeurism of "Nausicaa" has ultimately to do with narrative containment—"Gerty's presentation of herself as potential voyeuristic object for Bloom depends on her narrative structuring of the raw materials the scene presents to her."

This brings Shelton to the observation that "the most effective resistive mode is subversion rather than rebellion," the difference being that "subversion is not a different language from the dominant discourse it seeks to undermine; it is the same language spoken with a slightly different inflection" (45-6). Shelton ends this chapter on a note on biography, arguing that although the link between severe sexual abuse in childhood and "some forms of mental illness, including dissociative schizophrenia and multiple personality disorder" has already been firmly established,

> the question of whether Joyce abused his daughter is not merely unanswerable, but uninteresting, [since] the kind of incest Joyce might have committed with Lucia has little to do with their actual bodies and everything to do with narrative control of his texts and of his daughter; his use of her, however, differs little from his use of other people close to him, including many people he loved deeply. (49)

Lucia's problem, in her father's opinion, had to do with her being like Joyce, "a misunderstood genius" (50)—a comparative analysis of a July 1932 letter written by Lucia and an "Issy" passage from the *Wake* (*FW* 159) reveals an instance of "Lucia-as-text for Joyce" (52). The uncontrollability of which Sheldon spoke early on, and which has not been sufficiently demonstrated, begins to crystallize:

Although he could attempt to revise, edit, and translate [Lucia's] life for himself and for those around him, [Joyce] could not, finally, control the narrative she became. Lucia's madness put her beyond her father's narrative control and established her as a teller of her own tale. (52)

Thus, it was his own daughter's madness which confronted Joyce with a text he could not master—and the link to the *Wake*'s voices is therefore established on the basis of biography:

That failure of mastery evidently was a grievous burden to bear, judging from Joyce's letters. Yet at the same time that he was mourning his loss of control of his daughter [...], he was allowing his girl characters to challenge his mastery more and more. (52-3)

From here, Shelton undertakes several forays into various textual and intertextual realms. Having sketched her theoretical framework in sufficient detail, we can now follow these in a more schematic manner. Shelton first looks at how a girl's disobedience functions as a productive force, creating fathers as figures of authority where none existed before— examples of this are Eveline and Milly Bloom. Joyce's own appropriation of literary authority in the *Wake*, is exemplified by his use of Jonathan Swift and Lewis Carroll, both of whom were involved with young girls: Swift employed a private baby-talk in his correspondence with his nymphet Stella/Ester Johnson with whom he was rumoured to be married while Carroll proposed to Alice Liddell, the child who inspired *Alice* when she was eleven years old, causing public uproar. The cultural constraints of the "making of a girl" are then examined using the example of the adolescent girls of "Nausicaa." This chapter is bifurcated into female and male narrative voices and therefore best represents the manner in which the narrative structure of incest generates incompatible, mutually opposite voices. Finally, Shelton discusses the long footnote in II.2, where Issy interrupts the narrative, disturbing the masculine narrative of lessons and the boyish commentaries of her brothers. Issy's intervention is seen as the clearest example of the girl's "naughty speech" with which she undermines the narrative control of paternal discourse.

Shelton concludes by returning to Joyce's troubled relationship with Lucia:

Joyce's identification of his talent with Lucia's madness makes it easier to understand how Joyce could have given Issy—intentionally or not—so much power over language in *Finnegans Wake*. (123)

Joyce's unease about his daughter is seen to have been the generating force behind his "practice of creating powerful female characters who talk back to their creator, resisting the controlling impulses of his texts and providing a platform from which narrative experiment can be launched" in his last work. This Bakhtinian "talking back," need not be identified solely on the authorial level, but underlies the very process by which literature comes to be consumed—reading:

> Consuming Joyce's texts often may be a kind of contest, but reader and writer are at least always connected to one another, tumbling around each other in a double spiral that carries the meaning of the work. (124)

Thus, Shelton's low-key conclusion undoes what the work has done: it does away with the concept of incest-as-narrative-structure, or rather shows its substitutability with at least one other well-established narrative concept: Bakhtinian dialogism. However, Shelton's work has not been chosen for discussion here on account of its theoretical consistency, but rather as an example of the recent trend in this field of applying psychoanalytic tools and methods to a particular sexuality or gender-related issue, a trend that already points to the topic of the next chapter, where its conceptualization is examined within a new context.

XII

The last text examined here comes from Richard Brown's edited collection *A Companion to James Joyce*, which will supply the concluding remarks on some of the other approaches and topics discussed in this work. Luke Thurston's "Scotographia: Joyce and Psychoanalysis"[19] presents a suitable point of conclusion thanks to its lucid summarizing treatment of the three crucial psychoanalytic schools—Freudian, Jungian, and Lacanian—and what bearings they have on Joyce (as well as more importantly Joyce on them). Thurston revisits Joyce's "hardly disputable" hostility to "Freud and all things 'freudful' (*FW* 411.35) by placing it in contrast to the earliest *Ulysses* reviews, where

> confronted with the perplexing task of having to describe Joyce to the reading public in 1922, all reviewers could think of was to say "Freud," and that name would be enough to conjure up a whole world of unmentionable (and of course very un-English) "nastiness." (407)

However, a "Freudian Joyce" is by far not the most marked feature of the earliest, or early, Joyce psychoanalytic criticism, since for French Joycean theory, namely Philippe Sollers, the names Freud and Joyce became "equivalent, even somehow identical" in denoting what can "be still better expressed in French: *jouissance*." Thus, "Freud, Joyce" names "a single epoch-making outbreak of sexual joy, something exhilarating but also outrageous." Oddly or rather *uncannily* enough, Sollers' was an observation already made by Freud himself—*The Psychopathology of Everyday Life* features Freud's attempt at "translating his own name, Freud," into French as *Joyeux*, of which *Joyeuse* is the feminine form (408). This peculiar instance of uncanny doubling then bespeaks the practices of both

---

[19] Luke Thurston, "Scotographia: Joyce and Psychoanalysis," *A Companion to James Joyce*, ed. Richard Brown (Oxford: Blackwell Publishing, 2008).

psychoanalysis and Joyce's writing in that both are "self-conflicting participants in a 'clearobscure' (*FW* 247.34) coincidence of modernity and traditional morality, of enlightenment and obscurity" (409).

Returning to Joyce's avowed antipathy to psychoanalysis, Thurston illustrates how Freud-based Joyce criticism has tended to counter this by documenting the thoroughness of Joyce's reading of Freud and Freudians, which implies a clear interest on his part. However, to Thurston's mind, there are better and more substantial reasons for approaching Joyce by means of psychoanalysis: "the argument is based not on contingent historical circumstances, but on general claims about the nature of the human subject." Thus, the tradition in Joycean criticism that has adopted the negative tone of Joyce's anecdotal response to psychoanalysis is ill-grounded, attempting as it does "to hide the mutual strangeness, the fundamental discrepancy, of Joycean and Freudian worlds" (410). Such an anti-Freudian perspective, pointing as it does to "a long history of reductive psychoanalytic 'solutions' to aesthetic problems," can also avail itself of "another 'freudful' struggle to solve the problem Joyce, both in literature and outside it: that of Carl Gustav Jung," whose coming-to-terms with Joyce presents the next section of Thurston's paper.

The doubled nature of the Joyce-Jung encounter, taking place as it does both in history and theory, renders "our interest in Jung as a reader of Joyce [...] always supplemented and complicated by our knowledge of his role in Joyce's life," that of a psychiatrist attempting, unsuccessfully, to clinically treat Lucia Joyce (411). As concerns the historical side of their relationship, Thurston examines Jung's 1932 "hostile fan" letter to Joyce, one communicating to the author his impressions after having read *Ulysses* (and containing the memorable phrase about the devil's grandmother), impressions which read "almost as if," observes Thurston, "Jung were responding, with his anguished, writhing prose, not to *Ulysses* but to the work-in-progress Joyce had more recently been publishing in Eugène Jolas' *transition* and elsewhere." Moreover,

> when Jung speaks of the "infuriating disdain" shown by the book, it is the *clinical* resonance of the phrase—its implicit allusion to the clinical concept of "transference"—that is striking. (415)

Thurston then turns to Jung's 1934 treatment of Lucia, as part of which "Lucia's artistic gift, the creative urge to innovate in language which she inherited from her father [...], all of these treasured Joycean ideas were grimly negated by Jung's diagnosis," a negation which Joyce famously countered by quipping: "To think that such a big fat materialistic Swiss man should try to get hold of my soul!" (416). However, in another famous letter, Jung diagnosed Joyce's resistance to Lucia's psychoanalytic treatment by pointing to an Anima-like status his daughter had for Joyce, a *participation mystique* uniting the two of them, defying any attempt at a (even curative) split.

Of the Joyce criticism devoted to the Jung-Joyce relation, Thurston refers to Brivic's *Joyce Between Freud and Jung*, which posits the *Wake* as Joyce's "most Jungian book," one of the crucial concerns of which is to think of masculine subjectivity, not in terms of totality and nothingness (just as the youthful Joyce/Stephen did), but as compromised, hybrid, and supplementing its lack by the Other's feminine letter. Of this, Thurston rather cagily observes:

> If this transition finally takes place, according to Brivic, in Joyce's "most Jungian" book, it must correspond to the dynamic pursuit of destiny, the move beyond the limited perspective of the ego into some liberating engagement with the collective unconscious. We might however, consider this a rather rose-tinted view of a text that repeatedly insists, "We are circumveiloped by obscuritads" (*FW* 244.15). (418)

Accordingly, for "a less optimistic, and considerably more obscure," view on Joyce's assault on the "I," Thurston turns to the work of Jacques Lacan. Again, a real-life encounter is discussed, or rather the two encounters mentioned by Lacan in his 1975 Paris symposium address, one of which has since been proven to have been misremembered, while the other not to have taken place at all. However this misremembering for Thurston,

> is more than just a trivial biographical footnote; it can provide an insight into both Lacan's category of the real and his sense of how Joyce's writing can be seen as a unique manifestation of it. [...] It was just such a return of the real that Lacan would identify at the primal scene, the "epiphany" or vocation, of Joyce's writing, its unspeakable fantasmatic "root language." Lacan's misremembered encounter, then, can be seen as his own Joycean "epiphany": something irreducible to history, both impossible and yet overwhelmingly significant. (419)

Again, the implications of a real-life encounter are related to theory, Lacan's 23rd seminar of course entitled *Le sinthome*, a title "offered as a new *name* for Joyce—a literary hole-y man." Just as Jung, Lacan, too, "linked Joyce's singular creative gift to a fundamental pathology, but in Lacan's view that pathology could be precisely located: in a complete non-inscription, a radical foreclosure, of the Joycean paternal signifier."

Foreclosure, a significant concept of Lacan's early work, denotes an act of physical negation far more potent than that of Freudian repression, and comes from Lacan's early interest in and treatment of psychotics, whose foreclosure excludes "the name of the father, the normalizing guarantee of a successful escape from the Oedipal triangle." In Joyce's case, the foreclosure was still more radical:

> It bore not only on the paternal "metaphor"—disabling the instance of signifying substitution that gave rise to the normal-neurotic functions of the unconscious—but also on the imaginary, dislodging the very root of the ego. (420)

This concept of foreclosure, bound with the workings of psychosis in the early work, is in *Le Sinthome* expanded to apply to what confronts all human infants, not only those destined to become mad:

> The return of the real in Joyce's vocation or "epiphany," as now read by Lacan, thus recalls a universal confrontation by each human infant with what is foreclosed, what cannot be spoken; but the Joycean response to that confrontation is singular, does not go by way of the repressive Oedipal metaphor that leads to the formation of the neurotic unconscious. (421)

Instead, the Joycean (Borromean) knot points to the possibility of *nonrepressive structures*, and of the constitution of a subject "disinvested" from the unconscious that is not psychotic. Thus, turning to the question of the potential of Lacan's perspective for Joyce criticism, Thurston marks out "the Lacanian preoccupation with the various ways in which writing can encounter its own *limits*, the limits of its ability to make the world signify—in moments of unspeakable emotion or bodily abandonment, at points of mystical reflection or hellish violation" as resonating powerfully "with all of Joyce's work, from the first epiphanies to *Finnegans Wake*" (422).

Having sketched out the historical and theoretical circumstances of the three crucial encounters between Joyce and psychoanalysis, Thurston concludes with a note on the stakes of the current debates about Joyce and psychoanalysis, informed as they are by textual genetics (Thurston's examples are Daniel Ferrer's important 1985 article "The freudful couchmare" and its revisitation by Wim Van Mierlo twelve years later).[20] An examination of these reveals that

> What we learn from the work of Ferrer and subsequent genetic studies [...] is that Joyce responded actively, with the arcane methods he had developed to write *Finnegans Wake*, to the rich textuality of Freudian critical practice, and perhaps above all to the powerful *interrogation* of human meaning, its refusal of the self-evident. (432)

However, for all its potential usefulness, Ferrer's project of determining "precisely what caught Joyce's attention," remains problematic for Thurston in that it "risks returning us to a pre-Freudian—that is, undivided, self-consistent—subject." Instead, Thurston wishes (and manages) to present Joyce's perspective on psychoanalysis as "highly complex and inconsistent," which is aptly captured by Van Mierlo's stress on "the eminently *parodic* intention of these Joycean references." Moreover, an instance of transmissional corruption when the printer mistook the "x" in *cathexis* (itself Joyce's correction of a misreading of the word as *catheris*)

[20] Daniel Ferrer, "The Freudful Couchmare of L: Joyce's Notes on Freud and the Composition of Chapter XVI of *Finnegans Wake*," *James Joyce Quarterly* 22.4 (1985) 367-382; Wim Van Mierlo, "The Freudful Couchmare Revisited: Contextualizing Joyce and the New Psychology," *Joyce Studies Annual 8* (Summer) 115-53.

for a deletion mark giving rise to the "final" version *catheis*, further problematises, if not undermines, the relevance of authorial intention as such: an instance where "the letter that was supposed to mark the author's intended correction ends up as the mark of his conscious, parodic misspelling" (424).

In an uncannily doubling way—appropriate for the broad picture drawn here—it is precisely the issue of the untenability of authorial intentions that concludes the Oxford *Companion*'s piece on "The Joyce of the Manuscripts," written by none other than Daniel Ferrer. This, however, together with the other direction of the exchange, the potential that the field of textual genetics is offered by psychoanalytic theory, will be discussed in due course.[21] At this point, the discussion proceeds with what is markedly absent from Thurston's informed and lucid overview of the masculine psychoanalytic encounters with Joyce—Joyce's treatment within the field of feminist studies, a substantial part of whose theoretical framework has been crucially formed by psychoanalysis. The work analysed in the chapter's opening section comes from perhaps the most renowned theorist combining the two—Julia Kristeva.

---

[21] I.e., in Chapter X "Textual Criticism & Textual Genetics."

3. Feminism, Sexuality & Gender Studies

I

Nowhere is the antecedence of Alan Roughley's work, *James Joyce and Critical Theory: An Introduction*, more conspicuous in respect to the ground covered here than in this chapter. Indeed, the attention paid to feminist thought in his book could be described as disproportional: precisely one hundred pages, compared to slightly over forty on psychoanalysis, just over thirty on Marxism, and less than thirty on poststructuralist Joyce. However, both the scope and structuration of Roughley's treatment are well-justified. The scope bears testimony to the fact that feminism in general, and literary feminism in particular, has been one of the crucial intellectual movements of the modern (as well as postmodern) period, both within and without academia. The division of the discussion into two chapters on "Joyce and Anglo-American Feminism," and "Joyce and French Feminism" is indicative of one of the defining traits within its academic *Sitz im Leben*: its split into two distinct, and often antagonistic practices. Roughley traces the development of both (which is definitely not the case with all the other approaches discussed) almost up to his present moment of 1990, which leaves it for this work to focus on what has come afterwards (the case of Suzette Henke's study and beyond), thereby notably reducing its scope. Thus, for the collection *Women in Joyce*, or the work of Bonnie Kime Scott (in the former tradition), or Julia Kristeva and Hélène Cixous (in the latter), this study refers the reader to Roughley's informed, readable account. However, to make up for this necessary omission, it includes within the context of feminist discussions the enriching perspectives offered by broader theories of gender and sexuality, since it is precisely their impact on feminist studies — hand in hand with the increasing infiltration of French theory into Anglo-American positivist approach — that has marked it around the turn of the millennium.

For the third time, the present discussion returns to the 1984 Frankfurt symposium collection,[1] which includes discussions of feminist issues from the "Character and Contemporary Theory" panel, Derek Attridge's playfully deconstructive "Joyce and the Ideology of Character," and Bonnie Kime Scott's retro and prospectively evaluative paper "Character,

---

[1] Bernard Benstock, ed., *James Joyce: The Augmented Ninth* (New York: Syracuse University Press, 1988); Attridge's paper republished in *Joyce Effects: Language, Theory, History* (Cambridge: Cambridge University Press, 2000).

Joyce, and Feminist Critical Approaches," and a panel entirely devoted to feminism and gender, *Joyce's Women in Dubliners Re-Viewed*. The present focus will be on Attridge's and Scott's addresses, together with Julia Kristeva's plenary address.

Attridge's paper observes how "the term *character* crystallizes and enforces a number of assumptions about the human subject," the three most prominent of which are the wholeness of the subject, its composition of and inner division into parts, and the subject's uniqueness and self-identity, its being, says Aquinas, "that thing which it is and no other thing" (152-3). Hélène Cixous' paper, "The Character of 'Character,'" is evoked, maintaining that by means of "character" "is established the identification circuit with the reader: the more 'character' fulfils the norms, the better the reader recognizes it and recognizes himself." What is more for Attridge, in order for this identification to be effective, character "must be occluded in an illusory experience of unmediated access to knowable human nature" (153).It therefore follows that it is precisely this illusion that Joyce's writing in late *Ulysses* and *Finnegans Wake* subverts. A character, however, can also denote a written sign, "not a transcendent and transparent value but a historically produced, unmotivated, diacritical one." Attridge undertakes a synthesis of the two:

> By insisting that every time the term *character* is used to mean an "assemblage of consistent personal qualities" it should be thickened and coloured by the sense of character as "arbitrary sign in a conventional, historically determined system," we may be able to talk about characters in a novel without subscribing to the ideological premises which habitually underpin such discussions. (154)

The second, physical sense of *character* is also articulated in the *Wake*'s two "protagonists," an organization or co-occurrence of the letters HCE and ALP, as well as its employment of sigla. However, the repetition with a variation of the HCE and ALP occurrences is part of the *Wake*'s demonstration that the notion of the fixity of the sign is itself "yet another instance of the power exerted by centuries-old assumptions." In this sense, character

> is not so different from character in the other sense, and both demand *integritas, consonantia*, and *claritas* in order to perform what is demanded of them. [...] If Joyce is truly to undermine the character as personage, then, he must also undermine character as sign.

The most obvious example of this undermining takes the form of *Ulysses*'s variations played on the theme of the proper name Bloom; Attridge's examples include "greasebloom" (11.180), "Bloomusalem" (15.1548), "Boom" (16.1260), "Stoom and Blephen" (17.549, 541). Now, the point is that "*all* lexical items [...] are susceptible to this treatment," and what in *Ulysses* is staged as an occasional reminder becomes the rule of the thumb for the *Wake*'s radical destabilization of the word (155). At the same time as it subverts the character's self-identity, the *Wake* also signals to

> the strength of our own ideologically generated but inescapable design for the stability, coherence, and recognizability of character in both senses, and brings to consciousness the powerful tools we have inherited for the retrieval of personages and words [...] from even so decentered and shifting a text as this one. (156)

Scott's paper takes up Attridge's quotation from Pope concerning "women not having any character at all," in order to discuss the effects of "women's socialization upon their qualifications for character," as well as other properties relevant to gender such as "power, action, and speech, all similarly denied to women in the cultures of Pope and Joyce," the connection being the use of Pope's *Polite Conversation* as a resource for the "Nestor" episode (158). The aim of her brief address is "to chart only a few points on the map of feminist practices, and to suggest how they have treated and in the future might further address the critical category of character in Joyce" (159). Her mapping covers the region of traditional, Anglo-American gynocriticism, marked by its attention to Joyce's female characters and the gender politics and sociology of their era—an example of this tendency within Joyce studies would be the collection *Women in Joyce*.

From there, Scott moves to the "currently privileged" territory of "continental, post-structuralist, psychoanalytical theories, largely supplied by men," and focuses on "the least realist" text, one "least susceptible to traditional, empirical character analysis"—*Finnegans Wake*. Thus:

> Feminist post-structuralism encounters character more in the unconscious, dreaming or formative range than socially-oriented gynocriticism typically does. Feminist versions of Lacan hypothesize a divided object shaped by the socio-sexual experience of others. Gender marks the parents (significantly *two* parents), the mother first supplying semiotic flow, the father later imposing the authority and law of *logos*. (161)

Scott's is a generally welcoming acceptance of this state of affairs, concluding on a note of invitation of "scholars well familiarized with Joyce's texts" to "join feminist critics in investigating the varied, imaginative, and complicated manifestations of gender in Joyce" (162).

Finally, Kristeva's plenary address, "Joyce the Gracehoper or the Return of Orpheus," addresses an array of issues from its author's own psychoanalytically anchored feminist position. Kristeva begins by arguing that the symptomaticity of Joyce's writing resides in "the capacity of the speaking being to identify with another subject or object, or a part or a trait thereof" (167). If "the mechanism of identification" as the driving force of the Imaginary and "of the disquieting human adventure within meaning" can be said to underwrite the entire project of literature, then Joyce's specificity lies in the formidable superiority of having explored, mimed, known, and brought to light, through a knowledge perhaps ignorant of itself as such but nonetheless assuredly at work, the details of such identification's mechanism, one that presides over the Imaginary's genesis, and consequently over its realization.

As an example of this peculiar meta-position inhabited by Joyce's discourse, Kristeva chooses his "intense experience of Trinitarian religion," regarded as a mechanism that was "the motor of his fictional experience and which allowed him to concentrate his efforts of representation and elucidation upon the identificatory substratum of psychic functioning" (168). However, against the manifold insistence of Joyce on issues and motifs such as transubstantiation, Arius' heresy, or the consubstantiality of father and son, Kristeva notes a number of instances of "the displacement and realization of the topos of identification," for example Bloom's orality, the "vertiginous assimilation of knowledge" by Mulligan or Stephen, or the assimilation of the character of Molly by the narrator, "in a manner more striking than any other utilization by an author of the mask of a character." The most important of these are "the two variants of the amorous experience, Stephen's *Agape* and Bloom's *Eros*," regarded as "the most pertinent and analytically fitting attempt undertaken by Joyce to shed light upon the identificatory movement proper to artistic experience" (169). As two inseparable aspects of the identificatory process,

the amorous and the artistic experiences are our only means of preserving our psychic space as a "living system": one that is open to the Other, capable of adaptation and change. Such an integration of polymorphism or perversion is concomitant with a practice of language that [...] integrates pre- or transverbal representations, thereby embracing a vast semiotic range extending from gesture to colors and sounds. (169-70)

Kristeva then proceeds to reject both Jung's and Lacan's positions on Joyce, instead drawing a link between his writing and the myth of Orpheus. Claiming that "Joyce succeeds where Orpheus fails," Kristeva identifies Joyce's artistic adventure, with "the modern, post-Christian version of the Greek myth in which the hero-artist is forbidden to see something, forbidden to look for Eurydice in the underworld, forbidden to turn gaze upon the feminine mystery," with the important difference that "Dedalus-Bloom, on the contrary, never turns his look away from the infernal night in which Eurydice is engulfed" (170). Thus, Joyce's final backward glance, the "Penelope" chapter, is only mistakenly searched by the critics for its "recognition of, or alternately a censuring of, feminine sexuality." It is more correct to view "Penelope" as concerning "the male-artist who, sated with a final appropriation-identification, restores to us a menad swallowed by Orpheus" (171).

Before proceeding to further illustrate these points on concrete textual instances in Joyce's oeuvre, Kristeva pauses to specify her understanding of *identification*, which she sees as encompassing "various stages in the coming-into-being of the subject: narcissistic identification, hysterical identification, projective identification." In fact, identification underlies the whole of the individual's psychic operations:

> If I admit that, under the Law of the Other, I am never ideally One, my entire psychic adventure is composed of failed identifications, of impossible autonomies, in which narcissism, perversion, and alienation come to lodge. [...] Identification, then, is to be understood as this movement by which the subject comes to be, insofar as he makes himself one with, identical to, an Other. (171-2)

A type of identification particularly relevant to the theory and practice of psychoanalysis is what Freud terms *Einfühlung* as the fundamental moment of the cure, the "transverbal identification that undoubtedly goes back to primary identifications." In other words, the transference of the analyst's *affection* must be coterminous with that of his *word*:

> In order to guide my word to the psychic space where my patient undergoes convulsive crises, I must not only accompany him *affectively* in his suffering, but I must also enact a leap in the *language* of signs and give a name to our common affect which has—for a time—remained unnameable. (172)

A transfer must take place then on the levels of both the drive's representatives and verbal representations: body and soul. The artistic and analytic *Agape* of Joyce's works therefore leads "from identification to transubstantiation," as is illustrated by his numerous references to the Arian heresy, or indeed "the most striking passage condensing the Joycean obsession with the Christic mystery"—Stephen's reflection on Hamlet (174-5).

Opposed to the Christian *Agape* of transubstantiation was the Greek *Eros*, which was expressed in Plato's texts as "a violent, potentially fatal, sado-masochistic psychodrama between the lover and the beloved." Within the Oedipal economy,

> the amorous ingestion of the father that concludes the act of identification must not dissimulate the violence of the underlying aggression. [...] in the fantasy and within the movement idealizing identification with the father, it is the mother who bears rejection's wrath: for at least a while in everyone's case and, in the pervert's, for good. (176)

In this context, naturally, what receives attention are Stephen's guilt-ridden memories of his victimized mother, the cause of whose death he believes himself to be. However, in a typically Joycean deconstructive operation of a binary, the opposition of Stephen as the *Agape* of logos and Bloom as the *Eros* of the flesh breaks down, as Stephen's eroticism can be shown as centred around his mother, while Bloom's is ultimately a quest for filial love. Here, Kristeva summarizes the key points of her argument:

Love's two forms—which are two variants of identification, the one paternal and symbolic, the other maternal, having to do with the drive—are united in the artist's experience, leading him to transmute "consubstantially" his psychic life into his characters and their adventure. (177)

Returning to her incipit metaphor of Joyce the Orpheus, Kristeva concedes that the choice of Dedalus over Orpheus was "undoubtedly correct" in that it stressed "the labyrinthine complexity of discourse and psychic life, a name, moreover, finding itself thereby in unison with modern technicity." Nevertheless, she identifies the underlying motor of Joyce's writing in what she terms "Orpheus Complex," or rather "an Orpheus without complex":

Neither Oedipus nor Orestes, neither simply lover nor simply murderer of his mother, or his father: Orpheus—Stephen—Bloom, Agape-Eros—defies Apollo-Shakespeare and absorbs Eurydice-Molly. (179)

This neither/nor and both/and structure brings Kristeva's intriguing peregrinations to their end on a note of a possible norm for her approach, which she identifies with the postmodern paradigm. For Kristeva, even in their most abstruse forms, Joyce's "symptom and his obscurity bring into relief the objects of post-modernism's critical interrogation: identification, representation." The themes of *Ulysses*, ultimately,

illustrate perfectly this incandescence of the Imaginary space that, by reason of its bi-dimensionality (body and meaning), given this transcorporality, challenges the place of the sacred. (180)

II

The 1986 Copenhagen symposium gave rise to Morris Beja's and Shari Benstock's co-edited collection, *Coping with Joyce*,[2] which brought an important conceptualization of the potential consequences of the deconstructive discussion for the field of feminist studies.

Ellen Carol Jones' "The Letter Selfpenned to One's Other: Joyce's Writing, Deconstruction, Feminism" quotes Eugène Jolas' famous contention that "the real metaphysical problem today is the word" to argue that "Joyce's revolution of the word is part of the totality of our era, reflecting the revolutionary decentering of epistemology by nineteenth- and early twentieth-century thinkers" (180). MacCabe is also echoed in the connection drawn between Joyce's poetic revolution and its political agenda, consisting in his treatment of language as a material and social structure. Jones' feminist concerns come to the fore when she observes how "all deconstructive discourses are necessarily inscribed within the circle of a language based on the very metaphysical concepts they intend to sub-

[2] Ellen Carol Jones, "The Letter Selfpenned to One's Other: Joyce's Writing, Deconstruction, Feminism," *Coping with Joyce: Essays from the Copenhagen Symposium*, eds. Moris Beja and Shari Benstock (Columbus: Ohio State University Press, 1986).

vert." Feminist critiques of phallogocentrism are therefore seen as necessarily determined, if not outright limited, by the dominant male discourse (183).

Jones produces a sound critique of Luce Irigaray, who, despite addressing an issue of a similar nature to Joyce's concern—that "women lack access to a language appropriate to the expression of their desire, that female sexuality cannot be articulated within Aristotelian logic"—is seen to solve it by "locat[ing] her writing within the ideological space of female desire, within the pre-Oedipal or the post-patriarchal, *as if* we could remember or imagine a space before or beyond the phallic economy" (183-4). Irigaray's dilemma, symptomatic of much of theoretical feminism, has to do with the idiom in which her refusal of the patriarchal order and phallogocentric discourse is to be voiced without (since all semantic language is by definition masculine) having to fall back on them, or in Jones' words:

> to rethink the concept of woman without resorting to limiting or essentialist definitions enables her to critique the *conceptualization* of women in phallogocentric discourse, but also logically forces her to acknowledge as figurative and conceptualizing her *own* analogy between female sexuality and women's language. (184-5)

This in turn finds its anti-topos in the situation of *Ulysses* where,

> although Molly Bloom is characterized as an emblem of "otherness" [...], a figure for the otherness of the text as a whole, she never does and never *can* speak for herself as other [due to] Joyce's usurpation of the role of the other as he signs himself at once as spiritual father and mother of his text. (186)

However, this imperfect "feminization" finds its counterpoint in Stephen's theory of art (*U* 9.376-85), which presents the artistic creation in terms of a Penelopean weaving and unweaving. Moreover, Stephen's point about Shakespeare's emasculation by Anne Hathaway is a moment of undoing, which entails "the succumbing of the male body to sexuality, to female sexuality" – regarded as a fall into language, "it acknowledges female *jouissance* as writing." Thus, Stephen places the genesis of his art in the womb of sin of the fallen Eve, and his myth of paternity entails an origin, a first creation, *ex nihilo*, suspension upon the void. Jones concludes:

> Selfpenning a letter to one's other, then, is to recognize the limitation of the specular construct of the self as one, the coherence and mastery of "I," and to acknowledge the scene on which that self is produced: the body of the woman. (190)

III

Attridge's and Jones' papers mark a significant point of departure, within the framework of feminist studies, towards discussing the female no longer in terms of the veracity or mendacity of female character mimesis, but on the untenability of character as unity and self-identity, and the subsequent disintegration of the hitherto opposed male and female. The crucial importance for Joyce of the relationship and interdependence between these two indefinables, which on a fundamental level is manifested through sexuality, has received its first comprehensive treatment in Richard Brown's influential work, *James Joyce and Sexuality*.[3] Its groundbreaking status is enhanced in its introduction, surveying the so-far utterly insufficient treatment of sexuality in Joyce's works:

> Whilst the initial reluctance to give too much attention to these matters may be in part explained as a prudent defensive strategy, their continued neglect is more attributable to perennial characteristics of Joycean criticism. (2)

Dominic Manganiello's *Joyce's Politics*,[4] the acknowledged precursor of Brown's book, is mentioned as having "begun to piece together the implication of Joyce's fictions in the ideas of their time" (3). The type of implication that Brown's study seeks to piece together is the response of Joyce's fiction to the "felt importance of sexuality and sexual change," aiming to provide

> a means of establishing the relevant context of contemporary ideas, perhaps even a way of discussing Joyce that is partly independent of the dominant practices of Joyce criticism, whose tendency has been to play down exactly these issues which we wish to confront. To this end, the knowledge we have of Joyce's reading provides a real opportunity for investigation. (4-5)

The sources for Brown's investigation are "Joyce's letters, records of Joyce's personal libraries, and the works themselves"—in this very order, since

> [c]omments and references in Joyce's letters, his literary critical writings and the knowledge we have of his personal libraries, may provide reliable sources for the intellectual historian, but the works themselves are a more treacherous source since their allusions, references or parodic dependencies are introduced for aesthetic purposes. (8)

These aesthetic purposes have everything to do with "structural" allusion, since the degree of semantic and aesthetic dependence on earlier texts is unprecedented, and, in Joyce, reflected by the very titles of his works, whose "significance" and "appeal" derives precisely "from this doubleness

---

[3] Richard Brown, *James Joyce and Sexuality* (Cambridge: Cambridge University Press, 1985).
[4] For more, see Chapter VIII "Politics," section II.

of reference and it is an appeal which Joyce exploits throughout his writings" (10). As long as allusive dependence on other writing is what drives the semantics and aesthetics in Joyce's work, "it is the purpose of this study to show how Joyce's polemicism, the attitudes adopted by his fiction, may also express themselves by these means," and to argue for what Brown terms "a renewed sense of the importance of subject-matter in Joyce's fiction" (10). Thus, two aspects emerge as central to this work: one "tries to place Joyce's work in the context of ideas in which he participated," whereas the other "tries to show that it was by attitudes to and aesthetic exploitations of other works, more than by explicit comment, that Joyce's attitude's were expressed" (11).

Brown's analysis begins with a discussion of love and marriage. Apart from a biographical slant, Brown combines his focus on Joyce's private life (with his catholic upbringing at odds with his youthful practice of frequenting brothels) with a broader sociological investigation in the contemporary transformation of the institution of marriage:

> In his relationship with Nora, Joyce followed, in an accelerated form, the larger intellectual movement of his time, rejecting the theological in favour of a rational conception of the sexual relationship. [...] [I]n rejecting marriage and in forming his relationship with Nora, [Joyce] was echoing the larger shift from divine to humanistic authority. (15-6)

Joyce is thus linked with many prominent writers of the nineteenth-century Europe in that he "relies upon the affective power of adulterous situations for many of his most central scenes and most powerful emotional effects" in the earlier works such "The Dead," *Exiles*, or, to some extent, *Ulysses*, where to the question of Molly's lovers, "the answer that *Ulysses* offers is that there is always 'another chap in the case' and that no love nor any valid understanding can exist without a recognition of that fact." (17, 21). This broad literary interest is documented by Brown's analysis of Joyce's library and his wide reading of realist writers (relied on consistently throughout the book), as having to do with "Joyce's desire to replace romantic mystifications with biological certainties."

An example of this in Joyce's fiction is Gabriel Conroy's epiphanic recognition of Bloom's equanimity, both of whom realizes that "his wife is a separate being over whose actions neither he nor her lover have any direct form of control" (34-5). Thus, Joyce's treatment of the marriage institution and free love ideology in his early works is regarded in relation "to the 'progressive' theories of late nineteenth and early twentieth-century writers" (35). *Finnegans Wake* (the passage on *FW* 573-4) in contrast presents "Joyce's engagement with marital questions" as consisting in "adverting our attention to the language of the law itself and investigating or disrupting it through parodic and ironic means" (47). This double movement of both making manifest and subverting traditional structures accounts for, in Brown's opinion, "one of the best-known interests displayed by Joyce in the *Wake*," his interest in Viconian theory where "marriage arises suddenly and arbitrarily from human fears and runs in inevitable contradiction to biological desires" (48-9).

From this point Brown goes on to discuss the new science of sexuality as shaped by Freud, Krafft-Ebing and Ellis, and their *Three Essays on the Theory of Sexuality* which "provided the concept of a 'polymorphously perverse' sexual instinct, and a radical shift of attention away from *phylogenesis* (the development of the race) to *ontogenesis* (the development of the individual)"; *Psychopathia Sexualis*, with its familiar taxonomy of perverse sexual acts; and *Studies in the Psychology of Sex*, starting as an attempt to mount a defence of homosexuality (51). Joyce's readings of scientific and other literature of sexuality is further discussed as the "sources of his modernity," yet it is of a problematic status due to the fact that "his means of expressing it are not always straightforward" (54). For example, Garnier's *Onanisme* is seen as informing Joyce's frequent use of the motif of masturbation, especially in its notion of "generic onanism," according to which

> in the modern sense, almost all sexuality is to be understood as onanistic inasmuch as its goal is gratificatory not reproductive, [and thus] there seems to be an important similarity between the act performed by Bloom and Gerty and that performed simultaneously by Molly and Boylan. (61)

The other two important issues addressed by Brown include copulation without population which is linked to the Blooms' "limitation of fertility," the bold assertion here being that "their estrangement is hardly one which excludes sexual contact and should be enough to assure us that the formula is an 'Ithacan' way of describing a contraceptive sexual relationship rather than sexual abstinence" (67), and perversity where

> for all the attention to the perverse in Joyce, there is no single character, except perhaps the man in "An Encounter," who might be called sexually deviant in the Krafft-Ebing sense. On the contrary, Joyce is most keen to present his central characters with a variety of shades of sexual taste as if to suggest that such varieties are intrinsic to human psychology. (83)

Of relevance for Brown's argument here are Joyce's famous sexually charged letters of 1909, which "among a variety of sexual anomalies (such as coprophilia) which they uninhibitedly display, show a definite masochistic inclination" (87). Bloom's perversions (listed in "Circe") however do not prevent him from retaining his precarious normality:

> More than any physiological benefits he may derive from his solitary practice, it is the new onanistic concept of sexuality that saves him in the reader's eyes, permitting, even requiring, a degree of "perversity" in order to guarantee the "normality" of his deviation from the narrow traditional ideal. (88)

Brown's interest then centres around the female issue in Joyce's life and work. Joyce's early involvement with Emma Sheehy-Skeffington plays an important part in Brown's argument regarding *Dubliners*: "Emma's brightness and nationalism were traits that Joyce worked into the character of Molly Ivors in 'The Dead.'" The stereotyping of women has been noted by many, but Brown points out that "the male characters in *Dubliners* are just as constrained by their sexual identity" (92-4). This sexual dimorphism of Joyce's fictional world "clearly depends upon a strong sense of difference between the sexes," an example of which is the special language of 'Penelope,'" whose attempt at presenting a separate female identity "was by no means innocent" (98-9). However, the gender operations performed in *Ulysses* are ultimately seen as positive: Joyce's reliance on the famous Samuel Butler theory of the female author of the *Odyssey* enhances "the sense that *Ulysses* is a 'female' book and that a radical reinterpretation of masculinity and femininity takes place" (102). This is even further confirmed in Stephen's theory of Shakespeare presented in "Scylla and Charybdis," which has much to do with Joyce's experiments regarding ideas of "intermediate" or "androgynous" sexual identity, the first instance of which is the early epiphany of an older woman mistaking Stephen's sex: "It is from one's mother, Stephen claims, that one learns 'how to bring thoughts into the world'; the imagination is in this sense androgynous" (105).

Turning back to contemporary socio-sexual concerns, the Vaertings' *The Dominant Sex* which Joyce read, presented a radical revision of the theory of sexual difference in which a reconceptualization of Weininger's abstracted qualities "may not necessarily result from sexual difference at all but from the relative political dominance of either sex in any given society" (107). Thus, the Bella/Bello Cohen scene of female domination "reflects the atrocities of man's domination over women" and presents "a clear indication of the closeness of Joyce's view to that of [the] Vaerting[s]" (111). Of the female characters of *Exiles*, *Ulysses*, and the *Wake*, Brown observes:

> Joyce liked to present female characters with strong sexual desires. The sexual desires may be exposed satirically, [...] but when they are explicitly recognized and put into words in Molly's soliloquy they are among the most strongly-endorsed feelings that an ironized Joycean character may express. (115)

Brown then goes on to outline what he terms Joyce's sexual aesthetic, drawing a parallel between Joyce's abandonment of the Church and "a shift from belief in a God to a belief in the sexual instincts that make up the human spirit" (126). This has to do with Joyce's "pornography," literally "writing about prostitutes" (and here Brown notes it was from Balzac's infamous *Splendeurs et misères des courtisanes* that Joyce took his famous Stephen creed of "silence, exile, cunning"). Joyce's praxis is therefore at odds with Stephen's theory:

> To take too literally the apparently anti-sexual streak in Stephen's theory of art would be to misrepresent Joyce's own aesthetic achievement, since Joyce's fiction is quite evidently not one which seeks to reinforce the conventional distinction between serious art and sexual explicitness. (132)

Apart from the potentially grotesque flavour, Joyce's occasional explicitly pornographic details also draw "our attention to the fact that the world of the erotic imagination is governed by or transacted through the language and ideology of such kinds of literature." (135)

Brown's discussion of the censorship of Joyce's works takes into account Joyce's pre-programming, for "in trying to recount the history of Joyce's clash with censoriousness we are, in part, acting out a drama whose plot was written by Joyce himself" since it is to "Joyce's own conclusions about the necessarily alienated and condemned position of the artist" that we are bound when talking about censorship (150). In this respect, the Daedalus myth is a first instance of self-censorship:

> Daedalus's first task was to construct a wooden cow by means of which Pasiphae was able to commit the most notorious sexual transgression in classical mythology and his next job was, at the commission of King Minos, to construct a labyrinth at whose heart lay the product of the transgression, the Minotaur, could be concealed. (152-3)

Thus, in "Oxen of the Sun," the motivation of Joyce's art begins with a desire to go beyond realistic literature, by basing a portrayal of human relationships on a belief in the importance of sexuality. Just as Daedalus', Joyce's art is based on sexual transgression, developing as "a labyrinthine concealment more than as an explicit statement of transgression" (153).

Hence, apart from scenes of explicitly sexual content, Joyce's style conveys "literary pleasure" that is "as 'real' as sexual pleasure and also need[s] to be recognized" (154), where "literariness" is to be understood as "indirection" (157). Joyce's writing is one performing "conscious manipulations of previously written material" where "the importance of allusions and quotations is not merely secondary to the main intention or aesthetic statement of the work; as often as not they themselves constitute that statement" (159). An example of this could be Joyce's relation to Blake's artistic heresy, which taught Joyce "the practice of radical rereading" (163). Brown then concludes by observing of Joyce's art that it is one "whose novelty consisted in the fact that it was built out of heretical revision and re-reading of the orthodoxy it hoped to supplant" (164).

IV

Two important essayistic forays into the area of feminist Joyce studies appeared in the first issue of *European Joyce Studies*, the edited collection *Joyce, Modernity, and its Mediation*.[5] The editor's piece, "'The Lan-

---

[5] Christine van Boheemen, "'The Language of Flow': Joyce's Dispossession of the Feminine in *Ulysses*"; Jeri Johnson, "'Beyond the Veil': *Ulysses*, Feminism, and the Figure of Woman,"

guage of Flow': Joyce's Dispossession of the Feminine in *Ulysses*," poses as its crucial question the following: "What is the function of the image of woman for the coherence and prestige (the 'streamlining') of *Ulysses*?" (63-4) This reading, focusing on the rhetorical dimensions of the text, is involved in the feminist project of "break[ing] the enchanting mirror of seeming reality which keeps us locked in illusion," and instead calls for the need to "scrutinize the literary text with analytic objectivity and an awareness of its constructed nature." From this perspective, Molly Bloom "functions as warrant and proof of the authority of her author and his prestigious place in the tradition of the English novel as the writer who ended the realist tradition by carrying it to its limits" (64). Her Homeric archetype, Penelope is regarded as a possible model of authority for Joyce in that her example provides "a style of weaving which suggests and promises closure, but simultaneously postpones and subverts it, in defiance of full definition and definite choice" (65). Analogously to woman functioning as the complementary *other* to man, Joyce is seen as positioning himself as an *other* to the tradition of novelistic authority. Bloom's desire for the woman "to speak" expressed in "Circe" is satisfied in "Penelope," a chapter "of words instead of events, fantasy rather than fact, libido instead of ratio, seemingly Joyce's afterthought," which "may be central to our understanding of the nature of the text as a whole."

Analysing the text, van Boheemen notes its most dazzling stylistic quality—the scarcity of punctuation:

> Undermining the possibility of discrimination, distinction, and denial, "Penelope" suspends the either/or logic into a both/and (or neither/nor). But this unsettling preclusion of final meaning and identity is [...] also a characteristic quality of *Ulysses* as a whole.

This supplementary quality of "Penelope" is related to the question of authority, for the question presents itself regarding the nature of her otherness: might it be a projection of a modern and masculine desire for alternative authority? The real question for van Boheemen is "whether we think that alogical flow and physical secretion are (the) truly essential feminine qualities," the heart of the matter being the essential untenability of *the* or *a* essential femininity. As long as femininity is the other of man,

> then the connotation of "fluidity" may not be more than the counterpart necessary to give the masculine connotation of rationality self-identity and meaning—just as without the concept of death, the idea of life is meaningless. (69)

As regards the question of female essence, van Boheemen finds "ample evidence in *Ulysses* itself to warrant the conclusion that Molly is indeed to be regarded as the realization of hypostatic femininity," which despite its

Joyce and the Art of Mediation, ed. Christine van Boheemen (Amsterdam: Edition Rodopi, 1989).

striking explicitness still presents an "essentially true notion of feminine presence, not metaphysical but physical, not spiritual but fleshly, not phallic but uterine, not logical but flowing" (70). The consequence is momentous:

> Thus, even if *Ulysses* subverts the classic effect of discovery and knowledge implicit in the structuring effect of plot, and in the process avoids the mimetic representation of ultimate origin, Joyce nevertheless gives us the substitute revelation of Molly Bloom as an emblem of original otherness. (71)

However, it is exactly because of Molly's position of origin and essence that allows Joyce to portray her as a parody of received ideas and ideals. Here van Boheemen opposes what she regards as essentialising perspectives of MacCabe (Molly as liberating the speech of female desire, and Joyce therefore opposing George Eliot), Cixous' *écriture féminine*, or Irigaray's notion of woman's fluidity as model for her textuality. Instead she claims:

> However appealing this attribution of authority and transcendence to the feminine principle may be to the old-fashioned feminist type, I at least can no longer regard it the truth Joyce, Jung, or MacCabe hold it. And perhaps the fact they did ought to make us suspicious. French poststructuralism teaches that man's sense of full subjectivity is an illusion which he owes to his use of the medium of language. (72)

On closer scrutiny, Molly's image proves "a fallacious, ambivalent, in fact mythic construction, like the fetish made up from the conflation of contradictory qualities within the compass of one entity." Mark Shechner's *Joyce in Nighttown* is referenced as having made evident that it is precisely Molly's sexual ambivalence which turns her into the central agent of *coincidentia oppositorum*, or as van Boheemen puts it, "in her, the ontological contradiction between the masculine and feminine [...] is resolved" (73). In this connection, van Boheemen discusses the water imagery (traditionally female-associated) in *Ulysses*, which is revealed to be strikingly gender-ambivalent. The "great sweet mother" of Swinburne's as well as the "scrotumtightening" agent of castration in Stephen's imagination, the water imagery confirms the peculiarity of *Ulysses* in that "it combines two contradictory aspects which remain separated in *Finnegans Wake*" for "in *Ulysses*, there is no distinction between water as fertile sea [...], the source of life; and water as the cold and impersonal paternal ocean, the agency of death" (74). Thus, the notion of "flow" brings van Boheemen to call Molly a "flower" with the two possible pronunciation variations, the undecidability of which stems from *Ulysses* itself (*U* 11.861), and functions as "the imaginary fusion of notions of masculinity and femininity" (75). Here, the author revises her starting premise:

Indeed, my earlier surmise is wrong. *Ulysses* is not a text which tries to shift the *locus* of the idea of origin from the paternal to a maternal principle. It wishes to sublate sexual difference and banish alterity to turn everything into a mythic notion of flow which the fiction itself imitates and practices in its weaving/unweaving of the image of Dublin. (75)

This ideological nature of Joyce's novel, found "obtrusive" by van Boheemen, increasingly gives way to "the perverse oddity of Joyce's textuality," which thereby gains outline and clarity (76).

Instead of further pursuing this bizarre dichotomy, the author prefers to conclude on a general note about the general role of "the woman." Not only is writing herself into the text the "indispensable countersign to Bloom's passport to eternity," as Joyce argued, but it is also "the countersign of Joyce's passport to immortality as the author of *the* novel to deconstruct the self-presence of realistic fiction." However little this tells us about "the true nature of women," the question actually remains a different one: "whether any text can give us an image of true femininity or true masculinity for that matter." The feminist project must therefore remain "not *cherchez la femme*, but to study the mutual determination of notions of authority and connotations of gender" (77).[6]

In a similar vein, Jeri Johnson's "'Beyond the Veil': *Ulysses*, Feminism, and the Figure of Woman," also aims to investigate the conceptualization of gender as presented in the "perverse" textuality of *Ulysses*, if from a completely different perspective. First, however, Johnson surveys the complicated relationship between Joyce and feminism, noting that at the 1986 Copenhagen symposium (discussed above), "feminism burst onto the scene with all the force of the 'return of the repressed'" (203). The above-mentioned Anglo-American verses French divide remains for Johnson one of an "anti-Joycean" (Anglo-American feminist) attitude. This stands in opposition to the "useful projects" to be found in the Joyce of French feminism as represented by Julia Kristeva's work, which Johnson regards as useful in that it "suggests that a potentially revolutionary force which disrupts and displaces phallogocentric discourse can be detected in modernist or avant-garde writing."

More innovatively, Johnson ventures to ask the question: if where "before feminism divided Joyceans, now Joyce divides feminists," then "what is it about the conjunction Joyce and Woman that engenders such discord?" (204) This is followed by a careful examination of two examples: the work of Susan Gilbert and Julia Kristeva. Of the former, Johnson maintains that her reading rests on several assumptions, for example that

---

[6] What cannot pass unnoticed here is the striking similarity of van Boheemen's piece to Derek Attridge's essay, "Molly's Flow: The Writing of 'Penelope' and the Question of Women's Language," dating from precisely the same year of 1989, only published later in *Joyce's Effects* (93-116). The similarity consists in many of the crucial points of the essay, including those concerning Molly's style as a *written* one, a deconstruction of the gendered notion of her language as a "flow," and the double-reading of Molly as a "flow-er." A rare instance of critical telepathy, one should think.

"an adequate representation of women is possible; mimesis is not a problem because to her an *a priori* real exists (e.g. a real woman's experience unmediated by patriarchal ideology) which can be adequately represented in a language which in turn remains undisturbed by figurality" (205), assumptions which would be "anathema to Julia Kristeva," whose "Joyce the Gracehoper" (see above) is analysed later. More generally, Johnson observes that

> [f]or Kristeva, Woman is rhetorical trope functioning within a narrative economy as means to the end of revolutionary textual formation and a radically altered reader whose pleasure is not simply egocentric. The price one pays for such a reading is the disappearance of any signifying practice immediately relevant to women within culture, society or history. (207)

Thus, Johnson's own perspective turns out to be culturally historical—and a frequent invocation against deconstruction's a-historicism is played out here as well. However, in a similar vein to Derrida's, she also observes that an anti-Joycean as opposed to pro-Joycean feminist debate is "already conducted within *Ulysses*, a debate presided over, and rendered undecidable by, the 'figure of the Woman,'" who, "in becoming the ground of the struggle [...], becomes the sign of divided, irresolvable meaning" (208).

The particular locus from which Johnson revisits this debate is the frequently discussed tension between Stephen Dedalus and women, particularly the way Stephen's art theory as proposed in "Scylla and Charybdis" reflects these issues. For Johnson, the crucial questions are the following ones:

> Is Joyce, in acknowledging the truth of maternity, admitting the necessity of including or inscribing this truth in his art, or is he asserting this truth only to distinguish and exclude it from art which, like paternity, is fictive? Does Joyce give voice to the maternal or does he overwrite it? (209)

On one level, woman in Stephen's imagination associates itself with flesh, sin, and death, as in Anne Hathaway's example. On another level, she comes to represent the condition of a lived, bodily truth, incompatible with artistic creation:

> Woman's body may "know" the truth, but man's mind never can. And not knowing is the pre-condition of all art, which translates doubt into a greater truth through the imagination, the word, the Logos. If woman's word is unreliable, man's is ultimately artistically profound. (211-2)

In a similar manner, Stephen's view of the artist/creator as androgynous, anti-masculinist though it may seem, is revealed by Johnson as similarly inscribed within patriarchy. One must not, of course, conflate Stephen Dedalus with Joyce, nor does Johnson easily oppose Stephen's voice by the countering ones of Bloom and Molly. What the presented investigation aims at is to run across the tropological gamut of "Mother/Woman as flesh/truth, Father/Man as imagination/incertitude," and thereby to create "a countering discourse, one which controls Stephen in his attempt to master it" (216).

Regarding Stephen's famous meditation on the weaving/unweaving process whereby art comes about, Johnson notes that in falling back on this physical image,

> Stephen persuades himself of the persistence of selfhood through reliance on what he would identify as a paternal, insubstantial trace—memory. Molecules change and shuttle; bodies weave and unweave; moles, memories and entelechies persist. (218)

Later on in Johnson's argument, the mole-as-the-mark-of-the-Father comes to be re-marked via its allusion to Imogen's "mole cinq-spotted." In *Cymbeline*, explicitly alluded to at the end of the "Scylla" episode, it is "the masculine incertitude, fully in the grip of patriarchal distortion," that "turns a virtuous woman into a whore and displaces the responsibility for the violation of Lucrece's virtue from the male perpetrator onto the female who left him wounded" (222). Posthumus' error then lies in his assumption that the signifier (Imogen's mole) can only have one signified, her unfaithfulness. The mole, for Stephen, signifies betrayal, and Johnson observes betray it does:

> The only distinction between Stephen's mole and Imogen's is that his is dexter, hers sinister: the same mark, differently gendered, signified other to void the threat. [...] The only "Truth" signified by the sign of Woman is a truth that betrays. And it betrays at the very moment that one attempts to fix it. [... Thus,] in the language of rhetorical troping of *Ulysses* we see the only "Truth" of the "figure of Woman" revealed. This "Truth" is that the acts of reducing Woman to physicality, of mistaking language for materiality, of believing the sign of the thing is the same as the thing, are acts of reduction which language, Joyce's language specifically, will belie. And it is precisely in the figure of Woman that this drama is played out. (225-6)

Returning to the initial Gilbert/Kristeva discussion, both their positions are found to represent a split within feminist readings of Joyce that is generated in and by Joyce's text—or, "both Gilbert and Kristeva have been right for both have identified operations which do occur in *Ulysses*." More specifically, Gilbert has described "the elision of the sign of the physical with the physical at the locus Woman," whereas Kristeva has seen "Woman" as "functioning within the text to allow a masculine identity formation." However, Johnson insists, "this is not an either/or dilemma," but rather one "which can never be resolved because it is both/and" (227-8). Johnson concludes her informed reading by claiming that

> the extent to which any reading of *Ulysses* ignores the figure of Woman as that which prevents either Gilbert or Kristeva from speaking the whole

truth, is the extent to which that reading will fail to be other than a performance of an irresolvable debate already immanent in *Ulysses* itself. (228)

V

Looking back on the 1980s, Derek Attridge's edited *The Cambridge Companion to James Joyce*[7] featured a piece by the prominent Joycean critic Karen Lawrence devoted to "Joyce and Feminism." She begins by mentioning an instance of Joyce's own dream of Molly Bloom coming to chastise him for how badly he depicted her in *Ulysses*, this being an instance of the "numerous examples of women accusing men of misleading and misrepresenting them" contained in Joyce's recorded dreams (237). Lawrence expresses her reservations about the accusatory judgments of the likes of Gilbert and Gubar and their claim that women in Joyce are sentenced to a purely material existence, arguing instead that "Joyce's texts partly deconstruct the symbolic, encoded forms of their own representations and expose the workings of male desire" (239). Lawrence refers to the *Wake*'s expression for writing, 'squirtscreen' (*FW* 187.07), as denoting both "a burst of expression ('squirt') but also a 'screen.'" This dual nature of Joyce's writing of the feminine thus renders any "catalogue of misogynistic images or female stereotypes in Joyce's work" unable "to account for his undermining of the grounds of representation" (240).

For Lawrence, "increasingly, Joyce's texts unmask male anxieties of women's power" in that "in the earlier texts, these anxieties are represented as [...] the personal fears and desires of male characters like Stephen Dedalus or Gabriel Conroy" and "the later texts reveal these fears to be inscriptions of cultural anxieties" (241). Lawrence's own deconstructive slant is most outspoken when she observes that Joyce exposes "the power relationship suppressed within the binary oppositions that underwrite culture, i.e. the pairs of words like male/female and presence/absence in which one of the terms of the pair is privileged over the other," and it is in his unmasking of these binaries that Joyce is seen as "a precursor of deconstruction" (241-2). However, Lawrence is against the misconception of this unmasking as easily liberating in any way. She states that "to expose the workings of male paranoia, desire, guilt, and ambivalence in one's fiction, is not necessarily to free one from the same feelings." Indeed in Joyce's case, the representation of the feminine is "often double-minded, containing the traces of past desires and fears," an example of which might be Stephen's longing for the origin in the maternal body, transformed in *Finnegans Wake* into a search for a "natural" language—the desire "to see figuratleavely the whome of your eternal geomater" (*FW* 296.30-297.01) (242-3). What saves Joyce from a simply essentialising outlook is the double movement of his text, in which "the desire to lift the veil of Woman is everywhere portrayed," and yet "its impossibility is insistent." As examples even as early as the epiphanies

[7] Karen Lawrence, "Joyce and Feminism," in *The Cambridge Companion to James Joyce*, ed. Derek Attridge (Cambridge: Cambridge University Press, 1990).

show, in Joyce's works, "woman is not revealed but constantly revised." Woman functions for Joyce, not as "flesh-without-word," but as "allaphbed" figuring the erotic and material potential of language, offering "a way out of the discourse of Freudian rebellion, [presenting] instead a term for the Derridean 'drift' in language" (244). However, the anti-essentialist caveat resurfaces:

[One] must recognize the danger of the "genderization" of writing as feminine and of viewing the male avant-garde as writing the "feminine," for the undecidability that characterizes "feminine" writing might appear to reinscribe Woman in her old stereotypes. (245)

In the case of *Ulysses*, this degenderising perspective is exemplified in the well-known Stephen statements, according to which paternity is argued to be a legal fiction of origin and *amor matris* the only true thing in life, a product of nature rather than culture; and yet Stephen's theory of creation "pre-empts the role of the mother and leaves the male artist self-sufficient, free to create a world" (249), and the "Oxen of the Sun" chapter in turn, "represents the suppressed relationship between reproduction and textual production," the *womb* being the chapter's symbol (250). Writing, however, can also function as "skirtscreen," as "a defence against the power of woman's body," with male anxiety surfacing in a number of places. Two chapters in particular are seen as staging woman's subjectivity: "Nausicaa"—viewed, with reference to Derrida, as a postcard, "a romantic, anonymous, mass-reproduced fantasy, the caption, perhaps, reading 'love loves to love love'" (252)—and "Penelope," which presents the following particular problem:

how can [Molly] represent what is beyond Joyce's control, language emanating form somewhere else, and still somehow provide an ending of the book and a release from the stark, patriarchal abstractions preceding it? (253)

Molly thus represents "the *problem of woman represented by the male pen*," a problem refigured in the *Wake*, a book that "does not limit the sign of the unthinkable or the other to the interstices and final chapters" for "although Anna Livia, like Molly, has 'the last word', it returns us to the book's beginning" (253, 4).

Lawrence's paper draws to its conclusion by mentioning a famous passage from Joyce's letter to Nora, in which he claims that nothing fine or noble is to come out of his writing unless he listens "at the doors of [her] heart." This substantiates Lawrence's argument that "Joyce's works are letters of desire to the female that circulate through the texts of culture, letters published for all the world to see" (254). As one of the name's of Joyce in *Finnegans Wake* is "Shame's Voice," Lawrence points to Joyce's correspondence with Martha Fleischmann, addressed as it was to "Nausicaa" and signed "Odysseus." Moreover, it is written with Greek "e"s, which are taken as a synecdoche for all Joyce's writing, a postcard whose message with reference to Derrida "is both exposed to the world and yet curiously encoded for deciphering by its recipient" (255).

VI

Perhaps the most sustained attempt at theorizing the relation between Joyce and feminism has been written by Suzette Henke. Her *James Joyce and the Politics of Desire*[8] opens with a bold statement concerning the relation between the two:

> [A]lone, Joyce's artist is insufferably narcissistic, a logocentric creator awash in a free play of signifiers ultimately signifying nothing. For inspiration, and, indeed, for aesthetic grounding, he must turn to woman as both virgin and mother, creator of life and symbolic emotional savior. (1)

However, this clear-cut binary does not hold: Joyce's attitude to feminine desire is seen as "highly ambivalent" since

> the dichotomy in his mind was not...between virgin and whore, but between narcissistic virgin and phallic mother—between the untouched and untouchable *ingénue* and the experienced maternal female. (2)

After these preliminary presumptions, Henke turns to the representations of the feminine within the Joycean canon, observing that *Stephen Hero* and *A Portrait* present "extended delineations of Stephen's 'flight from woman,'" and regarding *Exiles* as the turning point in the development of Joyce's sexual politics." In *Ulysses*, despite her mythification, Molly manages to spin "a web of imaginative possibilities that allow her psychologically to inscribe herself in a complex polymorphous and polyphonic discourse of desire" (6). *Finnegans Wake* is seen then as crowning Joyce's feminist project in the sense that "nowhere is Joyce's anti-patriarchal obsession more evident than in his final *magnum opus*" (7).

Sketching the main sources of theoretical inspiration, Henke outlines how psychoanalysis informs her approach. Acknowledged are Freud's analysis of psychic longing in terms of physical need and emotional demand, which maps an economy of drives and satisfactions, as well as Lacan's revision thereof, introducing the important mirror stage of development as crucial in the formation of the "split" ego. This in turn brings about its psychological inscription into the register of paternal law and language, and the Other as an imaginary construction of the infantile psyche that refuses to acknowledge the self as a fragmented *corps morcelé*. Taking her cue from Lacan, Julia Kristeva further elaborated on his celebration of sexual *jouissance*, emphasizing the radical psychic and aesthetic differences "between the logocentric, symbolic register of the

---

[8] Suzette Henke, *James Joyce and the Politics of Desire* (London and New York: Routledge, 1990).

father and pre-Oedipal, semiotic attachment to the mother," the last distinction being "crucial to this study" (9). The term politics is used here "in the context of 'sexual politics' to delineate those struggles and maneuvers involved in the psychosocial construction of gender"; patriarchal ideology is seen in accordance with current neo-feminist theory, as "contingent on the humanist notion of a 'seamlessly unified self' [...] which is commonly called 'Man,'" but which is "in fact a phallic self, constructed on the model of the self-contained, powerful phallus." The purpose of Henke's study is then

> to show how Joyce, in the course of his career, became such a revolutionary writer, forging new psychosexual subject-positions in a controversial discourse of desire. (10)

Henke then goes on to analyse the whole of Joycean canon, with an eye sensitive to gender, sexuality and feminist issues in Joyce's polymorphous writing. Her "Desire and Frustration in *Dubliners*" sees the collection as "an anatomy of male hysteria over the paralytic fear of being feminized — a terror of Mother Church and Mother Ireland that gives rise to the psychological need for coldness, detachment, and logocentric control," depicting the citizens of Dublin as "demeaned by insatiable desires endlessly replayed on the body of Mother Ireland — a body defiled, raped, and adulterated by British authority," thereby bringing on board (post)colonial concerns (13). Henke surveys all the stories, examining "The Sisters" in connection with Lacan's theory of self-formation, "An Encounter" in terms of the pederasty implicit in pedagogy, or regarding the young Jimmy Doyle in "After the Race" as "an inverted replica of the naïve Eveline" (24). The "finely ambiguous ending" of "The Dead" receives careful attention with regard to the previous stories as "the author's ironic sensibility in stories such as 'Araby' or 'A Painful Case'" has taught us "to distrust swooning souls and self-deceptive epiphanies." Gabriel, imitating the Christ-like role of Michael Furey, "may well be trapped in a self-indulgent replication of romantic asceticism" (47). Gretta, by contrast, in touching "the semiotic rhythms of maternal love and erotic bonding," articulates "a spiritually redemptive aesthetics of desire," presaging "the future textual victories of Bertha Rowan [...], Molly Bloom [...], and Anna Livia Plurabelle" (48-9).

"Stephen Dedalus and Women" maps the simultaneously pervasive and elusive presence of women within *A Portrait*, who, "demonized by Stephen's childhood sense of abjection," stand as "powerful emblems of the flesh — frightening reminders of sexual temptation, the process of generation, and the inevitability of bodily decay" (50). The novel's opening is of utmost relevance here — Simon Dedalus appears "a bearer of the law and the word, instruments of the will that promise psychological mastery over a hostile material environment," and Stephen's mother "a powerful and beneficent source of physical pleasure," yet also "one of the women principally responsible for introducing [Stephen] to a hostile external world and to the repressive strictures of middle-class morality," as implied by her insistence that Stephen will "apologise" (50-2). Other key female characters include the virgin Emma, the prostitute, and the bird-girl.

Regarding Emma, Henke notes a parallel between Stephen's early interaction with her and the Freudian *fort/da* game, for what is at stake in both is catching hold of and assuming mastery over an essentially uncontrollable other. The perfumed prostitute of Stephen's first sexual experience "recalls his 'nice-smelling' mother at the same time that she functions as high priestess or vestal virgin in a contemporary phallic cult." In what is regarded as an oral-regressive encounter, "the prostitute becomes mistress of Stephen's lips and, through a lingual kiss that inaugurates a fantasy of pre-Oedipal bliss, temporarily appropriates the highly guarded powers of artistic speech" (66). The bird-girl, in Henke's psychoanalytic reading, comes to represent Stephen's self-projection of which he becomes enamoured in a fashion pointedly narcissistic: "The anima, the feminine aspect of the psyche, has won his passion and holds him enthralled." Just like Narcissus, "Stephen has fallen in love with his projected self-image clothed in female garb" (72). The Joycean irony here is his insistence on the erotic overtones in what Stephen would have a purely aesthetic encounter: "If Stephen feels incipient sexual arousal in the presence of exposed female thighs, he quickly sublimates erotic agitation beneath effusions of purple prose" (74). Finally, the discussion centres around Stephen's repudiation of women, at odds with his project of usurping their procreative powers for his artistic creation:

> Throughout the novel, Stephen has sought the evacuation of affect from language and a re-inscription of his filial self into the symbolic order and law of the Father. [...] The figure of woman as mother/temptress/whore is doubled in the many mirrors of art until she is apostheosized as the virgin goddess of a new artistic religion. [...Thus,] not until *Ulysses* will a new model begin to emerge—one that recognizes the need for the intellectual artist to make peace with the mother-lover of his dreams and to incorporate into his masterful work those mysterious breaks, flows, gaps, and ruptures associated with the repressed semiotic flow of male/female desire. (81, 84)

Henke's discussion of *Exiles* centres around its paradoxical ending, one which, appropriately for "a drama that deals prominently with the issue of libidinal desire" and thereby "titillates his spectator but denies him/her the satisfaction of climactic release." It therefore maintains life, in Joyce's own words, "suspended in doubt like the world in the void." (102).

Dealing with *Ulysses*, Henke divides her analysis into two chapters, the one focused on Bloom, the other on Molly. First, she notes Bloom's status as belonging to a racial minority which enables (or condemns) him to "inhabit those marginal spaces on the edge of social discourse usually reserved for women and for cultural deviants," and thus to emerge as "the new womanly man." But not only that—Bloom is seen as "androgynous not only in terms of psychological temperament but in libidinal orientation, as well" as "the Lacanian phallus is displaced in his symbolic imagination by a fetishistic concern with breasts and bottoms, feces, menses, urine, and other physical secretions" (106). Joyce's "heterogeneous representation of Bloom's masculine-feminine, active-passive character" is seen as participating in the process of "rewriting the text of turn-of-the-century sex-role enculturation in the discourse of polymorphously perverse desire" (107-10).

The phantasmagoria of "Circe" presents the climax of this process, questioning as it does the entire Oedipal triangular configuration, or the "Daddy-Mommy-Me" triangle defined in Deleuze and Guattari's *Anti-Oedipus*:

> Joyce seems to be suggesting, like Deleuze and Guattari, that cultural laws of gender are constant insofar as they are manifest in contemporary social representation. The whoremistress acquires all the accoutrements of imperialistic power as soon as she dons male trousers and sprouts a moustache. [...] When Bloom is transformed into a woman by Bella/Bello, he loses his dignity along with the accoutrements of masculine pride. The repressed female tendencies of this heroic androgyne erupt in a ludic play erotic madness. (112, 116)

What these gender-reversals reveal is that female gender confers parodic marginality, in which "feminine sexuality, represented as a hole or Freudian absence, absorbs a plethora of masculine fantasies that fill the castrated signature envisaged at the heart of female identity" (115). This reversal is even augmented in the scene of Rudy's apparition and Bloom's mothering (rather than fathering) of Stephen. Their ensuing interaction is viewed as subverting "the expected codes of Aristotelian denouement" in that Joyce "tantalizes the reader to interpret Bloom's meeting with Stephen through the epic grid of Homer's *Odyssey* as the triumphant reunion of Odysseus and Telemachus" (122). The nostalgia of the *nostos*, understood in Jane Gallop's sense of "a regret for a lost past that occurs as a result of a present view of that past moment" (123), brings Henke's argument to the remembered seedcake exchange in "Lestrygonians," a lyrical reminiscence where

> Bloom is both ravisher and ravished, Molly both lover and beloved. The repressed romantic sensibilities of the novel erupt in a representation of male/female bonding that imitates, for both partners, the pleasures of pre-Oedipal, oceanic union and captures the reciprocity of ecstatic *jouissance*. (125)

Molly, throughout the novel, embodies that figure of totalizing self-presence for which Bloom incessantly pines, or, in Henke's Lacanian vocabulary, "an unattainable object of romantic fulfilment sealed in the inaccessible world of the imaginary." It is to "Penelope" that Henke turns, where Molly is portrayed "from the standpoint of speaking/desiring subject rather than specular/desirable object, relates an entirely different (her)story of memory and desire" (125).

"Molly Bloom: The Woman's Story" opens with a blunt assessment of the current state of the critical debate, according to which Molly's character appears to be either "a fictional embodiment of the 'eternal feminine'" or "a middle-aged, cranky, and erotically-minded housewife frightened of losing her tenuous powers of sexual allure" (126). Henke's Kristevan position tends toward the essentialising perspective on Molly's fluidity:

> Molly has traditionally been excluded from male discursivity because she "speaks fluid," and her subvocal iterations imitate the amorphous and irrational utterances of hysterical speech. Her unpunctuated soliloquy flows out of Joyce's ficitional representation of a rich and capacious stream-of-consciousness that draws freely on those preverbal, prediscursive dimensions of language described by Julia Kristeva as semiotic—a threatening and subversive discourse associated with pre-Oedipal attachment to the body, voice, and pulsions of an imaginary maternal figure. (127)

The crucial word, here, of course, is "imitation," referring both to Joyce's fabrication of a feminine identity and Molly's own willed as it were imitation or in Henke's terms, "masquerade," which subverts any apparent aspirations for essentialism. However, not contenting herself with a mere identification of a masquerade subversive of priggish Victorian standards, Henke does attempt to claw her way toward what lies beneath it:

> As the Penelopean web of Molly's discourse transgresses the boundaries of Edwardian sex-role stereotypes, the voice of a lusty vamp gives way to the complaints of a destabilized ego—fluid and fragile, insecure and vulnerable. (127)

Molly's female self, "detached from the male-biased rhetoric of cultural inscription," is seen as "mentally split and schizophrenically fragmented" (127-8). Joyce's own declaration that Molly is "jealous of men" and "hates women" also implies that "she *also* hates herself—or, at least, struggles to handle the repercussions of diminished self-esteem." More concretely, the figure of the absent mother (who, Henke surmises, must have left the family early in Molly's childhood) "forms in Molly's narrative a psychological gap crucial to her understanding of sexual difference" (128). It is this trauma of maternal abjection, and the problems in ego-development therein entailed that have brought Molly to exhibit narcissistic tendencies. Thus, rather than Joyce's fantasies of Gea-Tellus, "Molly more closely resembles the legendary Persephone in search of a long-lost Demeter" (129). Her narcissism, with which she values herself and other women in terms of desirability, is viewed as due to the "complex web of Oedipal emotions" through which she is bound to her father, whom she reports herself to have courted (131). Her choice of Bloom as a husband then is symptomatic of her search for "the patriarchal signifier that will heal the gap of maternal absence," at whose end "Molly reverts to a pre-

Oedipal model of emotional satisfaction in her conjugal relationship with Leopold Bloom" (132).

The Molly-Leopold-Boylan triangle, seen from a psychoanalytic perspective, reinstates "the Oedipal relationship at the heart of familial association," with Bloom-the mother and Boylan-the father and Molly trying "to re-enact both the pre-Oedipal script of infant-mother attachment and the Oedipal drama of paternal seduction" (133). Molly's psychosexual quest thus entails obvious problems:

> while searching for the lost mother of childhood fantasy, she is simultaneously compelled to re-enact the family romance of Oedipal attraction. [...] It seems telling that every celebration of Boylan's penile prowess immediately gives way to expressions of anger and resentment over a conviction of female inferiority. (135-7)

Of the famous Ithacan lists of suitors, Henke notes that "it is surely one of the great curiosities of modern literature that readers for almost forty years persisted in a literal interpretation of the list of lovers dictated at the end of 'Ithaca'" (149). Another important topic touched upon in Henke's detailed account is the interaction between Molly and Milly. Again, Molly's childhood experience of an incomplete family is regarded as decisive: "Because Molly's notion of female parenting was defined negatively, by detachment and insouciance, she has a great deal of difficulty relating successfully to her own adolescent daughter" (154). The relation between Molly and Leopold remains crucial, as does how it was influenced by the banal, unique events of 16 June 1904:

> By presenting Stephen Dedalus in the "Ithaca" episode as a surrogate for Blazes Boylan, Bloom invokes a psychological strategy worthy of Homer's Odysseus. Having spiritually adopted Stephen to replace his son Rudy, Bloom finds it "only natural" to attempt to share his beloved wife with the poet/professor who might successfully distract her from the brawny suitor. (156)

And Bloom seems to have succeeded: "By the time she has fabulated a deliciously provocative liaison with Stephen, Molly is ready to judge Boylan a self-centered fool, an 'ignoramus that doesnt know poetry from a cabbage'" (157). This adoption of the "stray dog" of an author, though forever suspended in the never-actualized, does bring Molly closer to Bloom in Henke's view:

> A flower of Gibraltar and Howth, Molly says "yes" to Leopold and herself becomes a Bloom. She knows that sexual and marital consent are in this case identical, and her feelings about both suggest a strong attraction to Bloom's epicene personality, [for] on an unconscious, latent and symbolic level, the man-womanly Bloom satisfies Molly's repressed longing for pre-Oedipal (comm)union. (160)

Thus, what Henke allows Molly and Leopold to remain is their mutual belief in the other's all-roundness: "Both Molly and Leopold handle the Lacanian experience of radical 'lack' by nostalgically endowing one another with theological wholeness plenitude" (162). This mutualness and interdependence are ultimately what disturbs the generic hierarchy of Joyce's fiction.

Finally, Henke's discussion of *Finnegans Wake* focuses on ALP and how she, even more so than Molly Bloom, "captures the semiotic rhythms of the capacious unconscious and the free flow of fertile libidinal desire" (164). In what she treats as his most mythically charged text, Henke discerns that Joyce's invocation appeals to "a trinitarian deity whose emanation is both Catholic and Freudian. In her ancient identity as Annah, ALP embodies the archetypal female—Heva, Eve, and Lilith, mother of the race and the progenitrix of all the daughter-sons that presently people the earth" (166). Henke proceeds to follow the text and ALP's multifarious impersonations, from the Prankquean to Anna Livia the river to her Mamafesta, seen as "one of the central aporias of the book, an enigmatic document whose gaps and fragmented utterances reflect, in miniature, the polysemic discourse of its fabulative matrix" (185), and from here to the final nuptial scene of III.4. Finally, the ricorso part takes the stage, where "the lyrical voice of Anna, rejuvenating her husband and celebrating the dawn, gradually begins to emerge from the chaosmos of Joyce's *ricorso*." Henke's response to the final version of the key-riddle, "the first and last rittlerattle of the anniverse; when is a nam nought a nam," is "when he is dead or impotent (deprived of manhood), or when man (generic) is female (specific)" (197). This paradoxical tautology contends that a man is not a man when he is a god, a corpse, or a female. Eventually,

> It is with the fading utterance of ALP's definite article that we realize the endless, indefinite semiosis of *Finnegans Wake*. In a moment of epiphany that brings us back to the book's beginning, we are implicitly commissioned to re-read the entire text as an explosive extension of Anna's lyrical riverrun. (204)

Henke's "Ricorso: *Anna Livia Plurabelle and* Écriture Féminine" brings us back to the theoretical questions regarding feminist approaches to Joyce. Throughout her study, Henke has relied on the elusive concept of "feminine writing" as put forward by Kristeva, Cixous, Irigaray, and others, but also sought to align herself with the deconstructivist tradition (from Sollers to Norris to MacCabe), in whose perspective the *Wake* becomes "a linguistic subversion of the name and the law of the Father, a revolution of the word that disrupts the traditional symbolic order and challenges bourgeois practices allied with the repressed desires of a male libidinal economy" (206). In an Ithacan fashion, the question of how a feminist reader should approach Joyce is answered: "With care, certainly; with a sense of delight and appreciation; with skepticism and circumspection; and with a carnivalesque spirit of fun, play, amusement and curiosity." More seriously and relevantly, Henke asserts that "from certain parallactic perspectives, Joyce's postmodern *oeuvre* can be envisaged as contiguous with the projects of feminist fabulation" (211). Ultimately, Joyce's writing "flows sinuously, like ALP's riverrun, from the dramatization of repression in *Dubliners* and *A Portrait* to the exuberant affirmation of an unrepressed language of desire in *Ulysses* and *Finnegans Wake*," with the *Wake* ending "on a note of insatiable desire: the word 'the' reaches out, futilely, for a compatible term to introduce." A note of linguistic longing, the "the" of the *Wake*'s ending "remains unsatisfied, and the text refuses closure in a way that a scholarly study, or an individual life, cannot" (212).

VII

1990 was also the year of the conference "Miamafesta: Gender and Joyce," held at the University of Miami in 1990, which gave rise seven years later to another major contribution to the ongoing feminist discussion, a co-edited collection of essays called *Gender in Joyce*.[9] According to the editors' preface, one of the collection's aims is to cover a wide range of subjects reflecting "the recent increase in critical literary studies" that seek to "expose the constructedness of the very language that encodes all forms of social, ontological, and epistemological structures." In other words, the volume strives "to illuminate the process through which Joyce consciously and scrupulously [...] *constructed his language*—the vehicle of his criticism of the very ideologies he encodes and/or subverts through its use" (ix). The novelty of these approaches then lies in their combination of historical research, close reading, and most importantly their use of manuscript evidence. Here, two essays and Margot Norris' introductory piece have been chosen as illustrative of the general tendencies of the collection as a whole.

Mark Osteen's "Female Property: Women and Gift Exchange in *Ulysses*" investigates meaning as created in the always deferring, perennial movement of exchange. The exchange here is one of gift-giving and gift-accepting, and Osteen's argument relies on Lewis Hyde's contention (in *The Gift: Imagination and the Erotic Life of Property*) that a gift constitutes "female property." On both the biographical and more importantly artistic levels, the gift is how the male/female exchange comes to be conceptualized, both in its sexual and textual aspects (letter writing as a gift for both Joyce in his relationship with Nora and Bloom's with Molly). As the example of Molly suggests,

> when females become speaking subjects, the female economic condition becomes schizoid, as women are forced to play the roles simultaneously of exchangeable gift and gift-giver, being at once granted property rights and denied them. (37)

[9] Jolanta Wawrzycka, Marlene Corcoran, eds., *Gender in Joyce* (Miami: University Press of Florida, 1997).

A detailed analysis of the gift-giving motif in *Ulysses* reveals "the three objects [figuring] in most gift exchanges in *Ulysses*" to be "flowers, rings, and letters" (38). Given the focus on the "feminine" character of these exchanges, the question, for Osteen, remains whether Joyce's placement of real and fictional women into a gift economy signifies "his denial of their ability to function in a market (that is, 'normal') economy." Crucial here is Osteen's belief that "Joyce's linguistic economy derives from a principle of expenditure that is itself founded on gift-exchange" (41). In this light, "Penelope" appears, not as an appropriation of supposedly female discourse by the male pen, but as "the book's final offering, [...], a love letter, another text-as-gift-of-self, to both real and fictional women" (42).

Jean Kimball's "Eros and Logos in *Ulysses*" represents one of the volume's main foci—the varying psychoanalytic interpretations of gender, by moving from Jung's gendered categories of *Eros* and *Logos* to Joyce's balancing of male and female forces in the textual creation of the self, considering "the congruity between Jung's concept of the complementarity of masculine and feminine principles in the human psyche and Joyce's dramatization of the complementarity in *Ulysses*" (114). In the light of this congruence, Kimball's examination leads her

> to make a rough equation between the "bioenergetic" portrait of Stephen and the Jungian Ego, and to equate the "cybernetic" portrait of Bloom with the Shadow, Jung's personification of those alien elements of the personality that have been repressed or rejected by the Ego. (116)

Her discussion of the Stephen/Bloom encounter (and its manifold presages before its actual taking place) in terms of the Ego/Shadow rapprochement is complemented by looking at how Bloom in introducing (albeit indirectly) Stephen to Molly leads him to the second stage of the anima-figure, "the Anima proper as erotic and romantic object, named Helen by Jung ad Molly Bloom by Joyce" (118). It should be understood that this has relevance for Stephen as would-be artist, since Stephen's famous disquisition on the artistic "postcreation" as pre-empting the creative power of the mother implies in Kimball's Jungian view that

> in order to become capable of immortalizing his life—the flesh that passes—in art, the potential artist must first become a man, and this requires a rebirth, not through the spirit, as in religious conversion, but like the birth from the mother, through the flesh of the loved woman: "in woman's womb." (121)

This new kind of anima-relationship is enabled by the climactic annihilation of the horrifying apparition of the Mother in "Circe," making Stephen ready for a rebirth, which is textually accomplished midway through "Ithaca," in the scene of Bloom's insertion of "a male key" into "an unstable female lock," revealing "an aperture for free egress and free ingress." Indeed the whole image suggests to Kimball that "the 'rebirth into a new dimension' that Jung says may ultimately become available through the Shadow" (122). However, Bloom and Molly are not to be seen only as "potentially facilitating forces in Stephen's life," as

> they are also related to each other, and their fictional relationship shares in a complication that is a part of Jung's vision of the Shadow and Anima in relation [...where] the masculine Shadow takes on feminine characteristics while the feminine Anima takes on masculine characteristics. (124)

Kimball's final points therefore concern Molly Bloom and her variegated status of Gea-Tellus "in Joyce's text," Penelope "in his *schema*," Nora Barnacle "in his autobiography" and a comic Helen of Troy "in a Jungian scenario for *Ulysses*." However, Molly Bloom is still more than this: a prophetic figure, she foreshadows "a feminine insistence on sexual autonomy that has perhaps reached its height with the contemporary phenomenon of a single mother by choice" (125). This prophetic status links Joyce's Molly to the many conceptualizations of Jung's theory, both of whom "recognized the centrality of women in their own lives and translated that centrality into their work." Kimball concludes:

> Whatever the quality of Joyce's misogyny [...], his intuitive understanding of the significance of "woman's place" in a man's life and in his sense of himself is as sure as Jung's. [...] Thus, in *Ulysses*, though it is in no significant way peopled by women, Joyce has realized in symbolic terms the crucial interdependence and complementarity of the Masculine and the Feminine. (128)

Margot Norris' "Introduction: Joyce's Mamafesta" raises several issues relevant not only for further explorations into the field of Joyce and gender studies, but also for other approaches from the whole gamut of Joyce criticism. Norris sets out by contending that "modernism was more mothered than fathered" and aligns her article with criticism reconfigured "around new sets of gender and feminist paradigms," which gender "the very disposition of meaning in our discussions of the semiotic and the symbolic as we attempt to locate sites of authority in language and discourse." For these explorations, Joyce offers "an especially challenging frontier—a veritable textual no-man's-land in which phantom males and absent women speak each other's silences" (1). The figure of the "New Woman" that this criticism seeks to unveil is revealed to be what "Joyce himself might have called 'impossibilized'—a historically unrealizable construct" (2). Despite the tangible influence of the two kinds of Continental tradition that first gave woman her speech—social realism and the avant-garde—it is in Joyce that, to an unprecedented degree,

> the culturally silenced female voice of uncensored thought (Molly Bloom) or unbridled gossip (the washerwomen) becomes in the Joycean oeuvre the

privileged poetic language that drowns out the dominant discourses of all modern literature. (3)

Patrick McGee's notion of "the ideology of style"[10] is referred to as a fruitful area in which to study the workings of gender in Joyce's work and modernism as such. For as long as "Anglo-American feminism focuses on the rhetoric of language," French feminism "looks at the way language is itself figurated and subjected to a rhetorical logic" (4). Whereas Anglo-American feminism speaks of "a gender aggression" in Joyce, "a set of male elitist and occultive practices designed to exclude women as producers and consumers of modern art," the French feminists "construe Joyce's linguistic play as a way of rupturing language's own rhetorical figurations." Of crucial significance to this notion of language-as-rupture is Lacanian theory which endows these disruptions with a highly dramatic tone by following them in perceptual exchanges such as seeing and being seen, recognition and *méconnaisance*. Therefore according to Norris, Lacanian theory has become "a particularly favored tool for conducting thematic and narrative criticism freed from essentialistic or archetypal assumptions about gender" (5). Joyce's career is regarded as having run full circle, ending as it began,

> with address to the question of modern art's intertextual intervention in representing and criticizing the conditions of poverty, abuse, and oppression that kill girls and women, [with the awareness] that he must give dying girls and women voice even though they cannot speak, and that poetic experiments must be put in the service of articulating their silence.

Norris concludes by pointing to the repetition with a difference, to the quasi-advancement, that this full circle has performed from "the narrative elision that marks the place between the end of *Portrait* and the opening of *Ulysses*" to "the retrieval of the dying mother" at the end of the *Wake*. This also constitutes a movement away from the textual gap between the first two novels "that eloquently defines modernism's preoccupation with male mourning [...], at the expense of female dying" (6).

VIII

Another essay-collection from the late-1990s, the eighth volume of the "European Joyce Studies" series, edited by Ellen Carol Jones and titled "Joyce: Feminism/Post-Colonialism,"[11] brought an equally wide range of approaches, as my focus here on the editor's insightful introduction will attempt to show. In her "Borderlines," Jones views Joyce's writing as constitutive of "a postcolonial contramodernity" by which she means his use of "the cultural hybridity of Irish borderline conditions to translate—reinscirbe and thus reclaim—the social imaginary of both the metropolis

---

[10] See Chapter VIII "Politics," section IV.
[11] David Spurr, "Fatal Signatures: Forgery and Colonization in *Finnegans Wake*," *Joyce: Feminism/Post-Colonialism*, ed. Ellen Carol Jones (Amsterdam: Edition Rodopi, 1998).

and modernity" (7). This general postcolonial hybridity (Homi Bhabha's term) takes in Joyce's particular case the form of "a cultural translation" as a tropic movement that transforms the centrality of a dominant culture:

> It is that act of translation, that middle passage, that movement *between* that Joyce stages in his writing, estranging the languages of a totalizing imperial and colonial culture, reinscribing history through the writing of difference.

Joyce's intermediary position of re-inscription is marked by a remainder, both of imperial history and patriarchal canons, which "resists assimilation into the totalizing narratives of modernity, narratives whose concealed but central logic is imperialism" (8). Joyce's *in between* position is one of Derridean "Living On—Borderlines," in his case, those of "history and language, of race and gender":

> To live on the borderlines is to be located in the elliptical space between the self and the other. This border then becomes a place of negotiation between incommensurable cultural differences. (9)

For Bhabha, the "inter-" prefix signifies an opening; therefore international culture is one theorized not as a totalized epistemological object but rather as "a site of enunciation, translation, and negotiation: a site where objectified others can become the subjects of their own displaced and displacing histories." It is precisely this site of cultural inter-space that Joyce's writing, according to Jones, seeks to inhabit:

> The borderlines of language and history, the limits of race and gender, on which he poises his writing, have multiple fissures, fault lines that inscribe partition, migration, exile. [...] Joyce's texts are written out of those abysses. (11)

Jones brings "the subaltern," already used in a number of works of postcolonial Joyce theory, back to Bhabha's definition thereof as "the ambivalence in the structure of identification that occurs precisely in the elliptical *in-between*, where the shadow of the Other falls upon the Self" (12). It is from within that shadow that cultural difference emerges as an *enunciation* which in Joyce's works is made by and large by a female speaker as the extra-textual, extra-linguistic other of his writing:

> In an Oedipal economy, the border, the hymen, the (m)other is figured as abjected object, as that which has always already been lost, an elsewhere imagined beyond the present, but hallucinated in the present as an object who speaks of what eludes speech: the word known to all men, the word that can be spoken only by or through the (dead) body of the mother. (13)

Jones' Lacanian perspective is evident in her discussion of the mother as an "unsublimatable body, as remainder" in which she "survives for the subject as a constitutive loss," the border which gives the subject its frame and forms that subject. Abjection in this sense, "is the violence of mourning for an 'object' that has always already been lost: the mother. And it is on that inaugural loss of the mother that any being, meaning, language, or desire is founded" (14). Thus, the female, or in Jones' terms, "the sexual other," remains in Joyce's fiction imbued with a fantasy of certain knowledge that functions in Joyce as "forever the horizon, the unfolding, the boundary of difference." It is here however that Joyce's feminist and postcolonial projects clash:

> If Joyce's political project to write the incommensurable differences of colonial subjectivity founders in his writing [...], it would founder precisely because that writing retains the traces of the fantasy of an ontological other imagined as pure difference. (15)

Within the social context of this particular conflict which exists in Joyce's writing, commodity culture presents a locus where the imaginary (feminine) fullness encounters the real (postcolonial) lack, the essential truth of commodity culture being that "commodities are not so much material objects as their representations in fantasy." Consequently, objects are "like hysterical symptoms: a network of floating signifiers that perpetually incite desire, generalized unsatisfiable desire" (17). What is more "in fantasizing commodities that they of course can never actualize materially, the colonized attempt to actualize themselves. What they actualize are commodity selves" (18). Jones concludes by postulating that this "discursive doubleness" in Joyce requires the practice of "reading otherwise,"; in other words, a reading of the process of the emergence of a "postcolonial contra-modernity" which is "a form of cultural rediscription that moves, Bhabha argues, "back to the future, a future anterior" (21).

The volume's essays have been collected, Jones asserts at the end of her introduction, to bear witness to that "reading otherwise." The collection covers a wide array of approaches and themes. Jones' alignment of Derridean deconstruction with Bhabha's postcolonialism finds its echoes in Peter Hitchcock's "Joyce's Subalternatives," which posits that the subaltern prescribes the deconstructive, or Gregory Castle's "Colonial Discourse and the Subject of Empire in Joyce's 'Nausicaa,'" referring to H.L. Gates' observation that "what Derrida calls writing, Spivak [...] has renamed postcolonial discourse." This ahistorically theoretical position is complemented by historically-conscious papers such as Carol Schloss' "Behind the Veil: James Joyce and the Colonial Harem," or "Imperialism and the Rhetoric of Sexuality in James Joyce's *Ulysses*" by Gerald Doherty, which examines how a colonial poetics of the body comes to be identified with an erotic poetics in the official and literary discourses Joyce utilizes in *Ulysses*.

Here I shall pay attention to a paper combining the two above-mentioned approaches: "Fatal Signatures: Forgery and Colonization in *Finnegans Wake*" by David Spurr. In this essay, Derrida's theory of forgery as supplementary writing is brought to bear upon an historically oriented examination of Joyce's use of the famous forged Parnell letters within his *Finnegans Wake*. Spurr commences by distinguishing between three forms of transgression of forgery: "as an instrument of colonization, as a figure for the nature of writing, and as a metaphor for artistic creation." Forgery as a gesture of displacement and usurpation is for Derrida the unveiled character of writing itself "whose conditions of possibility are those of absence, and, ultimately, death." In typically paradoxical fashion, for Joyce,

> forgery also stands synecdochically for writing in a creative sense: writing is precisely that which is forged, wrought out of crude matter, like the conscience of his race that Stephen goes forth to create in *A Portrait*. (245)

Spurr proceeds to investigate this issue by analysing two figures associated with forgery in the *Wake*:

> *hesitency*, the misspelled word which exposed Pigott's forgeries in the Special Commission hearings of 1888-1889, and which recurs through the *Wake*; and the *signature*, which has what Derrida calls a "divided agency," testifying both to the absence and to the mysterious presence of the signatory. (246)

Joyce's concern with fraud and forgery bespeaks the broader context of his oeuvre: "far from destroying its context, the *Wake* remains deeply embedded in the ambiguities of modernity and the (post)colonial condition." It is not that the *Wake* destabilizes a historical context which is in and of itself coherent, stable, and intelligible, but precisely the other way round: "Joyce's writing reflects a historical context that is always already destabilized, itself a 'discontinuity in progress'" (248).

The connection between forgery and signature has been examined by Derrida most coherently in his famous "Plato's Pharmacy," a reading that reveals the mythical origin of writing as related in Plato's *Phaedrus* to be an allegorical rendering of patriarchal authority: writing, in Derrida's reading, appears to be "a highly ambivalent instrument whose mimicry of the Father can be used either to reinforce the structures of patriarchal power, or to expose the forged origins of such structures." It is precisely within the "parodies of such male authority" lies "an essential comic element of his text" (253-4). There is yet another significant ambiguity to the signature that has an important bearing on the *Wake*: "on one hand, it establishes a person's identity as authentic; on the other hand, it exposes the fact that, for legal as well as other purposes, such authenticity resides solely in writing" (254-5). Most specifically, the case of the "authentic forgery" of Richard Pigott

> shows how forgery and authenticity are not only complicit with one another, but also in a sense the same. In order for the letters to be proven forgeries, they must be proven authentic, that is, the authentic work of the

forger, bearing the unmistakable signature in [...] "the spell of hesitency." (258)

Insofar as the enforcement of distinctions is instrumental in maintaining imperial power (either/or questions such as "is it forged or authentic, is it literature or not, is it nationalist or unionist, is Parnell or Pigott guilty or innocent?"), *Finnegans Wake* subverts this power in its "great forge" (259). Spurr concludes:

> The subversive function of *Finnegans Wake* is thus closely allied to its co-medic function; its celebration of comic freedom is made possible by its power to render ideology ridiculous. (259-60)

X

To date, the most significant collection of essays addressing Joyce's oeuvre from the viewpoint of queer studies has been Joseph Valente's edited volume, *Quare Joyce*,[12] whose purpose as identified in the editor's introduction is threefold:

> to address and thus redress the compulsory heterosexuality that has en-cumbered even the most critically astute, theoretically sophisticated, and politically progressive Joyce scholarship; to reconfigure the economy of Joyce studies through the importation of a queer theory perspective [...]; and, correlatively, to take up the manifold question of homosexuality [...] as it pertains to the always slippery articulation of Joyce's life and his writing. (1)

A total of fourteen essays deal with queer issues in Joyce, concerning his representation, figuration, and dissimulation of homoerotic desire from diverse perspectives including psychoanalytic, sexological, postcolonial and feminist. The questions arising from this debate concern both the methodological ("whether a gay studies or psychoanalytic approach is the more productive in addressing the (homo)sexual dynamics in/of Joyce's texts"), as well as the hermeneutic level (the relationship between "the homophobia often represented in Joyce's work and the modes of narra-tion in which it is disclosed," or the implications of "Joyce's appropriation of certain received typologies of homosexuality") (2). The editor's ultimate aim is to present a project which

> taps into, prospects, and retrieves a whole other creative and critical his-tory for Joyce's writing, a framework of causes and corollaries, both mate-rial and discursive, that supplements, in the strong Derridean sense, the previously established patterns of Joyce's (af)filiations. (3)

The rest of Valente's introduction sketches out the double history, both creative and critical, of Joyce's gender positions. In assessing the impact

---

[12] Joseph Valente, ed., *Quare Joyce* (Ann Arbor: The University of Michigan Press, 1998).

of what he terms "the feminist and postcolonial turn in Joyce criticism," Valente observes that its main merit has been to "render the heterosexual imperative visible as an arbitrary ideological limit or constraint." However, Valente also points out that this has been done "*without* expressly addressing it as a problem or overriding the presuppositions that it mandates," an omission which the collection aims to amend. The *quare* of the title, an Anglo-Irish epithet denoting "odd" or "strange," is used as "a kind of transnational/transidiomatic pun," appropriated as it has been lately as "a distinctively Irish variant of queer." On a purely textual level then, the word is meant to allude, not only to "queer," but also to "square," denoting "straight"—in other words, what is taken for the very opposite of queerness. All these factors taken together,

> the epithet perfectly captures Joyce's inclination and aptitude for queering the dichotomy between the "queer" and the "square/straight," for unsettling the normative and hierarchical distinctions between different modes of sexual expression. (4)

When applied to the thematic of Joyce's texts themselves, particularly *A Portrait* and *Ulysses*, the dichotomy breaks down because "each sign or scenario of desire [...] can be construed to admit, evoke, even signal same-sex as well as cross-sex energies," as the sexual (or merely amatory) alliances in Joyce's fiction are seen in an almost exclusively triangular cast: "Stephen—E.C.—Cranly, Richard—Bertha—Robert, Bloom—Molly—Boylan, Bloom—Molly—Stephen, Shem—Issy—Shaun, Anna Livia—Humphrey—Issy, as so on." In this respect, Eve Kosofsky Sedgwick's transferential definition of homo and heteroeroticism might be regarded as informing the whole volume, particularly her conception of "male homosocial desire, the structural mediation of male-male relationships by an eroticized competition over and exchange of women," which occurs in the triangular structures outlined above (5).

Having sketched out the theoretical stakes, Valente historicises his discussion by turning to what he identifies as "a series of explosive events" in Joyce's lifetime, which operated "to enforce gender/sexual conventions and to reinforce the public obsession with them" in that they answered "a perceived crisis in British masculinity" with "a legal campaign against that newly constructed social species, the 'invert' or 'homosexual'" (6). The three cases examined include the scandal involving prominent officials in Dublin Castle, a legal response to it in the Criminal Law Amendment Act of 1885, whose section 11 outlawed male-male sexuality, and the first trials based on this amendment, the most prominent one being the so-called Cleveland Streets trial.

Most important in this respect of course is the trial of Oscar Wilde, which took place just when Joyce came to adolescence, fixing the image of the queer in the British popular mind. In order to appreciate Joyce's debt to Wilde, Valente goes on to discuss "the discourse of Hellenism that Wilde espoused and even embodied, a discourse whose history was a powerful determinant of the associations that homosexuality bore for Joyce as a young man" (9), tracing it back to Mill and Arnold, and identifying its further lineage with the figures of Pater, Swinburne, and Symonds. Joyce's high regard of and sympathy for Wilde is most conspicuously presented in the Stephen Dedalus of *A Portrait*:

> In bestowing a Greek surname upon the thoroughly Irish protagonist of his bildungsroman, Joyce could count on its contemporary audience to interpret Stephen's growth in the light of Hellenic ideals of self-development, particularly when the title of the novel [...] alludes to Wilde's two exemplary engagements with these ideals, *The Picture of Dorian Gray* and *The Portrait of Mr. W. H.* (11)

It was not only scandals impacting on the public consciousness which were instrumental in shaping Joyce's hetero versus homosexual dynamics, for Joyce's youth was an era of what Valente calls "the apex of classical sexology," whose "concerted attention to the phenomenon of same-sex preference helped to define homosexuality [...] as a distinct ontological condition" (12). Moreover, the era of Joyce's maturity and professional seniority in the Paris of the 1920s and 1930s was marked by "a fabulous confluence of aesthetic and sexual experimentation, owing in part to the singular tolerance offered homosexuality by the Napoleonic Code" (13). Sylvia Beach, Adrienne Monnier, Djuna Barnes or Natalie Barney, "Joyce's closest publishing and promotional contacts," were all without exception lesbians. In Paris then "Joyce participated for the first time in a culture, literary or otherwise, in which lesbianism was *heimliche*, a common part of the universe, so much so that the city was nicknamed Paris-Lesbos" (14). Valente's introduction as a whole points to the conclusion that with the variegated impact and importance of homoerotic possibility which his text so meticulously maps out,

> it is far less surprising that [Joyce's] work repeatedly turns heterosexual attraction inside out to discover its profound immixture with homosexual desire than that this methodology has gone largely unnoticed and its political import largely unappreciated to this point. (14)

Four essays from *Quare Joyce* have been selected for brief discussion here; with the aim of illustrating the volume's variety of approaches. Margot Norris' "A Walk on the Wild(e) Side: The Doubled Reading of 'An Encounter'" discusses the "puzzling and ambiguous gestures of both the story's writing and its telling," gestures which "further complicate [the] questions of Joyce's own time and our present moment" (19). Norris' reading, historicized by the importance of Wilde for Joyce and theoretically grounded upon Sedgwick's "ignorance effects," considers these gestures as displaying "certain provocative similarities in the rhetorical strategies of the pervert and the narrator":

Whether the story's narrative function is therapeutic (a psychoanalytic re-membering of a juvenile trauma for psychic relief) or testimonial (the author-ity of a victim serving prophylaxis, to protect children from pederasts), the reader is situated in the ethical space of the unexperienced child. (22)

This ethical space is marked first and foremost by an ellipsis. The elided perversion of the "queer old josser" has "an effect on the reader not unlike that of the unspecified 'sin' of *Dorian Gray*: the reader is pressured to supply a meaning at the risk of self-incrimination" (27). However, the boys of the story are not simply seen as innocently exposed, but also as oddly "experienced":

> The boy's averted eyes and lack of surprise symptomatize a knowledge that the narrative elsewhere shields, and the quickly contrived disguise the boy's understanding that the old man's irregular and provocative behavior — presumably masturbation — is intended for his and Mahony's benefit. The inconsistency in the boy's shrewdness and naiveté is striking and, I believe, intended to be suspect. (29)

Ultimately, the strategies of the story are revealed to position the reader into "a response whose disassociative reflexes align it with the symbolic power and coercive force of patriarchy," those reflexes that have pre-cisely contributed to the long-term suppression of a queer look at the "queer old josser" (31).

Jean-Michel Rabaté's "On Joycean and Wildean Sodomy" posits as its starting premise the belief that "the best approach to the sexual thematics underlying *Ulysses* is to link the strong undercurrent of homosexual im-ages to the issue of paternity" (35). The sundry "loves that dare not speak their names" involve zoophilia, as the mythical Daedalus' invention enabled Queen Pasiphae to enjoy intercourse with a bull — "Daedalus used all his genius in the deployment of *ignotas artes* that smack of perversity" (36). However, Rabaté's reading of Aquinas shows that "the name of love is never easy to utter, let alone define" because Aquinas' definition of love as "to wish someone's good" in one breath includes the qualification that one can wish one's own good as well as someone else's and lists among the causes of love *similitudo*, "similarity." Rabaté also turns to "The Sisters," where the alliteration of "the simoniac of his sin" possibly suggests "sodomy" as the name of the sin (or, in Rabaté's playful varia-tion, "the sodomic of his son"):

> It would be tempting to see in the repressed term of "sodomy" the fourth or missing corner of the "gnomon" evoked by the boy in the first paragraph of the story. [...] Sodomy would thus appear as the arch-sin, precisely be-cause in its inception it just describes a city in which human relations are perverted, without bringing a clear accusation against male homoeroticism. (38)

In a concluding discussion of the Wilde/Joyce intertext and influence, Rabaté stresses what he sees as the crucial heritage of Wilde's trials for Joyce—the discursive character of sin and sinfulness: "Joyce suggests that the Sin, if it is to keep its full value, cannot be reduced to a sexual content. The sin's meaning is produced by an interpretation that performs what it identifies" (41). Wilde's omnipresence in the *Wake* is thus related to its preoccupation with the "omnipresence of guilt," a guilt "that never denies sexual division, since it relies upon it, but transgresses infinitely all other boundaries so as to force all readers to admit a common legacy of sin" (43).

Valente's own contribution, "Thrilled by His Touch," deals with "The Aestheticizing of Homosexual Panic in *A Portrait*," with particular focus on the question of why Joyce "seems to have scrupulously avoided the use of terms that name same sex desires and relations directly," preferring elusive euphemisms instead (47). Relying on extended biographical research and Sedgwick's notion of homosexuality as emergent from certain modes of homosociality, Valente maps how Joyce's sexual unease exhibited in his correspondence is

[transferred] to his fictive alter ego, Stephen Dedalus, in a more extreme, explicitly "panicky" mode, which systematically shapes the most crucial decisions that Stephen enacts: his appeal to Conmee, his refusal of the priesthood, his assumption of an aesthetic vocation, his self-exile. (49)

Stephen's early delirious fascination with words like *suck*, *queer*, *cocks*, his fantasies about the thrill of pandying and being pandied, as well as his subsequent protest against the injustice of his thrashing—all are analysed very closely and in great detail by Valente as examples of "the resurgence of Stephen's 'homosexual panic'" which is seen as presaging, "in spite, and even because, of his social triumph," Joyce's treatment of the issue throughout the novel (57). Of particular importance is Valente's observation that Stephen's relationship with E.C. functions as a displacement of his affections for Cranly:

Surely it is no coincidence that this pivotal conversation [*P*, 247] with Cranly breaks off, assuring Stephen's departure, just when the possibility of homosexual attraction and involvement, which has been diverted, displaced, and misrecognized throughout the novel, is finally, if inconclusively, broached. Stephen's last unanswered question, "Of whom are you speaking," virtually epitomizes homosexual panic as a neurotic obsession with the identity, status and location of homo-hetero difference and virtually defines Stephen as its captive. (67)

Thus, Valente concludes, where Stephen's narcissistic anxiety proves essential to Joyce's narcissistic *jouissance*, "Stephen's homosexual panic is indispensable to Joyce's open closet." Joyce's strategy of disavowal (conspicuous in his elusiveness discussed as Valente's point of departure) then appears not so much "dissolved or transcended" as "internalized and sublated" in *A Portrait*. In other words, it is not the homoerotic-as-threat that Joyce's *Portrait* disavows, but rather the heterosexual identity-as-construct (70).

The variously historical-sexological-gender positions of these three essays can be aptly complemented by Garry Leonard's "The Nothing Place: Secrets and Sexual Orientation in Joyce," which addresses the issues at stake from an outspokenly psychoanalytic position. Noting the anaphoric, almost obsessively repetitive *it* from the opening of "The Sisters," Leonard relates it to Lacan's notion of the ego as intrinsically paranoid, "because the secret is the 'thing' around the universe to show where it stops, and 'the nothing place' [...] begins." The notion of the secret is crucial here insofar as

> to accumulate secrets is to feel an increase in interiority, which is also to feel like a subject capable of producing meaning and constructing interpretations. To have secrets discovered, or to feel pressured to confess them, is to feel increasingly subject to the Symbolic order in general, and the law in particular. (78)

The secret in turn is what marks the discourse of sexuality: sexuality is a secret in the Foucauldian understanding of the dynamics, according to which *positing* sexuality as a *secret* gives license to various "official" discourses to implant it, under the pretext of persecuting it out. Sexual "orientation," then, in the etymological sense of setting direction, appears as

> the way to assign the drive an itinerary, and then to chart its progress, on a "normal"/"perverse" axis, and thus create an excuse, and suggest a method, for accessing the subject's presumably sacrosanct "interiority" under the guise of merely accessing it in order to correct it. (79)

Applied to the official hetero-/homo-sexual divide, these Lacanian-Foucauldian dynamics of the secret reveals it is futile to speak of "latency" in one's sexuality, for it is always already publicly and officially constructed. More concretely, instead of "latent" homosexuality, Stephen's evident uneasiness around Cranly and Mulligan can be "looked at from the more nuanced perspective of him constantly shoring up fantasy of his subjectivity by trying to hide what he knows from Cranly and Mulligan, even as he tries to know what they hide" (79).

Lacan's reading of Poe's "The Purloined Letter" treats the movement of the letter from one person to another as allegorical of how the signifier moves from subject to subject. As long as "the subject may experience acquiring the signifier as the fortuitous possession of a secret others do not know," then "the precise content of the letter is irrelevant." In Poe's story then, "it is not the content of the letter that persuades the minister that the queen wishes to keep it secret from the king, but merely her furtive attempt to hide it." The queen's secret and the minister's theft ultimately have to do not with passion, but with power, "the power to constitute knowledge, to formulate discourse, and thus make things happen in one way rather than another" (82). Analogously, Oscar Wilde in Joyce's judgment was on trial not for anything he was or anything he did; "he was arrested because he refused to arrest himself" (84). Joyce's structuralist analysis of Wilde's trial, then, suggests that

> it is not necessary that secrets be interesting, or that they "be" at all, only that the fact of them be declared, for them to underwrite the mystery of interiority both intrasubjectively and intersubjectively (that is to say, both to one's "self" and others). Declaring a secret, and/or protecting one from disclosure , creates the inside/outside binary and creates a fiction of inaccessibility that can be misrecognized as psychological integrity. (86)

The point therefore is not mystery but "appearing mysterious," and the real secret becomes that there is none. This paradox is identified as "the retroactive 'essence' of both personality and the aura of the commodity" (87), as is amply evidenced by Leonard's analysis of some of the *Dubliners* stories (most notably, "An Encounter"), as well as his sustained interest in *Exiles*, where

> Richard Rowan makes clear that [...] what he fears is not that Bertha will have an affair, but that she will do so without telling him and that, still worse, this will prevent him from telling Robert that the knows, has known, and will always know what Bertha and he do or refuse to do together. In other words, content is incidental to form. (91)

Coming back to the analogy between the constitution of personal subjectivity and the aura of the commodity, Leonard draws a parallel between the Lacanian presentation of the ego and Marx's description of commodity fetishism, for "in both cases, the secret is that there is no secret" (93). This challenge to "sexual orientation" as an essential mode of being is also a challenge to the sense of the self as a "masculine" subject, which is in turn linked to the male confidence in himself as subject capable of signification, a confidence springing from "secrets kept in Stephen's secret cave." Leonard concludes,

> Steal from the cave and he becomes "feminine," not in terms of sexual orientation, but strictly in perceived phallic potential, which is an effect of relationship, not an essence. (95)

Put differently, the "masculine" subject produces a secret neither he nor anyone else can "know" (as does Richard Rowan) and demonstrates that the production of a secret and the production of the self "*are the same thing*." Heterosecrecy, then, "*succeeds to obscure this relationship*," while homosecrecy "*threatens to highlight it*" (96).

XI

Derek Attridge's seminal collection of papers already mentioned in our previous analyses, *Joyce Effects — On Language, Theory, and History*[13] also contains an essay relevant to queer studies as charted out in Valente's edited volume just examined. "'Suck Was a Queer Word': Language, Sex, and the Remainder in *A Portrait*" approaches the *Portrait* passage (with all due acknowledgment to the work done in *Quare Joyce*), aiming to "investigate the relation between implicit sexuality and overt attention to language, especially to single words," as its opening premise is that "the sexual suggestiveness in *A Portrait* frequently occurs [...] as part of Stephen's encounters with language" (64).

The question then becomes for Attridge one of the very possibility of language producing physical sexual effects, and what is more even without the sexual vocabulary by means of which to describe the subject's reaction. Here, Attridge makes use of the work of French linguist Jean-Jacques Lecercle, who in his study *The Violence of Language* posits four general propositions of language functioning:

1) Language is a material product of the body.
2) Language is an abstract system, independent of the body.
3) The speaker speaks the language, saying freely what he or she means.
4) The language speaks, and meaning belongs to the community before it belongs to the speaker. (65)

Now, "the commonsensical view" of language (which Attridge regards as represented by Ferdinand de Saussure's binary of *langue* and *parole* or Noam Chomsky's of competence and performance) combines propositions 2 and 3, conceiving of language as an abstract system of rules utilized by the speaker in order to form sentences. However, it is only when 1 and 4 "begin to transgress their allotted frontiers" that one becomes aware of "the *remainder*, that aspect of language's functioning which, in spite of its necessity, is normally suppressed from our conceptions of it," and which manifests itself most clearly in the language of delirium, schizophrenia, or glossolalia (66). On the basis of this distinction, Attridge draws a link between the language of delirium and the language of the feverish Stephen: "Stephen's bodily reaction to the word 'suck' does not belong to the linguist's domain of explanation and analysis" (67). On a general note then:

> Historically, it has been poetry which has found a variety of means to re-
> lease the bodily dimension of speech from its domination by language's ra-
> tional-communicative function, and it has been poets [...] who have testi-
> fied to a mode of composition in which the controlling consciousness of the

[13] Derek Attridge, "'Suck Was a Queer Word': Language, Sex, and the Remainder in *A Portrait*," *Joyce Effects: On Language, Theory, and History* (Cambridge: Cambridge University Press, 2000).

language user is relaxed in order to allow the language's own proclivities […] to determine to some degree the words of the poem. (69)

The parallel then for Joyce between the language of children and the language of literature lies in their shared "capacity to exploit the remainder, to allow the body and the language community to speak through and to some degree against the abstraction and instrumentalism of utilitarian employments, and most theories, of language" (73).

Attridge complements his reading of the word *suck* by Stephen's one other encounter with a single word, one which in his opinion "marks the changes in Stephen's relationship to language and to sexuality"—the word *foetus* which functions as a striking opposition to the word *suck* in a number of ways: "The former is Anglo-Saxon, the latter Latin; the former is spoken, the latter is written; the former evokes a memory, the latter a fantasy" (75). Together, or rather through the reaction provoked by them, they bear witness to Stephen's heightened sensitivity to the physical and erotic suggestiveness of individual words. Attridge concludes by noting how other instances of this process are scattered throughout the novel (e.g. *les jupes* of Chapter IV or *mulier cantat* from Chapter V); these, however, are marked by an increased sense of self-criticism and irony, as Stephen more and more consciously produces his artistic self, making use of "the spiritual-heroic refrigerating apparatus, invented and patented in all countries by Dante Alighieri" (77).

XII

Just as some of the later works discussed in the preceding chapter used psychoanalytic discourse in order to address gender issues, the penultimate work analysed here is one which approaches Joyce's treatment and depiction of perverse sexuality from a psychoanalytic perspective. It should follow that this symbiosis has recently proven most fruitful and presents the most common current practice within the Joycean feminist and gender studies. In *James Joyce and the Perverse Ideal*,[14] David Cotter examines "sexual masochism," which "runs like a core through the center of Joyce," as "the impetus of his writing" (1). Exemplary instances of what he considers the writing of masochism occur in the "Calypso" chapter's parallel between the cat and Molly, Bloom's voyeuristic fetishism (both in "Nausicaa" and "Circe"), Bloom's acquiesced cuckolding (here Cotter holds that the "other word" that Bloom wanted Martha to call him as well as the missing word of his sand-writing "I.AM.A." is—*cuckold*), or his painstaking evasion of carnality with Molly by way of masturbation. The received critical understanding of Bloom as an oppressed passive victim is powerfully challenged by bringing on board Deleuze's study of masochism, *The Cold and the Cruel*, which reveals the masochistic position of weakness as an outward perversion of the position of power from

---

[14] David Cotter, *James Joyce and the Perverse Ideal* (New York and London: Routledge, 2003).

which masochists take advantage of their partners' attraction in order to cast them in the leading roles in their project of self-torture, evidence of which can be seen in *Exiles*.

Cotter's examination of Joyce's and Nora's correspondence reveals his own interest in being cuckolded to be balanced by an inordinate fear of being cuckolded. The crucial question addressed by his study, and the suggested answer are outlined as follows:

> why does Joyce draw a perversity so extreme and so unusual into a character who is, in other respects, meant to be unremarkable; why such a perverse event in the center of a day otherwise like every day? This analysis will suggest that Bloom's masochism is not an anomaly, or an arbitrary obscurity, but an illustration of the extreme implications of an equation that is the bedrock of Joyce's writing. (5)

Cotter approaches masochism, quite justifiably, as a polymorphously perverse phenomenon, discerning apart from Bloom's type (the masochism of the cuckold) a whole array of other varieties from the more general ones such as female domination, bondage, sadomasochism, or fetishism to more refined ones some of which are of relevance to *Ulysses*. Thus, Cotter mentions *pageism*, in which the man acts as "a houseboy for a woman whom he loves, because he loves her, and she may or may not reward his devotion with sexual fidelity," *lancelotism*, according to whose scenario "the woman regularly engages in sexual intercourse with a third party, but continues to accept worship of the masochist," or *forced feminization*, where "the masculinity of the masochist is not negated but derided." This specification in turn reveals Joyce's age as one witnessing "the slow seismic shift from a perception of sexuality as serving the ends of reproduction to a perception of sexuality as in the service of pleasure" (7). The slowness of this shift is due to the influence of Christianity and its anomalous treatment of the taboo, which is regarded, not as sacred (as in primitive religions), but as profane—Bataille's *Eroticism* is referenced here. Cotter acknowledges the work done by Richard Brown in illuminating Joyce's interest in scientific and legal discourses on sexuality (Ellis, Kraft-Ebbing, Freud) yet in his approach Joyce's textual engagement is regarded as intending "not to speak around sexuality, but to speak from within, and for sexuality." This perspective allows for the following bird's-eye view of the Joycean corpus:

> in *Dubliners*, Joyce demonstrates the ways in which sexuality and the body become situated in ellipses. Through *A Portrait* and *Ulysses*, he learns to speak from within these ellipses, [and in the *Wake*], the speech of perverse desire [...] flows unrestrained. (9)

Unlike Brown's focus on the official sexological discourses, Cotter's regards Joyce's interest in pornography, an "alternative, underground discourse of sexuality," as perhaps "greater than his interest in the sexological and legal discourses on sexuality" (10). Stanislaus's observation that the bird-girl image from *A Portrait* was modelled on images of sexy girls given away on cigarette cards is recalled to substantiate this interpretation.

At this point, Cotter sketches out the theoretical grounding of his argument. Heavy use is made of Georges Bataille, offering an alternative perspective on sexuality to that of Freud in that "violence and sacrifice are more central to sexuality in Bataille's system, [speaking] from within a sadism implicit to conventional male heterosexuality." This position is utilized in Cotter's argument by inverting its perspective or point of reference. The argument is most heavily (apart from Freud, Foucault, and Lacan) dependent upon the works of Deleuze and Guattari: other theorists and works of influence of importance include Julia Kristeva's *Powers of Horror*, Leo Bersani's *The Freudian Body*, and Jonathan Dollimore's *Sexual Dissidence* (13). In Cotter's analysis, Bloom's adult sexuality and full-blown masochism are regarded "as a logical development of Stephen's adolescent sexuality," and so the sources of Bloom's masochism are sought in Stephen (18). Throughout the argument cuckoldry remains central to Joyce's masochism as confirmed by his letters and Nora's testimony. In this respect,

> Joyce is not simply spinning a yarn; in his work he is engaging with the dragons of his mind. His themes are the battles he has fought with his own conscience, his own desires, his own fears. (19)

Both Stephen's mourning and Bloom's passivity have a common denominator — excessive sympathy for the suffering female:

> Stephen smashes the lamp because the death of his mother is on his mind. Bloom becomes, not a woman, but a masochist's parody of a woman, because he has on his mind the fact that the most powerful component of his masochistic fantasy has passed from his dreams into life on this day. In both cases, the dreams are influenced by a kind of empathy for women, and by an excruciating sympathy for the sufferings of women. It is this sympathy, and not the memory of his mother, that Stephen tries to destroy. [...] Because of an excess of sympathy and love, Bloom distances himself from Molly, by encouraging his own cuckolding. [...] He makes her seem far off and untouchable to him, not possessed by him, in order to recharge his desire for her. It is humane, but it is also selfish. (20)

Insofar as, according to Deleuze, masochism entails a psychic dualism or multiplicity, in that the masochist must work against the interests of the non-masochistic self, then for this reason, "masochism serves liberty, in that it dismantles [...] the inauthentic interests of the socially constructed self," operating against "the construction of individual identity" (20). According to this rationale, it is a mistake to look for a "consistent stance" in Bloom, as long as masochistic rituals consist in a parodic in- and perversion of social constructs of identity; "the best we can do," Cotter insists, "is locate predominances in his character and in his attitudes. Bloom's masochistic traits offer perhaps the strongest impediments to our attempts to define Bloom" (21).

Cotter's main argument then evolves into a five-chapter structure, the first of which, "The Cracked Looking-Glass," discusses the patterns of dualism emergent in Joyce's presentation of sexuality (gradually identified with the masochistic duality discussed above). The second and third chapters then move from "Daedalus Desexualized" to "Icarus Resexualized," mapping out the development of Stephen's infantile, nascent masochism as depicted in particularly the earlier parts of *A Portrait*, to adult, full-blown masochism as practiced by Bloom. The fourth and fifth chapters discuss "The Rituals of Masochism" and "The Cuckold," respectively or the *Walpurgisnacht* at Bella/Bello Cohen's brothel in "Circe" and the domestic dynamics between Bloom and Molly of the bemoaned and desired adultery in the "Nostos."

The present account of Cotter's argument will end with a brief exposition of his conclusion, "The Emperor's New Clothes," which regards Joyce's masochism "as a structural device [...], written into the text when Stephen talks about Shakespeare's personal life, details of interest only to a parish clerk." The "shrewridden Shakespeare" and "henpecked Socrates" of "Circe" relate Bloom's masochism to Stephen's exile and artistry, with the connection between Stephen's exile and his idealism, subverted in Bloom's perverse idealism (220). Valente's *Quare Joyce* is referenced, displaying sexuality in Joyce as "a sexuality that eludes or disintegrates stability of identity"—Cotter's has been a focus on masochism as "the most resolute renunciation of the 'saleable' or 'normal' subjectivity of 'ego psychology,'" and as "the most pronounced rejection of the mental illness of the ego." Thus, masochism has provided Cotter with "one avenue through which sexuality becomes more than itself, and partakes of political, ethical and aesthetic constructs" (221). In Joyce, Cotter concludes, "masochism implicates itself throughout the text, creating meaning, and linking meanings," functioning ultimately as one of the possible metaphors for life, "in which life is a beautiful woman who is worshipped although (because) she denies satisfaction" (222).

XIII

The presentation of the range of feminist and gender studies approaches which deal with Joyce concludes with a brief discussion of a work whose concerns already align it with the next chapter, and therefore render it a suitable "bridging" piece with which to end: Katherine Mullin's *James Joyce, Sexuality and Purity*.[15] The discussion will focus on the introductory and concluding parts of the book, as these present the theoretical grounding of Mullin's approach, pointing to issues discussed under the rubric of "cultural studies," yet from a decisively feminist and gender

---

[15] Katherine Mullin, *James Joyce, Sexuality and Purity* (Cambridge: Cambridge University Press, 2003).

perspective. Mullin's "Introduction: provoking the puritysnoopers" opens by contending that "Joyce's publication history is a history of censorship" (1).

The watershed year critical to the history of literary censorship here is 1857 which "saw the publication of Baudelaire's *Les Fleurs du Mal* and Gustave Flaubert's *Madame Bovary*, the former convicted, the latter acquitted of offences against public morality" (3). Mullin's meticulous, well-researched historical overview of the many social, aesthetic, and political implications of the entry of Joyce's works into the public domain dominated by the discourse of social purity, reveals its various complexities as informing "the many imaginative, subversive, subtle and creative ways in which Joyce incorporates social purity discourses and campaigns into his fiction" (25). The crucial clash here takes place between the social purity campaigns and the sexually ebullient popular culture that Joyce so eloquently documents. The six chapters of Mullin's book explore this collision from the viewpoint of "two key issues of central importance to Joyce's subversive assault upon social purity," Joyce's portraits of several "young persons," children and adolescents in sexual danger, and Joyce's deliberate provocation and incitement of the eventual vice society intervention into the publication of *Ulysses* in 1921 "which would win him worldwide notoriety" (26-7).

Together, these two concerns of Mullin's argument aim to "dismantle the pervasive myth, so teasingly deployed by Joyce himself, of artistic martyrdom in the face of philistine prudery" (27). Thus, thematically, the book's first half concerns itself with Joyce's early fiction, approaching "An Encounter" in terms of an analysis of the broader historical workings of reading regulation in the service of colonial domination (Chapter I), presenting a compelling reading of the "Eveline" short story and its astute tapping into the contemporary propaganda discourse (II), and discussing the "true manliness" of *A Portrait* as policed by the colonial powers that be (III). The second half focuses entirely on *Ulysses*: its concern with subversive deployment of the sexual purity discourse, in particular, in "Scylla and Charybdis" (theosophical purity), "Nausicaa" (the feminine spectacle for the male voyeurism as a mutoscope), and "Circe" (brothel policing). Again, as with Cotter's book, it is especially in her "Afterword" that Mullin teases out the implications of her argument for the broader theoretical framework of Joyce studies, particularly the challenge posed to the received idea of the artist fighting against an oppressive philistine society. In Cotter's view, "this persuasive stereotype of artistic grace under fire carries overtones of passivity which cannot readily be applied to any aspect of Joyce's creative practice." Instead, the perspective proposed in Mullin's work is that

> social purity campaigns, in all their diversity, form part of the intricate cultural context of Joyce's fiction, whether those campaigns be to remove "penny dreadfuls" from schoolboys, deter young women from emigrating, prevent adolescent masturbation, raise the nation to a higher plane of celi-

bate spirituality, close down mutoscope parlours or police the dangerous and often exhilarating red-light zones of the metropolis. (204)

This has consequences for two fields of Joyce studies in particular: feminism and postcolonialism. First, Mullin proposes to regard the Joyce's frequently discussed aversion towards "emancipated" or "intellectual" women as a "hostility towards one particular and dominant strand, the purity feminist mainstream," whose prudishness is opposed to the dissident emancipated women who were "eager to engage with the taboo questions of sexual politics; contraception and abortion, women's capacities for orgasm and sexual pleasure, 'free unions' and marriage, homosexuality and the new science of 'sexology'" (206-7). Secondly, Mullin's research-based argument brings home the point that "there was no home-grown, Catholic, nationalist purity league to rival the Dublin White Cross Vigilance Association until after the foundation of the Free State," whose "National Vigilance Association's 'Dublin branch' sent reports back to London boasting of its close ties with the Dublin Metropolitan Police" (208). Hence,

> if Joyce's fiction, as Emer Nolan and Vince Cheng have so persuasively argued, explores the devastating effects upon Dublin's citizens of Ireland's status as a British colony, then social purity discourses and practices render the sense of colonial subjection they identify startlingly personal. [...] The colonial undertones Nolan and Cheng detect extend into the most intimate private spaces of all, those of the body and the erotic imagination. (209)

In the context of these two fields, to explore as Mullin attempts and manages to do, "Joyce's creative appropriation of the social purity crusades" is also to "assail this false dichotomy and demonstrate how the prolonged conflict with censorship does not stand outside his creative practice, but, rather, lies at its heart." The forgotten cultural ephemera with which Joyce's fiction is replete, "reveal a sustained, complex and politically freighted assault upon a movement responsible for the international proscription of *Ulysses*, and thus partly productive of his notoriety" (210). Mullin's argument ultimately reveals the threat or expectation of censorship as not incidental, but integral to Joyce's aesthetic. It is with Joyce's aesthetic as engaged in the retrieval and creative reworking of precisely the cultural ephemera discussed by Mullin that the approach discussed next concerns itself.

4. Cultural Studies

I

Widely regarded as the first sustained attempt at studying the Joycean canon from the perspective of cultural studies, Cheryl Herr's influential study *Joyce's Anatomy of Culture*[1] presents itself as the first critical examination which "addresses the impress of social history on the fiction of Joyce from *Dubliners* through *Finnegans Wake*" (ix). From within the whole gamut of the contemporary ideology of Joyce's time, Herr singles out three media instrumental in ideological dissemination and stabilization—the press, the popular theatre, and the Church. She then goes on to show how Joyce's texts, while treating these as "constituting the voices through which his characters find themselves speaking," arrive at exposing the institutional stylizations as such, steering clear of giving them "the status of persons even when they mimic the tones through which human voices acknowledge the profound influence of social institutions on individuality" (x).

Although the apparent all-inclusiveness of Joyce's creations (which Herr regards as neurotic) is to be seen less as "literature of commitment" than as "literature of exposure," the position held by many from which Joyce's fiction is viewed as apolitical still "calls for questioning" (6). With reference to Dominic Magnaniello's *Joyce's Politics*,[2] Herr considers the culture of Joyce's time and his texts as "parallel," as "reflexively related versions of an unrecoverable historical experience, which nonetheless expose the process by which social reality takes conceptual form" (8). It is the encyclopedic aspiration of his fictions that lends them the status of what Yuri Lotman has called "texts of culture" which are "universal"—the premise of Joyce's texts being that "they are not *only* fictions but also compilations of details emergent from the cultural *mythoi* dominant in their author's lifetime" (9). Crucial for Herr is Joyce's preoccupation with how social convention controls what individual subjects consider their private decisions. Drawing further on the Tartu/Moscow school of semiotics, Herr identifies four principles that define "culture in general and therefore Irish culture in particular":

---

[1] Cheryl Herr, *Joyce's Anatomy of Culture* (Urbana: University of Illinois Press, 1986).
[2] See Chapter VIII "Politics," section II.

1. The operations of culture take place at the level of signification, and all meaning depends on the frames of reference for those signs which the culture generates.
2. Culture is a mechanism which produces itself in texts—works of literature, newspapers, sermons, and the like.
3. Culture displays both unity and diversity on a number of levels and in a number of ways. It tends to assimilate new data into accepted or at least functioning ideological codes as well as sedimented ones, but it also accommodates countercodes and subversive ideas.
4. Culture forges the identities of individuals according to a system of constraints, standardization, and stereotyping. In the endless productivity of culture, there is mostly repetition of well-defined but often masked ideologically charged images and goals. Thus productivity becomes a kind of censorship. (14-15)

In Herr's focus on the involvement of Joyce's fictions with the institutional practices of culture, their subversive force appears to be twofold: they "critique the fundamental social relations of the middle class in Ireland" in that they define these relations as "ideological and their source as institutional" (16), and also "call attention to those cultural sites where ideological or semiotic conflict occurs" (17). Thus, in her discussion of the press, Herr deals with the clash between state and church on the issue of censorship. In her section on theatre, what gains prominence is the subversive potential of transvestism, while in the study of the sermon, Herr plays out the discrepancy between the envisioned Catholic social order and the harsh economic conditions of early 20[th]century Ireland. Crucial throughout her examination is the awareness of the importance of the uniquely allusive quality of Joyce's writing—not only do allusions in his texts reinforce the topicality of the narrative, but "they also bring into his works the fossilized forms of cultural activity, the bits and pieces of language that hardened into convention after emerging from the hotbed of cultural production" (18). Despite her focus on institutional practices, Herr's discussion ultimately sets out to document how these mould the individual into, in the Foucauldian double-sense of the word, "subjects."

After the preliminary caveat (apparent already from Herr's focus on the sites of ideological conflict), according to which both the institutional censorship and subversion thereof are generated not by any one individual institution alone, but rather by the complex relations among them, Herr goes on to carefully interweave "reconsiderations and contextualizations" of specific sections of *Ulysses* (particularly revealing is her discussion of "Circe" in Chapter 5) and *Finnegans Wake* (I.4. and III.2) with a meticulous documentation of the historical reality that shaped the three selected ideological discourses of Joyce's time (26).

Herr's afterword, then, presents an explicit critique of the critical movement with which her own approach has been at odds throughout—the New Critical practice of "scientific" textual interpretation isolated from historico-political contexts. What among other things her study sets out to achieve is to present a vision alternative to R. M. Adams's famous dichotomy between "surface" and "symbol"—as long as both the most banal detail of social reality and fundamental social relations can be revealed as related to a social institution as the site of their origin or reproduction, then the binary opposition ceases to hold, as well as the preference for the symbol as that which carries meaning in Joyce's fiction. Nor can one regard the cultural institutions as merely limiting Joyce's artistic vision—their binarisms provided the very stuff his subversive (deconstructive, one might say) writing was made on, engineering "in his texts what we might call a liberating vision of culture" where Joyce's "anatomizing undoes oppositions as absolutes and enables us to see that the institution, however formidable, is also man-made" (284-5). Ultimately, Joyce is seen as neither a victim of nor an isolationist from his day's popular culture, but rather as a voice which brings to the fore the underlying self-deconstructive forces of the conflicting ideologies of his time:

> Just as his society constantly created and constantly undermined its networks of conventionality, so Joyce's works both resolve and renew the nurturing conflicts of history. (285)

II

That Herr's book, for all its thematic innovativeness and theoretical commitment, was rather the tip of an iceberg than a solitary oddity, will be demonstrated in another section of the present study.[3] Here, the broader context of the mid-1980s discussions of popular culture, history and (post)modernity, can be demonstrated by a discussion of a well-argued paper included in the collection of essays from the 1986 Copenhagen symposium, *Coping with Joyce*.[4] The very title of Jules David Law's "Simulation, Pluralism, and the Politics of Everyday Life," manifests the essay's allegiance with what was then forming itself as the cultural studies of Joyce. Law focuses on "the metamorphosis of the quotidian into the historic" as "one of the great themes of *Ulysses*" (196). His example of the Greek nymph from the bedroom poster, animated and given her accusatory speech in "Circe," especially her status as a *photography*, not a painting, is seen as a preparation within the novel for "photography to become 'art' and for everyday life to achieve the status of an historical and aesthetic object." The crucial question posed by Law is the following one:

> The history and the culture of everyday life: are these parodic oxymorons, or modernist ideologies *par excellence*? And is if it *is* possible to write the history and the culture of everyday life, is Joyce's work an authentic—or even, perhaps, a unique—contribution to that project? (197)

[3] That is, in Chapter VIII "Politics," section III.
[4] Jules David Law, "Simulation, Pluralism, and the Politics of Everyday Life," *Coping with Joyce: Essays from the Copenhagen Symposium*, eds. Moris Beja and Shari Benstock (Columbus: Ohio State University Press, 1986).

Henri Lefebvre's celebration (in his seminal *Everyday Life in the Modern World*) of *Ulysses* as marking "the momentous eruption of everyday life into literature" is immediately restricted to what he regards as its *modernist* mode: its "exploration of subjectivity," its treatment of the everyday experience in representational concepts and modes that appear to Lefebvre as modernist clichés: ordinary and private language, stream of consciousness and slips of tongue. This "subject-centered" modernist concern is pitted against the postmodern "regime of the object" of Lefebvre's era (the 1960s). Thus, in order to properly evaluate Joyce's "revolutionary creation of a formal narrative from cultural bric-à-brac, it is necessary," in Law's opinion, "to emphasize how differently that bric-à-brac functioned in his time than in our own" (198). Bloom's "Ithacan" fantasies about the ultimate advertisement are shown to manifest this difference quite conspicuously:

> [O]urs is no longer an era of commodity production, and the objects of commercial culture no longer arrest us as the nymph does Leopold Bloom. Whereas at the beginning of this century, advertising images were still novel enough to be recognized as (pleasant or threatening) distortions both of everyday life and of history, now advertising presents a self-generating simulation of reality, without any historical dissonance or uncanniness. We like to think that if we scratched beneath the surface of contemporary everyday life, we would find the earthiness and uncanniness of Bloom's everyday life. But is this so? (199)

The difference becomes perhaps clearer in Law's use of Jean Baudrillard's distinction between the traditionally-capitalist economy organized around the *commodity* and the late-capitalist economy organized around the *simulacrum*. As long as in the world of *Ulysses*, "commodities are rarely consumed instantaneously, or once and for all, but rather decay through a series of use values, as if possessed of a radioactive half-life," the simulacrum on the other hand, "has no such uncanniness or sense of deferral about it; it exists to be experienced and used up at the same time, like a computer graphic, a television image, or a media event" (199). This opposition then, involving the postmodern abolition of the subject and of the referent in both literary mimesis and economic exchange, presents "a challenge to our attempt to recover the specific mode of representing everyday life which *Ulysses* itself represents." However, a still greater obstacle to a historical (and thus, for Law, political) understanding of *Ulysses* is posed by "the apparent simultaneity, in Joyce's work, of the mythic and the quotidian, of historicity and contemporaneity" (200). It is therefore thanks to Joyce and other modernists that the very notion of "everyday life" now "has a history, a psychological theory, and an unprecedented aesthetic evocation."

The question, for Law, still remains, "whose everyday life does Joyce represent?" (201). This calls for an elaboration:

If we were going to characterize Joyce's achievement, we would say that he exaggerates everyday life by making it denser and more complex than it "really" appears to the average consciousness. Thus it is his representation of subjectivity rather than of the physical world that we recognize as constituting his distinctive aesthetic deflection. [...] It is precisely because we think of everyday life as an unproblematic notion [...] that we think of *Ulysses* as being every bit as democratic in its accessibility as it is radical in its inaccessibility. (201)

This "myth of democratic accessibility" also accounts in Law's view for the easy admission of critical pluralism into Joyce studies. It follows then that if elsewhere in literary academia, "the concept and representation of everyday life are uncritically rejected as popular culture," within Joyce studies, "we are perhaps too uncritically receptive to the representations of everyday life." The task of a properly political reading, in Law's opinion, is

not to *choose* between Joyce, the chronicler of everyday life and Joyce, the mythmaker and esotericist, but rather to see how this very choice arises out of a historically specific conception of everyday life which *Ulysses* itself represents, and which contemporary criticism represents to us as still our own. [...] what *Ulysses* has to contribute to a politics of narrative is precisely its hold on the fundamental tension between the intentional and the unintentional, played out on the terrain of an increasingly anachronistic everyday life, whose image is still familiar enough to us to represent a powerful nostalgia. (202)

Only a critical attention to *Ulysses* that does justice to its self-contradictory treatment of the popular culture can turn this nostalgia into a "resistance to the simulations of everyday life in our world, simulations which cannot endlessly fend off the massive social dislocations on our horizon" (202).

III

If Herr's "atomistic" approach cleverly combined the heritage of the Tartu school of semiotics (Lotman, Boris Uspensky) with neo-Marxist theories of culture and power (Fredric Jameson, Michel Foucault), then the first of Brandon Kershner's major contributions to the studies of Joyce and popular culture foregrounds its theoretical anchorage in its very title: *Joyce, Bakhtin, and Popular Culture*.[5] A concise summary of this study would see Kershner combine a Bakhtinian analysis of the early Joycean canon (*Dubliners, Stephen Hero, A Portrait*, and *Exiles*) with a literary-historical research of the various texts that can be proven to have shaped these fictions, and thus to have set off the Bakhtinian processes of "dialogism" and "carnivalization."

---

[5] R. Brandon Kershner, *Joyce, Bakhtin, and Popular Culture* (Chapel Hill: University of North Carolina Press, 1989).

The grateful acknowledgment of Herr's pioneering work notwithstanding, Kershner still regards the vast amount of allusion to popular culture in *Ulysses* and elsewhere in Joyce as "daunting and often dismissed as either random bits of period 'furniture' thrown in to add historical verisimilitude or as evidence of an encyclopedic technique run amok" (2). Traces of this tendency can be found as early as *Stephen Hero*, where "Stephen, and probably Joyce as well, is something of an aesthetic Antaeus; he weakens if he goes too long without touching the earth," the implication being, obviously, that the ground on which Joyce's fiction gains its strength is—the popular text (4). In assessing the work done so far within the field, Dominic Manganiello's and Richard Brown's[6] approach is credited with "attempt[ing] to place Joyce within the social and intellectual context of his time, to present him as a participant in the heated dialogue regarding, respectively, politics and sex," while Richard Ellmann's reconstruction of Joyce's Trieste library in the appendix to *The Consciousness of Joyce* provides the material basis for Kershner's investigation, since it includes "some fifty works that might reasonably be regarded as popular literature" (9).

Kershner goes on to show how current critical theory of popular culture sets about dismantling the New Critical canon, undermining any aspirations to universal applicability of the "high" and "low" dichotomy as pertaining to literary art. Rather than as an aesthetic axiological polarization, cultural neo-Marxism comes to discuss this binary in terms of ideological allegiance. Louis Althusser's influential paper, "Ideology and Ideological State Apparatuses" distinguishes between state apparatuses which are repressive (such as the army or the police) and those that are ideological (e.g. the arts, literature, or sports). Whereas popular mass forms of culture operate "through ideology, in disguised, even symbolic forms, to buttress the prevailing power structure," genuine artists "'give us a view' of the ideology to which their work alludes and with which it is constantly fed, a view which presupposes a *retreat*, an *internal distantiation* from the very ideology from which the novels emerged" (12-3). In his seminal *The Political Unconscious: Narrative as a Socially Symbolic Act*, Fredric Jameson takes Althusser's argument a step further to distinguish among three stages of textual interpretation. In the first, the text is explicated merely as a symbolic act of its author; in the second, the text is regarded "as a single utterance within 'the great collective and class discourses' of the time,"; and in the third, "the 'ideology of form' within the work is examined" (13). It is then the ideology of allusion that presents the subject of Kershner's investigation into how literary and subliterary texts contributed to Joyce's writing.

It is here that Bakhtin's concepts of *dialogism* (which Kershner notes Bakthin also terms "polyphony" and which is closely related to "het-

[6] For Brown's *James Joyce and Sexuality*, see Chapter III "Feminism, Sexuality & Gender Studies," section III.

eroglossia") and *carnivalization* (often explored by Bakhtin through the notion of the "chronotope") come into play as the key concepts of a theory which, "although oriented to genre, allows for the stylistic and ideological analysis of texts of any social level" in that it regards "both written and spoken language and inner monologue [as] made up of a great variety of conflicting variants—'languages' of officialdom, vernaculars, occupational jargons, technical, literary, and subliterary languages, all polyphonically resounding" (15). Given the socio-linguistic orientation of Bakhtin's theory, Joyce's "striking absence" in the Bakthinian corpus is a puzzling omission, "since all of Bakhtin's major concepts seem best and most obviously illustrated by *Ulysses* and *Finnegans Wake*" (17). This obviousness however also accounts for why Kershner's book consciously avoids discussing either:

> Certainly Joyce's last two books are outstanding illustrations of heteroglossia and carnivalization, but the same concerns and techniques that animate those works are present in embryonic form in *Dubliners* and *A Portrait* as well. (18)

Kershner identifies three categories of dialogism in Bakhtin: one that takes place between the languages of the author and of the protagonist; one occurring between protagonist's language and other characters' idiolects; and one operating among the languages of entire texts, connected by means of allusion, whether implicit or explicit. Here it is not difficult to discern in the first type what narratologists have come to label *style indirect libre*; in the second what Bakthin also terms *heteroglossia* and regards as the key process constitutive of the novel genre; and in the third what Julia Kristeva (instrumental in introducing the West to Bakhtin's work) has termed intertextuality. The currentness of Bakthin's thought Kershner argues is still wider than that:

> Actually, Bakhtin's thought cuts across the grain of many current debates, since he allows no opposition between language and conceptual structures of an authentic, naked "self" and the surrounding society; the self "always already" finds language appropriated and ideologically dense. (21)

The ultimate similarity between Bakhtin and Joyce is that both see the world as "filled with conflict and opposition," yet neither denies the "joy and affirmation in its energy, dynamism, and continuity in the heart of change" (21).

The dialogical interchange in *Dubliners* as analysed by Kershner occurs on all of the above-mentioned three planes, of which the second and third prove the most fruitful. In "The Sisters," to take but one example, Kershner identifies "the massed chorus of Old Cotter, the uncle, the aunt, and Eliza, all of whom share a vocabulary, a syntax, and, in a specialized sense, an ideology," a voice which eludes plain characterization (though "Irish, lower-middle-class, turn-of-the-century, ill-educated" it undoubtedly is) a "popular speech" whose "most frustrating aspect [...] for the boy is the *rhetoric of ellipsis*" (25-6). The third intertextual type of dialogism comes to the fore in Kershner's discussion of "An Encounter" (read together with contemporary boy's magazines such as *The Union Jack* or *The Halfpenny Marvel*) and "Araby" (intertextualised with a variety of popular romance, such as *The Abbot* or *The Memoirs of Vidocq*). Kershner pays each of the *Dubliners* stories its due, analysing them with a sensitivity to their display of the dialogism, as well as engaging the four groups (into which they have been divided up by Joyce himself) into a dialogue between one another. He then proceeds to identify a general movement of the collection:

> The four stories of adolescence [...] lack the power and density of reference of the stories of childhood. They each feature protagonists very much unlike the author, whereas for Joyce's technique to be most effective, the implicit dialogue between author and protagonist must be close and intense. (60)

> The general movement of *Dubliners* is toward the hegemony of public rhetoric. While language is foregrounded throughout the volume, during the stories of "maturity" dialogue gradually supplants narration, until in the stories of "public life" [...] little but dialogue remains. (95)

In his section on *A Portrait*, Kershner identifies the crucial dialogical texts of its "narration that is radically destabilized, both dependent upon the protagonist's voice and unable to be identified with it" (151) in popular — for example Thomas Hughes' *Tom Brown's School-Days* — as much as in classical fiction — Alexander Dumas' *The Count of Monte Christo*, which *A Portrait* "echoes in theme, image, and language" (209). Kershner then goes on to distinguish between an "allusive dialogism" (pertaining to literary texts to which the text refers as being part of Stephen's reading) and "elusive dialogism" (Joyce's own reading at the time of the novel's composition).

Finally, *Exiles* comes to be seen as a text informed by the turn-of-the-century ideological discourse of marriage and sexuality. The major difference between the play's two principal male characters is believed to consist in their incompatible attitudes to the simultaneously constricting and choice-giving structures of ideology:

> Robert, the self-deluding egoist, is seemingly unaware of the problem, because he is so thoroughly the creature of popular ideologies. Richard, a far more honest egoist, finds that he cannot abolish by fiat either the constraints of his own nature or the society of which he is a reluctant member. (296)

In his "Conclusions," Kershner re-assesses the useful potential of Bakhtin's theoretical (non-) methodology for Joyce studies, and sees its main force in its "reinsertion of the man's writings, protagonists, and — we must suppose—Joyce himself into history" (297). Like Herr's before him, Kershner's is a voice contesting the New Critical alignment of Joyce with modernist ideologies, claiming that although his writings do invoke, or indeed even articulate these, they also demystify and criticize them—for example, his readings of the *Dubliners* stories with Bakhtin "foreground the struggles of protagonists against the systems of discourse that surround them, and there is unavoidably an air of heroism to such struggles," whereas the major interest of Stephen the would-be hero is "in the peculiar, conflicting set of languages and ideologies he encompasses" (299-300). Thus, not only has Kershner shown convincingly that "an important element in Joyce's literary genius is his appreciation of the importance of popular literature in the society of his time," but he has also managed to engage Joyce and Bakhtin in a fruitful dialogue, "in which the language of each would enrich that of the other, without any ascription of dominance to either" (301-2).

IV

After the "late" and "early" Joyce of Herr's and Kershner's books respectively, the next important publication within this field had an even narrower focus: the "Penelope" episode, the coda of *Ulysses*. The twelve essays (collected from various cultural studies panels at 1987 Joyce symposium and 1989 MLA conference) which form the volume edited by Richard Pearce and titled *Molly Blooms: A Polylogue on 'Penelope' and Cultural Studies*[7] present a veritable Bakhtinian *heteroglossia*. The central bone of contention of these studies is the ambiguity already sketched by Kershner: to what extent one can ascribe to a Joyce character (here, Molly Bloom) her own individual agency within what is presented as her socio-historical position—a strictly demarcated network of various restrictive social forces.

Richard Pearce's introduction emphasizes the interdisciplinary approach of the collection's polylogue, presenting "the first full-length study of Molly Bloom that attempts to restore Molly and her perspective on the world of *Ulysses*" by looking at "Penelope" through "the lenses of cultural studies which include feminism, new historicism, popular culture, postcolonialism, and postmodernism" (3). The crucial question addressed by these various approaches is "how Molly reproduces, negotiates, and resists" the narratives that shape her as she "shifts back and forth between what Mikhail Bakhtin calls 'authoritative' and 'internally persuasive discourse'" (4). The papers, often inter-referential, are grouped into five topics: "Molly and the Male Gaze," "Molly in Performance," "Negotiating Colonialism," "Molly as Consumer" and "Molly as Body and Embodied." Here the variety of approaches and the similarity of their results shall be exemplified by discussing three essays in some detail.

---

[7] Richard Pearce, ed., *Molly Blooms: A Polylogue on 'Penelope' and Cultural Studies* (Madison: University of Wisconsin Press, 1994).

Kimberly J. Devlin's "Pretending in 'Penelope': Masquerade, Mimicry, and Molly Bloom" re-explores the distinction drawn by Joan Riviere between female masquerade and female mimicry, a difference consisting in a passive and unconscious internalization of cultural images of femininity (masquerade) as opposed to a conscious repetition, parodying and appropriation thereof. Another way of thinking about this difference proposed by Carole-Anne Tyler, is in terms of flaunting versus flouting, where masquerade becomes "a potentially oppressive gender identity," whereas mimicry "a potentially playful one" (80). When dealing with the age-old question of *Ulysses* criticism concerning the "archetypical" status of Molly's femininity, Devlin unmasks the archetype versus stereotype dichotomy as virtually non-existent—archetypes being "stereotypes decked out as literary concepts or masquerading as inherent psychological categories" (82)—and instead argues for a Molly who "is represented as a character situated within representation, as a reader of popular culture, as a consumer of textual artifacts" who "participates in the female masquerade insofar as she often attempts to conform herself to cultural images of femininity, dramatizing them reflexively" (83-4). Molly can be seen to perceive herself through the identifications with the clichéd archetypes of "the pristine nymph" and "the dirty bitch," yet at the same time "the critical distance" she maintains from either allow for a reading of the final episode as "a savvy critique of gender performance, as Joyce's self-conscious anatomy of feminine as well as masculine roles" where roles are to be understood as theatrical personae (86-7). This theatre is ultimately aimed at the reader audience: "we are invited to see ourselves in Joyce-doing-Molly-doing-whoever, to recognize our own en-gendered inscriptings" as we witness Joyce's forged female voice which exposes the engendered linguistic codes of the entire culture (100).

Brian W. Shaffer's "Negotiating Self and Culture: Narcissism, Competing Discourses, and Ideological Becoming in 'Penelope'' begins by rephrasing the two interrelated questions of cultural determinism versus potential subversion as follows:

[H]ow is Molly "mollycoddled" into accepting a situation that many would find objectionable in the extreme, and yet how does she manage to extricate herself, at least partially, from the tangle of discourses that victimize her? (139)

To explicate the former, Shaffer uses the late Freudian theory (*The Future of an Illusion*) of the culturally provided narcissistic satisfaction; addressing the latter, he employs the Bakhtinian conception of the internally dialogic nature of language. The Molly who emerges from his careful intertwining of the text with the two theories is one whose "'narcissism of minor differences' limits her focus, helping her to evade, or at least to ignore, the dimensions of her victimization as a lower-class, female, colonial subject" (141), yet who also displays the ability to render "authoritative discourse internally persuasive" and thus is "in a state of ideological becoming" where the "official line of ideological discourse appears, not "untouchable," but rather "synthetic and alterable" (149).

Margaret Mills Harper's "'Taken in Drapery': Dressing the Narrative in the *Odyssey* and 'Penelope'" revisits the metaphor of text/texture/textile, frequently employed in poststructuralist criticism to denote the creative and destructive (self-deconstructive) forces within narrative. Here, however, it is employed in order to "look at fabric in the *Odyssey*, that well-worn text with which to dress interpretations of *Ulysses*" and in particular, the "Penelope" episode, a text "stretched out of ordinary shape in order to cover inadequacies in a form it suggests for itself, thus revealing the outline of the elements that trouble its proposed structures" (237-8).

The frequent association of Molly with textile production and consumption is clearly evocative of Penelope's art of weaving/unweaving the famous burial shroud for Odysseus' father Laertes, thereby perpetually deferring her forced decision to choose from among her suitors. This peculiar temporality of the *Odyssey* episodes featuring Penelope would seem to be echoed in a reading of the "Penelope" episode "as a novel-stopper, a web of associations that catches the narrative time in its mesh"—a reading which, however, has its limitations (243). Harper concurs with Patrick McGee's[8] view that the final chapter presents a radical de-centring of the whole novel's narrative, in the context of which Molly's counter-sign (Joyce's own metaphor) "stops Bloom, defining him as if her episode were a document sending him out of time 'to eternity,' placing him [...] as 'center' in a non-narrative orientation" (245). Although it might indeed stop Bloom, on no account does the episode's narrative do away with narrative temporality, which is seen to reappear "through the interstices left by the very parataxis that hides it, in the gaps between the grammatical and the intellectual or emotional connectives of the discourse," reminiscent of biblical narrative (251). Thus,

> [t]he discourse of "Penelope" strips away the story of *Ulysses* [...] partially by language that is stereotypically "female" and at first glance technically flamboyant in comparison to other episodes, and partially by a seeming retreat from diegetical time into timeless revery. (252)

V

Perhaps the most ambitious project of combining cultural theory with comparative analysis of the Joycean canon has been penned by M. Keith Booker. His *Joyce, Bakhtin, and the Literary Tradition*[9] presents a well-conceived attempt "toward a comparative cultural poetics" in detailing Joyce's relations to six traditionally canonical authors (Homer, Dante, Rabelais, Shakespeare, Goethe, and Dostoevsky), which in turn provides a

---

[8] For Patrick McGee's *Paperspace*, see Chapter VIII "Politics," section IV.

[9] M. Keith Booker, *Joyce, Bakthin, and the Literary Tradition* (Michigan: University of Michigan Press, 1995).

springboard for looking at the Joycean corpus through the prism of Bakhtin's theoretical concepts.

Surveying Joyce criticism in the introduction, Booker pinpoints the "almost uncanny ability" of Joyce's writing "to ride atop whatever crucial waves happen to be breaking at the moment" (2) and seeks to steer clear of the dichotomy between Joyce the apolitical aesthete and Joyce the subaltern postcolonialist in contending that perhaps the most striking aspect of Joyce's writing is "his ability to weave commentary on contemporary Irish social and political issues into the most seemingly 'aesthetic' aspects of his work" (5). Also noted is the trouble inherent in "applying" Bakthinian theory to Joyce, on account of the dangerous proximity between the best-known Bakthinian concepts and Joyce's writing:

> It may well be that Joyce's later novels match Bakhtin's ideas so closely and so obviously that most features of those novels that might be identified by reading though Bakhtin can be identified without Bakhtin. (9)

Booker's discussion of Joyce's relation to Homer brings up the question of Joyce's attitude toward cultural authority, and the modes of its transgression, whereas with Rabelais, Booker employs the term "inverse transgression" to associate transgression "not with violation of authority but with authority itself" (13). As for Joyce's attitude to Dante, the focus is on their shared semantic process of "sliding signification" by means of which their texts bring forth "richly polysemic structures of meaning" (13-4). Goethe serves as a springboard for examining the historicity of Joyce's texts, whereas Shakespeare provokes Joyce's most complex confrontation with authority. Finally, Dostoevsky's poetics enriches Booker's argument with the issue of human subjectivity in Joyce, and modern literature.

The chapter entitled "Joyce, Homer, and the Myth of the Mythic Method" casts the Homer-Joyce relation as a two-way exchange, one in which Joyce's transformation of Homer "shed new light on those texts, which causes us to read them in unprecedented ways" (24). Joyce's transgressive practices are then contrasted with T.S. Eliot's conservative cultural authoritarianism and paralleled with the political agenda of Mikhail Bakunin's anarchic politics.

Poorest in terms of direct allusiveness though the Joyce-Rabelais relation might be, there are still the affinities between the work of Joyce and that of Rabelais, "both in terms of the subject material and philosophical attitudes embedded in their texts and in terms of the exorbitantly heteroglossic encyclopedic styles that they use to express that material and those attitudes," have long been recognized by critics (46). The Bakhtinian link here of course is his famous reading of Rabelais in the context of the medieval laughter-culture and the carnivalesque. A link is drawn between Joyce's employment of parodic subversion vis-à-vis the Catholic Church and Bakhtin's own critical project which more or less covertly opposed the Stalinism of his time. The topos of the Rabelaisian feast as analysed by Bakhtin is paralleled with Joyce's employment of the meta-phor of cannibalism, which "embodies the ultimate lack of respect for the Other and the ultimate effacement of difference" and thus "functions as the ideal metaphor for the treatment of the Irish people by such forces as the Catholic Church, the British Empire, and Irish nationalism" (69). Asso-ciated with cannibalism is the motif of sexual violence, read by Booker (with reference to Bataille) as yet another means of Joyce's contesting the Church's authority. An especially strong connection is drawn between Catholicism and sadomasochism, "as when both HCE and Bloom undergo various torments while playing the roles of Christ figures," the implication being that "the Church as a whole is pleased that sin exists because the continuing existence of sin allows it to maintain its institutional power through ongoing threats of retribution" (74).

Dante's significance for Joyce is mapped on the basis of his fourfold exegetic technique, one combining the literal-historical meaning with alle-gorical, moral, and anagogical meaning(s). Analogously, "Joyce identifies the tendency to be locked into literality as one of the symptoms of the paralysis that he attributes to his fellow *Dubliners.*" Moreover Joyce also participates in the Dantean tradition of artistic renovation of language by means of the deployment of what is variously called the collage technique (here, Booker references Adorno's *Aesthetic Theory*), the mosaic piecing together of other texts (Kristeva's intertextuality), or *bricolage* (Lévi-Strauss) (84). Dante is further seen as perhaps the most prominent pre-cursor of Joyce's practice of allusiveness: his weaving allusions into a network of interrelated meanings. Thus, "Dante, too, gets considerable mileage from misappropriation of literary and linguistic materials. In fact, misquotation becomes a fundamental structural principle of Dante's hell, that land of misreading and lack of understanding" (92). The fundamental difference between the two, however, is no less relevant than their paral-lels—Umberto Eco[10] has pointed to the absence in Joyce's writing of the "transcendent God" of the Middle Ages. Reminiscent though it might be of the four levels of medieval biblical exegesis, "the sliding signification of Joyce the generation of multiple meaning is not under the ultimate control of a monological deity" (104).

The discussion of Goethe's presence in Joyce (and Bakhtin) centres around the former's *Wilhelm Meister* and how it might be seen to have informed the latter's *Portrait*, and more broadly the character of Stephen Dedalus. However tangential or even accidental the allusions to Goethe in Joyce, the palinodic, self-cancelling discourse of his epochal *Bildungsro-man* is seen as informing Joyce's own take at the genre, and in fact his whole oeuvre. Moreover, bluntly though he himself might have refused the character of Faust,

---

[10] Umberto Eco, *The Middle Ages of James Joyce: The Aesthetics of Chaosmos*, trans. Ellen Esrock (London: Hutchinson Radius, 1989).

it is Faust's assistant, Wagner, rather than Faust himself, who ultimately seems to resemble Shem — or even Joyce. Faust, who is displeased with his assistant's dogged devotion to the rational principles of secular Enlightenment science, anticipates Joyce the "scissors and paste man" when he castigates Wagner for his attempts to conscript the knowledge of others in the interest of his researches. (113)

Of the additions Booker makes to the much-discussed Joyce-Shakespeare relation, the most enriching one is his combination of the irreverence of the "how" with the respectfulness of the "that" — thus, "the attitude that Joyce displays toward Shakespeare in his fiction is certainly not reverential," and yet "the frequency of allusion to William Shakespeare in Joyce's work can certainly be taken as an acknowledgment of William Shakespeare's position at the center of the western cultural canon" (140-1). Furthermore, his Bakhtinian tack enables Booker to read the dialogue between the two as representing "an encounter between two different genres and a resulting clash between the ideologies they represent" (142). Booker then goes on to discuss the issues concerning Joyce's (post)colonial status, one in which

dialogues with the British colonial past of Ireland can occur not only through specific allusions to great texts from British culture but through very subtle linguistic effects due, above all, to the fact that he is writing in the language of the British Empire. (145)

An example of this is Gabriel Conroy's famous "journey westward" from the end of "The Dead," an echo of *Twelfth Night* whose intertextuality points to the connectedness of the destabilization of gender roles and the logocentric foundations of Western metaphysics. Throughout, Joyce is seen to approach Shakespeare "not with awe and reverence but with scissors and paste in hand, ever alert for bits and pieces of discourse that he can coopt for use in constructing his own modern works" (156), a process of fragmentation resembling the one discussed from various positions by both Eliot and Virginia Woolf, and an irreverence paralleled to Stephen Greenblatt's new-historicist analysis of Shakespeare's play-texts in the context of the Elizabethan society of the spectacle (167). Bakhtin's puzzlingly stubborn rejection of Shakespeare and the drama genre as lacking polyphony further helps to unearth the embeddedness of various literary genres within specific ideologies, and to expose Joyce's subversive use of Shakespeare as demystifying the contemporary modernist views of the bard as a representative of an idealized "whole" past.

Finally, Joyce's relation to Dostoevsky departs from Joyce's praise recorded by Arthur Power[11] of the Russian as the creator of modern prose, and from Bakthin's observations on Dostoevsky's construction of the human subject as a product of social interactions (172-3). This is documented in particular detail by close analysis of the trial scene in *Brothers*

[11] Arthur Power, *Conversations with James Joyce,* ed. Clive Hart (London, Millington, 1974).

Karamazov, where the officialness of the legal discourse is undermined by its literariness, and which outspokenly refuses to provide an authoritative perspective on the events related. More broadly, "Dostoevsky's novels are filled with illustrations of the notion that subjectivity is at base a narrative phenomenon." Booker's example are *Devils*, where "the superfluous man Stavrogin is largely superfluous because he is unable to find an effective narrative in which to participate" (191). A parallel is made between the characters of Raskolnikov and Stephen Dedalus, an exchange which is read yet again as happening in both ways:

> When read through Joyce, even the ending of *Crime and Punishment*—often criticized as being an overly reductive expression of Dostoevsky's Christian message—becomes potentially subversive of that message. [...] Raskolnikov's move from historical to religious narratives closely parallels that of Stephen Dedalus in *Portrait*. (197-8)

Booker's conclusion, "Modernism, Postmodernism, Joyce," contextualizes his dialogical study within the contemporary discussions of (post)modernity. Joyce becomes "a crucial figure for any exploration of the interface between modernism and postmodernism," chiefly thanks to precisely his in-between position combining that of the high-aesthetic modernist and that of the subversive, parodic postmodernist, therefore undermining the often-voiced neo-Marxist critique of the supposed modernist apoliticism. Joyce is even linked with Brecht in that his writing resists "the common critical view that literary modernism reduces art to a self-contained system that attempts to avoid engagement with the real world and that such art shows an elitist concept for the masses and mass culture" (206). This view requires that Joyce be dissociated from his alignment with the high modernist writers:

> Joyce's work has thus been particularly ill-served by the tendency to regard him automatically as one of the highest of all high modernists and thereby to assume that he shares certain characteristics usually attributed to high modernism, even though Joyce's work in many ways differs radically from that of most writers. (227)

It follows then that the very opposing categories of modernism and postmodernism are restrained to be applied, not to literary texts or authors, but to reading strategies, to the "warping processes" of the *Wake*'s self-description: "Joyce's work is particularly relevant to this process because of the central importance of his own 'warping,' or rereading of his literary predecessors." It is for such "self-consciously constitutive readings" that Booker's book ultimately calls, since these are "our best means of ensuring that culture and literature remain alive" (229). It is precisely the kinds of readings that Booker's intertextual study provides.

VI

The 1996 collection of essays edited by R. Brandon Kershner, *Joyce and Popular Culture*,[12] provides a useful introduction to the entire field's theoretical framework. R. B. Kershner's "Introduction" opens with the bold assertion that , today "Joyce and popular culture is one of the most dynamic and fruitful areas of modernist study," reflecting "the new theoretical consensus that the writing of Joyce is part of a continuous cultural fabric" (1). The recentness of this popularity is ascribed to the influence exerted by both the Frankfurt school (Theodor Adorno and Max Horkheimer who saw "the total effect of the culture" as "one of anti-enlightenment" where "the progressive technical domination of nature becomes mass deception and is turned into a means for fettering consciousness") and the Leavisian New Critical school of literary criticism (which "saw popular culture as the most deadening aspect of modern industrialized society, an agent actively undermining the possibility of genuine selfhood and moral responsibility") (2-3). The re-focusing was begun by Leslie Fiedler in the mid-1950s U.S., whose "increasingly stringent and enthusiastic defenses of popular cultural forms such as the comic book" was however still a "less radical a break with academic tradition than it appeared" Its full-fledged consequences emerged in the semiotic structuralist turn taken in the Western Europe of the early 1970s which turned to description and interpretation rather than evaluation. At the same time, beginning with Ann Douglas' *The Feminization of American Culture*, feminism furthered the idea that "popular culture, and especially popular literature, was culturally coded as feminine" (6). Kershner then goes on to survey the work done in the context of cultural studies and Joyce, and concludes on a general note by claiming that "elite and popular culture presuppose one another and even at the height of the modernist movement exist in a peculiar symbiosis" and later that "the distinction between the two cultural levels begins to dissolve under increasing interrogation," an interrogation which is precisely the volume's objective (13).

Three essays have been chosen for discussion here, capturing as they do the overall tenor of the collection. Derek Attridge's "Theoretical Approaches to Popular Culture" identifies the main goal of cultural studies with resisting the danger "that the notion of a homogeneous 'modernism' can come to be used without careful scrutiny" by introducing a "careful discrimination among those artists who have been obliged by our taxonomic insistence to wear that reductive label." The distinctive feature of Joyce in this respect is the democratic nature of his recherché material — in the *Wake*, "the reader unfamiliar with 'Humpty Dumpty' loses as much as the reader unfamiliar with the *Scienza Nuova*." With this in mind, Attridge speaks of "a principle of accessibility" built into Joyce's work as a

---

[12] R. Brandon Kershner, ed., *Joyce and Popular Culture* (Florida: University Press of Florida, 1996).

result of his "refusing the cultural hierarchies that most of his readers take for granted" (24). Attridge's poststructuralist slant becomes outspoken in his emphasis on the necessity of the abandonment of "the fundamental presupposition that reading is an attempt at *textual mastery*," one way of which is "acknowledging that texts are always in contexts, that contexts are always themselves contextualized, and that contexts are never exhaustible or predictable" (25). Studies of popular culture then can aim to show, not that there is no general preference for easy-to-consume texts, but that "this preference is itself a textual product, a reflex of, among other things, consumer capitalism's demands for instant profit and the anti-intellectualism it fosters," and Attridge's personal belief is that "one of our goals as scholars and teachers of Joyce should be to dispel the idea that you have to be a specialist to understand and enjoy his work" (26).

Michael Walsh's "A(dorno) to (Ž)ižek: From the Culture Industry to the Joyce Industry, and Beyond" discusses two important tributaries to the general flow of debate within cultural studies—the works of Theodor Adorno and Slavoj Žižek. His opening contention that "modernism was coterminous with mass culture" stresses the opposition between "the affection of some modernist writers, composers, painters, sculptors, and film-makers for the materials of mass culture" and "the critical writers of the period whom we retrospectively imagine as theorists," most prominent of whom was undoubtedly Theodor Adorno (40). If his "contempt for the masses" is regarded as "distressing," his "contempt for the commodity" is found "pleasing," and his co-authored central work, *Dialectic of Enlightenment*, is seen as transcending its own period: "deeply marked by the Nazi annihilation of the German left, it nonetheless anticipates the defeat of fascism and was actually most influential after its republication in German in 1968 and its translation into English in 1972" (42). This belated impact enables Walsh to make a link to the much more recent attempt at conceptualizing popular culture from a psychoanalytic perspective—Slavoj Žižek's *Looking Awry: An Introduction to Jacques Lacan Through Popular Culture*, which pursues a Lacan "who does believe that reality is predicated on the signifier, but who also believes in something else, the Real, which defies signification." The Real in this account appears as having a twofold function: "In one sense, then, the Real is whatever is beyond signification; in another sense, it is the black hole around which signification is organized." Thus, the famous Lacanian dictum according to which "the Real is the impossible" is not to treat the real and the fictional as indistinguishable, but rather to regard both as effects of the signifier, which for Lacan "works to retrieve a reality from the impossible Real" (44). Žižek himself regards Lacan's Joycean neologism *sinthome* as "a fragment of the signifier permeated with idiotic enjoyment," "the meaningless letter that immediately procures 'jouis-sense,' 'enjoymeant.'" For Walsh then the ultimate relevance between Lacan's analysis of the psychotic language and Joyce studies consists in that both the

Lacanian "lalangue" and Joyce's *Finnegans Wake* "remind us that symbolization is always exceeded by what cannot be symbolized, that language as meaning is secondary or tributary to language as material" (46).

Donald Theall's "Joyce's Techno-poetics of Artifice" opens by proposing two ways of looking at "the problem of '*Ulysses* in progress'": to see its process of composition as either "a learning process in which Joyce discovers his dissatisfaction with the purely narrative structure of the earlier stages of writing" or "a means of constructing a work that, following its author's original conception, is designed to provide its own thread to its conceptual labyrinth," and which brings forth the reconceptualization of "a literary work as a semiotic machine designed for a world where verbal language is being displaced by a growing multiplicity of communication machines" (139). Theall relies on textual genetic research to support his thesis that "Joyce wished to construct *Ulysses* with a conscious recognition that the contemporary literary work of art is a machine," arguing that for example the notorious late insertion of the newspaper headings into the "Aeolus" chapter exemplify "this increased attention to the machinery of communication, and to other machinic motifs" (140).

What Theall's techno-cultural approach brings to the cultural studies of Joyce is a heightened awareness of Joyce's involvement with the technological advances of his age, and how this bears on his late chef-d'oeuvres. Thus, the very ground plans of *Ulysses* corroborate that "Joyce wished to establish the same close connections between various electromechanical, scientific, and technological processes in *Ulysses*," and further demonstrate how "the complex connections he worked out between the various electromechanical, scientific, and technological processes, the organs of the body, and the multiplicity of styles and symbols" coexist in the text (144). As well as discussing the way in which individual instances of technology make particularly marked appearances (for example, the mechanical clocks of 17.1674-78), Theall also observes that the language of the gesture (envisaged by Stephen as the future means of communication in "Circe") is "a language inscribed by and in the senses and sensitivity of all bodies, human, animal, or nonorganic," generating "lines of striation and differentiation in space-time that through their effects machinically produce significance, so that the Joycean intellectual imagination is grounded in the memory." This intellectual imagination also necessarily confines speech and writing to a merely partial status in the general field of rhetorical communication (149).

Theall concludes by dividing communication technologies into three groups: "traditional sign systems (hieroglyphs, alphabets, icons, drawings); technologically mediated modes of reproduction (books, telephones, film); and crafted modes of popular expression [...] (sermons, pantomimes, riddles, comics)," all of which "are copresent in one integrated semiotic system that is integrated through the remembered copresence of the mnemonic pyrotechnics of 'Ithaca' (the last words of Bloom) and 'Penelope' (Molly's last words on Bloom's days)." This copresence hinges on the "transverse mode of communication with the reader's memory," which traverses "the rhizomic labyrinth that is created by the surface of the text," what Theall calls "a poetic machine" (151).[13]

VII

The 1998 co-edited collection, *Re-Joyce. Text, Culture, Politics*,[14] contains an essay by Cheryl Herr, which despite its completely different focus, departs from Theall's examinations of the Joyce-technology interface. Her "Blue Notes: From Joyce to Jarman" analyzes Joyce's exposure to African-American music, particularly to "blues, swing, ragtime, spirituals and early jazz" and maps its influence of the language of *Finnegans Wake*, given the "affiliation between Irishness and blackness" which "was honed in the Afro-Hibernian crucible of the minstrel show, where Paddy and Sambo interchanged roles, creating a matrix of longing that encompassed both the Irish lament and the Delta blues" (211). Closely examining several individual cases, Herr remarks that the appearance of the blues within the *Wake* is generally accompanied by "a recognition of sensory changes accompanying modernization, the beginnings of technological change that Joyce imagined in the later body-invasive capacities." This synaesthetic, intermedial aspect of the *Wake* is seen as "one of the major educative aspects of Joyce's writing," tutoring us as it does "about evolving social relations" (212). Donald Theall's *Beyond the Word* is gratefully acknowledged as informing Herr's essay, although her approach is analytic rather than synthetic—if Theall maps how Joyce depicts media machines and the discourses surrounding them as shaping the supposedly "human" society, for Herr, *Finnegans Wake* "dramatizes a dialectic between phenomenology and technology, between the immediacies of 'flesh'-ly embodiment and the impact of the machine eye…on all aspects of that flesh-of-the-world" (216). Joyce's last work also comes to be seen as "an act of warding off blindness, just as it is also an embodiment of visual failure," thus sharing with the blues the same paradoxical logic where "mimicry becomes rescue and depressive affect transmutes to pleasure." However, in the *Wake*, "the body becomes ever more fully caught up in information networks that are both technologized and in the service of the state apparatus" (219).

VIII

Garry Leonard's *Advertising and Commodity Culture in Joyce*[15] is a sustained analysis of how what Leonard calls "the history of the now" as embodied by advertising and commodity culture challenges the official metanarratives of history, imperialism, or canonical art. Leonard's intro-

---

[13] For more on Theall's work, see Chapter IX "Techicity, Media & Hypertext," sections I-II.

[14] Herr, Cheryl, "Blue Notes: From Joyce to Jarman," *Re-Joyce.Text, Culture, Politics*, eds. John Brannigan, Geoff Ward and Julian Wolfreys (London: MacMillan Press Ltd., 1998).

[15] Garry M.Leonard, *Advertising and Commodity Culture in Joyce* (Miami: University of Florida Press, 1998).

duction opens by discussing even Stephen's aesthetic theory of the epiphany in terms of advertising, where *integritas, consonantia, claritas*, and *quidditas* all become qualities of an advertised product:

> The object with a soul in Stephen's aesthetic theory is—despite his refusal to see it in these terms—a commodity. [...] That which is repressed from aesthetic theory, in the interest of defining "timeless" beauty, returns as the epiphany, which redefines the object in terms of immediate response. (3)

Leonard's psychoanalytic slant[16] comes to the fore in his analysis of advertising and commodity in terms of desire, delusional self-fulfillment, and the Lacanian Real—as long as the ephemeral and the trivial are ignored by hegemonic discourses, they "offer a glimpse of the Real—that unrepresented reality excluded by language in order to make the word appear to be an exact equivalent of the world" (6). Joyce's "epic treatment of the trivial" renders him "our historian of the soon to be forgotten and the not yet historicized." It is precisely his concern with the ephemeral that in Leonard's opinion stands as "one of the central reasons his work continues to grow in importance as we struggle to understand our own time" (11).

The theoretical background of Leonard's discussion of advertising is provided by Louis Althusser (specifically, his concept of "interpellation" as a way of ideologically "calling out to" individuals which shapes them into prepackaged subjectivities), Michel de Certeau (his notion of "negotiation" according to which a subject is an active agent vis-à-vis ideology), and Jean Baudrillard (his concept of simulacrum in the age of the spectacle in particular). Leonard's thesis on this topic is that well before de Certeau and Baudrillard, "Joyce understood that advertisements and commodities offer to the subject a wonderfully seductive type of pleasure that might be construed as positive or even welcome" (13). Of much importance for Leonard's argument is also Lacan's central thesis postulating personal identity as centred around a lack, compensated for by a symbolic self-understanding and by a construction of the "myth of the self," as well as Foucault's theory of sexuality as "an effect of discourse," a way of controlling the subjects' strivings for pleasure. Advertising within this context appears to act as "a sort of software that permits us to organize and print out 'pleasure scenarios' featuring our 'selves' as the focal point of a symbol-generated experience of 'pleasure'" (16). The crucial objective of this eclectic approach is ultimately to demonstrate

> how Joyce's fiction consistently asserts that what is disposable, insignificant, ephemeral, dead, or forgotten may nevertheless—may especially—influence and shape our sense of reality and self more profoundly than those objects, texts, and images that have been designated as worthy representatives of eternal truth. (34)

---

[16] For Leonard's psychoanalytic work, see Chapter II "Psychoanalysis," esp. section V.

The first cultural intertext of Leonard's discussion is the one between advertising and religion, where "modern advertising's promise of completion, redemption, and the attainment of paradise is the equivalent of holy scripture for Joyce" (35). Thus, in the famous "Lotus-Eaters" episode in *Ulysses*, Bloom's visit to the Catholic mass is explicated strictly in terms of "its brilliant marketing strategy," and further paralleled with the slogan for Plumtree's potted meat, with its promise of the completion of "home" and bliss (44-5). This mythic aura of completeness attached to the commodity is then linked with what Baudrillard calls "the deterrence machine" of commodity culture, feeding as it does upon the aforementioned Lacanian lack at the basis of human subjectivity (49).

Leonard then proceeds to discuss the commodity objects in the *Dubliners* stories (especially "Araby" and "Clay"), the sexual monetary exchange of *A Portrait*, and finally Bloom's summary of his day in terms of listing all the items he has purchased. Against Fredric Jameson's famous analogy between contemporary experience and psychosis, both stripped of a sense of historical continuity and stuck in a perpetual present, Leonard places Stephen's notorious reference to Ireland as "a pawnshop" in *A Portrait*. For "indeed, a pawnshop is where commodities go to die— stripped of all illusion, no longer packaged, no longer artfully arranged on the shelf, bereft of all the aura produced by advertising" (68). The metaphor of the pawnshop therefore exposes how Joyce's Ireland is stuck, not in the present of the commodity, but in the past-ness of its own present postcoloniality (68).

Pornography presents another popular culture discourse in that it advertises as commodities none other than its female protagonists. Through the medium of photography which made possible "the production of easily affordable sexual images," pornography serves Leonard's argument as "an example of the extent to which pleasure may be seen as a construct with a constantly fluctuating history," rather than "an innate and ahistorical byproduct of subjective experience" (75). Leonard subjects to careful scrutiny Gabriel Conroy's erotic reverie which concludes "The Dead," read in the context of the gospel annunciation story, where, "the female body's 'involuntary confession'" is "sought after by the masculine libido," and, in Gabriel's case, pitiably misunderstood (80-1). The pornographic overtones of Virgin Mary's "immaculate conception" are brought home once her "Be it unto me according to thy word" is seen as complying with "the 'masculine' fantasies depicted in pornography" which, "far from ignoring woman's pleasure, seem obsessed with discovering what it is" (84).

The religious/pornographic dimension to advertising and commodity culture is explored further through the female protagonist of the "Nausicaa" chapter in *Ulysses*, Gerty MacDowell, whose "personality is a product" in that she "carefully advertises and packages her sexuality as a complex masquerade of femininity designed to attract a male consumer" (99). Through this activity, Gerty complies (whether consciously or not) with the "male-defined standard of femininity" which Lacan has called "The Woman" (100). As long as Gerty's "femininity" remains a masquerade (and a question worth pursuing is whether it can ever be anything else), masculinity, as embodied in the chapter by Bloom remains indefinable: this at least is how Leonard reads his famous unfinished sandwritten message "I AM A" (103). This practice of masquerading has, for Leonard, the undesirable effect of transmogrifying woman into "some mythical species, the existence of which a man believes in as a way to confirm the myth of himself," and thus rendering her "dependent on the regard of men to assure her she exists" (111). Gerty's masquerade is shown to be so successful as to cause Bloom's "typical sensitivity to suffering" to be "lulled to sleep by her performance," mistaking her grim familial conditions with the cheap-romance idealized versions from her reading. Bloom's analogy of women and horses, according to which "Getry's 'self'-esteem is completely dependent upon the value she imagines Bloom has fixed upon her," as well as Milly's and Molly's practice of "marketing themselves," both serve to support Foucault's observation that

> [s]exuality is not the most intractable element in power relations, but rather one of those endowed with the greatest instrumentality: useful for the greatest number of maneuvers and capable of serving as a point of support, as a linchpin, for the most varied strategies. (139)

Leonard's discussion then turns to Molly's use of the word *style*, which "denotes 'a way of being'" and "clearly forecasts the intricate integration of identity and commodity objects currently celebrated or denigrated as a 'lifestyle'" (143). Bloom's famous sentence about women being flowers, "the most powerfully seductive line Leopold Bloom has ever spoken to [Molly]," appears under Leonard's magnifying glass as an advertisement slogan "about her body that she considers to be a 'true thing'" (156). Molly's yearning for the experience of "what its like to be a man" is shown to be an echo of Sacher-Masoch's *Venus in Furs* where "[t]he central dynamic of Wanda and Severin's relationship [...] revolves around the complex playacting of a man and a woman who blur the line between who is laboring and who is 'spending'" (166). In this sense Leonard concedes there is a possibility that "Bloom, relative to the affair of Molly and Blazes, is a man more sinning than sinned against" (167). An even more obvious literary analogy, that of Molly's famous namesake Moll Flanders, reveals both characters as "fairly adept negotiators," yet ones who "have only their physical looks and acting abilities with which to barter." Thus, "the 'capital' of a woman's appearance within a patriarchal economy [...] represents capital that inevitably depreciates over the course of time, no matter how wisely it is invested" (172).

Leonard concludes by revisiting his point of departure—Stephen's aesthetics of epiphany—and offers a reframing of modernism, "not as a representation of modernity, but as a symptom of it," in the light of which

"Stephen's modernist aesthetics must be viewed within the urban context that gave rise to them" (192). A rationalization, in Bourdieu's words, "of an ethos though this pure aesthetic might be, and purified of all sensuous or sensible interest," it is ultimately this insistence on its own freedom from these, its existence within an "aesthetic commercial-free zone," that relates it to what it defines itself against. Or, in Leonard's words:

> If Stephen's perfect work of art resembles not only a perfect kiss, or a perfect confession, but also Bloom's perfect advertisement, then the impulse to pay or pray, consume or worship, to lust after or to long for, all have much in common. (207)

IX

If Leonard's analysis re-identified the religious for Joyce with the desired and the commodified, an approach to religion in Joyce coterminous with Leonard's, yet treating its subject matter from a distinctly different perspective, deserves at least a brief mention at this point. Wolfgang Streit's *Joyce/Foucault: Sexual Confessions*[17] opens by discussing Joyce's overt hostility to Freud's psychoanalysis, taking its subject matter from his remark to Ettore Schmitz: "if we need [psychoanalysis], let us keep to confession" (1). Streit maps the area of commonality between the institutions of psychoanalysis and confession as follows: "the one promises to relieve the patient of his symptoms, while the other promises to redeem the Catholic believer from the tortures of hell." Inscribed into Joyce's texts beginning with the poems of *Chamber Music* are "both sexual discourse and references to the underlying compulsion as basic structuring principles." Here, a parallel is drawn with Michel Foucault's seminal *History of Sexuality*, which begins with the sacrament of penance as an "archetypal form of a whole network of forces and powers enmeshing the modern Western subject and resulting in an ever expanding movement of sexual representation, primarily in language." Analogously,

> [f]rom the very beginning, Joyce constitutes sexual confession as a result of power effects, and subjects it to the fundamental criticism that is addressed by the conditional "if" in his talk with Schmitz. (2)

What Joyce and Foucault share then is an awareness (textually negotiated) of the power effects of the confessional institution. Foucault's investigation deals, not so much with the erotic or sexual way in which human beings use their bodies, but rather with "desire and the sex act as they are spoken of, as they become part of an epistemological sphere by virtue of that speaking, and hence are transformed into language or discourse" (4). Thus, *sexuality* is not to be understood as having to do with the human body at all, denoting instead the speech-related, discourse

---

[17] Wolfgang Streit, *Joyce/Foucault: Sexual Confessions* (Ann Arbor: The University of Michigan Press, 2002).

version of sex. Its inception is placed by Foucault in the year 1215, when the Catholic procedures for the sacrament of penance were codified at the Fourth Lateran Council, procedures with which "the search for individual truth shifted in emphasis from issues of ancestry and heredity to personal confession, including, of course, one's private sexual behavior."

Turning to Joyce, Streit contends that

> [t]hroughout Joyce's oeuvre, no doubt one of the most exciting results of the analysis of sexual confession is the unearthing of the narrative representation of this movement from the confessional toward the profane realm of everyday life. (5)

Drawing explicitly on the work done in the field of cultural studies (by authors such as Manganiello, Herr, Kershner, or Leonard), Streit's study "does not exactly follow New Historicists' cherished method and does not offer crisp historical tidbits," and still, "by concentrating on one specific theme firmly anchored in history and on one of the foremost modernist writer's awareness of its productive impact and his attempts at resisting it," its methodology does share certain key features with this critical movement. Its attention to historical detail can best be exemplified by Streit's close analysis of the particularly Irish status of confession-as-institution, in which the 1885 *Maynooth Catechism* "permeated the lives of Irish Catholics with the imperative to reveal their sins" (7). Thus, throughout Streit's approach,

> the meaning of sexuality does not lie in opinions expressed by figures, or in obvious *contents*; the point is rather to reconstruct the specific *forms* in which, say, the various stances to the obligation to confess are expressed in speech-forming patterns or "orders" within the discourse of sexuality. (10)

From a structuralist perspective, Foucault's most interesting gesture in his *History of Sexuality* is his combination of the synchronous analysis of the structure of meaning within the discourse of sexuality with the diachronic examination of the development of its power: "Foucault tips sexuality, reconstructed as a horizontal table of meaning, onto a chronologically vertical corridor that traces the expansion of power" (11).

Streit's study of Joyce re-enacts this gesture by treating the individual works as already diachronic, in dialogue (whether confessional or not) with their preforms and inner transformations. After an initial discussion of *Chamber Music*, Streit's discussion of "The Sisters" focuses on its two publication variants (the late addition of the first paragraph being the most prominent difference), his analysis of *A Portrait* is conducted with an eye on *Stephen Hero*, and *Exiles* is treated in connection with *Giacomo Joyce*. Most fruitfully, Streit deals with *Ulysses* in its Gabler edition[18] which fa-

---

18 For more, see Chapter X "Textual Criticism & Textual Genetics," sections II-III.

cilitates a deeper diachronic understanding of the various versions of the text. In light of the complexity of the manuscripts, Streit's concluding analysis of *Finnegans Wake* and its thematization of "sexual uncertainty," is restricted to the published text. However, beyond their manuscripts or preforms, Joyce's works do exhibit a striking degree of mutual self-reference or re-writing:

> Just as narrative structures are re-actualized, according to Gabler, the cyclical form of the last chapter of *Ulysses* foreshadows the structure of *Finnegans Wake*; characters from *Dubliners* are adopted in *Ulysses*; or, in the case of Stephen, the character is transferred from *Stephen Hero* to *A Portrait*, in order to be rewritten for *Ulysses* in "Proteus." (11)

Carrying out its rigorous analysis of a motif running the length of Joyce's oeuvre from a fresh theoretical perspective, Streit's study presents the most sustained attempt to date at confronting Joyce with one of the key theoreticians and practitioners of cultural studies, Michel Foucault.

X

Volume 15 of *European Joyce Studies*, edited by R. Brandon Kershner, was entirely devoted to *Cultural Studies of James Joyce*[19] and presented an evaluation of the current state of the cultural debate within Joyce studies — it therefore makes a suitable point of conclusion for the present examination.

Kershner's introduction provides an historical introduction to the broader field different from that of his 1996 edited collection (see above), and thus deserves to be discussed here. Kershner begins with a familiar caveat that "no very clear definition or exhaustive description of the critical approach called cultural studies is available to us" to compensate for this definitional lack with identifying the crucial incentive for the popularity of the field as such:

> cultural studies makes available to the humanities a wealth of material that previously has been ignored or thought inappropriate for humanistic study, and brings to bear upon them techniques and methods developed during the rise of structuralism and poststructuralism. (10)

Kershner goes on to identify the familiar American/English divide in the theoretical conceptualization of the field, where the latter, under the forming influence of the Birmingham Centre for Contemporary Cultural Studies, took its theoretical anchorage in Marx and was marked by a leftist social activism, accepting only gradually (and sometimes reluctantly) the impact of French theory, while the former, informed by the Frankfurt School (and its seminal analysis of popular culture, Horkheimer and Adorno's *Dialectic of Enlightenment*), was heavily inflected by Continental thinkers throughout. However, during the 1970s and 80s, the divide petered out, with the

---

[19] R. Brandon Kershner, ed., *Cultural Studies of James Joyce* (Amsterdam: Edition Rodopi, 2003).

presence of Althusser, Barthes, Foucault, and Bakhtin achieving an informing status for both branches. In addition to these demi-gods of theory, Pierre Bourdieu's notion of "cultural capital" and his demystifying analysis of "taste," Jean Baudrillard's treatment of contemporary society as constituted by "simulacra," Julia Kristeva's blend of deconstruction with Freudianism, Michel de Certeau's broad examination of "everyday life," particularly in its "spatiality"—all these have proven immensely useful theoretical tools for examining modern and postmodern culture. Kershner is quick to add that

> [b]ehind all these figures, of course, is Jacques Derrida, whose interrogation of signification gave impetus to the entire poststructuralist enterprise and the correction of what now looks like idealist naiveté in earlier attempts at cultural analysis. (13)

Under this variegated influence of the polyvocal structuralist and poststructuralist critical theory, Kershner observes, the current cultural studies, despite its indefinability, does obtain a common denominator—its interest in "cultural practices and their relationship to power, with the intention of laying bare the ordinarily invisible conduits through which power flows," from which follows that "any criticism undertaken under the rubric of cultural studies should bespeak political commitment" (14).

In this respect, Kershner considers it unnecessarily limiting, or even crippling, to regard Joyce as "relevant to cultural studies only insofar as he and his work remain as a significant sign in today's cultural network," and sees this misconception as springing from "a denial of the way in which the evolving study of history over the past twenty years or so has impacted literary-critical studies" (14-5). Among the most influential developments of this period, often underestimated, Kershner discerns the French school of the *Annales* (and its recent turn to what Roger Chartier and others term *mentalités*) and New Historicism, or what its leading exponent Stephen Greenblatt preferred to call *cultural poetics*. On a general note, Kershner observes the striking degree to which

> the contributing strands that make up cultural are suited to discussion of Joyce: postcolonialism, feminism, gender studies, Marxism, cybernetics, popular/high culture investigations, and (yes, even) the New Historicism have all been extremely visible aspects of Joyce criticism over the past twenty years or so. (16)

The present collection, then, aims to "cover a broad area of contemporary Joyce criticism, not all of it strictly cultural studies (if indeed there is such a thing as strictly cultural studies criticism)" (18). For example, already the opening piece, Paul Saint-Amour's "Over Assemblage: *Ulysses* and the *Boîte-en-Valise* from Above" engages formally in what resembles deconstructionist typographical play to discuss the aesthetics of *cento* in both Joyce's novel and Marcel Duchamps' famous artwork. It is its historical grounding, shared by the following essay, "Stephen and the Venus of Praxiteles: the Backside of Aesthetics" by Valérie Bénéjam, the art-historical slant of which is combined with its treatment of nudity as a reluctantly accepted cultural theme, that justifies their inclusion in a cultural studies collection.

Margot Norris' "Critical Judgment and Gender Prejudice in Joyce's 'A Mother'" sets out to rescue the story's protagonist, Mrs. Kearney, from the prevalent critical readings that condemn her on the basis of the narrative's own condemnation of the *strong* woman. In doing so, Norris departs from a particularly insightful reading delivered by Joseph Valente[20] which deploys Jean-Francois Lyotard's notion of the *differend* as that which resists narration in order to discuss the story as the intersection of two forms of *differend* — the colonial and the sexual, while taking a different outlook on the sustainability of Mrs. Kearney's gender grievance that is regarded as possible, "if not inside the narrative then nonetheless extra-textually or critically" (79). Norris commences her own discussion of the story by identifying the critical dilemma posed by the weak male management of the strong woman:

> The difficulty with adjudicating this question is that the narration prevents the reader from approaching it impartially. A double judgment upon Mrs. Kearney is already inscribed into the narration both on the textual level of narrative event or plot and on the level of its telling. Indeed, the narrator pronounces judgment of Mrs. Kearney before the events unfold, thereby confronting us with a pre-judgment or prejudiced introduction to the case. (81-2)

Thus, even before the narration of the events taking place at the *Eire Abu* concert unfold, "Mrs. Kearney has already been condemned by the narrator not for what she says or does, but simply for what she is." In order to counteract this prejudice, Norris proposes to analyse the story backwards, "beginning with its ending when the negative judgment of Mrs. Kearney has been universally confirmed and approved" (83). Norris does this by means of the shared agency of Mr. Hendrick and Mr. Burke, the figures of reviewer and moral critic at the end of the story, whose conduct (what they *do*), as opposed to their presentation within the narrative (what is *said* about them), reveals "various contaminants of disinterested judgment" (84). Once the narrator's pre-judgment of the issue and attempt to adjudicate the labour dispute on its merits are set aside, "a much more problematic case emerges," one in which (and here Norris quotes Gifford's annotations) it is "Mrs. Kearney's violation of [an] *unstated* assumption about the improvisatory nature of economic agreements in the theatrical and concert worlds" that causes her condemnation (87, my italics). It is precisely this "unstatedness" that reduces the central dispute

---

[20] Joseph Valente, "Joyce's Sexual Different: An Example from *Dubliners*," *James Joyce Quarterly* 28:2 (Winter 1991).

to the realm of a *differend* for Valente, and which requires of Norris a final twist:

> We might give this reading of "A Mother" as a performance of gender prejudice a final twist by returning it to the specificity of Joyce's history, and by asking why Joyce would have turned his own most triumphant concert appearance into a performative allegory of gender injustice in the artistic and cultural marketplace? (88)

In this light, Joyce is seen as a socialist artist pondering the riddle of how artists may earn a living from their work, anxieties with are discovered to be prophetic of "a future experience when in 1912 Joyce would suffer the indignity and agony of a violated contract at the hands of George Roberts of Maunsel & Company" (88). In sum, Joyce's text stages gender as his "*lens* or *filter* for exploring the confounding of strength and weakness in the arena in which art, justice, and politics intersect" (89).

Two essays interrelate in their shared focus on the issue of the social control of madness and insanity, the one in the context of feminist studies, the other within the critical focus on Joyce's postcolonial condition. Tracey Teets Schwarze's "Female Complaints: 'Mad' Women, Malady, and Resistance in Joyce's Dublin," uses Elaine Showalter's feminist re-reading, in her *The Female Malady: Women, Madness and English Culture* of Michel Foucault's groundbreaking study, *Madness and Civilization: A History of Insanity in the Age of Reason*, in order to theoretically inform her critical discussion of Joyce's depiction of socially restrained women:

> Though Joyce does not allow any of his "nervous" women to be institutionalized in the sense of locking them away in lunatic asylums, he certainly does reveal their lives to be circumscribed by the inevitable scepter of male authority: husbands, fathers, priests, and popes preside over Victorian and Edwardian institutions with enough ideological power to shut women up as the asylum. (94)

Surveying the era's psychiatric discourse of insanity, Schwarze notices a clear-cut gender division:

> While Victorian psychiatrists theorized quite inconsistently about the causes of insanity in men, they were much more willing to confidently diagnose the "female malady." The female reproductive system was the culprit, according to the prevailing view: it affected women's nervous systems and rendered them more vulnerable to mental illness, creating a condition nineteenth-century physicians called "reflex insanity." (98)

What informs specifically Joyce's depictions of aberrant female behaviour though is the "theory that the body communicates, through the unconscious manifestation of hysterical symptoms, that which the voice cannot speak or cannot make heard," articulated with most momentum in Freud's and Breuer's work on hysteria (101). A glance at *Ulysses* and the *Wake* reveals their female protagonists as sharing "acts of defiance: Molly's affair with Blazes Boylan and ALP's quittance of her still-sleeping husband." However, "other women in Joyce's works appear much less capable of this kind of insubordination," and it is to these women speaking through their bodies that Schwarze devotes the crucial part of her argument (102).

Her two examples of Joyce's "foreground[ing] the plight of the emotionally distraught female" are "Eveline" and "A Painful Case," the former revealing "the plethora of male-orchestrated narratives at work in a young Dublin woman's life" (108), the latter dealing with "the ideological constraints Victorian relationships placed on women" (111). More specifically, in her reading of "Eveline," Schwarze shifts the focus from the recent critical attention to Frank's possible misrepresentation of his life in Argentina to what she terms the "narrative of entrapment," which "is not constructed around the veracity of Frank's claim to a home in Buenos Ayres," but rather represents Joyce's "most evident repudiation of the confinement that turn-of-the-century marriage mandated to women" (109). "A Painful Case," then, represents a case in point of what Schwarze has postulated as female speaking through her body, exemplified by Emily Sinico's desperate attempt to "make herself heard within the confines of this male-authored space" (111). In her gesture of catching Duffy's hand and pressing it to her cheek,

> Mrs. Sinico either has misunderstood him or has acted on an impulse independent of him; either way she is no longer capable of mirroring "Duffy" because she has dared to project "Emily." (112)

Taken together, both Schwarze's theoretical and textual analyses participate in the recent "shifting Joyce's studies toward the view that Joyce also portrays the lives of real women and men, rather than merely depicting archetypal figures." However, what is at stake in Joyce's short stories is not only the issue of a faithfully executed mimesis, but a clearly conceived critical engagement:

> Joyce's disturbed and disturbing women do not go quietly. In what may be his most powerful indictment of patriarchal structures, Joyce refuses to shut these women away from public view; they are neither quietly assimilated into the trappings of domesticity nor are they elided and forgotten by the text. Instead, they remain a haunting presence in his Dublin, a permanent and profoundly unsettling testament to the forces of social authority that confine them. (115)

The novelty of Cheryl Herr's "The Erratics of Irishness: Schizophrenia, Racism, and *Finnegans Wake*" lies in its departure from the numerous discussions of the relation between the language of schizophrenia and *Wakese*, centred as they are mostly around the role of Lucia or Issy in its motivation, and its attempt to interrogate schizophrenia as part of the persistent cultural stereotype of equating Irishness with mental illness. In this light, Herr begins by insisting that the Wakean "schizophrenesis," Joyce's own term for the style of his writing,

> must be viewed as an ironic commentary on the colonial stereotyping of Irishness that pulsed throughout eighteenth, nineteenth, and twentieth-century life on the island. (117)

Herr traces the genealogy of this stereotype back to the famous 1731 pronouncement of Jonathan Swift who "gave what little wealth he had / To build a house for fools and mad / To show by one satiric touch / No nation needed it so much." Less amusing, however, are the 1961 and 1968 WHO reports ascertaining that the Irish have the highest "hospitalization treatment rate for mental illness in the world" (119-20). Surveying the many medical, sociological, and historical accounts of and explanations for this phenomenon, Herr observes that

> there seems to be something in the Irish situation that combines with a genetic or other physical predisposition to mark the body in the distinctive ways characteristic of schizophrenia—with passivity and loss of volition; with overexcited, incongruous, or flattened affect; with dream-like and lethargic posing; with staring facial grimaces; and with other disturbances in bodily movements and repose. (123)

Turning to Joyce-the-man and the *Wake*, Herr establishes that "given the sufferings of his daughter, Joyce was himself intimately familiar with all manner of diagnostic tools and psychiatric theories in his time," most certainly acquainted with Emil Kraepelin's and Eugen Bleuler's work on "the oddities of schizophrenic language" (125). However, Joyce's achievement in the *Wake*, Herr emphasizes, tended toward neither an indication of a genetically produced disorder in himself/Lucia, nor a representation of his narrative/narrator as schizophrenic. Rather, Joyce's aim was

> to force upon the reader the experience of living within a linguistic field that systematically conditions her into the polysemous world inhabited by some schizophrenic patients. (126)

More particularly, the Letter passage, especially its exegesis by Shaun's alienating, dissociated medical discourse on the putatively Irish problem (*FW* 123), illustrates his acute awareness of schizophrenia as a disease stereotypically attributed to the Irish. Joyce's deployment of the "schizo" in the *Wake* is seen as taking place "some steps beyond deconstruction, where rupture and resistance produce a new cultural unconscious, structured as a different language, the vocabulary, syntax, and even grammar of which we cannot master" (129). One obvious candidate for this "not-yet" language would for Joyce be (with reference to Declan Kiberd) Irish in that "Joyce's insistence in the *Wake* on a degree of illegibility has much to do with positing the Irish social mind and social body as based firmly in the Irish language—that is, as contrary to Anglification" (130). Thus,

> [a]lthough Joyce is known to have had no great love for the Irish language, *Finnegans Wake* is full of Irish vocabulary and expression; Joyce was fully aware of the Gaeltacht as a space of alternative syntax and hence of alternative perception and strategies of verbal interaction. (133)

The example of Joyce's involvement with the peculiarity of the Irish language in lacking a word for the negative against the background of the 1882 Maamtrasna murders and the fate of the Irish-speaking Myles Joyce reveals the whole corpus to be

> penetrated and palimpsested by what the light writes, the capacity to "know" (hallucinate) instead of "no" (negate). So it is that Derrida has famously located ten categories or modalities of the word *yes* in Joyce, a kind of implosion of the Irish language's lack of the direct affirmative. (134)

Herr's informed and well-researched paper does not ultimately contend that no one in Ireland suffers from officially diagnosable disorders such as schizophrenia: it interrogates a critique of "mental colonialism implicit (and often explicit) in *Finnegans Wake*." One of the concluding paradoxes of Herr's argument is the way "the same language that so distressed [psychiatrists] in *Finnegans Wake* has been repeatedly claimed by Derrida as the inspiration for much that we have come to call deconstruction" (136).

The editor's piece, Kershner's "Playing for Keeps: *Exiles* and University College Dublin," as well as the concluding essay of the collection, Thomas A. Vogler's "James Joyce Meets Tank Girl," are both historically oriented and contextualize different points of particular importance, and will therefore only be touched on briefly here. For the sake of completeness, suffice it to say that Kershner's essay addresses the dynamics at the UCD of 1912 in relation to Richard Rowan's application for a professorship, the utter unlikelihood of which (given the contemporary state of affairs) seems to suggest a degree of Robert Hand's manipulation hitherto unnoticed by Joyce criticism, while Vogler considers the popular Tank Girl comics, focusing on a four-issue series of the comic called *Tank Girl: The Odyssey*, and provides some detailed comparisons with Joyce's novel and Homer's epic.

The other two remaining papers however deserve a careful examination, since both in their different ways present important new critical vistas on the whole framework of cultural studies, one from the viewpoint of Joyce's discursive involvement in the breakneck technological advances of his era and, more importantly, the technological nature of his writing, the other approaching the culture and ideology of modernity from a rigorously psychoanalytic perspective. Thomas J. Rice's "His Master's Voice and Joyce" explores the impact of the "talking machine" on the narrative presence of voice in *Ulysses*, to demonstrate that "Joyce was alive and responsive to both the aesthetic and the commercial challenges offered by the contemporary technology of sound reproduction." Rice's point of departure is his account of Walter Benjamin's "The Work of Art in the Age of Mechanical Reproduction" which attempts to do full justice to what it identifies as "the equivocal nature of Benjamin's response to the technology of reproduction or to the limitations in his analysis introduced by his nearly exclusive focus on visual media" (149), an equivocalness that lies in the way Benjamin's progressivist claims are found "tinged with a melancholia" located at "the heart of Benjamin's critical vision" (150). This melancholia is in turn connected to Benjamin's bemoaning, the end of the art of storytelling in another essay entitled "The Storyteller," which he regards as occasioned by the technological change occurring in modernity, and manifested in the literary realm by the rise of the novel. However, as Rice observes,

> [w]hat Benjamin elides in this argument is the fact that his recognition of the new beauty in the purportedly dying oral tradition is itself a concomitant symptom of the technological development of sound recording. (151)

In relation to Joyce and modernity, then,

> Benjamin's saturnine temperament, his conviction of the "impossibility of recovering what was lost," prevents him from recognizing that the age of mechanical reproduction brought to artists like Joyce a new awareness of the beauty that had vanished in the silent reading of the printed text; rather than disappearing, the voice of the storyteller becomes immediate in the "talking machine" of the new modernist novel. (152)

Rice's argument concentrates on Joyce's strategy of "approximating the heretofore unrepresentable sound of animals, non-human voices, in *Ulysses*" (153). To Rice's mind, "no one has put a name of Joyce's representation of such sounds in written text," and although one might here refer to Attridge's excellent discussion of non-lexical onomatopoeia,[21] which also includes an analysis of several of the textual instances mentioned here, Rice's technological outlook on this issue remains singular:

> We should probably call Joyce's orthographical strategy "phonography" or "gramophony," could we free these two terms from their immediate association with the mechanical reproduction of sound, misnomers that were already in general use by the beginning of the twentieth century. (154)

Derrida's Frankfurt symposium address is an obvious point of reference here, mentioning as it does "Joyce's 'dream of a reproduction which *preserves*' writing 'in the liveliest voice' as his 'gramophone effect,'" but Derrida's interest is in the ways Joyce's submerged voice can be heard in the text, and not in the particularly technological nature of this gramo-

---

[21] For Attridge's *Peculiar Language*, see Chapter I "Deconstruction," section V.

phonic writing (155). Rice follows both the invention (Edison's phonograph) and marketing ("His Master's Voice" trademark of the Victor Talking Machine Company) of technology in its historical particularity, in whose context Joyce's "gramophony" in *Ulysses* appears to be "his competitive attempt to realize the audio potential of the heretofore silent text of writing, to create a book that can be listened to, in a sense, as well as read, and thus to preserve more than the 'mental emanations of [his] brain.'" The cat's "Mkgnao" in the opening of "Calypso" heralds for the reader "Joyce's strategic representation of sound in text, his new technology of gramophonic sound reproduction" (161).

Throughout his paper, Rice relies on Friedrich Kittler's historical and theoretical assessment of the impact of technology upon the modern human sensibility. The phonograph, Kittler observes, "permitted for the first time the recording of vibrations that human ears could not count, human eyes could not see, and writing hands could not catch up with." To support this assertion, Rice adduces an account in Francis Arthur Jones, Thomas Alva Edison's biographer, of "one enterprising animal linguist's efforts to decipher [...] the speech of cats" by means of his utilization of the cutting-edge sound-recording technology (162). Joyce's accomplishment in *Ulysses*, Rice concludes, consists in his

> poising the readers [...] in the position of listening to the sound of the animal's voice, among the multiple voices and noises that resound in his book. It is now a commonplace to remark Joyce's mastery of many stylistic voices in his composition of *Ulysses*, to which we now add his representation of animal voice. (164)

Garry Leonard's paper, "Hystericising Modernism: Modernity in Joyce," departs from some of Leonard's previous observations on commodity and popular culture (see above), yet rethinks these from a particular psychoanalytic perspective, and within the wider context of modernism and modernity. Leonard begins by proposing that "the corollary of 'the age of anxiety' can be seen when we think of modernity as 'the age of the object,'" a corollary resulting from the way "the lack of assumed faith in transcendental certitude" has come to "put much pressure on secular object to serve as confirmation of identity and self-worth" (167-8). This process is reflected in how "objects become more and more animated as subjects feel less and less the center of cognition and the origin of meaning," and also in the corresponding way in which the twentieth-century theory of the object has become increasingly fractured—Leonard mentions "the object relation theory of Melanie Klein, the *objet a* of Lacan, the commodity of Marx and Benjamin, the 'thing' of Heidegger" (168). The innumerable examples of a Joyce character behaving in a consumerist fashion, buying or selling a commodity, or being under the influence of advertising, are too numerous to require reiteration here; what is noteworthy, however, is the conception of modernism Leonard teases out as their possible implication:

Modernism, as aesthetic theory, appears to try and find a middle ground between two different "modernities." But where these two modernities intersect is the object. The center of the onion of Stephen's theory of the
epiphany is a basket hanging in a marketplace, selected "at random," and
while he is at pains to say the language of the marketplace is not the language of literature, it is he who combines them in his aesthetics. Arguably,
this forging of modernism as a middle ground between the commodified
modernity of the marketplace and the supposedly private modernity of the
self-reflective "individual," is right there in the start in the concept of
Baudelaire's *flaneur*. (171)

By pointing to Breton's citation of Rimbaud's contention, "It is wrong to
say: I think. One should say I am thought," Leonard displays his Lacanian
position on human subjectivity as externally constructed rather than internally given. In other words, self-consciousness, in Lacan's theory, is "no
longer the conscious Cartesian arrangement of objects," but rather an
arrangement of "what the objects stimulate into something coherent, and
then the misrecognition of this coherency as intrinsic subjectivity" (172).

Coterminous with this dissolution of subjectivity is the rise of thought
that marks modernism's heritage within the field of critical theory: structuralism. Thus, part of the overall project of Leonard's essay is to "situate
Joyce's brand of modernism within the triangle of 'imperial,' 'semicolonial,' and 'colonial' subjects" (174). Within this framework then it is the
disintegration of imperialism and the subsequent de-colonization that
compel "imperial subjects" to turn "to the mysterious manipulation of
objects in order to effect a sense of internal coherence" (175). Leonard
then goes on to document exhaustively the various examples of such
manipulation in *Dubliners*, in the light of which modernity appears

> the fierce attempt to affirm identity and power over objects in the face of
> the impossibility of doing so, even as the amount and variety of objects in-
> viting us to try, escalates with unprecedented rapidity. If the "post-
> Imperial" subject eventually enters into this paradox, Joyce's "semi-
> Colonial" subject had already been surviving in this liminal world for some
> time. (177)

This "semi-colonial" mode, for Leonard, is "a way to think about any
historical crisis in white subjectivity," such as that of the Irish, "white"
people who "lost the social and economic privileges presumably guaran-
teed by 'whiteness,' and the British found themselves, later, unexpectedly
disinherited from this same assumption" (178). Leonard lists three "oddities" concerning the "Irish Question": whiteness (questioned or repressed
in the colonizer's racist discourse), the religion of the oppressed —
Catholicism, and consequently, its importance as a market for British
products (in a way neither India nor Africa could ever be), and thus a
primary target for, appropriately advertised, commodity culture. The particular balefulness of commodity objects to the situation of the semi-
colonial subject is due to "the way they appear to offer unexpected relief

from the daily tedium of social oppression and occasional self-loathing, but when the purchase is lost, or not made, or not right, the subject's ordinary defenses are in [...a] disarray," as Gerty McDowell's example shows very lucidly (182-3). In Lacanian terms, "there is something especially treacherous about 'the Other' in relation to whim the semi-colonial subject strives to experience a sense of identity" (184). These sudden lapses into the despair of non-signification are exemplified by the little boy in "The Sisters," Stephen's Cork epiphany, or Bloom's terror at the clouded Sun. Or, in yet another bird's-eye view of the *Dubliners* collection:

> There is no aspiration to rationality, nor even a confidence in a "prevailing economic system" for the semi-colonial people of Joyce's Dublin, and so the "mass ornaments" are broken (the harmonium in "Eveline," the chalice in "The Sisters"), enigmatic (the photograph in "Eveline"), missing (the corkscrew in "Clay"), destabilizing (the saucer of clay in "Clay"), lost (Maria's plumcake), or unimaginable (the non-purchase in "Araby"). (187)

Slavoj Žižek's observation about the "individual" and the "commodity" sharing their constitution as "effects of relationship," is seen as particularly apt for the post-Imperial condition, "where the 'immediate property' of an identity as an imperial subject is dwindling from the outside world, even as it is being shored up within." This process of shoring up commodities around oneself inevitably results in fetishism, aiming to offset the growing sense of alienation. However, Leonard concludes by observing that "sooner or later, when you play the game of fetishization, someone slips in the clay saucer, and you're confronted, once again, with whatever the game was designed to hide" (188).

Written in 2003, Leonard's paper did not bother to even reference the source of the deployed category of the "semi-colonial," which his essay theorizes quite originally and independently, so common had it become during the course of the 1990s to speak of Joyce's work in terms of the categories of the "colonial," "postcolonial," "post-imperial," or, in an appropriately Joyceanized manner, "semi-colonial." This should be seen as symptomatic of the general shift, culminating in the course of the 1980s and early 1990s, in sociological, historical, cultural, as well as literary theory, to issues related to the postcolonial condition of a major part of the world, whose critical and artistic voices were only gradually beginning to be heard in the Occident. The next chapter will outline precisely these concerns with the postcolonial aspects of Joyce's artistic career.

5. Postcolonialism

I

The "Irish turn" in Joyce studies of the 1990s was launched at their very beginning in the 1990 *Cambridge Companion*[1] containing Seamus Deane's essay "Joyce the Irishman," which opens by boldly asserting that although "Joyce's repudiation of Catholic Ireland and his countering declaration of artistic independence are well-known," he nevertheless "was formed by the Ireland he repudiated and his quest for artistic freedom was itself shaped by the exemplary instances of earlier Irish writers" who had "failed to achieve the independence which was at once the precondition and the goal of writing" (31). Among Joyce's Irish precursors rank prominently James Clarence Mangan, Joyce's preoccupation with whom displays betrayal as his obsessive manner of reading the Irish past, and Oscar Wilde, another example of Joyce's "translating an author into his own image" through his recognition of the issue of representation thematized in his *Dorian Gray* as "critical for the Irish artist" (35).

Deane proceeds to show how Joyce's concern with the specific restrictions placed upon his art by his own Irishness informs his writing. Thus, in his correspondence with Grant Richards, Joyce aims to persuade him that his *Dubliners* was "about a city that still had not been presented, or represented, to the world" (40), and his *Portrait* is marked throughout with Stephen's search for a unique mode of representation marked with "the notion of self-authorship, creation of one's self by becoming one's own father" (47), which belies Stephen's dream of origin that can never be realized. *Ulysses*, for Deane, is as concerned as is *Dubliners* with failure, with "the semiotic systems of Dublin, Irish history, literature," all of which are "read under the sign of betrayal which, while it exposes, does not reveal" (49). The *Wake* is marked with the belief that "the Irish had dreamt in their own language and then betrayed the dream into the English language in such a manner that the original had been lost, misread," and its Wakese takes the other direction of bringing English and as many other languages as is manageable "back to the literary equivalent of the Indo-European from which they had all sprung" (51-2). The peculiarity of the Wakean translation consists in the fact that "the text is never re-

[1] Derek Attridge, ed., *The Cambridge Companion to James Joyce* (Cambridge: Cambridge University Press, 1990).

vealed," that "this translation does not translate"—any recursion to an originary original is found to pursue an ever-receding mirage:

> The thousands of proper names in the text are so interwoven that even the minutest knowledge of Irish affairs [...] does not legitimize [...] a reading of the text as a version of Irish history in a Babylonian dialect. Names specify, but these names also typify. (52)

As early as *Dubliners*, possible readings as well as possible misreadings are purposefully implanted within the text, thus attesting to the obsessiveness of treachery as fundamental to his practice of writing—as for the Dublin represented by Joyce, Deane voices some necessary misgivings: "perhaps he was the first to represent it; or perhaps he was the first to show that it was not representable." Joyce is therefore ultimately taken as part of the larger cultural process of artistic remodelling of the idea of Ireland, in which "the country and culture he repudiated was also the country and culture he reimagined"—an absence that could become a presence (53).

II

However, the *crescendo* within the critical projects of bringing Joyce home such as Deane's notwithstanding, the field of postcolonial studies of Joyce had remained still relatively quiet by the mid-1990s, when a postcolonial bomb exploded in Enda Duffy's *The Subaltern Ulysses*.[2] Quite literally so (at least within the text), for Duffy opens his introduction with the question of whether there is anything an IRA bomb and Joyce's *Ulysses* might have in common, a metaphorical analogy that underlies his overall project of uncovering what he terms a postcolonial modernism, which aims

> to reclaim *Ulysses* [...] for Irish readers as *the* text of Ireland's independence, and by doing so, return it to readers everywhere as a novel preoccupied, in ways not suspected heretofore by its metropolitan critics, with both the means by which oppressed communities fight their way out of abjection and the potential pitfalls of anti-colonial struggles. (1)

In Duffy's view, it is not only the content, but also the period of the book's composition, "the crucial years of modern Irish history," which renders it nothing less than "*the* book of Irish postcolonial independence" (2). The strategies by which Joyce's text achieves this status is its constant emphasis on "mechanisms of the colonial regimes of surveillance and the panoptic gaze, as well as the secrecy they generate," exposing "nationalism and other chauvinist ideologemes of 'imagined community' chiefly as inheritances of the colonist regime of power-knowledge they condemn," and finally mocking "imperial stereotypes of the native" while "delineating their insidious interpellative power" (3). The most important

---

[2] Enda Duffy, *The Subaltern "Ulysses"* (Minneapolis: University of Minnesota Press, 1994).

of the questions raised by Duffy's project concerns the origin of postcolonial writing and its relation to literary modernism, a question answerable
by critical attention to a wide gamut of matters including "the particular
role of marginal national literatures within a supposed high modernist
monolith," "the parallels between guerrilla violence...and modernist textuality," the perception of modernism's treatment of common materials of
metropolitan culture, and finally, "the ways in which modernist textual
excess, and its mirror image in carnivalesque 'displaced abjection,' might
appear when transmuted from western literatures into their postcolonial
counterparts" (4).

Duffy proceeds to contextualize his postcolonial modernism with the
Jamesonian theory of a three-stage development of history/narrative,
according to which realism belongs to the moment of local or national
capitalism, modernism, to monopoly capitalism (or, imperialism), and present-day postmodernism, to our contemporary era of multinational capital.
The postcolonial in Joyce would then have to do with "filling the space of
and cries of the revolution's victims" (7), and its aesthetic problem would
be what Edward Said terms "adjacency," denoting the in-between space
between the ground of real experience and its aesthetic representation. In
this light, the adjacency between "the violence erupting in Ireland while
the novel was being written" and its complex homologization "by the
modernist textual strategies of estrangement" allows one to "read *Ulysses*
as a covert, cautious 'guerilla text'" (10).

Duffy goes on to survey Joyce's Irish politics in the examined period,
suggesting most contentiously that it is "Joyce's interest in Irish affairs"
which "might be the most immediate reason for the nature of the extended development of his novel" (12). Joyce's decision to set his novel
at a historical moment which precedes the time of writing by more than a
decade might be regarded as an elusion of the troublesome claims of the
contemporary condition, but on the other hand, Duffy maintains, the year
of 1904

> stands at a nadir of political development in modern Irish history, between
> the parliamentary agitation that saw its finest hour under Parnell in the
> 1880s and the War of Independence, which ended with the signing of the
> Anglo-Irish treaty in November 1921. (16)

Thus, Duffy concludes his exposition on a note of *Ulysses*' clandestine
subalterity: "a manifesto for postcolonial freedom" though it is not, it still
provides a powerfully subversive "representation of the discourses and
regimes of colonial power being attacked by counterhegemonic strategies," either modelled to parody the discourse of the oppressor, or presented in their nascent enunciative forms (21).

Duffy then goes on to document the various strategies of subalterity
as employed throughout the novel, beginning with the Telemachiad, in
which the tissue of texts within texts "slavishly tags its beginning as a
series of imitations in which these enclosed texts imitate each other"

(28). Duffy's discussion of these mock-*Bildungsroman* episodes focuses on the Haines character, whose presence in *Ulysses* "acknowledges at the beginning the degree to which all discussions of 'the Irish question' (itself a British phrase) are imitative of British models (of race, national pride, folklore) designed to condescend to colonial peoples such as the Irish in the first place" (51-2)., The significance of *traffic* in the streets of the Dublin of *Ulysses* is subsequently assessed, where *flanerie* is read as "aggressive, emancipatory, and the blueprint for a potential version of new postcolonial subjectivity" (63). As long as "the *flanerie* of metropolitan modernism was an education in consumption" (67) then for the subaltern, "the western flaneur's surrender to consumption [...] is the point at which he is finally won away from any ideology of 'self-determination' and can be fully and completely interpellated by the colonial regime" (70). Consumption, therefore, a topic whose importance for Joyce has been assessed by Joycean Culture Studies, comes to be imbued with a strongly ideological potential in service of colonial-imperialist forces. Consequently, Bloom's "response" to Emmet is seen as a reaction to, and an implicit critique of, not the Irish nationalist struggles, but their misappropriation at the hands of the oppressor:

> the reaction of the flaneur to the commodification of Emmet's statement in a junkshop window. For Emmet's words, like the rebel song, also concern telling [...]: they are an injunction to the Irish colonial population not to tell. (88-9)

It is, of course, in the "Cyclops" episode that what has been implicitly referenced or alluded to comes to the very centre—its frequently remarked on but never accounted for split into two clashing styles is interpreted as being due to the show of "the apparatuses of panoptic surveillance by which the colonial regime creates its split subject" (113). Thus, in Duffy's approach the episode's form is revealed as mimetic, since the two countering styles, "the realist narrative of the Nameless One and the heteroglossic hyperbole of the interpolations," appear to "correspond to the conflict between Bloom and the Citizen that is mostly described in the realist *récit*" (116). In Duffy's words, "The Cyclops"

> is a realistic rather than realist text: it purveys a hardheaded politics. It uncovers the hegemonic strategies exerted by the empire through its state apparatus of police, courts, and informers upon its Irish subjects, even if some of them professed to disavow that power. (121)

Also noted is the chapter's enigmatic mediator—the Nameless One, whose identity (a police spy, a newspaper reporter, or other?) is never revealed, and the episode's comic ending which, despite blending the two conflicting styles, offers no resolution. Bloom's "neither-fish-nor-flesh" identity, discussed as such rather one-sidedly by MacCabe,[3] is countered by Duffy's emphasis on Bloom's outspoken Jewishness, which "displaces the discussion of colonial oppression onto the question of the relationship of political power to the discourse of race" (127). Bloom's entrapment within the oppressive discourses of the chapter's style and narrative situation bring about within him "a glorious moment [...] of coming to consciousness," thus staging "Bloom's own potentially revolutionary moment, represented in such a way as to also open the reader's eyes" (129).

Duffy then turns to an exposition of "Circe" from the perspective of the complicity between terrorism in service of nationalism and the scapegoating of women, a complicity that is due to the contradiction between "the project of liberation, which aims to enable the construction of new subjectivities" and "terrorist violence that is willing to wreck any subjectivity in its path," a contradiction within whose space the figure of woman is often placed by masculinist discourses (132). "Circe" addresses this contradictory complicity, first by exposing "the inadequacy of realist representations of [terrorist] violence," secondly, by showing "the pervasive effect on terrorism in the subaltern culture" by means of "its modernist representation of the feminine as doubled image of both imperialist oppressor and as colonist native abject," and ultimately by calling on us "to discover in its radical form a narrative that homologizes a subaltern's response to terrorism as an issue of abjection" (140). Duffy then turns to Circe's depiction of realist terrorism (Stephen and Private Carr), particularly to its rendering of the "surreal terror" of the spectacular commodity fetishism, and to its scenes of "speaking subalterns" where Joyce's refusal to "realize the heroicization of the male subject in his realistic portrayals of violence" is paid for by his withdrawal from "a full realization of the figure of woman as the horror of either imperial or insurgent violence" (158).

Finally, Duffy's analysis of the concluding "Nostos" part of the novel focuses on the alternative to a tendency he sees as "a paranoid mimeticism, an eagerness to be correct with every timetable and house number on the one hand, and a desire to undermine every protocol of realist narrative on the other." This alternative, according to Duffy, is presented by a "second narrative impulse, modernist in form, which identifies more thoroughly with the subaltern predicament and which, significantly, is centered on a series of images of women" (169, 174). Of particular interest here is the character of Molly Bloom, whose contradictory nature splits her between "the image of the wholly interpellated subject, a type of the ideal colonial native" and "a shifting signifier that is at flash-moments deployed at a distance from the text altogether." It is, then, precisely in the in-between space dividing these two that "the voice of Molly as interrogator of postcolonial community operates" (183). Molly's is a complex use of the subaltern language:

<hr>

[3] See Chapter I "Deconstruction," section I.

Hers is not some lapse into the "flow" of the personal and the apolitical, but rather the subaltern's deft redistribution of forces in the language-economy of late-colonial power. [...] With her, the novel conforms the most sacred image of Ireland in the nationalist canon, the image of the nation as "pure" woman, as virgin or mother, and wholly subverts it, replacing the servile smile with subversive laughter. (187-8)

In his concluding remarks, Duffy returns to his Jamesonian slant in arguing for a consideration of Ireland's emergence into postcolonial statehood as the political unconscious of *Ulysses*, "a text that, written against the background of colonial violence in Ireland, meditates upon the forces of colonial rule that must be overcome" (189). His backward glance at the whole novel sees how the flanerie episodes thematize "the pervasive police presence in Dublin," the indoor episodes (such as "The Sirens") expose the colonizing power "[turning] its most developed colony into a consumer culture akin to its own." Indeed "Cyclops" in particular demonstrates "how colonist stereotypes of the natives [...] thoroughly interpellate the local population, so that its members' first impulse is to act out imperial stereotypes of themselves," and the novel's characterization of women particularly "amply documents the way in which the colony maintains the native population as an underclass" (189-190). As a whole, *Ulysses* "casts a cold eye on the subalterity wrought by the colonial administration, and invents forms to imagine ways in which this subalterity might be overcome" (191).

III

The year following Duffy's groundbreaking book saw the appearance of Vincent Cheng's *Joyce, Race, and Empire*,[4] a study combining postcolonial theory, minority discourse, and cultural studies of race in order to argue that Joyce wrote from the perspective of the colonial subject of an oppressive empire. Derek Attridge's foreword, apart from illustrating that Joyce "cherished no illusion that politics could be walled off in a domain of its own" (xi) using the famous example of the Christmas dinner scene, hails Cheng's work as the first devoted to

questioning the tendency to give an automatic privilege to the metropolitan view of the world, [...] developing theoretical tools to make possible alternative understandings of the relation between the metropolitan and the peripheral, and [...] exploring the role of art within the struggle against national and racial oppression. (xii)

Cheng begins by challenging the canonized view of Joyce as "the great Modernist writer whose stylistic and aesthetic innovations revolutionized modern prose style, but who remained steadfastly apolitical" by pointing to Jameson's contention that "this aesthetic approach to Modernism substitutes 'style' as a red herring ('style' is then the substitution of a

4 Vincent John Cheng, *Joyce, Race, and Empire* (Cambridge: Cambridge University Press, 1995).

spatial or perceptual 'meaning') for material and historicized substance"
(1-2). Among the precursors of his own "political Joyce," Cheng grants
Colin MacCabe the place of honour, re-identifying MacCabe's discussion
of Joyce's self-positioning on the margin throughout his work, and his
sustained dismemberment of the English language in the *Wake*, as having
to do with his "attempt to universalize the colonial relationship and struggle between an Ireland without Home Rule and the ruling British Empire"
(7). Cheng's general argument crystallizes in the following passage, according to which Joyce's works

> house, in carefully constructed intent, a symptomatic representation of the
> various ideological positions on these issues in turn-of-century Ireland — in
> very specific, cultural and historical detail and accuracy — and thus collec-
> tively can be seen as a dialogic locus for the many particular, historically
> based voices of the variant social discourses within the various levels of
> both hegemony and resistance. (9)

Postulated from Cheng's own "particular, subjective position of cultural
liminality," this thesis is elaborated upon via Cheng's cross-disciplinary
approach which strives to negotiate a simultaneous sensitivity to inter-
secting methodologies including minority discourse, cultural studies, and
postcolonial theory, with a particular sensitivity to the "dynamics of race,
culture, colonialism, and power" (12-4). The "race" of his title is used to
denote the "Irish Question" in the Anglo-Irish relationship, and the contextual specificities of the Irish experience of colonialism.

Drawing on a variety of critical writing from spheres as various as bi-
ology, history, sociology, and comparative ethnology, Cheng documents
the motifs behind and ramifications of the various derogatory labels applied to the Irish by their English colonizers ("white negroes" being among
the most notorious), which he divides into three categories. First, they
maintain the savage versus civilized (Other versus Self) dichotomy, serving to secure the colonizer's identity; secondly, they reduce the ruled
culture beyond history, beyond temporality and diachronic development;
and third, they turn the native culture, crippled as it is by its externally-
imposed identity of static primitivism, into essentially a dying culture (23).
Having shown the enormous extent to which the context of *race* (of ra-
cialized discourse and racial received ideas) informed the English colonizer's representation of its Irish colonized other in scientific as well as
popularly entertaining discourses, Cheng observes how Joyce went about
disrupting it. Joyce does this first in his critical writing, most notably
"Ireland, Island of Saints and Sages," and "Ireland at the Bar," with its
suggestive account of the Myles Joyce case, but then also in his fiction,
which Cheng follows chronologically, focusing on various topics as they
variously gain prominence in the individual works.

Dubliners is read as *colonialist symptomatics*, as the stories "provide
us with a *symptomatic* reading of the cultural and political histories and
tensions of Dublin at the turn of the century" (77). The concept of "other-

"otherness" in this chapter also acquires a sense different from the one it had previously—if "other" has hitherto meant "the constructed product of an imagined and absolute *difference* from the self," here it comes to stand for "the product of unacknowledged, unauthorized *desire*" (78). Edward Said's *Orientalism* is a formative influence on Cheng's reading of the stories of childhood:

> The Orientalizing/othering urge essentializes all the heterogeneous manifestations of difference (in nationality, race, ethnicity, culture, and so on) within the notion of a unitary, definable, knowable Other; this voracious concept colonizes all alien cultures and ethnicities under the banner of a homogeneous "Orient" (or, here, "Araby"). (94)

The "gratefully oppressed" protagonists of the middle stories are viewed, with the help of Frantz Fanon, as inhabiting "a hegemonic system" in which they "take on consensually the values of the oppressors," a process which leads to "a complex and nuanced hegemony in which the distinctions between the rulers and ruled are blurred" (122). Finally, Cheng's analysis of "The Dead" considers the story as an especially suggestive case study "of the clash between the Academy's institutional, canonizing practices / powers and an ideological reclamation of Joyce's works" (128).

The section of the book entitled "*Ulysses*: Imagining Selves and Nations" argues that Joyce's novel is founded upon an acute awareness of the discursive strategies by which the construct of the Irish other came to dominate the English attitude to their colonized subject. Whether focusing on the presence, both physical and discursive, of the English colonizers in the (mental) landscape of the novel's Dublin (in the earlier chapters), or on the stereotypical essentialization of its Jewish protagonist (especially in "The Cyclops"), or on imaginary constructs of future nations and selves (the phantasmagoria of "Circe"), Cheng displays an acute awareness of the many various realizations of the novel's overall project of

> [advocating] an acceptance simultaneously of heterogeneity and difference, on the one hand, and on the other hand, of a potential sameness and solidarity of shared similarities-in-difference [...] within a multivalent, internationalist perspective, rather than a binary polarization that freezes essences into poles of absolute and unbridgeable difference. (248)

Cheng's study culminates with his reading of the tropes of race and empire in the *Wake*, which is part of his project of turning "representations of racial and imperial/colonial relationships" into "one of the central and structuring topics of *Finnegans Wake*" (251). To achieve this, Cheng conducts his postcolonial forays along two lines: a study of the emphatic and frequently repeated trope of horses and horse races aiming to elaborate Joyce's developing positions about race, empire, and essence and a close reading of a selected passage (the "Museyroom" scene in I.1) designed to demonstrate the density of the texture into which such concerns are woven by means of the Wakean radical textual project. Taken together, these two forays stand as "exempla of the possibilities for the study of such topics in the complex and challenging but wonderful and moving text that is *Finnegans Wake*" (252).

Cheng's influential analysis succeeds in presenting the whole of the Joyce canon as a systematic engagement with the ideologies of racial and imperial politics in contemporary Ireland, presenting a Joyce who

> took very strong stances—a fact which becomes clearer when we look at their representations in his book in both detail and collectively—on such matters as: nationalism and especially Irish Nationalism; internationalism and multicultural politics; cultural stereotypes and racism; essentialism, whether racial, cultural, or linguistic; and alternatives to the problematics of all the above. (289)

What these concerns have all in common is that they all participate in one way or another in a discourse of (imperial) Self and (colonized) Other, a binary by which the psychological, linguistic, and philosophical implications the subversiveness of Joyce's writing is considered to be informed. Any discussion of a text's political impact needs to take into account the issue of its effectiveness, and here Cheng proposes two different modes of the functioning of Joyce's writing: as "fictional correspondences to cultural or social theories for a progressive literary art form" (responding to Homi Bhabha's call for "counter-narratives of the nation"), or as "practical applications of theoretical arguments for certain ideological positions and theories" (294)—such as those of Said, Anderson, Spivak, Fanon, or Bakhtin, whose relevance and usefulness for an exploration of Joyce's committed anti-imperialist critique Cheng's study has painstakingly documented.

IV

Both Duffy's and Cheng's books rest on the assumption of Joyce's essentially critical if not outright dismissive and derogatory stance toward the ideology of Irish nationalist movement. It is this, in her own words, "misconception" that Emer Nolan's study of Joyce and nationalism[5] seeks to redress, reconceptualising nationalism as deeply embedded within modernity, and thus an indispensable component of Joyce's art. Precisely on the basis on their shared ambivalence to modernity and modernization does Nolan reconstruct the polar opposition between modernism and Irish nationalism by viewing both "as significantly analogous discourses" (xii), thereby declaring war on many "pervasive and systematic misreadings of Joyce," which are due to a "failure on his critics' part to attend to the full complexity of nationalism in the political culture of modernity" (xiii).

In her "Introduction: Modernism and Nationalism," Nolan points to how "a certain reading" of Joyce has "allowed liberal critics to annex at

[5] Emer Nolan, *James Joyce and Nationalism* (New York: Routledge, 1995).

least some portion of modernist literature for their own values" and how "while he has been much praised," this "has not always been for innocent or well-considered reasons" (2). The central ambiguity is expressed as follows:

> For modernism, nationalism may be a symptom of cultural degeneracy, or a cure for it—both an aspect of the perceived crisis, and a way of resolving it. Nationalism is not, however, just an unattractive feature of the modern world, which could be transcended in art. (3)

This reading, tied later on specifically with poststructuralist (Attridge and Ferrer's collection) and Marxist (Franco Moretti, Terry Eagleton) interpretations, and criticized on account of its "lofty indifference to cultural or political specificity" (9), is pitched against a discussion of a few of Joyce's early-life alliances with nationalistically committed culture and art, such as the way he was read by Pound and Eliot—through their shared agreement that "Joyce's novels exhibit the immense modern panorama of futility and anarchy by faithfully depicting one nation, exemplary in its dishevelment and degradation" (5). Pound especially proves powerfully suggestive for Nolan's argument, maintaining not only the by-now-orthodox view that "Joyce repudiates his native culture," but also holding the more-often-ignored belief that "Joyce's critical assessment of the metropolis is *mediated through* his representation of Ireland." Thus, for Pound and for Nolan, the "bad" nationalism in Joyce, which "invokes tradition and community only to mystify petty-bourgeois self-interest," is nothing but "exemplary of the duplicity of the modern" (6). Here also lie the roots of Pound's dismissal of the *Wake*, according to which Joyce, "intoxicated with language and memory," falls into solipsistic obscurity and by the era of *Work in Progress*, "the provincialism which he once anatomized so dispassionately threatens to reclaim him." Pound's heritage for Joyce studies consists in the "several ways of theorizing the relation-ship between Joyce's writing and the metropolitan avant-garde," each of which "involves an interplay between localism and modernism which should be enough to thwart any attempt to co-opt Joyce as simply an uncritical advocate of change" (7).

After an incipient discussion of Joyce's relation to the Irish literary re-vival, the focal points of which are his relationship with Yeats and a discussion of "The Dead" in terms of nationality and literature, Nolan turns to the main subject of her study, the nationalist concerns as variously shaped by Joyce's writing in *Ulysses* and the *Wake*. Nolan proceeds to show by using the example of the confrontation between Major Tweedy and the Citizen in "Circe," that although it can serve to illustrate the critical case that this practice of writing erodes the grounds on which we could evaluate or seek to choose between the ideologies for which the pair stand (British imperialism and Irish nationalism, respectively), "such a view of *Ulysses*' 'anti-nationalism' is associated with a certain interpretation of Joyce's abandonment of narrative or plot in the text; in the next chapter, I explore these issues by considering chapter, I explore these issues by considering Joyce's representation of nationalism in relation to questions of style" (56). Her reading then focuses on "The Sirens" chapter, challenging MacCabe's stress on Bloom's isolation and privileging of Bloom over the other singers at the Ormond as a better *revolutionary subject* (62), and on Stephen's Shakespeare theory, where

> the moment of escape is the same as the moment of surrender to the maternal principle of life and death, and to the father's demand for death in life. The effort to escape history and abolish narrative in a vision of suprahistorical dialogue and interconnection finally succumbs to a recognition of the most final and inarguable narrative closure of all. (79)

She also discusses the often-made parallel between Jewishness and Irishness as exemplified by Bloom himself. Here, Bloom's historical memory of his race is seen as "flawed and homogenizing," and Nolan argues that while it "eradicates from the history of the Jewish people the promise of a better future," it also "proves insensitive to the similar messianic hopes of the Irish in the aftermath of Parnell" (84).

The "Cyclops" chapter receives extended discussion in Nolan's study, regarded as juxtaposing "colloquial invective and parody" with the styles of "modern journalism and advertising" (91). Her greatest challenge to the traditional accounts, which to her mind "are in general rendered incoherent by their refusal to attach *any* positive qualities to the citizen or the kind of language that he speaks," is her belief that the citizen's voice is "one of the most 'interesting' in literary terms, and probably the funniest in the book" (96). What is more, Nolan posits that the citizen's discourse in fact echoes "quite specific details of Joyce's" (in for example "Ireland, Island of Saints and Sages") (99). Attention to Joyce's language therefore reveals that the dialect deployed in the "Cyclops"

> bears the weight of crucial political questions [in that] his depiction of this vernacular as the medium of communication in a well-defined social group [...] obliges him to engage with the associated demands made from within that community for political recognition and autonomy. (113)

Thus, as opposed to "the usual binary between the multivocal dialogic interpolations and Bloom's speech as opposed to monological stream of Fenian shibboleths," Nolan's main concern is "to show the affinity between the speech of the citizens generally and the parodic interpolations." For, after all,

> at the simplest level, it is they, after all, who make jokes, talk excessively and compose their own parodies: in their more global interests in imperialism and in politics they actually transcend the narrow focus of the novel itself on the Irish situation (118-9).

Nolan's analysis of "Circe" in terms of its representation of political violence renders it analogous (through "its carnivalesque extravaganza and terrifying raising of ghosts, both personal and historical") to "the symbolism and theatricality of the 1916 Rebellion itself" (122). The central question posed by the *Wake*, for Nolan, is

> how to trace this potentially more sympathetic, dialectical and recognizably post-colonial response to nationalism in a work which so relentlessly dismantles all national languages and freely confounds historical epochs, events and individuals. (140)

The sympathetic character of this response, as Nolan documents, has to do with her belief that *Finnegans Wake* "does not in any sense set out to destroy the self-confident aura of modernist fiction" (146). In this connection, Nolan's ultimate concern is the "supposedly feminine word 'yes'" and how the feminine question ties in with the nationalist concerns of Joyce's modernity. She opposes feminist approaches that view Joyce's writing as *écriture féminine* by maintaining as an unanswered question the issue of

> whether Joyce genuinely surrenders authority to the "feminine," or whether his practice of modernism presents its final appropriation. For if modernism is among other things a response to a general cultural crisis of masculine authority, this invocation of "Woman" may be no more than a cunning strategy for maintaining dominion, rather than finally abandoning it. (164)

Joyce's extensive symbolic deployment of femininity is in turn viewed as analogous to how woman-as-nation was used within the discourse of nationalist movements (Gretta from "The Dead" is Nolan's example, here). Moreover, in the Bloom household, Leopold's "deconstruction of masculinity" is regarded as inversely proportional to what is in Nolan's view, "the 'defeminization' of the women, especially Molly, which Joyce portrays." Thus, "the 'feminization' of the public sphere is countered by the 'masculinization' of the private sphere" (179). Finally, it is ALP's character that "reverses the woman-as-nation allegory, in drawing a parallel between their repression and the repression of national community," and the last words given to her "undercut any such symbolic deployment of womanhood." The *Wake* then is a work in which any idea of an "emancipatory modernity is ultimately rebuked." Nolan's last remark concerns this rebuke in the context of the ambiguous transition to modernity, which does not bring only gains:

> When ALP-as-river joins the sea, something specific is lost in an oceanic chaos. As with her, so with Ireland. Both have entered the devil's area of modernity, liberated into difference, lost to identity. This is not a simple transition. Joyce both celebrates and mourns it; his readers have so far tended only to join in the celebration. (181)

V

The 1998 collection, *Re-Joyce: Text, Culture, Politics*,[6] discussed already as part of the advances in deconstructive Joyce criticism,[7] included an important essay written by Vincent Cheng, in which he revisits and questions the very assumptions which Joyce criticism informed with postcolonial theory (including his own work) has hitherto unproblematically taken for granted. "Of Canons, Colonies, and Critics: The Ethics and Politics of Postcolonial Joyce Studies" opens by reviewing the recent postcolonial re-evaluation of Joyce, a sustained attempt aimed against the "canonical" Joyce of former criticism. What Duffy's, Cheng's, and Nolan's studies share is "a view of Joyce's work as politically engaged and potentially subversive, a subaltern voice attempting to respond to colonial conditions and oppression" (226). However, questions still remain:

> Can the two [i.e., canonical and postcolonial] Joyces be somehow squared? Do these more recent critics manage successfully to un-canonize Joyce, allowing for the emergence of a new, subaltern, colonial voice speaking against the discourse of empire? (227)

The two questions immediately arising have to do with the expression "subaltern speaking": how is Joyce, and more broadly the Irish, postcolonial? And if they are, who and how can speak of their being so? Here, to Cheng's mind, the situation of Ireland and the Irish must be seen as one of a double-bind:

> essentialized as radically Other by the English imperial self, but denied the fraternity of victimhood by non-white colonials—in short, caught in a postcolonial no-man's-land, carrying on identity card with the identity politics of postcolonial discourse. (228)

If this indeed is the case, the question of "who can speak?" becomes even more pressing, for a plain refusal of the absurdity of denying the Irish this right only runs into another dilemma: "If anyone can potentially speak about Irishness, do we not risk robbing the colonial subaltern (once again) of his/her own voice?" (230) However unstable the concept of "Irishness" itself, the objectionably unethical "speaking *for*," which robs "the colonial subaltern once again of a voice" is even harder to substantiate (231). In our case, could it be denied that this recent critical project of de-canonizing and re-radicalizing Joyce has anything to do with the , practice of "speaking for," however noble its intentions? Or as Cheng asks:

> What happens to postcolonial studies when canonical authors (like Joyce) get recorded as colonial/native voices? Does postcolonial study then get diluted and lose some of its impact? Does it get appropriated and thus taken

6 John Brannigan, Geoff Ward and Julian Wolfreys, eds., *Re-Joyce. Text, Culture, Politics* (London: MacMillan Press Ltd., 1998).
7 See Chapter I "Deconstruction," section VIII.

over by "dominant" voices within academia, and thus get defanged of its subversive bite? (234)

This we have seen can be attributable to Joyce's subversive textual practice, whose allusiveness, pre-emptiveness, palinodic, self-cancelling movement, and above all the central and marginal positions it occupies, have turned it into the central testing ground of literary deconstruction, feminism, psychoanalysis, the modernism/postmodernism controversy: indeed, of the very possibility of critical meta-discourse at all. Here the paradox is one of "the postcolonial Joyce" coming close to being "another version of Marx's 'They cannot represent themselves, they must be represented'" (235). However consciously provocative and exaggerated this particular claim (for indeed the underlying belief here is that Joyce "should be read [...] from a postcolonial perspective"), Cheng warns against the potential consequences of this critical endeavour: "But then, what is next? Milton as postcolonial writer?" he asks with reference to the perverted logic of slogans such as "We are all ethnic" and "White is ethnic too" (237). Even more troubling is the possibility that "by privileging major 'minor' writers," one "may be helping to make neglected writers even more minor" (238).

In his conclusion, Cheng raises questions concerning one of the particular *how's* of postcolonial criticism—its entanglement with Western academia, the central blind spot which has emerged and thus allows a reading of Joyce the postcolonial or Joyce the nationalist to be the refusal to see that "the moment a topic is taken up enthusiastically by the academy, it is already 'safe' and neutralized, defanged, no longer threatening" (241). The particular predominance of American academics among postcolonial theorists is accounted for by two further blind spots of their own making: their concern with despotic cruelties forming part of the legacies of European imperialism conveniently occludes America's own troubled history of colonialism and neo-colonialism, and the "post" in the postcolonial can be seen as suggesting "an unthreatening 'past', [...] issues that an American can safely take sides on now because they carry no risk to one's *present* culture" (242). Not surprisingly, for Cheng, this "unrecognized blind spot" is caused and perpetuated by "the Western academy's own implication in Western colonialism" (242). What therefore emerges from Cheng's critique is not a Joyce who should not be studied as a postcolonial, politically committed writer ("for that would be an even more absurd disservice to the cultural/historical specificities of an Irish literary discourse"), but rather a postcolonial criticism of Joyce aware of its own ideological implications within the object of its study, and one that strives to subvert them by, in Gyan Prakash's words, returning "to the history of colonialism without rehearsing the naturalization of colonialism as History" (243-4).

VI

Derek Attridge and Marjorie Howes seek to capture the problematic status of Joyce within postcolonial debates in the title of their seminal collection of essays, *Semi-colonial Joyce*,[8] where the adjective "semi-colonial" is itself taken from the *Wake*'s address to "Gentes and laitymen, fullstoppers and semicolonials, hybreds and lubberds!" (*FW* 152.16). In their introduction, Attridge and Howes point to how in every single one of this series of binary oppositions articulated here—those of gender (ladies and gentlemen), religion (laity versus gentiles), class (high-breds versus low-breds), and colonialism (permanent versus temporary inhabitants)—is undermined as the very structure of opposition undergoes a deconstruction: thus, even though locals are "fullstopers," expatriates are only "semi-" colonials (1-2). Nolan's work is referenced to illustrate the central contention that

> in their dealings with questions of nationalism and imperialism, [Joyce's writings] evince a complex and ambivalent set of attitudes, not reducible to a simple anticolonialism but very far from expressing approval of the colonial organizations and methods.

The portmanteau identifying colonialism with punctuation testifies to how "Joyce's handling of political matters is always mediated by his strong interest in [...] language: the two domains are, finally, inseparable in his work." Moreover, in the context of postcolonial studies,

> the adjective *semicolonial* signals our sense of a partial fit between this set of approaches and Joyce's writing ... we believe that it is precisely from the limited compatibility between them that the most interesting lessons can be drawn. (3)

Not that the term "postcolonial" would be unproblematic in its own right: here as in the former section too, "efforts to characterize the relationship between the colonial and the postcolonial in terms of sequence" are found to only "rarely produce satisfactory results," and yet the question of *when* a postcolonial Ireland might have come into being (was it, ask Attridge and Howles, with the treaty of 1921, the 1937 constitution, the 1949 repeal of the External Relations Act, the recent peace accord, or perhaps it is yet to happen with some future final resolution?) is "inseparable from the question of what such an Ireland might look like" (5). A way out of the binary opposition between choosing either the "post" as marking a new departure, or the "colonial" as bespeaking continuity and aftermath, would be to define the postcolonial "as following the *beginning* of colonialism, collapsing any temporal distinction between the colonial and postcolonial" (6).

---

[8] Derek Attridge and Marjorie Howles, eds., *Semi-colonial Joyce* (Cambridge: Cambridge University Press, 2000).

These general (however fruitfully examined) concerns aside, the specificity of *Irish* postcoloniality raises further questions, the most contentious of which is the one whether it is "useful" or even "appropriate" for one "to call the relationship [between Ireland and Britain] 'colonial' in any or all periods of its history" (7). For as long as one version of the postcolonial rests upon "a dichotomy between the West and the non-West, and the other invokes an opposition between the colonizer and the colonized," then what this brings to attention is David Lloyd's contention about "the anomalous state of Ireland," for Ireland "clearly belongs on both sides of each dichotomy" (8-9).

Another way (especially productive in the case of Joyce studies) of defining postcolonial studies is by means of its ambivalent involvement with nationalism—since historically speaking, "most anticolonial struggles have been versions of nationalism," in that they have usually propelled the colonized nations "to migrate from the category of the historically contingent to the category of the historically inevitable" (10). In the increasingly sophisticated postcolonial examination, nationalism ceases to be "a simple nostalgia for the past or a straightforward defense of tradition," but comes to be seen as "an ambivalent response to modernity, like modernism, a connection that scholars of modernism have also begun to make." Thus, postcolonial studies "offers ways of articulating nationalism, both imperialist and anti-imperialist, and modernism as interdependent rather than opposed phenomena" (11).

The pitfalls of postcolonial theory identified by Attridge and Howes are largely due (and this has to do with its being an "academic discipline") to its need to work with "generalizations and abstract categories," a practice which jeopardizes it with "the danger of creating its own theoretical universalisms." Postcolonial theory is moreover seen as vacillating "between two ethical imperatives—the advocation of universal rights and the injunction to respect the other" where the first can merely replicate imperialism, and the second can relapse into an ethically unmanageable relativism. It is with respect to these conceptual difficulties that Attridge and Howes quote the contention from Livesey and Murray's *Postcolonial Theory*, according to which "the version of post-coloniality appropriate to an analysis of the Irish case has not yet been found" (13).

Yet the recent postcolonial boom within Joyce studies, or what has come to be termed "the Irish turn," has to do with the workings of the broader process of "the reconstruction of Irish studies in the light of postcolonial theory," and is marked by two inseparable tendencies: an "increasing attention to the Irish dimension of Joyce's writing," and a "reconsideration of that dimension in the light of post-colonial theory" (14). What all of the works of the complex genealogy of Joyce postcolonial studies (most of which have been examined above) have in common is

the conviction that the full measure of Joyce's achievement cannot be understood without relating it to the Irish struggle for independence—regarded

[...] as a bitter, complex, and protracted conflict, with a history still alive in Irish political memory.

However "ambivalent and shifting" Joyce's own approach to it, "the posing of questions about Ireland's status in relation to Britain" can still enable an understanding of some of the "aspects of Joyce's work occluded by previous approaches" (16). Finally, the collection as a whole is offered "not as a full stop but as, at most, a semicolon" as it hopes to be followed by further critical attempts at making the best of the potential of postcolonial theory for Joyce (17). Before looking at how postcolonial criticism of the new millennium responded to Attridge and Howes's appeal, a brief overview of the collection as a whole is necessary.

Seamus Deane's "Dead Ends" focuses on what he sees as a pervasive motif of the early *Dubliners* stories: "the sense of infantile repetitiveness that is the abiding feature of Dublin's condition, although the repetition involved also reminds us that immense psychic as well as rhetorical energy has to be expended on the production of stasis." Here, "repetition" takes on the various structuring forms of the echo, the epigone, or the parody, and extends "beyond persons to wider ranges of reference: there was the Eucharist, then there was sherry and biscuits; there was the sacred, now there is the secular" (21). It is this strategy of repetition which enables Joyce to indicate "how radical and yet elusive the state of being 'gratefully oppressed' can be," for repeated words "gain weight inexorably as they feed on their surrounding contexts and associations" (22). This Joycean method of juxtaposition via repetition acquires further postcolonial momentum when linked to his "counterposing that which is undeniably real [...] to something which is undeniably fake," which aims not so much to ratify the "real" as to show that it can be swallowed up in the illusory (23). This spectral haunting bears upon the very relation between Joyce's postcoloniality and modernity:

> For Joyce, the matter is both simple and involved. To be colonial is to be modern. It is possible to be modern without being colonial; but not to be colonial without being modern. (26)

Deane counterbalances these general observations with a close reading of "The Dead," the ending of which presents, apart from a supremely and self-consciously aesthetic moment, "a marvelous instance of the universalizing impulse in Joyce, the conversion, through highly cadenced repetition, of something solid into something spectral." This conversion, in turn, takes place by means of writing, of "an evocation of a world elsewhere, that of the aesthetic moment" (36).

Duffy's and Howes' essays take a narrower focus, examining the postcoloniality of *Ulysses* in terms of its politics of space and the issue of the geographical scale in the narrative of the nation, respectively—a feature of most of the essays in the collection (including Valente's piece on staging Irish manhood in "Cyclops" or Katherine Mullin's exploration of the discourse of emigration propaganda in "Eveline"). While they may be interesting in their own right, they hardly address the overall concerns of the field. For this reason only one other essay shall be detailed here— Emer Nolan's "State of the Art: Joyce and Postcolonialism."

Here Nolan considers the question of Joyce's rejection of anticolonial nationalism and of the state within the broader context of the issue of representation, central as it is

> to both modern aesthetics and democratic politics—demonstrated by a persistent stress on the "representativeness" of the artist and of the artifact, and on the capacity of the political representative to stand in for others, and to speak on their behalf. (80)

So the problem of "speaking on one's behalf" resurfaces, soliciting the *subaltern* critic "to dwell over and over on that (albeit important) moment in Joyce's text when the residual, or the voiceless, are granted speech," thereby participating in the Derridean *hypermnesis* in which Joyce's text pre-empts whatever critical position it can be addressed from. The commitment throughout *Ulysses* to "lending articulation to those who were previously inarticulate or unheard" is indisputable (85), but still raises further paradoxes. If the novel thereby accords with the paradigm of subaltern history, it already illustrates the irony of such a history: "in announcing that articulation has been denied to some, we necessarily articulate their case on their behalf." This raises the final unanswered question of Nolan's stimulating intervention: "Can a subaltern be aware of being so and remain subaltern?" (90)

VII

It will be remembered that toward the end of their introduction, Attridge and Howes voiced their belief in the particular need for "the posing of questions about Ireland's status in relation to Britain" in order to navigate a possible way out of some otherwise potentially paralysing theoretical impasses. Andrew Gibson's *Joyce's Revenge: History Politics, and Aesthetics in 'Ulysses'*[9] might be fruitfully read as an attempt at a response to this call and is one which would take full account of its complexity. His introduction begins by examining some of the early responses to Joyce; paired against each other are Ezra Pound (modelling an "international standard") and H. G. Wells, for whom Joyce is a nationalist. Further on, an exploration of Joyce's *Conversations* with Arthur Power reveals the depth of his involvement with the English cultural tradition, how the emphasis on "historical specificity is evident everywhere in his work, and asks the scholar "to respond accordingly" (8). The following statement may be taken to be the overall argument of Gibson's book:

[9] Andrew Gibson, *Joyce's Revenge: History, Politics, and Aesthetics in 'Ulysses'* (Oxford: Oxford University Press, 2002).

In *Ulysses*, Joyce works towards a liberation from the colonial power and its culture. He also takes his revenge on them. There is a will to freedom in *Ulysses*, and a will to justice, but also a recognition that the two do not necessarily coincide. (13)

It follows that within this project, the Jewish outsider Bloom functions as an extremely effective weapon against the various colonial discursive and ideological formations:

Stylistically, almost every chapter of *Ulysses* from the ninth onwards operates as a resistance to, a corruption or [...] a seditious reworking of [the dominant nationalistic] discourses. [...] The styles in *Ulysses* [...] are wicked practices upon the colonizer's culture. (14-5)

Joyce's own proclaimed hostility to official Irish responses to English nationalism are regarded as due to his awareness of "how far English nationalism had left its mark on Irish expressions of opposition to it," since "in the very act of combating English cultural nationalism, its Irish opponents were in danger of producing another version of it" (16). The crucial gesture performed by the text examined (*Ulysses*) and identified by Gibson is the "paradoxical movement in which the drive to liberation and the drive to revenge have a quite extraordinary momentum and yet always seem to be entrammelled" (17). The "Joyce revenge" of Gibson's title, then, becomes something *sui generis*:

The point becomes clearer with reference to the theme of *ressentiment*, [...] a key theme for current Joyce criticism. Joyce had a deep understanding of and deeply identified with Irish *ressentiment*. But he also had deep misgivings about it and worked to overcome it or leave it behind, [especially because] he understood how far *ressentiment* meant continuing in servitude and degradation. (18)

The three "self-evident and pre-eminent 'Joycean virtues,'" according to Gibson, are "historical specificity; work; and the clear-eyed recognition of difficulty of entanglement"—Joyce's "work draws its readers into a labour which knows no end" and thus "resembles what Joyce himself show to be the unremitting and unendingly ironical work of liberation" (18). *Ulysses*, with reference to Attridge and Howes, is "semicolonial" in a sense purely of Gibson's own: it is "a novel of the last years of colonial rule in Ireland" and thus also "a novel that moves towards conciliation and reconciliation, if intermittently and rather contradictorily" (19). However, reconciliation is not to be seen as the only way of managing political and cultural contradictions of the novel—"the most important one [...] is laughter," which "constitutes or *is* Joyce's political and cultural project" in that it "negotiates rifts and divisions that are historical, cultural, and inward at once." Stephen's laughing "to free his mind from his mind's bondage" (*U* 9.1016) is recalled to document that the lesson of Joyce's writing is a lesson in resisting, accepting, and transcending history at one and the same time. It is an artistic lesson, a political and an ethical one, and a lesson in negotiation between the claims of freedom and those of justice. (20)

That the key argument of one of the crucial works of recent historicist Joyce scholarship should come dangerously close to what Derrida's 1984 address managed to identify as the crucial countersignature to Joyce's signature is yet another break in the accepted division line between the supposedly a-historical deconstruction and the subsequent approaches seeking to supplant it.

Before turning to his theme proper—the latter half of *Ulysses*—Gibson discusses the novel's early chapters. In the progress of the Telemachiad, he observes a shift in Stephen's perspective, who becomes, from having been a self-absorbed priggish egoist, "an aspiring, colonial intellectual and artist whose project—and whose problem—is precisely independence" (22). Stephen is seen pitted "against the English presence in Ireland from the very start," especially in his interaction with Haines, whose "sentimental doublethink is English and of its time" (23, 25), and who sharply contrasts with the explicit victimization of Stephen's mother as a "victim of the system" (28). Haines then is regarded as "representing the cultural, even the psychological features of the 'constructive Unionist' project of 'equalization'" (30). Mr. Deasy's commitment to "Englishness" in "Nestor" is in turn recognized as indicative of his allegiance to the Ulster Unionist movement.

These two interactions motivate the intellectual performance of "Proteus," where Stephen "continues to resist the colonizer and his influence" by increasingly struggling "to think past that opposition and the history that produced it, or think it otherwise" (36-7). Proteus, in other words, is "very much concerned with the question of thinking change" (37). Turning to Bloom, Gibson notes of the sundry critical accounts of his Jewishness that they "have often not been sufficiently historically specific" (42). Gibson calls for a more refined approach, one that would do justice to the "range of complex and subtle practices" employed by Joyce who throughout the novel "seeks to repudiate and counter the Scylla of Irish Catholic anti-Semitism without identifying with the Charybdis of an 'enlightened' English and Anglo-Irish tolerance" (48). Generally, Gibson observes that

> In *Ulysses*, the habit of thinking determinate identities must collapse [because] it is inseparable, not only from the anti-Semitism depicted in the novel, but from a set of Irish political mythologies and their history. (59)

Gibson's discussion of "Scylla" identifies the chapter's principle in "opposition or fissure," and "the fissures spread and are perceptible everywhere" (60). The Dowden/Yeats controversy, which in the chapter comes to represent the relationship between English and Irish literature, allows Gibson to discern "a structural opposition [...] between what we might

call Fenian and Unionist readings of Shakespeare" (68). Stephen's icono-
clastic view, so often praised for its innovativeness, is seen within the
Irish context as partly stemming form "Shavian disparagement," G. B.
Shaw's "scathing critique of bardolatry" (74). In presenting this complex
critique,

> "Scylla" offers a miniature model to Ireland of how to settle for a feature of
> its history. So, too, [...] it might be even conceivably be read as offering
> white England a lesson in how to stop worrying and learn to love its lack of
> identity. (80)

"Wandering Rocks" functions as "an anatomy of colonial, Dublin culture,
and the relationship of the macro- and micropolitical within it," beginning
as it does "with one of Ireland's two 'imperial masters,'" and finishes
with the other. Church and State "enclose or contain the rest of the chapter," mapping "the effects of a colonial culture on the minutiae of psychic, social, and affective life" (81-2). The overall picture of Dublin which
emerges presents "a world of the fragile, handicapped, or ailing. Lack of
power is a literal, physical fact. Here, if anywhere, in Foucauldian terms,
is a stark, Joycean 'anatomo-' or 'bio-politics'" (89). As an example of
Gibson's skilled close-reading, one might adduce the attention he pays to
U 10.1198-9 as compared to *U* 11.67,70, the one depicting Miss Douce
and Miss Kennedy admiring the cavalcade, the other revealing them to
admire clothes and a man. This discrepancy Gibson reads as a gap between "an (English) form of representation and a clandestine set of indica-
tions as to 'what is really going on' in an Irish context," the result of
which "is subversive and wickedly funny." What is also significant is the
fact that the discourse at stake gets distorted, as though "its tie to its
origins were being 'corrupted' or radically loosened in a process of assimilation." From "Wandering Rocks" onward, "we move into a series of
chapters where such effects will be among the most notable features of
Ulysses" (102).

In his chapter on "The Sirens" and "Cyclops," Gibson illustrates how,
"having scanned the Dublin of 1904," Joyce "embarks on a particular
kind of treatment of English and Anglo-Irish discourses that is to a large
extent responsible for producing the famous 'styles' of *Ulysses*" (103). In
"The Sirens," by repeatedly deforming the word-forms, Joyce "reverses
the relationship between English and music" that was central to the revivalist project:

> Whatever music is or represents, it is not to be reconciled with English save
> through a process of anamorphosis of which the victim is English itself.
> (107)

It is in "Cyclops," however, that "Joyce's assault on Anglo-Irish revivalism is most pronounced," for the chapter "engages in a sustained assault
on Anglo-Irish, revivalist historiographies and constructions of Irish his-

tory, and the politics and aesthetics implicit in them" (107). The chapter is seen by Gibson as not so much a "parody" as "a massive recycling of a stock-in-trade [...] making light of a whole mode of discourse that speciously presented itself as a form of historiography." (117)

"Nausicaa" is preoccupied with the relation between individual and social discourse, or, "with the relationship between Gerty and a set of discourses that produce a serviceable model of English and colonial womanhood," in which "the British presence is a determining force" (133-4). In Gibson's meticulous analysis, the British *Lady's Pictorial* magazine is revealed to be constitutive even of the very "*particularities* of Gerty's mind" (137). This leads Gibson to regard the magazine as "the imperial, English discursive formation" and thus "treated cynically" by Joyce, but still also as "an important and even enabling feature of Gerty's development as a young Irishwoman at the turn of the century." It is by staging this aporia that

> Joyce identifies an inescapable double-bind in which the colonizer held the colonized: in many spheres of life, his culture was the chief if not the only source of anything resembling advanced cultural formations. (145)

On the lookout for liberating laughter, Gibson notes in conclusion that despite the painful irony of "Gerty's determination to live the 'untrammelled life' (*U* 13.673)," she is nonetheless capable of "moments of spontaneous release, like her 'joyous little laugh' (*U* 13.126-7)" (148).

Gibson's analysis of the "Oxen of the Sun" chapter opposes the received notion of Joyce's "advocacy of fertility," again placing Joyce's views firmly within the complex gamut of public attitudes, many of which were mutually contradictory. Of the tone of the chapter, he remarks that

> [it] designates its will to modern independence in its very insouciance. Its breezy cockiness or cavalier offhandedness is very important. So is its ease with itself, its capacity for making fun of itself. In Joyce's hands, an Irish discourse becomes so self-confident that it can afford not to take itself very seriously at all. (162)

The commonplace conception of the "Oxen" style as "a parody" is also challenged, for Gibson considers it more appropriate to regard the chapter's style as established "in a relationship of correspondence to (and therefore dependence on) the English writer," from which position it works its way towards freedom from it. In this gesture, Joyce "refuses the subservience of parody, its residual structure of fidelity to the master text." However, "the tie of the betrayer to the object of his betrayal remains," and so the "movement towards freedom is uncompleted" (178). Much of Joyce's practice in "Oxen" is seen as "actually an 'Irishisation' of things English," as "the invasion of the invader's preserve" (179). Gibson concludes his fruitful discussion:

"Oxen" is a tissue of contradictions: between history and modernity, the fertility trope and "inverecundity", a seemingly ineradicable, dominant culture and the imperative of resistance. Critics have often described the chapter as unified, as though everything in it could in principle be fitted together. In fact, it is an outlandish hybrid. As such, it not only exposes colonial history and culture as themselves productive of monstrous incongruities, but also negotiates those incongruities, in a manner that Joyce intended to be exemplary. (182)

The specificity of "Circe" lies in the fact that this chapter is not a reworking of "discourses that are traceable to printed texts," but rather a chapter of voices: "in 'Circe' people speak, and the effects of colonial power are heard in what they say, and how they say it" (183). From the postcolonial perspective, what the episode thematises most clearly is "British military presence [...] conspicuous on the streets of Dublin" (184), and yet "'Circe' is primarily concerned not with a military or political but with a cultural English presence barely noted by critics" (185). "Circe" foregrounds the invaded and adulterated nature of Irish culture "from the Bluecoat Schoolboy [...] to Bella Cohen's son at Oxford [...] to Bloom on the 'English invention' to quieten snoring [...] and Stephen's comment on 'the age of patent medicine'" (187-8). The phantasmagoria of "Circe" smacks of the Bakhtinian carnivalesque:

> Joyce very obviously took a gleeful, malevolent delight in twisting and perverting the forms of the imposed culture. The consequences are partly levelling or carnivalesque. Bakhtin certainly is relevant here. Like carnival in Bakhtin's description of it, "Circe" has its roots in popular laughter and parodies and travesties certain "high genres." (200)

The laughter evoked in the episode is manifold, from light giggle to savage jeer, but "the dominant laughter in the chapter is Nietzschean," a laughter that simultaneously "accepts and challenges historical circumstance, and triumphs over it, at least, in decisively transforming its proportions" (206).

"Eumaeus" is seen as an exercise in a mockery of "the English 'concern with language,' its purity, integrity, etc." (207). However, it is one that performs a carnivalesque inversion in that it "converts the blundering — that habit with which the English had long associated the Irish — into a bravura performance, and thus into a form of sustained, cultural triumph" (218). The reference to Lindley Murray (*U* 16.1475) is Joyce's avowal of his "massacring of the language" (226).

The "Ithaca" chapter, by engaging with contemporary scientific discourses, "also engages with the cultural politics of science in Ireland, and is partly to be understood as Joyce's intervention in that politics" (227). Throughout Joyce displays an awareness of "the contemporary emphasis on imperial science as a training for the mind" (239). The chapter's "sustained assault on science as an English and Anglo-Irish preserve" also "massively fleshes out the 'theoretical' nature of the nationalist commitment to science," and at the same time combats "the Anglo-Irish conception of Gaelic culture as impractical and dreamy" (241). By tearing science "from the stranger's grasp," the chapter presents

> another instance of Joyce's "Celtic revenge," sending science back to the strangers in a twisted or perverted form. Joyce "masters science" as one of the strangers' preserves, then goes beyond or "overcomes" it, interrogating its premises and displacing its emphases. (245)

Finally, Gibson's detailed discussion of "Penelope" focuses on Molly's Gibraltar, in other words colonial heritage. Gibraltar, Gibson stresses, was "a colonial possession with a very particular history and very particular political, military, and symbolic functions," as well as "with a history of relations with Ireland" of which Joyce "was clearly aware" (252). It should also be emphasised that, "the symbolism of Gibraltar as imperial British and Protestant stronghold was clear enough to Irish minds" (259).

As concerns the overall tenor of the chapter, Gibson discerns "two starkly contradictory practices or strands of thought […], one powerfully anti-imperial, the other, apparently, wickedly anti-nationalist" (267). According to Gibson," it is the relationship between the two practices" that "tells us something very important about both 'Penelope' and *Ulysses*" (268). However critical of the British imperial presence in Ireland, *Ulysses*

> repeatedly insists that, ultimately, the posture of antagonism or continued belligerence and indeed the historical obsession are chronically disempowering. They weaken, because they keep the wounds open and even allow them to fester, rather than letting them heal. Ironically, they therefore inhibit the growth of autonomy, of cultural pride and self-assertion. (271)

Thus, the chapter wholly given to a woman is also the one that "finally makes explicit a complex paradigm of cultural sanity and health that has been progressively emerging throughout the novel," by way of being "cheerfully *at ease*" with contradiction." "Penelope," is therefore regarded as the relaxation of "the structure of the titanic cultural struggle evident in *Ulysses* since Stephen first alluded to his imperial masters" (271). Gibson concludes:

> Gibraltar was a colony with a Catholic majority and a conspicuous British, military presence. It had a history of military conflict, discriminatory legislation, the imposition of alien, administrative, educational and legal systems, and devastating onsets of disease. In these and other respects, it closely resembled Ireland. Molly Bloom has grown up in such a world. Yet she has emerged from it averagely happy, averagely sane. It is an image of possibility of ordinary sanity and happiness that Joyce finally presented to Ireland in the year of its independence. (272)

VIII

Joyce's in-betweenness, already discussed in the contexts of psychoanalysis, feminism, as well as of some of the studies presented here, was foregrounded in the 2005 co-edited volume of essays, *Joyce on the Threshold*.[10] In the editors' introduction, the threshold metaphor is explicated as follows:

> In its radical commitment to innovation, Joyce's writing crosses many thresholds, and [...] as Joyce's readers we must prepare to encounter new systems of value and higher levels of difficulty. [...] If crossing a threshold expresses the sense of organic development in Joyce's writing, the idea of standing at or on a threshold captures its hybridity or "in-betweenness." (1)

However familiar the figures of the outcast and alien might be in modern literature, there is "a form of marginality more unique to Joyce" consisting in "the unusual power of the many peripheral figures in his works" (2). Whether these figures appear in the text as a result of "Joyce's naturalistic method" or as part of his "densely allusive narrative textures," they draw "the attention of Joyce's critics productively to his margins" (2-3).

The collection is divided into four sections. The first, "Joyce's Marginalia," consists of four pieces examining marginal figures and subjects in Joyce's fiction. This part includes Karen Lawrence's essay on the figure of the urban walker, Reed Way Dasenbrock's on the figure of "the Nolan"(Giordano Bruno), Mary Lowe-Evans' reading of "The Dead" (which unexpectedly assigns a central role to Freddy Malins), and finally Heyward Ehrlich's article which investigates Joyce's interest in the occult. The second part, "In the Shadow of English: Joyce as an Irish writer," includes four essays focusing on Joyce's liminality as a writer, more specifically as an English-writing Irishman. Andrew Gibson's piece echoes the argument he put forward in *Joyce's Revenge* which treats the "Oxen" chapter as an "anti-anthology." John Nash's essay deals with the "spectral presence" of Ernest Dowden in "Scylla," while Brian Caraher examines the two travel sketches and the unsigned newspaper editorial that Joyce composed during his last visit to Ireland in 1912. Finally P. J. Matthews assesses the young Joyce's superficially implausible association with George Russell's *Irish Homestead* magazine.

The third section, "On the Threshold of the Modern," is introduced as "[harking] back to the transition to another era, that of the last century and the distinctive period in art and literature of which Joyce's writing gives powerful representation" (7). It also contains Catherine Driscoll's essay, "*Felix Culpa*: Sex, Sin, and Discourse in Joyce's Fiction," to be discussed below. The last section, "On the Margins of Criticism," investigates "the wider context of Joyce studies, concentrating on uses of texts conventionally regarded as preliminary, ancillary, or marginal to the main critical task" (9). Here, Paul Saint-Amour's essay, "Ride 'em Cowpoyride: Literary Property Metadiscourse in *Ulysses*" will receive closer attention.

---

[10] Anne Fogarty and Timothy Martin, eds., *Joyce on the Threshold* (Miami: University Press of Florida, 2005).

Driscoll's essay returns to the frequently discussed entanglement of "sex and 'sin' as a ground for artistic production and subjectification." However, Driscoll does so within the not-so-often treated context of its interaction with "popular and public cultural discourses," as well as "dominant social institutions" (171). The most obvious connection between artist and art as "sinful," within Joyce's Jesuit background, is the Christian conception of art as both a mimicry of Creation and a fortunate sin: "All valorized artistic forms and moments are represented as somehow sinful, and these sins appear, moreover, as what make art possible" (172). Drawing on Martin Heidegger's important 1938 essay "The Age of the World Picture," Driscoll uses its parallel between an idea of the subject and a system of knowledge to argue that the modernist Subject, at least in Heidegger's understanding, "may be understood as 'split' or fragmented but is nevertheless linked to a locatable perspective on the world it produces," which in turn produces an "incitement to speak of a total system for knowing the world also particularly privileges access to the unknowable or imperceptible" (174). Among the fields for revealing the unknowable that acquired prominence in the modernist period, "sex education" is the focus of Driscoll's essay, representing the complex field of regulation which any discussion of Joyce's sexuality as "transgressive" should but does not always take into account. Sex education is also seen related to the institution of the confession, whose "incitement" to produce sex as "discourse" structurally resembles sex education, and "Joyce's alignment of the two in his later fiction is highly significant" (175).

Driscoll turns to the *Wake*, where Issy presents an obvious object of popular and public discourses on sex. Her participation in these lessons is contextualised in Driscoll's argument within the "newly dominant discourses on modern life in the 1920s, which held that girls should be educated about sex, yet cautiously so" (176). In this context, the section of the lessons chapter known as "Gramma's grammar" gains weight in that it is viewed as "a form of maternal advice inserting the traditional popular form of this contradiction between attractiveness and virginity in to the newly scientific and popular discourses laid out in the *Wake*'s lessons section." The whole of II.2 is seen as a representation of language as forms of knowledge, or discourses, whose ultimate interest lies in unveiling the maternal genitalia, a specular examination of a woman which "mirrors the desire to see and know, which Luce Irigaray, among others, links to Freud's taboo on representation of the Mother's body" (178). Heidegger's thinking of difference is brought on board here, helpful in conceiving of the revelation of difference as a double movement:

> fear in the face of difference that produces not *anxiety* but a sense of being "ill at ease" that has no object, and in the face of which "All things and we ourselves sink into indifference" (*Being and Time* 101). Heidegger argues that this experience, providing "nothing to hold on to," is what reveals being. It enables the transcendence Heidegger desires—and constitutes ex-

actly the double movement that Joyce's artists articulate in their failure. (179)

However, for all its subversion of the traditional distribution of gender roles, the *Wake* still "maintains the disciplinary power of the Blessed Virgin," and thus "subjects girls to considerably more surveillance than boys" (180). The splitting of Issy, often discussed in terms of schizophrenia, appears in Driscoll's argument as due to the "range of stark dualisms used to interpret and categorize girls, including a conflict between the virgin's significance as potential lover/bride and her inevitable devaluation once she becomes either" (181). Ultimately, then, the discourse of sex education is one of the "conflicting knowledge regimes" which is "constituted by competing discourses" and deployed in the *Wake* to contribute to the treatment of sex "not as an object of knowledge but as a limit-attitude, less through the transgressive daring of its artist-figures than through the self-reflection of girls who resist being known" (183).

Paul K. Saint-Amour approaches *Ulysses* from the viewpoint of literary property metadiscourse, which reveals at the very start a "Joycean antinomy" between "a collectivist model of intertextuality" and "an individualist model of authorial property," an antinomy which has so far produced a twofold critical reaction: one Joyce-based, the other language-oriented. However, Saint-Amour's aim is different in that he aims to show

> that the tension in Joyce's life and work between collective and individual models of literary property is symptomatic of a particular moment in the history of copyright law [... and that Joyce's] work [is] an extreme case of the general, rather than an exceptional case. (230)

First, however, Saint-Amour demonstrates how the literary property regime of its time "has left its imprint on more than the novel's colophon page—that it is legible in both thematic and structural elements of the text itself" (231). Several examples of this are adduced: the word "Usurper" at the end of "Telemachus," in the light of his previous conversation with Haines, appears to denote "not only Stephen's perception of Mulligan in having demanded the key to the tower but also Haines's would-be usurpation of Stephen's oral, and therefore legally appropriable, epigrams" (233). The irony here being of course that Joyce's alter ego accuses Haines of what it precisely is involved with in writing the novel, in other words appropriating the words of others:

> To link Joyce and Haines through appropriations across the oral/written interface is not necessarily to accuse Joyce of hypocrisy or to elide the difference between transcriptive texts that exploit or exoticize colonial subjects and texts that seek to [...] constructively criticize them. (234)

Still more complex is the issue of Joyce's text's intertextual dependence on other texts, ranging from "works still in copyright (such as the contemporary popular songs and the Dawson speech) and works now in the public domain (lines from Dante or Shakespeare, lyrics from *Martha* or *Rose of Castille*); the creative transformation of another person's literary property (in Joyce's improved version of John F. Taylor's speech); quotation for the sake of parody or criticism [...]; even that nebulous category of literary misdemeanor, the 'self-plagiarism'" (236-7). In an echo of the term *avant-texte*, favoured within the field of genetic studies, Saint-Amour coins the notion of the "*pendant*-text": the while-text, the through-text, which "comes into being with publication, but it does not at any point stop changing as the printed text usually does, nor does it congeal into a static intertextual state," but instead "continues to shift and coruscate as its intertexts join the public domain and as changes in the domestic and international copyright laws to which it is subject alter its various property-clocks" (238). From this *pendant-textual* perspective, the *Ulysses* chapter most interesting for a further examination is of course "Oxen of the Sun," where Joyce's "own seemingly transgressive acts of excision and collation" are seen as echoing "the similar but prior operations of anthologists" (240). Thus, "Oxen" differs from "parodies in that it travesties not only its source texts but also copyright itself" by "appropriating and transforming the terminal narrative of copyright in its own formal trajectory." "Oxen" ends as copyright ends: "in the intellectual propertyless condition of orality" (242). Taken as a whole, the chapter offers a re-thinking of style

> not as a rampart that protects private property from public trespass but as part of the legal container that transports expression to its final destination—that is, a delivery system of and to a public domain. (244)

IX

Among the most fertile fields, the recently re-visited studies of literary reception have proven as offering a still quite uncharted area, and therefore enabling criticism to bring forth many new insights. The most theoretically productive work so far has been John Nash's *James Joyce and the Act of Reception*.[11] Its purported aim is to show how "Joyce's work rewrites the responses of several actual readers and, in doing so, engages with the specific conditions of reception, notably in Ireland," and while implying that "reading itself is a performance," Nash's analyses "seek to place that action within particular contexts," showing "Joyce's engagement with the conditions of reception" to be "a matter of wider cultural significance since such issues carried particular social and political weight in Joyce's Ireland" (2-3). Joyce's works are said to be "also in part *about* reception" in that

---

[11] John Nash, *James Joyce and the Act of Reception* (Cambridge, London: Cambridge University Press, 2006).

by showing the ways in which reception was possible, [...] Joyce shows how a certain impossibility resides within the act of reading. Such an apparent "impossibility" [...] had particular political circumstances. (3-4)

Ellmann, Derrida, as well as MacCabe are referred to as promoters of the "idea that Joyce's readers are somehow lagging behind him" (6). MacCabe[12] is most radical in this, basing his critique of Joyce on the grounds of his texts being ineffective because "lack[ing] any definite notion of an audience to which they are addressed" (7). In general,

> [m]any readers of Joyce have noted the paradox of a difficult text that apparently requires patient study and guidance but yet also seems to undermine all readings, thereby defeating the very idea of guidance. (8)

Derrida's is singled out as the "most concerted reflection on the notion of reception as it pertains to Joyce's work," stressing the tension between "the competence necessarily sanctioned by the Joycean community and the undermining of this competence by the 'performativity' of Joyce's writing." The value of his analysis lies in its reminding us of "the significance of Joyce's 'unreadability', of the radical challenges that reading his work presents" (9). There is therefore a resulting split between the "unreadable" Joyce and the "historical" Joyce emerges, one which "the question of reception" might heal by "[clasping] them together" (11). The act of reception, for Nash,

> signals a "cultural dialogic" in which Joyce inscribed versions of particular readers and their responses. One important consequence of this manoeuvre is that later readers necessarily read in and through the responses of earlier ones. [...] It necessarily remains that to read Joyce is also to read (his version of) his contemporary readers. (12-3)

Nash's study thus aims to resituate Joyce "in relation to potential Irish audiences," demonstrating that "the practice of alluding to actual readers is more than an 'oppositional revenge' but is instead part of an examination of the sometimes oppressive conditions in which reading could — indeed, must — occur" (13). The particularity of the locus in Joyce is of much significance for Nash's study, for

> [in] grounding his work in the local,...Joyce also asserted the specific importance of his own background, split as it was between the partial "provincialism" of the Irish Catholic (and sometimes nationalist) and the uncomfortable "centrality" of the middle-class Dubliner (and British citizen). (15-6)

Clearly, Nash's approach defines itself against the German theory of *Rezeptionaesthetik*, whose status "has remained a problematic area in literary theory and criticism since Walter Benjamin's famous declaration in

---

[12] See Chapter I "Deconstruction," section I.

1923 that 'In the appreciation of a work of art or an art form, consideration of the receiver never proves fruitful.'" Following Benjamin's declaration,

> [it] is an informing premise of this work that a trans-historical reflection on
> reading—a theory of reading—is impossible and that, instead, any notion of
> reception must be part of the emphasis on reading as cultural practice and
> as textual process within and for his writing. (16)

Hans-Robert Jauss' concept of the "horizon of expectation," inspired by
Edmund Husserl's phenomenology of perception, places "emphasis on the
experience of reading as a constitutive element in literary history" (17)
However, it is criticized by Nash on account of its ignorance of "the specific historical conditions attending reading in any instance, being content
to allow for reading only as a form of textual affect," with "ideal" texts
"objectifying" the horizon of expectation. Wolfgang Iser's work, in comparison, has the advantage of "showing how readers simultaneously construct the text and are constructed by it, thus avoiding a naïve empiri-
cism," and yet "remains profoundly troubled by reading as a historical act
or by representations of actual acts of reading." To take a concrete example,

> [j]ust as *Ulysses* appears, for Iser, as the text *par exemple*, so Iser's notion of
> "the reader" is similarly universalised; yet this model of "the reader" is in-
> appropriate for Joyce's writing which focuses on the local and the specific.
> (18)

What is more, Iser's distinction between "reader-participant" and "reader-
observer" has much to do with the "criticism of modernism and privileging
of the later, future audience and a denigration of the 'participant' or
roughly contemporaneous (or politically 'inside') reader."

Nash summarizes his reservations by positing that "[s]tudies of Joyce
influenced by Iser have similarly tended to ignore reception as a significant *historical* issue in Joyce's writing" (19). Instead of the Husserl- and
Gadamer-based idealist reception theory, Nash derives his critical impetus
from the work of Michel de Certeau, Tonny Bennet, and most notably,
Pierre Bourdieu, with reference to whom Nash observes that "all reflections on reading at the level of theory risk falling prey to their own critique, further constructing an abstraction that bears little resemblance to
the practice of reading." According to this logic,

> the turn towards social and historical explanations of textual consumption
> suggests [...] that reception theory ultimately runs up against the fact that
> reading is performative or creative and so cannot be "accounted for" any
> more accurately than a text can: its "experience" cannot be recaptured, its
> "meaning" as elusive as that of the text it works on. (20)

In contrast to the criticized approach, Nash's study presents analyses that are "not so much concerned with the reading practices of Joyce's characters as with the texts' depictions of particular reading practices (including those of individuals)," and also examines "the ways reading practices exist in relation to various social discourses" (20). On the whole,

> this study takes the issue of Joyce's reception beyond the personal and into the wider political sphere. All the same, it does accept that reading is also implicated in bodily needs: the conditions of reading described here are not universal but particular states which often resonate with somatic effects. (21)

Joyce's writing, playing as it does upon the thin division "between fictional character and actual reader," emphasizes the relationship between the security and the performance of the reading subject, and thus represents "a *suggested* contamination between the historical and the textual." To R. Best's exclamation that "I am not a character in *Ulysses*!" Nash retorts, "He was not; but he is." Within the context of Joyce studies, Nash's study aims to further oppose the "universal" Joyce of the Ellmanites, while historicizing some of the implications of deconstructionist concept of unreadability:

> This study seeks to build upon the "unreadable" Joyce of Derrida and the Joyce critics he has influenced, by showing some of the cultural ramifications of this unreadability. At the same time, it offers a further resistance to the "universal" Joyce of another generation, influenced by Ellmann and others, by refusing to universalise the immanent speculation on reception that is found in Joyce's work. (25)

Ultimately, what Joyce's obsession with the reader implies is an "acute concern for the social expectations" conditioning his texts' reception, thereby opposing the wide-spread notion that "Joyce's texts are peculiarly self-obsessed" (27).

The first chapter places Joyce's *Dubliners* within the context of Revivalism and its concerns over the relation between an ideal and an actual audience. These concerns are exemplified by the short story "The Dead," which in Nash's view "results from a fuller and more serious engagement with Revivalism" and therefore forms "part of a concomitant development in Joyce's political views away from his former rather high-handed dismissal of revivalist ambitions and towards a more complex understanding of the generic and political ambitions of that movement" (29). Benjamin's essay "The Storyteller" is used to cast light on the generic importance of Joyce's story, where "Gretta's position and narrative, as well as Gabriel's response, resonate with the controversies that characterised the reception of revivalist theatre" (52). As concerns the famous lyrical ending, Nash remains sceptical, regarding it as "a textual exercise, a form of stylistic *bravado* that hovers somewhere between Gabriel and the narrator" (57-8).

From there, Nash proceeds with an analysis of how Joyce's works from *Stephen Hero* to *Ulysses* allude to some of their actual readers' responses. Crucial in this discussion is the 'Scylla' episode, seen as a key document of Joyce's "construction of a literary politics in general" (62). What Nash also notes as relevant here is the problematic of the literary genre of autobiographical confession, whose peculiarity consists in its construction of "a peculiarly specular form in which the younger subject is recreated, displayed and viewed by the later self," where this backward glance "introduces a double-time to the narrative" which Derrida calls a "contretemps." In this particular case, what is "at the fold in this structure in Joyce's more autobiographical work, between *A Portrait* and *Ulysses*, is a personal confession: Stephen's refusal to kneel at the deathbed of his mother [...] itself recall[s] the refusal to have confession at the end of the former book" (72). Thus, the contretemps

> signals a double-time, a disagreement and a paradoxical address. Joyce's inscription of his reception carries these meanings but it also situates that reception as a form of confessional in which a past response among local readers is replayed and transformed. In doing so, these scenes establish a notion of reception as a form of ongoing responsiveness between specific reader and the author but also between later readers and the historical moment. (73)

The thrust of Nash's argument examines Stephen's imaginary construction of his audience, a construct which is seen in many aspects incorrect or distorted, for example in Stephen's labelling of his hearers as Anglo-Irish, a label that actually fits none of them:

> By having Stephen construct his audience into a falsely homogenous group, *Ulysses* implies that reception is always in a sense a misrepresentation—not just a partial (in both senses) reading but also a means of categorisation. (84)

Nash then proceeds to discuss how Joyce's writing in *Ulysses* and *Finnegans Wake* contributed to contemporary notions of reception: how the writer contributed to the critical discourse of the ordinary reader. In general, Nash contends,

> Joyce's texts are just as unfriendly, though perhaps less aloof than Proust, since they display their scepticism with an open face, staring back at the readers looking in, acknowledging the difference. One point of this refusal of affability is to guard against the transformation of writing into Culture [...] and Joyce succeeded in this more than most by showing that the "fruits of culture" had far-off roots and spoke in many voices. (98)

The question of "who might read Joyce" was as much debated during his own lifetime as it is now. Nash notices that "the recent inflection" of the debate lies in the conflict between "an anti-intellectual denigration of the 'excesses' of modernist writing in defence of the ordinary reader" (whose proponents join in the claim made in John Carey's *The Intellectuals and the Masses* in the sense that "people like Bloom cannot read *Ulysses*") and "a celebration of those same excesses," where the contention is that "there is no model for *Joycean* competence," that there can be no "bad readings" of *Finnegans Wake*, in Derrida's words (98). Nash goes on to demonstrate that

> Joyce was deeply engaged with contemporary discourses of reception such as the very notion of an "ordinary reader" and the formation of specialist readers. This engagement continued Joyce's established concern with actual readers and their conditions of reading [...], allowing these conditions to inflect the production of his new work. (99)

Nash's scrutiny of Joyce's correspondence shows his "interest in subscriptions to *Ulysses* as well as its reviews" (most notably, the one by Shane Leslie in *Quarterly Review*) (105-6), as well as his understanding of "readers being in a hurry," and thus reading not thoroughly enough, an understanding which however, "did not extend to sympathy, much less empathy" (110).

> Despite the obvious difficulties of reading *Ulysses* and "Work in Progress," Joyce's rewriting of his reception implies that readers are already in the process of reading: even to say, with Leslie, that the "massive volume" of *Ulysses* "must remain impossible to read" is itself a reading of it. (115)

This re-writing is most conspicuously present in I.5 of the *Wake*, based as it was on notebook VI.B.6, where "Joyce had purposely compiled phrases from reviews of *Ulysses* in early 1924" (118). Nash's notebook analysis reveals that

> for Joyce, writing is a process of exhaustion, of the self and of the language. His sources are the well-worn archetypes of European Culture [...], but they are also the tired materials of everyday culture [...]. He even exhausted his own materials in the process of writing: often notebooks are filled "end to end hithaways" with lines "slittering up" and "slettering down" (*Finnegans Wake* 114.16-18). (122)

In this context, John Eglinton's "Glimpse of the Later Joyce" is notable for its recognition of a combination of "individuality and reproducibility in Joyce's writing: its desperate attempt to cling to the former while having to declare the latter is symptomatic of both Eglinton's own position and the challenge of Joyce's last work (127-8). Joyce's inclusion within the *Wake* of the receiving critical voices of his earlier work, and indeed of the *Wake* itself, provides for a historicity of reception:

> Later readers are reminded—or informed—of earlier ones; more than that, they cannot help but read through those responses (or versions of them). In one sense, earlier readers *are* the text that later ones read. In working through these, in our own readings, we repeat them: one result of our

competence is the identification of previous readers. [...] So the history of Joyce's reception is in part a fiction of his own writing. (130)

Finally, Nash's last chapter singles out one particular example of Joyce's inclusion of critical voices in and of the *Wake*, treated as particularly hypocritical, and yet casting a light on the intrinsic hypocrisy of *Finnegans Wake* as such, grounded as it is on the *hypocrite lecteur* who signals the dissonance of reception. The *hypocrite lecteur* passage (*FW* 489.15-28) serves for Nash's purposes as an illustration of how

> *Finnegans Wake* is a book that cannot have an epigraph. To do so would set up a relation, even perhaps hint at a genealogy, between text and predecessor, within which an implicit readerly position would also be assumed. An epigraph typically functions as a form of address to the "competent" reader. Instead, the *Wake*'s citations...are gestures and echoes that hint without stating. (131)

Baudelaire's address "Au Lecteur" of his volume of *Fleurs du mal* "announces a fundamental disjunction of modernity, between the apparently de-individuated crowd and the genetically-presumed individuality of the lyric poet," since "at the same time as depicting himself as one of the crowd, sharing their sins, his narrator addresses them through lyric with [...] the expectation of not being understood by these readers" (133). Joyce's departure from Baudelaire, then, rests in the fact that

> [a]lthough the poet names and addresses his *hypocrite lecteur* from the outset, in Joyce's text the hypocritical reader is instead already written onto the language and form of the text. For Joyce, there is no dedication or initial address "to the reader," only the motley assortment of phrasings that make little distinction. (134)

In the passage of *Finnegans Wake* focused on by Nash, Joyce's engagement with the specific terms of Yeats' invitation to Ireland is revealed as impacting his construction of the symbolic Letter "as both the Treaty and *Ulysses*," by means of which Joyce depicts "an already divided Irish reception of his work" (159-60). The act of reception as written into Joyce's text, then, is not only an informing historical moment, but also a constitutive feature of production:

> The point is not only that reading in the present is predicated on past readings but that overwriting, and reading between the lines, produce a reading that is, again, contrary, we are back at Beckett's impasse, in which performance (because reception is already built into it) is always necessarily "To be continued" and at the same time full of stops, points at which a hiccup and an expletive close the book. (163)

Nash's "Afterword" revisits Derrida's reading of Joyce by looking at how Joyce's writing of reception differs from Derrida's implicit "deconstruction of reception." He opens by noting the paradox that despite Joyce's avowed intention to keep the professors busy for hundreds of years, "generations of readers have been faced with the difficulty—perhaps even the impossibility—of 'saying something new' about Joyce," an impossibility seen as

> structured into Joyce's writing, not only in its play on the apparent exhaustion of the English language, but in its engagement with the question of reception. If reading Joyce is also reading in the conditions of contemporary readers, then the historicity of reception itself becomes a feature of the text. (164)

Nash associates his approach with the firmly established tradition of the contextualization of Joyce's work within varying social discourses (of nationhood, postcolonisation, gender, religious censorship), here underpinned by examining the extent to which the act of reading was itself a political issue in Joyce's Ireland. For example, "the early ambition of the Literary Revival to form a national audience, in its attempt to create an Irish pubic for art" is shown by Joyce's early work to have "misjudged the actual audiences available to it," and the increasing difficulty of Joyce's work appears "designed to render any communality impossible, as if all reading was already exhausted and inevitably hypocritical."

Yet, as Nash's reading of the contretemps of the non-address to readers in the Library episode of *Ulysses* has shown, "communities of reception are inevitable, if also problematically constituted" (165). Despite his early allegiance with deconstruction, Nash now regards the deconstructionist emphasis on demonstrating that Joyce's work anticipates all that follows it as "strangely comfortable alongside the older, humanist assumption of Joyce as a 'universal' writer whose work transcends its own time and place," and aims to counter both by outlining a theory of reception immanent in Joyce's writing (166). Nash especially takes issue with Derrida's "optimistic characterisation of both deconstruction and Joyce as the harbingers of a new form of audience," for while it can be speculated that "in a curious way Joyce's writing of reception looks ahead to, or perhaps preconditions, Derrida's own references to his readers and audiences," Nash insists that "they are not doing the same thing." The difference is the following:

> In Joyce, the act of reception is a more gloomy affair. Deconstruction implies a textual indefinite audience that is always deferred; on the other hand, Joyce never relinquishes a sense of the local and specific, especially with respect to the conditions of reception that are a part of that work. Without sentimentality, these scenes seem to implore the necessity of a context from which, nonetheless, they have been irrevocably split. [...] In Joyce, the historical has been "lost" even while it still casts its determining influence; in Derrida, it is always yet to come. (166)

In Nash's understanding of Derrida, both Joyce and deconstruction set the task for a "historical community" of "explaining" an infinite textuality, whose infiniteness "in turn inevitably undermines that community," and so Derrida's "deconstruction of reception" is seen to result "in an appeal to the possibility of a later, infinite and indefinite audience." Joyce, on the other hand,

> although also questioning the structure of reception, is more concerned for the social circumstances within which his writing circulates and the inevitable failure of any co-optation of it. (167)

What is at stake in Derrida's "denial of 'reception" is the "effacement of any apparently specific addressee within a future audience"—by implying that readers cannot be located, "Derrida dilutes specific readers into a universal notion of reading" (168). Derrida's appeal to openness to the future (in)definite audience is a call to an ethical responsibility to the other, one, however, which asks readers "to forego whatever broadly determinable audience they may [...] comprise (including any political community) in favour of an infinite and indefinite audience"; thus, the call to ethical responsibility "takes precedence over any socio-political community," and it has been Nash's purpose to show that Joyce maintains "the significance of those specific 'local' readers whose responses echo in his work" (169). However, at the same time, Nash's reading has operated with the assumption that "Joyce's writing moves towards ways of encoding reception into new generic modes—what might be called a form of responsiveness." It is clear from his argument that "Joyce does not address or imply any particular audience," that he has been merely "careful to record and transform some particular, historical readers and audiences."

Therefore, the fundamental difference of Nash's argument from Derrida's deconstruction of reception lies in its perceived limitation of "the orthodox critical presupposition that Joyce demands a future and better audience," as "such an audience can only be formed through the hesitations of those earlier readers and their conditions." The paradoxical movement of Joyce's work therefore displays two contradictory tendencies: "a concern for the historical situation of its own reading," as well as a displacement of "the very notion of reception in its critique of the priority accorded to an 'appropriate' audience" (170). Derrida's metaphor of a dream reader is therefore substituted by Nash's suggestion that Joyce's writing "is haunted by its contemporary readers," for reception "is by its nature a question of the past as well as the future" (170-1). Nash concludes his optimistic analysis by summarizing his key argument:

> The act of reception, then, should be seen as part of the context into which Joyce wrote. That his work came to be seen as "unreadable," and even promoted itself as such, is not a retreat into a purely textual realm, but forms its historical significance. [...] Joyce's refusal of an audience instilled the possibility of his readers. (171)

X

Most recently, Richard Brown's outstanding edited *Companion* featured an informed re-reading of the Joycean postcolonial criticism along with a sophisticated evaluation of the future potential of postcolonial theory approaching Joyce. Mark Wollaeger's "Joyce and Postcolonial Theory: Analytic and Tropical Modes"[13] shall thus form an excellent piece with which to conclude this chapter. Wollaeger's key argument has essentially to do with what we have seen as the case with Bakhtinian theory, Kristeva's *écriture feminine*, or to some extent traditional psychoanalysis — the easiness of "application":

> specific qualities of Joyce's work and several pre-existing trends in Joyce criticism made it possible, in the early years of postcolonial work on Joyce, for critics to re-dress a familiar modernist or poststructuralist Joyce in the vestments of postcoloniality without seriously engaging Irish history or substantially revising longstanding perspectives on Joyce as a high-modernist innovator. (174)

Wollaeger's aim then is to undertake "a simultaneous critique of postcolonial theory and its early appropriation in Joyce studies" where the blame is not entirely on Joyce critics, since "problems in postcolonial treatments of Joyce also throw into relief shortcomings in postcolonial theory itself."

In order to achieve this goal, Wollaeger distinguishes between two crucial modes of postcolonial criticism: analytic and tropical. The former is marked by its "deployment of a metalanguage that aspires to engage with the language of its object of study without becoming implicated in that language," and thereby "aims to establish a provisional set of stable truths in order to throw into relief particular features of literary texts and their contexts." The latter adjective applies to criticism that "self-consciously deploys metaphor as part of its practice" (175). This divide, it will be clear to the reader as it is to Wollaeger, is yet another variation on the *historical* versus *deconstructive* polarity, although the alignment is by no means perfect. *A Portrait* is evoked, where Stephen perceives words "silently emptied of instantaneous sense," thereby forming "heaps of dead language" (*P* 150). This in turn is the situation of many a reader of postcolonial theory, where

> the governing critical tropes [...] can seem excessively abstracted from the cultural and historical materials under discussion, and as a result the lives of historical subjects and the imagined lives of literature can disappear from view, turning the critical discourse into an entirely self-referential affair.

The reasons for this unproductive abstruseness are due to the setup and agenda of postcolonial studies *per se*. Given that "theoretical language

---

[13] Mark Wollaeger, "Joyce and Postcolonial Theory: Analytic and Tropical Modes," *A Companion to James Joyce*, ed. Richard Brown (Oxford: Blackwell Publishing, 2008).

always emerges from a particular historical situation, but it may not always transcend that situation," then, asks Wollaeger,

> [t]o what extent can models of post-coloniality derived from post-Second World War African or Anglo-Indian literature be mapped onto early century decolonization in Ireland? [...] Do issues of racial difference and geographic proximity inflect key terms? (176)

If Vincent Cheng's *Joyce, Race, and Empire* can be credited with showing how in the case of Ireland, racial similarity and geographic proximity produced a need to push the Irish away by transforming them into racial others, then it can be criticised for its transfer to Homi Bhabha's Indian context without addressing "the problem of transferability," an omission all the more regrettable since "valuable work such as Cheng's could counter the ungrounding of Bhabha's tropes by reflecting on what happens when they are imported into Ireland."

Here, Wollaeger relies on Arif Dirlik's critique of the embeddedness of postcolonial discourse in poststructuralism. Postcolonial theory is read by Dirlik as

> a discourse of self-legitimation for self-identified Third World intellectuals who are expressing not so much their "agony over identity" as their "new-found power" in the First World academy, all at the expense of analyzing the role of global capital in producing the very historical conditions post-colonial studies takes as its point of departure. (177).

The chief offenders, here, are Homi Bhabha and Gayatri Spivak (despite her self-inquisitive "Can the Subaltern Speak?"). Indeed, the marketable commodity that postcolonial studies have become under the influence of these and other key figures "makes it all the more likely that its ostensible political commitment to the victims of imperialism will be overshadowed by its promise of professional advancement."

This de-historicized appropriation of the body of postcolonial theory within Joyce criticism has been, to Wollaeger's mind, facilitated by two pre-existing developments: "the poststructuralist emphasis on Joyce's deconstruction of binary oppositions," and "the assimilation of Mikhail Bakhtin's theory of the novel into Joyce studies." In the case of deconstruction, its postcolonial appropriation has replaced "the architectural metaphorics of 'deconstructing' [...] by the politicized valences of 'subverting' and 'exposing,' and the targeted binaries are no longer speech/writing or inside/outside but self/other or colonizer/colonized." The space in between

> gets called "hybridity," a trope that wears thin when criticism does not acknowledge [...] that hybridity comes in many forms and operates differently in diverse historical situations.

For Wollaeger, to get involved in a mechanical politicising of Joyce's dismantling of oppositions in as a proof of his generally anticolonial subversiveness runs the risk of "obscuring the ways in which Joyce was am-
bivalently invested in the very forms of power he seems to subvert"—a
direct correlation between the two should not be taken for granted (178).
With Bakhtin, the dominant tendency in Anglo-American criticism was to
assimilate him into "a residual New Critical template that valued complexity, managed multiplicity, and a delicate counterpoise of contradictory
voices bound within the individual work." The postcolonial appropriation
of Bakhtin "made it easy to understand Joyce's polyphonic-
deconstructive-humanism as postcoloniality waiting to be named as
such." Bakhtin, as has been observed in the last chapter, can make the
appropriation of Joyce "seem inevitable, if banal," and more importantly,
notes Wollaeger, "Bakhtin functions to make an aesthetic claim look like a
historical one" (179-80). In sum,

> the formalistic nature of Bakhtin's reception and the persistence of decon-
> stuctive reading strategies that not only coincide with but to some degree
> derive from Joyce's own textual practice have contributed to the tendency
> simply to reuse existing theoretical templates under the rubric of postcolo-
> niality, a tendency further exacerbated by professional pressure to produce
> a steady flow of fashionable criticism.

Having elucidated the historical circumstances of postcolonial intervention, Wollaeger proceeds to re-apply his *tropical* versus *analytical* distinction onto specific works of Joyce postcolonial criticism. He distinguishes
the first-wave, tropical phase, represented by Duffy's *Subaltern Ulysses*
and Lloyd's *Anomalous States*, and their respective tropes of the IRA
bomb and adulteration, stating that the "relative strengths and weak-
nesses of these two tropes depend on a trade-off between defamiliarization and aptness." Thus, whereas Duffy's is seen as "defamiliarizing and
unapt," Lloyd's is "apt and yet too much in the service of Joyce's master
trope" (181). If "the first wave of postcolonial Joyce criticism coincided
with a surge of interest in race and modernism in 1994 that soon spilled
over into Joyce studies," then in the process of "the high theory of the
1980s immigrating into postcolonial studies," what Joyce criticism has
also seen was "an increasing number of highly theorized postcolonial
approaches, and these typically rely on a predominantly analytic mode."

Two examples of this are the psychoanalytically-feminist works of Boheemen-Saaf and Jones (ed.).[14] Since both *Joyce, Derrida, Lacan, and the
Trauma of History* and *Joyce: Feminism/Post/Colonialism* overtly rely on
the work of Homi Bhabha, Wollaeger subjects his work to a brief but well-
grounded critique, observing that especially "some of his early work reads
like a blueprint for the dehistoricized work of his followers" (184). The

---

[14] See Chapter VII, section IV, and Chapter III, section VIII, respectively.

playing down of history in Bhabha suggests why Fanon is such a rare presence in postcolonial treatments of Joyce:

> Why go back to Fanon, who never loses sight of actual social struggle, when you can get what you need from Bhabha, a theory of resistance which emerges from the aporias of writing and obviates the need to undertake historical research? (185)

It therefore remains for Wollaeger to show a possible route out of this analytic versus tropical double-bind. It definitely does not lie in any programmatic discarding of theory:

> Theory will always be crucial to opening up new ways to make literature matter to our own moment, but the routinized redeployment of theory untempered by new archives, new forms of contextualization, and a keen sense of rhetorical complexity — a kind of tone-deaf textual processing — tends to give theory a bad name by blunting its vision and wadding its ears. (186)

Wollaeger picks up Joyce's own trope of the voice, used "to suggest that individual consciousness is a cacophony of public voices inhabiting the seemingly private theater of the mind," in order to ask about the powers of voice within the colonial matrix Joyce maps in his texts (186-7). What Wollaeger argues for is a media-inflected perspective on voice, devoting a "growing attention to the place of acoustic experience in modernity" and exploring "how new sound technologies were changing the status of human voice at the turn of the century." Derrida's gramophone is mentioned here as "a metaphor for articulating the peculiar properties of the word 'yes,' which he traces throughout *Ulysses*." (187-8).

However, it is rather analysis than tropicality that Wollaeger's argument is ultimately in favour of, stressing as it does the "variability of embodied voicing." From this perspective, *A Portrait* might be seen as "a particular version of coloniality [...], one barely glimpsed through the inward gaze of Stephen's consciousness, but traceable through the text in the discrepant appropriations of English that followed the British Empire across the globe." *Ulysses*, with its greater polyvocality, in which voices tend to assert their autonomy, "the voices readers silently supply map a complex range of postcolonial differences in a world in which new communication networks, travel, diaspora, and migration place pronunciation and linguistic difference center stage as markers of national and transnational identities" (188). Ultimately, *Finnegans Wake* supersedes *Ulysses* "by evocations of simultaneous difference, or difference as simultaneity" where

> the eye registers multiple verbal possibilities as if seeing down through semitransparent strata, yet the readerly act of supplying a voice necessarily ousts multiple possibilities by regrounding the text in the body, which can supply only one text at one time in one place. The dizzying multiplication of

Joyce's voices-in-waiting thus offers the experience of locatedness in the moment of reading as a momentary stay against confusion.

It is precisely the historical embeddedness of voice which points toward a relatively untapped area of future research in postcolonial treatments of Joyce—his global reception:

> Given the complex voicing of Joyce around the world, the rapidly develop-
> ing field of transnational perspectives on modernism would benefit greatly
> from a comprehensive study of Joyce's global reception. (189)

However, with the co-edited two-volume tome devoted to *The Reception of James Joyce in Europe*[15] already in reader and critical circulation, Wollaeger's appeal to studying Joyce's "global" reception raises the questions of whether this comprehensive work has missed the target of settling the issues thematized in his illuminating paper—provided this was or could have been its target in the first place—or, if under "global" one should understand "non-European," how such a study could have any profound bearing on the postcoloniality of Ireland and Joyce. However, Wollaeger is quite right in claiming that one does need—as has been the case with some of the studies examined here—to discuss the issues to do with the locus of Joyce's Irish concerns in the context of their time dimension: the dawn of the twentieth century, flourishing technological modernity and its artistic counterpart, modernism. The next chapter shall look into precisely these matters.

[15] Geert Lernout and Wim van Mierlo, eds., *The Reception of James Joyce in Europe* (London: Thoemmes Continuum, 2004).

6. Modernism & Postmodernism

I

The first study to seriously engage in rethinking Joyce as a postmodernist writer (and what bearings that might have on an understanding of his modernist status) saw the light of day in the present work's year zero — 1984. Heyward Ehrlich's edited *Light Rays: James Joyce and Modernism*[1] brings together contributions both by prominent Joyceans (Hugh Kenner, Fritz Senn, Margot Norris) and "outsiders": theoreticians (Leslie Fiedler, Ihab Hassan) but also musicians (John Cage, Pierre Boulez). Ihab Hassan's contribution, hardly surprisingly, will be of great relevance as a starting point of our discussion.

The title, "*Finnegans Wake* and the Postmodern Imagination," is offered as an invitation "to place this most outrageous of books, this parodic myth of all myths, this endless sound of language and its echolalias [...] in the field of our consciousness." The crucial question, "How does *Finnegans Wake* accord with, how does it make itself available to, the postmodern imagination?" bespeaks the underlying conviction that the book "stands as a monstrous prophecy that we have begun to discover [...] but have not yet decided how to heed" (93). Hassan offers seven perspectives on this central question, each of which is punctuated by a counterpoint composed of "postmodern rumours and random reflections." The first, "A Death Book and Book of Life," conceives of the *Wake* as a book "more determinedly cyclical than Vico and the very seasons of the unforgetting earth." Its "presentiment of all ends" seems to portend "death of the self [...] of the old reader himself" (94). Speaking of "the secret threat of *Finnegans Wake*," Hassan asks, "Is *Finnegans Wake* outside literature? Or is it pointing the way for literature to go beyond itself? Or, again, is it a prophecy of the end of literature as we have come to know it?" He answers all three with a resolute "Yes. That is why I call *Finnegans Wake* not only a death book but also a book of life, not simply an end but a progress as well" (95).

The second perspective addresses the *Wake* from the viewpoint on its negotiation of "high art, popular culture, and beyond," addressing Joyce-the-writer from the supposed paradox of his being "among the most autobiographical of artists and the most impersonal, the most self-obsessed and also the most dramatically universal," a paradox that is argued to be

[1] Heyward Ehrlich, ed., *Light Rays: James Joyce and Modernism* (New York: New Horizon Press Publishers, 1984).

no paradox at all, for Joyce "simply pushed his subjective will so far that it became superfluous to distinguish between subject and object, self and world" (96). In *Finnegans Wake* then, "the distance between the sublime and the ridiculous is contracted into a pun and expanded into endless parody" and "pop, which Leslie Fielder identifies with postmodern, is never far from the edge of *Finnegans Wake*." But the *Wake*'s affinity with popular culture is still more complex. In view of the communal readings *Finnegans Wake* calls for, Hassan hails Joyce for having "revived the magical function of the old bards and shamans, in what by convention we consider a most unlikely place, the seminar room." In relation to the high art versus popular culture dichotomy, Hassan observes that

> *Finnegans Wake* carries the tendencies of high art and of popular culture to their outer limits, there where all tendencies of mind may meet, there where the epiphany and the dirty joke become one. If this still be elitism, it is elitism of a special kind. (97)

The third perspective, "Dream & Play (And Later Structure)," discusses the contradictions inherent to "the disorder of dreams, the purposelessness of play, the cunning of structure," contradictions on which "*Finnegans Wake* balances itself" (98). The paradox examined here is one of the *Wake* being "a dream book," and thus "an effort of huge wakefulness." However, this dream needs to be understood properly:

> Whether Joyce ever dreamt or not, we must recognize that his words constitute a metalanguage, not a dream. [...] The dream element in *Finnegans Wake*, then, seen from the point of view of its author, is simply his freedom [...] to alter language and reality. (99)

The fourth perspective, "Structure," notes with palpable irony that "all good structuralists go to *Finnegans Wake* on their way to heaven, and that is perhaps why they are so long in reaching their destination," for *Finnegans Wake*, "supremely aware of itself as structure" though it might be, is also "aware of the more obscure need to de-structure itself." Hassan's proposed pathway is to approach the *Wake* by means of "coincidence as structural principle," which denotes "both identity and accident, recurrence and divergence," implying "the frightening disorder that every fanatic order itself implies" (100-1).

The fifth perspective, "Eroticism," regards the "eroticism of *Finnegans Wake*" to be "as inclusive as its life, varied as its language," containing the following mystery of love: "the one coming from the many, the many becoming one again. The final point is not perversion but at-one-ment." By way of concluding this perspective Hassan asks, "Can it be so because final unity is always and wholly impersonal?" (104).

The sixth perspective, "The Language of Babel," echoes Frank Budgen's observation that "Joyce claimed to have discovered the secret of Babel," and makes its own observation that "Joyce senses that if reality can be identified with language, language can be identified with itself," and thus seeks "'words' that can become im-mediately pure meaning" (105). This Joycean project is viewed in the "Counterpoint" as having to do with postmodernism:

> The postmodern endeavour in literature acknowledges that words have severed themselves from things, that language can now only refer to language. And what book, or rather what language, calls attention to itself as language, as ineluctably verbal and quite finally so, more than *Finnegans Wake*? (105)

Finally, the seventh section, "Toward a Universal Consciousness," regards *Finnegans Wake* as aspiring "to the condition of a universal consciousness" (106), and the strategies deployed in the service of this goal "are as numerous as they have grown familiar." However, Hassan also discerns a sense in which "the totality of the book, its effort toward a universal consciousness, fails to parody or subvert itself, fails to ironize itself" (107).

Hassan's "Postamble" repeats the *Wake*'s status as "a monstrous prophecy of our postmodernity" (108), and yet takes a critical view regarding the "hollowness" of this prophecy:

> God created the world, and that, Joyce believed, was the original sin; for the creative act is always crooked. This flaw is in all generation, in sex as well as artifice. Thus Joyce could never see sex without the hidden taint and excitement of error. (109)

Having taken the pains to emphasise the prophetic sense of Joyce's master riddle, Hassan also confesses that "part of me cries […]: Human destiny may be larger than this vast, retrograde, and reversible riddle implies," and concludes by quoting Hélène Cixous' ambiguously eulogizing and deprecating comment on the out-standing character of the *Wake*, according to which "the world, in its blind lust to seek its own destruction, could wipe itself out, for *Finnegans Wake* had saved its symbols, its notations, and its cultural patterns." (109)

II

It was at the 1988 Venice symposium that the great theoretician of postmodernism Jean-Francois Lyotard gave his paper on Joyce, entitled "Going Back to the Return."[2] Although this paper does not explicitly deal with Joyce in terms of his (post)modernist status, some of its points are not without implications for the debate presented here.

Lyotard's meditation opens with the question of recognition—"how can one be sure that what returns is what disappeared, that its appearance is also re-appearance?—and turns to the *anagnorisis* scene in the

---

[2] Jean-Francois Lyotard, "Going Back to the Return," *The Languages of Joyce*, eds. Rosa Maria Bolletieri Bosinelli, Clara Marengo Valio, and Christine van Boheemen (Philadelphia/Amsterdam: John Benjamins Publishing Company, 1992).

Odyssey, where *Ulysses* is recognized by his dog Argos, the old faithful nurse Euriclea, and finally by his wife Penelope, on the basis of his smell, the scar on his leg, and his familiarity with the secret of their nuptial bed respectively. Lyotard notes:

> The signs, smell, scar, sex are physical proofs. Only Telemachus takes his father's word for it when he claims to be *Ulysses*. His name is sufficient proof. A son recognizes his father not by his body, but by his name. (193)

From this point, the argument turns to the issue of recognizing the *Odyssey* in Joyce's *Ulysses*: "But in what way? A god or a goddess has transformed it so as to make it unrecognizable. [...] There is no *Odyssey* perceptible in the various episodes of *Ulysses*." To be sure, the "correspondences" with the Homeric epic are legion, but what is crucial for Lyotard's argument is that "the assistance they give us is illusory because it is comparable to that offered to the observer of a classical painting by the knowledge of the structural principles behind its composition" (194-5). The pattern of these correspondences (what is meant here implicitly are the famous Linati and Gilbert "schemas") was not only rendered invisible, but Joyce took the effort "to cancel it, detail by detail, episode by episode." Thus, Lyotard's thesis slowly appears:

> If the *Odyssey* re-appears in *Ulysses*, it is by its absence. *Ulysses* wanders through an Ithaca inhabited by his family but deserted, peopled not only by ghosts. At home he is not at home. (195)

Turning to Homer and the Ancient Greek epic tradition, Lyotard presents a brief summary of its constitutive features (referring to the famous first chapter of Erich Auerbach's *Mimesis*), the most prominent of which is "the over-exposed identity of the role, the 'character'" of the ancient *Ulysses*:

> In particular, he does not grow old. Athena has to disguise him in order to make him unrecognizable twenty years after his departure. [...] His return offers a perfectly identical example of recurrence since the changes wrought in him by the goddess are purely circumstantial. (197)

However, we as moderns cannot believe that "an expedient, an exile, does not imply a change, an alteration." For us, "[t]he truth of *Ulysses* is not the same [...] at the end of his journey as it was at the departure." What is more, "with modernism what is true is no longer a place, a dwelling, *domus* or *oikos*, from which a non-essential circumstance, the external war, the Trojan war, has evicted the head of the household"—what modernism, in this respect, owes to Christianity, is "the internalisation of the war" (197). An example of this is the Helen/Eve pairing:

> Helen's beauty is undoubtedly the source of trouble among the Greeks. However, it merely gives rise to war far off. In the name of Eve, woman in-

carnates the figure of original sin: she is the permanent source of the secret war which prevents the soul from returning to the house of the father. (198)

In this connection, Lyotard voices his surprise at seeing how critics see in Molly Bloom and her final yes "the pagan/Christian leitmotif of the loving mother and the re-found refuge" and opposes this view with a reference to Claudel who, being "more receptive," sent back to Joyce "the copy he had dedicated to him, describing his book as 'diabolical'" (198).

After this Greek/Biblical excursus, Lyotard shifts his focus to *Ulysses* and Joyce's modernism:

> At the time Joyce was writing *Ulysses*, artists and writers knew, in their various ways, that the purpose of writing was, broadly speaking, the same [...] but henceforth, the writer's intention would not be so much to create a beautiful work of art as to testify to the possibility of something different, this voice which, in man, is greater than man, nature and the classical concordance between them. (200)

Lyotard identifies the city as the novel's leitmotif, to an extent unparalleled in either of Joyce's two great pre-modernist predecessors, Baudelaire and Flaubert. *Ulysses*, furthermore, is "written in the language of those outlaws who were the sons of Joseph in Egypt and are the sons of Parnell in Ireland." Following the "Aeolian" discussion of Moses "dying without having entered the land of promise" and "with a great future behind him," Lyotard observes the parallel between Moses and Parnell and reflects:

> The exodus is perhaps a return. It is at least a promise of a return. But this promise remains and must remain, kept as a promise, never fulfilled. [...] The future of the return remains concealed in the former promise. The time paradox is the element that controls the work of an anamnesis: what was announced in the past was that there would be a future to testify to it. (201)

Lyotard then carries his argument further to make three observations on how the subject of paternity concerns the leitmotiv of the homecoming. First of all,

> filliation obeys the general principle that it is reversible. The father is also the son of his son just as the son is the father of his father. They beget one another. One might say they are the same self-begetter. (202)

The father-son meeting, in *Ulysses* of course ends in separation which renders both paternity and filiation "suspended as impossible to achieve"—but, Lyotard insists, "it is precisely thanks to that failure of identification that the true principle behind generation becomes apparent. Real filiation requires a rupture, the interruption of the bond that links the father to the son" (203). Second, "consubstantial paternity is non-existent, except in the mystical sense which is that of the total uncertainty of filiation" and "filiation, that is, true paternity, is only what I have called the transmission of the call" — "there is no bodily filiation from father to son" (205). Lyotard's third point concerns the parallel between the father/son and author/reader relationships:

> What is true for the father and son is also true for the writer and the reader. The reader engenders the author, the author is the reader of his reader. But, also in this case, a sort of flesh interposes itself between them and prevents pure genealogy. This time the flesh consists of language, that whore which is language. (205-6)

Literary genealogy, in Lyotard's view, responds to the same need and faces the same aporia as filiation — "if one writes, how can one not abandon oneself to the water of language? Genius consists in writing what that water could not espouse. Water can't be sliced-up. Joyce-Dedalus macerates language."

Returning to the "Ithacan" catechism, the question concerning "the door of egress" being "a door of ingress" (*U* 17.1034-5), requires of Lyotard "one last return, then," "together with the cat [...] to and about sexual difference" (206). The cat (via its allusion to female genitalia) is "the passage through which the father has passed and from which the son will emerge." The cat argues that

> if the Lord has created us as sexual beings, divided and separate, and, if He has reserved to Himself the power of uniting us according to the fire in our loins, it is not only to test us, it is to reveal the mystery of His ways, and, in particular, the following one: that self-begetting, of which He alone is capable, is to be found, oh how palpably, *ad portas mulieris*. (207)

The question of return posed by *Ulysses*, the question of re-entering, in the small hours of June 17th, the door of no. 7 Eccles Street, is "not whether one can bathe twice in the same river," but rather "is sexual difference not ontological difference?" (207-8) Even though "certainly the return that is the *Odyssey* attempts to scar over the difference and the exodus narrated by the Pentateuch attempts to become free of it," yet "both attempts contain the confession of an initial and recurrent servitude. That is why we must award to sexual different a foremost position, prior to, and source of, any debate" (208). The omnipresence of sex in *Ulysses* is, then due to the fact that

> the text of the Homeric homecoming, even if it returns via the Biblical exodus, cannot avoid coming up against that difference, that most ancient, internal obstacle which hinders the return, prevents it and ceaselessly returns to it.

Lyotard concludes:

Going back to and coming up against the fact of sexual difference, which knows no site, no representation, which generates the most uncontrollable anguish, by rewriting this fact in language whose ductile power ceaselessly plunges us into that anguish and that impotence, Joyce's text affirms that the sin is unforgivable and the homecoming impossible. (209)

Frequently overlooked, because overshadowed by his theoretical work (which features Joyce in a place of honour), Lyotard's formally unconventional peregrination over the Homeric and Biblical intertexts of Joyce's *Ulysses* and its central concern with paternity and sexual difference remains a masterpiece in its own right, raising, adumbrating, or merely toying with, a number of issues crucial to the following "seriously theoretical" works of Joyce criticism.

III

The primary focus of the first issue of *European Joyce Studies*, discussed already in another context,[3] was at one, as its title implies, with Joyce's *Modernity and its Mediation*.[4] The editor's introduction posits Joyce's stature in the discussions about modernism—whether understood as "a style, a movement, or simply as a term referring to literature written between 1910 and 1940"—as always requiring "special attention" in that

Joyce is always already ahead of us, just as he was ahead of Pound, Eliot, Woolf, and Forster. An Irish writer, he seems to have made marginality into a strategic art of elusion, and preprogrammed elusiveness into the textuality of his writing. (3)

Unlike Eliot or Thornton, "we have lost some of our idealist innocence with regard to literature's power to embody the transcendent," and Joyce's importance rests elsewhere—upon the fact that he has made his readers "aware of the philosophical implications of textuality," of "the use of the medium of language," as well as "the effects of specific stylistic features such as citationality." To recapitulate, reading Joyce from our contemporary perspective,

[w]e find that the text, after our initial engagement with its portrayal of Dublin and its inhabitants which demands a complex moral, aesthetic, and emotional response, leads us beyond to ponder the nature of mimesis, the impossibility of representation, and especially the function and role of language (both written and oral) as the indispensable medium of human community, of selfhood, of artistic expression, and of thought itself. (4)

"Modernity," unlike its French prototype "modernité," is "not delimited by temporal parameters, and can refer to texts as widely divergent as *Frankenstein* and *Finnegans Wake*" (5), and Joyce's special place in the group

[3] See Chapter III "Feminism Sexuality & Gender Studies," section IV.
[4] Christine van Boheemen, ed., *Joyce and the Art of Mediation* (Amsterdam - Atlanta: Edition Rodopi, 1989).

of Modernist writers, for van Boheemen, may well have to do with the nature of his relationship with a (perhaps the) defining principle of modernity—its technologically mediated condition; or, in van Boheemen's words, Joyce might have been "the only one of the group whose work, in theme and technique, demonstrated a fascination with the nature of modern media—media of transportation, of communication, of entertainment, of expression" (5-6). Inherent to this "mediatization" of Joyce's artistic vision was its turn "towards reflection upon its own material substrate," culminating in *Finnegans Wake*

> with an inventory of discourses, of narrative- and other effects mockingly mediated through several media, and with a mediated inventory of the collective narrative memory of Western culture, highlighting nothing so much as the discontinuity between the real and (its?) representation. [...] All art can do, *Finnegans Wake* would seem to argue, is to testify to human limitation. (6)

Lyotard's concept of postmodernist art as bearing "witness to the unpresentable" and waging "war on totality" is seen as intrinsic to Joyce's notion of Modernity, which thereby also "implies an ethically demanding political program: to remain consciously aware of the insufficiency of human means" (6). The essays collected here are marked by their negative capability to treat Joyce's universe "founded upon the void" "without desire to proclaim or privilege a totalizing vision of either history or the text," focusing on "the limitations imposed upon representation by the necessity of mediation through the medium," whether "language in general," or, more specifically, "the ideological structures of 'secondary modeling' (Lotman's term) such as sexual difference and other conceptual configurations of opposition" (7). Within the context of the present discussion, two essays will be of importance, Marilyn L. Brownstein's "Against Mediation: The Rule of the Postmodern in the *Phaedrus* and *Finnegans Wake*," and Alan Roughley's "The Mediatization of Joyce."

Brownstein discusses the simultaneously "playful and serious meddling with the ordinary mediating function of language," characteristic of the linguistic subversions of both Plato's *Phaedrus* and Joyce's *Finnegans Wake*, in the context of the Lyotardian unrepresentable, the "lack of reality" within "reality," which also draws the division line between the modern and postmodern. In other words, whereas modern art presents "the solace of good forms," the postmodern "copes with reality's unrepresentability by attempting its representation" (79). For Lyotard,

> [p]ostmodern discourse, thus, abandons the linear, the hierarchical, the binary orderliness of an ideal form—the logic of language's forms—in pursuit of the real, of what "will have been done." It represents, after the fact, what has been occurring all along. (79-80)

The two texts juxtaposed in Brownstein's essay then share the common feature of "doubled forms of memory" which "offer respite from language's strictest mediations." As long as the postmodern project might be seen as engaged with "the remembering of what in fact the protective mediations of language conceal," then both *Phaedrus* and *Finnegans Wake* "turn away from the rationalizing proclivities of ordinary discourse, by presenting a particular view of memory as compensation and play" (80). This linguistic mediation anticipates "a Lacanian rather than a Freudian context" in that

> these lines yield a view of linguistic mediation—the replacement of desire for our mother with the symbols of our father—as a mixed blessing at best; for sorrow's gate opens to us all in language's utilitarian rejection of the real—as well in the (limited and limiting) solace of linguistic play with which these lines are marked. [...] Memory, in the postmodern text, survives as the urgency of a primary nostalgia reified, an etymological restoration, a reversal, in which *algos*, the grieving or longing for *nostos*, for homecoming, is renewed as a kind of corporeal eloquence—a speaking of the body through disruptions in the body of language (82).

Managing such a transposition involves "the reversal of the mediating role of language" - in Joyce, the alternative is located within "feminine or maternal memory, the recovery of the playful and dangerous (infantile) remembering of the origin of *eros* in direct relation to the maternal body." In that sense, the *Wake* "recovers all that is forbidden [in that it] reinscribes the activity of an infantile dynamic upon adult experience" (83). This figuration of feminine or sensational memory is found in Plato's notorious myth of the soul's constitution in a celestial chariot ride, where "sensational memory, remembering in the body" is also viewed as "ethical":

> love is divinely inspired; it only seems inexplicable, irrational, but in fact represents wisdom close to that of the gods, for the lover approaches the ideal [...] in the beauty of his beloved. (83-4)

The issue of "sensational memory" also surfaces in the famous examination of speech versus writing, which serves to display "the dynamic of the Socratic dialectic in all its erotic-ironic fluctuations" while also bringing home Plato's main point, "a celebration of the irrational, the mute or extralinguistic, as a means of knowing." It is "this reevaluation of the irrational" that is "key to Plato's postmodern position" (85). This special understanding of irrationality and sensational memory finally helps to bring the two texts examined by Brownstein together:

> So long as we understand that irrational simply means without benefit of the logic of linguistic mediations, then we can identify—and eventually, conflate—ethical memory in Plato and what Joyce calls the feminine in *Finnegans Wake*. In both cases, the special nature of sensory memory provides for a reenactment of an ambivalent (maternal) dynamic. (85)

Here, for further clarification of her main point, Brownstein turns to neurology, which "revises the notion of an unconscious in distinguishing languaged from sensational or spatial memory" in that it conceives of all experience as "stored both as linguistic and sensory memory," in "separate modules in the brain which are not randomly but idiosyncratically activated." This means that at "any given moment perception occurs as a series of linkages among a large number of locations in the brain" (86-7). The uses of mediation (understood as implementations of the rationalizing effect of language) are then "both individually and, very likely, culturally determined" (88). The primary individual determination concerns the constitution of humans as sexed as well as their construction as gendered beings. For an elaboration on how sexual difference impacts upon the uses of mediation, Brownstein turns to Lacanian theory of sexual difference. Her lucid summary deserves to be quoted at length:

> In Lacan's (linguistic) analysis of sex difference in Oedipal resolution, he concludes that women remain in the "real," that is, in relation to the maternal body while entering the symbolic order. Lacan distinguishes between "threat" and "nostalgia" as components of castration anxieties which activate the Oedipal struggle. "Threat" alludes to the male response, the agent of compulsory symbolic solutions, while "nostalgia," the feminine choice, represents a longing to return to the body from which she was born. In the masculine recoil from difference, in the opting for similarity even in the spectre of the large and threatening form of the father, lie the roots of the symbolic, a system which replaces the real with linguistic substitutions based in categories constituted out of similarity. The feminine version is one that both accepts the linguistic solution but also remains attached to the maternal body. (88)

Turning to the issue of Plato's and Joyce's postmodern status, Brownstein notes that both were working against a prevailing modernity: in Plato's case, against "the linguistically over-determined speeches of the Sophists," the crucial concern of his resistance being that "languaged memory obscures the sensational" (89). Joyce's project in the *Wake* is more complex: its "circularity surrounds us," and its "meaning, shape, pattern" can be assessed "from a distance, in a rereading." There is also one more psychological implication of the *Wake*'s occupation with sensational memory:

> [J]ust as text whose overdetermined or mediating forms would be paranoid—breaking the links between word and world—the text which functions exclusively in terms of sensational memory would be schizoid, blurring the distinctions between inner and outer. Texts made from languaged attempts to subvert the ordinary role of language shift intermittently between the two functions or entertain both possibilities simultaneously. (91)

Revisiting, by way of conclusion, the *Wake*'s postmodern status, Brownstein sees it as coming "both before and after, 'before' the literary postmodernism of this half of the century, temporally, and in the range of its inventiveness, and 'after' [...] as it attempts the representation of the unrepresentable (that which has already occurred)" (94). For Brownstein, our task as readers or teachers of Joyce, ultimately rests in a "demy-thologization" of the *Wake*:

> Perhaps for Joyceans, the time has come to ignore the setting, the mythol-ogy, the history—the literary aspects of the text—in order to confront the madness of the text, its schizophrenia, its destruction of boundaries be-tween what can be said and what is ordinarily unspoken. (95)

Roughley's essay is informed by his Derridean perspective (which obtains a book form later in his influential study of the relationship between Der-rida and Joyce)[5] on the issue of the process of mediatization of Joyce, an appropriately double-sensed genitive. Drawing attention to its own title, the essay opens with a coterminous interest in the titles of Joyce's works—the question of "[h]ow many of us still think immediately of a traditional Irish folk song when we hear the title *Finnegans Wake*; or of Homer when we hear '*Ulysses*'?," implies that the process of Joyce's titling itself involves a mediation of the textual predecessors, no longer signifying "the full control of its signified over the economy of which it was the ruling head," no longer guaranteeing, "as a capitalized proper name [...], the presence of immediate political control" (189). Thus, the double-genitive of Roughley's title is meant to denote two sets of textual operations: one, "Joyce's mediatization of the literary styles and textual fragments absorbed in his writing," and two, "the responses to Joyce's writing that we make as readers and critics who must attempt to annex our experiences of Joyce's writing to what is presumably a larger under-standing of language and writing in general." Whereas the former has to do with the Derridean concept of textual event "whose exterior form consists of a '*rupture* and a redoubling,'" the latter implies

> the various ideological and theoretical formations that have been set to work in critics' readings of Joyce's texts and then passed into the canon of received critical proclamations which determines subsequent readings of Joyce's writings.

Joyce's writings are seen as continually demanding this process: "They insist that we look at the ways in which we read those writings and re-think the *theoria*, the process of looking, that constitutes the *praxis* of our reading" (190).

Marquis de Sade is proposed as a possible "hinge on which we might hang our considerations of Joyce's and his critics' respective practices of mediatization" (191), a perspective in which "the critical project of con-verting Joyce's writing into a vast cataloguing array" functions as "a reversing mirror image of the procedure by which De Sade invented a

[5] For Roughley's *Reading Derrida Reading Joyce*, see Chapter I "Deconstruction," section VI.

paradoxical discourse from the classical forms which he inherited" (192-3). This cataloguing hunt, claims Roughley, marked as it is by looking beneath "the list of Joyce's characters, the so-called literary allusions in his texts, the recreations of Joyce's compositional techniques, the list of Dublin place names, and the stabilizing recitation of the literary themes" demonstrates a belief in finding "access to the meaning of Joyce's meaning" (193). This activity and belief bear a resemblance to New Critical practice, which, for Roughley, hinged on "the evaluation of literature through an assessment of its organic form and the appropriateness of this form to a content," in turn judged "from the narrow perspectives of the realistic psychological depiction of characters and the creation of a realistic, naturalistic, or symbolic setting" (196). In this context, Joyce's reinscription of one of the crucial New Critical works of literary and linguistic theory, Richards and Ogden's *The Meaning of Meaning*, as "maymeaminning of maimoomeining" (*FW* 267.03) is significant, not least because of its identification, in Roland McHugh's *Annotations*, with an allusion. Roughley opposes this since to his mind, in order for it to be an allusion, it would be necessary

> to create an identity between the two sets of terms by ignoring precisely those operations of decapitalizing and grafting that Joyce performed in order to destroy the identity created by the repetition of "meaning," and to introduce a play of difference into the repetition of the decapitalized as Joyce sets it to work within the play of *Finnegans Wake*. (198)

For Roughley, the double "maymeaminning of maimoomeining" engages in a deconstruction of a whole series of binary oppositions (preserved more or less intact by allusion), re-citing

> at the level of the letter and the "paperspace" precisely the double ALP, maternal/filial, permitting/denying assertion of the love given-to/claimed-by the self in relation to the other and the double experience of the loving/maiming that constitute the functions of oscillating desire on psychic cathexis. (199)

Roughley concludes his essay with a sharp assault on both the anti-feminist and anti-poststructuralist approaches warning against their "reactionary and potentially dangerous attitude towards reading and interpreting Joyce," which he fears could lead to "the sort of literary and cultural hegemony which would deny, or at least suppress, the fundamentally radical and revolutionary nature of Joyce's art" (200). This is an assault which, in the light of the presentations culled here, seems to be strangely at odds with the development of Joyce studies in the 1990s, where it was precisely approaches directed from anti-poststructuralist positions which claimed to have restored the radical and even political character of Joyce's artistic project. Roughley's assault, however, the concernment of which already evidences the shift against which it is aimed.

IV

Derek Attridge's *Cambridge Companion*[6] ought again here to be consulted on account of its inclusion of an essay by Christopher Butler titled "Joyce, Modernism and Postmodernism" which nicely documents the "anti-theory" turn of the Joyce (modernism) studies of the 1990s to which Roughley subjected such a scathing critique. Butler sets out to contextualize Joyce's revolution toward a "kind of skeptical relativism," the roots of which he traces back into the nineteenth century and Matthew Arnold's "confrontation with the customary" (262). The early Modernists are seen as having progressed from of working "through Symbolism and its derivatives" to moving "significantly beyond it by inventing radically new languages for art." Joyce is seen to first assimilate tradition, "producing a distinctly Chekhovian set of short stories," and then "manifesting in *A Portrait* the early modern metamorphosis of previous styles" in which "an ironic gap is opened up between Stephen's self-emancipating thoughts as an arrogant young man and his poetic mimicry of his predecessors" (264). However, Butler is careful to balance lines of connection with points of rupture, and discusses "the stylistic innovations of the opening and closing pages of *A Portrait* which launch Joyce into an original modernist experimentalism," which seem "almost unpredictable in terms of these earlier influences" (265). Furthermore, Joyce is regarded as resisting not only the past, but also the present, entering "the experimental mainstream of modernism by an extraordinary display of technique, and not by any anterior commitment to some avant-gardist doctrine" (266).

Pursuing his unique artistic project, by 1922 Joyce

> had challenged all who wished to write after him by producing a designedly encyclopedic epic, whose sustained mythical parallelism raised in an acute form the post-Nietzschean and post-Jungian questions of the nature of history as repetition (266).

Rather than being influenced by others, Joyce is regarded as an influence on Eliot, Pound, Woolf, Faulkner, Dos Passos, Doeblin, Broch, and Nabokov among others. The ideology of the contemporary avant-garde movement thus is found to be "irrelevant to his purposes," and an imperative is raised to place his work "within the modernist tradition by critical comparison rather than through the study of its direct influence" (269). Turning to the *Wake* requires of the critic the "concentration on the subjective" as the "aesthetic autonomy of the experimental work," as well as "a radical withdrawal from established modes of representation" prerequisite for its appreciation (274). The postmodern Joyce then emerges from the context of Kristeva's "revolution in poetic language" as an evasion of "that phallogocentric discourse of the Lacanian 'Symbolic Order' which

---

[6] Christopher Butler, "Joyce, Modernism and Postmodernism," *The Cambridge Companion to James Joyce*, ed. Derek Attridge (Cambridge: Cambridge University Press, 1990).

dominates our waking lives" (277). More broadly, the transition from modernism to post-modernism is regarded as

> concerned with the artificiality of modes of discourse, with intertextuality, and with that attack on mimesis which transforms "real Matter-of-Fact" into a "matter of fict" or "the matter of ficfect" (*FW* 532.29). (277)

A postmodernist avowal from one of Joyce's letters that "I know that it is no more than a game," substantiates Butler's view of Joyce as

> initiator of a new tradition, leading to writers like Ray Federman, Ronald Sukenick, Gilbert Sorrentino, and Donald Barthelme," in whose texts, like in *Finnegans Wake*, the "declamatory personality"... founders in the vacillation of the play of forms, sliding through them and retraceable only in the terms of sham, forgery, and citation. (278)

A postmodernist Joyce, Butler concludes, is "the parodist of the past styles in *A Portrait*, the inventor of eighteen new ones in *Ulysses*, and the celebrant of the occult orders hidden within that most subjective of experiences, the dream, in the *Wake*" (282).

V

The difficulties inherent to categorizing Jean-Michel Rabaté's kaleidoscopic readings have been already touched upon elsewhere.[7] Here his collection of essays *The Authorized Reader*,[8] will be introduced, organized as it is around the topics of modernity, authority, paternity, and the reader, which are therefore of relevance to the present discussion.

Rabaté's "Introduction" departs from the frequently mentioned peculiarity of the relation into which criticism is required to enter when dealing with Joyce:

> Perhaps more than any writer of this century, Joyce has forced criticism to acknowledge its theological nature. His ambitions [...] have driven his critics to repeat his gesture, to read and write "in memory of him," as Jacques Derrida aptly puts it. (1)

Rabaté, as Derrida before him, identifies this with the problem of authority, be it the author's or that of his/her work. This difficulty is seen as inherent in the modernist project:

> The common foundation of the new poetics, be they those of Flaubert's, Mallarmé's, or Joyce's, is the autotelic nature of the work's assertion. Its foundation upon the void and upon incertitude replaces the theological model of creation within a more human, but also more unconscious pattern, which uses another metaphor, that of paternity. (4)

---

[7] In Chapter II "Psychoanalysis," section VII.
[8] Jean-Michel Rabaté, *James Joyce: Authorized Reader* (Baltimore: Johns Hopkins University Press, 1991).

Rabaté goes on to focus on the "telegram" passage from "Proteus" (the notorious misprint of "nother dying"), which seems to him to illustrate that "any 'text,' any piece of paper with printed words or dates on it, constitutes an *alibi*—a proof that otherness is at work in a process that ineluctably entails the murder of some close relative," in which "the felicitous misprint of French telegraphists suggests the symptomatic resurgence of the 'other' in 'me' ('other me')." In a typically deconstructionist trope, Joyce's writing becomes a letter sent to its reader, which, if we accept to keep reading, forces us "to become either *lui* or *moi* and" and turns us "into the ideal addressees of a similar telegram sent by our new mystical father, Joyce" (8). Derrida's metaphor, in his "Two Words for Joyce," of Joyce's grandpaternity vis-à-vis his readers-grandsons, required to become the "fathers" of their reading, is mentioned as an instance of a most bizarre coincidence:

> a real-life Stephen Joyce, the actual grandson of James Joyce, should be mentioned in Derrida's texts, as it were, before he even knew of his existence. The actual presence of a grandson inevitably poses questions of jurisdiction, of legal control over texts, and of the laws of copyright which may set bounds to a given signature. (12)

This notion of a "fathered reading" brings forth the concept of the "perversity of literature," which Rabaté understands, not as "a negation of otherness," but rather as "the ineluctable return of the other in the self, an other that cannot be confidently ascribed to an identifiable place" (18). It is this perversity that Rabaté's essays set out to explore within the broad context of Joyce's modernity.

The first essay, "*A Portrait* of the Artist as a Young Dubliner,", deals with the issue of silence in *Dubliners*, bringing to mind Broch's and Pound's observation that it "may function like the silence of the analyst or the silence of the priest at confession, since it lets the symptoms speak of themselves" (20). Rabaté's main concern, given that "the question of the silence of interpretation is built within the text, prepared and foreseen in the deceptive game it plays with the reader," is to ask about the ways in which this book offers "a theory of its own interpretation, of its reading, of possible metadiscourse about its textuality" (20-1). "The Sisters" is an obvious starting-point, a text whose "symbolic realm of interpretation exhibits gaps which are soon filled by imaginary fantasies" (24). Rabaté's careful reading shows that

> [a]lthough the boy is urged by his uncle to "learn to box his corner"—which also alludes to the confession box in which the priest has been found laughing silently—this foolish assertion of the subject's autonomy and self-reliance is contradicted by the series of dichotomies the child faces. (28)

An etymological excursus into the famous trinity of *paralysis, simony,* and *gnomon* reveals a couple of interesting intersections, where Simon Magus corresponds to Persia as the locus of the boy's dream, and *paralysis* (from *para-lyein*, "to release, to unbind," coupled with *paresis*, "to let fall") seems highly relevant for the priest, whose "paralysis" is "both a dropping of some holy vessel (a chalice) in a parapraxis (a slip or lapsus) and the untying of the knots which paradoxically constrict the cramped movements of the protagonists" (29). The story's elusive obsession with perversion is shown as coterminous with its depiction of the dividedness of subjectivity:

> [T]ruth implies a certain concern for division, whereas heresy thrives as perversion on the body of dogma; nowhere is perversion more virulent than in a discourse which attempts to articulate the truth of the subject in his own division, and this is where psychoanalysis and religion exhibit their common logic, a logic Joyce merely displaces—or, rather, warps. (32)

Rabaté regards "The Dead" as a supplementary addition to the series of stories of *Dubliners* which, "added one year after the completion of the rest, not only mirrors the earlier stories, but modifies them retroactively, pushing them into a new mode of writing." Rabaté's focus on silence draws his attention to

> [t]he uneasy silence of this parodic last supper is transformed into the general silence marking the signal for Gabriel's speech. His empty rhetoric soars on the background of a willingness to forget the silence of vanished ghosts. (42)

The movement of the final story completes and subverts the movement of the collection as a whole: as long as "the first fourteen stories try to set up the possibility of an ethical discourse criticizing the paralysis of Dublin," this is ultimately "left outside the scope of the subject's discourse in 'The Dead,' as in *Finnegans Wake*" (46). The practice of rereading Joyce's works in the light of his later texts, of which Rabaté is undoubtedly a staunch advocate might be helpful in yielding some clues "to the symbolic strategies he employs, and such is the case with the parody of all the titles of the stories in *Finnegans Wake*" (*FW* 186.12-13) (47). The Wakean perspective then allows for a view of "The Sisters" as a text which stages the paternal hesitation "between the paralysis of heresy and sexual sin," figured in Rabaté's playful conclusion

> by the GPI, or syphilitic "general paralysis of the insane" affecting Father Flynn, and the paralysis of mute orthodoxy, the GPO, or General Post Office, the pure ballast of an empty symbolic structure, defining the void center of the capital. (49)

"Thy Name is Joy" is preoccupied with "the narrative functions" of paternity in fiction, which "constitutes one of the major themes of *Ulysses*" (50). Lacan has much to offer here, as for him, "the paternal function is the key to the metaphors which underpin our Unconscious," and is divided into three modes:

1. the real father, or actual genitor, who is the historical father inside or outside the family, always inadequate to his role or to expectations;
2. the symbolic father, who is reduced to the pure agency of the Father's Name through which the Law and castration come into play;
3. the imaginary father (or the invested substitute father whom children may evolve in infantile dreams, fantasies, or wish-fulfilments), who occupies the space of the paternal "fantasms" between the symbolic structure and the real lack or absence. (51)

Against the widespread view of Stephen in search of a father, Rabaté remarks that "Stephen is obviously looking for a substitute mother much more than for another father, at the psychological level of the fiction at least" (52). Even on the symbolic or imaginary levels, Stephen's longing for a return to a father as a point of origin appears misconceived since

> if a subject wants to create durable art that helps him to awake from the nightmare of history he has to pursue the circle of his writing, returning not to his father, but to a displaced origin (or, more precisely, the displacing of origins in a movement of quest for ultimately wanting origins) that lies in language. (55)

Analogously to Lacan's triad of paternal levels, Rabaté summarizes his observations into his three remarks on paternity: the first positing that a father "is not simply an 'individual,' but mainly a function; paternity is that place from which someone lays down a law, be it the law of sexual difference, the law of the prohibition of incest, or the laws of language"; secondly, that a father "is not a 'problem,' but a nexus of unresolved enigmas, all founded on the mysterious efficacy of a Name, which in itself remains a riddling cipher"; and third, that "if a father is defined by his absence, paternity and patriarchy are set adrift in a world of substitutes, in which everybody is endlessly elsewhere" (58). As a countercurrent to the novel's thematic preoccupation with fatherhood and paternity, Rabaté notes that it begins "in the atmosphere of the pervading presence of the mother," and ending "with a hymn to femininity" (59). Always on the lookout for lessons taught by the *Wake*, Rabaté concludes by contrasting the father of "legal fiction" in *Ulysses* with the father in *Finnegans Wake*, a door-opener "to the laws of fiction as 'truthful structure.'" "True," that is, "to the joy of naming" (61).

"The Figures of Incestitude" complements Rabaté's meditations on the issue of paternity with a discussion of the theme of *incest*, the specific meaning of which "entails a pun on blindness and insight contained in the verb *to know*." Thus, in the phrase "wise child that knows her own father," which "echoes proverbially and also recalls *The Merchant of Venice*," Rabaté notices instances of failures of recognition, especially those in which "Simon Dedalus fails to recognize his son several times" (e.g. *U* 11.254) (67). The father-son bond rests in the wife-mother, their shared "unmentionable privilege of having crossed in person, once at least, the threshold of her womb. 'What links them in nature? An instant of *blind* rut' (9.859)." Mother is identified with the "true 'genitive' subjective and objective" of *Amor matris*; father, with the 'ablative plural' of *Caecitas patribus*, which implies "desire and castration, places and replacements" (69). Castration and incest, Rabaté observes

> are thus played off one another to define the symbolic order of the written text. Paternity is reduced to being a name, which can be separated from the bearer and transmitted to an heir, as Shakespeare did when he trans-ferred his power to Hamlet, who was "disarmed of fatherhood, having de-vised that mystical estate upon his son" (*U* 9.835-36). (70)

Stephen's "voice of Esau" (*U* 9.927-28) is found twice to be absent: "a first time because it has been usurped by Jacob's voice, a second time because it has been replaced by his handwriting" (72). Turning to the Bible proves relevant here especially the motif of Jacob's obedient follow-ing of (and standing-in-for) his mother Rebecca's voice:

> When, later, the blind father feels his son's body hidden beneath a goat-skin, he seems to renew a sensual contact with his wife. His lyrical bene-diction takes the form of a fresh alliance with a feminine earth: "*See*, the smell of my son is as the smell of a field which the Lord hath blessed."

In Isaac's benediction, "something is inexorably written, a signature which becomes a fate: *fari fatum*. Speech is a production entailing irreversible action as soon as it is undersigned by a name: 'Speech, speech. But act. Act speech. They mock to try you. Act. Be acted on' (*U* 9.978-99)" (72). The unsteadiness of Stephen's balancing between a father's and a son's name is even heightened in the fundamental instability of Bloom's own signifier, due to which, "a prey to transformations," 'Bloom' "will never acquire the status of a symbolic signifier." This instability lies in the obvi-ous legal action which turned "Virag" into "Bloom":

> The transformation of the name and the suicide can then arise from similar causes; a suicide like that of Rudolph Bloom is a desperate act, committed in isolation, while the *deedpoll* that ratified his new name is a deed exe-cuted "by one party only." (74)

The concluding note, here, is on Bloom's own filial encounter with Virag in "Circe," who "appears as Bloom's real father in this scene, since he at least is an authority on sexual matters" (75).

"Circe's Stagecraft" picks up the threads of the conclusion of the pre-vious essay, noting that another father/son encounter takes place, here, by means of Stephen's imitation of "the mannerisms of Simon Dedalus when singing and playing the piano, thus meeting him in spite of himself, thanks to a symptomatic and deliberately willed blindness" (78). The only method discerned within the chapter's madness is "the hallucinatory blooming of fantasies: Bloom meets his parents; all his messianic and masochistic wishes come true with a vengeance; he becomes a woman, is prostituted, witnesses the love scene between Boylan and Molly" (81). The perversity of the chapter and its "symbolism" which "Bloom acts out without being conscious of doing so" is determined by fetishism, "a key strategy in the technique of the episode" (83). This is particularly conspicuous in Circe's "theatricalization of the natural world, in which the objects have a stage turn at the expense of the 'actors,'" where fetishism plays the role of "staging post in the crystallization of fantasies—fantasies of castration, transsexuality and prostitution" (84). The "baroque dispersion of all the motifs" of the novel occurs however at the important cost of the loss of psychic economy: neither Bloom nor Stephen gain anything in this scene: "they do not learn any deeper truth about themselves and never mention their fantasies when dialoguing after the episode" (89). Shakespeare's appearance at the climax of this psychic tempest is all-important:

> The act becomes paralyzed when it passes through this booby-trapped echo chamber: Shakespeare says "ago" (I act) in order to discover the self (I), the eye; but the performative splits into two, divided between the agent and the actor of the act, between Othello and Iago; Iago must be repeated *à gogo* (ad libitum), reiterated in a derisory parody, "Iagogogo." (91)

Ultimately, however, fetishism is renounced in Stephen's refusal of "the stick Bloom wants to give"—Stephen

> does not need any weapon, since he has already shouted "Nothung!" in the brothel to indicate that he has not been hung like the Croppy Boy of the Irish song, that he calls upon the Sigfried's sword to defend himself, but also that this sword would be invisible and imponderable. (93)

"Spinning Molly's Yarn" imaginatively and innovatively revisits the Homeric intertext. First, in "The Sirens,"

> Bloom's Homeric ruse amount precisely to this: he asks the waiter to leave the door open so that he can hear the songs while looking at the fascinated and fascinating barmaids. He sees their ears in order to hear the songs without falling prey to the power of music, uses this visual mirror as a relay between emission and reception. If he misses the vision of the singers' faces, the distance allows for a better audition. (97)

Homer's story posits yet another paradox: Circe the sorceress tells Odysseus how to resist the Sirens, adding "tell them is you should shout out and command them to let you loose, they must tie you tighter with a few more ropes" (98). However, asks Rabaté, "how do the sailors know that the ship is out of range of the fatal song if they really can hear nothing and if *Ulysses* cannot move?" Similarly to the strategy within Joyce's text, the resolution of the critical aporia comes from the way the sailors, at least in the *Odyssey*, open their eyes wide and see; they even judge by seeing — that is to say, by struggling in their turn with this ineluctable modality. (99)

Proceeding to discuss Molly's chapter, Rabaté remarks that to "cancel an omission may asymptotically approach the shortest route to a direct statement, which is "precisely what Molly achieves, in an idiom that keeps contradicting itself in order to assert her supreme 'indifference.'" Moreover, Molly "concludes" a text that "seemed to have exhausted its possibilities as she subverts its written status by an unexpected return to oral discourse" (105). It is also in Molly's concluding meanderings that Bloom's name, whose instability has been symptomatic of his uncertainty as a deceived husband throughout, seals his victory over all his rivals, whether real or imaginary:

> In a sense he signs Molly's text, dominating its imaginary world not by bringing into play the power of the conquering male, like Boylan, but by acting parasitically upon the flowers of her rhetoric through the bloom of his name: his name is diffracted and disseminated into a multiplicity of signifiers. […] His victory over Boylan does not depend on his having "more spunk" than the other, but on his name's ability to be combined, translated, and inverted and to frolic with complete liberty in the voice which accepts it. (109)

Finnegans Wake, then, begins as "a sort of sequel to *Ulysses*, just as Molly, having become 'adult' for the first time through adultery, delights in her name, which she writes in her imaginary works, and just as Bloom frees himself from the paternal metaphor." What the *Wake* heralds is the relationship between writings and languages which works toward shifting "the question of the 'author' and of interpretation" and renders perversity as marking "a stage in the relation between the text and the reader" (115).

"Idiolects, Idiolex" departs from positing a binary between a *code* and an *idiom* which frames the whole spectrum of textuality:

> Every text probably falls between the absolute, utopian objective of total communication of its elements — in short, a code — and the creation of an individual language that is not to be found anywhere else — in other words, an idiom.

What the so-called "modern" text tends to do, caught as it is between the two extremes, is to "tighten the bonds between the code and the idiom" and thereby "establish the inner necessity justifying all its presuppositions; it is the road to the idiomatic code — that is to say, the idiolect" (117). This subversive creation of the idiolect, a rebellion against the normative either/or of textuality, is akin to the rebellion of the son against paternal tyranny, with which Rabaté paves the way for his analysis of the theme of incest in the next chapter, as by killing the father, the sons "unwittingly violate the most prohibited of the incest taboos: when they murder him, strangle him, shoot him, they are in a way having sexual intercourse with him" (131). To elaborate on this startling analogy, Rabaté turns to one of the *Wake*'s exemplary stories—the one of Buckley and the Russian general. "Language of Earse" provides a biographical account of the story's genesis and inclusion within the *Wake*:

> Joyce, who had heard this story narrated by his father, had enormous difficulties in inserting it in the *Wake*, despite the straightforward relevance of the classical Freudian themes. He could do so only after Beckett had given him a nationalist key to its conclusion: Buckley shoots the general because he wipes himself with a "sod of turf," offering "another insult to Ireland."

Beckett's suggestion gave Joyce "a convenient relay, enabling him to move from the murder of the mythical ancestor to a wider interrogation about a role and place of the mother in language" (136). Hence, in the *Wake*, the incestuous economy of the sons' rebellion against their father undergoes a considerable transformation in that "their libidinal places are interchanged: the brothers attack the father's anal perversions in the name of the mother's honor, only to repeat the same shift from orality (Shaun) to anality (Shem)" (138). A look into Stanislaus' *Dublin Diary* proves quite revealing:

> James and his father seem already linked in an ambivalent inheritance of anal abuse, while Stanislaus, instead of being accused of homosexuality, stresses his own femininity. (142)

These symptoms, however, matter not because they shed new light on Joyce's private biography, but rather as "the seeds of a future textual scene that will appear in full only with the episode of Butt and Taff." Stanislaus' notes are "relevant as literature, for we know that Joyce kept reading them and used many details in his later fiction from *Dubliners* to *Finnegans Wake*" (143). Here, conversely, a backward glance at paradoxes identified in earlier fiction is fruitful in that the "initial paradox of *Ulysses* in which the dead mother is living and the living father is dead" undergoes a further twist in *Finnegans Wake* which "asserts the primary function of a dead symbolic father who allows for all the substitutions around his name, his 'normative letters' (32.18), H.C.E." (148). A final touch is Rabaté's recalling Lucia's exclamation when told of her father's death: "What is he doing under the ground, that idiot? When will he decide to come out? He's watching us all the time" (149).

Finally, "*A Portrait* of the Author as a Bogeyman" (originally a paper delivered at the Frankfurt symposium) recapitulates the "voyage in search of the subject in the text and in history," and voices a demand that the recurrent question in both *Ulysses* and the *Wake*—Who the hell could have written all that? (as present in e.g. *FW* 107.36)—is "interlinked with the problematics of reading itself" (150). The Joycean paradox identified in the issue of authority is that Joyce's demand of a "birth of the reader-as-writer" can only be complied with by means of "a philosophy of authority."

> Joyce's phenomenology of the mind repeats and mimes the totality of empirical culture, a gesture which, for Husserlian phenomenology, still smacks of empiricism and of historicism. In that sense, Joyce might well stand as our last author in the sense of *auctor*, the one who augments, adds to: he has clearly enlarged our notion of literary totality, a notion which [...] is never far from that of the monstrous. (153)

This monstrous totality is related to Derrida's noted resolution of Levinas' Jew versus Greek dichotomy in Joyce's formulation that *Jewgreek is Greekjew. Extremes meet*, which on the one hand, is "a neutralization of all differences in the circle of reason," yet on the other also "a declivity, an abruptness, a towering height." Or, to go one step further, "on the one hand, the Author, on the other, the Other: is the alternative too simple?" (154) To do away with the binary, Rabaté claims, one needs to "understand how the writer—not an author yet—has to acknowledge his debt to the Other prior to any self-authorization"—and, to do so, he returns to the figure of Stephen in *Ulysses* (155). Stephen's famous mental response to A.E., his "A. E. I. O. U." (*U*, 9.197-213) is related to Dante's *Convivio*, where "author" is derived from the Latin verb *auieo* ("I tie, I bind") or from the Greek form of *autentin* ("worthy of trust and obedience") (160-1). The implication then is a connection between authority and debt:

> authority is not limited to a "power"—the power to be obeyed [...] which generally opposes reason and authority; it also signifies a "credit," the consideration or weight a theory carries, the credence held by a witness or a historian. Authority is founded at the intersection between the force of an enunciation and the credit given to it. (164)

Stephen's pondering of "things that were not" (*U* 9.347-58) reveals not so much a reduction of Platonism to idle speculation as an attack on "the structure of speculation as such," regarding "the dialectics of life and death inherent in writing in the paradox he formulates: writing is a 'still life' but also a living death, which urges the reader to act" (165). In the psychoanalytic configuration slowly unfolded by Stephen, "analytic judgements would be restricted to the mother's side, since certitude dominates, whereas the fathers all appear condemned to the realm of the probable: *pater semper incertus*." This dichotomy taps into what Freud in *Moses and Monotheism* identifies with "the move from hieroglyphs, still pertaining to the triumph of material evidence in claims for affiliation, to the Semitic alphabet," in which "*maternal* and *material* are quasi-synonyms that are displaced by the law of the Father and a transcendent principle that finds its sure guarantee in writing" (166). Rabaté poses the question, "how can a subject divided by his guilt and debt repossess this divinized projection of himself into two dialoguing ghosts?" to which he offers the following response:

> Simply because the skilled dialectician, aware of all the artful dodges evolved by the artist, soon learns how to use and to abuse double negations: neither son nor father, he is both at the same time; neither Plato not Aristotle, he enacts the drama of his own death and dispossession, uniting Jesus with Socrates drinking hemlock. (167-8)

Paternity, Rabaté's account demonstrates, "points to the void, the unconscience of origins, the unconscious hoarding of signs or letters, and yet it remains the model of any creative gesture" (171). More specifically, however, one needs to also attend to the particularities of Stephen's character as presented in the novel:

> What are we to think of this young, arrogant prig who, although clearly aware of Bloom's race and origins, thanks him for his hospitality by singing an old ballad conveying a crude anti-Semitism? [...] Moreover, why should Stephen, who is the first-born of his family, see himself as Esau, ready to bargain his theories for a glass of beer? (174-5)

Answering the latter question first, Rabaté observes that just as Shakespeare, Stephen "secretly desires his dispossession, a disinheritance in favour of more cunning rivals, in order to enact an exile ensured against all calls back home." The above-mentioned doubleness of authority however also assures that Stephen is also a Jacob in the cunning with which "he has even managed to disguise his own voice, which points toward a still-future writing in which he cannot yet find his bearings" (175). Stephen's song then is seen as part of the "Ithacan infinity," used as a weapon against "the reassuring promises of synthesis or atonement which are endlessly deferred, set adrift in the spatial transmigration affecting everything" (176). This is an infinity the type of serialization of which "cannot be ascribed to Hegelianism any longer," but only referred back to Vico. The perspective brought to bear on the issue of aesthetics and authority by *Finnegans Wake* is "the abandon of Joyce's aesthetic discourse as such: there cannot be any hope of holding a discourse describing the function of the artist or of the creator; the versions and perversions are so numerous" (179). The *Wake*'s uniqueness, then lies

> in that anyone who wishes to penetrate it must [...] arrive at the point when a reader's authority is established. The reader has to authorize himself to the status of reader [...] also because this provides an experience of reading which then radically alters any subsequent reading. (183)

The final missed encounter in "Ithaca" therefore seems anticipatory of the linguistic abandon of *Finnegans Wake*. Rabaté concludes his brilliant reading thus:

Stephen Dedalus gains a sense of authorship only when he refuses all the shelters and ruses of a cunning feminine reason, fleeing from Molly's deep night, into which Bloom is smothered at the end of "Ithaca." Stephen is sent like a wandering missile on an unforeseen orbit, and nothing announces that he is going to sit down at some makeshift table and immediately start writing the book one is still holding. Perhaps he is authorized only to keep silent, for he may well be the first reader of *Finnegans Wake*. (184)

Rabaté's "Conclusion" recirculates back toward the issue of the "theology of criticism" discussed in the preface, linking it to the issues of perversity and modernity that co-formed the riverrun of Rabaté's whole argument:

Perversion is founded on a structure of thought which is overhauled despite a lack of belief in its efficacy; the efficacy of language will be left to divided speaking and writing subjects. (186)

It follows then that Joyce's sense of being a modern is inseparable from a crisis in faith, "a crisis that took the very name 'modernism' and developed a debate within the Catholic and Protestant churches at the end of the nineteenth century." Commenting on the Stephen-Mother encounter in "Circe" (*U* 15.4188-92), Rabaté sees in it a typical example of Joyce's "perverse strategies":

one cannot hear what is already written, one cannot see what is merely spoken. The "tell me all" of the washerwoman gossiping [...] must indeed stay a frustrated demand, endlessly disappointed, for there can be no "bridge" between the two talkers. (189)

The burning of this bridge in *Finnegans Wake* "completes the work accomplished by *Ulysses* in that it 'hastens' all the more the changes it tried to bring about," putting an end to "the dichotomy between reader and author," abolishing "the opposition between text and commentary, novel and criticism" (191). Despite this abolishment however criticism remains, in Rabaté's concluding point, *ineluctable* as "it can be called 'wholesome' and even nourish the reading — and the writing." Indeed, criticism "engages in a systematic dismemberment that creates its own memory while opening up to the alterity of authority" (192).

VI

A herald of the great transformation within Joyce studies toward a historico-politically committed scholarship, Margot Norris' 1992 study *Joyce's Web*[9] approaches his works in terms of their "social production," thereby also reflecting the author's avowed "shift away from the ahistoricism of my earlier approach to Joyce." This ties in with

---

[9] Margot Norris, *Joyce's Web* (Austin: University of Texas Press, 1992).

the increasingly historical perspective of the contemporary critical and theoretical debates on the nature of the avant-garde and modernity, of modernism and postmodernism, that center largely on the relationship of modern
art to social practice. (3)

The crucial question of these debates for Norris is whether linguistic and
philosophical disruptions "can or should be thought of as harboring revolutionary potential of a kind that can properly be called 'political,'" that is to
say, as bearing on "the relation between the symbolic order (an ontopsychological conception of social power) to history conceived in the more
structural materialist sense of traditional Marxist philosophy." Norris'
argument relies heavily on Peter Buerger's *Theory of the Avant-Garde*,
which for her construes "modernism's noninstrumental aestheticism as
signifying the artistic autonomy that makes modern art the institutional
collaborator of modern bourgeois ideology" (4). Joyce's historical locatedness at the precise moment when "the avant-garde's self-critique was
made possible by its confrontation with aestheticism's disavowal of art's
social origin" seems sufficient justification for deploying Buerger's political
plotting of the art of modernity as a means of "rehistoricizing *Finnegans
Wake* to restore its significance as a text of the politically volatile thirties"
(5).

In this study, Norris is most mordantly opposed to one of the "effects"
of Joyce's canonization for "an ahistoricism and apoliticism that appears
to repeat Stephen's heroic *Non-Serviam* from *Portrait*" (6). Her crucial
argument is that the Joycean text is capable

> of an ideological self-correction aimed specifically at the socially empower-
> ing features of its own aesthetic modernism. The strategy of this self-
> critique is to implicate the very qualities in which Joyce's emplacement as a
> modernist resides [...] in domestication of the oppressive history, colonial
> and continental, he is believed to have transcended with his art. (7)

However, Norris does not intend to treat these textual self-corrections as
the effect of historical contradictions that inscribe themselves into all
textual discourses; rather, she aims to "adopt the more dramatic, but
theoretically retrograde, practice of personifying these effects as Joyce's
intention":

> Like a modern Penelope, Joyce imbricates and interweaves the life of the
> art in ways that ravel modernism's myth of aesthetic and artistic autonomy.
> (8)

At this point, Norris takes issue with both strands of feminist thought.
The Anglo-American tradition is criticized on account of its "privileging of
representation over performativity, of realism over *écriture*, a faith in the
presence and unity of the subject rather than delight in its disruptions,
and a commitment to the authority of the authorial voice rather than to an
unmasterable play of styles." The French feminists, despite their political

and anti-phallogocentric slant, are critiqued for their lack of historical grounding and the consequently "ontopsychological, rather than material or historical," revolutionary potential of their discourse (10-11). To recapitulate,

[t]he danger, for feminism, in politically valorizing a writing like *Finnegans Wake*, is precisely that of producing feminism without women—a feminism of no benefit to historical or material women. [...] Both feminist traditions practice a polemically mandated ahistoricism that, in each case, erases, elides, or 'forgets' its male intellectual antecedence. (11-2)

Despite the ground-laying work of Dominic Manganiello's *Joyce's Politics*,[10] Norris regards "the full range of possibilities for historical progress that might have been produced in male consciousness by a variety of oppressive conditions and their intellectual effects in the late nineteenth and twentieth centuries" as remaining still largely unexplored (13). She takes *Stephen Hero* to show that this early text "explicitly thematizes and dramatizes Joyce's early obsession with the critical uses and functions of modern art," thereby substantiating her argument that the young Joyce "began with a highly developed and clearly demonstrable sense of, and commitment to, the social function of art" (15-7). The commitment to the social functioning of art in this manuscript avant-text, however, stands in stark contrast to what Joyce's officially published novel figurates as the aesthetic gesture: "Stephen's theorizing of beauty as a set of formal relations in *Portrait*," which "explicitly performs aestheticism's excision of material and social labor from the aesthete's idealistic concerns" (18). To be sure, Norris emphasizes that the techniques used for her exploration of the social and political effects of Joyce's texts

retain much of the textualism of my post-structuralist and postmodernistic training. Only I hope to give the postmodernistic features I will uncover in the texts, their fragmentariness and patchiness, for example, an etiology that is more political and less hypertextual and logopoetic than that of de-constructive approaches. (20)

The frequently discussed self-referentiality and self-reflexivity, taken to stand as the defining principle of Joycean aestheticism and the author's interest in style at the expense of politics, is re-identified in Norris' argument with an avant-garde intention "of criticizing, rather than reinforcing, the autonomy, separatism, and ultimate transcendentality of modern art" (20). Nor does she simply align her approach with the proper tasks of ideological criticism as defined by Eagleton, as it "largely displaces focus from Joyce and his production of the text in history to Joyce's narrative discourse and its ideological formation within the Joycean text" (22). The title of her work, *Joyce's Web*, might thus also be seen as bearing on her own critical "raveling of Joyce's raveled text,"

---

[10] See Chapter VIII "Politics," section II.

a teasing apart and reknitting of writing intertexted with itself as gaps in early works become visible only when they are sutured by extended narratives in later works, as later works rewrite and revise earlier texts that themselves give the later ones a different significance. (22)

The weaving metaphor, associated primarily with Penelope, also applies to Joyce's textuality—the particular kind of weaving which Norris' reading tries to unravel is the "larger narrative maneuvers of self-repeal and sub-textual counterreadings that allow the Joycean text to incriminate and indict itself—both for its aesthetic effects and its bourgeois values" (23-4).

Norris' critical readings and unreadings are organized around three my-thologized tropes of the Joycean canon—artist, woman, and child—and aim to track "both their representations, especially their aestheticized and epiphanic figurations, and their mutism, what they can't say, in order to articulate their dialogical occupation of the Joycean text" (24). The analogy between such textual ravelling or weaving and Joyce's art is fairly obvious: the *Wake* manuscripts (Norris singles out the most famous one, *Scribbledehobble*), which bear "similarity to the psychoanalytic textuality of dream formation: the dream's raveling and reweaving of discarded and trivial psychic material into new and significant [...] dream texts." Whereas in *The Decentered Universe*, Norris sees herself lacking "a wak-ing referent, a source for the manifest content," now this absent referent has emerged, "and can now be found, in the early Joyce works them-selves" (25). For example, the fact that *Scribbledehobble* identifies in "Nausicaa" a precursor to the 'Nightlessons' of II.2, turns it in Norris' view into an account of Joyce's "preparatory moves to interweave a fantasy of happy childhood" with a "historical reality of poverty, disease, hunger, and mortality among the Irish young of the turn of the century" (26). Her approach to this particular topic also seeks to emend what she regards "a troubling elision" in Derrida's "Two Words for Joyce," where he "fails to [refer] to the children at all" (27). The general plan, beyond the Nausicaa-children parallel, is then

to retrieve other marginalized and suppressed figures, or certain features of their aspects, that weave themselves through the Joycean texts; [... how-ever, the intention is] neither to restore these submerged figures to repre-sentation, nor to show Joyce giving them muted voice, [... but rather] to explore their subversive function in pressing against the aesthetic style and bourgeois ideology of the narrative effects. (27)

In the final part of her introduction, Norris' project is said to be "enabled by the benefit, and spurred by the cost," of the specifically modern-ist/postmodernist discussion, or in Norris' terms, "postmodernization of modernism," whose "removal of writing from history" Norris hopes to redress (27).

Since the issue of children was the ground of Norris' critique of Der-rida, it will be on the last chapter of her study, "The Politics of Childhood in 'The Mime of Mick, Nick, and the Maggies,'" that my presentation of Norris' influential study shall focus. Her discussion of this chapter conceives of its object as an *anti-Bildungsroman* in that the educative lesson fails to take place, and in that "the Enlightenment ideal in which childhood, education, and maturation is implicated, is subjected to an artistic self-critique" (183). In this, the Mime "represents the possible paedocentric rewriting of many Joycean plots," in which

> it is especially consequential to explore its revision of *Portrait*, because its dialectical movement in simultaneously demystifying the artistic legitimation myth and restoring infantile social reality to a plane of serious consideration can be foregrounded with this maneuver. (190)

In its exploration of the politics of childhood, Norris' argument focuses on three moments: "the tea party, exile, and home" which "this chapter relates narratively in a way none of Joyce's individual works do" (191). Of the children games played at the tea party, Norris observes that their "seemingly 'innocent' courtship, marriage, and kissing games teach them the commodification of sex they will later encounter in both the marriage market and the brothel," and sees them as crucially informed by the short story "Clay" and "Nausicaa" episode (194). Moreover, with a reference to Horkheimer on courtship, Norris also notes that "the kissing, courtship, and marriage games they play imbue children with an ideology of class distinction, desire, and transgression" (196). Therefore throughout, "the utopian vision of childhood represented in the game of 'tea party' is repeatedly revised through the Joycean tea party" (199).

"Exile" deals with the domestic tribulations of the 1904 Joyce household (to be sure the "Mime" brims with references to Joyce's own Irish ancestry and relatives), to which Joyce reacted by going into exile, the demystification of which was launched already in the "Proteus" chapter. In the "Mime," artistic exile "takes on the features of criminal transportation rather than Icarean flight," which Norris relates to the fact that "behind the romantic exile of Irish writers there are more tales of banishment, incarceration, isolation, futility, and failure than there are tales of triumph like Joyce's own" (202). On a more general level, Norris notes that "the kind of magical transformations both Bloom and Stephen practice on women in their imaginations, Joyce uses in the 'Mime' to mark the dialectical relationship between their symbolical and their socially real versions" (204).

Finally, "Home" deals with the end of the games at dusk and the children's return home, and also with the parents (especially fathers)-children relationship, as the children are called home by a powerfully paternal voice reminiscent of all the dominant paternal figures of earlier stories (in *Dubliners*) and episodes (in *Ulysses*). Here Norris' critique of Derrida's famous reading of "He War" surfaces as the context of the words is the children's Passover prayer. Furthermore, in Derrida's essay the children of this chapter too are displaced by the dispersed voice of god, as language becomes the focus of concern at the expense of the children who eat air or breath or wind, and who flee, perhaps from their parents' creditors, like the Dedalus children, or from their parents, like the Farrington boy. (211-2)

"The Mime" as a whole, in Norris' concluding global perspective, entails a rewriting of "some of Joyce's most famous textual terrain: the paedocentric visions of childhood with which he opens *Dubliners* and *Portrait*." However, these early works, as Norris' prior argument strove to show, "establish the legitimation myth of art, the story of the sensitive child apart from its culture, able to transform suffering into infant martyrdom." Standing in opposition to this tendency then is "The Mime," which in Norris' reading,

> retroactively challenges and critiques this myth of art and the artist by producing an art of childhood that reintegrates the child into its social and political matrix. "The Mime" revisits childhood with a dialectical perspective on its utopian and dystopian versions, its function as the colonized site of adult desires and hopes that suppress and conceal the social and class reality of children's lives. (212)

VII

One of the most important works of literary theoretical scholarship aiming to conceptualize the specificity of literary postmodernism, Brian McHale's *Constructing Postmodernism*[11] devotes a whole chapter to "The Case of *Ulysses*," and is thus of relevance for the present examination.

McHale commences by observing that in spite of its traditional alignment with High Modernism, *Ulysses*, together with some other founding texts of High Modernism, "has lately entered upon a strange second career as a *post*modernist text" (42). This is due to its being composed of "two differentiable texts placed side by side, one of them the hallmark of High Modernism, the other something else," a something else that has recently been called "postmodernism" (43). The doubleness itself is an observation with a long critical lineage, and even the early Joyce criticism abounds with accounts thereof, most influentially in Karen Lawrence's *The Odyssey of Style in Ulysses*,[12] according to which the normative style of the early episodes is abandoned, beginning with "Wandering Rocks" and "The Sirens," for a "diverse series of extravagant stylistic performances." The relation between these two, for McHale, is "one of *excess* and *parody*: the poetics of the postmodernist chapters *exceed* the modernist poetics of the 'normal' chapters, and the postmodernist chapters *parody* modernist poetics" (44).

---

[11] Brian McHale, *Constructing Postmodernism* (London and New York: Routledge, 1992).
[12] Karen Lawrence, *The Odyssey of Style in 'Ulysses'* (Princeton, New Jersey: Princeton University Press, 1981).

McHale proceeds with a discussion of these two *halves*, one after the other. He examines the "modernist *Ulysses*" by means of two formal methodological sub-categories, *mobile consciousness* and *parallax*. Quoting Fredric Jameson's contention (in *Fables of Agression*) in the sense that "the most influential formal impulses of canonical modernism have been strategies of inwardness," McHale discusses the varieties of interior discourse techniques and their common aim — to render the mind more *mobile*, "quicker to seize on objects of external reality and then to abandon them for others, freer to digress along associative pathways and to produce 'subworlds' of its own making." He then immediately posits a necessary corollary for such inner mobility: the "stability of presented world." This duality has an important ramification for the doubleness on the representational level: the modernist part of *Ulysses* engages us "in a constant, microscopic collation of the two world-versions, the authoritative one and the one constructed by the character's consciousness" (45). The other narrative strategy, parallax (related to the perspectivism inherent to interior discourse) involves a "multiplication of versions," both serving "to confirm the stability of the world outside consciousness," as well as exposing "the similarities and differences between different minds" (46). McHale's examples of these two strategies at work are the cloud in *U* 1.248 and *U* 4.218 on a smaller, and the "Wandering Rocks" episode on a larger scale.

McHale's "other, postmodernist" *Ulysses* is regarded as both pushing "the modernist poetics of mobile consciousness and parallax to a point of excess where it topples into something else," and parodically undermining that modernist poetics (47-8). For his examination, he chooses the categories of the *mobile world* and *discursive parallax* (to match the *mobile consciousness* and *parallax* of his previous discussion). Of the "mobile world," McHale observes that in the late chapters of *Ulysses*, "reality itself has become fluid, metamorphic, not merely as a function of the consciousness — but *in its own right*" (48). One examples of this is Haines' "appearance" in the maternity hospital (*U* 14.1010-32), where the source of uncertainty is "the pastiche style which interposes here between us and (fictional) reality," a style which "brings with it its own complement of realia" (49). Another example brought to bear by McHale is the "Circe" episode as a whole, where (with reference to Kenner's *Ulysses*)[13] "nothing distinguishes 'real' from 'hallucination,'" or more specifically, Boylan's appearance in Nighttown (*U* 15.3726-810). Here,

> the disorienting mobility of the world in "Circe" is the more readily seen if we contrast it with the pseudo-mobility of the world, which is actually the mobility of consciousness [...] in "Proteus." (50)

A parallax of discourses, for McHale, is palpably present especially in "Cyclops," "Oxen," "Aeolus," "The Sirens," and "Ithaca":

[13] Hugh Kenner, *Ulysses* (Baltimore: The Johns Hopkins University Press, Revised edition, 1987).

if in the "normal" chapters of *Ulysses*, there is an effect of parallax between adjacent sentences of a character's interior discourse and authorial discourse, there is even a finer-grained parallax *within* a character's discourse, a kind of micro-parallax. (51)

McHale's example is "Eumaeus," where the perspective (or in McHale's term, focalization) "is predominantly Bloom's, but not *entirely* his," as there are passages which "cannot be attributed to Bloom's consciousness" (52). Derek Attridge[14] is cited as having brought home McHale's point that "the ways in which the language of this episode permits slippage and uncertainty, deception and detour" go beyond "a particular character's mental condition and spring from the propensities and liabilities of language itself" (53). This postmodern undecidability springs from the fact that "a discourse implies a world," encoding a particular version of reality; and thus, encoded by different discourses, the different versions of reality end up being "inevitably [...] mutually incompatible, incommensurable" (54). The modernism emerging from MacHale's account is therefore according to one of his titles (quoting Helmut Lethen), "cut-in-half," and *Ulysses* appears to be "a founding text of 'High Modernism' and a postmodernist text, a 'demonstration and summation' of modernist poetics and a parody of modernist poetics; it defines and consolidates modernism yet at the same time exceeds and explodes it." This, however, is countered by another claim that "the transition in *Ulysses* is not from modernism to postmodernism at all, but rather from the early phase of modernism reflected in Joyce's preceding works" to "the full-fledged 'High Modernism' of the 'narrative norm'" (55).

The problem identified by MacCabe has clearly more to do with critical terminology and reading methods rather than with anything "intrinsic" to Joyce's text. McHale refers to Lethen's *Modernism Cut In Half*, which argues against the officially presented modernism, in other words the one of Thomas Mann, which he terms "conservative" in that it excludes its avant-garde and consequently projects it onto postmodernism. In this context, Lyotard's contention that postmodernism presents modernism in its native state, and therefore *precedes* modernism, makes good sense: postmodernism "thus precedes the consolidation of modernism—it is modernism with the anomalous avant-garde still left in." This process, as Lyotard remarks, is constant; McHale argues that what Lyotard means by this is, in effect, "not the particular history of the phases of the twentieth century but a general historical principle whereby each successive cultural phase recuperates what has been excluded and 'left over' from the preceding phase and bases its 'new' poetics on that leftover" (56).

Contrary to this modernism-cut-in-half view is the tendency of assimilation as found in John Frow's 1986 *Marxism and Literary History*, which defines a "postmodernized modernism" as characterized by

[14] For Derek Attridge's *Peculiar Language*, see Chapter I "Joyce & Deconstruction," section V.

1) its attention to the status of the utterances it produces [...]; 2) consequently an antimimetic impulse: the realities it constructs have a discursive rather than an ontological foundation; and 3) an antiorganicist impulse, working typically through the fragmentation of textual unity, through the play of contradictory genres of discourse, and through a splitting of the subjects of utterance.

Frow's definition, McHale observes, "does not seem very adequate to the conservative, by and large mimetic and organicist modernist poetics" but it is "easy to see how it would apply to the more radical modernists" (57). McHale concludes that "the choice between the two constructs [...] can only be made *strategically*, that is, in the kind of work which [...] the construct could accomplish" (57-8). However, as is obvious from his account of *Ulysses*, McHale's preference is "for the modernism-cut-in-half scenario," which he chooses on account of its exclusion of the most radical avant-garde wing of modernism. McHale's reason for this is that "it seems the construct likeliest to shed light on the regularities of modernism and the specific 'otherness' of postmodernism" (58).

VIII

The study presented in this section approaches the issues of literary (post)modernism from its viewpoint attending to the physical form of the novel in its printed form. Thus, Michael Kaufmann's *Textual Bodies: Modernism, Postmodernism, and Print*[15] presents a fresh outlook on how the aesthetic and political stakes of modernity and postmodernity have been crucially informed by the influence of print technology.

Kaufmann begins by observing that strict attention to the physical form of the novel, such as his study engages in, "runs counter to much of novelistic tradition and most of critical tradition," for we as readers "have been trained not to see the print, but to see what it 'means.'" However, many modernist works "flaunt their bodies and invite the stares of their readers." Such works, in literary terminology, are *metatextual*—"they 'show' themselves and comment physically on their material existence in the way that metafictional works comment on their fictiveness" (14). In this metatextual process, "the printed form of the book becomes a part of the narrative," so that ultimately, "the narrative occurs not only on the 'other side' of the page but directly in front of the readers' eyes on the surface of the page itself" (15). Kaufmann's theoretical apparatus is defined at this point:

> Modernist writers intuited the phenomenon that Marshall McLuhan and, more recently, Walter J. Ong have explored: the format and conventions of print are part of the information conveyed; [...] this work examines how those modernist writers used the printed bodies of their books. (16)

[15] Michael Kaufmann, *Textual Bodies: Modernism, Postmodernism, and Print* (London and Toronto: Associated University Press, 1994).

Other critics dealing with metatextuality and informing Kaufmann's study include Gerard Genette and his concept of the book "as a total object", Terence Hawkes' notion of *iconicity*, Joseph Frank's notion of "spatial form," and Carl Malmgren's *iconic space* (17).

In terms of literary genres, the first to undergo the transition from "the work of art" to "text," and the first inherently tied to the print technology was the novel. Kaufmann maps out a whole genealogy of the novelists' meta-dealings with the form of their texts, spanning the early device (deployed by Defoe or Richardson) of the authorial self-presentation as an "editor," singling out Stern's *Tristram Shandy* as the first novel to actively engage with its material book-status on the thematic as well as narrative levels, and the gradual shift toward the "naturalization of the print to the voice" (Kaufmann's example is *Huckleberry Finn*) (24-8). In regard to the early 20th century, Kaufmann speaks of a "crisis of print and metatextuality," when the appearance of thousands of newspapers and cheap books made it "impossible to maintain" the "transparent language theory" as proposed by the seventeenth- and eighteenth-century linguists (29). In the modernist period, writers became divisible according to their allegiance either to the spoken (Yeats, Frost) or to the written language (Pound, the Imagists) (30). In this respect, Yeats is seen as championing "Irish poetry and stories which 'were made to be spoken or sung,' over English literature 'all but completely shaped [...] in the printing press,'" whereas Pound seems a staunch adherent to "Mallarmé's injunction that 'the rhythm of a sentence about an act or even an object has meaning only if it imitates them, and, enacted on paper, conveys in spite of everything some element of that act or that object'" (31). Thus, "unlike Eliot's fretting, early modernist footnotes to *The Waste Land*," high modernism aimed to explode "the conventional text" and expose "the 'deep' structure of early modernism."

It is precisely this problematic that Kaufmann's study sets out to examine, trying to "show the gradual opening of iconic space from William Faulkner and Gertrude Stein to James Joyce and William Gass," treating these as "various extremes of metatextuality." Joyce, in particular his *Wake*, Kaufmann argues,

> overuses the conventions of print until they become visible as conventions [...] more spectacularly, he brings the narrative not only *into* the page, but *onto* it. The *paginal space* becomes a narratival space; the printed characters on the page *are* the fictional characters and they interact literally [...] across the page. (34)

Kaufmann's Joyce-devoted chapter, "James Joyce and the Body of the Text in *Finnegans Wake*," departs from Kenner's contention that "*Finnegans Wake* is inconceivable without the mediation of print. Print [...] is its very form" (68). However, a backward glance at *Ulysses* reveals its deep-rooted interest in its own form as well. Bloom, upon watching a printing press in "Aeolus," "notes that everything speaks in its own way," and in

"Circe" this is enacted in the scene where "flybills (advertising syphilis cure) begin to speak." However, "not until 'Aeolus' does the text overtly reveal itself as text," and it is only the high modernism of *Ulysses*'s later chapters that "opens fully in the explosion of *iconic* space in *Finnegans Wake*—*alphabetic*, *lexical*, *paginal*, and *compositional*" (69). In the *Wake*, the very initial word reveals the text's metatextuality by means of its small-case opening letter. In chapter II.2, the page is "composed of 'geological strata,' attesting to the fact that "print has created an environment in which all eras are somehow concurrent" (72). The alphabet, as Kabbalah shows, is not merely "a collection of signs but a group of mysterious entities, each with its own story to tell"—here, Joyce's "characters" as "written characters on page," his HCE and ALP, the Doodles sigla, the 608.6-8 aleph, bet, gimel and daleth, make obvious points of reference (73).

Discussing the perforated letter in *FW* 124.7-12, Kaufmann notes that in the *Wake*, "what we see of characters on the page is all of them [...] everything in *Finnegans Wake* is paper-thick," and in instances like the above, "the signs literally point and name themselves. They look like they mean" (74-5). Returning to II.2, its iconicity lies in the literal "marginalization of the children," a position from which they attack and subvert "the dominant parental position, undermining the usual 'order' in language," an attack which exposes the primary text to the "danger of being taken over by its commentary," resulting in the concluding childish scrawl on page 308, displaying the joy at domination (79). Kaufmann concludes his chapter on the print in the *Wake* by pointing out that the most "dramatic moment" in *Finnegans Wake* takes place also iconically, when on page 279 Issy inserts a Nightletter to herself with the diagram of ALP's genitals, also Issy's double, introducing "a disorderly scrawl into the right-justified world of print" (83).

IX

Perhaps the most sustained attempt to date at re-theorizing the Joycean corpus by means of "a postmodern reading" is Kevin Dettmar's book-length study *The Illicit Joyce of Postmodernism*.[16] Its wide-ranging, if also sketchily presented and internally inconsistent, theoretical framework, its many insightful and productive readings, the plethora of stimulating points relevant for the whole modernist/postmodernist controversy, as well as its bold concluding gesture "to ignore *Finnegans Wake*" (more of which below)—all these makes Dettmar's book worthy of close examination here.

Dettmar's introductory chapter posits modernism as "not just a style of creative writing, but equally a style of critical writing, even critical thinking" (5), and argues for a potential usefulness of a shift:

[16] Kevin Dettmar, *The Illicit Joyce of Postmodernism* (Madison: The University of Wisconsin University Press, 1996).

If the official language of Joyce criticism is, has always been, modernism, then postmodernism provides one alternative avenue of inquiry, one somewhat different language in which we might attempt to (re)articulate Joyce's texts. (6)

A postmodern reading of *Ulysses*, then, "might begin by looking at the incommensurability of these two narratives [i.e., of *Ulysses* and its criticism]—approaching *Ulysses* with a scepticism regarding those critical narratives which have grown up around it" (8). Accordingly, the two chapters devoted to *Ulysses* in Dettmar's argument argue that "while the novel is obviously one of the pillars of Anglo-American literary modernism, its postmodernism is at the same time bustling all over" in the way "the skilful narrative consistently overflows its ostensible mythic framework; the language is increasingly ludic as the narrative progresses" (11). Dettmar's manifesto of postmodern reading states the following:

> For a critic like Ellmann, the ne plus ultra of literary criticism would be to replicate within oneself the mind of Joyce, or as one of his titles has it the consciousness of Joyce; Joyce's characteristic posture, on the other hand, was to remain apart, to wage guerrilla war, both on those things that he hated and on those he loved. Surely the time has come for his critics to do the same. (11)

The second chapter derives a working definition of postmodernism, particularly a description of stylistics, drawing heavily on the work of Mikhail Bakhtin, Jean-Francois Lyotard, and Roland Barthes, as well as the synthetic work of Ihab Hassan. Dettmar sets about postulating his definition by identifying two possible modes of inquiry. The first is an "inductive" one, which asks about the stylistic features shared by a preestablished canon of texts, and finds as its representatives Brian McHale, or Linda Hutcheon (13), with the important limitation that "in deploying it one would never question the workings of a text were it not beforehand considered a postmodern text" (14) The second is a deductive method which "produces noticeably different results," with the necessary limitation that "while the range of texts it may interrogate is in theory unbounded, its definition of postmodernism cannot be—one of the unknowns in this equation must be fixed before a solution can be attempted" (14). Thus, Dettmar's syncretic treatment of postmodernism aims at not so much a definition as a *description* of postmodern stylistics, which it then goes on to apply to Joyce's works.

From Barthes, Dettmar takes the (non)concept of Text, or the *scriptible*, or the text of bliss which he unproblematically identifies with the Postmodern on the grounds of its being

> a timeless literary phenomenon which, once our perceptual apparatuses have adjusted themselves to its workings, we can see animating the quirky textual antics of texts through the ages—afterimages of postmodernity cast over the range of modern texts. (18)

Furthermore, the postmodern text (that is, Barthes' text of bliss) is "a text which to some degree thwarts the author's creative ego" in the sense that in the text of bliss "it is language, and not an Author, that speaks" (23). Indeed, the very Protean nature of Barthes' playful theorizing can itself be seen, "not as the byproduct of methodological sloppiness," but rather as "a symptom, or better the sign, of a joyously postmodern celebration of the possibilities inherent in language" (26).

Bakhtin's aesthetics of carnival, Dettmar argues (again, rather contentiously), "constitutes Bakhtin's most important contribution to the emerging aesthetics of postmodernism," which in turn is linked to "concepts of heteroglossia and the carnivalesque" at the heart of "Bakhtin's theory of the novel, of that unique impulse he calls novelness" (29). Dettmar even goes so far as to identify Dostoyevsky's use of heteroglossia as "part and parcel of the postmodernism seething beneath the surface of his texts" (32). What Bakhtin shares with Barthes is that his voice as much as Barthes', "was [...] crying out in the wilderness, announcing the arrival of an anonymous postmodernism" (37).

Lyotard's *Postmodern Condition* is credited for its idiosyncratic use of the term "avant-garde," according to which, in Dettmar's view, what is meant is "not a specific artistic movement," but rather "the very essence of 'the artistic' in that the function of the artist, from [the 1920s] on, is "no longer to produce *good* forms, new good forms, but on the contrary to *deconstruct* them systematically and to accelerate their obsolescence" This is, of course, one of the underlying principles of the historical avant-garde, as well as other artistic movements (38-9). Also of import for Dettmar's argument is Lyotard's concept of "the evanescence of the addressee," which

> frees the writer to indulge the critical function of her writing, for in the postmodern condition there is no possible consensus of taste, no possibility of writing for an audience of one's peers. (43)

Also, Lyotard's crucial distinction between the modern and the postmodern in their treatment of the sublime has its bearings in consequent discussion of Joyce's stylistics: according to Lyotard, the modern "uses all the equipment at its disposal to insist that 'the unrepresentable exists,'" whereas the postmodern is what "puts forward the unrepresentable in presentation itself; that which denies itself the solace of good forms, the consensus of a taste which would make it possible to share collectively the nostalgia for the unattainable" (45). Quite aptly, this contrast is thematized by the difference between Joyce and Proust:

> For Proust, an intuition of the unpresentable—the sublime—has changed the very nature of his vision, but not the means of its expression; for Joyce, however, the awareness that the unpresentable exists has an effect not just on his message, but much more profoundly on his medium. (46)

To summarize then, the theorizing of Barthes, Bakhtin, and Lyotard, as presented by Dettmar, seems to share a number of salient characteristics, which are enumerated as follows: all three are "markedly idealistic, even utopian, about the nature of postmodernism," all "celebrate postmodernism," all three are "utopian," while two of the three are "essentially mystics" (47). For all three, "the 'shock of recognition' is all the justification necessary for the project of postmodern rereading" (48). Thus, in the light of Dettmar's concept of postmodernism willed by the reader, *Ulysses* "'contains' postmodernism; and I, as a reader of *Ulysses*, can choose to make much or to make little of that nascent postmodernism" (50). Needless to say, Dettmar's study makes of it as much as it can.

In a chapter devoted entirely to "The Sisters," "From Interpretation to 'Intrepidation,'" Dettmar further refines his emergent conceptualization of a model postmodern reading. The unsettling quality of the story lies, for Dettmar, chiefly in its "calling into question the hermeneutics of reading that we bring to the text, and those structures of desire with which we control what that text will be allowed to say to us" (56). By the story's end

the boy has learned, as others (like Old Cotter) will never learn, that mystery is not opposed to life, but is at its very heart; it is, as well, one of the motive forces behind postmodern art. (58)

As "a mystery story in which the mystery is not solved, indeed is not soluble, a mystery story faithful to the character of real mystery" (65), "The Sisters" performs a gesture of "saying yes to mystery," a gesture which,

is one of the hallmarks of postmodernism, and "The Sisters," perched on the brink of the Joycean oeuvre, stands as a (typo)graphic manifestation of Joyce's untimely postmodernity. (69)

What then would be the appropriate critical response to a story that seems engaged in resisting, subverting, or even effectively forestalling interpretation? Dettmar terms such a response "intrepidation" and describes it as emphasizing "not the solution of mysteries, but rather an acceptance of and openness to the essentially mysterious nature of existence," a style of interpretation that is "both 'intrepid' and filled with 'trepidation' in the presence of its object" (74).

The next *Dubliners* chapter, "The *Dubliners* Epiphany: (Mis)Reading the Book of Ourselves," deals with one of the underpinnings of Joycean modernist critical apparatus—the notion of Joycean epiphany, which, however, never was used by Joyce himself to describe his stories, the preferred metaphor being that of *epiclesis*:

The difference between the two terms [...] is this: an epiphany evidences one's ultimate mastery of a situation, while epiclesis is instead the moment of submission to mystery. (82)

Thus, in spite of their original spirit, "the name epiphany has become one of the Joyce industry's tactics for dealing with these wilful and unruly stories" (84). Dettmar's survey of the collection ultimately reveals that *Dubliners* "contains no psychological epiphanies for its protagonists—not even for Gabriel Conroy":

> Finally, epiphanies are equally a characteristic of Joyce's texts and an experience of their readers; we see epiphanies because we *need* to see epiphanies—the characters are enlightened because we need them to be. (99)

What the stories do contain, almost without exception, is their dramatic demonstration of "the connivance of interpretation with desire"; as long as "the texts cooperate with their narrators' (or protagonists') desires," then we as readers "read the stories through the lenses of our own desire" (103). What Dettmar calls, in a playful pun, "mistyreadings," then result from "an intricate pas de deux in which, when we discover our 'errors,' we simultaneously find that Joyce has anticipated and cunningly prepared them." Hence,

> *Dubliners* is a text that implicates us in the deadly work of paralysis, and reveals to us our own paralysis. [...] *Dubliners*, beginning with "The Sisters," whispers: Give up the flattering project of interpretation; give in to the mystery which is life. (104)

In "Dedalus, ~~Dead Alas!~~ Dead At Last," Dettmar elaborates on his incipit belief that *A Portrait* is "the Joycean text that fares least well in a postmodern age" (10). Within the Barthesian dichotomy between *work* and *text*, "*Dubliners* emerges as Joyce's first text, while the later *Portrait* turns out to be Joyce's first—and only—work" (107). This "lapse" from the early postmodernism of *Dubliners* to the self-important modernism of *Portrait*, in Dettmar's view, is due to Joyce's own personality, harboring within himself "these two contradictory spirits: the high modernist purpose and the low postmodern play, a belief in the work as creation of the Artist as God, and an awareness of the Text as the construction of the Artist as *bricoleur*—the co-creation of a Text and its readers" (108).

However, apart from merely re-staging old critical notions within a new postmodern garb, Dettmar also enhances narratological vocabulary by coining the term "free indirect prose" denoting "prose which is an unacknowledged cipher of the subject's own prose style" (119). The Telemachiad, for all its formal innovation, does not to Dettmar's mind add much significance to the prevalent view of Stephen from *Portrait*:

> When all is said and done, Stephen is the only genuine object of his own pity; as the "Telemachus" episode opens Stephen is in mourning for a particular kind of heroic artist, the Romantic poet-hero—Lord Byron, for preference. (130)

The thrust of Dettmar's argument, and the focal point of his whole book, is to be found in the two chapters of *Ulysses*. The first, "Toward a Non-Modernist *Ulysses*," opens by likening Modernist literature to Euclidean geometry on the grounds of their shared "creation of the structures through which [they] had been scrutinized." Just as Euclid himself has come to be considered to have been "the first non-Euclidean geometer,"

> [i]t is perhaps time that critics began experimenting with a nonmodernist poetics with which to examine the modernist's texts. Just as mathematicians currently countenance two distinct non-Euclidean geometries [...], we can imagine a number of different nonmodernist poetics, which would violate various of the central tenets of modernist poetics and perhaps violate them in different ways. (139)

The main argument of the present chapter is therefore that "[t]he vital impulse behind Joyce's stylistic experiments in *Ulysses* is not [...] *mimetic*, expressive, but rather carnivalesque—imitating *not* the *Ding an sich*, the 'matter' of the episode, but primarily previous literary attempts at expressive form, and subtly mocking their naiveté" (150). The proposed shift in vocabulary is one from the modernist expressive form toward the postmodernist excessive form. The illustration of this argument is threefold: the "Aeolus" and "The Sirens" episodes and the issue of Homeric parallels. In his analysis of "Aeolus," Dettmar distinguishes three salient stylistic hooks. Of the accumulation of the chapter's headlines, he notes that their effect

> is not to enhance the representational or "expressive" character of the text, nor even [...] to evoke the ethos of the newsroom, given the extreme distance between real newspaper headlines and those in "Aeolus"; rather, the patent artifice of these late textual supplements serves to highlight the highly conventional, artificial nature of the text they would introduce, and to mock any notion that form can be made consonant with content. (154)

Secondly, he remarks that although "Joyce most certainly did embellish the episode with numerous references to wind," it is just possible that "setting out as we do to find references to the wind, we may find some that were not 'planted' there." Moreover, Dettmar claims that "here Joyce does not try to make his words work, in the way that the characters in "Aeolus" do, but instead allows them to play" (156). Third, the much-discussed catalogue of the episode's rhetorical tropes does not pose, for Dettmar, an established fact, but rather raises the question of whether "those tropes are a product of Joyce's desire for the episode," or rather "an after-the-fact product of the interpretive framework Joyce published for the episode" (156). He then goes on to demonstrate this by locating, within the first ten lines of the overture to "The Sirens," the total of thirty-two different rhetorical figures. Last but not least, regarding the issue of Homeric parallels, Dettmar recasts the modern/postmodern divide as a confrontation between Eliot and Joyce on the issue of myth:

> [W]hile Eliot believed that myth inheres in the substance of contemporary history, and must be uncovered and made explicit by the writer, Joyce [...] saw it rather as an artificial construct—simply one writer's way of working. (164)

This constructedness of the Homeric scheme should not, however, be confused with some sort of secondariness or randomness as it was of a profound bearing on Joyce's own artistic practice:

> Throughout his career, Joyce searched for—indeed, *created*—problems to overcome in his writing. [...] Composition was for Joyce a process of discovery, the uncertainty of which he often found frightening. [...] At the same time, writing was for Joyce the act of overcoming obstacles; whether the obstacles were "natural" or "artificial." (167)

Thus, while Joyce established his *Ulysses* schemata as a way "to concentrate his energies," they are revealed as malfunctioning, which is corroborated by a glance at the facsimile page proofs of an episode like "Aeolus," brim as it does with further insertions, corrections, and elaborations:

> Appropriately enough, it seems to have been Joyce's superstitions [...] that finally convinced him to surrender the manuscript. Without that deadline [of his fortieth birthday] pending, every time he received the "final" version of his novel from the printers Joyce had another go at it—a process of compositional accretion that in theory need have no end. (172)

Dettmar's other *Ulysses* chapter, "James Joyce and the Carnivalesque Imagination," takes a broader look at the novel, reading its peculiar rift as a result of a particular instance of its carnivalization. Dettmar opens with the observation that

> much of the carnival atmosphere of the late episodes of *Ulysses* could equally be attributed to a wake—not a wake properly celebrated, like Tim Finnegan's, but paradoxically the emotionally impoverished *Wake* of Paddy Dignam that proves insufficient to placate his restless spirit. (174)

Many critics (McHale being one) have commented on the "seemingly abrupt stylistic shift that occurs between the 'Hades' and 'Aeolus' episodes of *Ulysses*." However, even before the intrusion of the formal gadgets of newspaper headlines, the seemingly smooth flow of the early chapters' narration presents instances of radical rupture. Indeed, already in the Telemachiad, Dettmar shows that Stephen remembers phrases and words ("shafts of light" and "barbicans," to be specific) *belonging* to the seemingly objective, third-person narrative, and is thus revealed as "responsible for [its] language" (179).

However, there is one event that occurs *in between* the "Hades" and "Aeolus" episodes, and is seen to trigger off much of the postmodern misrule that is to follow—the interment of Paddy Dignam who is to resurface as a ghostly presence haunting Dublin later on (in "Cyclops" and

"Circe"). Dettmar's hypothesis then is that the stylistic carnival of the latter half of *Ulysses* is meant to celebrate the improperly, insufficiently celebrated (because not *waked*) passing of Paddy Dignam. Here Dettmar's socio-historical research pays off, as he discusses the "two worldviews colliding in 'Hades,' two different attitudes toward life and death, two different approaches to mourning: these two views, the English and the Celtic, are everywhere in conflict in the episode" (195). The difference is this:

> The English tradition implicitly encourages [...] a posture of "moody brood-ing" in the "bereaved"; the *Wake* tradition encourages a larger, almost cosmic view of the death, a perspective that helps the "bereaved" to tran-scend the limitations of narrow egotism. (200)

The Church's restrictions and pronouncements against the Irish *Wake* have a clear enough substantiation: the threat of communal merrymaking in the face of death—"when a people no longer fears death, those who seek to tame it have lost a very significant part of their control" (202). The "wake" as a linguistic sign is traced through the text in the "various permutations" it undergoes, "unsettling the text wherever it appears." This "wake" is further related to what "Derrida described as *différance*, "the movement by which language, or any other code, any system of reference in general becomes 'historically' constituted as a fabric of dif-ferences" (207). Concluding his postmodern revisitation, Dettmar states the most general reason for a postmodern Joyce:

> to bring to the dock the works of our modernity and to try to discover wherein lies their freedom—to discover within the works of the modernists themselves the antidote to their sometimes "authoritative discourse." When we do look, we will find that it is, in many cases, there; our postmodern glosses might then help us to confer on the great works of modernism an altogether different legacy. (208)

Dettmar's most shocking and unsettling, indeed, postmodern gesture is reserved for the very end of his book—his "Afterword: On Ignoring *Finne-gans Wake*." Agreeing implicitly with Nabokov's famous dismissal of Joyce's last text, Dettmar notes that "the *Wake*'s stylistic upheaval is, paradoxically enough, a less revolutionary stylistics than that which Joyce produced in *Ulysses*." Whereas *Ulysses* "merely obeys the letter of the law; it is a spiritually lawless text, concerned with getting out from under the tyranny imposed by a unitary voice or style," *Finnegans Wake* "estab-lishes its own law outside the received law once it has broken free—becomes a law unto itself" (210). Thus, in Dettmar's heterodox view, "*Ulysses* would be the postmodern work which clears a space for the untimely modernism of *Finnegans Wake*." More specifically within post-modern theory, the superlanguage of *Finnegans Wake* "attempts to over-come the inherent limitations of any national language, or any dialect, or any sociolect, as Bakhtin would call them," but "Bakhtin, Barthes, and

Lyotard would all find such a gesture utopian" (211). In addition to Nabokov's, Faulkner's reservation about the *Wake* and Joyce himself ("James Joyce was one of the great men of my time. He was electrocuted by divine fire [...] He was probably—might have been the greatest, but he was electrocuted. He had more talent than he could control.") is recalled, perhaps to add justification to Dettmar's exhortation:

> If there's one obvious area in which Joyce studies has thus far refused to postmodernize itself, it is this: that very few, if any, commentators on Joyce's work are willing to resist the powerful influence of Joyce's promotional apparatuses and reputation. (214)

The *Wake* is also as "a conceptual novel," related to Cage's conceptual music, and "as such, it suffers the occupational hazard of conceptual art: it's more interesting as a concept than as art" (216). The reason finally given by Dettmar for the *Wake*'s inferiority to *Ulysses* is the following:

> *Finnegans Wake* is industrial-strength postmodern stylistics; it's 99 and 44/100 percent pure. But in writing, that's not finally a very fulfilling blend. [...] *Finnegans Wake* itself has become a kind of museum exhibit of postmodern stylistics, a touchstone for the purity of those postmodern texts that live in the shade. But it's those shady texts, finally, that we hanker after. (216-7)

X

The point of revisiting Derek Attridge's *Joyce Effects*[17] in the present context lies in his piece (first published in 1995) titled "The Postmodernity of Joyce: Chance, Coincidence, and the Reader," where the issues of (post)modernism in Joyce's writing are explored through his deployment of the concept of "coincidence." Attridge examines the "Ithacan" question (*U* 17.611-41) concerning the three modes of knowledge ("information or coincidence or intuition?") out of which Bloom choosescoincidence: "to the two modes of *knowledge* that might explain the chiming between the worlds of narrator and audience [...] Bloom prefers that unaccountable falling together of events that we call coincidence" (117). This scene, in Attridge's opinion, has broader implications in that it "draws attention to an aspect of Joyce's art that is becoming more and more evident as we look at it in retrospect, from a cultural platform for which 'postmodernism' seems the best name" (118), and which is understood throughout as

> an art in which the very complexity and heterogeneity of the forms and representations crafted by the artist produce possibilities of connection and correspondence when they engage with an individual consciousness at a given moment. [...] The features of recent art in a variety of media could be thought of as producing not the sense of *necessary* cohesion that charac-

[17] Derek Attridge, "The Postmodernity of Joyce: Chance, Coincidence, and the Reader," *Joyce Effects: On Language, Theory, and History* (Cambridge: Cambridge University Press, 2000).

terizes most modernist and pre-modernist art, but a sense of the constantly renewed *possibility* of connection. (118)

Attridge goes on to distinguish this recent phenomenon from modernist works (*The Cantos*, "The Waste Land" and *The Waves* are his study cases), which he regards as "attempts to secure permanence, purity and absoluteness" which ultimately entail "a resistance to ungrounded effects of meaning, even though we may now be able to read them against the grain of their grand projects, finding in their failure a success of another and more relativist kind." This fight for necessity against arbitrariness, moreover, is seen by Attridge as underwriting the whole modernist project — he speaks of "the superb certainty of a Mondrian painting, the self-authenticating power of a Mies building, the assured self-validation of every note of a Schoenberg twelve-tone composition" (119).

Even though both *Ulysses* and *Finnegans Wake* have similarly 'modernist' pretensions, Attridge stresses that

the particular manner in which Joyce accumulates details, multiplies structures, and overdetermines interpretation achieves something [...] that sets his texts apart from most other modernist works [... ;] it makes possible, and relishes, the random, the contingent, and [...] the coincidental. (120)

Thus, their postmodernist quality would seem to be due to the extreme, *ad absurdum*, level to which both novels drive their modernist projects: "it is the rich systematizations of *Ulysses* and *Finnegans Wake*, their ordered heterogeneity and multiplicitous coherence, that render their meanings forever unsystematizable" (120). This unsystematizability is also largely due to what Attridge discerns as both texts' active engagement with coincidence, "an internal and fully thematized principle in these works." In *Ulysses*, the exponent of coincidence, functioning "as Virgil to the reader's Dante as they explore the world of the coincidence," is Bloom, and the word *coincidence* itself is something of a Bloomian leitmotif — Attridge maps its fourteen occurrences in the book, all of which are associated with Bloom's consciousness (122). Bloom would therefore be the playful postmodern force disrupting Stephen's modernist aspirations: while Bloom "is always on the lookout for connections across time and place, verbal echoes, patterns in the heap of fragments that characterize his consciousness," Stephen "seems driven by the traditional (and modernist) artist's need to *make* connections [...] rather than to find and celebrate them in passing." The *OED* definition of coincidence as "a notable concurrence of events or circumstances having no apparent causal connection" reveals in Attridge's attentive reading the curiosity of the adjective *apparent*, for "part of the fascination of coincidence is that it always *may not be* a coincidence." Attridge asks with an explicit reference to Pynchon, "who can say of any apparent coincidence that it isn't in fact the punctual culmination of a vast and perhaps ancient system of connections?" Turning to the *Wake* to make his concluding remarks, Attridge offers a view of its portmanteau style as "a continuous exploitation of this potential in language and culture, languages and cultures" toward the chance, the coincidental (123). A comparison with Joyce's great Irish contemporary proves illustrative:

> One has only to compare Yeats's use of the gyre with Joyce's use of the Viconian cycle to gauge the difference between an attempt to wrest coherence from the chaos of history and a rejoicing in the patterns of repetition thrown up by the chaos of history. (124)

For Attridge, *Finnegans Wake* is "one great co-incidence, 'falling together'" (124).

XI

Providing the coda to the highly selective polyphony of the modernist/postmodernist critical treatments of Joyce, David Spurr's *Joyce and the Scene of Modernity*[18] is chosen as an example representative of a broad and fertile tendency in recent Joyce criticism to approach Joyce's modernity in relation to its specifically postcolonial condition. His book is a collection of a total of seven (largely republished) essays centred around a variety of topics, interrelated and contextualized through his well-grounded introduction which deserves to be discussed in its own right.

Spurr's "Introduction: Altereffects" views the collection as an attempt to bring together two "distinct critical movements in the recent study of literary modernism": one studying "the relations between works of modernism and contemporaneous historical events," the other reading "the texts of modernism, and Joyce in particular, in the light of the questions posed by literary theory" (1). One of the aims of Spurr's theoretical project is

> to demonstrate that this theoretical project, far from being abstracted from questions of historical context, is in fact motivated by the specifically modern situation [...], and that it has gone a fair distance in helping to explain the precise nature of the relation between the texts of literary modernism and the objective conditions of modernity. (2-3)

For Spurr, the Joyce of Lacan is relevant in his notorious concept of Joyce as *symptom*, referring to "that element of Joyce's writing which sacralizes the human body and in which language itself functions as fantasy, that is, as the symbolic manifestation or symptom of bodily desire." Joyce, for Lacan, "has recourse to an 'epistemic babble' (*bafouillage épistémique*) that deliberately resists this [symbolic] order in the name of a being-in-speech (*le parletre*) that Lacan proposes to substitute for the Freudian unconscious." Spurr notes in reverential passing that Joyce's "binding of the real onto the symbolic" understood as a "mimesis of loss" has been related to the historical trauma of Irish colonization in van Bo-

---

[18] David Spurr, *Joyce and the Scene of Modernity* (Miami: University Press of Florida, 2002).

heemen-Saaf's recent work[19] (3). The complementary yet opposing approaches of Lacan and Derrida nicely surface in Spurr's observation that

> If Lacan's figure of the symptom is essentially synecdochic—seeing Joyce as the manifest part signifying the pathological whole of being—then Derrida reads Joyce from the other direction.

For Derrida, "Joyce constitutes the 'great memory,' a vast software containing all languages and cultures in which the reader's own frame of reference is revealed to be a small and rather insignificant part," a universality which, in Derrida's purposefully ambivalent analysis, evokes "a certain 'admiring resentment'" within the reader (4). This universality, for Spurr, has also another important dimension, posing yet another problem for the reader

> in that [...] his text also tends to deny or subvert whatever it affirms, so that every positive meaning in Joyce is subject to self-cancellation, as if written in the mode that Derrida renders as "*sous rature*" (under erasure). (4-5)

Acute though it may be, Spurr's understanding of the *historicity* of Derrida's reading of Joyce goes against the grain of common critical misconception, relying as it does on a concept of *historicity* that "differs from that which is ordinarily invoked in making the charge that poststructuralist criticism is ahistorical and that it fails to examine the circumstances of literary production in terms of its objective, material contexts." However, for Derrida,

> the semantic content of language is historical insofar as linguistic meaning is produced in actual human contexts, and that the signifying function of any expression relies on the history of that expression's use. [...] By exploiting the historically latent forms of signification within every utterance, the Joyce of *Finnegans Wake* produces a "pure historicity" of language. (5)

Nevertheless, Spurr's is also an approach informed by the Frankfurt School of Criticism, and thus "historical" or "historicizing" in the more usual sense. Georg Simmel's definition of the modern city's "subjective and somewhat incalculable effects on human relations and consciousness," for example, the phenomenon of eccentricity, the cult of originality, and "the manifestation of the intellectual life as an intensification of the nerve system of urban movement and communication," is of much importance for Spurr's exposé of Joyce's modernity. Walter Benjamin's notion of *Erlebnis* contributes in his project of historicizing the notion of experience, and "defining it in terms of human life in society rather than in the relation to nature or myth" (6). Theodor Adorno, "perhaps the most rigorous in his analysis of modern literature as an effect of the conditions

---

[19] See Chapter VII "Historicism," section IV.

of modernity," demonstrates "its inevitable rootedness in contemporary reality, even at those points where its subject matter is turned away from the social or historical." Spurr quotes Adorno's example of Proust, through which Adorno shows

> the degree to which modernism calls into question the conventions of nov-
> elistic representation, with their reassuring qualities of a stable point of
> view on a more or less coherent object. (7)

Observations such as these, in Spurr's view,

> help us to conceive of literary modernism as more than a series of technical
> innovations; more than a preoccupation with image, myth, and conscious-
> ness; and finally more than simply a response to the alienating effects of
> modernity.

Modernism, for Spurr, can best be described as "the encounter with *otherness* variously conceived or marked as beyond conception" (8). To stay with Adorno's example, Proust located alterity primarily in the self, but other modernist works, "and especially those by Joyce," extend this alterity "to the world at large in a manner that surpasses the familiar phe-nomenon of alienation" (9). For example, the already discusses "pure historicity" of *Finnegans Wake* consists in "a language that, through its extreme condensation and synchrony of meanings, purifies itself of adul-teration by the ideological and epistemological constructs of history," yet "what Joyce affirms is precisely that which remains in doubt, that which cannot be calculated and resists meaning." (10) Furthermore, this aspect of Joyce is seen as an important "corrective to the critical tradition that sees in the encyclopaedic character of his work a kind of totalizing knowledge" (10-11).

Turning to his book itself, Spurr makes the point that the "scene" of the title refers to "a modern tradition that conceives of contemporary history as something seen," and therefore including both "the spectacle of imperial power as manifested in parades and exhibitions, as well as the visual space of the modern city," and modernity's "inner scene as well," which produces "effects of anxiety, nervousness, fantasy, and the un-canny within the individual psyche" (11). The *basso continuo* of the col-lection as already mentioned is *alterity* around its response to which mod-ernity constructs itself.[20] Thus, Spurr's first three essays for instance, "address the effects of certain forms of power and knowledge character-istic of the early twentieth century: colonial domination, nationalism, and anthropology."

The first chapter, "Colonial Spaces in Dublin," dramatizes the intrinsic incoherence of colonial domination by looking at the final scene of "Wan-dering Rocks" in which the viceregal cavalcade parades through the

---

[20] Here, I follow the author's own summary of the collection on 11-16.

streets of Dublin to a heterogeneous and heterodox series of reactions from the citizenry. The double-function of Irish nationalism, combining its resistance to British colonial domination with its repressiveness toward Jews and others designated as foreigners in Ireland is addressed in the second chapter, "The Comedy of Intolerance in Proust and Joyce." The third chapter, "Anthropologies of Modernism: Joyce, Eliot, Lévy-Bruhl," turns from colonialism and nationalism to the shifting senses of alterity that arise from the complicated relation between anthropology and literary modernism. The argument here is that, anticipating Blanchot, Joyce exhibits his affinity with the nomadic aspect of Jewishness, the condition of being exiled, on the move, at or beyond the limits of a pagan, rooted experience. The fourth chapter, "Joyce, *Hamlet*, Mallarmé," documents a modern crisis of mimesis on the example of the problem faced by any actor playing Hamlet of how to interpret a character who is both there and not there, a mere ghost of his ghostly father. The fifth chapter, "Scenes of Reading," records a crisis in the representation of reading: traditionally regarded as a sort of participation in a fairly homogeneous cultural or national formation, twentieth-century writing comes to represent the act of reading as a more solitary, more heterogeneous, and more ephemeral undertaking. Chapter VI, "Fatal Signatures: Forgery and Colonization in *Finnegans Wake*," already discussed elsewhere,[21] demonstrates Joyce's linguistic texture of history, understood as a signification of historical events with all the ambiguity and unpredictability of language, and a taking place of history as occurring *in* language, within the space of language, insofar as it has any meaning at all. The final chapter, "Writing in the *Wake* of Empire" displays this proliferation through the example of Joyce's parody of colonial discourse as manifest in the alleged indecency in Phoenix Park, a discourse penetrated by male sexual fantasies, which exposes both the erotic formations of empire and the imperialist dimensions of masculine desire. Spurr concludes:

> *Finnegans Wake*, and to a great extent all of Joyce's work, may be seen precisely as a series of acts of sabotage from within the structures that make of language an instrument of power, be it political, historical, or literary. Joyce achieves this by opening up within those structures the space of the uncolonized, unrepresented, and incalculable: the space of the other. (16)

The synthetic, both theoretically and historically-grounded (in fact providing sound evidence *against* this binary), character of Spurr's essays renders them not only a paradigmatic example of the current trend in Joyce studies, in which Joyce's modern or postmodern status is approached from a framework creatively (re)conceived as part of the critical project itself, but also a presage of what follows in the next chapter: approaches

---

[21] See Chapter III "Feminism, Sexuality & Gender Studies," section VIII.

dealing specifically with the complex issue of history in Joyce and Joyce in history.

XII

2006 saw the re-publication of a very significant co-edited volume whose variegated focus (of the names reappearing elsewhere in the present work, one can name Fritz Senn, Joseph Valente, Sheldon Brivic, Richard Brown, Hélène Cixous, Gayatri Spivak, or indeed one of the editors, Louis Armand) falls best under the overarching rubric of modernism studies — Louis Armand and Clare Wallace's *Giacomo Joyce: Envoys of the Other*,[22] which will provide a suitable concluding piece for this chapter. The sundry theoretical concerns of the individual contributions make it impossible for the collection to be covered here in its entirety, the present account will therefore focus on just the collection's "Introduction," from whose delineated ground all the contributions seem to depart in their own directions.

Armand opens his "Introduction — Through A Glass Darkly: Reflections on the Other Joyce" pointing out that since its publication in 1968, "the critical reception of *Giacomo Joyce* has been defined largely by a concern with biographical placement, stylistic transitions and the vicissitudes of authorial intention," all symptoms of the "novelty" presented by this late addition to the canon, novelty which inherently entails a sort of "marginalisation." It is this marginalisation that the volume seeks to redress, as one of its premises is that "it takes seriously the claim that *Giacomo Joyce* should be treated on its own terms" (1). Contrasted with Richard Ellmann's biographical delineation, influential in regarding *Giacomo Joyce* as a kind of secondary vignette from Joyce's life located on the margin of his canon, is the "supplemental nature of *Giacomo Joyce* which, in light of the textual theories emerging at the time of its publication, lends it a particularly deconstructive force" (2). An example of such a reading is Cixous' 1968 *Le Monde* review where the "deferral to the assertions of biographical facticity give rise to a set of questions regarding textual authority which need to be addressed" (3). Going on to sketch the care with which the publisher and first critic of *Giacomo Joyce* Richard Ellmann sought to contextualise and explain away the anomaly presented by this text, Armand turns such a contextualisation back on the critic, claiming that "a significant challenge facing Joyce critics is to effectively extract Joyce's work from this overly determined placement" and treat it as effectively *other*: "if Joyce's later writings are any measure of this, it is the otherness of the text itself, as fugitive, subordinated, bastardised, suppressed, which most demands accounting for" (5). Armand proposes to view *Giacomo Joyce* as a type of "ghost writing," a "counter-portrait," that mirrors *A Portrait*, "the model mirroring the portrait-artist — 'forged' or plagiarised from an already confabulated artificer," and insists that the

[22] Louis Armand and Clare Wallace, eds., *Giacomo Joyce: Envoys of the Other* (Prague: Litteraria Pragensia, 2006 [2002]).

text's "transitional" quality be taken into account (9). The text's transitional nature manifests itself not only within the context of Joyce's oeuvre. Cixous' description of its genre as a "poem in prose" points towards a transitional effect of its structure. Furthermore, *Giacomo Joyce* is "not merely transitional" but also "translational," both in the sense of "a writing simultaneously between and across genres," and in "the projective 'presencing' of other texts in which it is constantly deferred and 'returning'" (12). Armand echoes the work of textual geneticist Daniel Ferrer:

> In textual genetics this effect is ascribed to what Daniel Ferrer and others term *avant-texte*. This does not refer to what might otherwise be thought of simply as preparatory drafts or notes, but rather to a text "in advance of itself," a type of haunting which is also an alterior discourse "within" [...]. Maurice Blanchot has similarly described this effect in terms of discursive emplacement and of the "fragment" as an element of metonymic recursion. (13)

In itself a text concerned on the thematic level with appearance and disappearance, *Giacomo Joyce* might be thought of as "not a single work bounded by the covers of a book," but instead as "a matrix of textual fragments, whose traces and tracings through other texts [...] describe a type of ghost writing" (13).

This matrix effect, seen as a type of virtuality, points to how *Giacomo Joyce* could "also be thought in terms of hypertext, anticipating the cybernetics of Joyce's later work, which Jean-Michel Rabaté has described as a 'perverse semic machine'" (14). A textual machine, *Giacomo Joyce* also suggests, via the possible dates of its composition, a particular historical placement within the development of European avantgarde, whose aesthetics were very much invested in, and preoccupied with, the machinic, or what Donald Theall describes as "techno-poetics."[23] About the much contested relation of Joyce to the avantgarde, Armand observes:

> Writing almost contemporaneously, it would be difficult to believe that Joyce was unaware of the technological undercurrents in these works, all of which were informed in one way or another by the ideas of Marinetti and the Italian Futurists, whose *Manifesto* (of which Joyce possessed a copy) had appeared in *Le Figaro* in February 1909, the year Joyce established the first cinematograph in Dublin.

Within the context of the avantgarde aesthetics of the fragment, it is also inviting to consider that the abandonment of *Giacomo Joyce* "might in fact have been a calculated element of the work itself, anticipating the 'discarded' works of the Dadaists and of Duchamp's abandoned, occulted, vanished, destroyed and yet highly fetishised objects of the 1920s onwards" (15). The broad avantgarde context of the work might also account for the typograpical arrangement of its fifty textual fragments—

---

[23] See Chapter IX, "Technicity, Media & Hypertext," section II.

and Armand manages to persuasively link this feature of the text to the modernist occupation with simultaneity as a "verbal analogy to the technology of film," for "the visual arrangement of the textual fragments and the blank spaces between them might also be seen as a type of filmic notation, montage effect, or 'script-writing'" (16-7).

Therefore, the "transitional" character of *Giacomo Joyce* appears in Armand's lucid account as "not an after-effect but rather a pre-condition," an experiment "not only in advance of the Joycean project, but already, as it were, 'in place of it.'" It seems to Armand that the poetic economy of Joyce's fragmentary envoy required "the expansive edifice of *Ulysses* and *Finnegans Wake*" in order to achieve anything like "a sustained formal expression" (18). If this is indeed the case,

> then there needs to be a re-evaluation of the way in which *Giacomo Joyce* constitutes a formal experiment which can manifestly be shown to have "proceeded," then it is not enough to attribute its marginalisation to an effect of oversight. What it suggests, rather, is a type of clairvoyance, a foresight or before-sight of what the "present" in Joyce must always return to."

7. Historicism

I

Among the first studies to attempt to combine a Derridean interest in the (con)textuality of history and Joycean subversion of the possibility of historical "re-presentation" with critical attention to the specificity of Joyce's own socio-historical situation, James Fairhall's *James Joyce and the Question of History*[1] views Joyce's works as "grounded in a dense historical reality, yet at the same time free-floating in a universe of endlessly signifying, interconnected words" (xi). Throughout Fairhall's study, history is understood as enacted ideology; in other words,, as socially derived beliefs and values put into work within a specific place and time, which necessarily mould it into one particular shape. This is why Joyce in his fiction might be said to attempt to "subvert history, which he saw as both a chronicle of violence and oppression, and as a fixed past that had ousted other possible pasts and thus delimited the present" (xii). As long as both Joyce's late masterpieces defy the very basis of history by destabilizing the linguistic base of ideology, the critic's goal "is to analyze not just the success of Joyce's rebellion against history but its limitations" by examining its assumptions, by asking "those questions which his art does not acknowledge as questions" (xiii).

Fairhall's introduction maps out the Jamesonian perspective from which he approaches the theme of history, especially, his frequently quoted injunction against taking history as past events (despite its dependence on their narrative (re)construction) for a *text*, for a *narrative*, and his reminder that the referent of history as an account of past events is not merely imagined but real. The three questions asked by Fairhall throughout his dealings with Joyce are the following:

> First, how do we gain knowledge of past events when we can no longer experience them? Second, how do we gain knowledge of aspects of the past which have shaped our lives without our awareness and which make themselves felt to us as givens, as Necessity? Third, how does the discourse of history mold those events which it attempts to represent? (2)

Jameson's concept of the "collective unconscious" is taken on board here, having to do with history in that "we cannot look at this uncon-

[1] James Fairhall, *James Joyce and the Question of History* (Cambridge: Cambridge University Press, 1993).

scious directly as an object of study, yet we can infer its nature from the inevitable signs and symptoms of repression" (6). Fairhall's understanding of ideology is also Jamesonian, especially its informative influence upon interpretation: "We cannot read narratives without interpreting them, and interpretation cannot occur without a framework provided by ideology." (7) Where Fairhall departs from Jameson is in his repudiation of the latter's Marxian master narrative, which cannot solve the issue of historical representation, as all histories, just like stories, remain trapped within the hermetic closure of language. His most daring gesture is to abandon this linguistic perspective, breaking open the gates of the poststructuralist prisonhouse of language:

> Instead of closure, we might see an infinite semiotic openness; instead of entrapment, we might see freedom—at least a freedom from absolutist concepts and ideologies. [...] It is this idea of freedom or liberation which links Joyce's attitudes toward history and language, and provides a common ground for both Jamesonian and Derridean perspectives on his work. (9)

This combining approach does not and indeed cannot do away with the critical impasse between Marxist activism and deconstructivist intervention discussed even today "in a debate that Joyce's art prefigures." Fairhall himself leans toward ideological activism, based in part on Jameson's theories, "that aims to change our lives [...] by changing the way we think about history," yet refuses to accept its Marxian essence and is perfectly willing to assign deconstruction its own political implications which inform it with a potential for left-wing activism. Thus, no discourse is accorded ontological privilege in Fairhall's approach, which regards all positions as self-divided and their claims to authority as self-contradictory. It is against the background of these far-reaching implications that Fairhall sets out to trace

> the evolution of Joyce's own narrative interventions in history, which began with the word's attempt to change the world and ended with the collapsing of the world into the word. (10)

Fairhall's discussion opens with a convincing demonstration that there is no account of the infamous 1882 Phoenix Park murders, whether that of a participant and an imaginative memoirist (Tynan), or that of a historian (Corfe), or that of a literature professor (Brown), which could raise substantial claims to definitiveness or "truth," laying bare "the slippery, protean nature of the thing—history—which they try to capture and render into a fixed form" (19). From the few appearances of the incident in *Ulysses*, Fairhall induces a general quality of Joyce's fictionalized history:

> Joyce [...] delighted in having his characters display their imperfect historical memories, especially when they come to the right conclusions anyway. That is how the Phoenix Park murders enter *Ulysses*—through the faulty

recollections of the aging editor, Crawford. [...] The Phoenix Park murders lie at the center of *U*, at least insofar as Joyce uses the novel as a vehicle for a meditation on the nature of history and of Irish history in particular. (22, 26)

On a theoretical note, against the received Aristotelian notion of privileging poetry over historiography on account of the latter's being restricted by objectivity, Fairhall posits ideology as an important means of restraining the poet's far-from-free fancy, due to which meaning is "not a given monolithic system of beliefs, but rather an ongoing dialectic among various coexisting and historically determined ideological practices" (32). An example of Joyce's thematization of the very process by which history-as-events becomes history-as-accounts-thereof would be the depiction of the character of Skin-the-Goat, "assuming he was he" (*U* 16.985), as a "historical figure who may be a fiction within a fiction," acting "as a potential maieutic device that begins by making the reader a little uneasy through its subversion of traditional notions of history and fiction and even identity" (37). While attentive to Joyce's subversive treatment of history *in general* as a slippery process of discursive construction and reconstruction, Fairhall remains clear about his inescapable entanglement within history *in particular*—his own and Ireland's.

Fairhall proceeds to discuss what he sees as a crucial connecting point of these two histories—Joyce's *idée fixe* of betrayal, both in his own life and in Ireland's national life: "Parnell had been betrayed; he, too, would see himself as having been betrayed by friends, colleagues, his wife Nora, and Ireland herself" (42). Through this linkage, the theme of Joyce's political outlook comes to the fore, characterized as a blend of his early-day socialism, pacifism, and "his bedeviled nationalism," seen to recede into background "as his fame [as an esthete, an apolitical artist] developed," yet never in the least abandoned (49-51). An example of this is the Myles Joyce case thematized in the *Wake* as the problem of "having one's history misrepresented in the hegemonic narrative of a conquering power" (58). No discussion of the *Wake* can understate the import of Vico's combined theory of history and language, conceived by Fairhall as

a forerunner of Nietzsche and Foucault: all three set about "decoding" or deconstructing the established historical traditions in their respective Ages of Reason. [...] Joyce followed Vico's example in turning to mythology as a liberating counterreality, [which, being] both real and imagined, breaks down Aristotle's distinction between poetry and history. (62)

Ultimately, what matters for Fairhall is not the *how* of Joyce's politics (whether nationalist, left-wing liberal, socialist, anarchist, Viconian, and so on), but the *what* of it: Joyce's status as "a literary revolutionist for whom writing represented the supreme political act" (63).

Here, Fairhall commences his textual analysis of all of Joyce's major works. Of *Dubliners*, he notes that the previous ahistorical critical tradition has underestimated the warping process of Joyce's "polished looking-glass" and thus blurred or even elided "the difference between Joyce's Dublin and its historical referent" (67). Fairhall's approach reveals Joyce's stories as of an inevitably restricted outlook on the Dublin they describe:

> Apart from his preoccupation with paralysis, one limitation of Joyce's stories as a historical picture of Dublin stems from his focus on the Catholic petty bourgeoisie to the virtual exclusion of other important classes—not only the slum-dwellers but also the Anglo-Irish. [...] Precisely because relations stop nowhere, and because the magic circle of Joyce's art is an illusion, we must look beyond the circle of history and historical narratives in order to better understand that art. (71, 73)

What this "look beyond" allows Fairhall to see is that Joyce's portrayal of Irish Catholicism's paralysis was undertaken from his own middle-class perspective, and therefore was necessarily negligent in regard to what fell outside of it, for example the Dublin poor.

The process depicted in *A Portrait* is described as *growing into history*. A careful analysis of the opening reveals, with the help of the example of the 'moocow' as both an Ovid allusion and a reference to traditional Celtic mythology mediated by the father, the very first sentence to encompass elements of many stories: "Greek and Irish myths, the story of Stephen's development into an artist, John Joyce's retold tale of the magical cow, and James Joyce's story of his own development into an artist" (113). This development is depicted as springing from fear:

> Stephen's rhyme, embodying his ability to make art out of a frightening experience, ends the first section of Chapter 1 on a mixed note. Conjuring up a green rose as baby tuckoo was a joyous exercise of imagination. The rhyme is creative, too, but its regular, rigorous shape and incantatory sound imply its function as a counter-charm against evil and reflect the rhymer's changed relation to the world. (115)

This childhood reply to a conflict with authority (hiding and making a rhyme) is regarded as foreshadowing Joyce's adult decision to pursue his art abroad. The particular overtones of the Parnellite drama (played out in the famous Christmas dinner scene) are discussed here against Joyce's background of middle-class Catholic morality, and also as symptomatic of his attitude to women: "The historical drama of Parnell's downfall features an all-male cast of major characters except for the offstage siren, Katherine O'Shea" (146). Crucial in this sense is Stephen's encounter with the prostitute, revealing "a complex dualism that extends to other women, mothers and virgins as well as whores" in that "his wish to impose his will on a female typifies males in a repressed society who resent the female's, especially the whore's, supposed sexual power over them" (154). Of note in this connection is the often lamented "loss involved in the reduction of Emma Clery, who shows signs of a life of her own in *Stephen Hero*, to the shadowy E.C. of *A Portrait*" (158), regarded as typifying (in its downplaying of Hanna Sheehy's real-life importance) Joyce's involvement, whether conscious or unconscious, in "many of his culture's assumptions about women" (160).

In his discussion of *Ulysses*, Fairhall immediately calls attention to the huge discrepancy between the Dublin of *Dubliners* and the Dublin of this novel, accounted for by the fact that for all of its author's seeming aloofness,

> *Ulysses* does inevitably reflect the era and circumstances of its making. It constitutes a response, in content and form, not only to WWI, the Easter Rising, and other upheavals, but to the preceding quarter of a century—a period of intensified imperial and national rivalries, of technological innovation, of social change, and of the emergence in art of modernism. (164)

The anachronistic reading of World War I as present in a 1904-based novel is substantiated by stating that in *Ulysses*, "there are remembered, reported, or imagined events which remind us that Dublin 1904 belongs to a world marked by violence past and present" (165). The nationalistic concerns of the "Cyclops" chapter are examined with the help of Benedict Anderson's definition of a nation as "an imagined political community," according to which

> [a]ny nation differentiates its citizens from those of other nations in terms of certain shared traits, while it ignores inconvenient facts that tend to subvert the illusion of unity. (173)

Thus, the Citizen cannot tolerate debate "because he is actuated not by reason but by mystical concepts of race and nationality," concepts which are "intertwined in *Ulysses* with violence and the cult of death" (178). However, again this particular perspective of nationalism, bespoken by "the absence from *Ulysses* of any Irish nationalists except those who are grotesquely funny, pernicious, or ineffectual," is indicative of the limitations of Joyce's own viewpoint (182).

The *avant-garde* form of his novel goes hand in hand with Joyce's fascination, throughout *Ulysses*, with technological innovation, which is seen as having to do less with the Dublin of 1904, "a border outpost of European culture" whose tram system was the only *avant-garde* feature, than with his stay on the Continent, particularly its Paris period (201). Joyce's *avant-garde* technique is regarded as spanning his celebrated stream of consciousness, in which his innovation was to do away with the individuality of any single mind and explore instead its linguistic make-up (e.g. Hayman's "Arranger"), camera eye technique (e.g., in "Proteus"), or film-montage, most prominent in "Wandering Rocks" which therefore "represents a response to the acceleration of history in Joyce's era and its attendant danger for the artist of pathetic anachronism" (211). The Great War, which "symbolized a combined destruction and liberation which long had been the goal of *avant-garde* art," becomes most palpably present in "Circe," which seems to be stage-managed by its own version of the organizing mind of the war—that omniscient intelligence, indifferent to human well-being, whose bizarre logic [...] many soldiers and civilians alike sensed in the weird unpredictable twists and turns of the fighting. (212)

Thus, Fairhall insists on viewing Joyce's narrative innovations as serving the double goal of "recreating the Dublin of 16 June 1904 and saving his narrative from pathetic anachronism." In his historicizing approach, the structuring principle of "Cyclops" reflects "a suprapersonal consciousness," which was brought into being by the scientific and technological advance of prewar Europe and culminated in the Great War:

That an analogue to this mind should be embedded in the very form of *Ulysses*—an antiwar novel concerned with depicting the richness of individual consciousness—is one of the novel's great contradictions. (213)

Finally, Fairhall turns to *Finnegans Wake*, centred as it is too around some "foul act" perpetrated in Phoenix Park:

But is it fact? And whether fiction or fact, what exactly happened? Who are the malefactors? Who the victim? Why did they do it? If they did it. Do we have evidence to convict? Whom? Of what? Such questions arise when we try to define the central event in *Finnegans Wake*. (214)

Again, no definitive history can be told. Before exploring the potential meanings of this narrative motif, Fairhall glances at other prominent instances of Irish history present within the *Wake*, including the many battles of I.1, the career of Parnell (together with the issue of forgery, the famous "hesitency" textual motif) linked with the Dreyfus affair, the recent Irish Civil War, as well as the already mentioned unfortunate Myles Joyce, whose last words, "I am going" (*ta mé ag imteacht*) are revealed as echoed in Anna Livia's fade-away ("I'm going!" *FW* 215.7) and other key moments of departure (215-9).

On a general note, Fairhall proposes to read the *Wake*'s "slipperiness of identity" as "an attack on essentialism" (221), one whose stakes are made clear in the pub scene in *Ulysses* where "the chauvinist Citizen first questions Bloom's Irishness and then amid echoes of the great artillery barrages of WWI" (224). The *Wake* is also from another perspective regarded as a work embedded within its time:

In *Finnegans Wake*, composed during the menacing period of *l'entre deux guerres*, Joyce takes his critique of the undivided subject much further. The *Wake* does not simply destabilize identity; its centripetal force whirls away the elements of any narrational center, such as Festy King, almost as soon as they come together. (228)

In his reaction to the difficulties of this period, Joyce is seen to have gone "immeasurably beyond any other artist," such as Owen, Sassoon, or Hemingway: "he set about creating a new, self-deconstructing language in which binary oppositions such as honor/dishonor, virtue/sin, and right/wrong could find no purchase" (234). Joyce's advancement can best be seen through a comparison of Molly and ALP. As long as the extent to which the former is capable of escaping her society's received notions of femininity remains dubious, in the case of ALP, "we can hardly speak of self-possession or conventionality since she is not a distinct character situated in a finely articulated social setting. But Joyce's concept of ALP and other feminine figures in the *Wake* certainly has a historical component, some aspects of which may be recoverable" (238). The *Wake* and *Ulysses* also reveal some of the earlier works' limitations:

> *Ulysses* reveals the superficiality of Stephen's emancipation from his mother and reminds us, through Molly, that Joyce took a woman with him when he left Ireland to forge his identity. Both novels counter masculine artistic and intellectual power with a subversive feminine force. (239)

This perhaps simplistic binarism notwithstanding, Fairhall's study ends more pertinently on a note about Joyce's deconstruction of the opposition between history and language. As long as "*Ulysses* suggests that the dark annals of Irish and world history coexist with those 'possibilities they have ousted' (*Ulysses* 2.51)," then in *Finnegans Wake*, "the possibility of ideareal history centers not so much in imagination as in language. Language itself becomes the prime creative and deconstructive force, acting as such whether generated by artists (Shem the Penman) or solid citizens (Shaun the Post)" (244). The language of the *Wake* then is seen as pointing to "the possibility of freedom from mastery by being that force which reveals any unitary identity, whether that of master or servant, to be an illusion" and which renders the linguistically constituted subject "divided [...] from the moment of self-awareness." This division in turn bears on historiography, since every weaving of a historical narrative contains, imprinted on the material, "the marks of our own dividedness." Fairhall enumerates three consequences for a Joyceanized understanding of history: "no history [...] can be authoritative or objective"; "our dividedness can be read historically, so that any narrative about history becomes itself a historical document"; and, "we need to be adept at reading the subtexts, or the latent content, of histories" (245). The fall into history is a fortunate one in Fairhall's opinion as long as one can "move away from the illusion of an unchanging self, predestined to have its fixed desires disappointed, toward a more flexible subjectivity" (246).

This vision of freedom based on language as offered by the *Wake* contains, nevertheless, an important paradox:

> However exhilarating it may be to read the *Wake*, and whatever it teaches us of potential liberation, the book tends to become a prisonhouse of words in the very endlessness of its play of meanings. [...] Thus *Finnegans Wake*, that meditation on freedom and limitation, has its own limits as a history lesson. Far ahead of its time, perhaps immune to pathetic anachronism, it offers us radical insights into the problem of historicity. Yet, as a historical

product itself, it remains rooted in its own time; and it conveys thoughts on language, history, and gender which are conditioned not only by Joyce's subject position but by our own positions as readers within history. (247)

Fairhall's "Afterword" revisits the central concerns of his work, questioning both the specificity and generality of Joyce's resistance to the constraints of history by means of a liberating language, exerted in his last novel. However, Fairhall turns to earlier (in fact the earliest) - texts as well: the inefficacy of the three floating signifiers of the opening of "The Sisters" is implied when the boy "must rely on his dreams—on nonverbal dream language—for a felt response to Father Flynn's death" (248). The boy is not alone in his failure to recognize the potentially liberating effects of a deconstructive use of language: in fact, "none of the characters in *Dubliners* avoids entrapment in historically determined modes of language and thought." Yet the artist himself does make an escape "in that we cannot identify him with a single voice or level of discourse among the many marking the stories" (251). This in turn is seen as the key reason behind Joyce's abandonment of Daedalus as an authorial persona: his project of "developing concepts of language, history, and subjectivity, incompatible with phallocentric mastery" was much better suited for a novel of the scope and structure of *Ulysses* rather than the stories or the autobiographical novel. Fairhall makes three important summarizing points about *Ulysses*:

> First, it sets about deconstructing the notion of a stable, unified subject. [...] Second, it deconstructs the boundary between history and fiction. [...] Third, *Ulysses* suggests and embodies a creative mode based not on phallocentric mastery but on a feminine generative principle, similar to the creative aspect of Derrida's *différance*, that subverts all forms of mastery. (252)

Finally, the *Wake*'s heteroglossia (adopted for Joyce in the sense of "a development of the ever more varied voices of the earlier works") undermines positions of dominance among national languages "much as its deconstructive use of words in general undermines phallocentric privilege" in that the artist seems to assume throughout a "feminine" position of subversion and of perpetual resistance to history. Fairhall's alignment with deconstruction reaches its climax here:

> Joyce thus discovered the political potential of *jouissance* and *différance* long before deconstruction was a gleam in Derrida's eye. The playful, anarchical elusiveness of language threatens all fixed, hegemonic positions. (255)

However, echoing his reservations from the "Introduction," deconstruction remains for Fairhall hopelessly inactive when it comes to the possibility of intervening in history: "if we need narratives to live by," he contends, "then we cannot adopt a politics pure and simple of deconstructive resistance." Joyce's literary politics is seen as pitiably flawed by the incapacitation vis-à-vis action it entails:

> To be perpetually marginal and subversive [...] is to close off certain historical possibilities by limiting our ability to intervene in history. [...] Such a position also inevitably reflects the historical circumstances of its production, and is no escape from history; it harbors its own political unconscious. This is a major limitation of Joyce's politics, particularly in *Finnegans Wake*.

This limitation notwithstanding, "the deconstructive openness of all Joyce's fictions encourages the opening up of other narratives, especially those of history," and therefore provides sufficient reason for Joyce's works being worth "the effort of introducing them to nonspecialists and nonacademics, since it is all of us who will shape future history together." (256)

II

The year following the publication of Fairhall's work marked an increase in the study of Joyce's historicism and saw the publication of another significant work on the subject—Robert Spoo's *James Joyce and the Language of History: Dedalus's Nightmare*.[2] Here, a study of Joyce's historiography is undertaken, spanning *Dubliners* through *Ulysses*, with a special emphasis on Joyce's early intellectual formation shaped crucially by 19th-century ideas of history, which are found to be variously resisted in Joyce's writing.

Spoo's "Introduction" opens by positing that history, "a provocatively complex word whenever Joyce uses it," carries "an especially heavy, shifting freight of meaning in *Ulysses* that makes it the verbal counterpart to Stephen, who personally labors under the burden of the past" (3). History, in Spoo's view, is more than just a theme in the novel: "it is to an exceptional degree a condition of the novel's aesthetic production" in that "Joyce became the compulsive historian of the Dublin of June 16, 1904, drawing his details from contemporary newspapers, maps, and city directories, and poring over histories of the capital" (4). Spoo aligns his approach in the book with an array of critical movements including "New Historicism, cultural poetics, popular culture studies, materialist feminism, metahistorical theory," whose common denominator has been

> to rescue literature from deconstructive strategies of reading, which [...] have become to seem abstract and self-indulgent, totalizing in their epistemological claims, but curiously blind to the ways literary texts process nonliterary discourses and institutions and are in turn shaped by those forces. (6)

---

[2] Robert Spoo, *James Joyce and the Language of History: Dedalus's Nightmare* (New York: Oxford University Press, 1994).

Part of this "rescue mission" from the deconstructionist effects (curiously regarded as "totalizing") is also Spoo's rehabilitation of "Stephen Dedalus as the novel's hero," this by demonstrating that

the persistent historiographic concerns of *Ulysses* are ultimately *his* concerns, that his intellectual attitudes, though seemingly remote from the styles of the later episodes, continue to shape the text's contestatory stance toward history long after he has receded as a character. (8)

The theoretical framework of Spoo's interest in Joyce the historian and historiographer is informed by "recent theorists such as Hayden White, Dominick LaCapra, and Michel Foucault," as well as by "historians and philosophers of history whose ideas formed part of Joyce's intellectual culture." Spoo's metahistorical readings of *Ulysses* aim not only to "show how dominant notions of history are both figured and resisted in the Joycean text" (9), but its Stephen-focusing perspective turns the novel into

a book about a restless, unhappy son, an overburdened Telemachus, a young artist seeking to flee what Gerontion calls the "decayed house" of his personal and cultural past, but realizing that he must reenter history through the window or the back door before he can achieve anything of value. (10)

The first two non-*Ulyssean* chapters[3] function as a contextual prologue, the one isolating Joyce's Rome sojourn as a text resonant with his ambivalent thinking about history, and the other providing another textual context to Stephen's nightmare of history through an examination of his overdetermined metaphors for historical experience in *A Portrait*. The third chapter examines how *Ulysses* challenges the Hegelian teleological models of history, as well as their near kin, monocausality (history as full presence), by means of the a-teleological movement of its narrative as a whole, a global perspective counterbalanced in the following episode-focused chapters. The examination of the "Nestor" and "Proteus" episodes in Chapter IV, importantly establishes what Spoo regards the basic historiographic rhythm in Joyce: a thematic revelation of the nightmare of history ("Nestor"), followed by a textual resistance to it ("Proteus"). The fifth chapter pursues the relationship between language and history in the theme of rhetoric in "Aeolus" and relies on both Vico's and LaCapra's insistence on the inseparability of historiography from the persuasive, performative aspects of language. Chapter VI views "Oxen" and "Circe" as a repetition, though one with vast ironic and stylistic difference, of "Nestor" and "Proteus." Finally, in "Conclusion," Spoo focuses on the *Nostos* part of the novel, where what Joyce himself called the "spectral language of myth and symbol" comes to dominate and eventually to displace Stephen's nightmare.

---

[3] Here, I follow the author's own outline of the book on 11-13.

However, Spoo's is not a cheap substitution of myth for historiography, in that neither is "immune to textual scrutiny" of its own ideological grounding. Spoo observes:

> There is ultimately no escape—for Stephen or for Joyce, antihistorical Icarus or pragmatic Dedalus—from the nightmare, only the ceaseless effort to awake from history's oppressive texts through the weaving and reweaving of alternative ones. (13)

It follows from the brief outline of the entire work that Spoo's central discovery, informing the thrust of his overall argument, takes place in the fourth chapter which deals with, as its title implies, "'Nestor' and 'Proteus': History, Language, Intertextuality," and therefore it is on this chapter as a *pars pro toto* of the entire book that the present discussion focuses. First, following a brief discussion of Virginia Woolf's *The Mark on the Wall*, Spoo recognizes in its image of waking from a nightmare "a characteristic trope of modernist historiography, a figure for the desire to break through received textualizations of the past to an unwonted authenticity," an appropriate starting point for his discussion of "Nestor," where "the unreality of the past almost overwhelms the young artist" (90). Spoo regards the entire chapter as dramatizing

> a complex allegory in which history and art, personified by Deasy and Stephen, respectively, are pitted against each other in a struggle for cultural supremacy. Deasy embodies what Nietzsche called the "malady of history," the burdensome dependence on the past which he feared was sapping intellectual and moral vitality in the nineteenth-century. Stephen represents the modern artist newly arrived on this scene of intellectual belatedness, struggling to establish a healthy relationship to history a usable past that will inform but not deform his aesthetic sense and art. (91)

"Proteus," on the other hand, presents Stephen alone at Sandymount Strand, where his "obsession with human solutions and formulas, with total explanations of the past and totalized projections of the future, is relaxed in an undulant symbiosis of word and world" and "nightmarish economies" thus give way to "linguistic ecologies" (91).

Spoo's treatment of "Nestor" centres around what the chapter's opening presents as Stephen's crucial concern with history; on the one hand, as "fabled by the daughters of memory," and yet also as "it was in some way if not as memory fabled it." Given that "some belief in the signifieds of historiographic discourse, in the 'real' content of history, must be preserved," the key questions present themselves,

> how far should credulity extend? Where does fact end and fabulation begin? And how—in what "way"—should this content be expressed in language? What governs the choice of signifiers and the stories they cumulatively tell? (93)

Spoo's view of Stephen's pedagogy as founded on repetition brings him to viewing the "Nestorian" history as a whole as "caught up in a repetition compulsion which, far from leading to the manifestation of God or any other glorious, pious, and immortal telos, seems likely to end by killing the spirit of historian and artist alike" (94). Attention is paid to Stephen's Christ-like, silent thrusts at Deasy which at times go beyond the framing of clever, bookish retorts, engaging instead in a strategy resembling the Foucauldian counter-memory, "an assault on 'the theme of history as reminiscence or recognition' designed to reveal and revitalize 'the buffoonery of history'" (97). Of crucial interest, of course, is Stephen's catchword phrase about history being "a nightmare from which I am trying to awake," which, "disturbing as a metaphor, overdetermined as a concept, problematic even as a rhetorical gesture in the dialogue with Mr. Deasy," has attracted "much scholarly attention, especially among source-hunting critics" (98), whose critical project, however, has not yielded any conclusive results as no single textual source has been revealed so far—Spoo's effort aims to document as a "strong intertext" the writings of Jules Laforgue (99). Deasy's pretension to English penny-wise philosophy is revealed as subscribing to the baleful pragmatic history written by the victors whose violence and injustice are fully in the service of the workings of the "one great goal," the revelation of God's will in history. His anti-Semitic, unhistorical quipping about Ireland "never letting Jews in" is also shown as turned on him, "for Joyce is the teller of this particular tale, and only a few pages later he will welcome into his narrative the outsider whom Deasy's history and story exclude" (102).

"Proteus," as if "in calm, unhurried response to the historical crises of 'Nestor,'" offers "counterimages of benign natural flux, replacing a claustrophobic sense of time with the undulant rhythms of the nearing tide" (107-8),. It thus presents a "repetition of 'Nestor' with a difference—a movement from rigid actualizations to rich potentialities, from history as closed, man-made system to the alternative rhythms of a feminized seascape" (109). Moreover, "Proteus" (just as "Circe") functions within the broader structure of the narrative as a 'threshold episode' in that it not only presents an obvious passageway leading from the Telemachiad to the *Odyssey*, but also in that its "natural, nonteleological rhythms [...] are a preparation for the advent of Bloom, who is associated throughout the novel with the body and its functions, the flowing properties of water" (111). The chapter is also of relevance for Stephen himself, for if "his historical sense coalesce[s] impressively, perhaps for the first time, in his 'Parable of the Plums,'" then the raw material for this tale first presents itself in the two "*Frauenzimmer*" he spies on the strand. Spoo concludes,

> The Parable is Stephen's first genuine effort to wrestle down the protean city of Dublin and make it yield historical and political meanings; it is also, in counterpoint to the nightmarish opposition between art and history, the first step in their rapprochement in the persons of Stephen and Bloom, hydrophobe and waterlover. (112)

III

A widely influential collection of essays, the co-edited volume *Joyce and the Subject of History*,[4] sprang from the "need to rethink historicity" which was in the introduction said to obligate and enable Joyce "as never before" (1). Felt at the time of its publication as acutely as at the time of its inception (the 1990 Yale Conference on "Joyce and History"), "the gap between history and theory" is what the collection attempts to bridge "without settling into any of the easily routinized conventions of established models for literary historical scholarship." Thus, while necessarily in dialogue with cultural studies, New Historicism, and post-Marxism, "the book's broader aim is to reconceive the field as a whole" (2). The prominence of Joyce's fiction in any discussion of Joyce and history springs from the fact that Joyce's personal relation to history remains shrouded in mystery, as he—unlike his fellow modernists Yeats, Pound, or Eliot—displays a distinctive status of aloofness:

> If we wish to pursue the topic of Joyce and history, then, we inevitably find ourselves at the mercy of Joyce's fictions, and here we are in danger of being overawed or misled. (2)

As opposed to the anti-historical bias of early critics (led by Eliot's myth of a-historical modernism), what the collection as a whole aims to emphasize is "an honest assessment of our critical heritage" which "should help us to recognize the limitations of our own critical positions and the importance of preserving [...] a lively dialogue between history and aesthetic form" (3). Stress is lain on what the editors view as the mid-1980s "revision of poststructuralist assumptions [...] when a group of critics trained in critical theory began to explore Joyce's use of popular culture." What was new in the work of critics like Cheryl Herr or R. Brandon Kershner was their "determination to theorize the implications of their discoveries and therefore to bring to bear on the empirical data of history a conceptual rigor previously reserved for questions of language and textuality" (4). This confluence of disciplines, theories and movements have rendered historicity one of the major thematic issues of Joyce criticism and its variety of conceptualizations "is not likely to be invoked to limit the multifarious play of Joyce's language," as ultimately it is Joyce's language that presents historicity with the most interesting challenges: "however evasive Joyce himself may have been in relation to historical categories, his texts ceaselessly enact and reenact the problems of history and history writing" (8). The collection as a whole is meant to bear witness to this ceaseless process, not by issuing in some simple consensus, but rather by giving an idea to "just how open that subject is" (9).

The collection falls into three sections. Part I, "Critical and Theoretical Prospects," contains three essays whose critical perspectives we have

---

[4] Mark Wollaeger, Victor Luftig and Robert Spoo, eds., *Joyce and the Subject of History* (Ann Arbor: University of Michigan Press, 1996).

already mapped out. Garry Leonard's "The History of Now: Commodity Culture and Everyday Life in Joyce" was discussed as part of Leonard's informative study of *Advertising and Commodity Culture in Joyce*[5]—here, Leonard conceptualizes commodity within Joyce's fiction as "the-not-yet-historicized," the epiphanic object and moment that eludes the narratives colonial ideology. R. Brandon Kershner's "History as Nightmare: Joyce's *Portrait* to Christy Brown" presents yet another foray into the Joyce/Bakhtin relation,[6] using the Bakhtinian notion of dialogic difference to present an intertextual reading of two *Bildungsroman* novels, unveiling implications of historical difference within generic sameness. Joseph Valente's "James Joyce and the Cosmopolitan Sublime" offers some fresh departures from the author's work within postcolonial studies,[7] using Homi Bhabha's theory of colonial ambivalence to argue that Joyce's articulation of the "perennial frustration" of decolonization is indicative of his search for "the underlying possibility of political agency." Finally, Fritz Senn's is a classical example of the author's work, aiming to combine the specific, a close reading of a selected passage (here the opening of the "Nestor" chapter), with the general, observing how *Ulysses* treats history as a polyphonic blend of variously authoritative voices. Senn's "History as Text in Reverse," with its usage of the neologisms "nuncing," the "now-ing" of the past, and "tuncing," the "past-ing" of the present, is a lucid exploration of the many ways in which the "historical" eludes its consignment to the past.

Of the essays that follow in the other two sections devoted to *Ulysses* and *Finnegans Wake* those deserving at least a brief mention feature Mark A. Wollaeger's reading of *Ulysses* in terms of the ideology of the novel genre. According to Wollaeger, its discourse is seen as having potentially the policing effect akin to British colonial presence in Dublin, and yet several strategies can be detected within Joyce's novel that seek to liberate the novelistic mimesis from this repressive force. Also worthy of note are Robert Spoo's piece discusses how historical events contemporaneous with the writing of *Ulysses* (those of World War I) are inscribed into the text, rupturing the naturalist mimesis of a day in June 1904; Vicky Mahaffey's article on "Nomadology and Female Piracy in *Finnegans Wake*," juxtaposes the historical accounts of Grace O'Malley with a reading of the Prankquean tale in the *Wake* which draws on the radical micropolitics of Deleuze and Guattari, revealing ALP as an equally powerful and duplicitous match for HCE; and finally Margot Norris' piece rethinks the critical history of *Finnegans Wake* through the prism of Peter Buerger's distinction between the historical avant-garde and modernism,[8] where the *Wake* comes to subvert the widespread modernist assumption

---

[5] See Chapter IV "Cultural Studies," section VIII.
[6] See Chapter IV "Cultural Studies," section VIII.
[7] See Chapter V "Postcolonialism," section IV.
[8] Thereby, Norris' article aligns itself with her earlier work done especially in *Joyce's Web* – see Chapter VI "Modernism & Postmodernism," section VI.

about the autotelic nature of texts by serving as the "historical unconscious" of Joyce's oeuvre.

IV

The variegated Protean nature of the discussions of Joyce from a historicist perspective (reenacting the very nature of Joyce's writing of history),
such as we have seen here so far, has been further enhanced by perhaps
the most sustained synthesizing attempt at bringing Derrida's deconstruction and Lacan's psychoanalysis to bear on the postcolonial condition of
Joyce's history, Christine van Boheemen-Saaf's *Joyce, Derrida, Lacan,
and the Trauma of History*.[9] In the words of the introduction, this book is
"a study in the informative presence of what Freud called the 'death instinct,'" and what is seen as "the peculiarly traumatizing and uncanny
effect of Irish historical experience in the rivalry for truth of three disciplines: deconstructive philosophy, Lacanian psychoanalysis, and Joycean
Irish modernist literature." Van Boheemen-Saaf's central claim is outlined
as follows:

> Joyce's encrypting of the experience of destitution in the material location
> of his text opens up a new, intersubjective realm of communication which
> may help to make it possible to work out the heritage of the past and trans-
> form the ghostly uncanniness of the "death instinct" into full discourse. (1)

This, in turn, has important consequences for the treatment of the individual theories themselves: poststructuralist theory is historicized as "itself a product of a certain resistance against the trauma of history," a
position made possible by Jean-Francois Lyotard's concept of "discursive
trauma (the Holocaust)," which allows one to see

> Joyce's dramatic materialization, or literalization, of the possibility of failure
> of symbolization itself as a "death-in-life of discourse," or an unconscious
> *within* history and discourse which adds a psychic dimension to textuality.

Joyce, as an Irish writer growing up in the English language, has to allude
allegorically "to what can never be voiced with immediacy: the loss of a
natural relationship to language, the lack of interiority of discourse and
coherent selfhood" (2). This specifically postcolonial lack at the heart of
Joyce's writing is brought to bear on the different notions of "materiality"
at work in Joyce, Derrida, and Lacan, rendering "Joyce's materialization
of the spectre of nothingness of colonial experience in *Finnegans Wake*
[...] different from Derrida's 'writing' or Lacan's 'materiality of the letter'"
(3). For an emblematic image of this Joycean "mimesis of loss," van Boheemen turns to the *Portrait* epigraph from Ovid's *Metamorphoses* which
stops short of the words "*naturamque novat*," "and he renewed nature."
On the grounds of this impossibility of renewal, Joyce is compared to

[9] Christine van Boheemen-Saaf, *Joyce, Derrida, Lacan, and the Trauma of History* (Cambridge:
Cambridge University Press, 1999).

Ovid's raped and muted Philomel, "who managed to communicate by indirect means—color and texture—a story which could not be told in words." This indirection, in turn, is found resonant in relation to James Joyce, in whose works "the symbolic event of the entry into language as a disruptive and violently fracturing moment splitting body from discourse" brings about "an endlessly repeated attempt at arriving at a signification of itself" (4). Joyce's texts, in this light,

> work in that split, and in that affective gap, writing in an English which, in its defamiliarization and slips of the tongue [...] evokes the continuous spectral presence of what [...] we may denote as the felt presence of the lapsing of the mother tongue. (5)

In its development, then, Joyce's writing increasingly opens the void gaping between the "foreign" and the "familiar," only to end up giving "the materialization of that void a local habitation and a name in *Finnegans Wake*," through what van Boheemen terms the strategy of "storytelling in the oppressor's language" (5). This renunciation of any locus within the specific socio-historical condition of postcoloniality "dramatically enacts the presence of a condition that in its extremity questions a facile generalizing use of 'the castration of truth as the truth of writing'" in that "the muted suffering of colonial oppression may be understood as an actual historical event which inscribed the experience of death-in-life into history and subjectivity, encrypting an ontological void." Lacan regarded this new, specifically Joycean dimension of discourse "as a confluence of the 'real' (denoting the unpresentable, death, sexuality, in contrast to the everyday use of the term which understands 'real' as referring to the existent) with the symbolic of language," while also conceding that "the historical example of Joyce's textuality upset his conceptualization of the relation between the imaginary, the symbolic, and the real." As Chapter II has shown and van Boheemen reiterates, "it was his confrontation with the symptom of Joyce (Joyce as the telling symptom of what supports human subjectivity) that led Lacan to revise his earlier schema, and admit that the symbolic, imaginary, and real, tied together in a Borromean knot—a fourth agent—may also be kept from psychotic fraying through a peculiar form of symptomaticity" (8). However, van Boheemen's is not solely a psychoanalytic perspective, for her study aims to show how "Joyce's historical example re-aligns the place of poststructuralist theory in current postcolonial studies," thereby refining Homi Bhabha's claim that "postcolonial writing 'occupies that space of double inscription, hallowed—no, hollowed' by Jacques Derrida." The intention here, "is not to demonstrate the applicability of Derrida or Lacan to Joyce," but rather to show how "their abstract concepts have a concretely embodied textual precursor in Joyce's complex textuality" (9). The book's thesis is that Joyce's work will remain misread, enlisted in the service of transcendent truths or narcissistic play, unless we learn to receive and confront it in its sensuously embodied form as the "art of trauma." [...] This book contains [...] an ethical appeal to read differently and read whole. (11)

To read differently in the first place entails rethinking Joyce's modernist context. This van Boehemen does by arguing that

[t]hough Joyce's drive to be modern and metropolitan is an incontrovertible fact, that appearance of modernity seems to me to have been a strategy to ensure the transmission of his work. Underneath that modernity, that work, I propose, participates in the sense of the traumatic nature of Irish experience of those who now write in Irish; but in a tragic mode, without its revivalist "dreamy dreams." (13)

Lyotard is fascinated, in *The Differend*, with Auschwitz as a deadlock of signification—apart from exterminating the Jews, the Germans also destroyed a vast amount of their records, the documents indispensable for the validation of the genocide. Lyotard asks, "Should we then have to conclude that history has no means of establishing its occurrence?" Thus, in Lyotard's text, the place name "Auschwitz" functions as the signifier of that which has been declared unutterable. When transposed to Irish history, this question has a twofold referent: "there is the sign of the absence of the language, and the non-figurable feeling, which travels through history divorced from a referent." In other words, the lapse of language functions as "a sign that something which ought to be or to have been expressed cannot (yet) be uttered discursively" (14-5). The parallel between Joyce's presentation of Dublin and Lyotard's "Auschwitz" lies in the former's function as

a secondary positivization, a material substitute in the shape of the representation of a place and its people, offered to take the place of the story which happened there but which cannot be articulated directly.

As long as in *Dubliners* paralysis affects the object of representation and the *Portrait* relates it to "the traumatically violent entry into subjectivity and naming of the artist-figure himself," then *Ulysses* "splits the self and stages the asymptotic double quest of two protagonists [...] and unravels the unity of the text into two gendered layers between which gapes the cold emptiness of 'interstellar spaces'" (16). This darkness of unmeaning opened up in *Ulysses* is in the *Wake* staged as the allegory of its own condition of impossibility, and Joyce's career is thus seen to end with "the blatantly demonstrative, heroic assumption of the dark stain of meaninglessness and racial denigration as the cross of *Finnegans Wake*" (17).

Here a meditation follows concerning the contradictory responses to Joyce as an *event*—and how Joyce's writing has divided his readers within Joyce studies into "the Ellmanites"—Joyce "as a humanist genius whose work advocates perennial values"—and "the Kennerites": Joyce "as an ironist, a genius with words and literary conventions whose playfulness delights us and outwits us" (22). Not only is this curious polarity of the positions pre-programmed by Joyce's text itself, but it is also seen reduplicated in two famous responses from outside Joyce studies: Derrida is considered a Kennerite, and Lacan, an Ellmannite. Van Boheemen's approach strives to steer clear of either and re-conceptualize the notion of representation: for "if we reflect on the nature of trauma as by definition an unclaimed and perhaps unclaimable experience, it becomes clear that the representational side of Joyce's works is *ersatz*, counterfeit, 'Shem'" (24). Thus, Joyce's work performs a paradoxical "literalization of the original Platonic notion of mimesis: as in a mirror, in his work reality appears *where it is not*." As long as the mirror of mimesis is "deceptive because it displaces, and lets language appear in a place where it did not originate," then van Boheemen envisages her reading as "an attempt to tear through the screen of representation itself, and make the text concretely present" (26).

Derrida's revisionary readings of older texts, "presented as a correction of the lack of attention to "writing" in classical philosophy," are acknowledged as informing van Boheemen's study with a few of its crucial theoretical notions, which are in turn seen as marking and re-marking individual Joycean texts: "*différance* proves to be the textual pattern of *Portrait*, 'dissemination' the mode of 'Cyclops,' and 'supplementarity' the structural pattern of the text of *Ulysses*." Lacan's theory of the split subject, which points to its "determination by an other—language or the symbolic system" is used as "most poignantly appropriate a description of the split sense of self-awareness of subaltern consciousness" (27). Van Boheemen's syncretic approach thus follows Joyce's example whose lesson is that

> we do not need to choose between either Derrida or Lacan in their attribution of truth to literature—psychoanalysis locating the "truth" in the textual example, philosophy in the act of writing. (28)

Her polymorphously shaped approach is also meant to respond to Joyce's dramatization of reading as "an activity which may emotionally affect the reader, and involve him or her in a processual dynamic which restructures subjectivity itself, not just our cognitive *understanding*" (29). Van Boheemen concludes her theoretical preliminaries by presenting the Joyce of her book:

> Blurring the boundaries between art and litter, realism and allegory, high and low, ink and excrement, metadiscourse and cry, Joyce's art is both mirror and symptom, both icon and index, about our world as well as a product in and of it. The unique distinction of Joyce, and his terrible beauty, is that he increasingly opted for the second term, relinquishing the first and sacrificing meaning, referentiality, the acclaim of fellow writers

and friends, driven to express in and through words the violence history has suppressed, and the death-in-life of colonial experience. (30)

Chapter II, dealing as it does with *"Representation in a postcolonial symbolic,"* opens appropriately—with a meditation on Stephen's metaphor for Irish art, "the richly suggestive" cracked looking-glass of a servant:

> A cracked mirror is a flawed object to be discarded or handed down to a servant: Irish art makes do with the outmoded models of representation of the master culture. Moreover, when we look into a cracked mirror, we see a redoubling and splitting reflection. We never see ourselves whole. (31)

Here, the postcolonial tenor of van Boheemen's argument gains momentum as she discusses the "contradictory nature of Irish subjectivity"—its being "part of the United Kingdom but perceived as racially and culturally different by the English" and "English-speaking while aware of the loss of the mother tongue"—as allegorized in a 'cracked lookingglass' "which can never achieve wholeness" (32). However, an immediate switch takes place, the exposition turning to poststructuralism and "its re-absorption of the citationality, or non-firstness, of the first word into the projective act of the constitution of linguistic subjectivity itself." Joyce's peculiarity consequently lies in how "he pre-inscribes the sublation of the poststructuralist strategy of reading as a feature of his work" (34). Especially, or rather most prominently, *Finnegans Wake* engages in this process of blurring the margins and boundaries in that it "also includes citations of newspapers that Joyce read, and even quotes from the critical reception of *Ulysses*," thereby blurring the distinction between life and text, metalanguage and object language.

Another subversive practice of Joyce's is highlighted "in his habit, after 'The Dead,' of ending the text with a personal postscript," in which "work and life, text and self, reality and fiction, the objective and subjective" are deliberately fused (35). This Joycean preoccupation of collapsing seeming binaries into undecidable supplementary dependency or at-one-ment brings to mind Jung's perceptive objection to the world of *Ulysses* as one in which

> [o]bjective and subjective, outer and inner, are so constantly intermingled that in the end, despite the clearness of the individual images, one wonders whether one is dealing with a physical or a transcendental tapeworm. (41)

The crack in the Joycean mirror is also contextualized along the lines of the modern versus postmodern division. Critical dealings with Joyce from some of the most prominent theorists of postmodernism (e.g. Ihab Hassan, Jean-Francois Lyotard, or Brian McHale) bear witness to the manner in which Joyce's textuality seems to challenge the very dichotomy[10]—or,

---

[10] For more on the work on Joyce by Hassan, Lyotard and McHale, see Chapter VI "Joyce, Modernism & Postmodernism," esp. sections I, II, and VII.

in van Boheemen's general observation, the crack in the looking-glass "subverts attempts to fix Joyce in neat categorizations" (42). Even *A Portrait*, regarded as in a sense Joyce's most traditionally modernist work, can be "actualized in two different ways—depending on which voice in the text we hear most loudly," as either an unconventional *Bildungsroman*, or as a sequence of repetitions in which every chapter "begins with the depiction of Stephen in a new role," and concludes with the abandonment thereof:

> Read thus, Stephen's artistic vocation can no longer be regarded as the brand and seal of the identity of the protagonist, or the grand aim of this novel. [...] It certainly seems impossible to keep seeing Joyce's text as only a modernist work [...] We must also [...] see the other half of the mirror, where the text appears as a poststructuralist serial construct. The text provides an image with a double exposure. (45-6)

This doubleness of exposure brings van Boheemen to the psychoanalytic theme of transference, described as "a spilling over of unconscious content beyond the frame of the individual self," and therefore fundamentally changing the status of the critic. Quoting Jane Gallop, van Boheemen observes that in the relation of transference, "the critic is no longer analyst but patient," a position which can be terrifying in that "it represents, to the critic who in her transference believes in the analyst's mastery, a position of non-mastery" (51). From the psychoanalytic perspective, Joyce's peculiarity lies in that "his work illustrates the presence of a hole in the other which Lacan himself would eventually acknowledge," a hole with which Irish history left Joyce in the form of "a traumatic discursivity always locked in the attempt to come to terms with the violence and treachery of language" (52). Consequently, Joyce's text has a functioning similar to that of the child in Freud's *Beyond the Pleasure Principle*, whose "reliving of trauma of the parent's absence" is also his "attempt at learning to cope." In Freud's parable, "the boy learns to symbolize the mother's absence, and thus bear it, through a repetitive gesture which gives a sense of mastery" (57). Furthermore,

> [s]uch a structure of involuntary repetition is what Freud defined as the effect of a wounding moment which can itself not be symbolized. [...] Even more curious is the fact that while memory of the original event has disappeared, it apparently survives in the body. Unclaimed memory is staged as involuntary mental activity by the body. (60)

Crucially important in this respect is the prelude to *A Portrait* which presents "the impossible record of the moment of trauma which establishes Stephen's at once tenuous and over-cathected linguistic subjectivity" (62). Moreover, this scene

> suggests a moment of wounding constitution of the self which locks it in a perpetual struggle to escape, while binding the self to that event in an end-

less repetition of undoing, of acting out and being and denying that trauma. (63)

In the particular case of Stephen Dedalus, this working out must take place "in the discourse of the oppressor," thereby entailing "an inescapable bondage to the voice and the ear" (64). The unconscious being textually inaccessible, the *text* can "only speak the repetitive effect of the trauma rather than the trauma itself" (67). However, a semiotic treatment of *A Portrait* implies something markedly different:

> The notion that *A Portrait* functions as index, as pointer to something not-presentable, suggests that there is more to textuality than just language, that the poststructuralist attempt to circumscribe the world as text, the psyche as language, may paradoxically backfire to draw our attention precisely to what it excludes in its originary repression. (71)

Turning to *Ulysses* in "*The language of the outlaw*" complicates things yet further for if in *A Portrait*, "Joyce still offers an image which seems to represent a world we know," in *Ulysses*, "for all its realistic precision of detail, Joyce deliberately set out to frustrate the reader's expectations of encountering a unified and naturalizable representation." It is the chapter's main contention that this is done in order "to maintain a position outside western ideological preconceptions in order to dramatize the impossibility of an authentic Irish voice" (74). Van Boheemen focuses on "Cyclops" as not only "one of Joyce's most direct parallels to Homer," but also "the focus of discussions of Joyce's nationalism and postcolonial poetics" (78). Her reading reveals the narrative interpolations to unveil the narrative itself as "bugged" and with "a virus" (79). This virus can be traced with reference to the semiotics of narrative, where

> narratology, a structuralist approach to narrative based on the ancient distinction between mimesis (dramatic enactment) and diegesis (verbal summary), untwines the strand of the narrative text into two component threads, which I shall here refer to as "fabula" ("a series of logically and chronologically related events that are caused or experienced by actors") and "story" ("a fabula that is presented in a certain manner").

In this light, the peculiarity of "Cyclops" is that it "sabotages this critical distinction, thus vitiating the hierarchizing priority of fabula over story which grounds the objectivity of representation" (86). David Hayman's widely adopted suggestion that "we see the 'implied author' as a split-subject, sometimes manifesting himself as an 'arranger'" is ultimately refused as "*a defense against Joyce's meaning*: Joyce hopes to puncture the illusion of the possibility of voicing an ontological Irish presence [...] within hegemonic realist representation" (87-8). In other words if we following the metaphor, "the 'bugs' and 'strangers' already inhabit the self; they have also invaded authorial subjectivity" (89). Van Boheemen's thesis on "Cyclops," then begins to emerge:

In "Cyclops," Joyce deliberately leads his reader into the maze of a world in which a discursive or semiotic logic seems to have ousted realistic referentiality, because the traumatic condition of imprisonment in the hegemony of the oppressor's language entails such a preclusion of the priority of fact. (91)

There is no stable "self," no consistent personal voice in *Ulysses*, primarily "because all elements of human experience are already deprived of identity by the reader's awareness of the clichés of a collective cultural discourse which anticipatingly contaminates the self-presence of any narrative" (92). "Cyclops," more specifically, is composed of the discourses of the collectivity of written media which constitutes the self-mirroring image of culture, the language which constitutes cultural community" (94). Hence, van Boheemen finds "the presence of the void" at the heart of the Joycean text:

> *Ulysses* and *Finnegans Wake* are best understood as attempts to encrypt "castration," or the ontological void, *into* textual structure. [...] Thus [Joyce] stages the non-representability of the traumatic experience as the real condition of narrative—all narrative. This move is part of what Lacan speaks of as Joyce's "sinthome." (98)

This movement also has to do with what has already been defined by Derrida[11] himself as one of the crucial responses elicited by Joyce's text— laughter: "Not only is Joyce hilariously funny, his comedy rests in the suggestion that the symbolic order itself is structured around a lack, around an unclaimable, unassimilable moment just as Joyce's own traumatic texts" (103). This Derridean laughter is in turn "postcolonialised" in van Boheemen's argument in terms of hybridity:

> In Joyce's laughter a space opens up between identification and rejection, a hybrid location "between" where, as Bhabha puts it "culture's double returns uncannily—neither the one or the other, but the impostor—to mock and mimic, to lose the sense of the masterful self and its social sovereignty." (108)

Importantly related to this is Joyce's project of "somatization of reading," biographically (as well as textually) documented by his interest in Marcel Jousse who van Boheemen informs us, "held that the liturgy of the Church encodes a form of embodied knowledge which the student can only acquire through memorization and identification with the combination of gesture and word" (111). Analogously, "Joyce himself called *Ulysses* an epic of the body more 'than of the human spirit,' centering each of the chapters on an organ, and figuring the text as a whole as a human body" (115). Revisiting the issue of postcolonial agency, Homi Bhabha at last receives more than a passing nod from van Boheemen's argument:

---

[11] For more, see "Introduction," section III.

Joyce's text is regarded, with the help of a Bhabha quote, as opening up "a possibility for 'the emergence and negotiation of those agencies of the marginal, minority, subaltern, or diasporic that incite us to think through— and beyond—theory.'" Bhabha's notion of "writing outside the sentence" sounds "as if he were describing Joyce's praxis"—another example of the often noted proximity of theory to Joyce's writing (118):

> It is as if Bhabha theorized Joyce's revolutionary example. Perhaps it is a pity that we need Bhabha to recognize what some of Joyce's contemporaries may have understood clearly. (119)

Chapter IV, "*The primitive scene of representation: writing gender*," asks how Joyce could face the terror of meaninglessness identified in his works, and addresses Joyce's strategy of coping with the "castration" which he in turn "inflicts on representation and the reader." An argument is also made for a historical perspective on his "fetishistic handling of the possibility of diminishment, loss, or difference" (120). After this digression, the notions of representation and theory return in the fifth chapter, "*Materiality in Derrida, Lacan, and Joyce's embodied text*," first in connection with Nicolas Poussin's painting *Et in Arcadia Ego*:

> The question Poussin's representation brings into this inquiry is not just the reminder of our mortality, but the relation between representation (writing or reading) and death/castration. As the reading figure traces the letters, his arm throws a shadow on the tomb which takes the form of the traditional symbol of the scythe which cuts human life. Thus the very act of reading— and by extension the act of writing—itself brings the shadow which denies the permanence we traditionally attribute to the medium: *ars longa vita brevis*. (155)

Joyce's *Finnegans Wake*, it is repeated, is "best understood as the next step in [his] self-dialectical trajectory of attempting to catch up with the non-figurability of the moment of trauma (158). Its triumphant laughter, its *jouisssance*, "is based on the phantasy of the primal and undifferentiated (anal) materiality of writing, the redoubling of the flow of ink ('**p**ee') as graphic mark ('**P**opo'), which creates a location for the inscription (the **P**en) of the alienation of self-identity" (161). Joyce's sublimity then rests in his having "have made a location for the presence of the Nothing to which colonial culture reduces the subaltern" (162). Jean-Francois Lyotard's paper "Going back to the Return"[12] is referred to, conceptualizing the gendered "unconscious" as "a past without memories." Time and again, the ambivalent manner in which Joyce's writing both conforms to and transgresses the Lacanian and Derridean theory brought to bear on it:

> Joyce's *writing,* then, seems to partake of a different affective mode, that of witnessing and testifying (rather than signification)—and it more closely

---

[12] See Chapter VIII "Modernism & Postmodernism," section II.

follows a phenomenological outlook, although it seems to confirm the "truth" of either Lacan or Derrida.

A re-visitation of both follows, one which is worth pursuing here, as it too centers around Lacan's and Derrida's conception of the letter in Joyce. With Lacan, his fascination with Joyce was due to

> the latter's play with writing as graphic inscription—the "littering" [Lacan's term] of the letter, its brinkmanship and virtual destruction of meaning. However "psychotic," Joyce's text keeps a *modicum* of meaning beyond its nonsensicality. (167)

Among the crucial points of further interest are Lacan's focus on "the odd inscription of and in *Finnegans Wake* as the *graphic* truth of the existence of the 'sinthome,'" as well as "the Real persistence of pleasure as *jouissance* (elsewhere in his theory related to the feminine and outside the Symbolic)," his "enthusiastic imitation of Joyce's punning and graphic experiment," his shared "interest in supplementarity" (168-70). In van Boheemen's understanding,

> [t]he "sinthome" as the limit of psychoanalysis may also be the symptomatic indication of what the theory of psychoanalysis cannot engage or address: the affect of the trauma; or, in words abusing Lacan's term: the suffering encrypted in the "letter in sufferance." (176)

Derrida, just as Lacan, "partakes of Joyce's fetishization of the signifier." What is of primary interest for Derrida, however, is "latter's seeming strategy of radical *Aufhebung* and transcendence" with which "Joyce lifts himself by his own bootstraps." Derrida, moreover,

> is transferrentially involved with an ambivalent, Shem-like Joyce who laughingly eludes the split between signifier and signified, and endlessly makes signification its own signified in the act of signifying. (177)

Derrida's *Acts of Literature* frequently mentions of Joyce as "sharing *Joyce's dream*"—of which van Boheemen notes that gone is Derrida's "earlier emphasis on Joyce's design to 'compute,' 'control,' and 'program' us," and what remains is "the lack of demarcation within Derrida's construction of 'history' as an echo-chamber of intertextuality, an archival universe of textuality" (178). Van Boheemen's project of postcolonializing the Joyce of Derrida and Lacan is summarized as follows:

> Joyce's text allegorizes both Derrida's and Lacan's placement of the sexual other, owing to his splitting of the representation of the feminine. [… S]ome of Lacan's and Derrida's contributions to the discussion of postcolonial textuality have their grounding in the Joycean text. Différance, dissemination, supplementarity, *jouissance*, the Thing, these abstract concepts might have made less impact if the literary work and the lived experience to ground and illustrate them had not existed. (190-1)

However, there is for van Boheemen also a profound disjunction at work between the theorizing of literature and Joyce's postcolonial writing:

> If colonial practice arose out of the failure to imagine and experience the reality of the other as equal, theory, which splits fetishized intellectualization from emotional engagement, is complicit in that act of splitting repression.

Both Derrida and Lacan are criticized on account of "ignoring the fibula and story of literary works," which leads them "to disrupt the imaginative totality of the work, and fail to engage the full charge of its force." In sum,

> [i]f the "true otherness" of the work of literature is its function as conduit of conscious and unconscious affect, we "castrate" literature if we understand it as just a form of performative "writing." (192)

What then has been the primary purpose of van Boheemen's pairing of literature and theory, given how different or even incompatible they turn out to be in her account? Her project, she contends by way of conclusion, aimed to introduce

> a way of healing the breach which threatens to separate the reading of literature from theoretical reflection; it is also an attempt to relocate theory in the affective context from which it has struggled to escape on Daedalian wings. (193)

Van Boheemen's "Conclusion," in an appropriately commodius vicus-like fashion, recirculates back to the metaphor of the mirror which is here, "anamorphic" due to its deployment of "strategies of resisting textuality and linguistic inventiveness which unsettle the mirroring function of western representation" (194). The resource-richness of Joyce for theory is seen as owing to how the way "his work stages the dilemma of our understanding of consciousness: is it one or two, single or divided?" However, Joyce's writing, and this is its feature emphasized most consistently throughout van Boheemen's book, "holds an ethical appeal to the reader which theory as such lacks" (195-6). This appeal is essentially twofold:

> In packaging the mute appeal for recognition and subjectivity as a joke, Joyce enlists our involuntary, physical response to his writing—the pleasure it gives serving as lure to attachment.

However, beyond our laughter, *Finnegans Wake* "also demands and needs the imaginative act of our witnessing empathy," its agonized "mememormee!" positing a demand for "symbolizing remembrance after death [remember me] as well as [...] a desperate plea for the witnessing recognition by the reader [me, more me]. Perhaps," concludes van Boheemen, "we need to learn to read in a wholly new way" (210).

Van Boheemen's crucial trope, "the trauma of history," proves fruitful in that it enables her to include within her scope both issues specifically Joycean (English as a language profoundly alien to his Irish heritage) and strictly textual (the traumatic opening of *A Portrait*, the "bugged" narrative of "Cyclops"), along with literary theoretical (*mimesis*, narratology, literary semantics) and critical theoretical ones (the Derridean *différance* or *supplementation*; Lacan's split ego and textual *jouissance*; Bhabha's *hybridity*). However, her syncretic approach poses at least two fundamental problems: first, the peculiarity of her "trauma of Irish history" is that in her Lacanian/Bhabhaian approach, there is nothing particularly "Irish" or "historical" about it. In the context of the present chapter on Joyce and history, the absence of both appears especially striking: "Irishness" denotes the loss of Irish language (to which Joyce himself surely harboured far more ambivalent emotions than a mere mourning of its loss), and "historicity" is reduced to a simply given Irish postcoloniality, conceived of, moreover, within the Lacanian purely textual model of subjectivity, and thus perfectly de-historicized. This also ties in with a second possible objection: the effect of the trauma—the acutely sensed "loss of Irish authenticity" (see above for the many instances thereof), which not only oddly opposes van Boheemen's poststructuralist and postcolonial approaches—both of which strived to primarily do away with essentialism of this sort—but also, more importantly, is at odds with Joyce's artistic project (accordingly, it is in her dealing with "Cyclops" that she finds all "elements of human experience deprived of identity" and "always already contaminated"). Oddly enough it is her concept of historical trauma that brings her to take issue with theory for "castrating" literature. Nevertheless, her study remains beyond doubt the most ambitious project to date which attempts to re-think the potential of poststructuralist theory for postcolonial and historical studies of Joyce, offering an insightful reading of the latter, and an informed, original recontextualisation of the former.

V

Attridge's collection of essays,[13] a veritable treasury of material for this examination, palpably present in almost every single chapter so far, will here make its last appearance with two essays devoted to the history-related issues in Joyce's work. These complement each other well as the first one presents an attempt to think Joyce's historiography in relation to, and contrast with, the influential theoretical position of Fredric Jameson, while the other strives to tease out the particular *Wake*-an theory of history by looking at its peculiar mode of temporality and some of its textual practices.

Attridge opens his "Joyce, Jameson, and the Text of History" by evoking Jameson's postulation from his *Political Unconscious*: "[h]istory is

[13] Derek Attridge, *Joyce Effects: Language, Theory, History* (Cambridge: Cambridge University Press, 2000).

what hurts." There are, to both Jameson's and Stephen's mind, two kinds of history, present within human life "as that which, operating from outside the human capacity to construct and construe signs, imposes limits upon [...] thought and action; and on the other hand as that which communities make and remake under the shifting pressures of ideological and material needs" (78). History in the former sense of limitation essentially resists any conceptualization, and goes by many other names in the various strands of theoretical thought such as Jameson's "Necessity," Lacan's "Real," or Althusser's "Absent cause." The other sense of history as not only man-making but also man-made, "provides more possibilities for discussion—indeed, the unbounded scope it offers for verbalization constitutes one of the major difficulties in dealing with it" (79). Jameson's argument, followed at some length by Attridge, involves the project of treading the middle ground between two contrasting ideologies which deal with the two above-mentioned understandings very differently: the ideology of structuralism, which "would deny the existence of the first history or of the referent of any historical, or narrative, text," and the ideology of vulgar materialism, which "would reduce the second, textual, history to a mere mechanistically determined reflection of the first." Jameson's middle course would then, "*not* be an instance of ideology, since it would be an acknowledgement both of the real contradictions that constitute History [...] and of the constitutive function of the texts in which those contradictions are represented."

As opposed to this view, in Joyce's writing *all* versions of history as regarded as "made in language" and thus "ideological constructions, weavings and reweavings of old stories." In this respect, *Finnegans Wake* achieves the status of "the fullest statement in the world's archive of this view of history, exploiting the properties of the linguistic signifier to mix and conjoin narratives from a multiplicity of cultures" (80). This process is seen to have been launched in the *Ulysses* project of "extended dismantling of all the traditional assumptions of realistic fiction," and consummated in the *Wake*, which "give[s] language and its chance patterns and echoes absolute primacy over non-linguistic reality" (81). Thus, for all their difference, Joyce might be seen as a dramatization of Jameson's argument from his *Political Unconscious* that "although history is not a text, it is 'inaccessible to us except in textual form, and that our approach to it and to the Real itself necessarily passes through its prior textualization.'" (82) However, in a typical twist, Attridge proposes the other direction of exchange, reading "Jameson in the light of Joyce," as potentially more fruitful. Consequently, Jameson's book is revealed to rely on "the progression from point *a* to point *b*, where *b* preserves but subsumes, and thereby transforms, *a*," bespeaking the Hegelian and Marxian position of Jameson's argument, in whose dialectic the irreversibility of the progression is given particular emphasis. Joyce, by contrast, although he does use the same narrative scheme, does so "partly to draw attention to it *as* a storytelling device" and undermines the unidirectionality of the process. Ultimately, in the *Wake*,

> Joyce fully resists the linear, progressive, subsuming structure at the level of *discours* as well as at the level of *histoire*: no amount of ingenious analysis can make the language or the content of the later chapters encapsulate, transcend, or dominate that of the earlier ones. (83)

The particular usefulness of Joyce's writing for approaching Jameson's text consists in the way it

> enables us to challenge the separation of the two senses of "history" implied in Jameson's argument [...] by questioning the division of the world into signs and referents, language and existents; it reminds us that signs are referents and existents too, and history as text or ideology is as real as the unfathomable history that hurts us or gives us a back kick. (84)

Thus, it is not any clear dichotomy of the Real and the Text, or an irreversible progress from sheer signification to an apprehension of Necessity that one can learn from Joyce, but rather "an appreciation of *difference*, which resists the narrative of progress and the claims of transcendence." A preservation of this difference requires of us to "continue to find ways of rewriting ourselves, our history, our future, one another, in a constantly reworded engagement with the non-textual Real" (84).

Attridge's other essay discussed here, "Wakean History: Not Yet," revisits the conceptualizations of history as presented in both *Ulysses* and *Finnegans Wake*. If the Ulyssean conception is one which "minimizes the gap between two radically different uses of the word 'history,' on the one hand as the totality of events as they have occurred through time, and on the other as a story told about the past" (86), in that its being set on a dateable day and in specifiable location "situates it firmly in the mainstream tradition of the novel," which is "seen as the ficitional counterpart of the historiographical tradition," then *Ulysses* as a whole can be said to "leave the conventional concept of history as the union of events and language intact, if somewhat shaken." However, the *Wake*

> breaks decisively with that concept, [...] insisting that the multiple and endless accumulation of events and beings in the world and the equally endless telling of stories belong to two quite different orders of reality, whose relationship is deeply problematic — as much so for the historian as for the novelist. (87)

For Attridge, *Ulysses* leaves the reader with the impression that "the representation of the world in language is a matter of free agency," which for him implies that "behind all the variation is an unchallengeable, neutral base [...] from which these alternatives derive and against which they are measured," whereas the *Wake*, by contrast, "offers no such metatextual or paratextual solace" (87). What the *Wake* seems engaged in instead is shattering "the model of the novel as simulacrum of history," and to-gether with it "the model of historical writing as simulacrum of the novel." Provided that the language of the historian possesses all the prop-erties revealed in *Finnegans Wake*, "then the dream of capturing in words 'what really happened' must be abandoned" (88). Here, the "passencore" or *not yet* temporality of the very first page of the *Wake* is relevant in that

> [it] both parodies the tendency in historiography to present events in terms of what they lead to and at the same time demonstrates the centrality of this mode to any historical writing, which must always reconstruct after the event and never bear witness to it in its own time and place.

Elaborating on the French "passencore," Attridge notes the ease with which *encore* passes "from 'yet' to 'again,'" and how "the cyclical view of history so prominent in the *Wake*" operates as another device for un-settling our secure linear perspectives:

> if history comes to us only as narrative, it happens as often as it is told or retold, its repetitions stretching endlessly into the future. (89)

This repetition-with-a-difference process is related to Joyce studies them-selves, where "each International James Joyce Symposium prolongs the existence of Joyce's writings, but also changes them, even if what the participants claim to be doing is restoring them to their original or real selves," a case in point being the 1984 Gabler edition, the hitherto "not yet" text. It would, however, be to err in a Stephen-like fashion if one were to bewail the loss of some sort of imaginary historical real and blame it on its textual translation. As a matter of fact, there is no real, or rather the "original" is always already translated:

> Texts make history; history makes texts. *Finnegans Wake*, in dramatizing this cycle-wheeling process, manages to make it an extremely funny busi-ness. The joke, finally, is on Stephen, whose meditations on the subject of history in "Nestor" [...] fail to engage with the productive potential of the past's inevitable textuality. (91)

VI

The latest and last critical examination of the issue of history within the Joycean oeuvre (and Joyce studies) discussed here has been recently penned by Margot Norris as part of Jean-Michel Rabaté's edited volume of essays, *Palgrave Advances in Joyce Studies*.[14] Norris' piece attributes the consensus as to the centrality of the question of history in Joyce studies to the fact that "the issue of history is not restricted to Irish history any more":

---

[14] Margot Norris, "Joyce, History, and the Philosophy of History," *Palgrave Advances in Joyce Studies*, ed. Jean-Michel Rabaté (London: Palgrave Macmillan, 2004).

Irish history is the nightmare from which Joyce scholars have awoken, but only to find themselves facing the even more loaded issue of Joyce's philosophy of history. (203)

A rapid review of the genealogy of the surged interest in these issues, spanning both cultural studies and postcolonial approaches and including Joyce scholars such as Herr, Kershner, Duffy, Cheng, Spoo, Nolan, and others, is meant to suggest

> a remarkable coherence, except for a striking disjunction between this panoply of work on the subject of history and the simultaneous — if less conspicuous — scholarly interest in Joyce and the philosophies of history that preoccupied him in his own day. (204)

This disjunction is precisely what Norris' essay aims to overcome, by focusing its discussion of the subject not only on Joyce and his relation to the Irish past or present, but also and more relevantly on Joyce *as* a historian and historiographer. From the array of possible etymological definitions of history presented by Norris, "Joyce emerges as a historian chiefly in the archaic sense, as one who narrates events or incidents that relate to real or imaginary objects, persons, and careers" (205). Thus, she seeks to complement the Joyce (the historian of the everyday) of Garry Leonard[15] or the Joyce (the border-zone occupying cosmopolitan) of Joseph Valente[16] with a Joyce engaged with "philosophers and philosophies of history, particularly those that were themselves oppositional and marginal to their own intellectual moments" (206) — here, Norris' argument focuses on Joyce's interest in Giambattista Vico, Edgar Quinet, Jules Michelet, and Friedrich Nietzsche.

Vico presented, for Joyce, a philosopher of cyclical history dissident both to the Christian orthodoxy and to the official rationalist Enlightenment thought; drawing on a variety of secondary material, Norris documents the crucial features of the Viconian conception of history and the crucial impact it left on the Joyce corpus. The assumption of many critics that Joyce would have learned his Vico not from the original, but through the translation by Jules Michelet (which launched his career of historian in 1827), swerves Norris' discussion in the direction of Joyce's relation to French historical thought, which, in Michelet's designation of "the historian as archivist of the people's forgotten texts," was one of great appeal to Joyce. Of even greater influence was Michelet's famous colleague, who was co-instrumental in their launch of the revolution in historical studies in the France of 1820s — Edgar Quinet. Quinet's role in Joyce's thought "remains troubled by the paradox of its startling prominence in his writing, and the lack of context for Joyce's focus of [his] famous lyrical sentence," which famously remains the only formally appropriate

[15] For Leonard's *James Joyce and Commodity Culture*, see Chapter IV "Cultural Studies," section VIII.
[16] For Valente's *James Joyce and the Problem of Justice*, see Chapter VIII "Politics," section VI.

quotation in the whole of *Finnegans Wake* (211). Then, Joyce's French-discovered Hegelianism is touched upon, and Hegel's model of history, "with its emphasis on the spirit's drive for self-transcendence in the historical process," is regarded a possible refutation for Haines' defensive comment in "Telemachus" that "It seems history is to blame" (214). Marx's work in this respect is important not only as Hegel's most important critical revision, but his *Capital* contains a quite significant footnote to Vico in its contextualization of one of its key beliefs that "men make their own history" (215). In the genealogy of thinkers of history as a non-teleological process, Nietzsche stands prominent, referred to directly in "A Painful Case" and "Telemachus." Of the twentieth-century philosophers of history, Joyce is known to have read with respect the work of Benedetto Croce (216).

Norris' contextualization, however important in the particularities it brings together, only becomes truly relevant when she attempts to tease out of them a set of principles of historical conceptualization characteristic of Joyce's historical thought. Norris identifies three characteristics common to all the above-mentioned projects. Joyce seems to have been attracted to "historical theorists who were themselves intellectual outliers or experimentalist, able to imagine worlds [...] that are cosmically unimaginable," as well as to "philosophies of history that posit human agency in the production of history, and human possibilities for change and development aimed toward increased freedom," and finally, to "philosophies that collapse past, present, and future—either by positing recurring cycles or by assuming the saturation of the present with the past and the present pregnant with the future" (219-20).

Norris concludes on a skeptical note concerning any claim as to the exhaustibility of historical context. As long as "history, and the philosophy of history, vastly exceeded the matter of the merely thematic in the Joycean text," then

> [h]istorical excavations of the philosophies of history Joyce may himself have encountered, understood, and transmuted in some form in his writing are themselves doomed to speculative modes and methods with compromised rigor. We can only gesture toward what sort of historical principles might have guided Joyce in transforming the paralysis of Irish politics in the *Wake* of the death of Parnell into varieties of desultory or sentimentalia in *Dubliners*, *Portrait*, *Ulysses*, and *Finnegans Wake*. (221)

In mentioning the potential of Marx's influence on Joyce's thought, and in dealing with the broader theoretical implications of Joyce's sustained treatment of the historical within his work, Norris' essay and this chapter as a whole already point to the crucial concern of the next chapter—Joyce-the-man and Joyce-the-text in relation to the political.

8. Politics

I

For the third and last time, if only in passing, the present overview reverts to Colin MacCabe's pioneering study,[1] as its explicitly political position and concerns have turned it into an indispensable study for most of the later engagements with the ideology and political commitments of Joyce's writing examined here—the reader is thus referred back to Chapter I, which discusses MacCabe's treatment of the political nature of Joyce's writing in considerable detail. Here, I focus only on a brief presentation of a chapter purposefully excluded and reserved for the present context. "Joyce's Politics" observes that "[i]t is little realised, and never stressed, that James Joyce's life before 1914 gave him the very rare opportunity to observe two of the most important political developments of the twentieth century [..., i.e.] anti-colonialism and Fascism," whose major component was "nationalism" (159-60). MacCabe is perceptive in specifying the *kind* of nationalism against which Joyce waged his artistic war:

> In so far as nationalism persists in "familiarising" the relation of the individual to a community or to a State, persists in making us "sons" or "daughters" of the "mother" or "father" land then it must be combated. [...] Such a nationalism confers identity and belief there where we would find desire and knowledge. (167)

From here, MacCabe turns to Joyce's post and inter-war political stances, focusing on Joyce's "refusal to visit the Free State," which he regards as "based on sound political judgment," or Joyce's engagement in a process (meant to counter his lack of "audience that would allow his texts to function politically") of constructing his writing as an increasingly "desperate attempt to deconstruct those forms of identification which had allowed the triumph of the national revolution to mean the very opposite of a liberation of Ireland" (169-70). It follows that the ensuing works very much follow in the line of inquiry of MacCabe's seminal book, providing his merely sketched observations with the well-deserved and also much called-for elaboration.

---

[1] Colin MacCabe, *James Joyce and the Revolution of the Word* (New York: Palgrave, 1978; 2003).

II

Already hailed in a number of instances as a pioneering study of Joyce's personal political beliefs, Dominic Manganiello's *Joyce's Politics*[2] is most valuable as a comprehensive, historically-oriented analysis of Joyce as a *zoon politikon*.

Manganiello opens his discussion of the political commitment of citizen Joyce by surveying the political situation of the Ireland of Joyce's youth. The beginning of "*A Portrait* of the Artist as a Young Parnellite" adduces several instances about Joyce's verbal dismissal of politics on several occasions from which Manganiello concedes, "it would be possible to construct a picture of Joyce as a writer totally detached from his century." However, "to regard Joyce as a dweller in an ivory tower," would not be in accord with another of his statements, according to which his art presented "the attempt to picture totally the situation of man and woman" (1). The somewhat enigmatic nature of Joyce's relation to politics has been due to the fact he "does not present a vision of the social order in accordance with a strict ideological line" (2). Paradoxically, it was politics that presented the subject of Joyce's first piece of writing, his (now lost) poem "Et tu, Healy," dedicated to the memory of the betrayed Parnell;

> Beyond Parnell lay seven centuries of Irish struggle for Home Rule. Like his fellow countrymen, Joyce considered his long-sustained English presence in Ireland an occupation. He would have agreed with Robert Dahl's standard definition of "political," that it treated "any pattern of human relationships that involves, to a significant extent, power, rule, or authority." (8)

In his treatment of the issue, Joyce was very well aware of "the role the indigenous population and the Church had played in the Anglo-Norman invasion and in the series of betrayals against the revolutionary patriots," which still did not alter his outspokenly critical view of English misdeeds in Ireland (13). Equally two-sided was Joyce's relation to nationalism, which for him "exemplified political delusion in the secular sphere" (16), and yet the thrust of Joyce's critique seems to be rather of the practical than ideological nature: several of his early political papers imply that the reason he takes issue with the Nationalist party is due to its subservience "as during the Parnell crisis, [...] to the British government" and its being "still haunted by the 'shade of Parnell'" (22).

However, in "Literature and the National Consciousness," Manganiello further elaborates and expands Joyce's main political project—a critique of the "tyrannies that kept the heart prisoner"—to also include the Church "which through its ministers imposed a rigid sexual morality" (37), or indeed the narrowly negative, oppositional notions of freedom as proponed by nationalists and socialists. In Manganiello's view, Joyce's deployment of literature as "an instrument for altering men's minds" (39)

[2] Dominic Manganiello, *Joyce's Politics* (London: Routledge & Kegan Paul, 1980).

with which to "challenge the social and political order of his country" verged on "revolutionary." Manganiello insists that

> Joyce did have a perspective, despite his "silence" or veiled intentions. His response to these radical ideas, and the way that they influenced his views of later events in Irish history, are the politics I propose to examine here. (42)

Manganiello's biographical account follows Joyce around the politically dynamic and radical times of his Europe, pointing however to how Irish-based his political views remained: "in whatever part of Europe he resided, Joyce, like Dante, carried with him a consciousness of the political situation of his city and of his country" (43). In Trieste, resolving to consider contemporary Italian political thought, Joyce became particularly interested in the work of historian Guglielmo Ferrero:

> Joyce takes up Ferrero's point that the debasement of love is an index to the national temperament, and relates it to the socio-political situation of Ireland. Joyce indicates that the absence of gallantry in relations between male and female results in the exploitation of women. And this degradation of women in turn signals the degradation of Ireland. (51)

In Rome, where his political views were famously characterized by a chance acquaintance as "un po' di tutto," "a bit of everything," Joyce became influenced by the Marxist political philosophy of Antonio Labriola. At this point however Manganiello turns to Joyce's works themselves and teases out their implications for the political views of their author.

Echoing Whitman's invocation that poets should be the voices of liberty, Manganiello first discusses Joyce's early liking for Bakunian anarchism, as present in *A Portrait*. What fascinated Joyce about Bakunin was what repelled him, at least anecdotally, from Marx: "whereas Marx dictated an impersonal class warfare, [Bakunin] sought to liberate the individual from those forces that smothered human potentialities." The artist's word, according to anarchism,

> is not only tinged with Marxist ideology, but it is also delivered in the anarchist spirit by subordinating immediate political success to the fashioning of a "new man" in the womb of the old society. (71)

The political stance reflected in both *A Portrait* and *Stephen Hero*, then is Joyce's conviction that Ireland is unfree under the joint despotisms of Church and State, as well as the ineffectual enthusiasm of patriotism:

> In both these books Joyce implies that the artist's perspective will emancipate a future generation from these excesses, so that the children conceived by the daughters of the nation will no longer be imprisoned. (94)

Manganiello then turns back to "The National Scene" and discusses Joyce's engagement with, or rather dissociation from, the emergent nationalist and separatist movements in the early 20th century. Of Joyce's relation to *Sinn Fein*, Manganiello notes his support of its abstentionist policy, "paradoxical in view of Parnell's career as a parliamentarian," and Joyce's main objection to Griffith's Sinn Fein—its "avoidance of the social question" (126-7). Two more reservations about *Sinn Fein*, though perhaps not voiced, must have been felt: "Joyce could not have agreed with Griffith's strictures on literature," nor could he have endorsed "the racism he detected in *Sinn Fein*" (129). Apart from this, Joyce's interest in *Sinn Fein* and its leader was of a primarily supportive nature:

> Joyce insisted that his work was a patriotic undertaking. Many critics have argued that Joyce remained aloof from politics even while in exile. Joyce's work as an Italian journalist bears witness to the contrary. Not only did he keep abreast of the Irish political scene, but Joyce staunchly defended Griffith's line of argument on key issues. (139)

On a general level, "Joyce's views dovetailed with Tolstoy's at many points. Tolstoy's political writings, along with those of Tucker, were the ones Joyce admired most" (155), especially because of their shared belief that "patriotism is an 'unnatural, irrational, and harmful feeling' and the cause for a great part of the world's ills" (157). As should be clear by now, of the non-violent and terrorist aspects of anarchism, the former was the most congenial to Joyce, war being utterly devoid of its perverse Futurist appeal in his view:

> For Joyce, [...] war never benefited mankind. He never considered brute force to be profoundly human. As an artist, he repelled the theory of physical force in life and in literature by adopting a "suave philosophy" which permitted him to use only the non-violent weapons of silence, exile, and cunning. (160)

What was of much appeal to him, on the other hand, was the project of the Irish nation's reawakening, in whose service he delivered much of his public performance, and which surfaces quite powerfully in *Ulysses*:

> The desire to bring Ireland to a new self-awareness is matched by the equally urgent need of preventing its acceptance of any rigid control by Church and State. (166)

Still, the fact that "Molly makes two references to Griffith" does not obliterate in Manganiello's argument the reservations harboured by Joyce as regards *Sinn Fein*, as well as some of Griffith's views (170). Thus, of an Irish Free State which still "paid homage to what he considered spiritual tyranny," Joyce remained skeptical, while nevertheless remaining "loyal to the conscience of his race which he had just forged and which alone safeguarded individual sovereignty over mind and body form the stranglehold of external authority" (174). Not even after 1922 did Joyce's political views alter too much, as his repetitive association in the *Wake* of de Valera with Shaun might imply:

> Although Joyce told Stanislaus that he was not interested in politics but only in style, it becomes clear that the two are interrelated. Joyce would not replace English with Irish but would at once extend his language beyond national boundaries. Yet he wished his work to be looked upon as deeply Irish. [...] Writing, therefore, becomes the most important activity in the *Wake*. (179)

Just how important the *Wake* became is illustrated by a letter Joyce wrote to his friend Curran "saying that he would not consider returning to Ireland before he had completed his book" (186). From this and other remarks, Manganiello contends that for Joyce, to be Irish "did not mean bloodthirsty involvement in the movement for independence or the narrow nationalism" represented in the *Wake* by the "dogmestic" Shaun. Instead, Joyce preferred to be outward-looking:

> As a young man he had aimed to Europeanise Ireland. In this sense, it can be said that in the end Joyce hibernicised Europe too, since he had accomplished as much as Irish politicians in drawing the attention of people from all countries towards Ireland. (189)

The last part of Manganiello's argument is focused on Joyce's "literary politics." Joyce's early aliveness "to how his predecessors had treated politics in art" is meticulously documented by an extended discussion of William Blake's revolutionary artistic project, the late 19th century anarchist art (Gabrielle D'Annunzio, Ibsenism, Wagnerism), Joyce's rivalry with George Moore (as staged in the Library scene), his complicated relationship with W. B. Yeats, and the informing influence of Oscar Wilde, particularly his *The Soul of Man under Socialism* (190). In conclusion, and most importantly, Manganiello turns to the political implications of Joyce's own artistic project. Noting how early "Marxist critics have misconstrued Joyce's position as merely factitious unconventionality," Manganiello stresses the unrecognized political potential of Joyce's message that "*any* external system burdens the human spirit simply because it is a yoke and therefore tyranny" (225; 6). Moreover, Joyce's avowedly apolitical personal stance is all the more valuable and admirable in the context of his era, in which "European intellectuals generally expressed dissatisfaction with parliamentary democracy, claiming that it meant in effect rule by vested interests or rule through corruption," and many of them "turned to Fascism, or the rule of the Few, as a viable alternative to representative government" (228). Unlike them, Joyce, shaped by the above-mentioned influence, could not have but rejected these extreme right-wing alignments:

> Joyce inherited from Dante the sense of moral and political intrepidity of the artist who, in rejecting all party affiliation, constitutes a party by him-

self. From Blake Joyce learned to combat tyranny through the imagination, and to assert the liberty of mind and body. In Ibsen Joyce found not only the independence of the modern artist who stands alone politically, but one who reinforced his own socialistic views as well.

Instead of the two crucial ideologies of his later life, fascism and communism, what Joyce proposed to achieve in his art "was a political vision which consisted of a socialism without Marx, and an anarchism without violence" (232). What saved Joyce from the Icarus fall of his artists like Pound was the fact that "he distinguished, as Pound did not, between the aesthetic and the political" (233). Manganiello concludes:

> That his motives were indirect reflected his desire not to coerce other individuals into accepting his point of view and not to interfere with their liberty. The Dedalean policy of silence, exile and cunning had stood him in good stead. (234)

III

It has been observed before[3] that Cheryl Herr's *Joyce's Anatomy of Culture*, frequently seen as pioneering in its interest in Joyce's treatment of popular culture from the viewpoint of the cultural analysis of the Frankfurt School or Foucauldian conceptualization of discursivity, is in fact better viewed as part of a broader surge of interest within the mid-1980s Joyce studies in the political commitment of Joyce's writing. This observation can be corroborated here by yet again going back to the Frankfurt symposium proceedings[4] (here, also complemented by a paper from the following symposium in Copenhagen), and their section of "Joyce and Marxism," which was unsurprisingly chaired by Herr herself.

In her "Prefatory Note" on "Joyce and Marxism," Herr points to the fact that the effort of the two Frankfurt Marxist panels was "to benefit from the analytic tools that Marxism provides for those interested in issues of identity, class, and culture as they occur in Joyce's works." Although Herr concedes that "there is not as yet even a consensus on what the principal issues are when we bring together Marxism and Joyce," there were some points of contact among the diversity of papers presented in Frankfurt. For instance, commonly found in Joyce's works were "varieties of resistance [...] to the supposed paralysis of Irish culture," and also Joyce's "struggle against ideological containment even in [his] reproduction of the voices and texts through which his society carried out its ideological practices" (309).

In the first paper, "Dominant Ideologies: The Production of Stephen Dedalus," Trevor L. Williams aims to treat *A Portrait* as, "above all, a history," of *the* artist forsooth, yet an artist who, "like every other human being, is being 'produced' by a specific social context," in which Stephen

---

[3] In Chapter IV "Joyce & Cultural Studies," section II.
[4] Bernard Benstock, ed., *James Joyce: The Augmented Ninth* (New York: Syracuse University Press, 1988).

"never ceases to be socially constructed" (312). Williams goes on to identify the "main forces underlying the production of Stephen's consciousness" in "the state (its colonialist form), the Roman Catholic church, and Stephen's family," and notices that this production comes about through "a reciprocal process whereby the human subject re-produces those forces, is a willing accomplice in the work of self-subordination" (313). Williams then focuses on how "*A Portrait* demonstrates the construction and internalization of ideology" (315)—here, the concluding image of chapter one, the brimming bowl, the ironic overtone of which is an allusion to the game of cricket, rings with "a neat irony," as this reference "recalls the presence of the British in Ireland" (316). A far more obvious example however of how the public discourse of religion is internalized by the private consciousness would be the hell-fire sermon in the third chapter where "language seems to dominate to the exclusion of all else, even, at moments of pressure, to seem to be *writing itself*" (317). What then are the consequences of this colonization?—"Not only [...] is consciousness thoroughly penetrated, but the consciousness of Joyce's bourgeois Dubliner dialectically produces a physical, intellectual, and moral world *in cooperation with* the two dominant forces" (319). However, subtle examples such as the one of Stephen "wondering at the multitude of corks" (*P* 66) suggest that "this is also the Stephen who has begun, obscurely, to resist the ideology that would suppress his individuality" (320). This is a resistance, Williams concludes, which will take an outspoken shape in the "Nestor" chapter of *Ulysses*.

W.J. McCormack's "James Joyce, Cliché, and the Irish Language" takes an explicitly linguistic stance on the issue of Joyce's political commitment, departing from Philippe Sollers' famous 1975 declaration about the non-existence of the English language ever since the *Wake* was written. Sollers' contention is taken as a springboard for a discussion of the general issue of an "exhaustion" of language, exemplified by the Eumaean cliché: "Who or what exhausted the language? What reward or result did the exhausters get for their efforts? What has been exhausted from the language? In what service did it become exhausted?" (325) McCormack goes on to trace the etymological derivation of the word "cliché" from French, derived from the verb *clicher* meaning "to click," which ties it with the technology by whose means it came into being: "The history of *cliché* is therefore clear; it emerges within the increasing sophistication and industrialization of printing during the romantic period" (326). Hence, "cliché" comes to be associated with what Marx's *Capital* speaks of as "the processes of reification and animation," processes "which are everywhere evident in the styles of Charles Dickens and Alfred Tennyson" (326-7). This machinic dimension of the cliché is due to how machine printing "already held within it the possibility of self-generating, desocialized, and unexperienced language," an example of which is Bloom's observing the typesetter in "Aeolus" (327). The very strategy of naming this process is not without its implications:

The English language masks this process by employing a foreign term to negotiate the transfer between technology and humanity. The hidden dimensions of cliché organize the repression of the process by naming it exotically, and thus frustrating its exposure at home. (328)

Turning to the other half of the paper, McCormack notes that "a central stylistic element in the Irish language is known as *na cura cainte*, literally translatable as "'the runs (or throws) of speech.' One should emphasize the definite article [...] which indicates their normative status within the language" (328). This phenomenon of formulaic elements in Irish is not devoid of political implications either, as it points to "the language's survival orally during the prolonged period of suppression which Gaelic culture endured" (329). Thus, whereas the ideology behind *cliché* is one of concealment and exoticisation, obscuring the underlying complicity of technology with an exhaustion of language, *na cura cainte* manifests its own fossilization and normativity, pointing to how the language's present has been crucially formed by its past. Turning to Joyce, McCormack traces the instances (always highly disruptive) of the "dead" Irish language surfacing in Joyce's texts (most prominently in "Eveline" and "The Dead"), noting that what comes together in them is "sexual crisis, death, and 'language difficulty'" (333). This leads to McCormack's final and crucial question, "What modes of production are we dealing with in Joyce?" Far from able to answer it in full, he claims that by reading Joyce,

> the reader is obliged to see the affability of word and object as phony and violent, is obliged to engage in elaborate exercises in translation to liberate from the domination of mass-produced language what Dante described as both an action and a passion.

McCormack's specific approach has, to say the least, revealed that Joyce "stands alert to recollections of another language's death-cries," which at once "informs his sense of Edwardian Dublin as a colonial simulacrum and destabilizes the concept of a base-language within which he could not have redeemed the commonplace from the cliché" (335).

Finally, Mary C. King's paper, entitled "*Ulysses*: The Dissolution of Identity and the Appropriation of the Human World," focuses on Leopold Bloom as "a man with a vacancy in his life, the gap left by the death of his son Rudy" (337). Thus, "if Bloom is an adman and consumer-at-large in the city of Dublin, he is also an alien in his own city, and not merely because he is a Jew. His alienation is unequivocally objective [...], but it is also deeply subjective"—Bloom "repeatedly seeks reassurance that his being has not dissolved, that it has not melted away into the flow of objects and events in a city at whose heart is a gusty bag of wordy winds" (338). This preoccupation with objects bespeaks, for King, "a deeply historical affinity of imagination between Marx and Joyce, to which this shared momentum and related metaphoric intensity bear witness" (341).

King then asks: "what has the alienated demotic world of nighttown and *Capital*'s parallel underworld of vampires to do with the dissolution of the person and the social appropriation of the human world?" The answer is obvious: "the fetishism of commodities," to which Bloom has recourse "in his hard labor of a strenuous sympathetic effort to appropriate, as a sensuous, language-using subject, the world in which he searches for identity" (342). King concludes:

> As a man of his, and our, time, a time when the disciples of Milton Friedman still hold sway over almost half of the world's population, Bloom can encounter *only* in the form of commodification the objective sensuous expression of his own subjectivity. [...] His struggle involves a renunciation of the ultimate in fetishistic possessiveness, his claims over Molly, his wife, as private property. But in this most profound and most humane act of renunciation lies the inspiration for Molly's "Yes." (345)

Patrick McGee's "Joyce's Pedagogy: *Ulysses* and *Finnegans Wake* as Theory," included in a collection of essays from the next Joyce symposium in Copenhagen,[5] deserves an extended analysis at this point, not only because of its retrospective assessment of the two major poststructuralist interventions into Joyce studies (i.e., the Derridean and Lacanian), but also due to its focus on a topic with particularly interest, if not for the politics, then definitely for the practice of literature — Joyce's pedagogy. It shall also provide a suitable introductory piece for the ensuing discussion of McGee's central book-length contribution to the field.

In this paper, McGee departs from Wyndham Lewis's observation about "the schoolmaster in Joyce" to discuss "the pedagogical effect of Joyce's work," the way "it sets out to inform and reshape the reading subject." The scenes of teaching in *A Portrait* and early *Ulysses* depict "the teacher, like the father" as "doomed to failure, especially for Stephen" (206). Thus, for all its complex ironies,

> *A Portrait of the Artist* is *only* a novel; [...] it remains faithful to the convention of the novel and refuses to problematize the relation between the writer and the reader. It does not require the extensive restructuring of the reader through self-analysis and the overcoming in the reader of resistance to the act of reading. (207)

The "Nestor" episode in *Ulysses*, however, engages in a more ambiguous rendering of the teaching practice. Derrida's contention from "Living On" that "education in its traditional forms 'has as its ideal ... the effacement of language'" is seen as challenged in Stephen's teaching, drawing attention as it does to "a use of language that resists effacement" (207-8). In this view,

[5] Patrick McGee, "Joyce's Pedagogy: *Ulysses* and *Finnegans Wake* as Theory," *Coping with Joyce: Essays from the Copenhagen Symposium*, eds. Moris Beja and Shari Benstock (Columbus: Ohio State University Press, 1986).

[t]he troubled gaze of Stephen's students after hearing the joke is a symptom of their traditional education, of their lack of knowledge about language as language, about its rhetorical dimension Knowledge of such a dimension entails the ability not only to tell jokes but to make the figures of speech that are crucial to the construction of both literary texts and persuasive arguments. (208)

What Stephen's unorthodox teaching methods demonstrate to his students is that "understanding involves more than effacing words in order to grasp their referent," for it also involves "seeing or hearing words as iterative, self-reflexive." What Cyril Sargent learns from Stephen is not to solve the problem in his own fashion, for he merely repeats Stephen's performance. What he does learn, however, is "not to fear the problem — not to fear a certain language," since "Stephen's refusal to finalize knowledge on the blackboard forces Cyril to teach himself" by way of a repetition of repetition, for "contrary to what Cyril thinks, Stephen is not the one who knows but the one who repeats the steps of a formula that were already a repetition in the first place" (209). "Scylla and Charybdis," then, dramatizes another aspect of Joyce's pedagogy — contrary to what Eglinton asserts, Stephen's Shakespeare theory was not intended to compel belief, but rather to show a problem:

Stephen does not teach his audience the truth about Shakespeare; he shows them the shape of the desire for truth, a French triangle. [...] This geometry of desire destabilizes the relation between self and other by insisting on the structural possibility of a third position (which may or may not take the form of a third party), the position of the other as subject or the subject as other. (210)

This third position is postulated by Lacan as the desire of the capital Other, a desire inherent in the use of language. Stephen's pedagogy, then, occupies this position in that it "destabilizes the position of authority from which he only pretends to speak; it foregrounds the rhetorical dimension to such an extent that it forecloses the possibility of any stable referent as the object of his thought" (210).

The structure of the French triangle, McGee goes on to observe, is inherent to the whole of *Ulysses*, in that it "triangulates the desire of writer and reader by foregrounding language itself, by perpetually undoing the grammar of narrative and the logic of content through rhetorical displacement." Derrida's remark that "Joyce laid stakes on the modern university, but he challenges it to reconstitute itself after him," in "*Ulysses* Gramophone" is recalled, which McGee's pedagogical perspective translates as "the book must be taught in order to be read; reading must become self-teaching." Of relevance here is also Paul de Man's concept of "resistance to theory," which is due to "a resistance of the use of language about language" (211), also reformulated, importantly for McGee's purposes, as "a resistance to the rhetorical or tropological dimension of language, a dimension which is perhaps more explicitly in the foreground in literature

[...] than in other verbal manifestations." In this respect, Joyce's work "operates like a theory, that is, as language about language forcing us to recognize reference as one function of the rhetorical." In other words, "the pedagogical effect of Joyce's writing constitutes it as a theoretical discourse." This resistance, launched in some parts of *Ulysses*, is brought to its climax in *Finnegans Wake* which

> tends to resists any institutional framework—no matter how radical—founded on the principle of reason. I say that it resists, not opposes. Joyce's last work is not a celebration of the irrational [...]; it offers no alternative, no counterculture, no counter university. I don't believe that it is unreadable or unteachable, though its resistance to teaching and reading exceeds that of any other book in our culture. (212)

It is ultimately this resistance to reading that presents the lesson of *Wake* pedagogy, teaching "how to recognize, manage, and write about this resistance." McGee also thinks of the *Wake* as an extension of the French triangle: if in *Ulysses*, Stephen explores it from within the house of reason—the library, the boundaries of which are more or less respected—then in the *Wake*, "the library is engulfed by the triangle, an opening to the abyss that the principle of reason desperately tries to fill" (213). What the "Night Lessons" chapter teaches Shem/Dolph and Shaun/Kev is that language's dimensions can be defined in the pun "dimention" (*FW* 299.6):

> For in the "dimentioning" of language, in doubling it so that we read it grammatically and logically [...] even as we undo its "grammatical cognition" through a rhetorical reading of its figurative play—in this double speech or double writing, we discover the dimensions of language, its materiality or spacing. (214)

This in turn is related to the Lacanian psychoanalysis term "la bêtise," according to which "le signifiant est bête," the signifier is stupid, beastly, animalistic. Beyond its meanings inscribed in the imaginary register, "language is *en corps* [...], 'in or of the body,' and Lacan considers this relation to be 'the foundation of the symbolic dimension that alone permits us to isolate analytic discourse as such.'" The parallel with "dimentioning" becomes striking in Lacan's pun on "dit-mension," signifying "the priority of the signifier over the signified in speech." Both Joyce and Lacan therefore "use the pun to collapse the distinction between 'use' and 'mention' into a single rhetorical act" (215). What then is the most hidden truth that any teaching worthy of the name, including the Joycean and Lacanian pedagogy, discloses?

> After Lacan's seminar on "The Purloined Letter," we should be able to guess that the most hidden truth of psychoanalysis is out in the open where everyone is free to misconstrue it. It is language itself, or rather the rhetorical dimension of language, the field of operation of what Lacan calls the Unconscious. Lacan, like Joyce, theorizes by giving play to the Unconscious in the disfigurations or dislocations of style. (216)

"The seim anew" as the often-mentioned structuring principle of the *Wake* as a repetition-with-a-difference, could be taken as an impasse; perhaps, McGee argues, even the poststructuralist impasse:

> As many have stressed, Joyce's work anticipates poststructuralism, antici-
> pates the impasse of repetition that poststructuralism identifies as its first
> principle. But I think there is a way of reading Joyce that goes beyond the
> impasse, beyond poststructuralism—though I don't mean to say that post-
> structuralism itself is without knowledge of this "beyond." (217)

The "pedagogy" of the *Wake*, therefore, is the pedagogy of enactment, and thus essentially rhetorical, offering itself "as a form of resistance to the university's totalizing functions, to the encyclopedic unity of its knowledge, to the social and intellectual hierarchies into which it is organized," and positing "self-teaching" in the above radical sense as "the only teaching worthy of the name." This pedagogy as *theory*, McGee concludes,

> points beyond its own institutional framework, even beyond poststructural-
> ism as the still-emerging critical institution of our time. We should not be
> afraid to go beyond poststructuralism or to fail in teaching it. As Joyce
> urges, we should not be afraid to teach ourselves or, like Issy in *Finnegans
> Wake*, be ashamed to be "selfthought" (*FW* 147.9). (218)

IV

Referred by many as a crucial work in the field, Patrick McGee's work *Paperspace: Style and Ideology in Joyce "Ulysses"* [6] presents itself as a reading which conducts "a dialogue with the positions of Lacanian psychoanalysis, deconstruction, feminism, and contemporary Marxism." However, it does not function as "a strict application of the methods currently in use," but rather "finds that in reading *Ulysses* from the position of a postmodern historical subject, such discourses are the most pressing, the most unavoidable" (1). Exactly how McGee negotiates these various positions will be the focus of my presentation here.

McGee's "Introduction" also describes its own approach as "a historical reading," however, one that is understood as involving "more than uncovering the relation of a text to its context, [for] it also acquires taking into account what could be described as the transferrential effect—the way in which the reader positions a text in relation to his or her *own* historical context" (2). Joyce is further seen as occupying "a special place in the history of postmodern thought," often functioning "as a bridge between the modern and the postmodern"—Eco's "open work," the discovery of Lefebvre's "everyday life," Sollers' contention that the political effect of Joyce's writing "situates him as the most anti-fascist force in literature between the two world wars," Lacan's cryptic remark that

[6] Patrick McGee, *Paperspace: Style as Ideology in Joyce's 'Ulysses'* (Lincoln and London: University of Nebraska Press, 1988).

"Joyce the symptom illustrates the psychoanalysis that Joyce the subject refuses," Derrida's comment that "the Joycean literary machine already comprehends in advance everything we say about it," Jameson's implication that "Joycean parody approaches postmodern pastiche"—all these point to the fact that "at every phase in the development of recent literary theory, Joyce appears as an example and an authentic symptom of his and our historical moment" (2).

Coterminous with this proliferation of critical voices is "a focus on the indeterminacy of meaning." Here McGee launches a critique of *Post-structuralist Joyce*,[7] and the editors' contention regarding "'a proliferation of meaning' inherent in the critical text itself that is only contiguously related to the work on which it comments," which "stylizes the act of interpretation so that it becomes self-conscious and parodistic" (4). McGee points to the absence of any mention of the fact that "the use of this concept can be traced back to the influence of Wolfgang Iser, whose criticism locates the indeterminacy of meaning in a determinate relation between the reader and the text" (4-5). This omission he attributes to the difference between Attridge and Ferrer's approach and Iser's project, which upon closer scrutiny reveals the text, "despite its gaps," as "a stable entity" to which "the reader has a relatively privileged relation." *Post-structuralist Joyce*, however, in McGee's opinion, engages in a "radical "defamiliarization" of the text. This critique forms a preamble to McGee's formulation of his profoundly anti-poststructuralist stance:

> Terms like "unreadability," "infinite productivity," "perpetual flight of the Subject," and "deconstruction of representation" or their analogs have lost a lot of their radical aura. Calling a book unreadable […] is a reading of it; and I would go a step further to argue that it is the most hegemonic reading practicable on a text [in that] [t]he reading that excludes all readings withdraws from the political and social space in which textual productivity is realized in practice. It retreats into the idealism or fetishism of the text. (6)

A postulation of his own reading position follows shortly thereafter:

> Works like *Ulysses* and *Finnegans Wake* are interminably readable because no historical code of signification can ever fully exhaust their semantic possibilities.

The aim then of McGee's approach is to "try to go a step beyond most approaches made to [*Ulysses*] during the last ten years: beyond the indeterminacy of meaning to the indeterminacy of value itself." (7) This, hardly surprisingly, is related to Lacanian psychoanalysis which has enabled this kind of reading

> by positing the instability of the subject situated in the realm of language where it circulates in search of a meaning that can only be arbitrarily fixed.

7   See Chapter I "Deconstruction," section III.

[…] [T]he subject is not a being but a signifier whose only life is the effect of displacement along the metonymic chain of signifiers that compose the symbolic order. [...] reading inscribes, then, not simply the meaning of the text, though that is its imaginary effect, but *the relation between the reading subject and the text subjected by its critical history*. (8)

This relation in turn, "presupposes gaps in the reader that are symptoms of gaps and silences in the symbolic order itself." The theory of reading derived from this model ultimately aims at "demonstrating the political effects of such semantic instability." Colin MacCabe's work[8] is credited with being the first "to elaborate a theory of reading based on the Lacanian model and to give extended treatment of the 'political effect' of Joyce's writing," but also is criticised on account of MacCabe's "contemporary critical bias against interpretation." This seems absurd given that "the positions [of MacCabe's argument] from which meaning becomes possible" can be arrived at "only through interpretation." McGee's shift from MacCabe's ground then lies in his intention "to show that interpreting Joyce is not *politically* negligible" (8). Instead, a politically motivated interpretation assumes that "criticism cannot afford to remain innocent of interpretation as a ground of contention between the radically different political perspectives." With reference to Althusser's famous definition of ideology as "the imaginary relation of [...] individuals to the real relations in which they live," McGee observers that it is "in giving definition to these imaginary relations" that "art inevitably induces the experience of the real as 'something missing' in art, the meaning that escapes every interpretation." Here, Lacan's conceptualization of Joyce's writing as a symptom of Joyce's refusal of psychoanalysis is recalled and elaborated on:

Lacan says that if Joyce's work illustrates psychoanalysis as a symbolic progress, it also refuses it as an ideology, just as it refuses the ideologies of the church, the nation-state, art, and so on, from which it nevertheless draws all of its symbolic material.

Joyce's symptom, or rather Joyce the symptom, would then stand for the "contradiction between the structure of art and the desire of the artist, between the constituted subject and the subject-in-process, between the law binding the subject and the law's other, the process of symbolic exchange" (9-10). Finally, McGee concludes his introduction by evoking Derrida's deconstructive critical practices which suggests that "it means something else to deconstruct a work of art, for art does not claim truth value or mastery of concepts but a more elusive aesthetic value." This in turn calls for the necessity in deconstructing a literary work, of deconstructing "the system of values, the literary standards and conventions that make up the ideology of literature" (10).

---

[8] See Chapter I "Deconstruction," section I.

Given the subject topic and overall structure of McGee's book—the *ideology of style* followed in a chapter-by-chapter fashion through *Ulysses* and concluded by a summative theoretical epilogue (the very core of the book's argument)—one chapter has been chosen as representative of McGee's approach to the novel as a whole, followed with an extended discussion of the epilogue. Appropriately, my illustration is McGee's chapter on the "Oxen of the Sun," which foregrounds the "ideology of style" in ways more conspicuous than perhaps any other. "The Ends of Style: 'Oxen of the Sun'" focuses on the implications of Joyce's own avowed "idea behind the chapter—crimes committed against fecundity." However, unlike traditional criticism, McGee reads this contention, not as a point about art's transcendence of nature or art being "like" nature in any simplistic organic way; rather,

> it seems more likely that Joyce articulates a fictive point of view than cites a moral law or takes a position from which he can determine the relation between art and nature in terms of absolute criteria as to what is good or bad, fecund or impotent, in writing.

In this perspective, the history depicted within the chapter's genealogy of styles is one which

> identifies the fecundity of writing with its sterility and wastefulness; it is the history of transgression and transgressed boundaries in which the crime described by Homer [...] is repeated with a difference as a double murder: first, the murder of nature by art; second, the murder of the opposition between art and nature by writing (100).

In harmony with this technique to McGee's mind is Joyce's organ for this chapter—the womb, "the organ of gestation, whose surfaces self-infold and fold into the body of woman." This is McGee on the womb and its procreative function:

> The fold in woman's body that frames the production of sexual difference signifies itself in the exclusion of what remains at (as) the end of its labor; the human body is the remainder of woman's body, itself the remainder of itself, the frame framing itself. Woman's body is the unfinalized frame of the body of man and woman, of the unfinalized human body (101).

As opposed to this, medical science founded on "the act, the privilege, of making the decision, of making the surgical cut that removes ambivalences from the relation between life and death." The "art of medicine," despite its relation to objective science, "is founded," McGee points out, "as a symbolic practice dominated by men, on a theology" (102). If the womb, as productive of sexual and semantic difference, and as structured as Derridean fold, can be considered a metaphor for the structure of language, then "it also precedes language as one of its conditions, as the ground of the perishable word. Between the human word and the eternal word lies the womb and closes the gap between structure and structure, stricture and stricture" (103). This has obvious bearing on paternity and filliality, for here, the excluded feminine "truth" undermines, because triangulates, the binary relation:

> Bloom may want to father Stephen, and Stephen may want an eternal father. But this paternity desired from different angles of the triangle is a fiction (just as Joyce's fathering of all the English styles is a fiction) disclosing a truth, the same truth underlying the Christian trinity. The truth is a woman who transgresses the law of the father in being more and less than Mother, in being one of the mothers. (106)

Bloom, whose paternity (of Milly and Rudy) has been questioned by the citizen and others, and whose response "has been the hesitation of the onanist" (107), stands the "caricature of everybody's daddy, Theodore Purefoy," who

> discloses the function of contraception as a figure in masculine discourse, an ironic symbol of male identity. I refer to the obscene talk of the medical students, who define themselves as free subjects in relation to one another on the basis of woman's difference and clearly delineated objectification. (112)

What, then, are the ideological implications of the chapter's style? McGee asks

> Is "Oxen of the Sun" Joyce's revenge? Is it his attempt to father English literature, to reverse the violence of colonialism, to expropriate the expropriator linguistically?

The answer for McGee is, "on the contrary," because to him, Joyce's writing suggests that "an author cannot dominate language, or its effects, through his will to power or the authority of a personal style." Thus, McGee opposes Kenner's view that "in *Ulysses,* all is words," as, with his underlying metaphor of the ideological site of *paperspace,* much more is at stake than words, words, words:

> In the stylistic fractures of the history of writing, the matter of language, its maternal space of differentiation and process (or the paperspace into which the mothers have been exiled), asserts itself not as a return to a natural origin but as a challenge to the historical foundations of patriarchy. (113)

Although every style in the episode is revealed as a mask, "the arch covering, the supreme fiction," for McGee, "is the chapter as a whole," presenting as it does "the Viconian vision of language as a temporal sequence of styles alternating between two poles, form without content (the ritual words and Latin-like English at the beginning) and content without form (the sexual explosion of dialects and slangs at the end)" (113-4).

Finally, McGee's "Epilogue: Style, Ideology, and Beyond" summarizes as the aim of his book to go "beyond the positive references of the words those gaps and absences that constitute *the eccentric text*," where *eccentric* has a twofold sense: first, "ex-centric" reading that purposefully misses the centre to follow the margins of the book, privileging the micro over the macro-text; secondly, "to refer to those aspects of a text that are [...] odd, whimsical, even frivolous" (182). It is only in reading the eccentric that "we are confronted with the paperspace, a space that expands and divides beyond the limits of the book, that includes the history of its criticism, its reception, its social context, and so on" (182-3). The particular eccentricity of McGee's reading lies in his focus on the relation between language and power in the narrative itself, which can be illustrated on the difference with which Stephen and Bloom approach language. Whereas in the opening scene of *Ulysses*, "the effect of the word cannot be separated from the power of the subject who speaks it," this desire for artistic power on Stephen's part "is in contrast with Bloom's more dispersed desire, reflected in his playful point of view and slightly perverse sexuality." Bloom thus

> finds his medium of expression in the postal system, in the play of letters, [...] as both an advertising canvasser and a linguistic fetishist, Bloom is enmeshed in the modern symbolic order and the configuration of power constraining it. He is the *Ulysses* of the postal era. (183)

The chapters which follow "Lestrygonians" are regarded as exploding the traditional novel *from the inside* "as Joyce's writing stylistically mirrors conflicts and contradictions within the narrative itself" (183-4). For instance, in "Scylla and Charybdis," Joyce is doubling himself in Stephen doubling himself in Shakespeare doubling himself in Hamlet the father doubling himself in Hamlet the son:

> Stephen stands in the space of [the name of the mother], which neither authorizes him as subject nor positions him as object, the space of neither subject nor object but the abject—the self thrown away. (184)

In each of the latter half episodes, "style manifests its ideology through the disclosure of some fundamental contradiction between form and content." Examples of this abound: "Wandering Rocks" displays a disjunction between style of representation and technique of arrangement, where the wandering rocks become "words themselves, detached from their referents through the arbitrary will of an author who subverts the intentional structure of his own work"; "The Sirens" produces "a musical style that seems to privilege signifier over signified, sound over sense"; "Cyclops" explores "the conflict between story and discourse, between narrative and the word of a speaking subject"; the styles of "Nausicaa" demonstrate "the inadequacy of form to content in the ideological representation of sexual difference"; while "Oxen of the Sun" studies "*literature against itself* in presenting the history of literary style as the history of its ideological fractures, eruptions and displacements" (185). "Circe" is regarded the premature climax of *Ulysses*, featuring "a fictive or imaginary space which functions in relation to the whole book as its unconscious, the condition of its writing, an image of the process erased by the fixed positions of narrative." Both Bloom's and Stephen's resolutions are "illusory and premature, based as they are on the repressed desire animating patriarchal ideology: man's desire to be other, to be what he imagines a woman to be" (186-7). The *Nostos* episodes, in turn, provide an anticlimax, a recollection as the book "drifts into the night of history." The book's ending, for McGee, depends on one's reading of "the last word" and one's answer to the question, "Whose desire is being expressed?" Of this, McGee has the following to say:

> Certainly, after feminism it is not in any simple sense woman's desire, but after poststructuralism it is not entirely certain that it is Joyce's desire either—at least, not that of Joyce the autonomous subject. [...] Molly forces us to go beyond the text proper of *Ulysses* to the marginal space that her word broaches, for "Penelope" is neither a conclusion nor a return but an opening [of] the void into which *Ulysses* falls, into which the reader falls: the void of temporality, of the backward glance with its endless retrospective rearranging. (187)

In sum, McGee's reading presents a *Ulysses* whose political force goes "beyond Joyce's conscious political understanding, an intentional structure independent of Joyce's conscious intention and indistinguishable from the effects of what Fredric Jameson calls the political unconscious." Joyce's work is seen as a response "to the failure of his father, the early death of his mother, and the general breakdown of the Irish family; to his ambivalent passion for the language and literature of his conqueror and his hatred of English imperialism in general; to his equally ambivalent refusal of the Catholic church, the Irish patriarchy, and the Irish nationalist movement" (189-90). As has become clear in McGee's discussion of "The Oxen," the instability of Joyce's position as "an Irish writer of English" resolves itself in his "strategy of an imaginary conquest of the English language and its literature in *Ulysses* and *Finnegans Wake*" (191).

Paternity and patriarchy become a synecdoche for "all hegemonic relationships, so that even the domination of capital, the real social relation underlying the Irish colonial experience, is only another instance of ruthless patriarchal law." Bloom's longing for maternity and his sexual ambivalence as the womanly man then

> registers utopian social desire that would break through hegemonic social codes and linguistic conventions to the constitution of a new collective— that is, androgynous—subject. It turns out that reinventing man means reinventing woman, reinventing man as woman, which Joyce does in writing the discourse of the abject: Molly's monologue. (192)

Molly's final word represents in this light, "the voice of marginality itself" which "destabilizes all the other styles of the book" in that it marks "the limit of the stylistic illusion, by dramatizing the unrepresentability of sexual difference." Finally, the styles of *Ulysses* encode the class conflict through their dialogical relation to one another, through their reconstitution of social hierarchy as a variable in the history of symbolic forms. Taken as "a timeless and self-contained unity of signifier and signified, each style is an ideology, a victory of the imaginary over the real" (192-3).

The dynamics of Jameson's conception of the text as a field of force which makes apprehensible signs from distinct disparate modes of production make up, for McGee, "what can be termed *the ideology of form*, that is, the determinate contradiction of the specific messages emitted by the varied sign systems which coexist in a given artistic process as well as in its general social formation" (193). An example of these dynamics would be Joyce's deployment of Homeric structuring, offered as "a formal pattern whose thematic import is the historical continuity of patriarchal law and its binding necessity for modern man." Yet at the same time this strategy (the much-criticized strategy of inwardness) "is almost immediately challenged" by the "mechanical influx of stylistic transformations that effectively dismantle the subject" (193-4). In Lacanian terms, *Ulysses* deconstructs and demystifies the symbolic order "in order to reveal a space beyond the horror and the nightmare—the space of the collective subject," which "exists not in some distant future but in the present, in the symbolic order not as a process but as a structure—the structure of a symbolic exchange between each of us, of our being in language as the collective ground of all subjectivity," and precisely "between the process and the structure" appears "a difference without division: the collective subject is also the abject" (196). The effect of Joyce's writing therefore is the following:

in translating the styles of Western literature into Joyce's personal abjection, it exposes the historical abject underlying the illusion of style. No longer the pure object of our literary discussion as pure subjects, writing becomes the abject ground, the political ground, from which we emerge as subjects.

It is as constitutive of this abject ground that we should, in McGee's opinion, understand Joyce's famous retort to Stanislaus, "don't talk to me about politics, I'm only interested in style." McGee concludes on noting how the political in Joyce is the repressed, re-identifying it as Joyce's symptom proper:

Every style, as the performative dimension of *Ulysses* proves again and again, occupies political space and contains political content, for the politics that Joyce seemingly disowns comes to signify through repression: it signifies as the disclosure of those stylistic illusions grounded in the fiction of the autonomous writing subject. That is Joyce's symptom, and that is what signifies for those readers who come to reinvest and reinform his work with their collective desire. (197)

V

Dating from the same year as McGee's study, one of the "new alliances" of Bonnie Kime Scott's edited collection[9] was Joseph Valente's paper, "The Politics of Joyce's Polyphony," the presentation of which here shall provide a suitable introduction to next section's preoccupation with Valente's crucial book-length contribution.

The *polyphony* of Valente's title is to be understood in its Bakthtinian sense, as a model for novelistic prose, which is regarded as Bakthin's "attempt to negotiate between the Scylla and Charybdis of modern critical thought: the ground of historical determinacy and the vortex of rhetorical dissemination," in that the polyphonic model is seen by Bakthin as "socially determined 'not from without but from within,' that is, as integrating anew the ideological contradictions and idiomatic diversity at work in its social context" (56). Furthermore, Bakthin's notion engages in a general dialogue of order and disorder within language, a dialectics of its "centrifugal forces," the natural, given conditions of human intercourse gravitating toward heterogeneity, contingency, and freedom, as opposed to its "centripetal forces," imposed amid this primordial cacophony and establishing absolute social hierarchy, conformity and control. Just like the Derridean *différance*, "these dueling forces simultaneously hold discourse together and pull it apart." Implicit in this dynamic, in Valente's view,

> is a socially wrought division of that last hope of self-identity, the conscious subject. Instead of the signifier splitting the psyche at the opening of desire, as in Lacan, its contending uses and possibilities stratify the mind at the moment of intention. (57)

There are, to conclude Valente's Bakhtinian overture, two especially fertile social conditions for the development of the polyphonic model, the capitalist social formation—which serves "to destabilize specific languages by bringing into free and equal contact social groups segregated in the more rigid class structure of the late feudalism"—and "verbal-ideological decentering," which occurs "when a national culture loses its sealed-off and self-sufficient character" (58-9).

Turning to examples of the dialogical technique in Joyce, his *Dubliners* deploys it most noticeably in the tension created by Joyce "within the narrative voice, between the narrative language *per se* [...], and what Bakhtin calls the 'character zones', places in which this background tone is modulated by the accents of the dramatic figures." Joyce's depiction of the "acquired speech" of the characters' voices as replete with echoes of

[9] Joseph Valente, "The Politics of Joyce's Polyphony," *New Alliances in Joyce Studies*, ed. Bonnie Kime Scott (London: Associated University Press, 1988).

the banal discourses constituting popular Irish culture marks, for Valente, that "Bakhtinian threshold between the individual and himself," presenting the mind of his *Dubliners* as "at once a colony and a combat zone" (61). However, in *Dubliners*, "multi-voicedness does not yet convey a true plurality of values," but rather operates "to exalt the artist-figure relative to the world he creates," which, at least from a political viewpoint, is a highly retrograde ethos (62). Thus, the real challenge is posed in *Ulysses* by its contestation of the "historically entrenched economies of power, eschewing as [Joyce] does violent means or authoritarian imposition" (63), since social revolution in *Ulysses*, to Valente's mind, is "ultimately removed to the plane of [...] *carnival*" in the "Cyclops" episode (64). The subversion in *Finnegans Wake* is one of "the Trinitarian basis of authority." First, of "the notion of a distinct or unique self-identity (the Name of the Father)," which is found "supplanted by the 'writer-complexus'" (*FW* 114.33); secondly, of "the object-form or reified image (the body of the Son)," which is "to be replaced by the 'in imageascene all'" (*FW* 331.30); and thirdly, of "the effectively calculable utterance (the Force of the Spirit)," by means of "the word whose *specific* contextual variability in practice answers to the task of regulation" (65).

Recalling Joyce's famous self-comment that with him, "the thought is always simple," Valente observes in conclusion that "what is difficult is the de-reifying language necessary to render [Joyce's] straightforward political truth metaphysically irresistible" (67). In the light of Valente's argument then Joyce's "declaration that he cared nothing about politics, only about style," appears brimming with "the sort of iridescent irony we are accustomed to finding in his fiction" (68).

VI

A different approach to the political potential of Joyce's writing, one informed by poststructuralist and psychoanalytic theory and centered around the issues of law and justice, has been undertaken in Valente's *James Joyce and the Problem of Justice: Negotiating Sexual and Colonial Difference*.[10] The extended first chapter, "Justice Unbound," contains the work's theoretical preliminaries as well as its broader overview, and will thus inform its presentation here.

Valente begins by referring to Derrida's remark from "The Law of Genre," according to which the "mark of belonging does not belong" to the corpus so demarcated. In Valente's view, the concept of justice "can be said to represent the mark of belonging or propriety of the law; to be just is the imperative whose perceived fulfillment translates tyrannical force into legitimate authority" (1). In other words,

> the law of genre presides over the institution of the law as such. The su-
> preme authority of the law can neither be simply *a part of* the ethico-

[10] Joseph Valente, *James Joyce and the Problem of Justice: Negotiating Sexual and Colonial Difference* (Cambridge: Cambridge University Press, 1995).

juridical edifice, in which case it could not found the law as a whole, nor simply *apart from* this edifice, in which case its pertinence to the law would always remain to be demonstrated, and so remain dependent on yet another authority. (3)

Theorizing this aporia further, Valente makes use of Jean-Francois Lyotard's concept of *differend*, classifiable as "an unstable state or instance of specifically moral or juridical discourse, wherein a claim, grievance, or point of view that needs to be registered cannot be registered, at least not effectively" (8). In this light, "the appositeness of Lyotard's use of the holocaust to illustrate the *differend* haunting Enlightenment discourse becomes evident" in showing that "what mainstream liberal jurisprudence has attempted, in theoretical terms, is something like an Original Solution" (10). Illuminating is Valente's application of the "Freudian construct of deferred action" to "the domain of liberal jurisprudence":

> Just as no meaningful order or consciousness can emerge except in a belated relation to some other-scene which it proceeds to occult and transfigure, so no other-scene or unconscious can properly be said to exist except in the pressures it exerts and the effects it registers upon that meaningful, occulting order, i.e. as its retrospective condition. (16)

Justice, in Valente's account, emerges as marked by its "counterfactual logic" — "the way its descriptive aspect, the respect for what is, and its prescriptive aspect, the projection of what should be, both inform and contaminate one another" (19). Valente's "Historical Developments" seeks to historicize and contextualize the preceding theoretical preamble by focusing on the particular colonial aspect of justice and law in the Ireland of Joyce's time, identifying it, on account of "the structural convergence of modern feminism and modern jurisprudence" (25), as a profoundly feminine, and, in our time, feminist issue, related as it also to "gender justice." Noting how "the imperialist enterprise of the West was [...] filtered through normative tropologies of gender disjunction, exclusion, and stratification" (28), Valente regards Joyce's Ireland as in the grip of "colonial hypermasculinity," in which

> [t]he hybrid construction of subject positions crossed and recrossed by significant social differences and the explicit political articulation of these differences enables an amphibious ethico-political stance toward the forms of authority and resistance alike, a posture especially attuned to the double inscription of justice. (30)

Joyce then experiences this double inscription first and foremost as "an insistent ambivalence concerning his own cultural identity and allegiance." His position was quite peculiar:

> He occupied a border zone between a minority, irredentist society he repeatedly avowed, and an imperialistic civilization, in whose language he conceived and framed such avowals, upon whose liberal ideology he para-

doxically based them, and from whose literature he drew many of the standards to which they refer. (35)

There is palpable textual evidence of this ambivalent in-betweenness in both *Stephen Hero* and *A Portrait*. When in *Stephen Hero*, Stephen concedes the obvious—that he is "an Irishman after all and not one of the red garrison" (*SH* 51)—Valente observes: "[he] is immediately converted into an injunction to support the language movement and a radically defined national autonomy" (36). Thus, if "much has been made of Stephen's rejection of Ireland and the Irish cause," Valente suggests it would be truer to speak of

> a mutual polarization, in which the nationalist refusal to tolerate analysis or ambivalence, let alone opposition, helps to push Stephen toward a stance of elitist apostasy. (37)

Although Joyce's creation of the Citizen in *Ulysses*, might reflect "his disgust with colonial hypermasculinity as regards the bigoted exclusivism and repressiveness of its ends and the violence of its means," Stephen's refusal to sign the peace constitution and calling Davin "my tame little goose" for doing so (*P* 202) still signals to Valente that "Joyce was not so dislocated from or ambiguously determined in his primary gender position as to escape anxiety over colonial feminization and the loss of male entitlement it implied" (43). Thus, all things considered, Valente can say that "from the beginning of his career, Joyce saw the artist as properly engaged, even in his most lyrical moments, with questions of social organization" (45). What his deployment of the idea of justice as an interpretive key affords is

> not just a relatively new angle on Joyce but a relatively new Joyce—not an undiscovered Joyce to be sure, but an *underdiscovered* Joyce, a corpus that has yet to receive the extensive scrutiny to which his more standard works have been subject. (48)

A further exposé of Valente's book deals with its last "Epilogue: Trial and Mock Trial in Joyce," which comes after Valente's discussions focused on *Dubliners* (Chapter II "Joyce's sexual *differend*: an example from *Dubliners*"), *Giacomo Joyce* (Chapter III "Dread desire: imperialist abjection in *Giacomo Joyce*"), *Exiles* (Chapter IV "Between/Beyond men: male feminism and homosociality in *Exiles*"), *Ulysses* (Chapter V "Joyce's siren song: 'Becoming-woman' in *Ulysses*"). It then surveys the whole of the Joycean corpus from the perspective of its depiction of trial, focusing on the following scenes: "the impromptu trial of Father Dolan in *A Portrait*, the double trial of Bloom in 'Circe,' the Festy King trial and the Anita-Honophurious trial in *Finnegans Wake*." Each and every one of these, Valente notes at the start, "represents a strongly parodistic moment in the text, and is represented as a site of comic excess and carnivalesque exaggeration" (245). Valente's survey reveals both the juridical and the comical to "partake of a structural symmetry," which is due, as shown by Valente's preliminary chapter, to the "evacuation of the ultimate site of social and political authority" (a consequence of the democratic revolution), which results in the law being "deprived of any ultimate or ultimately secure grounds of legitimacy" (247). In this light,

> Joyce's representation of a trial like Bloom's, which is to say his parody of a trial like Wilde's, would seem to suggest that liberal jurisprudence rests not on a fixed set of oppressive values but on the repressive dissimulation of the relativity of all values. Such an ideological formation, being inherently defensive, is tremendously vulnerable to comic parody at one level. (249)

This "one level" reservation has to do with a different temporality of the juridical and the comical. As long as "the law splits against itself in order to facilitate and authorize decision, even as this split inflicts each decision with a liablility to interpretive self-revision," the comic parody, on the other hand, "splits against itself in order to impede decision, to trigger the possibility of oscillating self-revision at the *moment* of decision" (250). Looking at the Festy King or "Maama" trial scene in the *Wake* (*FW* 85-6, which explicitly refers to the Maamtrasna trial of Myles Joyce),[11] Valente notes the oedipal confusion of the principals, due to the bizarre nature of name confusion also at work:

> Not only were the defendants, Myles and others, predominantly Joyces, but the murder victims were Joyces and certain of the Irish informers to the British constabulary were also Joyces. Whether conceived in terms of ethnic, sept, or national allegiances, to be a Joyce *qua* Joyce in this case is to be divided against oneself and complicit with one's most intimate adversaries. (254)

In Valente's conclusion, this issue of complicity is also applied to the parodic genre, since parody is "at once a counter-song and a beside-song" (255). Analogously, Joyce remains "at once a counter-Joyce and a beside-Joyce" to the "bitterly opposed Joyces of Maamtrasna." What Joyce's Wakean parody works toward revealing, for Valente is that Myles Joyce, "in appealing for justice in a foreign language, the language of otherness,"

> not only symbolized the Irish nation at the bar, he exemplified the appeal for justice as such, insofar as this appeal can only be answered by that *in* language which is most foreign *to* language, by the otherness of language to itself. [...] [T]he appeal to justice can never really be answered at all, which is why it must be repeated endlessly and in endlessly variable forms. (256)

[11] See Fairhall's discussion in Chapter VII "Historicism," section I.

VII

A study whose title is perhaps the most explicitly tied to political re-readings of Joyce's ocuvrc, and which presents both a retrospective overview of the past and prospective outlook on the possible future of Joyce's politically committed criticism, is Trevor L. Williams' *Reading Joyce Politically*. [12]

Williams' *Preface* commences by pointing out the special importance of two words for his argument: "political," and "ideology." It still seems to him necessary, due to what he perceives as a general hostility to the subject, "to reassert the Marxist claim that 'social being determines consciousness, that all our acts, including that of literary criticism, have an ultimately political origin.'" The "political stance" of his reading, then, comes to denote "a stance that seeks wherever possible to analyze the power relations that exist within a text, whether at the level of content, the most obvious place to look, or as expressed through technique" (xi). The other word, *ideology*, of course has a very long complicated genealogy, and in recent times has stood at "the core of the debate centered on the question of 'false consciousness,' the negative connotation which Marx seemed to assign to ideology throughout most of his writing." For Louis Althusser, whose position in the debate was crucial, "ideology served to secure the adhesion of the individual to a system opposed to his or her fundamental interests and thus to preserve the power of the dominant class in society" (xii). *Hegemony*, a third frequent notion of his analysis, has the double meaning of a "fact of domination," but also in Gramsci's sense of persuasion of the whole society that the ruling class's "system of values, its ways of perception, its apportionments of energies, its approaches to the future, constitute reality" (xiii). In Joyce studies, Williams contends, "the hegemonic view" is one of "an apolitical Joyce"—here, Williams recognizes Manganiello as his only counter-hegemonic precursor.

Williams' scrutiny as presented in the book is therefore political in the following ways: in raising the questions of "power relations and the role of intellectuals within the state apparatus of education" and in attempting "to interweave them with some broad themes in Joyce's work" (Chapter I); by examining and aligning itself with "the important, though few, critical responses to Joyce from the left" (Chapter II); in identifying the "problem" of *Dubliners* with the dominated consciousness of citizenry suffering under repression (Chapter III); by analysing Joyce's *Portrait*'s "production of one consciousness (Stephen Dedalus')," and asking "how, if ideology is so pervasive and so effective, it is possible for any individual to stand outside it"[13] (Chapter IV); in attempting "to place Joyce in a wider colonialist dimension than the Irish by examining just one book in his Trieste library and relating its contents" to Joyce's work (Chapter V); and finally, by revealing "how resistance is built dialectically into the system

---

[12] Trevor L. Williams, *Reading Joyce Politically* (Miami: University Press of Florida, 1997).
[13] For this chapter, presented as a paper in Frankfurt, see above, section III.

by revealing "how resistance is built dialectically into the system of repression and how the very technique of [*Ulysses*] constantly works to unveil or demystify ideological thinking" (xiv-xv).

The second chapter, "Joyce from the Left: A Brief History" presents the focus of the present exposition, not only because of its metacritical value as a useful overview of leftist approaches to Joyce, but also because it stakes out Williams' own argument developed throughout the rest of the book. The two focal points of his overview are the First Congress of Soviet Writers of 1934, with the famous condemnation of Joyce as "a decadent" by Karl Radek, and the Paris Joyce Symposium of 1975, with the famous eulogy of Joyce as an arch-priest of the perverse textual *jouissance*. The early reception of Joyce from the left, in Williams' account, was hardly a political one: "Whatever political value Joyce's earlier texts may have contained as insights into the sources of the paralysis then afflicting much of Europe, no contemporary critics appear to have read (or politicized) them in this way" (15). Ironically, the only positive response to Joyce from the Soviet Union, coming only a year before Radek's scathing critique, was that of Sergei Eisenstein. However, Radek's speech, entitled "James Joyce or Socialist Realism?", brought, apart from the famous "heap of dung" metaphor for *Ulysses*, very little relevance to the debate, and doubts linger whether Radek had even read the novel (17). However, for all its oversimplifications, Radek's address, and the 1930s criticism in general, did voice one important point in its "condemnation of Joyce for his world outlook," a discrimination deriving its particular urgency "from the rise of fascism in Germany" (25). Turning to the 1970s and to the new alliances taken up by Marxism, especially poststructuralism and psychoanalysis, Williams notes that it was appropriately in Paris, the city of the *Tel Quel* magazine, as well as the most progressive stream of neo-Marxism of the era, that "the various strands of the political Joyce were first drawn together" (28). Summarizing critically the keynote addresses by Ellmann and Lacan himself, as well as a crucial (and much-overlooked) intervention of Philippe Sollers, on the French side, and Seamus Deane's or James Atherton's contributions, on the English one, Williams presents the Paris symposium as a veritable "landmark in the history of Joyce criticism":

> Whatever the differences of approach to the political Joyce—between those who would explain in terms of the historical background the choices, artistic and personal, that Joyce made, and those who would see the Joycean text (in effect, the *Wake*) as continuously revolutionary in its effects—the complexity of "social relations" was never far from the surface of the discussions. (35)

Moving on to MacCabe's *Revolution*, Williams sees some of his arguments as occupying "a position diametrically opposed in the last resort to the customary Marxist approach to a literary text." Furthermore, to hope that the answer to "the first question a Marxist is likely to ask" as regards

Dubliners (and which MacCabe never raises), "how precisely did these *Dubliners* come to *be* so paralyzed?", would be "produced by the reader's own activity" is to, in Williams' view, "risk an entirely arbitrary response and a backsliding into the kind of mystification in Joyce studies which MacCabe deplores" (36). Thus, the veritable "turning point in Marxist criticism of Joyce" came only in the mid-1970s with Franco Moretti's "The Long Goodbye: *Ulysses* and the End of Liberal Capitalism" (42), which is looked at in great detail, and whose blatant dismissal of Bloom is read as implying that "what is important in Joyce is not what happens to Bloom (or any other character) but what happens to the reader" (47). Williams' overview ends in 1982, at the Leeds Joyce conference, entitled "James Joyce and Modern Literature," the high point of which was Fredric Jameson's contribution "*Ulysses* in History" with its focus on the processes of reification as characteristic of modernity, and the opposing processes of de-reification as symptomatic of the novel's refusal to "solidify into an achieved and codified symbolic order" (51). Jameson's "brilliant" demonstration of "what is involved in the politicization of the text" presents the final point of Williams' survey (52). Rather than rehearsing Williams' rehearsing of leftist Joycean criticism, the rest of the present discussion will be devoted to Williams' own conception of a political, Marxist reading.

Williams, finally, presents his own view of the response which a "political" reading should provoke, and charts out the project of his book. Political criticism, for Williams, should lead to one fundamental question: "How does all this relate to you and the way you live your life now in your particular society?," a method which "passes beyond the ethical moment (the recognition of an evil) to the political moment when one asks":

> Now, having seen how oppression comes about, how false consciousness is constructed, what then am I prepared to do to combat similar forms of oppression and false consciousness in my own society? (53)

For the Marxist reader more specifically, two questions are paramount: "what are the material conditions required for social and personal change to take place; and how would I, the individual confronting this text, react if placed in a similar [...] circumstances to Leopold Bloom and other *Dubliners* in my own (different) society?" (53). Clearly, only the first question can be addressed theoretically and yield empirically verifiable and applicable results. Posing this question about Joyce's *Dubliners, Portrait,* and *Ulysses*, Williams' book seeks to propose the following. The "general paralysis" of the Dublin of Joyce's stories is in fact far from general, but pertains only to the petit bourgeoisie, a class to which all the characters depicted belong. The reason for this foregrounding, is not that "there is no working class worthy of note," but that "they are part of the problem" in that "they are fearful and visionless." Given that "as a stabilizing force within the state the petit bourgeoisie is invaluable," the whole petit-bourgeois world of the stories will necessarily be stabilized into paralysis (54). Unlike the broadly conceived panoramic view (although restricted to one class) of *Dubliners*, *A Portrait* "begins to demonstrate what sort of society produced these people by examining in detail the production of one consciousness in Dublin" (54-5). Williams' analysis ultimately serves to follow "the process of mystification and demystification in the production of Stephen's social being."

The unique value of *Ulysses* from Williams' materialist perspective is "its enactment, through the indeterminacy of narrative time and space, of the constant dialectic between past, present, and future." In other words, *Ulysses* can (or, must) be seen "as an act of demystification," raising the questions of "how do we view the world?", "how do we deal with the problems raised throughout the text?" questions that require of the answerer to "[enter] into politics" (55).

VIII

A study of major import, revisiting some of the author's earlier claims in *Paperspace* from a variety of theoretical perspectives (most prominently, an explicitly Marxist one) that reflect the major advances in Joyce studies in the interval between the two works, is Patrick McGee's *Joyce Beyond Marx: History and Desire in Ulysses and Finnegans Wake*.[14]

McGee's introduction is useful precisely in its revisiting, not only *Paperspace*, but most of the trends and fashions that have come to shape the area of Joyce studies since the late 1980s. First, however, comes a presentation of the work itself, which approaches Joyce's work from the following four key positions: as "both a theoretical articulation and an example of the politics of textual production and transmission," in terms of its "critique of gender and sexuality as the object of social constructions that produce critical authority," from the perspective of "Joyce's materialist ethics and the critique of private property that derives from it," and, finally, focusing on "Joyce's deployment of literature as an instrument of social intervention aimed at transforming [...] the capitalist mode of production" (1-2). Thus, in place of the presentation of Joyce in terms of his "polyvocal or multivalent discourse" as delivered in *Paperspace*, the political meaning articulated by this "constellation" of the different approaches lies in the term "communism" taken up in the last chapter, referring "not to a state or a utopia but to a desire that runs through both the work of Joyce and my own attempt to render that work meaningful," ultimately coming to denote "the desire for something more than what can be named" (2).

Looking back on *Paperspace*, McGee singles out one discovery achieved in this book—that "Joyce was a colonial subject" This is understood in the two following ways:

[14] Patrick McGee, *Joyce Beyond Marx: History and Desire in 'Ulysses' and 'Finnegans Wake'* (Miami: University Press of Florida, 2001).

First, Joyce was a subject, that is, a construction that derives from history through the mediation of culture or the symbolic order; second, Joyce was a *colonial* subject because the Ireland that stamped his social formation was a de facto colony under the political rule and military occupation of the British empire. (3)

For McGee, the fact that Joyce "was a subject," meaning that he could not strictly be an autonomous self, was "just as important and required just as much explanation" as the fact that he was "a *colonial* subject." His account aimed to present history, not as "the exclusive form of chronological events," but rather viewed "human subjects and the discourses that articulate them, including history itself as a discourse," as "symptoms of historicity" (3). In this light, McGee criticizes Vincent Cheng's *Joyce, Race, and Empire*[15] and its claims to "firstness" by contending that although "Cheng's is among the first book-length studies of Joyce to incorporate much of the language and insight of the burgeoning field of postcolonial studies," Cheng's study also "represents a moment of institutional consolidation within Joyce studies"[16] in that it "articulates the moment in which Joyce's historical identity as a colonial subject has been normalized as a matter of common sense." Here is McGee on Cheng:

> Cheng's book makes an excellent introduction to Joyce, even at the undergraduate level [...] yet the finality of the claim to "firstness" [...] belies the actual process of critical production, which is never quite so simple. (4)

Instead, in *Paperspace*, McGee's reading of Joyce's text which aimed to address the larger context (including everything from Joyce's immediate experience of Ireland as a colonial subject to McGee's own contemporary experience of the critical context of his own writing) was informed by his belief that "it was historically rigorous to assume that the past never enters the present in an unmediated form" and "decidedly unhistorical to imagine that one could ever see the past in its own terms or that one could privilege the theories and critical assumptions of an earlier period over contemporary theories through an appeal to common sense" (5). Thus, *Paperspace* comes to be re-recognized as a proto-postcolonial work, which associated its interest in Joyce the colonial subject, not with postcolonial theory (which, in McGee's view, did not really exist in its radically theoretical form then), but with

> a Marxist commitment to the analysis of individual consciousness in relation to the determinations of social, political, and economic structures. In retrospect, I realize that I treated those structures as monolithic and uniform in their social effects.

---

[15] See Chapter V "Postcolonialism," section III.
[16] However, as I have tried to show in chapter V, this is done with full (and rather disturbed) awareness on Cheng's part, as is clear from section V of the same chapter.

The possibility of re-writing *Paperspace* in postcolonial terms without doing much harm to its theoretical integrity is demonstrated in how McGee's use of the Kristevan term "subject-in-process," would, were he to write this work "today after the interventions of Spivak and the rise of postcolonial studies," be most likely substituted by the term "subject-constituted-in-contradiction," a substitution spurred by the necessity to "analyze the internal structures of the text as a symptomatic articulation of the contradictory formation of the subject" (6).

McGee singles out four studies with which his book engages in dialogue: Duffy's *The Subaltern "Ulysses"*, Nolan's *James Joyce and Nationalism*, Norris' *Joyce's Web*, and Valente's (ed.) *Quare Joyce*.[17] Duffy is credited with carrying "to a new level the political reading of Joyce" begun by MacCabe, especially by means of his use of Marxist cultural theory (Fredric Jameson in particular). Norris' work is praised for "a series of utterly brilliant close readings that drive home the concrete social facts that animate Joyce's work," yet also criticized for its simple dismissal of poststructuralist approaches to Joyce to which, McGee observes, it is indebted "for having raised questions about the political effect of Joyce's writing in the first place." Valente's collection is hailed as "a fundamentally new critical development in Joyce studies that concretely reveals the material links between gender, sexuality, and political economy," and Nolan is gratefully acknowledged as a powerfully challenging voice of "all the simplistic portrait of Joyce as a pacifist internationalist with no commitment to the liberation of his homeland" (6-9).

The present book then composed of a series of essays with only the last one written exclusively for this publication aims at a general view of history as "a formal discourse" which "speaks from the viewpoint of the dominant forces in a society and consolidates that viewpoint through the official construction of a social reality which becomes a block to certain forms of human desire" (10-11). As a mythological metaphor for the two prevailing approaches to history, McGee speaks of "the Narcissus and Echo of history," where the former is "the ultimate objectivist [who] imagines that the images and values he projects onto the screen of history are the simple unmediated facts," as opposed to the latter, the *other* of history "that can subvert the dominant discourse through the subtle manipulation of its own words [...], the subaltern who cannot speak in her own words and still be heard by Narcissus" (11). Since the present exposition of McGee's book will primarily focus on its last, most explicitly "political," chapter, it is appropriate that his own mapping of the traversed field[18] be followed briefly before proceeding with detailed readings. After Chapter I, "Pedagogy and Theory,"[19] the following two chapters, "Is There a Class

[17] See Chapter V, "Postcolonialism," sections II and IV, Chapter VI, "Modernism & Postmodernism," section VI, and Chapter III, "Feminism, Sexuality & Gender Studies," section X, respectively.
[18] As presented on 11-12.
[19] Discussed in detail above, section III.

for This Text?" and "The Value of Error" discuss the ideological elements and conflicts entering into the process of editing the text of *Ulysses* and will be dealt with in the appropriate place.[20] The fourth and fifth chapters, "Reading Authority," and *"Ulysses* as 'Profane Illumination'" regard feminism and queer theory as Joyce's productions aiming to pin him down to historical meanings in the service of specific social narratives. Chapters VI "Errors and Expectations in *Finnegans Wake*" and VII "Nationalism and Decolonization" focus on Joyce's critique of private property and the ethical value of desire; while the concluding triad of chapters, "Cultural Revolution in 'Aeolus,'" *"Finnegans Wake* as Historical Document," and finally "'Politicoecomedy' and Communism" negotiate the value of Joyce's writing as social critique and engagement which purposes to critically name and analyze the historical players and institutions of his time, foregrounding the fictionality of history and its interpretive ground.

McGee concludes his stimulating introduction by further contextualizing and concretizing the relationship between Joyce and history:

> History is what I write about, because Joyce's words can only be history, but it is a history that constantly subverts itself through the manufacture of echoes. (12)

Derrida's crediting Joyce for everything we say about him, in this respect, is not due to his godlike or all-knowing capability

> but because he manufactured us—that is to say, because he created the ground of our cultural industry [...] by creating a text that produces an echoing effect, that demands or produces its own subversion by creating or seducing those echoes that are nothing but human desires seeking material form or expression. (12-13)

Complementary to this all-inclusive historicity is the refusal of Joyce's language "to be pinned down by the mirage of historical truth." Instead he makes "history into an open text, which only means that he writes history that will continue to have a history." This inversion of history onto history itself, in Joyce, happens materially in order to demonstrate that "each inversion is not just a reproduction of the same relation," that "history's echo always involves a subtle displacement of the voice it takes over, just as Joyce took over the English language, which history had already imposed on the people of Ireland" (13). As long as, according to McGee's argument, desire plays the role of history's echo, then

> as long as there is capitalism, there is a political economy of desire, a process for manufacturing echoes that breach the authority of the dominant system in its own language. This is what Joyce called "politicoecomedy"; it

[20] See Chapter X "Textual Criticism & Textual Genetics," section III.

>349‹

represents not the end of history as salvation but the ongoing reproduction of desire as the condition of hope. (14)

This "refusal of the final truth" is, to be sure, "not the refusal of all truth." Should the present work be the history of McGee's errors,

> it also maps out the desire for truth as its sublime object. The truth lies inside history's echo, the unexpected voice that gives to authority its true image. Desire is the truth about history. It is "the clash of our cries till we spring to be free" (*FW* 627.31-32). (14)

Here, besides the other already indicated locations in which McGee's essays are contextualized, and the already mentioned final essay which most trenchantly conceptualizes the possibilities of Marxist criticism within Joyce studies, the two feminist and queer theory essays will be briefly presented, on account of their close involvement with other critical texts, and the particularly politically-minded critique to which McGee's forays exposed them.

"Reading Authority" opens by showing how (the examples being Kristeva, Spivak, Butler, and de Lauretis) the revolutionary effect of Joyce's work is not immanent but institutional:

> It emerges from its dialectical relation to the discourses of feminism, Marxism, psychoanalysis, deconstruction, postcolonial studies, cultural studies, queer studies, and so forth. Joyce is the effect of historical processes, but those processes do not come to a halt with the completion of his work. His authority and value are reconstituted—and sometimes deconstituted—in different critical and historical arenas to produce uneven and heterogeneous effects. (70-1)

Surveying the work of Anglo-American feminism in particular (Gilbert & Gubar, Bonnie Kime Scott, and others), McGee's overview of feminism regards it as "the most effective oppositional criticism to emerge in the university during the last thirty years," one that has been "particularly sensitive to the traces of effaced and self-effacing subject-effects that are left in the *Wake* of the canonized masterpieces of Western literature." However, this praise is qualified by one serious reservation, according to which even its most radical forms "take [Joyce's] authority for granted and indeed take their construction of his authority through reading for granted" (81). As an antidote to this, McGee suggests that "we read authority as a text, not as a given or natural fact. Authority is a simulacrum and must be read in terms of the simulation models that construct it" (81-2).

"This Man Who is Not One" is McGee's response to *queer theory* in Joyce studies, which seeks "to determine the radical nature of Joyce's desire, a desire that continues to live after Joyce, that continues to demand theoretical reformulation as the expression of its aim rather than its object" (83). Here McGee discusses the frequent response to the "Nausicaa" chapter as having to do with Bloom's (and Joyce's) "male feminism." McGee voices his objection to these discussions on account of their lack of a proper contextualization of "imaginary identifications that dominate the political representations in *Ulysses*," for in Joyce "it is impossible to separate the question of gender politics from other sociopolitical questions, including that of imperialism" (88-9). The "queer theory" presented in Valente's collection, in turn, is criticized for presupposing and totally relying on "the very binary logic they claim to be challenging"—in *Quare Joyce*, according to McGee, "the binary relation heterosexual/homosexual is being criticized and naturalized in the same gesture" (93). Rather than being constituted by (the breaching of) binaries, McGee views sexuality in *Portrait* as one "in formation, which is being constituted through acts and feelings and through interactions with social categories and stereotypes" (98). Of the Wilde-Joyce relationship that informs the collection, McGee observes that any homosocial relation, in his view, "operates through the disavowal of homoerotic feeling and thus, ironically, of the fact that the sexual relation between men does not exist" What can therefore be seen *beyond* homosociality is nothing more than "the realization that there are erotic impulses behind every relation between men, between women, and between men and women" (107).

These meta-critical readings, intriguing and polemical in their own right, serve to pave the way to McGee's last chapter, which presents a final elaboration and summing-up of the Marxist arguments that are most diffuse and limited in scope in the earlier chapters, and consequently functions as "the logical end of a thought process that took place in historical time" (10). "Politicoecomedy and Communism" opens with the radical contention that the spectre of Marx can be seen as "haunting *Finnegans Wake*" and that, although not a Marxist, Joyce's work "contributes to Marx's value and to the Marxist theory of value." In the light of the anecdote recorded in Gorman's biography about Joyce dismissing *Das Kapital* after having read its first sentence (quoted by McGee: "The wealth of societies in which the capitalist mode of production prevails appears as an 'immense collection of commodities'; the individual commodity appears as its elementary form.") and finding it "absurd," both *Ulysses* and *Finnegans Wake* come to seem to "constitute a massive return of this repressed knowledge" (221). Thus, the society of the Dublin of *Ulysses* is regarded as "an immense collection of commodities," and Bloom's "monetary value" in 'Ithaca' is pointed out as telling, whereas the *Wake*'s opening "commodius vicus of recirculation" comes to represent the circulation of commodities (222). Bernard Benstock's *Joyce-Again's Wake* is considered "the single best book ever written on *Finnegans Wake*," and its emphasis on Bruno's coincidence of contraries, seen as a synthesis of Marxian dialectics, emphasize, in McGee's view, the shared commitment of Joyce and Marx to "changing the word" (227). An obvious link between the two would also be their shared interest in Giambattista Vico's theory of history,[21] especially its reference to "the mind of mankind, not God, as the supreme agent behind human history" (230), a shared interest that evidences the way in which

> [f]or Joyce and Marx, human history is driven by the material contradictions of the different social systems or modes of production. These contradictions give rise to antagonistic social desires that lead to direct confrontations between the classes. (232)

Vico's particular interest for Joyce, then, lies in his image of "permanent social change through the dialectical interaction of contraries that are ultimately manifestations of one social process" (234). McGee then goes on to broadly conceptualize the possible usefulness of Marxist theory for Joyce, consisting in its view of Joyce's work "as the refusal of work and the refusal of value" (243). What McGee refers to as Joyce's communism is his insistence "that the condition of art is human labor and production," which is illustrated by Shem's example of making "art out of the waste from his body," reflecting "the material condition of his physical existence" (248). For McGee, what the *Wake* poses as "the antithesis of exchange-value or value in general, which ultimately embraces use-value as its counterpart," is grace (250). McGee observes in conclusion that

> [l]ike it or not, Joyce calls on the Finnegans of Ireland and the world to *Wake* and rise; but his work evades the closure of a final utopian goal, and the stones that rise up eventually become the monuments that fall down. The hope nevertheless lies in the desire for change itself as the continual reproduction of desire. (281-2)

The often disappointed bridge "between the national and the international," ultimately, consists in "the dialectical image of social desire that cannot be reduced to a form of property." And, McGee insists, "it is this desire that *Finnegans Wake* manifests and that we must learn to call communism" (282).

---

[21] For more, see Chapter VII "Joyce & History," esp. section VI.

9. Technicity, Media & Hypertext

I

At once a pioneer and already a classical figure within the field, the late[1] Donald F. Theall played a crucial role in the Joyce criticism engaged with the technological aspect of Joyce's "revolution of the word," as criticism itself came to be increasingly technologized with the advent of the World Wide Web in the early-1990s. Here, my presentation focuses on Theall's two book-length contributions to the technology and media studies of Joyce, his *Beyond the Word: Reconstructing Sense in the Joyce Era of Technology, Culture and Communication*[2] and *James Joyce's Technopoetics*.[3]

The broad subject of Theall's examination in *Beyond the Word* is what he terms the "new poetic age," whose beginning is traced back to Mallarmé and the consummation of which was the publication of Joyce's *Wake*, "*the* major poetic achievement of the decades between the two wars" (xiii). Perhaps the most fitting definition of Theall's project comes at the very start, when he speaks of "inventive cultural productions," denoting "the means by which the limits of and the boundaries between semiological systems" come to be "transformed or surpassed." Humour, drama, film, comics, poetry, storytelling—all these form part of a process identified as "the groundwork of an ecology of communication," which Theall, following Gregory Bateson's "ecology of mind," calls "the ecology of sense," for

> it is through playing with signs and signifiers and their relation to people's perceptions of embodiment that the communicative repertoire is extended and deepened, permitting people to cope with changing reality and construct artificial realities. (xiv)

Thus, it is with "inventive cultural productions" in Joyce's era of rapid social and artistic technologization, and with the peculiarly modernist "ecology of sense," that Theall aims to engage. The premise of Theall's work, then, is that "the poet or artist in her or his practice can simultaneously be a theorist," by means of "the complex dialogue that occurs between poets, artists, other cultural producers, and technology that is simultaneously directed towards developing a critical, yet reconstructive, theory of techno-culture" (xiv). It is precisely with this dialogue that Theall's study sets out to engage, with its constant emphasis on Joyce's *Ulysses* and *Finnegans Wake*, which he views as

> key texts, if not *the* key texts, for understanding this complex interaction of the new modes of technological reproducibility with cultural production. (xv)

Theall's opening essay, "The Poetic Body in the New Culture of Time and Space: Communication, Art, and Technology in the Twentieth Century," identifies the "controversy over modernist indifference to communication," and communication in its broadest (most prominently technological) implications, as the crucial concern of Joyce's last text. The inherent link between (not only) modernist art and technology is brought home by Theall's understanding of the art work "in machinic terms as an assemblage" (4), a link so firm as to bring a further rapprochement among other terms:

> poetry and poetic will be used to speak about designed assemblages of expressive elements whatever the medium or genres within which they are constructed [; the term poetic] will entail the theoretical exploration of this act of assembling in and of itself. (8)

In the context of assemblage, the specificity of modern poetry lies in its poetic machines that "depend upon breaks, gaps, disjunctions which invite ambivalence and negativity" (8). More specifically still, the assemblage in *Ulysses* is one of "the symbiosis between the person and the *city*." This urban space, for Joyce, itself operates as "a text, a communicating machine, just as all the meaningful action within its precincts is also textual" (10-11). *Finnegans Wake*, in turn, presents

> one of *the* key contemporary texts for a theoretical understanding of the struggle between the primacy of oral and written language and the hyperlinguistic semiotics of the new electronic media [...], also a self-reflexive book about the role of the book in the electro-machinic world of the new technology. (12)

HCE, "Here Comes Everybody," or however else one can refer to the *Wake*'s protagonist, is, for Theall, "a communicating machine [...], an electric transmission-receiver system, an ear, the human sensorium, a presence 'electrically filtered for all irish earths and ohmes.'" Joyce is argued to have anticipated the relationship between the technologically mediated production and distribution of communication with reference to his speaking, in the Bar-room scene in the *Wake*, of "'bitts' in relation to TV broadcasting in this pub scene where the customers watch a fight on TV (possibly the first fictional TV bar room scene in literary history)" (13).

Thus, both the *etym*, "Joyce's imaginary unit for the true source of a word in historic terms," and the *atom*, "the basic unit of matter until 1931, when the possibility of atom smashing arose" are seen as "based on a conception of assemblages of different bits" (14).

The next broader topic thematically dealt with in Joyce's fiction, "technologized" and recontextualized by Theall within the broad frame of modernity, is "gesture," the notion of the rhythm as the future universal language (known to Joyce from the work of Marcel Jousse):

> partly as a result of ethno-linguistic studies and partly as a factor of how consciousness was being changed by communication technology, twenti-eth-century artists developed a hyper-sensitivity to the importance of gesture. (16)

At this point, Theall investigates modern dance (Isadora Duncan), modern theatre (Brecht's epic theatre, Artaud's theatre of cruelty), film montage, or abstract collage art, as the art forms of Joyce's era that engaged, in the variety of their means of mediation, with the issue of communication-as-gesture. In this respect, the romantic doctrine of *synaesthesia* "assumed a new importance" in the interwar period, inherent to the heritage of the integration of the arts which gained new momentum in the technologized modernism. Joyce's achievement, especially in the *Wake*, is regarded as

> the culmination of a period; though, as most such culminations, it is prospective as well as retrospective, since it transcends most of the work of the period. [...] Joyce's practice encompasses a theory of communicative action [...] directed to a festive, dialogic, encyclopaedic, and bodily-oriented conception of the process of communication which moves beyond the conception of differentiated media of communication. (20)

Theall's second essay, "The Micro as the Medium and the Message: Synaesthesia, the Harmonization of the Senses, and the Mechanics of Art" conceives of the development of modernist aesthetics in terms of the "prehistory of cyber-space" (21). Marshall McLuhan is hailed, in this context, as the prime prophet of the VR (virtual reality) era, which "while encompassing the traditional audio-visual media, offers the potential for expanding these to include the tactile, the olfactory, and intrasensory and intersensory phenomena" (23). With the first new modes of technological (re-)producibility of the late 1830s (the telegraph, the Morse code, the daguerreotype), synaesthesia emerges as the increasingly dominant mode in artistic works which are syntheses, integrations, or orchestrations of the arts" (24), with its "overt theoretical recognition" in Baudelaire's 1857 *Fleurs du mal* (25). Together with this,

> there emerged a greatly heightened consciousness that communication is a continuum of which language is only one significant component [...for] when vowels could be imagined as generation colours and the idea of a

colour organ could become a product of the imagination, the fluidity of the interaction of sound, image, sign, and gesture had come to occupy an intrinsic place in artist practice. (26)

What in the light of the above occurs in the *Wake* is a creation of "a comic-satiric machine for exploring distorted communication." Joyce's play with the multiplicities of sense in language "deliberately exploits gaps to force the exploration of what creating paths across those gaps will reveal about our culture and its future" (27). Sense, in this respect, can be considered a fourth dimension in that it is not "the body or object; it is not the word; and it is not a sensitive or rational representation," but rather "it is the node where the sign and the material spasmodically and temporarily span a gap" (33). Joyce's wordplay on the very word *sense* opens up "rambling networks of connections (rhizomes, lianas)" which "generate simultaneous multiple meanings." This multiplexity for Theall typifies the operation of sense and how it establishes "an ecology of sense essential to the processes of communication" (34). Deleuze's concept of a condition of transversality is evoked, relating to "the discontinuity and fragmentation that confronts the artistic process in the contemporary world," and thus marking the technological assemblage that is the *Wake* (37). Synaesthesia, understood as "an archetype of the transformation achieved through the spontaneous perception of momentary connecting links between differences," also prefigures the inherent possibility within communication for the transformation from one code system to another:

> If synaesthesia is involved in playing with the transmutability of the effects of the senses resulting from the perceiving of transient resemblances that are actually momentary connections between differences, it is concerned with the surface of meaning, the play of the signifier, which is the domain of what we describe as sense. (37)

Just as synaesthesia, related as it is with sensory experience, is a matter of "surfaces which we encounter," so the spoken or written sense is a matter of "the encounter with the surface," and thus, for Theall marks the very "act of reading or listening," which involve "an unconscious acceptance of the metamorphoses on which synaesthesia takes place" (38).

Theall further examines this issue in "From Sense to Nonsense: Gesture, the Body, and Communication" by looking at the "dream communication" of Carroll's *Alice* books, which

> while staged in the world of dream and the imaginary, are directly involved with human communication, for dreaming is an action in which the mind-body that constitutes a person undertakes to produce a way of communicating its suppressed content to the ego of the mind-body which is the dreamer. (40)

Joyce's and Carroll's use of semiotic devices such as dream-language, nonsense, but also metaphor, is regarded as "foreshadowed in the work of earlier writers confronted with rapidly shifting social, cultural, and technical worlds," such as Rabelais, Swift, Sterne, William Shakespeare, and the *symbolists*. Theall's discussion of Rabelais is refreshingly non-Bakhtinian:

> Rabelais uses a wide variety of doublings and multiplicities to open up the petrified language of sixteenth-century scholasticism, in a manner suggestive of strategies Carroll and Joyce were to use. One such strategy has to do with playing with print itself. [...] One of Rabelais's most far-reaching strategies is the extensive exfoliation of the language of the body achieved by a contrapuntal action between the individual organs or parts of the body and the unified body as a surface unity — an imaginary body without organs. (49)

Joyce's writings, in this connection, embody "an advanced twentieth-century transformation of the comic grotesque that so fascinated Bakhtin," which in Joyce's case, is aimed at "regenerating the processes of communication" (50). However, a closer examination of the modernist period is necessary to substantiate this.

"The Joyce Era: Modernity and Poetics" provides just such an examination, opening with the summative contention that

> decades before the writings of Barthes, Deleuze, Derrida, Eco, or McLuhan, Joyce wrote books that were pivotal for examining relationships between the body and poetic communication and for exploring aspects of such items on the contemporary intellectual agenda as orality and literacy; the importance of transverse communication in contemporary discourse; the role of transgression in communication; the role of practical consciousness in everyday life; and the relationship between the events of everyday life and their embodiment and materialization in the sensory nature of the contemporary interior monologue. (56)

Joyce's critique and expansion of the Freudian-Jungian conception of the "unconscious" is detailed, demonstrating how Joyce considered Freud's version of it as having failed to deal with many significant roles of the unconscious in ordinary daily social life. Accordingly,

> In his construction of the interior monologues of Stephen, Molly, and Bloom, Joyce combines aspects of the repressed content of the Freudian unconscious [...] and of the idiom of primary processes involved in mammalian interaction, such as the varieties of signals associated with hunger in the "Lestrygonians" episode (peristaltic rhythm, gastro-intestinal rumblings, preoccupation with smells, obsession with food). (58-59)

The uniquely Joycean adaptation of stream of consciousness is characterized by three essential developments: first, a presentation and illustration in action of the role of "unspoken words, unacted thoughts"; second, a

materialization, despiritualisation, and embodiment of the interior monologue; and thirdly, a merging of the internal and external, "the dialogic and
the monologic, into a medley of intertwining and interactive voices" (59).
Ultimately, Theall observes, Joyce's satiric mode of his modern poetic
imagination "probes the complexity of communication through comic,
satiric, and parodic techniques that are nomadic and transgressive, strategies the nature of which pose major difficulties for a transparent communication" (64). The particularly technological nature of these techniques is
ambivalent, as they are perceived as both determining and to be determined by artistic creation. However, the ancient traditional prophetic
function of the poet is palpably present, in that

> the artists and writers working in the first half of the twentieth century
> forecast the advent of the communication era that began after the Second
> World War, [... foreseeing] the trend of increasingly mediated and multi-
> media communication and the ultimate merging of media through the de-
> velopment of computerization in the post-mass-mediated age of telematics.
> (70)

Thus, what in the modern era commences as "an exploration of technology and its implications for changing concepts of time, space, and communication" rapidly comes to pertain to "cultural, social, and political
questions which transform the very way people regard poetic activity in
the individual arts" (72).

Chapter V, "The Book, the Press, Eisenstein, and Joyce: Changing Relations in Culture, Technology, and Communication," uses the example of
the "Aeolus" episode of *Ulysses* to discuss the newspaper as "a cultural
phenomenon affecting all poetry and arts that shape language and communication." Theall sees its function in the era as being to accomplish the
kind of "rhetorical liberation which literary language and the visual arts
required at the turn of the century," examples of which are Brecht, Pi-
casso, and Welles (78). Theall goes on to comment extensively on the
exchange between Sergei Eisenstein and Joyce, the former's *Film Forum*
citing Joyce on a number of occasions, claiming for example that Joyce
had "reached a limit in reconstructing the reflection and refraction of reality in the consciousness and feelings of man." Eisenstein, in Theall's account, regards Joyce essentially as a failure (84-5). However, with reference to László Moholy-Nagy's *Vision in Motion*, where Joyce's project is
allotted a unique role in the process of "orchestration of the arts," Joyce's
work appears as publicly resonating, and at least to some extent positively, with the artistic concerns of its era (86). Theall goes on to draw "a
direct line from this type of artistic thinking [...] and the current intense
interest in the arts among scientific and technical communication re-
searchers" (89).

In "Beyond Media," Theall maps just this contemporary interest by
drawing on McLuhan's analysis of "the information environment" which
has "become so all-pervasive that it became invisible." This is an impor-

tant source, especially given that "the media's contribution to the creation of this all-pervasive milieu is largely unconscious," and therefore McLuhan's writings are instrumental in dramatizing "the importance of the effect of *any* medium on how and what people communicate" (91). In this chapter, Theall documents how "the evolution of communication has broken down the definition of media," with references to Baudrillard speaking of "a hyper-real world lost in an ecstasy of communication where simulacra are the reality," Eco, of "hyper-reality," Arthur Kroker, of "hyper-aesthetic," or Marc Angenot of "paraliterature" (103-4).

In "The Comic, Wit, and Laughter: Dramatic Engineering of Communication," Theall returns to the concept of "the poetic work" as "an assemblage of bits" in order to discuss the devices deployed in Joyce's comedy. Ranking prominently among these, of course, is the pun:

> the pun is a node of semantic energy where the material realization of the pun (e.g., in print) is an entity which radiates and disseminates signification. Therefore, it is a major example of the process of the "abnihilisation of the etym." (110)

Kenneth Burke's aesthetics are referred to here, his heuristic technique "joycing" as a tool for examining how Joyce, or literature in general, "tease communication theory out of social praxis through the use of the pun and other polysemic devices" (112). Here, the particularly "dramatic" engineering of communication of interest for Theall consists in its "juxtaposition of multiple actions," a juxtaposition underlying "the way we read a story, see a play, watch a film, or listen to a poem":

> The primary meaning of jest (or gest) is that of a legend or a tale, from which it derives its later meaning of a joke. It shares a common root with gesture, both being related to performance. [...] Polysemic devices, particularly pun and portmanteau, address the immediate material basis of communication, while drama addresses that ritual aspect of communication which is spoken about by using terms such as "participation" and "communion." (124-5)

This brings Theall further to conceptualize his "Dramatic Theory of Communication," where dramatic action involves experimentation with an exploration of precisely "human communication [which] involves non-verbal forms, such as gestures, visual and auditory elements, an kinaesthetic rhythm" (128). This is explored in the realm of cinema, both of Joyce's (Chaplin's *Modern Era*) and postmodern (Kubrick's *Clockwork Orange*) eras, both artistic and overtly ideological/propagandistic (Riefenstahl's *The Triumph of the Will*), which directs Theall's argument to address the notion of mimesis. Here, Joyce's specific understanding of the Aristotelian *e tekhnē mimeitai ten physin*, not as "art is an imitation of nature," but that "art imitates nature" in that "the artistic process is like the natural process," is redefined by Theall as "the artist assembles as the *bios* assembles" (133). Theall's "dramatic communication" involves the following "mimetic and imaginary aspects":

1. the representation of actors [...] and their motives;
2. the movement of thought both within the action and between the actors, as well as in the interaction between the drama itself and the audience;
3. the flow and ebb of speech and its rhetorical and poetic shaping;
4. the visual and gestural language of spectacle;
5. and sound, rhythm (including music) and kinaeshesia. (138)

From this point, Theall goes on to discuss a broad range of topics, some of which have to do with Joyce (most prominently, further explorations of "satire" as "secular communion," tactility in communication, or "memory" as the "crux of communication"), others with the broader (post)modern contexts such as cinema, information theory, computing, or electro-mechanization. However, the crucial concepts of *Beyond the Word* having been already mapped out, the present exposé will cease here, moving on to Theall's other book. The two are connected by their preoccupation with the issue of Aristotelian/Joycean mimesis. It is with precisely this topic that Theall's other book opens, which is more directly Joyce-oriented, and therefore calls for a more thorough discussion in view of the present purposes.

II

Theall's *James Joyce's Technopoetics*, a sequel to *Beyond the Word,* provides the understanding of Joyce's work which informs the exploration of "the common productive activity" of all cultural production undertaken in *Beyond the Word*, thus "serving as a complement, supplement, and foundation to it" (xxi).

The "Introduction" also posits the aim of Theall's second book independent of its precursor: to explore the "entire range of everyday culture, science, and technology in *Ulysses* and *Finnegans Wake* to establish how Joyce transformed poetics in the new techno-scientific era and the new age of communication" (xvi). As has been shown in *Beyond the Word*, mimesis is "developed by Joyce in relation to the performative and to a modernist, post-Aristotelian reading of the relation of mimesis as mimicking the operation of the natural world" (xvi). The important supplement presented here is the issue of "Joycean allegory," which will be revealed to be "a radical modernist transformation of the potential of baroque allegory through the multi-layered, polysemic transformation of language itself, which enabled Joyce to adapt and metamorphose Dante's levels of meaning" (xvii). The theoretical grounding, though in many aspects similar, is nevertheless marked by the heightened presence of Walter Benjamin and Georges Bataille, whose meditations on technology, the theory of allegory, a fascination with the Kaballah and the esoteric, and theorizing of the avant-garde (in the work of the former), along with the theory of excess and inebriation, of the nature of the sacred and of the depth of laughter (the latter) inform this work to an unparalleled degree (xviii). A renewed importance is accorded the work of Deleuze and Guattari, especially their assertion that

> the material or machinic aspect of an assemblage relates not to the production of goods but rather to a precise state of intermingling of bodies in a society, including all the attractions and repulsions, sympathies and antipathies, alterations, amalgamations, penetrations and expansions that affect bodies of all kinds in their relation to one another (*A Thousand Plateaus*, 90).

In this light, Joyce's *Ulysses* and the *Wake* are investigated as "'machinic assemblages' and in the case of the *Wake* as a more complex machinic assemblage that incorporates its own abstract machine: first, in incorporating its own meta-levels; and secondly, in being in one of its aspects a meta-commentary on *Ulysses*" (xix).

"James Joyce and the 'Modern': Machines, Media, and the Mimetic" opens the discussion by examining the modern trope of poet-as-engineer, whose prototype is to be found in Leonardo the polyhistor. Mapping the overall technological context of Joyce's era, Theall observes in the *Wake* the resulting "major emphasis on the mechanics of composition entailed in references to tailoring and weaving; building and constructing; and writing tools and their tool-like products, such as the early runic alphabet, hieroglyphics, or oghamic scripts." Theall regards these references as related to Joyce's conviction, as early as 1903, of the importance of "the Greeks having used the word *tekhnē*, for art, poetry, crafts, and the production of artifacts" (8). Joyce's association of art with *tekhnē* has to do with his concept of "the artist as a constructor," and his recognition of "the classical affinity of the arts and the proto-technology of the crafts," with which "he carries his conception of the artist as engineer forward into the post-Enlightenment eras of mechanization and electrification" (9).

In a sense, Theall's project aims to carry out Joyce's unrealized sequel to *Our Exagmination*, which he envisaged would be composed of four parts, three of which were to deal with "the treatment of night; mechanics and chemistry; and the humour of the *Wake*"—hence already *Beyond the Word*'s emphasis on technology in relation to the comical, satirical and dramatic (10). There are, to Theall's mind, three crucial aspects to Joyce's engineering. First, "he viewed his books as types of machines and approached their construction as an engineer"; secondly, *Ulysses* and the *Wake* "refer to many aspects of professional engineering"; finally and most importantly of all,

> Joyce realized that the arts and modes of communication of the period [of] 1915-1939 were extensively mixed up in new modes of social organization and of technological production, reproduction, and distribution that required a new exploration of the relation of all poetic communication to the "machinic." (11)

Joyce's art, with reference to *Stephen Hero* (*SH*, 186), is an "art of vivisection," a process clearly "experimental in nature and surgical in technical execution," which "permits the satiric poet to demystify religious illumination and to reveal the arts by which people are being ruled" (14). Throughout the *Wake*, the vivisective project of Joyce's art is his reconstruction of English "as a polylingual language that is simultaneously lavish, over-abundant, inclusive, and immoderate—a language of excess [...] and transgression, which, like Bataille's linguistic vision of excess, is constructed within a theory and practice of cultural production in a technological era." Both Benjamin and Bataille emerge as informing theoretical sources in the final contextualizing conclusion:

> Linking the concept of intoxication to that of a dream and profane illumination is an aspect of Joyce's project which is similar to Benjamin's account of the programmatic of surrealism. The deliberate blasphemy made possible through the blending of orgiastic levels, the symbolic eating of the corpse, communal inebriation, and the Eucharist opens up an exploration of eroticism, sacrifice, and the sacred similar to Bataille's account of eroticism as an individual/collective awareness of death and the basis for "an-other" type of ontology. (15)

Proceeding along similar lines is Theall's "Art as Vivisection: The Encyclopaedic Mechanics of Menippean Satire," which draws the link between the laughter and the machinic from Wyndham Lewis' argument that "laughter arises from seeing people as machines" (17), as well as from Joyce's preferment for the comico-satiric literary tradition, and goes on to demonstrate Joyce's "unique radical modernist revision of Menippean satire" (18). Here are its constitutive features:

> [Joyce's] carnivalesque, allegorical satire, a metamorphosis of Menippean satire, consciously utilizes the "machinic" nature of laughter to mould a satiric machine and to investigate what Joyce found to be the inadequacies of the episteme admired by [...] *l'art-pour-l'art* movements in comprehending the centrality [...] of the newly emerging techno-culture. (22)

Joyce's transformation is further recontextualized as part of the English classicist tradition of "Varronian" satires, featuring most prominently Dryden's "Absalom and Achitophel" and "Macflecknoe," as well as the work of Swift, Pope, and Sterne, all of whom are seen as further exploring "Cartesianism, Newtonianism, and other manifestations of the 'mechanical operation of the spirit,' such as the advent of printing as a mass medium" (23). Joyce's interest in the satirical literary tradition is related to his engagement with science and the techno-cultural via the following connection:

> Radical modernist Varronian satire provides a deliberately engineered or designed language that permits writing to occupy a new, unique role in probing and critiquing the social unconscious which is complementary and sup-

plementary to the new technological means of production, reproduction, and dissemination. (24)

Thus, for example, the "Lestrygonians" episode is seen as technologising the Menippean particularized body:

The particularities enumerated in each example underline the body's encounter with things and the impact of these things […] on body and image interpenetrating with technology. […] Bloom provides a natural, tactile basis for consummating a modernized metamorphosis of the Menippean vision. (28)

The satire moulded by Joyce on the Varronian-Menippean model is therefore of a "carnivalesque, allegoric" nature. In other words, Joyce utilizes the "'machinic' nature of laughter" in order to "investigate what he found to be the contradictions in the epistemic conflicts arising from the new techno-culture's impact on romanticisms such as the Celtic Twilight" (29).

This impact is further elaborated upon in "Electro-Mechanization, Communication, and the Poet as Engineer," where the textual criticism of *Ulysses* written by Michael Groden[4] — which maps the history of the composition of Joyce's novel — is seen as confirming "Joyce's techno-poetic theory, which regards the writer as co-producer with his consumers, acting as a literary, or perhaps more precisely, a poetic engineer," showing also "how Joyce progressively works towards developing a techno-poetics" (31-2). Theall revisits the Linati and Gilbert ground plans on the lookout for "the complex connections" Joyce worked out between "various electro-mechanical, scientific, and technological processes, the organs of the body, and the multiplicity of styles and symbols that coexist in his book" (33). Here, particular significance is attributed to the central episode's ("Wandering Rocks") art of *mechanics*, which is instrumental in the chapter's establishment of "the importance of the spatio-temporal shape of Dublin to the epic geography of *Ulysses*." Another chapter of special import is "Aeolus," the significance of which lies in its "first engaging the reader's ongoing attention with the electromechanical and technological complexity of *Ulysses* and its social grounding in Dublin" (34). The crucial question that Joyce's art is seen as addressing is *What is the role of the book in a culture which has discovered photography, phonography, radio, film, television, telegraph, cable, and telephone?* The answer, for Theall, is to be sought in the already examined problematics of gesture ("in the beginning there was the gest"):

Joyce intrinsically relates writing to a conception of gesture as the universal language, […] a language inscribed by and in the senses and sensitivity of all bodies, human, animal, or non-organic. (42)

4 See Chapter X "Textual Criticism & Textual Genetics," section I.

For Theall, such a gestural mnemomnic, in a Deleuzian reformulation,

> generates lines of striation and differentiation in space-time which through their effects machinically produce significance, so that the Joycean intellectual imagination is grounded in the memory, which is itself physically and dynamically grounded in the body and its electro-mechanics and electro-chemistry. (42-3)

Thus, to relate this to *Ulysses*, while the "Circe" episode, as the novel's climax, reminds the reader of "the mechanics of the Freudian dream work," the book's conclusion, counterpointing "the almost science-fiction-like mathematical catechism of 'Ithaca,'" as well as "the intense desiring machine produced by Molly's closing soliloquy," is for Theall "the only possible resolution" in that it "shows that only through the machinery of memory can communication as communion occur" (48).

In "Singing the Electro-Mechano-Chemical Body," Theall revisits the issue of the scientific comic akin to Lewis Caroll's exploration of nonsense, noting that

> Joyce's interest in the technical surface and the machinic provides him with a natural route to wit, humour, and the comic since encounters between the machine-like and organic life frequently dramatize discontinuities in the flow of life. (51)

Turning to the *Wake*, Theall observes how "key passages at the beginning, near the mid-point, and at the conclusion of the *Wake* all involve motifs of engineering or popular mass media technologies" (57), due to Joyce's awareness of the crucial influence exerted by technology on the very nature of communication. For a fuller appreciation of the *Wake*'s involvement with technology, it is necessary for Theall to turn to the close of *Finnegans Wake*, whose "description of the 'vicocyclometer' provides the most abstract and extensive passage about the body, the book, and mechanical, electro-chemical, and electro-mechanical processes" (61). This is examined in depth in "Books, Machines, and Processes of Production and Consumption," an extended demonstration of how Joyce's engineering, mathematical, and scientific interests make it possible for Theall to speak of *Finnegans Wake* as "a poetic machine" (72).

The following two chapters, "The Machinic Maze of Mimesis: The Labyrinthine Dance of Mind and Machine" and "Mimicry, Memory, Mummery, and the Multiplying of Media," explore how the relation of Joyce's work to global techno-culture reveals "the important interplay between memory, metamorphosis, mimesis, the mechanics of meaning, and their relation to alterity ('otherness')" (73). This interplay is underwritten by the *Wake*'s "dream web" which "generates complex comic and parodic intermixtures of technology, theology, mimesis, and bodily sensuousness and sensuality" (80). The Daedalian project of creating this labyrinthine structure had already been recognized by Marshall McLuhan in the 1950s as "a mimesis of the process of cognition, arguing that it was associated with symbolist theories of Poe and Mallarmé" (86). An extended analysis of the Mutt and Jute episode serves as an illustration of a broader point that "Joycean dream language is consciously mimicking audio, visual, and audiovisual media (phonograph, radio, film, photography, television)," this with the intention of reintroducing "the magic of mimesis and sensuosity into the oral and the printed word" (92). Joyce's play with "cultural objects as leitmotifs," omnipresent in the *Wake*, is already at work in *Ulysses*, as Theall's discussion of the famous Lenehan pun reveals: its fourfold iteration renders it "ultimately permeated with echoes of commerce and technology," a permeation that "reveals the mimetic relationship between the people, their traditions, their everyday world, and their techno-culture" (102).

Turning to the very title, *Finnegans Wake*, opens up a new pathway for Theall's argument, in particular its indication of Joyce's "probing the secularization of the sacred in a rationalized techno-cultural world":

> This is why he uses an Irish wake, a specific folk mortuary custom involving comedy, intoxication, and transgression, as a major component of the title of his book. [...] Moreover, since the new techno-culture is itself an extension of the person and a transformation of nature, it can also be the ground for new modes of ritual and sacrifice and for elaborating the play of eros. (103)

It is in this complex interplay that Theall's section entitled "Secularizing the Sacred: The Art of Profane Illumination" approaches issues already discussed with a new concern with "Joyce's view of the social function of the poetic in the new pre-millenial techno-culture, which provides him with a new, deliberately engineered or designed language" (116).

"Assembling and Tailoring a Modern Hermetic Techno-Cultural Allegory" returns to Benjamin's analysis of the *Trauerspiel* (in terms of Baroque allegorism), which provides "some important motifs and linkages in exploring Joyce's allegorical technique in treating the multiplicity of interlaced tales in the *Wake* and its strategies for adapting the allegorized Homer to a contemporary *Ulysses*" (117). This allegorical technique ultimately consists in the poet functioning as both "an interpreter and meta-commentator on—coder and decoder—the poetic origin of every night's dream vision" (129).

"The Rhythmatick of Our Eternal Geomater" then goes on to discuss this "night's dream vision" as crucially informed by mathematics (for example Henri Poincaré's concept of the evolution of numbers). In the *Wake*, Theall suggests, Joyce

> returns *mathemata* to its original sense of a learning, a learning about things we already know, but a learning that leads to the understanding of the abstract, so that the two parts of the liberal arts coalesce. (141)

"The New Techno-Culture of Space-Time" broadens the discussion of Joyce's interest in science with a sustained analysis of the ways the reconceptualization of time and space in modern physics could have impacted upon Joyce's artistic techno-cultural project. Indeed the result as with any possible "influence" on Joyce is one of radical recontextualisation and reformulation:

> For Joyce the complexity of times and spaces also includes "physical space," "visual space," "acoustic space," and "architectural space" [...]. This permits him to develop complex analyses of modes of communication, as in his recognizing a role for light both in his discussion of manuscript and of television [...] and to place these analyses in their social context, while at the same time linking them discontinuously with the past. (152-3)

"Cultural Production and the Dynamic Mechanics of Quante and the Chaosmos" takes these issues a step further, by linking Theall's early interest in the interrelation of production and consumption with the contemporary advances in "chaotic" modern physics, both of which are seen as hinging on the principle of complementarity:

> Producers are consumers because the prime manifestation of self-consciousness is communicability, intersubjective interaction. [...] While quantum theory is not properly speaking chaotic, nor was it recognized as such when first articulated, the implications of the uncertainty (or completementarity) principle coupled with the crisis in contemporary mathematics probably permitted Joyce [...] to intuit that the cosmos could be regarded as tending towards an orderly disorder. (154-5)

The conjectures about what Joyce might or might not have intuited are drawn from his observations recorded by Jacques Mercanton, which, apart from revealing "Joyce's interest in non-verbal communication," also emphasize "two important theoretical aspects of his work: the belief that every person is a poet and, secondly, his conception of poetry as the foundation for a 'new science'" (162). Finally, "The Relativities of Light, Colour and Sensory Perception" textualizes Theall's forays by looking at two specific *Wake* passages from its concluding chapter, the discussion of the window triptych, and the ensuing Patrick-Archdruid conversation, both of which stage the importance of "physics, mathematics, mechanics, and optics" for Joyce's composition.

Theall's "Conclusion" presents a well-executed theoretical synthesis of most of the wide-ranging interests of his whole approach, here carried a step further in associating it with "Joyce's pre-millenial vision of importance for cyberculture." Theall sets out by bewailing the general under-appreciation of Joyce's importance for McLuhan, or indeed "other major figures [...] who have written about aspects of communication involving technological mediation, speech, writing, and electronics." Of these,

McLuhan provides the most specific bridge linking the work of Joyce and his modernist contemporaries to the development of electric communication and to the prehistory of cyberspace and virtual reality. (185)

The critique of McLuhan undertaken from the position of the orality/literacy dichotomy (as proposed by Walter J. Ong, Harold Innis, or Eric A. Havelock) is charged by Theall with having

> failed to comprehend the fact that McLuhan was disseminating a Joycean view which grounded communication in tactility, gesture, and central-nervous-system processes, rather than promulgating the emergence of a new oral/aural age, a secondary orality. This emphasis on the tactile, the gestural, and the play of the central nervous system in communication is a key to Joyce's literary exploration. (187)

In this context, it must not be forgotten that Joyce's *Finnegans Wake* is "not only a polysemic, encyclopaedic book designed to be read with the simultaneous involvement of ear and eye: it is also a self-reflexive book about the role of the book in the electro-machinic world of the new technology" (187).

Echoing a point already made early in *Beyond the Word*, Theall again insists that "the hero(ine) in the *Wake* [...] is a communicating machine [...] an electric transmission-receiver system, an ear, the human sensorium, a presence 'eclectrically filtered for allirish earths and ohmes'" (*FW* 309.24-310.1). He goes on to bring together the many remarks consistently made about the importance of gesture:

> The originary nature of gesture [...] is linked with the mechanics of humour (i.e., jest) and to telling a tale (gest as a feat and a tale or romance). Since gestures, and ultimately all acts of communication, are generated from the body, the "gest" as "flesh-without-word" (*FW* 468.5-6) is "a flash" that becomes word and "communicake[s] with the original sinse" (*FW* 239.1-2). By treating the "gest" as a bit (a bite), orality and the written word as projections of gesture can be seen to spring from the body as a communicating machine. (188)

Not only that—the *Wake*, throughout Theall's argument, is regarded not only as a retrospective summa, but also a prospective anticipation. Hence, the language of the *Wake* is considered "a poetic anticipation of hypertextuality and hypermedia" in that its "mnemonics of paronomasia, portmanteau, and other verbal play establishes transverse nets of association above and beyond the ongoing flow of the printed and spoken text" (190). As Kenneth Burke realized as early as the 1930s,

> Joyce's grounding communication and language in gesture is distinctly different from an approach which privileges oral language, for it involves a complete embodying of communication. While the oral only embodies the speech organs, the entire central nervous system is necessarily involved in all communication, including speech. (191-2)

Thus, "the emerging technological capability to create the 'artificial reality' of cyberspace" is seen as having been prefigured by Joyce's deployment of dream and hallucination for the creation of "virtual worlds within natural language" (193). Most importantly, Theall concludes by enumerating six reasons why communication history and theory ought to take account of Joyce's poetic project:

1) Because he designed a new language [...] to carry out an in-depth interpretation of a complex socio-historical phenomenon, namely new modes of semiotic production [...];
2) Joyce's work is a critique of communication's historical role in the production of culture, and it constitutes one of the earliest recognitions of the importance of Vico to a contemporary history of communication and culture [...];
3) His work is itself the first "in-depth" contemporary exploration of the complexities of reading, writing, rewriting, speaking, aurality, and orality [...];
4) He sees the importance of the "poetic" as a concept in communication, for the poetic is the means of generating new communicative potentials between medium and message [...];
5) Joyce develops one of the most complex discussions of the contemporary transformation of our media of communication [...];
6) And finally, his own work is itself an exemplum of the socio-ecological role of the poetic in human communication. (194-5)

Theall's immense erudition and skill at combining textual analyses with broad wide-ranging contexts and theoretical frameworks bears witness to all this, and much more.

III

Eric McLuhan's study *The Role of Thunder in "Finnegans Wake"* [5] presents—in what can be seen as a direct (if also unwitting, because contemporaneous) application of Theall's broadly delineated framework onto an analysis of a particular textual passage—a detailed exposé of the set-up of the ten famous thunderwords. In the first part of his study (on which the present account prefers to focus), McLuhan offers a comprehensive overview of the Menippean, or Cynic, satire as a genre and poetics and then addresses the question whether *Finnegans Wake* classifies as one. He identifies the Menippean "jolt" with the effect of the *Wake* requiring of its reader active participation in its audio-realisation where "the reader-cum-performer is forced to shift (irrationally) from one posture of sensibility to another, without any one of them being allowed to dominate" (16). Another Menippean feature is the concept of the *Wake* as "a text writing itself," harking back to "the common Menippean pose that

[5] Eric McLuhan, *The Role of Thunder in "Finnegans Wake"* (Toronto Buffalo London: Toronto University Press, 1997).

the satire is writing itself, or that the pen is doing it, or the readers, etc."
(17). In a summarising fashion, McLuhan observes that

> In writing *Finnegans Wake* as he did, Joyce adopted a particular configura-
> tion of stylistic techniques and tactics quite different from those he used in
> his other, more "literary" Menippean satires, *Ulysses* and *Dubliners*. These
> tactics were not chosen in a haphazard quest for novelty but carefully pat-
> terned after the new sensibility his generation had learned from the new
> electric media. (19)

McLuhan then proposes to read the *Wake* as a complex grammar, a system of signification, showing how "Joyce's concern in the *Wake* with
media and technology and their reconfigurations of culture was integral
with his grammatical concern with language" and how he "went much
further than any previous Menippist or grammarian in exploiting language
as the storehouse or midden-heap of cultural experience," illustrating this
by a particular passage from the *Wake*, *FW* 183.10-184.10 (21-3). This
conception of language is regarded as part of the Viconian heritage, which
must be to McLuhan's mind reckoned in terms of the following matters:

> Both works are grammatical, both entirely concerned with language and the
> effects on it and the senses of human technologies and artefacts. But
> whereas Vico propounded theories and reported the results of his studies,
> Joyce forges the language directly to probe sensibility and awaken and re-
> tune the sense of his readers. Vico wrote a report, as it were; Joyce, a sat-
> ire that makes us do the exploring. (29-30)

It is ultimately Joyce's insistence on the material properties of language,
on words-as-things, that ties him with the Menippean tradition. And it is
also why McLuhan's study chooses to focus its exegetical attention on
the ten thunder words which "are conspicuously *things* in the text, more
than just words undergoing mutation by pun or portmanteau." Hence,
McLuhan's study attempts "a reading of *Finnegans Wake* as a Menippean
and grammatical satire, based on an examination of the verbal landscape
and in particular on the oddest features of that landscape, the ten thun-
derclaps," the underlying conviction being that the *Wake*'s language and
style "are particularly concentrated in the thunders, and hence it is with
an examination of the thunders that a reading of *Finnegans Wake* should
begin" (34).

IV
Simultaneous with Theall's broadly cultural framework for Joyce's interest
in, and "poeticization" of, the technological advances of his era was an
attempt at presenting Joyce as actively engaged with, and his work as

responding to, the coterminous revolution in the field of physics: Thomas Jackson Rice's *Joyce, Chaos and Complexity*.[6]

Rice departs from Joyce's claim recorded by Budgen, according to which "any difficulty in reading what I write [is due to] the material I use. In my case the thought is always simple." It is this "interplay of simplicity and complexity" that Rice's study aims to pursue "both locally and globally" (1), especially in connection with the discovery of modern physics of "order out of chaos," its "new recognition of embedded design or spontaneously occurring patterns of organization in systems previously considered to be random, lawless and incomprehensibly complicated." The connector here is Joyce's fiction which "well represents [the] symbiotic relationship of the 'two cultures,' the literary and the scientific" (2).

Thus, Rice directs his argument against C.P. Snow's conception of the two distinct cultures (in *The Two Cultures and the Scientific Revolution*), the artistic and the scientific, which Snow regards as "accelerating in opposite directions of specialization within their distinct cultures," claiming instead, with reference to Katherine Hayles (and her *Cosmic Web*), that the governing assumption of his book is that "the models of physics and mathematics, the theories of the philosophy of science and [literature], and the structure and strategies of literary texts" of an era constitute a broad "cultural field" (3-4). It is precisely the model of *the field* that remains central to Rice's study in its discussion "of the interactive relations among Joyce's fiction, his cultural context, his readers, and their context" (4). The Joyce of Rice's book, in his wide reading and lasting interest in physics comes to resemble, not the "Stephen who "ineluctably constructs meaning upon the incertitude of the void," (*U* 17.1013-15) but rather "his character Leopold Bloom as "a conscious reactor against the void of incertitude." (*U* 17.2210-11) Joyce is seen as having begun "his career as a realist," accepting the "'scientific' conception of naturalist fiction, 'the experimental novel' tradition of Zola," in which "writing becomes a mix of empirical observation and diagnosis of symptoms." Although Joyce does clearly move "away from the conventions of literary 'realism' as early as his second work of fiction," still for Joyce, "reality exists 'without you' (*U* 3.27)" (7). Following on from the implications of this, Rice's general thesis on Joyce's art emerges according to which it is the "nature of reality, but not the real itself," that "changes during the course of Joyce's career." Hence, the four chapters of Rice's book aim to show

> 1) that recent developments in mathematics and science had penetrated mass culture by the turn of the century; 2) that a reasonably intelligent and educated individual of the era was certainly [...] likely [...] to be scientifically "literate"; 3) that Joyce [...] exploited the current developments in mathematics and science for his fiction; [and finally that] the chaos and

[6] Thomas Jackson Rice, *Joyce, Chaos, and Complexity* (Urbana and Chicago: University of Illinois Press, 1997).

complexity theories [... provide] new vantages on the nature and significance of Joyce's achievement in his last two works. (10)

Analogously to "the transferrential effect," Patrick McGee's term[7] for the reciprocal relation underlying the process of reading, Rice argues for a "critical *relativity*," which postulates that

> the object scrutinized by the text, the "real," does not shift and change under the influence of the act of observation; the transformations take place in the community of observers, the field composed of the text, its author, and its audience. This is what the "naïve realist" Einstein was saying; this, too, is what the scientific "realist" James Joyce has to say. (11)

Rice's first chapter on "The Elements of Geometry in *Dubliners*" inevitably departs from the association of "the exotic word *paralysis*" with "the word *gnomon* in the Euclid and the word *simony* in the Catechism," which for Rice reflects "the equivalent status of Euclid's *Elements* and religious doctrine in both secular and Catholic education" (16). Rice's illustration of the prominent status that Euclid played in Joyce's Jesuit schooling points to how geometry in general, and the Euclidian in particular, "restored an earthly equivalent to the logical and coherent order of Christian doctrine" (18), and to how both St. Augustine and St. Thomas Aquinas," on which this doctrine relied, accept "the Euclidean assumptions that reality [...] exists and can be understood and described" (23). Illustrating Joyce's "art of arrangement," Rice presents a syllogistic logic of the development of the first tetralogy of stories:

> A. a boy learns that paralysis is the condition of the Dubliner ("The Sisters"); B. a boy learns to appreciate that he is a member of the community...which he had to this point "always despised a little" ("An Encounter"); C. a Dublin boy is paralyzed in and by his attempt to achieve integration with this community ("Araby"). The fourth story, "Eveline," embodies a straightforward syllogism: A. in Eveline's experience, relationships between; B. Frank offers Eveline a relationship; C. Eveline withdraws in terror from a potentially abusive relationship with Frank (who may not be altogether "frank"). (25)

The overall organization of *Dubliners* is indeed marked by "an essentially geometric" *construction* and "the specifically mathematical roots of Joyce's four-part arrangement of *Dubliners*," as Joyce's correspondence—a September 1905 letter from Trieste to Stanislaus—testifies to the organization of the original twelve stories in the following progression: childhood ("The Sisters," "An Encounter," "Araby"), adolescence ("The Boarding House," "After the Race" and "Eveline"), maturity ("The Clay," "Counterparts" and "A Painful Case") and public life ("Ivy Day," "A

---

[7] See Chapter VIII "Politics," section IV.

Mother," "Grace"), with the additions of "Two Gallants" and "A Little Cloud."

However, Rice opts for a different approach to Joyce's construction, one based on Euclidean geometry, and focusing on the joint composition of "Grace" and "The Sisters" (Sept. 1905—May 1906). Here Joyce's use of the term "quincunx" on the last page of "Grace" provides a "convincing association with the first paragraph of "The Sisters," the quincunx being ironically used as "the fulfillment of a gnomon and a sign for the completion of his collection" (32-4). The overall scheme for *Dubliners* seems to Rice to parallel Euclid's arrangement of his opening books of the *Elements*. Just as Euclid proceeds "from the line and angle to rectilinear figures, to circle and to problems of inscription," Joyce focuses "on individual figures of childhood, adolescence, and maturity, and then turns to relations *among figures* in Dublin's public life" (36-7). The concluding example of the many "failed acts of perception in [the] stories" (42), one of Gabriel's drowsy perception, in which the symbolic vision of "the vast hosts of the dead" is revealed as "the shadows of snowflakes, projected through the window against an interior wall by an external source of light" (49), shows that Joyce's

> exploitation of the Euclidean structural model for *Dubliners* as a whole prepared him to recognize and respond in his next major work [...] to the increasingly intense contemporary critiques of Cartesian and Euclidean subjectivity (51).

The second chapter, "The Ailments of Jumeantry in *A Portrait of the Artist as a Young Man*," connects Joyce's further education in science with the coincidence of his 1906 Rome sojourn overlapping with Roberto Bonola's publication of his classic critical and historical survey *La Geometria Non-Euclidea*. Joyce's acceptance of Bonola's radical revision of Euclid had been facilitated by his education, which had taught him to view Euclid as synonymous with his Catholic catechism and therefore ready to see as "an absurdity which is logical and coherent" (*P* 244) (59). An excursus into geometry, and Euclid himself, reveals the inherent flaw in his famous "fifth," his postulate of *parallelism*, which immediately reveals itself to be "curiously complicated and not as general as the previous postulates," which Rice explains is due to how "the fact that parallel lines never meet introduces the concept of infinity," which is an abstraction that Euclid "would have found to be a repugnant defect in a mathematical science grounded in experience" (60). Thus, Stephen's rejection of Catholicism as "ab-surd" requires a corresponding shift in critical perspective—Rice introduces "the Riemannian parallel" which allows him to view Joyce's irony "as providing a counterbalance to the inherent identification promoted by his narrative techniques" whereby he moves his readers away from "an initial identification with Stephen as an 'everyboy'" toward the final "equidistant relation between the character and the reader." What Joyce does by creating "parallels" that diverge, that curve away from an initial point of contact, "establishes a non-Euclidean geometry for the readers" (67). Just as Riemannian parallels, the narrative parallels of *Portrait* "invariably meet, diverging from one point of contact [the beginning of the novel Stephen = reader *"once upon a time"*] to reconverge at another point [reader = the artist in maturity = Joyce himself in the novel's final words, the tale of his telling: Dublin 1904/Trieste 1914]" (68). However, geometric aspects can be discerned in more specific places than global narrative schemes: Rice notes, for instance, the geometric aspect of Stephen's aesthetic theory (lyric (line) — epic (circle) — drama (3-D)), which he regards as due to scientific and mathematic emphases within Stephen's education (77). Also of interest is how Joyce's reconception of *Stephen Hero* as *Portrait*

> transcends the dualism of self and other by "conceptualizing each in terms of the other," simultaneously presenting the subjective subject objectively (irony and authorial detachment) and admitting the subjectivity of the purportedly indifferent artist ("A" Portrait, not "The" Portrait). (80)

Moving on, Rice notes that "although Joyce was very much of his time in *Dubliners* and *A Portrait*, he was so much ahead of his time in *Ulysses* and *Finnegans Wake* that we are only now [...] 'learning to be his contemporaries'" (80).

Chapter III, "*Ulysses*, Chaos and Complexity" departs from the "messenger interpolation" in the "Aeolus" chapter (*U* 7.760-5) which in Rice's view reminds the reader of the following four facts of human existence:

> (1) minute causes can have momentous consequences; (2) events appear to be purely accidental and contingent in the present moment of their occurrence; (3) these same events, once displaced into the past and reviewed [...] seem to have been fully deterministic; and (4) in the real world [...] we can establish *with certainty* that determinate effects result from determinative causes. (83)

The correlation between "the fundamental premises of chaos theory [...] and the four facts above" is the following: "(1) minute causes may have momentous consequences; (2) everything in the world of the present [...] is accidental; (3) the dynamic systems most characteristic of life [...] behave in a deterministic fashion; and (4) it is possible to arrive at "*objective truth about the world*" (83). Chaos theory as such in Rice's account

> springs from the discovery that chaos is *ordered*, that a vast array of complex and purportedly random phenomena [...] reveal deeply embedded patterns. (84)

This discovery makes chaos theory applicable to such complex systems as weather, earthquakes, evolution, viruses and politics (in Rice's order) as the famous "butterfly effect" in Edward Lorenz's paper shows (see below). The paradox inherent in this is that in studying chaos, chaos theory "reaffirms certainty in the realm of science," and thus reverses "the increasingly skeptical 20th-century conviction [...] that all orders that the individual *discovers* are merely ideological *covers* subjectively imposed by the observer," restoring "the realist's picture of a reality that exists 'independently of observers'" (85).

Joyce's "stochastic determinism," then, his "dialectic of chance and determinism, analogous to that of chaos theory," manifests itself in the three principal characters of *Ulysses*: "throughout the novel Stephen expresses a deterministic view of the world," whereas Molly Bloom "confirms her husband's assumption that women 'believe in chance because like themselves,' it is unpredictable (*U* 13.808-9)," and Leopold Bloom mediates between "the deterministic Stephen and aleatory Molly," while repeatedly seeing himself as "inhabiting a world where things happen 'accidentally by design'" (89). What Joyce and chaos theory share then is "a unique resolution of the [fortune vs. fate] antithesis that accepts both," suggesting (Joyce) or showing (chaos theory) that "what is unpredictable in prospect will be seen, in retrospect, as the result of deterministic initial conditions" (90). Rice's argument goes on to single out four important features of chaos theory which "offer intriguing applications for the reading and criticism of an orderly chaotic literary work like Joyce's *Ulysses*":

> (1) the principle of sensitive dependence, (2) the role of feedback in sensitively dependent dynamic systems, (3) the emphasis on scientific explanation rather than prediction, and (4) the concept of design, either innate or emergent, in chaotic systems. (93)

As concerns the first, the notion of "sensitive dependence" came into being in Edward Lorenz's 1979 paper "Predictability: Does the Flap of a Butterfly's Wings in Brazil Set Off a Tornado in Texas?" which brought about "a massive reorientation of contemporary thought in the sensitively dependent system of the sciences, a new analytical focus on the complexity, irregularity, and unpredictable muddle of the world as we experience it." This massive reorientation manifests itself in *Ulysses* as follows:

> [I]n *Ulysses*, Joyce sustains and builds on his conception of the epiphanic significance of the "triviality," the capacity of a "vulgarity of speech or of gesture" or of action to trigger "sudden spiritual manifestation" wherein the "soul of the commonest" event "seems to us radiant" with meaning: the event "achieves its epiphany" (*SH*, 211, 213). (95)

Examples of such "significant trivialities" abound. Rice singles out a textual one: Joyce's use of the period punctuation mark in both the "Penelope" unpunctuated monologue and Martha Clifford's letter in "Lotus Eaters" in which "bad headache. today." makes Bloom think, "has her roses probably" (*U* 5.285). Generally,

[Joyce] fosters the readers' recognition of the importance of trivial things uniformly along the continuum from the smallest issues of typographical conventions to the large concerns of the novel's meanings (98).

As regards feedback and description, Rice characterizes the former as marking "all sensitively dependent phenomena, vastly intensifying the effects of even the most humble of causes" (100), and the latter as a means of discerning it. Therefore, whereas "prospectively, much in the cosmos is unpredictable and accidental," in explanation, "in description by a kind of retrospective arrangement," we can see that "this cosmos is designed and determined" (102)—an example of this from *Ulysses* is the great recirculation of the preceding whole—the "Circe" episode. What chaos theory also shows is that "indeterminism is not enough"—even though holding that "apparently simple nonlinear dynamic system can generate phenomena of extraordinary complexity," the reverse is also true (106). Thus, to turn to *Ulysses* again, the "conscious reactor against the void of incertitude" (17.2210) is marked by another quartet of features: he

(1) holds in one conception [...] the unity of chance and determinism; (2) rejects the reduction of complex phenomena to the half-truths of simplicity [...] (3) accepts the reality of immanent and emergent design [...] and (4) recognizes that even the infidelity of his wife [...] is as natural as any and every natural act. (109)

Even critical traditions can, in Rice's witty account, be rewritten according to their "geometries" and "physical laws": hence New Criticism in Todorov's words pursues the analytic "geometry of meaning"; formalism and structuralism are governed by a deterministic concept of law, and yet structures of literature appear contingent, not absolute (Einstein); post-structuralism is preoccupied with intense subjectivity (Copenhagen interpretation); and finally, the contemporary return to the context of New Historicism and culture studies, closes the temporal gap, and runs parallel to chaos theory (110). To recapitulate,

Ulysses [...] strays from the ordered and static world of the stable system, not into chaos, but to the borderline of complexity, the edge of chaos, where small causes have large effects and where both life itself and great works of literature are found. (111)

Finally, "*Finnegans Wake*: The Complexity of Artificial Life," opens by contending that in reading *Finnegans Wake*, chaos theory "forces us to adjust our overly linear view of cultural influence as merely a direct matter of proportional action and reaction, linear cause and effect" (114). Rice undertakes a foray into neurology; specifically, its PDP (*parallel distributed processes*), which he presents as follows:

(I) the multiple connections among neurons allow information to move in many directions; (2) feedback seems to be at the root of the brain's ability to retain, store, and recover information; (3) a nonlinear complex system like the brain is capable of manifesting globally a "behavior"—the phenomenon of *emergence*—that is not attributable to any single element of the system acting in isolation. (117)

Touching upon an array of variously related issues, including the Wakean collapse of Cartesianism, its complex network of mutually interacting forces and the border zone between simple order and pure randomness inhabited by the text, Rice conceives of his chapter as "a prolegomenon for the study of the *Wake* as a complex literary system, not itself a full reading of Joyce's work in terms of complexity" (123). *Finnegans Wake*, in his account, emerges as a dream "not in Freudian terms, as overdetermined by consciousness," but one that is "analogous to a reality processing an immanent design as yet uninformed by a mediating consciousness" (139). In conclusion, Rice argues for a widening of "the boundaries of our own hierarchical system, the discipline of literature, to learn from what our contemporaries are doing" with the purpose of becoming able to "finally attack the difficulties of negotiating the distance between a genetic, bottom-up study of *Finnegans Wake* and a broadly interpretive, top-down analysis of the novel's 'meanings'" (140).

V

Aiming to direct Rice's attempt to make chaos theory and the discourse of modern physics into possibly fruitful perspectives from which to explore Joyce's writing toward an analysis of his central novelistic text's protagonist, the point of departure of Peter Mackey's *Chaos Theory and James Joyce's Everyman*[8] is the conviction that "a contemporary field of mathematics popularly known as 'Chaos Theory' provides a revealing metaphor through which to understand Leopold Bloom" (1).

From the physicist discourse, Mackey extracts four ideas of possible relevance for one's personal life:

(1) a trivial decision can wholly change a life; (2) a chance encounter can dramatically alter life's course; (3) a contingent nexus exists between consciousness and environment; (4) a way of thinking [...] helps us to interpret life's chaos. (1)

Ulysses, in Mackey's view, presents "a narrative that promises the ready plot line of the Homeric myth yet that experiences the chaotic subterfuge of Joyce's language and Bloom's surprising day" (2). As regards the issue of indeterminateness, Mackey distinguishes between two opposing views:

[8] Peter F.Mackey, *Chaos Theory and James Joyce's Everyman* (Miami: University of Florida Press, 1999).

one holds that nature only appears indeterminate because we do not know any better [...] If we could find these temporarily hidden variables, nature would seem causal and determined again. The second view says nature itself is indeterminate [...], possess[ing] superpositions of qualities. [...] God *did* create a universe of law and order *and* left the dice rolling. (5)

Among the examples of influential postmodernist treatment of science within the humanities, Mackey features Katherine Hayles (*Chaos Bound*), and Philip Kuberski's application of the Copenhagen model of quantum indeterminacy to non-quantum reality but not without adding a caveat warning against the postmodernist seriousness about its own non-seriousness, akin to the "blind faith in the mechanical model of the universe" (13). Chaos theory, in this respect, "provides the fruitful middle ground between the extremes of the postmodern and mechanical models" in that it accepts "the indeterminateness and interrelationships emphasized in postmodernism yet affirms the existence of an aboriginal reality" (19). As opposed to Rice's critique of the postmodernist application of the tenets of modern physics to the non-physicist realm, Mackey lays emphasis on "the interrelations of science, literature, and even daily life" by viewing "Bloom's world" as permeated by chance which maintains a "dynamic, liberating potential" (26). The argument of Mackey's study proceeds along the following lines: his first chapter elaborates on the fundamental tenets of Chaos theory, "indicating their general relationship to *Ulysses*, especially to Bloom's development." Chapter II studies the importance of the "Ithaca" chapter to a general appreciation of pattern in chaos and life. The third chapter examines "the overlap of Bloom's evolving stream-of-consciousness, through which we come to know him," and the fourth investigates "the similarities between the flow of Bloom's identity and flow in complex systems." Chapter V exposes the similarities between the trivialities in Bloom's aboriginal life and trivialities in complex systems. Finally, in Chapter VI these ideas merge to expose the hope and freedom that *Ulysses* reveals the everyday hero's ultimate courage (27).

However, not only does Mackey's book not differ in any substantial way from the theoretical framework already mapped in Rice's study (following in no significantly different way than Rice, Hayles, Lorenz, Poincaré, quantum vs. wave undecidability, etc.) it also follows very similar textual instances (for example the messenger moment in "Aeolus," or the "triviality of epiphany") and narrative characteristics (Bloom-as-chance-lover, "Ithaca" as "the clearest indication in *Ulysses* of its correspondence with chaos theory" (62) the water-stream of consciousness parallel), and thus unfortunately cannot be said to present the sort of follow-up that Rice's book calls for in its conclusion, and will not be followed in any detail here.

VI

Revisiting (in a much more productive way than we have just seen do Mackey with Rice) Theall's brilliant wide-ranging recontextualisation of

Joyce's art within the various theoretical discourse and artistic practices of his increasingly technologized era from a yet broader theoretical framework that includes, most prominently, Derridean deconstruction, Lacanian psychoanalysis, hypermedia theory, cybernetics, computing, and postmodern poetics, Louis Armand's *Technē: James Joyce, Hypertext & Technology*[9] presents the most comprehensive and theoretical attempt at rethinking Joyce's work as not only in a dialogue with the contemporary technology, but anticipating, "soliciting," the digital technology to-come in the post-war period.

In his "Preface: Instigations," Armand points out that the concern of his study is "the question of technology in its relation to the work of James Joyce and theories of hypertext" as much as "a concept of technology arising from the language of *Finnegans Wake*." Echoing Theall, Armand aims to show that "Joyce's writing provides a model for rethinking the relationship between technology and 'all forms of cultural production.'" The relation between Joyce's writing and hypertext is, Armand argues, one of *solicitation* (as theorized most influentially by Jacques Derrida)—denoting "the extent to which Joyce's text can be said to both *call for* and *motivate* a hypertextuality irreducible to a stable field" (xi). Furthermore, hypertext is situated within the context of twentieth-century philosophical discourses on technology, in order to "elaborate a number of implications for hypertext which touch upon our fundamental understanding of language." In this respect, the notion of *enframing* and the parallel drawn between *technē* and *poiēsis* via their common belonging to "bringing forth" as theorized in Martin Heidegger's seminal essay "Question Concerning Technology" is pertinent.

More broadly speaking, Armand's study orientates itself around the three following objectives:

> Firstly, to trace the historical development of communications technologies in the context of Joyce's writing [...]. Secondly, to trace some of the effects of communications technologies upon scholarship generally, and upon Joycean scholarship in particular. And thirdly, to investigate the ways in which technology *per se* is involved in a "communication" with Joyce's language in *Finnegans Wake*. (xii)

Presenting his argument in a Theallian fashion of a historico-theoretical peregrination across the broad ground of several intellectual fields, with several points being revisited more than once from various directions, Armand departs from a thorough mapping of the modern and modernist context of Joyce's era. The art of this period is viewed throughout as one (mostly, but not exclusively avant-garde) of the *machine*, the technological character of cultural production presenting, however ambivalent the responses of the individual artists, the very prerequisite for some of the

---

[9] Louis Armand, *Techné: James Joyce, Hypertext & Technology* (Prague: Karolinum, 2003 [1997]).

most radical experimental artistic advances. This broad avant-garde context is even further expanded by reference to Jean-Francois Lyotard's (echoing Peter Buerger's) link between the pre-modernist and the postmodern—the critical theory of the 1970s postmodern era comes to creatively deal with its social and political as well as technological status in ways not dissimilar from those of the pre- and interwar avant-garde. The technological status of postmodern theory is first and foremost the advent of cyberspace and the hypertext which necessitated a whole array of important (resistances to) reconceptualisations:

> What, until recently, has been called for alternately empirical and mystical reasons *the book* is entering a distinct epoch in which it will no longer be possible to limit the range of a material body of writing by enclosing it within a published volume, as, for instance, something we could call a definitive or even standard edition. (31)

Drawing upon theorists of hypertext such as the pioneering figure of Theodor H. Nelson or more current theorists Jay David Bolter and George P. Landow, Armand proposes a whole variety of possibilities for rethinking Joyce's Wakean project in terms of contemporary technological advances, one of which is its implication for textual genetics:

> Similarly, in the genetic process of reduction and recuperation, what have heretofore been considered distinct, if problematic, features of Joyce's writing [...] would thus be brought within one another's sphere of signifying influence, as it were, as "material" parts of a single, if contradictory, hypertextual apparatus. (38)

This solicitation of hypertext though, for Armand, is not to be located somewhere within the thematic or specifically formal organization of Joyce's work, but rather "in the structure of possibility itself" (39), which is explained by means of a reference to the Aristotelian nut cracked by Stephen, the question whether *anything is possible that does not actually take place*, and to an often-used phrase of Derrida's—"calculated and by chance," a paradox inherent to possibility as such, in that

> something implies the possibility of its being realised at some unspecified time or place, or in some unspecified way as a form of destiny to which it is tied regardless of whether such a possibility will ever be realised or not. (44)

In a theoretical gesture important for his purposes, Armand, speaking of Derrida, reidentifies his crucial concepts underlying language functioning as signification—of *trace*, *différance*, and *iterability* among others—in broadly mechanical, technological terms, presenting Derrida's *iterability* as "the possibility of repetition, which is mechanical" (54). Bringing some of his observations to bear on among other things the *Wake* notebooks scholarship, Armand speaks of "a certain perversion" which is due to the enormity of the *Wake* corpus and the challenge this poses to traditional modes of communication (re)production on the one hand, and the desire "to resolve this challenge in a way that might affirm the truth and/or limits of normative experience" (56). Surveying a number of critical studies of the *Wake*, ranging to the most apostate (such as John Cage's "Roaratorio") to some of the most canonical (Clive Hart's *Structure and Motif* or Roland McHugh's *Sigla of Finnegans Wake*), Armand stresses the need

> to consider how signification in *Finnegans Wake* turns about an indefinite "double axis," between linguistic and non-linguistic operations. That is to say, in a broadly semiotic way whereby a marking on the page may function linguistically on one hand, and non-linguistically on the other, yet in both instances signifying in a meaningful and interdependent fashion. (70)

Of the textual geneticism that comes to inform Armand's concern with the technological, it is Daniel Ferrer's[10] work preoccupied with how *avant-textes* come to exercise a certain influence over the text itself in a fashion akin to that of the Freudian unconscious that appeals to him most, dealing as it does (when related to Derrida's *grafting* and *citationality*) with the possibility of "signifying 'states,' whose structural translatability underwrites what we might call 'the *technē* of inscription,' as a form of articulated palimpsest" (76). The psychoanalytic slant of Ferrer's approach further links it with Armand's, as his is one markedly influenced by Lacanian psychoanalysis, both its early (the mirror) and its very late (*le sinthome* and the Borromean knots) stages. Of the other ITEM-ists, Jean-Michel Rabaté, especially his "Lapsus ex Machina," is a continual point of reference. His contention that the *Wake* "begets only beginnings but invalidates all origins" stimulates the following disquisition on the opening of the text:

> At the very "beginning" of Joyce's text there appears a scission which, despite all efforts, cannot be assimilated within a system, whether dialectical or grammatical, on the basis of which it might be substituted for by a signifier of sense. [...] the apparent absence of a formal grammatical logic in the text's opening passage cannot simply be supplied by joining the first and last lines of *Finnegans Wake* together. (104)

Armand's technological perspective and his primary attention to the *Wake* allows him to address other often invoked issues, not only the obvious (and disputable) "circularity," but also the Derrideo-Lacanian "unreadability," the Lévi-Straussian bricolage, or the reading/writing transversal effect. In a passage crucial in terms of the Heideggerian underpinning of the study, Armand discusses his re-identification of Plato's *aletheia* as *a-lēthē-ia*, denoting both "unconcealment" and "non-forgetfulness." For Armand, the intrinsically "mnemotechnic technology" of truth "resides in the topical reversion of memory as 'writing.'" According to this logic,

---

[10] See Chapter X "Textual Criticism & Textual Genetics."

the mnemotechnic of *a-lētheia* marks a certain defilement of *Erinnerung* (as "riverrun") in a way that would characterise memory as the recurrent affirmation of concealing-forgetfulness, but also as a kind of recursive apparatus—what Heidegger terms *Ge-stell*, or *enframing*, as a technological form of disclosure or "revealing." (127)

The "lapsus" motif, itself recurrent within Armand's study as prominently as within the *Wake*, can be, in this light, re-identified not only with the many "falls" of HCE, but also with Nietzsche's theory of eternal recurrence and the Viconian cyclical model of history:

> what becomes evident in *Finnegans Wake*, as it does in Nietzsche's concept of *eternal recurrence*, is that this apparent "negativity" masks an "affirmation," and that this affirmation comes "before" *logos*, inscribing it within, and according to, the limits of its own discourse, as a kind of "lexinction" [...] of the word (*FW* 83.25). (141)

The *Wake*'s obsessive recirculation of the "seim anew" is furthermore related to Freud's fort/da game, the concept of "redundancy" in Claude Shannon's modern information theory, or the "strange attractor" in Edward Lorenz's dynamics of complex systems. These numerous "departures" lead in the end to "Destinations," the book's third segment. Here, some of Armand's continuous concerns are brought home, most importantly with the "altereffect" of the Wakean writing in which its textual elements are "articulated in terms of a certain *mark*, or absence of a mark, of differentiation"—an articulation which "does not take place linearly or diachronically [...] but synchronically and synoptically, so that the text appears to be structured like a palimpsest." However, what is in Armand's view most often ignored, is that

> in order to being reading *Finnegans Wake* in either of these ways one is required to perform violence against the text, effectively defacing it in order to constitute or reconstitute the text that it supposedly represents in a confused way, or at least that it poorly preserves. (188)

Turning to hypertext, Armand warns against viewing the supposedly non-material cyberspace text as a "disembodied signifier of a *deus ex machina*, which would be nothing more than logocentrism under another guise." Instead, he suggests that theorists examine the "paradox of material non-materiality" of the hypertext "in terms of what Derrida has called the 'trace,' or 'arché-writing,' or again 'différance'" (189). In this connection,

> Joyce's "endless play of substitution" might also be posited as a finite *probability*, and so affirm the metaphysical dimension of hypertext as a totalising movement. These problems, however, can themselves be situated as so many *topics* of transversality. Indeed they can be said to be genera-

tive of transversality itself, and for this reason it is not simply a question of determining where such problems "come to rest." (190)

Ultimately, in itself "a network of topics," hypertext is viewed by Armand as describing "a transversal between what we might call topological charting, between the topical mask of narrativity and a narrative of *topos*." However, if one is to speak of a *solicitation* of hypertext, as has been the case in Armand's study,

> it would be in the sense of its "activating" a certain non-reserve "at the origin" of a system of signification, an "originary *différance*" at the point at which the rupture technology invades the universal problematic. (194)

In itself a topological charting of a "network of topics" so wide and rich as to include most of the important philosophical thinking of and artistic creation from within technology in the markedly technological condition of both the modern and postmodern eras while maintaining an acute awareness of the positions and agendas of Joyce and Joyce criticism within the modernist artistic and postmodernist theoretical discourses respectively — Armand's study manages to deliver a vast philosophical-critical synthesis, unparalleled in its ambitions and achievements.

VII

Louis Armand is also the editor of a collection of essays aimed at bringing the discussion of Joyce's "hypermedia" — or to borrow a term coined by one of its contributors, Mark Nunes, "Joycemedia," — in dialogue with contemporary advances in textual genetics: *Joycemedia: James Joyce, Hypermedia & Textual Genetics*.[11]

In the preface, Armand traces the genesis of the collection back to Daniel Ferrer's keynote speech on Joycean hypertext at the 1995 Brown University Joyce Conference. This speech was one of the first attempts to theorize the outburst of publishing activity that had occurred during the period between 1990 and 1993 (during which Joyce's output had for a brief moment moved out of copyright before Britain and the USA revised their copyright laws in accordance with the EU standards), seeking to implement hypermedia studies for various pedagogical or editorial purposes. Despite the lengthy ten-year process of the volume's formation, Armand insists that its arrival should not be seen as taking place "after the event" — instead, the collection is to be seen as coming "in advance of itself," since Joycemedia still has "a quite rarefied existence" (xii).

In his introduction, Armand maps out the development of the internet together with the evolution of Ted Nelson's term "hypertext," with the focus on its first practical applications within Joyce studies. Even in some of the most prominent Joyce criticism, Armand detects an acute sense of what he calls "a nostalgia for the text as artifact," noticeable in both the

---

[11] Louis Armand, ed., *Joycemedia* (Prague: Litteraria Pragensia, 2003).

theoretical approach of J. Hillis Miller and the practical project of Hans Walter Gabler whose 1984 "corrected" *Ulysses* edition sought, in Armand's view, "to fix the text forever" (5). Also mentioned is the implication of genetic studies in the issues of legality, ownership and copyright vis-à-vis the Joyce estate, exemplified by the "emendated" re-issue of Brenda Maddox's *Nora*.

However, proceeding with the theoretical part of his argument that draws from the originary conceptual rootedness of textual genetics in post-structuralism, Armand argues that "hypertext emerged at a time when textual theories had already reconfigured the way we think about the book and about what it is that constitutes a text" (9) and goes on to demonstrate how twentieth century theory (whether the early phenomenological approach of Ingarden or the later project of deconstruction in the writings of Derrida or Rabaté) in many ways prefigured the contemporary challenges posed by the hypertext to the traditional concept of textuality. That even the earliest *Wake* criticism can be seen as Joycean hypertext studies *avant la lettre* is exemplified by Hart's 1963 *Concordance* or McHugh's 1976 *The Sigla of Finnegans Wake*, the former presenting "one of the earliest prototypes of a Joycean hypertext" (15), the latter conceptualizing hypertext by engaging "the way in which textual elements in Joyce's writing signify otherwise than linguistically" (17).

Armand's introduction is useful in that it provides a theoretical framework within which many of the contributions operate. The whole collection then can be said to address the various modes of "reconfiguration" required by Joyce's supreme experimentation with the possibilities of textuality, materiality and mediality. What follows is a brief account of some of the more stimulating possible reconfigurations.

Donald Theall's "Transformations of the Book in Joyce's Dream Vision of Digiculture" positions Joyce within the larger context of the avant-garde exploration of the interface between the artistic and the technical, the human and the machinist. By focusing on the "poetic prophecy of *Finnegans Wake*" (28) as rendered by its language, "Wakese … hyperlanguage [and] paralanguage" (31), the essay seeks to provide an understanding of "how Joyce came to occupy a unique role in what … [is] called the 'prehistory of cyberculture'" (29).

In "Gaps and Convergences in the Joycean Network," Mark Nunes investigates how, in G.P. Landow's words, Joyce's texts can be viewed as "*implicit* hypertexts in nonelectronic form" (44). Apart from poststructuralist approaches to hypertextuality, Nunes mainly bases his theoretical argument on Eco's concept of semiotic networks which according to him provide "a final point of convergence by foregrounding a set of cybernetic principles in the context of literary studies" (49). In the "practical" part of his essay, Nunes examines what he sees as one of the "gaps" in Joyce's text—the famous "come in" incident, locating the possible instance of it with the use of electronic search engines.

Louis Armand's essay "From Hypertext to Vortex / Notes on Materiality and Language" seeks to provide a notational framework within which one can engage with the question of materiality and move toward "a theory of hypertextuality" (73). The most striking quality of *Finnegans Wake*, in his view, is "the power of its resemblant quality" (77).

In his contribution, first presented as a paper at the 2003 Prague James Joyce Colloquium, "The Work of Joyce in the Age of Hypertextual Production," Daniel Ferrer draws a parallel between chronophotography and genetic criticism. Both seek to reconstruct the dynamics of a (creative) process from what was originally meant to constitute a fixation—a frozen movement in the first case, a fixed textual object in the latter. It is this fixedness that genetic criticism challenges, with the danger however of fetishising, via its focus on the creation, the author. Instead, Ferrer invokes Derrida's statement that Joyce's texts exist "in memory" of other texts. In his opinion, it is the due to the peculiar type of intertextuality presented in the thousands of pages of Joyce's obscure and mostly undetectable notes that genetic criticism should strive to account for, a striving much facilitated by the possibilities of hypermedia.

The volume *Joycemedia: James Joyce, Hypermedia & Textual Genetics* presents a major attempt at theorizing the fusion of hypertext and textual genetics, news of which, now in 2009 sadly just as much as in 2003, to revert to Armand's preface, "remains to be received." For, as the next chapter shall demonstrate, sadly enough only very little of the technological potential of Joycean *avant-texte*-as-hypertext as theorized by both Armand's book-length study and this edited collection has been actualized by Joycean textual geneticists.

VIII

Louis Armand returns to Joyce in the sixty-page coda to *Literate Technologies—Language, Cognition, Technicity*,[12] a book concerned with the question of technology, conceived in its broadest sense, and its relation to language, discourse, mediation, and art. The breadth of this concept of technology, or *technē*, allows Armand to engage in an analysis of some of the very fundamental issues in the human sciences, for example the operations of thinking, the character of consciousness, and the general condition of a system that underlies all human experience. Armand engages with the work of Derrida (to which he is similar in that he pursues the underlying conditions of possibility), Freud, Lacan, Roman Jakobson, Ludwig Wittgenstein, Martin Heidegger, Maurice Merleau-Ponty, and many, many others in order to posit a "technological" field of operations prior to the common human activities of thinking, desiring, speaking, and so on.

[12] Louis Armand, *Literate Technologies: Language, Cognition, Technicity* (Prague: Litteraria Pragensia, 2006).

The final, extended essay, "Constellations," provides the most consistent investigation into the literary significance of Armand's arguments. His point of departure is the following conviction:

> That we believe ourselves to experience the world as a conscious continuum shaped by causally defined events, and as authors of our own actions, does not require or even imply that the *means* of experience (or experience itself) should equally be constituted in these terms. There is no reason to suppose that even the "experience of consciousness" should be founded upon a conscious agency within the apparatus or phenomenon of experience. (165)

Instead of these commonsensical notions of consciousness, all of which fall under a closer scrutiny, Armand proposes to speak of consciousness as "a constellation-effect" which is "an effect of relativity" coming about in "the way in which otherwise unrelated terms are brought into signifying relation by way of an arbitrarily 'imposed' schema," which extends along the co-relational and co-referential axes (166). The broadly syntactic and schematic nature of these signifying relations allow one to recognise the constellation-effect as essentially textual or *hypertextual*, or indeed what Armand terms *vortextual*:

> And despite its appearance as describing a condition of stasis, or inertia, in which each of its signifying terms is closed in a fixed relation to every other term, the provisional nature of any constellation requires us to account for certain structuring "processes"—even, or especially, where such processes appear to be invisible or contained within an act of perception. (167)

Having introduced this conceptual framework, Armand can now deploy it in a series of discussions of artistic works exploring precisely this constellation-effect: John Cage's Joyce-inspired musical compositions and writings on music, Georges Perec's mathematical layout for *La vie: mode d'emploi*, and most prominently, the late works of James Joyce—*Ulysses* and *Finnegans Wake*. Departing from Shklovsky's aesthetics, Armand sets out from the following observation:

> Textual automation, based upon signifying materiality, can be seen as underwriting the entire discursive infrastructure of the later work of Joyce [...]—from grammar and syntax, to latent semantic features and so on (i.e. the general problem of a certain logic).

The prominent feature of Joyce's writing under Armand's scrutiny is "the formal articulation of the variance and invariance of structuring 'codes' represented, among others, by the trigrammatic figures ALP and HCE" which are seen "to represent certain probabilistic co-ordinates of lexical and sublexical combination or permutation in Joyce's text" such as anagram, acrostic, or acronym (178). Armand delves into the semiological work of Gregory Bateson, Umberto Eco, or Algirdas Greimas, among others, in order to show that as long as the trigrammatic figures HCE and

ALP are treated as a generative matrix of significations, then "the 'hierarchical' relation that may be attributed to sequential coding/decoding processes and their outcomes [...] is never anything but provisional, or rather virtual" (179). The challenges of Joyce's *Finnegans Wake* reside, for Armand, in the following questions:

> How do we situate the probabilistic limits of meaning or signification? How do we determine qualitatively the effect or object of constraint? Moreover where do we locate the *agency* of constraint (its "switching mechanism") vis-à-vis the assumption of a system of signifiers *in the first place*? (180)

In the *Wake*, such questions are posed in initially thematic terms with regard to novelistic convention of plot and character. As "figures of constraint," the ALP and HCE trigrams "describe a nominal probability of any sequence of terms in the *Wake* being related, structured around the constellation-effect described through repetition and permutation of these triadic figures" (181).

However, the diagrammatic transposition of ALP in *FW* 293.23 draws attention beyond the purely normative function of these three letters representing an algorithm of textual relations toward "the fundamentally normative character of the letters themselves, posed [...] at the very limits of signification" (182). This is made yet more explicit in Joyce's use of the sigla whose non-linguistic function "can also give rise to other translational processes of ideographic summation or *literalisation* through their material 'resemblance' to other signifying 'scriptsigns'" (183). As opposed to the view expressed in Lévi-Strauss' *The Savage Mind* which places proper names "on the margin of classification," in Joyce's *Wake* this margin "finds its iteration at every level of the signifying relation, and not simply as a 'special case'" (185). Underneath this concept of proper nouns is "a particular nominalism in the distinction between signifying function and materiality, on the one hand, and between the specific and generic, particular and universal, on the other." Moving from the concept of "indexical discontinuity or *contiguity*," Armand finally arrives at

> a hypertextual edifice, in which each letter or combination of letters in this "grouptriad" (*FW* 160.04) would be capable of virtually infinite subscriptions across the entire field of language without any one subscription assuming the unique role of *indexical* value.

Joyce, in Armand's account, is ultimately seen to locate this aspect of signifying materiality "within the materiality of language (and cognition) itself" (186).

10. Textual Criticism & Textual Genetics

I

The first book-length study of the pre-publication history of *Ulysses* to draw critical conclusions relevant for its interpretation was *Joyce's Ulysses in Progress* by Michael Groden,[1] which departs from the intention to illuminate one major obscurity about *Ulysses* — "its complicated and bizarre prepublication history" (3).

The four chapters of Groden's argument proceed very logically from Chapter I where he identifies the "three stages" of *Ulysses.* He then moves on to three subsequent discussions of each one, focusing on how the compositional process of a chapter is representative of the whole stage ("Aeolus," "Cyclops," and, though not exclusively, "Circe"). Thus, in Groden's terms, the "Early stage" from "Telemachus" to "Scylla and Charybdis," is marked by a development of "an interior monologue technique"; the "Middle stage" from "Wandering Rocks" to "Oxen of the Sun," is where Joyce's experiment with the monologue is abandoned "for a series of parodic styles that act as 'translations' of the story"; and finally the "Last stage" from "Circe" to "Penelope" is when Joyce "created several new styles and revised the earlier episodes" (4). The general complexity of the whole creative process is illustrated by Groden's schematic "Stemma of *Ulysses*," which features no fewer than nine stages through which the text had gone prior to its final form — a complexity intriguing and unique in its own right, but also with one significant, unwelcome effect: a high incidence of textual error, of which there are, to Groden's mind, four major factors: "the printer's lack of English, Joyce's difficult handwriting and weak eyesight, and the pressures of time." Groden also adduces one example thereof — an instance in "Nausicaa" when the printer skipped, and failed to print, a whole line (8). Groden's stand on the matter is as follows:

The present exposé shall follow a rather anomalous — because thematic rather than strictly chronological — course, split in response to the division in the field itself; here, of a thematic rather than methodological nature (though that would, indeed, be a possible option were not the most recent praxis of Joycean textual criticism and genetics marked by its syncretism rather than divisionism). It shall first present the textual criticism devoted to Joyce's penultimate text, *Ulysses*, focusing especially on the "*Ulysses* wars" of the 1980s (sections I-IV), and then proceed with an exposition of *Wake*-based genetics which, given the plethora of critical material produced in this branch, shall restrict itself to the most current contributions, beginning only in the 1990s.

[1] Michael Groden, *Joyce's 'Ulysses' in Progress* (New Jersey: Princeton University Press, 1977).

However, considering all the complications involved in writing and publishing *Ulysses*, it is amazing that the text is not more corrupt than it is. Still, there is no doubt that the numerous prepublication transcriptions introduced unfortunate errors that were never corrected. (10)

Chapter I further presents the entire work, and shall therefore be the focus of the present exposé. It opens by making the important observation that, rather than really finishing his *Ulysses*, Joyce "had to stop writing it," by which time "he had spent eight years on the work, lived in three cities, changed his address nineteen times, suffered several eye attacks and subsequent operations, and, at a distance, experienced a world war." It was a revolutionary period both externally and personally for Joyce, during which "his artistic goals changed to such an extent that a book that in some aspects began as a sequel to *A Portrait* ended as a prelude to *Finnegans Wake*" (13). Surveying the early criticism of the novel, Groden notes that what it struggled most to come to terms with were the

> opposing tendencies in *Ulysses* — compression and expansion, verisimilitude and literary parody, "centripetal" and "centrifugal" writing — that achieve a state of resolution, remain locked in unresolved conflict, or are simply thrown together in a witches' brew that is proudly termed "allincluding." (18)

Against the one-sidedly positive/negative readings of Gilbert, Goldberg, and others, Groden contends that

> [c]ritics who enter Joyce's "workshop" through his notesheets and drafts and through his revisions of *Ulysses* repeatedly find themselves in trouble with a unilateral interpretation of the book, since they find evidence of a dichotomy in Joyce's intentions that a single approach cannot subsume. (21)

The dichotomy in "The Early Stage," comprising the first half of the episodes, is one between *The Little Review* versions, as opposed to the final forms of the episodes, where "in style as well as character, the fair copy-*Little Review Ulysses* is more 'novelistic' than the final version." "Aeolus" is chosen for an extended discussion since here the differences are most pronounced. "The Middle Stage," marked as it is by an abandonment of the previous method, presents a dichotomy in its own right:

> It is tempting to speculate on why Joyce first violently distorted and then replaced the monologue method. For one thing, he probably grew tired of it. It served his initial purposes well; it provided a unique view of character and a consistent style on which he could play his variations. (34)

The dichotomy is also re-identified in a less convincing manner as one of individual and national specificity as opposed to archetypal vision: the transition is one from "individual and even national history" toward "a larger view in which any specific individual or situation recreates archetypal patterns form the past" (35-6). A closer look on the "Sirens" episode reveals a more pertinent view on the logic of composition applicable to all other middle-stage chapters:

> In texture they tend to be loose and rambling; they achieve their encyclo-pedic dimension primarily in their cumulative effect. They represent Joyce's attempt to filter his story through established forms of narration [...], al-ways distorted by his instinct for parody. (51-2)

"The Last Stage," is again a period of further transition and abandonment, in which the work on "Circe" seems pivotal in that Joyce "seems to have begun it as an episode similar in scope and length to the previous three, but by the time he finished it he had left the middle stage behind for new developments" (52). "Ithaca" and "Penelope," "balanced at the end of the book as they were in Joyce's composition process, together represent the conclusion of the book." For Groden,

> the gradual expansion of all aspects of *Ulysses* since the end of "Scylla and Charybdis"—a proliferation of possible perspectives and readings, all of which are valid to some degree—makes inevitable such an ambiguous, un-resolved, "allincluding" ending (63).

II

The *annus mirabilis* of 1984 also saw, as if in response to Groden's be-moaning the flawed condition in which *Ulysses* has been preserved for posterity, the publication of the much-discussed new edition of *Ulysses*,[2] edited by a team under the supervision of Hans Walter Gabler. In his "Afterword," Gabler first surveys the compositional process the novel, from its early conceptions to the first edition of 1922, then examines Joyce's manner and habits of writing, before finally introducing the editorial procedures for establishing the critical text.

In his discussion of the process of composition, Gabler distinguishes five stages through which it proceeded: from preliminary notes and first drafts to final draft, from there to fair copy, further to typescript, and finally, through the multiple-layered revision process on the typescripts and proofs, to the final 1922 publication (1859-1891). However, this publication "does not present the text of the work as [Joyce] wrote it," and the Gabler edition's whole rationale is "based on the assumption that the legal act of first publication did not validate the actual text thereby made public to the extent of lending authority to its high incidence of corruption" (1891-2). In the edition's pursuit to recover the ideal state of development, it seeks to redress the corruption of the 1922 edition by first turning its attention to the composition (Joyce's autographs) and pre-publication transmission (the *Little Review* and *Egoist* serializations) mate-rial. Crucial here is the question of textual authority—which of the many versions (autograph, typescript, proof, serial version, final version?) is to

[2] James Joyce, *Ulysses: A Critical and Synoptic Edition*, Vols. I-III, eds. Hans Walter Gabler, Wolfhard Steppe and Claus Melchior (New York & London: Garland Publishing, 1984).

be accorded primacy over all others, and on what grounds (the issue of authorial intention)?

> Since by their autograph overlay the typescripts and proofs partially acquire the status of documents of composition, the question arises of how far the authorial presence affects, and penetrates, their basic level of transmissional transcription. [...] Conversely, the authorial overlay may touch text proper to the relevant typescript or proof, that is, its textual deviations and corruptions. (1893)

Of help here is Joyce's "almost pedantic insistence on what he had once written to his own satisfaction," which allows the editor to attach much weight to "a felt restorative tendency in part-corrections." However, "authorial interventions reacting to a transmissional departure may at times incorporate the corruption and revise the text in consequence of it," challenging the status of both "corruption" and "revision." Also of difficulty is Joyce's repeated failure to attend to transmissional departures and corruptions — here, Gabler took the usual editorial decision to dismiss the issue of "passive authorization," and not to regard the uncorrected mistakes as "willed" by Joyce. The notion of authority implies the necessity of choosing the *copytext*, a "text of highest overall authority" (1894). Gabler's crucial gesture is to "[eliminate] the first edition of 1922," since "the analysis of the manuscripts, typescripts, and proofs reveals just how extensively it presents a non-authoritative text," and to appoint Joyce's autograph notation "the text of highest overall authority on which to base a critical edition of *Ulysses*." Nevertheless, the rub lies in that this "autograph notation" is a non-existent text, imaginatively constructed by Gabler as a "continuation of the holograph inscription of the Rosenbach Manuscript," the continuity of which "derives immediately or mediately from the Rosenbach Manuscript, the typescripts, the serialisations, the proofs for the first edition, and the fist edition itself" (1895). This construct, what Gabler calls "continuous manuscript text," is both "assembled to present *Ulysses* in compositional development," at the same time as it "serves as the edition's copytext and is edited accordingly." It thus simultaneously presents the process of writing and the product of its finalization, with the *synoptic* text on the left-hand and the *reading* text on the right-hand side (1896), to be followed two years later by the *corrected* text.

The scale of the controversy aroused by the *Gabler* edition, sometimes dubbed *Ulysses* wars, came uncannily close to the *Ulysses* scandals following its 1922 publication, and kept scholars busy for the next decade. Michael Groden's "Afterword" from the 1993 Bodley Head reprint of the Gabler edition almost ten years later,[3] shall serve us as a witness to the sound and fury of these conflicts, as well as to the sounder and less furi-

---

[3] Michael Groden, "Afterword," *Ulysses*, eds. Hans Walter Gabler, Wolfhard Steppe and Claus Melchior (London: The Bodley Head, 1993).

ous theoretical assessments of its import. Groden insists that the critical and synoptic edition be "understood in terms of the assumptions and methods of most Anglo-American editing today, because it both follows them and departs from, even challenges, them in important ways" (647-8). This editorial practice relies on the choice of a copytext, "usually the first edition or, if available, the author's manuscript," as the basic text to follow for textual variations within the different editions:

> In the terminology of editing and textual criticism, the words are called "substantives," spelling and punctuation are matters of "accidentals," in-conclusive readings are "indifferent" ones, and the editor's alterations of the editor's alterations of the copytext are called "emendations." (648)

It follows that the peculiar textual situation of Joyce's *Ulysses* required of Gabler some significant departures from common practice. Groden lists three basic reasons for Gabler's decision: first, the manuscript "does not provide a beginning-to-end version in Joyce's hand" and is "too far removed from the extensively augmented text that *Ulysses* eventually became"; secondly, "the typescripts and proofs are steps along the way in the process of expansion"; and finally, "the first edition is too filled with errors" (649). Gabler's "continuous manuscript text" is based on two following premises: any text handwritten by Joyce, unless proven faulty, is deemed superior to any transmitted text, and a word or passage from an earlier document could be admitted into the text on the basis of the invariance of its surrounding context. This has led to an important, and much-contested, aspect of the edition:

> Several words and passages appear in the Rosenbach Manuscript but pre-sumably not in the final working draft that was used by the typist and is now lost; these words and passages thus were never typed or printed. When Gabler judged them to be Joyce's revisions as he made his fair copy of the working draft […], he admitted them into the continuous manuscript text on the grounds that they represent the fullest development of the text. (651)

The goal of this complex procedure was the creation of a parallel text to the historical first edition, its "ideal" version restoring what has been lost in transcription and transmission. Groden concludes his evaluation as follows:

> In being a text-based, rather than an author-based, edition; in its use of ge-netic editing theories and methods; and in its synoptic presentation, this edition of *Ulysses* offers an alternative to dominant Anglo-American meth-ods of editing that questions and challenges the accepted paradigms. (654)

Gabler's procedure was bound to cause much controversy. Among his defenders, Jerome McGann linked his methodology with "all the central questions that have brought such a fruitful crisis to literary work in the postmodern period," and Vicky Mahaffey contended that most of the attacks against the edition are led from within the framework of traditional textual criticism, and consequently incapacitated to come to terms with Gabler's edition, which "does not share many of the premises on which the critique is based" (654-5). His most virulent critic, John Kidd has employed various effective strategies of public enunciation to make his voice heard, thus capturing a great deal of attention. However,

> all his pages of supposed analysis, and the sixty pages of tables and charts of Gabler's alleged errors and inconsistencies in his "Inquiry" into the edition, managed finally to demonstrate only two errors [...] and point to one reading that resulted from the editor's inconsistency in following his edition's own stated rules of procedure. (655)

In conclusion, Groden voices the hope that, Kidd's vociferous campaign having now subsided, the time has come for the kind of inquiry that McGann and others have called for.

III

It is just this kind of inquiry, undertaken from a clearly defined perspective, yet attentive to how Gabler's project requires a radical reconceptualization of the received textual-critical practices, that has been performed by Patrick McGee's recent Marxist study of "history and desire in *Ulysses* and *Finnegans Wake*."[4]

McGee devotes two chapters of his study, "Is there a Class for This Text?" and "The Value of Error," to the Gabler edition and the heated controversies surrounding it, significant since it is "for the political economy of social desire" (32), and therefore also for his critical project of reading *Joyce Beyond Marx*. He positions his inquiry as a follow-up to McGann's article, considered here as "one of the most significant commentaries on the Gabler edition of *Ulysses*" and praises it for its stressing "that it is more than an example of innovative textual criticism" in that its synoptic edition "accuses recent literary theory of failing to grasp its own historical object." To turn again to McGee:

> Gabler's edition implicitly criticizes those interpretative approaches to *Ulysses* and other texts that locate indeterminacy in an idealized relation between reader and text. (33)

What McGee adds to the debate is his view of Gabler's copytext in terms of the Derridean *undecidable*: "Gabler's copytext is both copy and original; its authority as copy lies in its originality as signature." Rather than a simulacrum of an original that it enables us to recover, "it is the original from which all other reading texts, including the one Joyce must have intended for the first edition, are derived." Yet at the same time as "the

[4] Patrick McGee, *Joyce Beyond Marx: History and Desire in "Ulysses" and "Finnegans Wake"* (Miami: University Press of Florida, 2001). For more, see Chapter VIII "Politics," section VIII.

projection of everything Joyce wrote onto a single *imaginary* document," the copytext of the Gabler edition of *Ulysses* "is a simulacrum—not *of* but *as* an original. The original *Ulysses* is a simulacrum." Thus, "the continuous manuscript text does not claim to be Joyce's final intention; it claims to be *what Joyce wrote*"—hence also Gabler's insistence that his text is "non-corrupted," and *not* "corrected" (36). Gabler's synoptic edition must be also faced when teaching Joyce, in view of the arising predicament "of having to teach a text that is not the text [the teacher's] students are reading" (40). McGee echoes McGann's points about the inherent postmodernism of the Gabler edition:

> In true postmodern style, the synoptic text cannibalizes on the compositional origins of *Ulysses*; it situates the composition process within the realm of social value as a simulacrum [in which] the relation of postmodern pastiche to Baudrillard's simulation model cannot be ignored. (47)

This process within the realm of social value McGee terms *symbolic exchange*, which he sees discoverable in the classroom text-teacher-student dialogue where the lesson is that

> meaning is not in the text, not in the reader, but in the dialogical relations between reader, text, and the larger contexts of culture and history. Thus, the individual text is demystified as students recognize the social values invested in it as an object of aesthetic or scholarly consumption. (47)

What the Gabler edition bears witness to is "the incorporation of the autonomous work of art into a new social formation," the message of which for McGee is: "nothing without its value, nothing outside of the system of values, nothing outside of the commodity" (47). The final paradox, for McGee, is that Gabler, "in attempting to save Joyce's writing from historical interference," has actually worked to demonstrate "the authority of history over Joyce's writing." It is precisely this "reversal of value and meaning" which inserts Gabler's project within "the space of symbolic exchange" (48).

"The Value of Error" departs from Kidd's key objection that "a cardinal rule of critical editing—*Check all transcriptions against originals*—was not observed," and its flat dismissal in Gabler's "What *Ulysses* Requires" and "Text as Process." Kidd's critique, as based on W.W. Greg's influential essay "The Rationale of the Copy-Text" and its focus on the issue of deciding for an original versus copytext in editing, is hardly applicable to Gabler's text, the central problem with *Ulysses* being that there is "no *whole* manuscript" which "the author intended for publication." In other words, "Gabler did not select a copytext—he constructed one" (54), albeit one that is "notional" in that "it is not a document but a set of relations between documents," or more specifically, "'a more critically edited version' of the original manuscript documents" (55). What Kidd thus rejects in this light is "Gabler's heavy reliance on the Rosenbach manuscript for authoritative readings of what Joyce wrote" (57), and the Kidd/Gabler opposition becomes one of "the publication as the final act of the author's intentions" as opposed to "the instability of the text in process" (58). It follows then that, neither the synoptic nor the reading text is meant to fullfill Joyce's final intentions of any sort—in fact, they both "call any such authority into question" (61). However, what both display is an expression of the *editor's final intentions*, and here McGee comments on what he perceives an inconsistency in Gabler's own theory between the 1984 "ideal" text and 1986 "non-corrupted counterpart" to the 1922 edition. This in turn serves to bring home McGee's key observation:

> The text may be determinate as a collection of traces, but the relationship between the textual variants depends on the theory of the editor and the institutional framework within which the editorial event takes place. (62)

In conclusion, McGee contends that Gabler's edition has transformed "the language of the text [...] into the discourse of theory," which to him means that "every 'public text' is, to some extent, hypothetical." Whatever the tensions and ambivalences, both Gabler and Kidd have succeeded in rupturing "the naiveté of Joyce scholars about the transparent authority of the text they teach." (63)

IV

It was also Hans Walter Gabler who wrote the general introductory essay on "Joyce's Text in Progress" for Attridge's *Cambridge Companion to James Joyce*.[5] Here, the Joyce of Gabler's approach is regarded as being "as much a reader as a writer of texts":

> anticipating long in advance the conceptualizations of present-day text theory, he discovered the structural and semiotic analogies of language-encoded texts and experience-encoded reality. [...] Learning to read the world in this way was an act of intellectual self-liberation, and reading it in this way was a new experience. (213)

For Gabler, the notion of "writing as a process of transubstantiation" springs from the fact that "to circumscribe, and thus make readable, the wholeness of things means to unlock them, in a kind of deconstruction, out of their apparently amorphous contingencies" (215). His analysis of the notes and drafts for *Exiles* brings him to view the play as an example of "the process of transforming reading into writing" (217) In *Portrait*, Joyce's "epiphany-texts" are used as "pre-texts from within his own *oeuvre*," this without any "indication of representing the order of composition" (218), whereas the author's life as a pretext is removed from the text of the novel as a result of Joyce's "intervening reading and writing processes" (219). Of *Ulysses*, Gabler observes that it is prominently "in a

---

[5] Hans Walter Gabler, "Joyce's Text in Progress," in *The Cambridge Companion to James Joyce*, ed. Derek Attridge (Cambridge: Cambridge University Press, 1990).

mode of rewriting within Joyce's own oeuvre, as well as on the level of concerns about structure that predate the actual writing," that "the beginnings of *Ulysses* first manifest themselves." The parallel between a Martello Tower fragment and Stephen's recognition of himself as a fallen Icarus as late as "Scylla" shows that "that the earliest writing for *Ulysses* from the autobiographical fountainhead originated in Joyce's endeavors [...] to define a line between *A Portrait* and *Ulysses*" (223). Surveying the individual episode manuscripts, Gabler discerns "a suggestion" in their appearance of "a descent from a pre-existing text." What this suggests is "a manner of composition by which Joyce thought out at length, and in minute detail, the structures and phrasings of whole narrative sections before committing them to paper" (224). Also of note is "the unwavering structural stability of most of the novel's episodes [...] with the exception of 'Aeolus'," a stability in which "no episode changes shape, but retains the structural outline it possesses in the fair copy" (226).

The famous antiphon from "The Sirens," appears to Gabler as an instance of "a typically Joycean set of notes" entering "the published writing so as to render explicit a dynamic dependence of text upon a pre-text" and by the manuscript evidence reveals that "the antiphon was prefixed to the entire chapter when the latter was already extant in fair copy" (228). Crucial in the process of Joyce's rewriting is the "Circe" episode, implying that "the preceding narrative of Bloomsday is made to function as if it constituted not a fiction, but itself an order of empiric reality." In "Circe,"

> Joyce may thus be seen to embrace the full consequences of his creative artistry: by no other pre-text than from within his own *oeuvre* could he have rocked the foundations of traditional narrative. (232)

The *Wake* notebooks, finally, present mere "preliminaries to all subsequent constitution of compositional text" (233-4). For the second half of Joyce's writing years, "we possess in abundance sketches and working drafts, fair copies, typescripts, segment publications and multi-revisional proofs that [...] relate in a far more complex ways than anything to be observed in the organization of the writing for *Ulysses*." Gabler ends on a prospective note, claiming that

> indeed, to do justice to Joyce's creative artistry in Work in Progress, Joyce scholarship may yet require a new critical outlook and a new corporate experience. (234)

As will become evident, it was also in the year 1990 that this "new critical outlook" began to form itself.

V

Jean-Michel Rabaté has been a major presence within this work, whether in respect to his deconstructionist formation, Lacanian erudition or focus on the broad mechanisms of modernism and modernity. Hence, without including in this chapter at least a brief illustration of how his complex approach to matters Joycean is informed by his continuous and expert study of the notebooks, I would be guilty of a serious omission. As Rabaté's *Joyce upon the Void* states in its subtitle, its main concern is *The Genesis of Doubt*.[6] Published in 1991, the book concentrates on a main concern, and also includes a collection of essays culled from a period no shorter than a decade. It also marks the end of the highpoint of deconstructive practice in Joyce studies.

The theme around which the individual forays are centred is identified with "the idea of doubt seen in a genetic perspective" (xi). Doubt, via a reference to the doubting Thomas and from there to Thomas Aquinas (marking the emergence of an Eliotian "strange third"), is regarded as having "always retained a functional value for Joyce" in that it "provided him with his major faith: his faith in himself, which alone could underpin his faith in the real world." This theme, Rabaté makes explicit, is approached from "a genetic perspective"—which the author associates with the methodology of the Paris genetic school formed around the ITEM (*Institut des Textes et Manuscrits Modernes*)—aiming to destabilize the old notion of text (referenced is Louis Hay's famous maxim that "the text does not exist") and open up "the traditional fixity of a given text" by including within the critical discussion "the multiple layers of all the drafts, proofs, manuscripts," so as to face the critical task with the necessity "to confront a semantic multiplicity" (xvii). Or, in an etymological explanation,

> a *text* has therefore to be understood as the unstable product of an act of *texture*, *textus* had to be understood as the past participle of *texere* (to weave, to braid); *text* became synonymous with *weft* or *web*, and [...] [all] implied an author looking more and more like Penelope, undoing in the night of his or her unconscious what he or she pretended to write by day. (xvii)

Still in the introduction, Rabaté acknowledges the importance of the recent Gabler edition, and notes how, significantly for his concern with doubt, "the recent controversy over the new edition of *Ulysses* has centred around the reintroduction of the word 'love'" (xix), referring to the notorious passage in *U* 9.427-31. The question for him exemplifies "what stands out so symptomatically in current discussions about the meaning of textuality, and the loss of single, identifiable text" (xxi), in that doubt, and not necessity, "offers a key not only to obsessional neurosis," as in the case of Freud's "Rat-man," whose doubt of love was "diffused over everything else," but, "because of the great 'suspension' it affords," to "the essence of Life" (xxv).

My major concern in presenting Rabaté's book here, as has been stated, is to show the ways in which his genetic perspective informs

---

[6] Jean-Michel Rabaté, *Joyce upon the Void: The Genesis of Doubt* (London: MacMillan, 1991).

Rabaté's forays into the theme of doubt, of which one chapter will serve as a suitable example. It is in Chapter IV on "Wakean Cryptogenetics" that Rabaté's genetic interests surface in his argument most clearly and productively. Rabaté begins by discussing what is often considered a first artistic self-applied *avant-textual* analysis—Edgar Allan Poe's *Philosophy of Composition*. In this text, Poe allows his "readers a 'peep behind the scenes,'" which yields "an idealized reconstruction of his intentions" and of the composition process, "whose redaction is then no different from the solving of a mathematical problem" (71). The artificiality of the process described by Poe is derived from his conception of "an inverse genesis," in which "the words must be chosen and deployed in terms of their formal properties, not their meaning" (72). The text invoked by Poe is essentially of a "cyclical nature," in which "stereotypic repetition of identical phonemic units supposes a complex drama of interlocution, which situates dialogic tension within the character." Invoked both by structuralists like Jakobson and more recently genetic critics,

> Poe's theories are capable of overcoming a too-rigid distinction between formalism and geneticism, since he introduces the very modern notion of a text understood as the field of all its drafts, preparative schemes and authorial variants, and relates this expanding textuality to a sequential practice of composition. (73)

Rabaté then proceeds to note the point of resemblance between Poe and Joyce, both of whom held true art to be a process of composition in which, "by an extremely elaborate calculus," the artist "produces a 'model' of the universe which aims at a precise *effect* on the reader"; for Joyce then, "the effect lies in the totality of impression produced by an experience of the limits of language, and by a pleasurable awareness of the subject's swooning and fading presence" (77).

Just exactly how this effect was "composed" is illustrated in Rabaté's discussion of a February 1923 letter to Shaw Weaver in which Joyce remarks on the "heaps of notes about the *Odyssey* which I could not fit in," and on "sort[ing] these out according to a brand new system I have invented for the greater complication and torment of myself." This, Rabaté notes, is "how Joyce came to devise his 'sigla,' an invention which [...] must be seen in its proper context: the sigla are a kind of Lullian mnemotechnics designed to prevent Joyce from forgetting what he himself has written, what he had meant" (78). Relatively soon, however, these sigla were to undergo a considerable shift in purpose:

> Joyce's sigla, originally mere "abbreviations" for the main characters, soon came to designate those parts of the book devoted to them; the narrational calculus indexing linguistic units and attributing items [...] turned into the underground logic controlling the balance of individual chapters and books (80).

However, if from a classificatory convenience they end up as complex ciphers which are glossed as if they were ideograms, this must have in itself been due to a complex process of reidentification, or, in Rabaté term, "remotivation" of the sigla's function. Of this "iconic remotivation," Rabaté observes that here, "the mimetic language only imitates itself, comments upon itself, refers back to itself because it is never identical with itself"—the sigla, in other words, are "not identities, but pigeonholes for functions which can be occupied by a vast variety of real or imaginary persons" (89).

At this point, Rabaté turns to Chapter II.2, whose combination of "a history lesson and a geometry lesson" also includes a demonstration of the sigla "in full view" (90). His analysis focuses in particular on a passage beginning in *FW* 264.15, its point is being "to show how the most complex textual work can be founded on extremely simple principles which pertain to an almost mechanical borrowing from sources which have no literary merit whatsoever" (91). The chapter's composition, testified to by Joyce himself as "the most difficult of all," reveals "a certain break [...] linked to growing personal problems and also to the logic of the *Wake*'s wordmachine" (101). The textual dismemberment, in Rabaté's psychoanalytic reading, is "the answer to textual incest," which "creates a dynamics of centrifugal versus centripetal movements which cross and recoup themselves around the letter" (105). Issy's leave-taking with the phrase "kissists my exits" (*FW* 280.27) is found to echo Goetz von Berlichingen's famous taunt of "kiss my arse," betraying the fact that "there can be no central signifier in her idiom that would not have been immediately subverted" (111).

In "conclusion," one of the noteworthy points made by Rabaté is his question after "a thinking" implicit to Joyce's writing:

> Is there then a thinking at work in Joyce's writing? Does he really "think" or is he only a master of style [...]? Does he redefine our concepts, reshape the world, or does he merely let his word-machines make their own calculations? [Depending on one's answers], one will opt either for a Joyce seen as a systematic artificer who masters all the styles and languages, who aims finally at calculating even the undecidable [...] or for a Joyce who invests language as a pure medium, never allowing any foreign consideration to interfere and prevent him from experiments, however daring they may be, who is impelled by his logic to the creation of an autonomous universe; [...] on the one hand, the Joyce described by Derrida; on the other, the Joyce seen by Cage. (217)

Crucial, in this respect, is the notion of the "epiphany," usually conceived as the main building-block of Joyce's writing. However, in the case of the *Wake*, Rabaté warns that

> [i]t would be idle to look for "epiphanies" in Joyce's drafts and notebooks for *Finnegans Wake*, although the term is still used in most presentations of their contents. What is there which allows one to distinguish between a

quotation and the account of a dream, between a sequence of foreign terms and a moment of personal vision? (221)

The concluding question of how Joyce, "being more a 'sceptic' than an 'idealist,'" could write a universal history, is answered by reference to the central thematic concern of Rabaté's book, but also to the essence of Joyce's creative method:

> The answer lay in the deeper comprehension of what *skepsis* meant, and implied a synthetic approach to universal culture which alone might enable him to overcome the limitations of a doubting Thomas [...], enclosed in a maze of private fictions and puns. (222)

VI

The "new critical outlook" called for by Gabler before a rewarding digression toward Rabaté's book began to take shape in David Hayman's influential *The Wake in Transit*,[7] published in the same year as Attridge's edited *Companion*. Introducing the term nodality, Hayman's is among the earliest studies to combine an extensive analysis of the *Wake* notebooks with an attempted theoretical conceptualisation of Joyce's method of note-taking, as well as his creative artistic methodology. The present overview will focus on the "Introduction" and first chapter of Hayman's groundbreaking study.

In his "Introduction," Hayman states as one of the goals of his study "to disclose how Joyce managed the transition from the diurnal to the nocturnal, the waking to the sleeping, the individual consciousness to the universal subconscious." In doing so, he also intends to

> address the question of the seeming randomness of Joyce's notetaking, establish relationships, study contexts, and attempt to draw rational conclusions concerning Joyce's methods at different moments in the book's early development. (2)

Acknowledging Danis Rose and John O'Hanlon's *Understanding Finnegans Wake: A Guide to the Narrative of James Joyce's Masterpiece*[8] as "the first *Wake* study based on the manuscripts," Hayman also voices the reservation that "Rose's expertise in manuscript details is not always matched by his critical acumen." Rather than revealing some fundamental "understanding" of the final text, Hayman's present aims at making sense of the manuscripts themselves, countering the prevailing tendency to perceive them "as random and chaotic jottings" (6). Hayman then goes on to provide "a bare-bones account of the major developments in the manuscript history of *Finnegans Wake*," meant to "situate the argument of this book in relation to the novel's full structural evolution" (8). Commenting

[7] David Hayman, *The Wake in Transit* (Ithaca and London: Cornell University Press, 1990).
[8] Danis Rose and John O'Hanlon, *Understanding "Finnegans Wake": A Guide to the Narrative of James Joyce's Masterpiece* (New York: Garland, 1982).

on the process in general, Hayman thinks it best to see it "in relation to turning points, those rare and revealing lapses in the writing process, moments of indecision and choice foregrounded by both notebooks and manuscripts" (15). He then proceeds to situate eleven such moments:

(1)   note-consolidation and notetaking for the large "Scribbledehobble" notebook under headings taken from Joyce's earlier work (late 1922-early 1923);
(2)   the shift from theme-motivated notetaking under headings to more passage-oriented preparations in the small and more portable note-books (early 1923);
(3)   the drafting of the early sketches destined to be the armature of the *Wake* (spring-summer 1923);
(4)   the abandonment of plans to make "Tristan and Isolde" the parodic focus of the book (summer 1923);
(5)   the gradual discovery through the notetaking process of the everyday (or night(couple and the earliest version of HCE's crime (spring-summer 1923);
(6)   the drafting of the Here Comes Everybody sketch followed by the composition of the three male chapters for Book I (fall 1923);
(7)   the composition of ALP's Letter counteracting the fall of the male ego and reconceptualizing the book into a balanced male/female develop-ment (winter 1923-24) [...];
(8)   the composition of the situating catechism that comprises chapter I.6 (spring 1926);
(9)   the composition of the geometry lesson at first called "The Triangle" for II.2 and the conceptualization of Book II (summer 1926);
(10) the composition of the overture for the *Wake* or I.1 (fall 1926);
(11) the drafting from previous notes and the reformulation of the first half of II.2 [...]. (15-6)

Following these turning points, Hayman's argument (as presented on page 16) is set off with a discussion of the "Scribbledehobble" ink notes (Chapter I), traces the development and role of the early sketches (Chapter II), and proceeds with a detailed analysis of the sources and evolution of the crucial Tristan and Isolde theme (Chapter III), together with its accompa-nying notes which trace the early development of HCE and ALP (Chapter IV). The fifth chapter deals with HCE's crime and its narrative conse-quences, followed by an account of the seminal dreams in Chapter VI. Finally, Chapter VII traces the composition of ALP's Letter, initiating the *Wake*'s powerful feminine plot. As a whole, the book stands as a testi-mony to Hayman's conviction

> that we can and should use manuscript evidence as an extension of the text and that by retracting the meanders of the creative process, we can deepen our understanding of the proliferating and open-ended textual envi-ronment that is *Finnegans Wake*. (17)

Clearly, the concept that has proven most influential in subsequent ge-netic *Wake* criticism has been the one of *nodality* as noticed and theorized in the first and second chapters, respectively. It will be on these two chapters, then, that the present exposé will focus.

Chapter I "Preparatory to Anything Else" deals with the "Scribbledehobble" notebook as reflecting "the writer's attempts to bridge the gap between the earlier imaginative efforts and the prospective one" (19). That for instance the development of "Pop" under "Eveline," but especially under "A Painful Case," prefigures "the crime of HCE by alluding to voyeurism and incest and hinting at scandal" is due to two complementary tendencies:

> On the one hand, the writer was using his early work to point himself toward unexplored regions. On the other, he was mining it for profound psychic echoes, attempting, that is, to psychoanalyze or perhaps to "deconstruct" his own creative impulses. (23)

The "Scribbledehobble" notebook is also the locus of the total of seven "sketches," which include "a drunken scene and a semi-adulterous seduction" (the Roderick O'Connor & Tristan skit), followed by "the two mockhagiographic sequences: a broadly portrayed dumb show (Kevin) and a farcical disputation (Patrick and Berkeley)," the seed for the fifth sketch "Here Comes Everybody" dealing with the "defense of the ur-HCE, Pop," a "sixth passage, Mamalujo" and "Anna Livia's famous and truly seminal Letter" (29-30). Hayman proposes to view these sketches as "prime nodes," noting that "whatever Joyce's enthusiasm for the book's title, his secretiveness about its structure and especially about the five unpublished sketches is of greater moment." Given that he arranged for separate publication of every other set piece, Hayman asks after the reason "why he never thought to publish these entertaining and relatively accessible snippets." (32) The answer he gives is that these provided the very pattern, the "nodal infrastructure," of his work's narrative framings:

> The existence of important chains and interlocking systems of allusions to these passages suggests that, in casting those disparate but profoundly symbiotic sketches as the contact points of his fiction, Joyce set in motion the nodal procedures that would guarantee coherence. (35)

The second chapter "Nodality: The Disposition and Reverberations of the Sketches" proceeds from the concluding statement of the previous one by defining the term "node" as applying

> to a more or less clearly developed and displayed cluster of signifiers to which reference is made systematically in the course of the novel. Such clusters tend to generate, above and beyond the structure of chapters and sequences, a coherent but unhighlighted system of relationships.

This nodal perspective has a crucial bearing on any understanding of the work's composition:

Joyce's goal was to produce the effect of the random in a work that was in fact meticulously controlled and crammed full of interactive (and often conflicting) patterns. Ultimately, the nodal infrastructure is only one of many sorts of patterns, but the manuscript evidence suggests that it figured among the earliest and was decisive in the later development of the book. (37)

Hayman proceeds by distinguishing among four levels of nodality: "a well-articulated, free-standing textual circumstance" (first level) which will find "strong secondary resonances strategically located elsewhere" (second level). A "weaker allusion will be more broadly scattered" (tertiary level). This last one is usually found "supplemented by a fourth level composed of highly stylized and broadly scattered allusions." Taken together, "these materials constitute the fully articulated nodal system" (37-8). The privileged role of the early sketches as "prime nodes" is due "partly to Joyce's decision to unite them, but ultimately to their placement at the beginning, middle, and end of the book" (38), examples of which would be what Hayman calls "mini-systems" such as the Jute and Mutt/Butt and Taff/Muta and Juva dialogues or the two Shaunish fables that coalesce around the geometry lesson of II.2 (39). What the nodal system guarantees is

the constant presence of varieties of narrative experience in the absence of coherent threads of narrative discourse. [...] Joyce's determination to build the *Wake* around the early sketches clearly enabled and conditioned the networks of echoing and interacting passages. (41)

Further analysis unveils each secondary node as "in turn the source of at least one further nodal system." One example of this is "the professional account given in I.5" which, by pointing up the sacred book analogy, "[turns] the text dug up from the kitchen midden by the neighborhood hen and rescued by a schoolboy into a fragment of the lost past, a mysterious scripture" (45). The various examples of the different stratifications of nodality reveal that "because the nodal systems were not preplanned, but rather grew into and with the text, each of them sets its own rules" (48). This can be seen in the Tristan and Isolde nodality which is markedly different from the one of the Letter in "its generative function" and its "integrity and omnipresence" (50). Further explorations finally yield a list of nine categories of the nodal infrastructure, presented in an "order of importance":

(1) The early sketches through the Letter.
(2) Passages devoted to character exposition: the profiles and monologues.
(3) Symmetrical passages such as the brother confrontations and the fables.
(4) Expositions of major themes: the fall, the flood, the crime, historical decay, sexual activity, sexual deviance, writing, language, etc.
(5) Exposure of aspects of the landscape: river, mountain, tree, stone, city, park, sea, fauna and flora.

(6) Allusive parallels drawn from history, religion, and literature.

(7) Allusions to Joyce, his work, and his family.

(8) Key rhythmic clusters: the tonality of the river, the legalistic "tion" references […], the Quinet passage, HCE's stutter, the thunder words, song and poetic tags, etc.

(9) Foreign-language word clusters. (54-5)

Hayman concludes by observing that in "composing *Finnegans Wake*, Joyce was neither filling in the blanks of a prefabricated structural plan nor indulging in free association." Instead, his effort was "partly to make language obey *his* rules rather than its own, partly to exploit the potential of words and syntax, partly to discover and disclose the quintessential 'givens' everywhere." In other words, his was

> an effort to assert a self (by imposing a pattern or a flux of patterns) or rather to win a self back from the language over which he repeatedly gains and as often loses mastery. (55)

VII

One of the most stimulating while also (as will become evident later on) controversial versions of "the story of the formation of *Finnegans Wake*," was penned by Danis Rose and published under the title *The Textual Diaries of James Joyce*.[9]

The controversy of this particular account is foregrounded already in the preface, for it is a story of how *Finnegans Wake* "began as another book entirely, *Finn's hotel*, and of how it grew and changed not once, but several times" (viii). The first chapter provides "A brief history of the diaries," presenting the whole study as "a retrospective and prospective overview of this massive detritus [in the critical examination of the notebooks]: to consider and set forth what we do know, to repudiate misconceived models and theories, and to delimit what we do not yet know" (8). The co-edited (with Rose's participation) 1978 publication of the *James Joyce Archive*[10] was coterminous with Rose's work on *The Index Manuscript* of the *Wake*. In the "General Introduction" he outlined the arguments as to the fundamental nature of both the text of *Finnegans Wake* and the extra-textual material contained in the notebooks, which "crystallized in three logically separate propositions: in modern parlance, in a theoretical matrix, which can profitably be restated here:

1. *Finnegans Wake* is primarily an ordered assemblage of units (words and phrases) taken from the notebooks.
2. The notebooks are primarily compilations of units derived from external sources.

[9] Danis Rose, *The Textual Diaries of James Joyce* (Dublin: The Lilliput Press, 1995).

[10] Michael Groden (general editor), Hans Walter Gabler, David Hayman, Walton A. Litz and Danis Rose, eds., *The James Joyce Archive* (63 vols., New York & London: Garland, 1977-79).

3. The translation of each unit from notebook to draft was intermediated by referring that unit to one of a small number of contextual invariants. (16-8)

In Rose's own general view, the *Wake*, "famously the world's most idiosyncratic, eccentric and creative work," appears "in truth an *assemblage* made up of bits and pieces of sentences freely plagiarized by Joyce from the writings of other men and women" (18).

After these preliminaries, Rose proceeds with the space-time axis, providing a chronology of the notebooks (containing a total of forty-nine primary extant notebooks and eighteen transcriptions), "the only" of its sort "which takes seriously the idea [...] that the set of notebooks as a whole constitutes a continuous sequence of notetaking" (22). The extended list of notebooks, running over 15 pages,

> comprises one long continuous allincluding diachronic integument, Joyce having paid no heed to the documents as documents in themselves. It is for this reason that the whole tale that this meta-diary relates remains for a total edition to tell. (37)

What the subsequent detailed cataloguing and accompanying discussion drive at, therefore, is an outline of the chronological arrangement of documents deployed in the composition of *Work in Progress* as well as *Finnegans Wake*. Rose details the compositional process, which involved copious notetaking, sketch-drafting along with further revisions and interrupted by several bouts of writer's block, that occurred when Joyce transferred the notes from his notebooks onto the drafts. These transfers, Rose takes pains to point out, resulted in a re-deployment of a word, sentence, or textual unit, far removed from its original source. It is in the last section, "Technical," that some of the theoretical implications of Rose's chronological approach reach the surface.

First of all, Rose intends to "avoid an anarchic and ultimately meaningless proliferation of interpretations" by "*restricting* (in the work of exegesis) the meaning of a unit to that which it originally carried" (147). Stated even more radically, "it is solely through the index connection that we can analyse the larger patterns of Joyce's work in progress" (148). Supplementing these two implications to do with questions of hermeneutics and interpretation, and lacking nothing of their radicalness, Rose concludes by a reference to Joyce himself and his creative project by stating firmly that "we can exclude Joyce's knowing involvement" from the *Wake*'s creative process:

> our clarification of this last point should be of some considerable concern to those who struggle to oppose what they view as the usurpation of the Creator Joyce by Joyce the Assembler. (170)

The notebooks are not "a part of the draft record," but rather "belong to a purely compilational phase of the work in progress antecedent to the act of composition," or, put differently, "the words were not yet Joyce's until they left the notebook page" (180). The implications of Rose's analysis for Joyce's art ultimately lie

> not where the writer suggests that we should seek them—in imagined dream representation—but rather in Joyce's engagement in the cold, premeditated act of appropriation itself. (180-1)

IX

The fifth issue of *European Joyce Studies* brought a volume edited by David Hayman, and devoted entirely to *Genetic Studies in Joyce*.[11] Its broad range of topics and excellent introduction shall therefore make it one of the crucial works of textual genetics to be examined here.

Hayman's "Introduction" opens by contending that

> a careful study of the notes taken when Joyce was preparing to write a passage can legitimately spawn a whole range of approaches to both the creative process and to the completed text, approaches that would not claim to be authoritative (in any sense) but which would bring us closer to the procedures of the writer and the text. (5)

It is necessary to note that this "careful study" has been made possible by the monumental publication of the 63-volume *James Joyce Archive* released in 1978 by Garland Publishing, itself "a memory bank to which we can go for information unavailable from other sources," the presence of which "has effectively changed the face of Joyce criticism" (6). Hayman aligns the contemporary genetic Joycean discourse with the French tradition of *la Critique Génétique*, which he insists should not be viewed as a new phenomenon, nor should it be equated with philology, "which has always used manuscript materials to establish lost or flawed literary texts" (7). As a "good candidate for the title genetic criticism" Hayman considers "the new bibliography," the method pioneered by Hans Gabler for his edition of *Ulysses*. Hayman's view on the Gabler edition is the following:

> As it is, the edition shows at times editorial hubris, claiming to be saving Joyce from himself by restoring words and punctuation he omitted and ignoring the fact that Joyce tended to write around such omissions where they were unintended. (8)

Genetic criticism in general, to Hayman's mind, can be best used "not to prove any preconceived truths," but rather "to disclose by the scrupulous use of evidence and theory what manuscripts have to tell us about the composition process and hence the creative procedures" (10). The genealogy he draws dates back to the mid-1950s, and early 1960s, which saw the publication of Hayman's own *Joyce et Mallarmé* and A. Walton

[11] David Hayman, Sam Slote, eds., *Genetic Studies in Joyce* (Amsterdam: Edition Rodopi, 1995).

Litz's *The Art of James Joyce* respectively, both widely considered to be "the first two works using the genetic approach to Joyce." As a special branch of textual geneticism, Hayman singles out the Joyce Studies Group associated with ITEM (*Institut des textes et manuscrits modernes*) founded by Claude Jacquet following the 1978 *Archive* publication, and featuring such prominent Joyceans as Jean-Michel Rabaté, Daniel Ferrer or Laurent Milesi, whose production, for Hayman, is marked by "the extent to which they have digested contemporary theories of all sorts and applied them intelligently to manuscript studies" (11). Surveying the present collection, Hayman sees it as reflecting the current variety within the discipline, as well as pointing to its key split:

> it is a characteristic of our genetic critical enterprise or perhaps of the state of the discipline [...] that different critics come to different conclusions about the same piece of evidence. [...] Since few of us make our principle focus the identification of sources, the work of the theoretically oriented ITEMists and my own work and methods, along with that of some of my students, tends to antagonize my more philologically-inclined colleagues. (16)

This difference is ascribed, rather too simply perhaps, to "the nature of the manuscripts and notebooks," which provide critics with "grounds to form different patterns as aids to the comprehension of aspects of the macro-text," This is in turn related to the *Wake* itself, which "too lends itself to multiple rereadings, and there is ample evidence that Joyce was continually exploring such avenues as he exploited the implications of his own procedures in both notebooks and text" (17). The overarching belief of Hayman on the issue of the "usefulness" of the manuscripts is that

> [a]fter all, even for Joyce, the manuscripts were more than inert pieces of paper. They are featured in the treatment of ALP's letter, Shem's scrivening, and elsewhere as part of the matter of the *Wake*, its poignantly written substance. I believe that this volume indicates how that substance helps enlarge and illuminate the years of gestation as well as their result.

In essence, Hayman concludes, each of the following essays forms its own theory, and performs its own application thereof, since the two crucial concerns he perceives as forming their common grounding are

> the nature and theoretical underpinnings of genetic criticism of Joyce and especially of *Finnegans Wake*, and some of the many ways that theory can be applied to the creative situation reflected in the notes and manuscripts. (18)

The presentation of the volume here will focus on some of the more theoretically-grounded pieces, seen as providing the theoretical underpinning of other, no less worthwhile or interesting, but simply more practically oriented papers. Three essays have been selected on these grounds: two are almost overtly engaged in a theoretical dispute while the third presents a productive revisitation of the *Ulyssean* genetics.

A crucial, if not *the* crucial, formulation of an idiosyncratic theory comes already in the first paper of the collection. Geert Lernout's "The *Finnegans Wake* Notebooks and Radical Philology" begins with an historical survey of Joycean genetics, including the two early studies by Hayman and Litz, the 1978 publication of the *Archive*, and the ensuing formation of the ITEM group. Following this introductory overview, Lernout moves on to apply the crucial argument of his *The French Joyce*, "a radical contextualization of Joyce criticism," to Joycean genetics, a contextualization which is necessary due to the fact that

> national and/or critical approaches to Joyce's work differ so much that it is not just useful but also necessary to consider them as separate paradigms in need of reciprocal translation. (26)

Rose and O'Hanlon's *Understanding Finnegans Wake* presents "an explicit theory about the nature of the notebooks that is radically different from that of David Hayman or the French." The difference lies in that "both Hayman and *ITEM* start their discussion with the special position of *Scribbledehobble*, which is seen as a channel between *Ulysses* and the new book, whereas "Danis Rose and John O'Hanlon [...] have shown that *Scribbledehobble* cannot be the first of the post-*Ulysses* notebooks" (31). On a more general level, the difference is that in Hayman's and ITEM's work "the notebooks are read as a literary text which is at the same time a record of the creative process and that process itself," whereas for Lernout, "any serious study of the notebooks leads either to a consideration of their status in the chronology of Joyce's work on *Finnegans Wake* or to the search for sources." Thus, Lernout opposes what he calls the maximalist conception of "text" such as the one found in Hayman's *The 'Wake' in Transit*. The reason posited is that

> [a]s long as we do not know exactly when the different handwritings in *Scribbledehobble* were entered, it may well be a waste of time and energy to speculate on what Joyce was meditating on in the first year or so of writing *Finnegans Wake*.

It is at this point that Lernout's thesis begins to emerge:

> The problem with reading notebook material in the way in which we read *Finnegans Wake* is paradoxically that we will create context and coherence where there is none. [...] When we take human life (in casu our present understanding of the *Wake*) as the ultimate purpose of the evolution of the world, we are forced to misunderstand the nature of evolution (the hits and misses, the changes of direction, the whole haphazard business that the writing of the *Wake* undoubtedly was). (34)

The procedure practiced (and argued for) by Lernout therefore lies somewhere "between David Hayman's elegant readings" and those of "the *ITEM*-group," which are charged (specifically in the work of Daniel Ferrer) on account of their quests for "absolute certainty" in their attribution of meaning to the notebook entries; it thus ends up being "far less coherent than that of Hayman" and devoid of "the *absolute certainty* of Daniel Ferrer" (38). This procedure is termed "a radically historical study" and also comprises, apart from "tracing sources," the study of "the exact link between the source and Joyce's notes, in order to establish the reason(s) why Joyce was reading this particular text and what he planned to do with the material" (41).

An example of this is Lernout's recognition of some of the VI.B3 entries on Wagner and Mathilde Wesendonck as originating from the French translation of Schuré's *Femmes inspiratrices et poètes associateurs.* Lernout's "tentative conclusions" foreground that what is at stake in the notebooks controversy is "the role and importance of the notebooks in our reading of the *Wake*, and this importance is not so self-evident as the practitioners of the discipline have made it appear" (45). In other words, unlike for David Hayman or some of the *ITEM* scholars, for Lernout, "the notebooks are not diaries or journals," nor are they "a writer's journal" (46). The "radical philological approach" advocated by Lernout may well constitute "a theoretical dead-end," but Lernout prefers to hope that

> it signals the end of a certain type of theory and the beginning of a practice that will require the concerted efforts of scores of Joyceans on both sides of the Atlantic for most of the next decade. (48)

Daniel Ferrer's "Reflection on a Discarded Set of Proofs" discusses a set of "Circe" corrections from the last days of 1921 which "represent the last throes of a process of accretion that resulted in the transformation of two lines of dialogue into a 20 page long scene," while also enjoying "a particular, *marginal* status," and thus providing "a good vantage point for some general remarks about genetic criticism" (49). The "particular marginality" of the set is due to their being marked, not by the traditional *bon à tirer*, but by a plea: "corrections supplémentaires si encore possibles JJ," thereby voicing

> the desperate effort to keep open the possibilities of *writing* [...] and to postpone the closure inherent to the *written* text, [which] is representative of the Modern predilection for potentialities and processes over the finished work of art [...] the current development of genetic criticism is undoubtedly part of the same tendency. (50)

Due to the fact that the set arrived "too late" to be included, it remains peculiarly marginal—willed by Joyce, and yet never accepted due to the temporal restraints of its particular moment. Ferrer concludes by pointing to how incidents like this one can provoke genetics into refashioning its own critical tools:

> [Groden] has shown how *Ulysses* as a whole is the result of the layering of three different large temporal contexts, corresponding to what he calls the *Early, Middle* and *Last Stages*. Here, we have a chance to observe an interference between two micro-contexts with the Last Stage. [...] This example raises in an unusual but very acute way the problem of the interpretation of genetic paradigms. (52-3)

In discussing the current genetic approaches, Jed Deppman's "Hallowed Chronickles and Exploytes of King Rodericke O'Connor from Joyce's Earliest Drafts to the End of Causal Historie" follows Lernout's dividing line, while occupying, and arguing for, the very opposite side. Deppman distinguishes between "practical" and "theoretical" geneticism.

Outlining the former first, Deppman characterizes *practical* geneticism as one seeking to "uncover the source material for notebook entries, or to demonstrate that certain notebook material has been incorporated into the *Wake*." He immediately proceeds by pointing to its difficulties: "obstacles such as Joyce's hand, the fragmentary nature of the notebooks, the multiplicity of source materials, and the complexity of the *Wake* itself," all these make it "an understatement to say that practical geneticism is painstaking and challenging." Moreover,

> purely practical projects are apt to be unsatisfying, as the goal of such devoted research remains ambiguous: practical geneticists always run the risk of resembling the hands-on archaeologist who turns up endless artifacts and then leaves them unexplained, preferring the practical work of the detective to the theoretical murk of the inductive. (179)

On a final note, Deppman observes that since the practical work consists "solely in the *act of finding* itself," its value thus lies in "its use in future criticism," a rationale according to which "practical geneticism ultimately depends upon the more theoretically-oriented criticism which it tends to view as uncertain and even superfluous."

"Theoretical geneticism," for Deppman seems to "revel in precisely that ineluctable modality of speculation most abjured by practical geneticists." Hence, it constitutes

> an attempt to give another dimension to the finished literary text by interrogating the documents which make up the work in progress [... aiming to] evaluate in theoretical terms both the components and the composition of the evolving text.

The difficulty inherent in this approach is that "theoretical criticism must also wager and then demonstrate *that* the text evolves in a way susceptible to study," and the verb *evolve* is "already too much to say, for the very word a theoretical critic chooses to describe the movement of the

Wake is through time is already an ante—i.e., in what sense does the text 'evolve'?" Unwilling to go into this debate, Deppman claims instead that textual criticism

> does better to defer decision on questions of this kind, and gamble, rather, that something can be learned by rereading/redeciphering the notebooks and manuscripts along with the *Wake* itself.

The following essay, then, is "just such a project for the oldest member of recorded Wakean history. Roderick O'Conor, next" (180). The underlying assumption in "II. Roderick O'Conor, Text," is that

> emendations and additions are always signals of discontent, and markers of the intending of the text; it is for these textual intentions, inscribed in each successive version of the sketch, that I will look. (181-2)

The question, "why does Joyce return to Roderick?" (one of the earliest sketches to be composed and among the last ones to be actually integrated within the *Wake*), is tentatively answered by establishing a link "on the basis of narrative experimentation" between this textual snippet and the "Cyclops" episode from *Ulysses*; for

> in order to grasp what Joyce is doing in Roderick, we need more than a thematic idea of what he's done in "Cyclops"; we need a precise idea of the narrative technicity of that chapter, for it is on the order of technique, and not theme, that the Roderick sketch diverges from "Cyclops." (185)

As long as "the narrative techniques Joyce employs in Cyclops may satirize and compete," but still "they grant access to direct, opposing statements of historical interpretation" (186), then analogously

> while it may seem that Joyce was concerned primarily with the transposition of the events of the fallen king's life into a contemporary pub, *he wasn't actually*. The *materia prima* for the Roderick sketch is thus not the king, but all the accounts of him. (191)

What the 1923 Roderick sketch shows then is that "although Joyce is interested in the pure *techné* of narration, there is already a move toward freeing this *techné* from the service of historian and narrator." Expression in the absence of a trustworthy narrator becomes "the free activity of received forms, none of them pure, all of them always already encountered as ready-to-hand" (194). At the other end of the process, "the late stages of integration" of the Roderick sketch into the *Wake*" can help to "illuminate the links to ALP, the letter, and the crime plot" (201). Which they, in Deppman's conclusion, do—with reference to ALP's "traumscapt" (*FW* 623.35-624.05), echoing as it does "the 'rased' voice of Roderick, raised, razed, and never erased, a forwarding phrase from the 'ancient days'—the earliest dreams of a *Wake*" (202).

X

Responding to Lernout's critique of Ferrer's article and seeking to recuperate Derrida's conception of the sign as of importance for textual genetics is a section from Louis Armand's *Incendiary Devices*,[12] whose psychoanalytical thrust is discussed elsewhere.[13] Armand points out to the evident irony that Lernout should be critiquing Ferrer by quoting his Derrida quote from "Singature Event Context" concerning the "possibility of disengagement and citational graft which belongs to the structure of every mark, spoken or written" (xiv). However, taking it seriously, Armand rephrases the gist of Lernout's objection as contending that "whatever stands 'before and outside every horizon of semio-linguistic communication' constitutes [...] 'that whereof we cannot speak,'" and treats the opposition in question as one of "methodology or rather of *method*." That is, whereas Derrida views the anteriority of signification as an indication of a necessary relation of the instantaneousness of the present to some sort of *technē* as a generalised condition of signification elsewhere termed "iterability," Lernout seems to insist that "whatever stands as an object of anteriority, and hence of 'intuitive' knowledge, is unverifiable; it is not an object of knowledge at all and is therefore irrelevant to the science of philology." However, Armand is careful to point out that the renunciation of linguistic anteriority for the sake of scientific verifiability runs into the issue of "prediction":

> If anteriority is purely a matter of intuition, as Lernout argues, the verifiability itself succumbs to the indeterminacy inherent to all forms of predictive modelling. What is significant is not that this indeterminacy arises as a consequence of the "incompletion" of philology [...] but that it is structural and structurally inherent; which is indeed the point of Derrida's statement regarding "possibility." (xv-xvi)

Lernout's "radical philology," in Armand's critique, appears nothing more than "an approximative method" or rather an "approximative system of knowledge," where approximation is "a condition bound up with the materiality of 'knowledge'—that is, semio-linguistic or *signifying* materiality." This view on knowledge is crucial to understanding, for Armand, why Lernout's argument regarding the intuitive character of semio-linguistic anteriority does not hold—and instead presents a wholly other problem for thought, one of the nexus between *praxis* and *poiēsis* in a common materiality. The predictive limits of philology require the impossible double bind in which "all recourse to context [must] be provisional" yet at the same time "the probabilistic feature of this 'recourse' [must] NOT be regarded as provisional." Armand concludes:

> Indeed, probability invests the philo-genetic project at every level, consequent upon precisely the "possibility of disengagement and citational graft,"

12 Louis Armand, *Incendiary Devices: Discourses of the Other* (Prague: Karolinum, 2004 [1994]).
13 In Chapter II "Psychoanalysis," section X.

as Derrida says, "which belongs to the structure of every mark, spoken to written, and which constitutes every mark in writing before and outside every horizon of semio-linguistic communication." (xvi)

XI

One of the two most recent influential studies in the field of Joycean genetics, indebted to many of the findings and methodology of approaches and works already mentioned, while also breaking some unexplored and potentially very interesting ground, is Finn Fordham's *Lots of Fun at Finnegans Wake: Unravelling Universals*.[14]

Fordham's broadly retrospective as well as prospective introduction presents the book's project as an analysis of "how Joyce wrote *Finnegans Wake*" conducted by way of "interpreting what he wrote through a method [called] 'genetic exegesis.'" Before illustrating this method, Fordham introduces several different approaches that *Finnegans Wake* has invited from readers and critics, divided up into a total of seven forms (6-7), only some which, due to lack of space, will be followed here. First, the *structural approach* aims to offer "bird's-eye views and provide skeletal outlines of the overall form," with frequent recourse to Vico's 3&1 structure (Hart), dream theory (Bishop) and the collective unconscious (Budgen) (7). The *theoretical approach* is introduced via its shared reservation regarding the practice of the previous approach, for "to uncover a transparent narrative in *Finnegans Wake* is to be untrue to its project of apparently undoing or reformulating storytelling conventions and everyday language."

Such was the viewpoint of many of the *Tel Quel* theorists, who

> were keen to speak generally of its radical project, to reflect in particular on its language and even to emulate [...] its difficulty and complexity, its non-referentiality and non-communicability [as part of] an attack on "language" as a tool of instrumental reason, as a structure fixed to reality and natural phenomena. (16)

Against this Fordham pits Lernout's *The French Joyce*, "a partisan book and a concerted attack on the influence of 'theory,' especially in so far as theory has detracted from the traditional philology that Lernout wishes to reinvigorate" (17). Fordham's slightly ironic attitude to theorists is evident in his concluding observation that "it is one of the most enduring universal myths about *Finnegans Wake* that it is about enduring universal myths" (18). Fordham's treatment of the issue of cultural studies' Wakean explorations is informed by calling into question not the *what* but the *how* of Joyce's use of the popular cultural ephemera:

> Is he creating a protective archive for cultural ephemera, or locking them into a context of obscurity which is alien to them, where, like fish out of

---

[14] Finn Fordham, *Lots of Fun at Finnegans Wake* (Oxford: Oxford University Press, 2007).

water, they lack the oxygen of publicity and popularity and public consumption that allowed them to live in the first place? (19)

Fordham is appreciative of "that branch of cultural studies interested in technology," for it has to his mind, "produced interesting work through the notion of the *Wake* as a machine and an examination of writing technologies," albeit, "relating it to the everyday or to the contemporary [...] has been less successfully carried out" (19). The *genetic approach* is seen as forming "a large and growing part of a renewed philological practice." It is said to involve "leafing through Joyce's manuscripts, with their notebooks, drafts, fair copies, printers' copies and proofs of 'Work in Progress,' all reproduced by the Garland Press in the sixty-three volumes of the *James Joyce Archive*" (22) which is

> extraordinary, partly for the survival of its contents but more centrally as an unprecedented set of witnesses of illustrating the creative processes behind one of the most extraordinary texts ever conceived. (23)

The chronological account of Joyce's chapter-by-chapter compositional process, provided on pages 24-7, proves just like any synopsis of the whole of the *Wake*, "reductively commonsensical" in that it brushes away the tiny turns that Joyce made as he wrote his way along:

> Just as the tales of the book can be examined in greater and greater microscopic detail, so can the narrative of its telling. My project in this book is to bring these micronarratives together: the details of what is written, when it is written, and how it is written. (27)

This book takes up the genetic approach in that it shows how "a given passage, of a page or three in length, grows over its numerous drafts"— this at the intended expense of the notetaking process. Of the privileging of the early notebooks over the later drafts (as is the case with Rose's approach), Fordham notes that "the notebooks cannot tell you much about the methods of applying the materials within them," because for that one has to go to the drafts. The study is envisaged as

> a complement to the current excellent notebook work, in the hope that one probably quite distant day ahead they will be brought together. [...] As well as using a genetic approach, this book will be exegetical, the last of the seven "approaches." (28)

The *exegetical approach* finally presents "not necessarily a clarification" as much as "extension and accretion":

> Reading *Finnegans Wake* one is constantly tempted to apply the hermeneutics of suspicion—to doubt your own interpretation and then question the prejudices that have led you to them. It is a work which seems to contain its own opposite, so you can only ever say half-truths about it. (31)

Hence, the "genetic exegesis" employed with the aim of "unravelling the universals," has as its method the selection of "a short, relatively self-contained passage of between half a page to three pages," and the scrutinisation of "how it grew from its earliest draft of perhaps just fifteen to twenty words, through the many draft levels, up to the form of its appearance in the final version, the third edition of 1975" (33). The purpose of such forensic analysis is to (re)introduce the *Wake* by means of its manuscripts, revealing it to be

> an object of many endings and beginnings, of points of transition, transmutation, and transfer which, like a tree and its leaves, reaches out via multiple surfaces, each one feeding back into the whole. (35)

The method here is also the message: "the proliferation of meanings and stories in and next to the *Wake* unravels universals—the universals that it seems to set up through its mythic coincidences and reproductive analogies." Part IV of Fordham's book (which I will examine in some further detail) argues

> that the elaborate character of Joyce's writing methods is reflected in the elaborate characters of the writing themselves [...] The principal characters represent principles of composition. [...] These primary "forms" have an effect of limiting within their "frames," the people as "types." (35)

Ultimately, Fordham's argument in favour of this correlative between composition and meaning aims to endorse a comic optimistic vision of *Finnegans Wake* as "a symbol for a secular collective—not divinely individual—Resurrection" (36).

The passages subjected to Fordham's "genetic exegesis" include the six stages of Shem's "cyclewheeling history" (*FW* 185.27-186.10), the seven transformations of Anna Livia's "very first time" (*FW* 203.17-204.05), and the scenes with "Butt: I Shuttm!" (*FW* 351.36-355.09) and the "Nircississies" (*FW* 526.20-528.24). The last chapter, "Revising Character: The Maggies and the Murphys" will be discussed as a representative synecdoche of the whole of Fordham's fine book. In this chapter, Fordham "continue[s] this focus on character" by tracing the genetic development of "the 'people' embodied in the 'Maggies' and the 'Murphys'" (217). This character-focused approach yields the following insight:

> All the characters of the *Wake* can be seen [...] as projected figments of a single man's imagination. And if it is any single person's dream, with determining contexts round that person, it is the dream of James Joyce, dreaming, perhaps of the version of himself he might have become, his other life passing before him, interred not far from the river Liffey, maybe something like his father. (219)

This radical unravelling of character is brought back to Joyce's rewriting procedures described in a useful summary which deserves to be quoted at length:

> Initially, Joyce drafted particular characters that are peculiar in being dehistoricized, their social contexts unspecified, as a rule absurd, with an inconsistent mixing of historical allusion. They are carriers of Joyce's exercises in style, rather than self-consistent entities. [...] Over time, rather than becoming more specific, they proliferate, change name, sex, nation, class, period. [...] The consequent multiplication of temporal and spatial contexts means that the delineating limits of character blur. It is through revision that character is refracted and multiplied, stretched across incompatible and incongruous realms. (220)

The concluding concern of Fordham's argument has to do with intention: an intention, if ascribable at all, applies to "Joyce's compositional processes" in that "intention produces processes, and as these processes develop new intentions are produced" (243). However, the progression of reworkings is not to be seen as simply a causal derivation of one reworking after another:

> Each one has some external source lying outside the internal source of the text to which it is added. The details do not derive from that to which they bring themselves. [...] Each one represents the supplement of a different narrative, creating in sum a mass of half-concealed stories of difference. (243)

It is, according to Fordham's concluding remarks, precisely by being attentive to the details of these processes, by "tracing them through the many levels of Joyce's drafts, gradually releasing the contents of the work of the *Wake* as revealed in the *Archive*," that one can remain alive to them. "For 'here are the details' (601.03). And for further details apply within" (243).

XII

Hailed by some as the most complete and accurate account of Joyce's compositional process in the *Wake*, and undoubtedly the most ambitious genetic critical project of the past three decades, Sam Slote and Luca Crispi's edited volume *How Joyce Wrote Finnegans Wake*[15] presents the grand finale (prior to a recapitulative coda) of the present genealogy of Joyce's genetic criticism. Given the vast scope and variegated nature of the work, my remarks on it shall restrict themselves to the triple introduction, and a brief overview of its general framework.

The "Introduction," co-authored by the two editors and Dirk Van Hulle, opens by the *Wake*'s famous epigraph after the last "the"—*Paris, 1922-*

[15] Sam Slote and Luca Crispi, eds., *How Joyce Wrote Finnegans Wake* (Madison: The University of Wisconsin Press, 2007).

1939. The collection's main aim is then put forward: "to show what might be gained from recognition of what is implied in this epigraph, that is, from reading *Finnegans Wake* in the context of its prepublication manuscripts," the particular situation within the field being that "the manuscripts for *Finnegans Wake* are no longer a vast and daunting uncharted landscape," which is related to "the past decade's consolidation of Wakean genetic studies" (3-4). Tracing the *Wake*'s compositional history, the notetaking is taken as being responsible for "a great deal of the *Wake*'s verbiage":

> In some cases, especially with the later notebooks, Joyce took the notes for specific purposes, and in others he merely jotted down random words that were then subsequently used because they struck his fancy a second time, when he was going over his notebooks and preparing drafts. (6)

The editors mention as particularly beneficial the recent (March 2006) acquisition, by the National Library of Ireland, of previously unknown drafts of the early sketches, which "changes our understanding of the earliest genesis of *Finnegans Wake*" (10). A comparison with *Ulysses* reveals just how far more important pre-publication material becomes in the case of Joyce's last book. Whereas the *Ulysses* template included "Homer's *Odyssey* and certain events in Dublin on 16 June 1904 from the perspective of three clearly defined characters," in the case of the *Wake*, the book "from its beginning [...] lacked such clear points of contact," which resulted in the *Wake* operating as "a concatenated series of *intratextual* echoes that proceed from the sketches," in which its "scaffolding is generated internally"—what Hayman's study (see above) calls "nodality" (14). The machine metaphor is used here too: "In a sense, the sketches were but the initiating spark for a perpetual motion text machine" (15). Rose's study is also given a nod of acknowledgment, albeit with (as has been mentioned) an important reservation: Rose's argument that the early sketches should be viewed as originally autonomous units, resting on the sketches' "thematic congruity and on the fact that they were only incorporated into the text of the *Wake* in 1938," which even leads him so far as to claim "that the project of the sketches differs enough from *Finnegans Wake* that they should be considered as separate yet not absolutely unrelated entities," is ultimately proven wrong by the recently discovered new notebooks. These documents show that "Joyce considered these sketches to be interchangeable and malleable rather than as discrete units to be published in short story form" (16).

What follows at this point is a detailed survey of the compositional process spanning the early 1923 sketches, the *transition* period, the *Exagmination* collection, Joyce's late 1920s/early 1930s writer's block, and the final years of "piecing the book together out of a jigsaw puzzle-like state" (27). In a section on "The *Finnegans Wake* Manuscripts," the editors produce a useful categorization of the draft manuscripts to be deployed in the collection:

early drafts (the most basic drafts); several stages of later drafts (each usually more legible than its predecessor); fair copies (more legible manuscripts produced from his drafts, most often so that they could be typed); typescripts (usually prepared for printers); galley and page proofs for serial and deluxe publication; printed texts that Joyce further revised for another publication; and the galley and page proofs for *Finnegans Wake* itself. (33)

Finally, "A Brief Introduction to Genetic Criticism" written by Van Hulle departs from Hay's notion of "avant-texte" to ask three interrelated questions about its character, "where does the *avant-texte* end, how does it progress, and where does it start?" Its key contention is that "the confrontation of a published text with all its previous versions gives the reader an idea of what they might have become," and it is "this attention to the text's potential energy" that informs textual genetics (37). In particular, Daniel Ferrer's work is credited with having "shown how every artifact inevitably involves a project, which means that it constantly 'oscillates between an anticipatory perspective [...] and a retrospective vision.'"

The list of contributors, with perhaps the sole omission of Laurent Milesi, reads like a "who's-who" of Joycean textual genetics, from Hayman, Ferrer, Rabaté, to Lernout, Van Hulle, Van Mierlo, to the two editors, Fordham, or Deppman, each of whom has been allotted one of the *Wake*'s chapters. Despite this variety, the collection's approach (bestowing the place of honour, the opening chapter, upon Lernout) exhibits a clear preference for the sort of source excavation and gradual process-of-becoming documentation of the radical philological sort which Lernout advocates. In other words, there is very little in the book to complement the *how* of the title with some sort of *so what*, especially given the volume's unique status.

This might come close to what Jean-Michel Rabaté (whose theoretical approach standing poles apart from the postulates of the radical philology which has been exemplified above) states in the opening of his own contribution to the volume:

> The idea of "genetic" approaches to chapters of *Finnegans Wake* is bound to promise more than it can hold: what is often tantalizingly proffered is the disclosure of new meanings, of deeper and more thorough annotations, even as a revolutionary interpretive horizon bridging the gap between original hermeneutic strategies and an array of verifiable empirical and textual data, whereas what is really given is a little more "sordid," or perhaps I should say "sordomutic" (*FW* 117.14). Sordid, because in the end we only get another story, for the new "understanding" sends us back to that useful but predicable reminder: "There are sordidly tales within tales, you clearly understand that?" (*FW* 522.05-6). (384)

Rabaté is right—the collection's title speaks of nothing but the *how*, and of its own being *A Chapter-by-Chapter Genetic Guide*, both of which it accomplishes with distinction.

XIII

Most recently, the excellent *Companion to James Joyce* has included a retrospective summarizing piece by Daniel Ferrer which shall provide a recirculative coda to this chapter.

Ferrer's essay, "The Joyce of Manuscripts,"[16] observes of the 63-volume *James Joyce Archive* that it has, in addition to the sufficient obscurity of Joyce's published canon, "provided us with an inexhaustible story of supplementary obscurity" (286). The published / unpublished binary, like many others we have seen, does not completely fit the Joycean canon, as works normally read in their published form, such as *Epiphanies, Stephen Hero*, or *Giacomo Joyce*, "were never published by Joyce: as far as he was concerned, they never went beyond the stage of manuscripts," which do not become works of art "until the moment of final publication." Until then, a manuscript is to be viewed as "an instrument towards the elaboration of a projected work, not a literary text but a protocol for the fabrication of a text" (287).

Another common project of textual criticism, one which uses the manuscripts in order to *establish* the text, is proven to be "an impossible task" through the example of "Circe," which contains a textual instance where "the corrupted text could be considered to be, in some respects, superior to the version of the fair copy" (289). The often observed "accretive" mode of Joyce's is illustrated by an episode from the final period of the novel's composition, when Joyce's last addenda, created after the deadline set by his printer, arrived too late for inclusion—an episode that shows how "a writer's purpose is not an absolute, but a fluctuating, time-bound transaction between a series of writing events and a series of external constraints." Thus, even though it may not always provide one with easy editorial solutions, retracing the genesis of some passages can be productive in several ways. As opposed to *Ulysses*, where the threefold stylistic development constructed by Groden's analysis still holds, in the case of the *Wake*, "we cannot assign major 'styles' as convincingly as we do in *Ulysses*, and given the nature of the published book it is not so easy to detect in it the traces of the process of evolution" (293). However, even here, the accretive character of Joyce's writing, as well as the general trait of the relatively late creation of formal chapter specificities, are both clearly discernible on the example of the ALP chapter, the three informing features of which (the multi-lingual aspect, the density of colloquialisms, and the interweaving of river names) are all genetically discovered to be "later additions to former versions" (294). According to Ferrer's concluding observation, what the textual genetic practice proves is that

> Authorial intention cannot be the last word on the text: it is something that
> we should not neglect, something that we should pursue through its fluc-

---

[16] Daniel Ferrer, "The Joyce of Manuscripts," *A Companion to James Joyce*, ed. Richard Brown (Oxford: Blackwell Publishing, 2008).

tuations and nuances by a rigorous interpretation of the extant documents, but it cannot be a limitation of our powers of interpretation. (297)

(XIV)

An "authorial intention" to be *pursued*, yet *also abandoned*: an imperative to remain faithful to Joyce, to the point of betraying him by way of the interpretation which his writing solicits as well as forestalls, requiring one to write in its very own memory. The "yes" that criticism has telegraphed back to Joyceville, just as the one to which it was responding in the first place, contains as many confirmations as it does negations of whatever was intended by that first and unique Joycean "yes."

Bibliography

JOYCE-RELATED

ARMAND, Louis. *Techne: James Joyce, Hypertext & Technology* (Prague: Karolinum, 2003 [1997]).

ARMAND, Louis, ed. *Joycemedia* (Prague: Litteraria Pragensia, 2003).

ARMAND, Louis. *Incendiary Devices: Discourses of the Other* (Prague: Karolinum, 2006 [1994]).

ARMAND, Louis, WALLACE, Clare, eds. *Giacomo Joyce: Envoys of the Other* (Prague: Litteraria Pragensia, 2006 [2002]).

ATTRIDGE, Derek & FERRER, Daniel, eds. *Post-structuralist Joyce: Essays from the French* (Cambridge: Cambridge University Press, 1984).

ATTRIDGE, Derek, *Peculiar Language (Language as Difference from the Renaissance to James Joyce)* (Ithaca, New York: Cornell University Press, 1988).

ATTRIDGE, Derek, ed. *The Cambridge Companion to James Joyce* (Cambridge: Cambridge University Press, 1990).

ATTRIDGE, Derek. *Joyce Effects—Language, Theory, History* (Cambridge: Cambridge University Press, 2000).

ATTRIDGE, Derek & HOWLES, Marjorie, eds. *Semi-colonial Joyce* (Cambridge: Cambridge University Press, 2000).

BEJA, Moris & BENSTOCK, Shari, eds. *Coping with Joyce: Essays from the Copenhagen Symposium* (Columbus: Ohio State University Press, 1986).

BENSTOCK, Bernard, ed. *James Joyce—The Augmented Ninth* (New York: Syracuse University Press, 1988).

VAN BOHEEMEN, Christine, ed. *Joyce and the Art of Mediation* (Amsterdam - Atlanta: Edition Rodopi, 1989).

VAN BOHEEMEN-SAAF, Christine. *Joyce, Derrida, Lacan, and the Trauma of History* (Cambridge: Cambridge University Press, 1999).

BOLLETIERI BOSINELLI, Rosa Maria & MARENGO VALIO, Carla & VAN BOHEEMEN, Christine, eds. *The Languages of Joyce* (Philadelphia/Amsterdam: John Benjamins Publishing Company, 1992).

BOOKER, M. Keith. *Joyce, Bakthin, and the Literary Tradition* (Michigan: University of Michigan Press, 1995).

BRANNIGAN, John & WARD, Geoff & WOLFREYS, Julian, eds. *Re-Joyce. Text, Culture, Politics* (London: MacMillan Press, Ltd., 1998).

BRIVIC, Sheldon. *The Veil of Signs: Joyce, Lacan and Perception* (Chicago: University of Illinois Press, 1991).

BROOKER, Joseph. *Joyce's Critics: Transitions in Reading and Culture* (Madison: University of Wisconsin Press, 2004).

BROWN, Richard. *James Joyce and Sexuality* (Cambridge: Cambridge University Press, 1985).

BROWN, Richard, ed. *A Companion to James Joyce* (Oxford: Blackwell Publishing, 2008).

BUDGEN, Frank. *James Joyce and the Making of Ulysses* (Oxford: Oxford University Press, 1972).

CHENG, Vincent J. *Joyce, Race, and Empire* (Cambridge: Cambridge University Press, 1995).

CHENG, Vincent J. & MARTIN, Timothy, eds. *Joyce in Context* (Cambridge: Cambridge University Press, 1992).

COTTER, David. *James Joyce and the Perverse Ideal* (New York and London: Routledge, 2003).

DETTMAR, Kevin. *The Illicit Joyce of Postmodernism* (Madison: The University of Wisconsin University Press, 1996).

DEVLIN, Kimberly J. *James Joyce's "Fraudstuff"'* (Miami: University Press of Florida, 2002).

DUFFY, Enda. *The Subaltern "Ulysses"* (Minneapolis: University of Minnesota Press, 1994).

ECO, Umberto. *The Middle Ages of James Joyce: The Aesthetics of Chaosmos*, trans. Ellen Esrock (London: Hutchinson Radius, 1989).

EHRLICH, Heyward, ed. *Light Rays: James Joyce and Modernism* (New York: New Horizon Press Publishers, 1984).

FAIRHALL, James. *James Joyce and the Question of History* (Cambridge: Cambridge University Press, 1993).

FOGARTY, Anne & MARTIN, Timothy, eds. *Joyce on the Threshold* (Miami: University Press of Florida, 2005).

FORDHAM, Finn. *Lots of Fun at Finnegans Wake* (Oxford: Oxford University Press, 2007).

FRIEDMAN, Susan Stanford, ed. *Joyce: The Return of the Repressed* (London and Ithaca: Cornell University Press, 1993).

GABLER, Hans Walter. "Afterword" to *"Ulysses": A Critical and Synoptic Edition* (Vols. I-III, New York & London: Garland Publishing, 1984).

GIBSON, Andrew. *Joyce's Revenge: History, Politics, and Aesthetics in "Ulysses"* (Oxford: Oxford University Press, 2002).

GRODEN, Michael. *Joyce's 'Ulysses' in Progress* (New Jersey: Princeton University Press, 1977).

GRODEN, Michael (general editor), GABLER, Hans Walter, HAYMAN, David, LITZ, Walton A., and ROSE, Danis. *The James Joyce Archive* (63 vols.; New York & London: Garland, 1977-79).

HART, Clive. *Structure and Motif in "Finnegans Wake"* (Evanston, Illinois: Northwestern University Press, 1962).

HAYMAN, David. *Joyce et Mallarmé* (Paris: Lettres Modernes, 1956).

HAYMAN, David. *The Wake in Transit* (Ithaca and London: Cornell University Press, 1990).

HAYMAN, David & SLOTE, Sam, eds. *Genetic Studies in Joyce* (Amsterdam: Edition Rodopi, 1995).

HARARI, Roberto. *How James Joyce Made His Name: A Reading of the Final Lacan*, trans. Luke Thurston (New York: Other Press, 2002).

HENKE, Suzette. *James Joyce and the Politics of Desire* (London and New York: Routledge, 1990).

HERR, Cheryl. *Joyce's Anatomy of Culture* (Urbana: University of Illinois Press, 1986).

JONES, Ellen Carol, ed. *Joyce: Feminism/Post-Colonialism* (Amsterdam: Edition Rodopi, 1998).

KAUFMANN, Michael. *Textual Bodies: Modernism, Postmodernism, and Print* (London and Toronto: Associated University Press, 1994).

KENNER, Hugh. *Ulysses* (Baltimore: The Johns Hopkins University Press, Revised edition, 1987).

KERSHNER, R. Brandon. *Joyce, Bakhtin, and Popular Culture* (Chapel Hill: University of North Carolina Press, 1989).

KERSHNER, R. Brandon, ed. *Joyce and Popular Culture* (Florida: University Press of Florida, 1996).

KERSHNER, R. Brandon, ed. *Cultural Studies of James Joyce* (Amsterdam: Edition Rodopi, 2003).

LEONARD, Garry M. *Reading "Dubliners" Again: A Lacanian Perspective* (New York: Syracuse University Press, 1993).

LEONARD, Garry M. *Advertising and Commodity Culture in Joyce* (Miami: University Press of Florida, 1998).

LERNOUT, Geert. *The French Joyce* (Ann Arbor: The University of Michigan Press, 1990).

LERNOUT, Geert & VAN MIERLO, Wim, eds. *The Reception of James Joyce in Europe* (London: Thoemmes Continuum, 2004).

LITZ, Walton A. *The Art of James Joyce* (Oxford: Oxford University Press, 1961).

MACCABE, Colin. *James Joyce and the Revolution of the Word* (New York: Palgrave, 1978, 2003).

MACKEY, Peter F. *Chaos Theory and James Joyce's Everyman* (Miami: University of Florida Press, 1999).

MAHON, Peter. *Imagining Joyce and Derrida: Between "Finnegans Wake" and "Glas"* (Toronto, Buffalo, London: Toronto University Press, 2007).

MANGANIELLO, Dominic. *Joyce's Politics* (London: Routledge & Kegan Paul, 1980).

MCGEE, Patrick. *Paperspace: Style as Ideology in Joyce's "Ulysses"* (Lincoln and London: University of Nebraska Press, 1988).

MCGEE, Patrick. *Joyce Beyond Marx: History and Desire in "Ulysses" and "Finnegans Wake"* (Miami: University Press of Florida, 2001).

MCHALE, Brian. *Constructing Postmodernism* (London and New York: Routledge, 1992).

MCHUGH, Roland. *The Sigla of "Finnegans Wake"* (Austin, Texas: Texas University Press, 1976).

MCLUHAN, Eric. *The Role of Thunder in "Finnegans Wake"* (Toronto Buffalo London: Toronto University Press, 1997).

MILESI, Laurent, ed. *James Joyce and the Difference of Language* (Cambridge: Cambridge University Press, 2003).

MULLIN, Katherine. *James Joyce, Sexuality and Purity* (Cambridge: Cambridge University Press, 2003).

MURPHY, Sean P. *James Joyce and Victims* (London: Associated University Press, 2003).

NASH, John. *James Joyce and the Act of Reception* (Cambridge, London: Cambridge University Press, 2006).

NOLAN, Emer. *James Joyce and Nationalism* (New York: Routledge, 1995).

NORRIS, Margot. *The Decentered Universe of "Finnegans Wake"* (Baltimore: Johns Hopkins University Press, 1974).

NORRIS, Margot. *Joyce's Web* (Austin: University of Texas Press, 1992).

PEARCE, Richard, ed. *Molly Blooms: A Polylogue on 'Penelope' and Cultural Studies* (Madison: University of Wisconsin Press, 1994).

POWER, Arthur. *Conversations with James Joyce*, ed. Clive Hart (London, Millington, 1974).

RABATÉ, Jean-Michel. *James Joyce: Authorized Reader* (Baltimore: Johns Hopkins University Press, 1991).

RABATÉ, Jean-Michel. *Joyce upon the Void: The Genesis of Doubt* (London: MacMillan, 1991).

RABATÉ, Jean-Michel. *James Joyce and the Politics of Egoism* (Cambridge: Cambridge University Press, 2001).

RABATÉ, Jean-Michel, ed. *Palgrave Advances in Joyce Studies* (London: Palgrave Macmillan, 2004).

RICE, Thomas Jackson. *Joyce, Chaos, and Complexity* (Urbana and Chicago: University of Illinois Press, 1997).

ROSE, Danis & O'HANLON, John. *Understanding Finnegans Wake: A Guide to the Narrative of James Joyce's Masterpiece* (New York: Garland, 1982).

ROSE, Danis. *The Textual Diaries of James Joyce* (Dublin: The Lilliput Press, 1995).

ROUGHLEY, Alan. *James Joyce and Critical Theory: An Introduction* (Exeter: Harvester Wheatsheaf, 1991).

ROUGHLEY, Alan. *Reading Derrida Reading Joyce* (Miami: University Press of Florida, 1999).

SARTILIOT, Claudette. *Citation and Modernity: Derrida, Joyce and Brecht* (Norman and London: University of Oklahoma Press, 1993).

SCOTT, Bonnie Kime, ed. *New Alliances in Joyce Studies* (London: Associated University Press, 1988).

SENN, Fritz. *Joyce's Dislocations*, trans. John Paul Riquelme (Baltimore: Johns Hopkins University Press, 1994).

SHELTON, Jen. *Joyce and the Narrative Structure of Incest* (Miami: University Press of Florida, 2006).

SLOTE, Sam & VAN MIERLO, Wim, eds. *Genitricksling Joyce* (Amsterdam: Edition Rodopi, 1999).

SLOTE, Sam & CRISPI, Luca, eds. *How Joyce Wrote "Finnegans Wake"* (Madison: The University of Wisconsin Press, 2007).

SPOO, Robert, *James Joyce and the Language of History: Dedalus's Nightmare* (New York: Oxford University Press, 1994).

SPURR, David. *Joyce and the Scene of Modernity* (Miami: University Press of Florida, 2002).

STREIT, Wolfgang. *Joyce/Foucault: Sexual Confessions* (Ann Arbor: The University of Michigan Press, 2004).

THEALL, Donald F. *Beyond the Word: Reconstructing Sense in the Joyce Era of Technology, Culture and Communication* (Toronto: University of Toronto Press, 1995).

THEALL, Donald F. *James Joyce's Technopoetics* (Toronto, Buffalo, London: Toronto University Press, 1997).

THURSTON, Luke, ed. *Re-inventing the Symptom: Essays on the Final Lacan* (New York: Other Press, 2002).

THURSTON, Luke. *James Joyce and the Problem of Psychoanalysis* (Cambridge: Cambridge University Press, 2004).

VALENTE, Joseph. *James Joyce and the Problem of Justice: Negotiating Sexual and Colonial Difference* (Cambridge: Cambridge University Press, 1995).

VALENTE, Joseph, ed. *Quare Joyce* (Ann Arbor: The University of Michigan Press, 1998).

WAWRZYCKA, Jolanta & CORCORAN, Marlene, eds. *Gender in Joyce* (Miami: University Press of Florida, 1997).

WILLIAMS, Trevor L. *Reading Joyce Politically* (Miami: University Press of Florida, 1997).

THEORY-RELATED

ALTHUSSER, Louis. *Ideology and Ideological States Apparatuses* (New York and London: Monthly Review Press, 1971).

ARMAND, Louis. *Literate Technologies: Language, Cognition, Technicity* (Prague: Litteraria Pragensia, 2006).

ASHCROFT, Bill & GRIFFITHS, Gareth & TIFFIN, Helen. *The Empire Writes Back: Theory and Practice in Post-Colonial Literatures* (London and New York: Routledge, 1989).

BAKHTIN, Mikhail. *The Dialogic Imagination*, trans. Michael Holquist (Austin, Texas: University of Texas Press, 1982).

BLOOM, Harold, ed. *Deconstruction and Criticism* (New York: Continuum, 1986).

DERRIDA, Jacques. *Of Grammatology,* trans. Gayatri Chakravorty Spivak (Baltimore: The Johns Hopkins University Press, Corrected edition, 1998).

DERRIDA, Jacques. *Dissemination*, trans. Barbara Johnson (Chicago: University of Chicago Press, 1983).

EAGLETON, Terry. *Literary Theory* (Oxford: Basil Backwell, 1983).

FELMAN, Shoshana. *Jacques Lacan and the Adventure of Insight* (Boston: Harvard University Press 1987).

FIEDLER, Leslie. *Love and Death in the American Novel* (New York: Stein and Day, 1966).

GODZICH, Wlad, ed. *Paul de Man: The Resistance to Theory* (Minneapolis: University of Minnesota Press, 1986).

GRODEN, Michael & KREISWIRTH, Martin, eds. *Johns Hopkins Guide to Literary Theory* (Baltimore and London: Johns Hopkins University Press, 1994).

HOLLAND, Norman N. *The Dynamics of Literary Response* (New York: Oxford University Press, 1968).

HUTCHEON, Linda. *A Poetics of Postmodernism, History, Theory, Fiction* (New York and London: 1988).

KRISTEVA, Julia. *Revolution in Poetic Language*, trans. Margaret Waller (New York: Columbia University Press, 1984).

LOOMBA, Anita. *Colonialism/Postcolonialism* (London and New York: Routledge, 1998).

DE MAN, Paul. *Allegory of Reading* (New York: Yale University Press, 1982).

SAID, Edward. *Orientalism* (London and New York: Penguin Classics; 25th Anniversary Ed., 2003).

DE SAUSSURE, Ferdinand. *Course in General Linguistics*, trans. Roy Harris (London: Open Court Classics, 1998).

STRINATI, Dominic. *An Introduction to Theories of Popular Culture* (London and New York: Routledge, 1995).

WILLIAMS, Raymond. *Culture and Society: 1780-1950* (New York: Columbia University Press; 2nd edition, 1983).

Index

Fairhall, James, 14, 288-96, 342
Fanon, Frantz, 24, 204-5, 236
Felman, Shoshana, 19
Ferrer, Daniel, 4, 6, 37, 113-4, 206,
    286, 331, 380, 382, 384, 406,
    408, 411, 417-8
Fiedler, Leslie, 23, 177, 238
Fordham, Finn, 3, 412-5, 417
Foucault, Michel, 106-7, 153, 158,
    163, 166, 181, 183-9, 217,
    290, 297, 299, 324, 423
Freud, Sigmund, 18-20, 28, 31, 68-
    9, 72-5, 80-1, 83, 88-9, 92, 94,
    98-9, 101, 103-7, 110-13, 119,
    124, 133-4, 136-7, 140, 157-8,
    171, 184, 189, 222, 246, 258-
    9, 281, 302, 307, 340, 357,
    364, 376, 380-1, 384, 396
Friedman, Susan Stanford, 79-81,
    327
Frow, John, 268-9
Gabler, Hans Walter, 185-6, 316,
    382, 389-6, 399, 403, 405
Gallop, Jane, 137, 307
Genette, Gérard, 270
Gibson, Andrew, 214-8, 220-1
Gilbert, Susan, 21, 88, 129, 131-2,
    241, 251, 350, 363, 388
Godin, Jean Guy, 74
Gramsci, Antonio, 23, 343
Greenblatt, Steven, 175, 187
Groden, Michael, 16, 363, 387-92,
    403, 409, 418
Guattari, Félix, 19, 102, 137, 158,
    301, 361
Hall, Stuart, 23
Harari, Roberto, 91-5
Harper, Margaret Mills, 172
Hart, Clive, 175, 380, 383, 412,
    423
Hassan, Ihab, 26, 238-40, 272, 306
Hayman, David, 292, 308, 399-
    403, 405-8, 416-7
Heath, Stephen, 23, 37, 52
Hegel, G.W.F., 38, 49-50, 63-4, 76,
    297, 314, 318
Heidegger, Martin, 3, 62, 72, 194,
    222, 378, 380-1, 384
Henke, Suzette, 22, 115, 134-40
Herr, Cheryl, 162-4, 166-7, 170,
    180, 185, 190-2, 300, 317, 324
Hillis Miller, J., 17, 382

Hogan, Patrick Colm, 70
Horkheimer, Max, 177, 186, 265
Howes, Marjorie, 211-5
Irigaray, Luce, 20-1, 121, 128, 140,
    222
Jacquet, Claude, 406
Jakobson, Roman, 39-41, 384, 397
Jameson, Fredric, 166-7, 182, 202,
    267, 288-9, 313-5, 331, 336-7,
    345, 348
Jauss, Hans Robert, 226
Johnson, Barbara, 54, 424
Johnson, Jeri, 126, 129
Jones, Ellen Carol, 120, 144
Jones, Ernest, 18
Jung, Carl Gustav, 74, 100, 111,
    112, 118, 128, 142-3, 306
Kaufmann, Michael, 269-71
Kenner, Hugh, 5, 108, 238, 267,
    270, 334
Kershner, R. Brandon, 166-70, 177,
    185-7, 192, 300-1, 317
Kimball, Jean, 142-3
King, Mary, 126, 293, 326, 341-2,
    409
Kristeva, Julia, 20-2, 48, 114-20,
    129-31, 134, 138, 140, 158,
    168, 174, 187, 233, 250, 350
Lacan, Jacques, 4, 6, 18-23, 28,
    33, 54-5, 68-103, 110, 112-3,
    117-8, 134-5, 137, 140, 144-5,
    153-4, 158, 178, 181-3, 194-6,
    235, 246-7, 250, 253-4, 281-2,
    302-3, 305, 307, 309-14, 327-
    32, 337-8, 344, 378, 380, 384,
    395, 420-4
LaCapra, Dominick, 297
Landow, George P., 379, 383
Law, Jules, 119, 149, 164-66, 254,
    339
Lawrence, Karen, 132-3, 221, 266
Lefebvre, Henri, 165, 330
Leonard, Gary M., 79, 82-6, 89,
    153-4, 180-5, 194-6, 301, 317
Lernout, Geert, 5-7, 9, 37, 55, 71-
    3, 237, 407-9, 411-2, 417
Lévi-Strauss, Claude, 4, 174, 380,
    386
Litz, A. Walton, 403, 406-7
Lotman, Yuri, 162, 166, 245

Lyotard, Jean-Francois, 25-6, 188, 240-5, 268, 272-4, 279, 302, 304, 306, 310, 340, 379
MacCabe, Colin, 23, 27-33, 37, 68-9, 120, 128, 140, 201, 203, 207, 225, 268, 319, 332, 344, 348
Mackey, Peter F., 376-7
Mahon, Peter, 45, 63-7
Marx, Karl, 23, 154, 186, 194, 210, 318, 321, 324-6, 343, 346, 351-2, 392, 422
McCormack, W.J., 325-6
McGee, Patrick, 76, 144, 172, 327-38, 346-52, 371, 392-4
McHale, Brian, 266-9, 272, 277, 306
McHugh, Roland, 103, 249, 380, 383
McLuhan, Eric, 368
McLuhan, Marshall, 26, 269, 355, 364
Milesi, Laurent, 8, 11-5, 24-6, 62-3, 406, 417
Millot, Catherine, 73, 100
Mullin, Katherine, 159-61, 213
Nash, John, 221, 224-32
Nelson, Ted, 379, 382
Nolan, Emer, 13, 161, 205-9, 211, 214, 221, 317, 348
Norris, Margot, 4, 28, 140-1, 143-4, 150, 188, 238, 261-6, 301, 316-8, 348
Nunes, Mark, 382-3
Ong, Walter J., 26, 269, 367
Osteen, Mark, 141-2
Pearce, Richard, 90, 170
Pound, Ezra, 5, 47, 206, 214, 244, 250, 252, 270, 300, 324
Rabaté, Jean-Michel, 3, 6, 37, 72-3, 86-9, 151-2, 251-61, 286, 316, 380, 383, 395-99, 406, 417
Rice, Thomas Jackson, 192-4, 370-7
Rose, Danis, 224, 399, 403-5, 407, 413, 416

Roughley, Alan R., 4, 6, 21, 37, 53, 57-61, 63, 67, 74, 115, 245, 248-50
Said, Edward, 23, 25, 199, 204-5
Saint-Amour, Paul K., 187, 221, 223-4
Sartiliot, Claudette, 46-53, 63
Saussure, Ferdinand de, 4, 16, 19, 39, 43, 76, 155
Schloss, Carol, 146
Schwarze, Tracey Teets, 189-90
Scott, Bonnie Kime, 37, 115, 117, 338, 350
Sedgwick, Eve Kosofsky, 149-50, 152
Senn, Fritz, 3, 12, 98, 238, 285, 301
Shelton, Jen, 104-6, 107-10
Showalter, Elaine, 21, 189
Slote, Sam, 3, 62-3, 405, 415
Sonnenfeld, Albert, 70
Spivak, Gayatri Chakravorty, 21, 25, 146, 205, 234, 285, 348, 350, 424
Spoo, Robert, 14, 81, 296-301, 317
Spurr, David, 3, 144, 146-8, 281-4
Streit, Wolfgang, 184-6
Theall, Donald F., 179-80, 286, 353-69, 377-8, 383
Thurston, Luke, 20, 91-2, 95-102, 110-14, 421
Valente, Joseph, 15, 148-50, 152, 155, 159, 188-9, 213, 285, 301, 317, 338-42, 348, 351
van Boheemen-Saaf, Christine, 35-6, 38, 53-5, 57, 126-9, 235, 240, 244-5, 302-9, 311-3
Van Hulle, Dirk, 415, 417
Vico, Giambattista, 51, 64, 67, 123, 238, 260, 281, 290, 297, 317, 334, 352, 368-9, 381, 412
Wawrzycka, Jolanta, 141
Wenzel, Hélène, 21
White, Hayden, 161, 210, 297
Williams, Raymond, 22
Williams, Trevor L., 324, 343
Wollaeger, Mark, 233-7, 300-1
Žižek, Slavoj, 178, 196